Who's Who
OF TWENTIETH-CENTURY
NOVELISTS

THE ROUTLEDGE WHO'S WHO SERIES

Accessible, authoritative and enlightening, these are the definitive biographical guides to a diverse range of subjects drawn from literature and the arts, history and politics, religion and mythology.

Who's Who
OF
TWENTIETH-
CENTURY
NOVELISTS

Tim Woods

London and New York

First published 2001
by Routledge
11 New Fetter Lane, London EC4P 4EE

Simultaneously published in the USA and Canada
by Routledge
29 West 35th Street, New York, NY 10001

Routledge is an imprint of the Taylor & Francis Group

Typeset in Sabon by Taylor & Francis Books Ltd
Printed and bound in Great Britain by TJ International Ltd,
Padstow, Cornwall

British Library Cataloguing in Publication Data
A catalogue record for this book is available from the British Library

Library of Congress Cataloging in Publication Data
Woods, Tim.
Who's who of twentieth-century novelists/ Tim Woods.
p. cm – (Who's who)
Includes bibliographical references and index.
1. Fiction–20th century–Bio-bibliography–Dictionaries.
I. Title: Who's who of 20th century novelists. II. Title: Who is who of
twentieth century novelists. III. Title. IV.
Who's who series.
PN3503 .W66 2001
809.3′0403–dc21
2001019313

[B]

ISBN 0–415–16506–7

Contents

FOR GEOFFREY WOODS, *IN MEMORIAM* (1939–1998)
AND JUDITH WOODS

Preface

What makes one writer 'in' and others 'out'? Anthologisation always runs the risk of substituting selection by the one for appointment by the many. Compiling a guide such as this *Who's Who* is less a process of judiciously winnowing the chaff from the wheat, and more of keeping one's finger in the dyke for fear of drowning in the multitude of potential candidates for entries. Consequently, a guide to twentieth-century novelists will beg criticism for erecting canons where only authors exist, for polemicising rather than objectively collecting, and for imposing significance where other people see blandness.

However, it is not intended that the possession of this guide becomes a substitute for reading other books. Rather, it is hoped that it will act as a quick reference guide, including as it does short and accessible entries on important novelists drawn from throughout the world in the twentieth century, outlining biographical details, social context and, at times, offering thumbnail sketches of significant works by those novelists whose writing has formatively influenced the trajectories of twentieth-century fiction, across a range of countries, genres and styles. By 'formatively influenced', I mean writers who have shaped genres, markets, audiences, forms and perspectives. A second and allied aim is to chart those writers who have been omitted by many other accounts of twentieth-century literary history, as well as areas of fiction which have been overlooked. The writers in this volume fall into three main categories: (i) anglophone writers, many of whom may be deemed 'canonical'; (ii) writers whose work has been translated into English, who have had a measurable impact in English-speaking countries, and who have remained in print for the past ten years; and (iii) the formative writers in popular fiction (science fiction, romance, thriller, detective fiction).

Since this is a vast undertaking, and one which will inevitably raise questions about inclusion and omission, the book has been compiled with some basic ground principles:

1 The emphasis is on post-1945 writers. It is recognised that there are many significant pre-Second World War writers, many of whom may be deemed

'canonical' in the past fifty years. However, I wanted the principal focus to fall upon writers in the post-war period, in order to reflect the fact that much pre-war fiction, although currently undergoing critical re-evaluation, can already be found in many existing guides and companions.

2 The dividing date of the Second World War is not arbitrary. Such an emphasis allows for entries on the 'canonical' pre-war writers, against whom so many post-war writers pit their writing strategies. However, it also means that a substantial part of the book can chart the proliferation of the multiplicity of literatures which emerged with the national independence movements after 1945.

The purpose of this world coverage is to allow the volume to extend the focus of literary importance, to include those areas, countries and languages which have hitherto remained forgotten or marginalised in a predominantly Anglocentric selection of the world's 'best' writers. Hence, the book includes entries on writers from Commonwealth countries, as well as increasingly significant African, Asian and other postcolonial writers. It also includes many writers from non-English-speaking countries, for example from South America, who have nevertheless had a major impact on the world literary scene in the twentieth century. Thus, this book aims to provide a new context for the literatures of non-English speaking countries, as well as centring attention on writers who have been excluded from any serious critical readership.

To anthologise is not to eulogise. Since some writers – like Barbara Cartland, Agatha Christie or Michael Crichton – sell more novels and have a broader readership than many of the widely regarded 'serious' novelists, it would seem inexplicably conservative and elitist to exclude them from a book which purports to be a guide to the formative novelists of the twentieth century. Furthermore, I am conscious of the intellectual and cultural efforts to recontextualise the traditional 'canon' of major writers of the twentieth century, and this guide reflects the popularity and influence of many non-canonical writers who have previously been excluded on the grounds of some conservative aesthetic criteria, rather than that of class, race or gender. Therefore, Chicano writers like Ana Castillo and Sandra Cisneros, and Asian-American writers like Amy Tan and Jessica T. Hagedorn find a context; while the major writers from such genres as detective fiction, science fiction, romance and thrillers find a place. The inclusion of such novelists also demonstrates the increasingly agonised debates in cultural studies, postcolonialism and postmodernism about what is deemed to be 'central' to national literary cultures. Thus, for example, as the political and cultural reorientation occurs in South Africa, notable non-white writers like Lewis Nkosi, Peter Abrahams and Mbulelo Mzamane are beginning to emerge alongside more established writers, such as Nadine Gordimer, Alan Paton and J.M. Coetzee.

This opens the volume to a vast number of possibilities, and its aim is not to cover every twentieth-century writer who has been translated into English (many of whose works are now out of print). Instead, as mentioned above, the book includes writers who have had a significant impact upon the anglophone world, and who have remained in print during the last ten years. Significant impact by a writer can be measured in a variety of ways. One, admittedly crude, method is references in academic search tools, like the Modern Language Association Bibliography. Another gauge is in the 'cultural' impact of certain authors. For example, the translated novels of Jean-Paul Sartre and Albert Camus have had a considerable influence on the popular understanding of existentialism; while the writing of Aleksander I. Solzhenitsyn and Arthur Koestler has profoundly shaped the West's understanding of social life in the former Soviet Union. This again places the emphasis on writers of the later half of the twentieth century.

The main criterion for compiling the entries has been 'usefulness' to readers: the book seeks to maintain a (delicate and difficult) line between those authors who will be familiar to readers and those who languish in certain obscurity. This has meant taking a risk with some entries concerning lesser-known writers, or writers who currently have little fiction to their credit but appear to have future potential. Here, it is important to note that this work is conceived of as a guide, and not as a compendium or a database. Although I have aimed for maximum coverage, the book is limited by the boundaries of a manageable single volume. Thus, a working principle was to include a range of novelists about whom readers were likely to have questions, and thus to be generally useful to as broad a readership as possible. And while the majority of the entries are from non-English-speaking countries, the book does reflect a cultural dominance of English-speaking writers. This sets an ambitious series of tasks for this reference work; but by the same token, it opens up the possibility of an exciting, innovative and provocative introductory companion to twentieth-century world fiction.

Producing a reference work of such diversity is a daunting task, and inevitably leads to some contentious decisions. For example, I have omitted Thomas Hardy on the basis that none of his novels were written in the twentieth century, despite the fact that many twentieth-century writers might derive influence from Hardy. In addition to the major novelists whose reputations would secure them a place in most reference works on twentieth-century writing in English, I have also included novelists about whom people may have questions owing to their fame or literary prominence, once more on the criterion of 'usefulness'. Yet in order to create a balanced and fairly comprehensive account of a broad range of nationalities, emergent writings and new authors, popular literary merit has not been the only consideration. National and ethnic identities, as well as a representation of the various periods of the twentieth century, have played an important part in the selection procedure. Again, on the criterion of 'usefulness', where a novelist writes in a language other than English, I have given the translated title of his or her work and omitted the titles of (albeit numerous) other as yet untranslated works. The original publication date is given in brackets, followed by an English translation date; and where only a translation date is noted, it also refers to the original publication date. As a rule of thumb, in order to be included, an author must have published at least three significant novels within the twentieth century. Inevitably, I have had to break this rule at times, since I have included novelists whose reputation exists solely on one novel (for example, Harper Lee and John Kennedy Toole). Some risks have also been taken with younger and more recent writers who have shown promise to date, especially where they have only published one or two widely acclaimed books, or if they significantly represent a literary culture in its formative phase. I have excluded writers who are deemed to be solely children's fiction writers.

Each entry seeks to give succinct biographical details, outlining typical characteristics of the author, placing his or her work within a social context, listing literary achievements, and offering a brief description of his or her significant novels. In addition, selected important bibliographical source material is listed at the end of each entry, thus providing further guidance to readers who wish to pursue unfamiliar writers. Authors are cross-referenced throughout the entries, signified by their surname in small capitals. The Appendix includes chronological tables of the winners of the most prestigious literary awards: the Booker Prize, the Pulitzer Prize, and the Nobel Prize for Literature.

I have been greatly aided by my editors at Routledge, Kieron Corless, Roger Thorp and Hywel Evans. I would also like to thank Helena Grice and Matthew Jarvis, both of whom either wrote entries or helped with the checking of the entries. Helena also provided enormous 'invisible' help in terms of ensuring that I had the time to complete this project, for which I am extremely grateful. Finally, I want to acknowledge the help of my father, Geoffrey Woods, who worked enthusiastically and knowledgeably upon many of the entries, and died of a heart attack on his way to Reading University Library to check information for the book. Although a distinguished diamond physicist, he nevertheless proved an invaluable source of literary information throughout my life. This book is dedicated to his memory.

Tim Woods
Aberystwyth, Wales, 2000

A

Abbas, Ahmad (1914–1987) Born Khwaja Ahmad Abbas, in Panipat, in the Punjab, India, he attended the Aligarh Muslim University in the 1930s, after which he worked for the *Bombay Chronicle* until 1947. He then worked for *Blitz* magazine in Bombay, and later became involved in film production. He was a prolific writer of novels, short stories, plays and Hindi film scripts. An extremely popular writer in English, aspects of his novels have been inspired by real historical events, causing some people to criticise the 'journalese' style of his fiction. His novels describe the Second World War, religious riots and killings, the partition of India and Pakistan, the post-Independence years of disillusionment in India, and cultural and social prejudices, such as in *Tomorrow Is Ours* (1943), which celebrates the bold opposition of a 20-year-old heroine, Parvati, to the Indian caste system. Other novels include *When Night Falls* (1968), *Maria* (1972) and *The Walls of Glass* (1977). His non-fiction includes *I Am Not an Island: An Experiment in Autobiography* (1977), *The Naxalites* (1979) and *Bombay, My Bombay!* (1987). His utilisation of popular forms and 'Bollywood' scripts has added to the academic and serious attention paid to his writing in later years. Often accused of being too political, too journalistic, too crowded and undisciplined as a writer, he was nevertheless guided by the desire to represent and include all experiences in India.

A. Habib, *The Novels of Khwaja Ahmad Abbas* (1987).

Abe, Kobe (1924–1993) Born in Tokyo, Japan, he went to Tokyo University (MD 1948), and became a widely honoured novelist and playwright. His first novel was *Inter Ice-Age Four* (1959, trans. 1970). This was followed by, among others, *The Woman in the Dunes* (1962, trans. 1964), which centres upon a man and a woman who are trapped by a tribe and forced to live at the bottom of a deep sand shaft, and their new relations and identities, *The Face of the Author* (1964, trans. 1966), told in the episodic style of letters and a journal, *The Ruined Map* (1967, trans. 1969), which uses the conventions of the detective novel as flight and pursuit merge, and *Secret Rendezvous* (1977, trans. 1979), again in episodic form dating back to tenth-century Japan. More recent works include *The Ark Sakawa* (trans. 1988), about a hermit's preparations for nuclear disaster, and *The Kangaroo Notebook* (trans. 1996), a strange surrealistic work in which the narrator wakes up one morning to find radishes sprouting from his legs and continues with horrific experiences. A collection of short stories, *Beyond the Curve* (trans. 1991), merge real and surreal events, exploring the fragility of identity. Many of his novels remain untranslated into English, as do several plays, lectures, short stories and essays. He became a director and producer of the Kobo Theatre Workshop in Tokyo in 1973. Resisting his country's nationalism in the 1930s and 1940s, his existential themes, bizarre situations, and metaphysical overtones are reminiscent of BECKETT or KAFKA, with whom he is often compared for his explorations of modern human displacement.

H. Yamanouchi, *The Search for Authenticity in Modern Japanese Literature* (1978).

Abish, Walter (1931–) Walter Abish was born in Austria, the son of prosperous Jewish parents. The Abish family fled to Nice in 1938, and then to Shanghai in 1940. He lived in Israel in the 1950s, where he served in the tank corps, and then worked as an urban planner, a job which he continued to do in New York City upon his arrival in 1960. He published two collections of early short stories entitled *Minds Meet* (1975) and *In the Future Perfect* (1977), but is best known for his experimental, postmodernist novels. His first novel, *Alphabetical Africa* (1974), is an accretive alphabetical structure of twenty-six chapters from A to Z until chapter 27, from when first Z and then the other letters of the alphabet are gradually subtracted and reversed chapter by chapter, making fifty-two chapters in all. *How German Is It* (1980), which won the PEN-Faulkner Prize (1981), is a detailed exploration of German national identity, collective consciousness and history. His pervasive playfulness with language, suggesting its general incapacity to refer to anything other than itself, recurs in *99: The New Meaning* (1990), which comprises five 'ready-made' texts, and *Eclipse Fever* (1993), which continues to explore reduced narratives. He has published a collection of poetry, entitled *Duel Site* (1971), and his current novel in progress is entitled *As If*.

Abrahams, Peter (1919–) Born in Vrededorp, Johannesburg, in South Africa, Peter Henry Abrahams was educated at several Church of England schools and colleges. He became a merchant seaman (1939–1941), and then lived in England, working as a reporter for the *Observer* and the *Herald Tribune*. His early work was influenced by Marxist ideas, and through a mainly naturalist style mixed with traditions from African oral culture, such novels as *A Song of the City* (1945), *Mine Boy* (1946) and *The Path of Thunder* (1948) explore the social, racial and cultural consequences of urbanisation and industrialisation on the lives of young black migrant workers in South African cities. On the strength of these novels, he became one of the first African writers to receive European and American critical attention. He went to Jamaica in 1957, where he worked for the *West Indian Economist*, before moving into radio journalism, eventually becoming the chairman of Radio Jamaica (1977–1980). During this time, he continued to write novels about South African society: *Wild Conquest* (1950) tells of the Afrikaner 'Great Trek', *A Wreath for Udomo* (1956) explores the consequences of African states gaining independence, and *A Night of Their Own* (1965) is about the underground politics of resistance groups in South Africa. His last two novels, *This Island Now* (1966) and *The View from Coyaba* (1985), focus on the racial tensions, politics and histories of Africa, the Caribbean and the American Deep South. He has also published a collection of short stories, *Dark Testament* (1942), and an autobiography entitled *Tell Freedom* (1954), while *Return to Goli* (1953) recounts his experiences as a mulatto in South Africa.

K. Ongungbesan, *The Writing of Peter Abrahams* (1979).

Achebe, Chinua (1930–) Born Albert Chinualumogo, in Ogidi, eastern Nigeria, he is considered to be the foremost Nigerian novelist of the twentieth century, and is a strong spokesman for African literature in the postcolonial period. After studying medicine and literature at the University of Ibadan, he worked for the Nigerian Broadcasting Corporation in Lagos. Following the Nigerian Civil War, he taught at many universities in Nigeria, Canada and the United States. His first novel, *Things Fall Apart* (1958), received widespread critical acclaim, and focused on the rise and fall of Okonkwo, an important man in the Obi tribe, in the days when Europeans were first arriving in West Africa and colonialism imposed itself on local villagers' perspective of history. He then wrote *No Longer at Ease* (1960) and *Arrow of God* (1964), both of which consider the various debilitating effects of white colonialism on Nigerian culture and society, albeit in an unsentimental fashion. *A Man of the People* (1966) was followed by *Anthills of the Savannah* (1987), a devastating critique of oligarchic power, which was shortlisted for the Booker Prize. Characteristically, Achebe makes use of oral narratives and folk tales, as he attempts to endow Nigerian culture with its own historical significance and to rescue the narratives of generations whose stories were submerged by colonial rule. In addition, he has written a number of essays on literature, culture and politics in postcolonial African writing, collected in *Morning Yet on Creation Day* (1975), *Hopes and Impediments* (1988) and *Home and Exile* (2000). One of his most controversial essays, 'An Image of Africa: Racism in Conrad's *Heart of Darkness*', has set the tone for many recent re-evaluations of CONRAD's work; while as a cultural critic, he has continually advocated that fiction must engage with social realities rather than an abstract universalism. He has also published a number of short stories and collections of poetry.

S. Gikandi, *Reading Achebe* (1991).

Acker, Kathy (1948–1997) Born in New York City, US, she studied Classics at Brandeis and the University of California at San Diego, followed by graduate work at New York University. Acknowledging the influence of the poets David Antin and Jerome Rothenberg, she initially published with small independent presses, and has since achieved international fame as a 'postmodernist' or 'punk' writer. Frequently compared with the experimental work of William BURROUGHS and Jean GENET, her writing juxtaposes violence and pornography with childhood reminiscences and narrative segments in a shifting framework of fragmented voices, perspectives and character portrayals. Her early works, written under the pseudonym of 'The Black Tarantula', and collected in *The Adult Life of Toulouse Lautrec* (1975) and *Kathy Goes to Haiti* (1978), feature graphic descriptions of sex acts, reflecting her previous employment as a porn actress. She received wide acclaim for *Blood and Guts in the High School* (1984), which is an account of Janey Smith's trials and tribulations, incorporating gritty realism and fantastical meetings. She moved to London in 1984, but returned to the US in 1989. Pastiche recurs in *Don Quixote* (1986), and other novels – including *Empire of the Senseless* (1988), *In Memoriam to Identity* (1990) and *Eurydice in the Underworld* (1997) – often negotiate an intertextual relationship with other works. She has also written poetry, plays, art criticism and a screenplay entitled *Variety* (1985). *Spectacular Optical* was published posthumously in 1998. By disrupting discourses, destabilising identities and turning plagiarism into a creative technique in her work, Acker became something of a literary *enfant terrible*, marked by her transgression of cultural and social limitations and barriers.

R. Siegle, *Suburban Ambush* (1989).

Ackroyd, Peter (1949–) Born in London, England, he studied at Cambridge (MA 1971) and Yale (1971–1973). An accomplished and versatile writer, he has won acclaim as a biographer and for writing novels which fictionalise the lives of famous historical figures. His first novel, *The Great Fire of London* (1982), whose plot and characters hinge upon a film production of Charles Dickens' *Little Dorrit*, was followed by *The Last Testament of Oscar Wilde* (1983), purporting to be Wilde's autobiography, written in Paris during the final months of his life. Other novels in the same semi-historical vein are the prize-winning *Hawksmoor* (1985), which fuses detective and horror genres in a battle between rationality and passion, involving the investigation of mysterious murders in interwoven parallel plots between the present and the eighteenth century; *Chatterton* (1988), a multiple narrative about the seventeenth-century poet exploring authenticity and originality; *First Light* (1989), about archaeology and astronomy; *English Music* (1992), which boasts another time-twisting and reality-bending plot; *The House of Doctor Dee* (1993), about the Elizabethan intellectual John Dee who practised black magic, and the contemporary Matthew Palmer living in Dee's house who investigates the lurid past; *Dan Leno and the Limehouse Golem* (1993), about mysterious murders in London in 1881; and *Milton in America* (1996), which depicts the picaresque adventures of the English poet John Milton transposed to the New World. Among several volumes of poetry is *The Diversions of Purley* (1987), and his non-fiction works include *Notes for a New Culture* (1976), condemning the intellectual trends of literary realism, empiricism and positivism, and *Dressing Up: Transvestism and Drag*

(1979). His acclaimed biographies consist of Ezra Pound (1980), T.S. Eliot (1984), Charles Dickens (1990), William Blake (1995) and Thomas More (1998). His latest work is *The Plato Papers* (1999), a blend of science fiction and fantasy set in AD 3700, with Plato the orator in London narrating the past epoch of Mouldwarp which occurred in AD 1500 to 2300. Often regarded as a postmodernist for his explorations of the way past fictions work their effects on the present, Ackroyd's novels consider the nature of art, temporality and spatiality, 'truth' and fiction, reason and emotion.

Acosta, Oscar (1935–1974?) Born in El Paso, Texas, US, Oscar Zeta Acosta has proved to be a controversial author, whose narratives focus upon the cultural history and ethnicity of the Chicano people. As a lawyer, he defended members of the Chicano movement, and as a friend of Hunter S. THOMPSON, provided the basis for his sidekick 'Dr. Gonzo', the attorney, in *Fear and Loathing in Las Vegas* (1972). He is best known for *The Autobiography of a Brown Buffalo* (1972), a fictional autobiography describing a development from an alienated lawyer to a man of prominence in the Chicano movement in Los Angeles. *The Revolt of the Cockroach People* (1973) follows the active exploits of the Chicano people as they develop their own cultural identity. In May 1974, Acosta mysteriously disappeared while writing an article on cocaine smuggling from Mexico to the United States.

Adair, Gilbert (1944–) Born in Scotland, he became a freelance writer, novelist, critic and journalist. His first novel was *The Holy Innocents* (1988), which evokes Jean COCTEAU's novel *Les Enfants Terribles* and includes references to French New Wave directors such as Jean-Luc Godard and Jacques Rivette, as it depicts the sordid pastimes of movie-loving twins and their American friend. More degradation followed in *Love and Death on Long Island* (1986, filmed 1997), in which an ageing man is obsessed with a young idol, and *The Death of the Author* (1992), in which Leopold Sfax attempts to obscure his controversial past by his own theories on the texts in question. Recent novels include *The Key of the Tower* (1997), about an unusual exchange of cars in France leading to a mysterious adventure centred upon a tower, and *A Closed Book* (1999), involving a symbiotic relationship that moves towards an increasingly disturbing and unsettling conclusion. In addition to children's books, his non-fiction includes *Hollywood's Vietnam* (1981), looking at how mainstream cinema distorts the Vietnam conflict; *Myths and Memories* (1986), which is a dissection of British cultural life; *Flickers* (1995) and *Movies* (1999), both of which are guides to the history of cinema; and essays on culture in the 1990s in *The Postmodernist Always Rings Twice* (1992) and *Surfing the Zeitgeist* (1997). He has translated French film director and critic François Truffaut's *Letters* (1989), and the *A Void* (1995) by the French novelist Georges PEREC (which does not contain any words featuring the letter 'e'). A versatile writer of intelligence and playfulness, he reveals a multiplicity of allusions in his works.

Adams, Alice (1926–1999) Born in Fredricksburg, Virginia, US, and educated at Radcliffe College (1946), she subsequently worked in publishing in New York, and later moved to California. Her novels include *Families and Survivors* (1974), *Listening to Billie* (1978), *Rich Rewards* (1980) and *Superior Women* (1984). Her work frequently portrays women's emotional and financial struggles in family relationships, as they attempt to define their work and emotional lives. *Second Chances* (1988) portrays long-time friends having important relationships in later life. Subsequent novels include *Caroline's Daughters* (1991), *Al-*

most *Perfect* (1993), *A Southern Exposure* (1995), *Medicine Men* (1997) and *The Last Lovely City* (1999). Her last book, *After the War* (2000), is a sequel to *A Southern Exposure*, set in North Carolina during the Cold War years. Her short stories are collected in *Beautiful Girl* (1979), *You Can't Keep a Good Woman Down* (1981), *To See You Again* (1982), *Return Trips* (1986) and *After You've Gone* (1989), and show the imprint of rural life and farm culture. Known for her frank depiction of female sexuality, her novels have received mixed reviews, and are often criticised for their coincidental plots and soap opera style.

Adams, Douglas (1952–) Born in Cambridge, England, Douglas Noel Adams graduated from the University of Cambridge (MA 1974) and became a novelist and scriptwriter (1978). He is best known for the incredibly successful 1978 BBC cult radio series (later adapted for television), *The Hitchhiker's Guide to the Galaxy* (1979), and continued with *The Restaurant at the End of the Universe* (1980), *Life, the Universe and Everything* (1982), *So Long, and Thanks for All the Fish* (1984) and latterly, *Mostly Harmless* (1992), published in the omnibus volume, *The Hitchhiker's Trilogy* (1984). A comic satire, it tells of the outlandish space adventures of Arthur Dent, a bewildered Englishman, and his alien friend, Ford Prefect. In its bizarre and zany perspective, its gift for characterisation and eye for humour, it upsets all science-fiction clichés. Other books include *The Meaning of Liff* (1983, rev. 1990), and he does for the detective genre what he did for science fiction in two detective novels, *Dirk Gently's Holistic Detective Agency* (1987) and *The Long Dark Tea-Time of the Soul* (1988). Author of numerous television scripts, including episodes for the BBC's *Doctor Who* series, he has also written a travelogue about the endangered species of the Far East, New Zealand and Zaïre in *Last Chance to See* (1990). He has recently published a science fiction adventure on CD-ROM entitled *Starship Titanic* (1998).

Adams, Richard (1920–) Richard George Adams was born in Newbury, Berkshire, England. After service in the British army during the Second World War, he went to Oxford University (MA 1948) and joined the British Civil Service, when he turned to writing in 1974. He is best known for *Watership Down* (1972, filmed 1978), an extremely popular juvenile book and enjoyed by adults, about the adventures of a group of rabbits looking for a new warren. This was followed by further books centred upon animals, with *Shardik* (1974), an allegorical treatment of religious belief, set in a mythical time and place, in which the natives worship a greatbear, Shardik, *The Plague Dogs* (1977), an anthropomorphic tale of two dogs that escape from a research laboratory, and *Traveller* (1988), which sees the American Civil War through the eyes of General Robert E. Lee's horse. Other novels include *The Girl in a Swing* (1980, filmed 1989), a haunting tragedy and gripping ghost story about a marriage, and *Maia* (1985), a magical tale of romance and adventure. In addition to *The Tyger Voyage* (1976), *The Bureaucrats* (1985) and *A Nature Diary* (1985), he collected folktales in *The Unbroken Web* (1980), and wrote an autobiography, *The Day Gone By* (1990). Recent works include *Tales from Watership Down* (1996) and *The Outlandish Knight* (2000).

Agee, James (1909–1955) Born in Knoxville, Tennessee, US. After graduating from Harvard University (1932), he began his literary career with a collection of poetry *Permit Me Voyage* (1934). He served on the staffs of *Fortune* and *Time* magazines, and later the *Nation*. An article on Alabama sharecroppers in the Depression, which was published with photographs by Walker Evans as *Let Us Now Praise Famous Men* (1941), departed from ob-

jective reporting, adopting instead a more subjective, impressionistic style, and was widely acclaimed. *The Morning Watch* (1951), a novel about a day in the life of a 12-year-old Tennessee schoolboy, was a prelude to his principal novel, *A Death in the Family* (1957, Pulitzer Prize). Part autobiography, this was a story about a happy, secure Tennessee family wrecked by the father's accidental death. His cinema reviews are collected in *Agee on Film* (1958), while *Agee on Film: II* (1960) includes his screenplays of Stephen Crane's short stories among others. His correspondence with a family mentor was published as *Letters to Father Flye* (1962), and *Selected Journalism* (1985) gathered unreprinted articles. His *Collected Poems* were published in 1968.

A. Spiegel, *James Agee and the Legend of Himself* (1998).

Agnon, S.Y. (1888–1970) Born Shmuel Yosef Halesi Czaczkes Agnon, in Buczacz, Galicia, in the Austro-Hungarian empire (now Poland). He lived in Palestine between 1907 and 1913, after which time he became a lecturer in Germany, before returning to Palestine in 1924 where he held various academic posts. Although widely honoured, he is not well known outside of Israel, despite being awarded the Nobel Prize for Literature in 1966. His first published work was in 1919, and he continued to publish prolifically in Hebrew under the pen-name Agnon. His novels include *The Bridal Canopy* (1931, trans. 1937), which portrays the Old World culture, and the adventures of a Jewish man travelling in search of dowries for his daughters, *A Simple Story* (1935, trans. 1985), about a man's thwarted love, his psychosis and his gradual return to normality, *A Guest for the Night* (1939, trans. 1968), about a man trying to adjust to the changes in a Polish village upon his return from Palestine, and *In the Heart of the Seas* (1935, trans. 1948), a vivid sea adventure from Galicia to Palestine. Other works include *Tehilla* (trans. 1956), *Twenty-One Stories* (trans. 1970), *Shira* (1971, trans. 1989) and *A Dwelling Place of My People: Sixteen Stories of the Chassidim* (trans. 1983), and various short stories, letters and commentaries. A man of two worlds – his ancestors' Judaic tradition and the realm of modernity – his works return to the traditions and laws of the ancient sources of medieval Hebrew, and revive ancient forms of storytelling eschewing the modern 'realist' tradition. The epitome of Jewish folk-literature for some, his fiction pivots on a feeling of loss and a blend of Judaic and Yiddish realism and mysticism.

D. Patterson and G. Abrahamson, eds, *Tradition and Trauma: Studies in the Fiction of S.Y. Agnon* (1994).

Aidoo, Ama Ata (1942–) Born near Saltpond, Ghana, she graduated from the University of Ghana in 1964. She has held fellowships in creative writing at Stanford University in California, the Institute of African Studies, and has worked at universities in Ghana, Kenya and Nigeria. She began with *The Dilemma of a Ghost* (1965), a play which examines the social and cultural dislocation of young, western-educated Ghanaians returning to their village communities. Another play, *Anowa* (1969), focuses on marriage, women's assertiveness, masculinity and slave ownership. Her experimental novel, *Our Sister Killjoy* (1977), considers the interrelationship of gender and race, and was followed by *Changes: A Love Story* (1991), an exploration of the conflict of value-systems in marriage. Poetry collections like *Someone Talking to Sometime* (1985) and *An Angry Letter in January* (1992), engage with the continent's problems of poverty, ethnicity and the idealist politics of radical ideologues, while collections of short stories like *No Sweetness Here* (1970) and *The Girl Who Can* (1996), show identity and role to be the subject of fierce negotiation. Like many other West African writers, the art of oration is an important source in her writing.

Aiken, Joan (1924–) Born in Rye, Sussex, England, Joan Delano Aiken is the daughter of the American poet and critic Conrad Aiken. She has worked for the BBC, the United Nations Information Office, and was a journalist between 1955 and 1960, before turning to full-time writing. She is most famous for her children's fiction, and is credited as having invented the 'unhistorical romance', in which fairy tale is combined with romance, myth and history in fast-paced narratives of action and humour. Often set in an imaginary period during the reign of James III in England, among her books are the well known *The Wolves of Willoughby Chase* (1962), *Black Hearts at Battersea* (1964), *The Whispering Mountain* (1968) and *The Stolen Lake* (1981). She has also written a plethora of adult fiction, including detective novels in *Trouble with Product X* (1966) and *Hate Begins at Home* (1967), and horror and suspense in *The Windscreen Wipers* (1969), *A Whisper in the Night* (1982) and the short stories, *A Touch of Chill* (1979). However, she has also written several fictional treatments of characters from Jane Austen's novels, including *Mansfield Revisited* (1984), *Jane Fairfax: Jane Austen's Emma Through Another's Eyes* (1990), a sequel to *Emma*, *Eliza's Daughter* (1994), a sequel to *Sense and Sensibility*, *Emma Watson* (1996), continuing Austen's unfinished *The Watsons*, and *The Young Miss Ward* (1998), in which she imagines the early history of three basic characters from *Mansfield Park*.

Alain-Fournier (1885–1914) Born Henri-Alban Fournier in La Chapelle-d'Angillon, France, he was educated at the École Normale Supérieure, Paris, and killed in action in 1914. He was a journalist, poet and novelist who wrote under the pseudonym Alain-Fournier. He is principally known for one novel published before his death in the First World War, entitled *The Wanderer* (1913, trans. 1928, also as *The Lost Domain*, trans. 1959). This follows the nostalgic quest of the protagonist, trying to recapture the lost love and dreams of youth. It is based upon a romantic episode in the author's own life, and is characterised by a simple, uncomplicated style and intense lyricism. A posthumous collection of prose and poetry was published as *Miracles* (trans. 1924), together with several volumes of correspondence.

R. Gibson, *The Quest of Alain-Fournier* (1953).

Aldington, Richard (1892–1962) Born in Hampshire, England, Richard Edward Godfree Aldington was educated at University College, London, and rose to prominence in several literary capacities. A founder poet of the Imagist movement around 1912, notable for its free verse and vivid images, he befriended Ezra Pound and married the Imagist poet Hilda DOOLITTLE in 1913 (they divorced in 1937), and his *Complete Poems* was published in 1948. Serving with the infantry during the First World War, he became a noted novelist who depicted the horror of the conflict; although after the war, disillusioned with the British literary scene, he moved to France and lived as an expatriate. Indeed, his postwar writings are deeply pessimistic, such as the firsthand account of the war in his most significant novel *Death of a Hero* (1929), which is partly autobiographical and depicts the alienating impact of war on civilian life. Several further novels followed, including *The Colonel's Daughter* (1931), *Stepping Heavenward* (1931), which is a caricature of T.S. Eliot, *All Men Are Enemies* (1933), *Women Must Work* (1934), the comic farce *Seven Against Reeves* (1938), *Reflected Guests* (1939) and *Romance of Casanova* (1946). A prolific translator and editor, especially of Oscar Wilde and D.H. LAWRENCE,

many of his critical writings, essays, and volumes of letters have also been published. Short stories occur in *Soft Answers* (1930), *At All Costs* (1930) and *Roads to Glory* (1930). In addition to the memoir *Life for Life's Sake* (1941), he wrote critical biographies of D.H. Lawrence (1950) and of Lawrence of Arabia (1955) after having moved to the US during the Second World War. Despite lacking the same degree of popularity today as some of his contemporaries, his writing is still a good example of the preoccupations of his generation.

C. Doyle, *Richard Aldington: A Biography* (1989).

Aldiss, Brian W. (1925–) A prolific English science fiction writer, Brian Wilson Aldiss was born in East Dereham, Norfolk, in England. He served with the British army in the Far East during the Second World War, and then worked as a bookseller in Oxford, England. After *The Brightfount Diaries* (1955), his first science fiction novel was *Non-Stop* (1958), set in the enclosed world of a spaceship. During the 1960s, he was associated with Michael Moorcock and his *New Worlds* magazine, and his work at this time is characterised by innovative literary techniques and an open treatment of sex. His better known novels include *Hothouse* (1962), linked stories set in the tropical abundance of an expiring Earth, *The Saliva Tree* (1966), the bleak novels of *Greybeard* (1964) and *Earthworks* (1966), and the linguistically experimental novels of *An Age* (1967), *Report on Probability A* (1968) and *Barefoot in the Head* (1969). In the 1970s, a collection of novels entitled *The Horatio Stubbs Saga* explored the adventures of a young soldier in Burma (now Myanmar). Later fiction includes *Frankenstein Unbound* (1973), acknowledging the influence of Mary Shelley's novel on science fiction, *A Rude Awakening* (1978), *Moreau's Other Island* (1980), which alludes to

H.G. Wells' novel *The Island of Dr. Moreau*, *Life in the West* (1980), *Dracula Unbound* (1991) and *White Mars, or, the Mind Set Free* (1999). His 'Helliconia Trilogy' (*Helliconia Spring*, 1982; *Helliconia Summer*, 1983; *Helliconia Winter*, 1985) is an epic encompassing the history of an entire planetary system. In addition, he has edited many anthologies, for example *The Best Science Fiction Stories of Brian W. Aldiss* (1965) and *A Brian Aldiss Omnibus* (1969 and 1971), and published a number of short story collections including *The Canopy of Time* (1959), *Intangibles Inc.* (1969), *Neanderthal Planet* (1970), *Foreign Bodies* (1981) and *The Secret of This Book* (1995). He has also written a history of science fiction in *Billion Year Spree* (1973), *Cities and Stories: A Traveller's Jugoslavia* (1966), as well as autobiography in *The Hand-Reared Boy* (1970), *A Soldier Erect* (1971), *Bury My Heart at W.H. Smiths: A Writing Life* (1990) and *The Twinkling of an Eye* (1998).

B. Griffin, *Apertures: A Study of the Writings of Brian W. Aldiss* (1984).

Aldridge, James (1918–) Born in White Hills, Victoria, Australia, he became a successful journalist in Europe and a war correspondent during the Second World War. His early novels, *Signed with Their Honour* (1942), *The Sea Eagle* (1944) and *Of Many Men* (1946), were war stories set in Greece, Egypt, Finland and Russia. *The Diplomat* (1950), about an Anglo-American-Russian dispute over Iran and its oil, was a best-seller in Russia, and established him as a major political novelist with Marxist persuasions. His other novels include *Heroes of the Empty View* (1954), *The Last Exile* (1961), which focuses upon the British rule in Egypt and the Suez Crisis, *The Stateman's Game* (1966), *My Brother Tom* (1966), about small-town life and religious factions in Australia, *I Wish He Would Not Die* (1957), about the war in Egypt and the

Western Desert, *A Sporting Proposition* (1973), *Mockery in Arms* (1974), *The Untouchable Juli* (1975), *Goodbye Un-America* (1979) and *The Broken Saddle* (1982). Short stories occur in *Gold and Sand* (1960), non-fiction in *Living Egypt* (1969) and *Cairo* (1969), and he has also written several books for children.

Aleichem, Sholom (1859–1916) Born Sholem Rabinovitch in Pereyaslev, Ukraine, Russia, he was a Yiddish novelist whose pseudonym is a traditional greeting in Hebrew, meaning 'Peace be unto you'. He has become one of the most widely read and translated Yiddish writers of all time. With the publication of his first story in 1883, he devoted himself to the dissemination of Jewish culture. The first episode of the epistolary series *Menahem Mendl* (1892), was followed by the first story of *Tevye der Milkhiker* (1894). These two characters are most famously associated with his name, especially his tales of Tevye the dairyman, which were adapted into the highly successful musical *Fiddler on the Roof*. His principal translated works include *The Old Country* (trans. 1946), *Teyve's Daughters* (trans. 1949), *Adventures of Mottel, the Cantor's Son* (trans. 1953), *The Tevye Stories* (trans. 1959) and *The Adventures of Menahem-Mendl* (trans. 1969). Owing to the stories' humour and their ability to capture the lifestyle and traditions of the Yiddish communities of the eastern European shtetls, Aleichem became known as 'the Jewish Mark Twain'.

Alexie, Sherman (1966–) Born Sherman Joseph Jr. Alexie, in Spokane, Washington, US, he graduated from Washington State University (BA 1991), and quickly gained high praise for his poetry and fiction of contemporary Native-American life. He draws heavily upon his experiences as a Spokane/Coeur d'Alene Native-American, who grew up and still lives on the Spokane Indian Reservation in Washington. His early volumes are poetry, including *The Business of Fancydancing* (1992), *I Would Steal Horses* (1992), *First Indian on the Moon* (1993) and *Old Shirts and New Skins* (1993). His latest poetry occurs in *The Man Who Loves Salmon* (1998) and *One Stick Song* (1999). His fiction writing first appeared in the short story collection *The Lone Ranger and Tonto Fistfight in Heaven* (1993) which, like much of his poetry, depicts the despair, poverty and alcoholism that often pervade Native-American life. The various characters in these stories were picked up again in his first novel, *Reservation Blues* (1994), in which the young Native-American friends come into possession of the legendary blues musician Robert Johnson's magical guitar, and form a rock band, their trials and tribulations bringing the Native and Anglo cultures into conflict. This was followed by *Indian Killer* (1996), a controversial murder mystery novel about a killer in Seattle scalping his victims which leads to racial tension and violence in the city. More recently, he has written the screenplay, *Smoke Signals* (1998), and the short stories in *The Toughest Indian in the World* (2000).

Algren, Nelson (1909–1981) Born in Detroit, Michigan, US, he grew up in a poverty stricken Jewish family in the Chicago slums. After a degree at the University of Illinois at Urbana, he managed the Illinois Writers' Project for the Works Progress Administration (1936–1940). His literary career based on novels of social protest and proletarian realism began with *Somebody in Boots* (1935), about a poor white Texan boy during the Depression, and continued in *Never Come Morning* (1942), about a Polish hoodlum in Chicago who dreams of becoming a prizefighter. His famous novel *The Man with the Golden Arm* (1949), depicts the life of Frankie Machine among scenes of gambling and drug addiction in Chicago, showing how the corrupt environment frustrates people's lives. It earned

Algren the distinction of being the first recipient of the National Book Award, and the screen adaptation (1956) starred Frank Sinatra. *A Walk on the Wild Side* (1956) presents an erotic and bohemian underworld in New Orleans during the Depression. A collection of stories appeared in *Neon Wilderness* (1947), and *Who Lost an American?* (1963) sketched life in New York and Chicago and travels abroad. Other occasional writings include *Conversations* (1964), *Notes from a Sea Diary* (1965) and *The Last Counsel* (1973). His romance with Simone de BEAUVOIR is treated in her autobiography *Force of Circumstance* and, to an extent, in her novel *The Mandarins*.

M. Cox and W. Chatterton, *Nelson Algren* (1975).

Ali, Ahmed (1910–1994) Born in Delhi, India, he was educated at Lucknow University (BA 1930, MA 1931), and lectured in English at various universities (1931–1942). In his early days, he formed the Progressive Writers' Association (1936), which caused some political discontent by bringing modernist aesthetics and Marxism to Indian literature. He moved to Pakistan where he served in the diplomatic service and held various government positions. In addition to various stories, plays and poems in Urdu, he has written several novels in English. *Twilight in Delhi* (1940) was a highly acclaimed novel and is now regarded as a classic, depicting the decay of the Muslim élite in India in the early twentieth century. His other novels include *Ocean of Night* (1964) and *Rats and Diplomats* (1985), whilst his short stories in *The Prison-House* (1985) experimented with new techniques in combining realism with symbolism and introspection. Other works include *Mr. Eliot's Penny World of Dreams* (1942), *The Failure of Intellect* (1968), *The Shadow and the Substance* (1977), which collects essays on art, literature and philosophy, and he edited

Under the Green Canopy (1966) and *Selected Pakistani Stories* (1988), anthologies of writing from Pakistan. He also translated the Koran from Arabic (1984).

Allen, Paula Gunn (1939–) Born in Albuquerque, New Mexico, of Laguna Pueblo, Sioux and Lebanese descent, she grew up in Cubero, New Mexico, a member of the Laguna and Acoma Pueblo Native-American communities. She gained a doctorate from the University of New Mexico, and has taught at a variety of universities and is currently at the University of California at Berkeley. She began writing poetry in the 1960s under guidance from Robert Creeley and has published several volumes including *Shadow Country* (1982), *WYRDS* (1987), *Skins and Bones* (1988) and *Life Is a Fatal Disease* (1997), often about tribal consciousness, the pueblos and deserts. In her first novel, *The Woman Who Owned the Shadows* (1983), the racially mixed protagonist, Ephanie, validates her own lesbianism through a spiritual and emotional quest, by forging links between her personal past and the mythic aspects of her tribal heritage. In addition, Allen has steadily pursued scholarship and been central to the extension of Native-American Studies, such as with the two edited anthologies of essays in *Studies in American Indian Literature* (1983) and *Spider Woman's Granddaughters* (1989), and her study *The Sacred Hoop* (1986), which seeks to unearth the feminine aspects of tribal cultures erased by Anglo-European representations of Native-Americans. Her collections of Native-American myths and stories central to women's spiritual condition are gathered in *Grandmothers of Light* (1991), and there is a two-volume study entitled *Voice of the Turtle: American Indian Fiction* (1994) and *Song of the Turtle: American Indian Literature* (1996). *Off the Reservation* (1998) collects essays, criticism and personal reflections. An anti-nuclear, peace and environmental activist, her interests have centred upon Native-American feminine rituals and traditions.

A. LaVonne Brown Ruoff, *American Indian Literatures* (1990).

Allende, Isabel (1942–) A Chilean novelist born in Lima, Peru, she is the niece of the late Salvador Allende, who was the President of Chile from 1970–1973. She worked for the UN in Santiago (1959–1965), and then as a journalist and editor of *Paula* magazine (1967–1974). She has subsequently been a television interviewer (1970–1975) and an administrator in Caracas (1979–1982), before turning to fiction. Her first novel was *The House of Spirits* (1982, trans. 1985 and filmed 1994), which adopts the format of the family saga, narrating modern Chilean history from a broadly socialist perspective, and criticising the right-wing government. This was followed by *Of Love and Shadows* (1984, trans. 1987), about a young woman possessed by spirits and denouncing the abuse of human rights by the Pinochet government in Chile, *Eva Luna* (1987, trans. 1988) about a glamorous transsexual, *The Stories of Eva Luna* (1990, trans. 1991), *The Infinite Plan* (1991, trans. 1993) and *Daughter of Fortune* (trans. 1999). One of South America's best-known female writers in the English-speaking world, other works include *Paula* (1994, trans. 1995), about the death of her daughter, and *Aphrodite: A Memoir of the Senses* (trans. 1998). Her work blends magical realism with idealised romantic love, strong female characters, exotic notions of South America and the worlds of soldiers, army camps and revolutionary governments, resulting in critically acclaimed best-sellers.

P. Hart, *Narrative Magic in the Fiction of Isabel Allende* (1989).

Allingham, Margery (1904–1966) A detective novelist, born in London, England, Margery Louise Allingham wrote her first novel, *Blackkerchief Dick* (1923), at the age of 19, and four early novels under the pseudonym Maxwell Marsh. She became the most pre-eminent British detective story writer between the wars, and among her vast output, she is best known for her 'Campion' series, from *The Crime at Black Dudley* (1929) to the posthumous *The Return of Mr. Campion: Uncollected Stories* (1990). Arthur Campion is a modest, aristocratic man, who matures over the years of the series, and is ably supported by the characters of his wife Amanda, his valet Magersfontein Lugg, and two police officers Charlie Luke and Stanislaus Oates. The stories have been collected in *Mr. Campion and Others* (1939), and *The Tiger in the Smoke* (1952) is often considered the best Campion novel. With zestful, eccentric though credible characters, and innovative, devious narratives, she continually devised new forms for the detective genre.

J. Thorogood, *Margery Allingham: A Biography* (1991).

Alther, Lisa (1944–) Born in Kingsport, Tennessee, US, and educated at Wellesley College (1966), she was catapulted to fame by her first novel *Kinflicks* (1976). Partly autobiographical about leaving Tennessee to move north, it offered a bleak overall vision, in which the protagonist searches for meaning in a post-nuclear environment. After publishing stories and articles in magazines, her second novel *Original Sins* (1981) concerning people who leave Tennessee for the north and gather at a funeral, presents a satirical account of a corrupt and indifferent social structure. In the face of her typical black humour and dark pessimism, *Other Women* (1984) surprisingly offers an optimistic account of a lesbian relationship which renews creative vigour, a theme that was pursued in *Bedrock* (1990), which examines a new direction in the life of a middle-aged woman bored with middle-class success and security, and *Five Minutes in Heaven* (1995),

which also explores loss and mourning in a tale of sexual awakening during the 1960s, set against the backdrop of the Stonewall gay rights riots.

Aluko, T.M. (1918–) Full name Timothy Mofolorunso Aluko, born in Ilesha, western Nigeria, he studied engineering and town planning in Nigeria and England. After various positions in public works in Nigeria, he lectured at the University of Lagos until 1979, since when he has been a consultant engineer and writer. His novels are flavoured with the Yoruba oral tradition, and he has achieved wide popularity within Nigeria as a powerful humanist-satirist exploring the various transitions of indigenous to modern modes of existence. In *One Man, One Wife* (1959), he satirises African Christian converts who spurn all aspects of their cultural heritage, while in *Kinsman and Foreman* (1966), he focuses upon the impediments of the African extended family system in contemporary society. His disillusionment with the problems of adapting to a new social structure inform *Chief, the Honourable Minister* (1970), while other novels, such as *One Man, One Matchet* (1964), *His Worshipful Majesty* (1973), *Wrong Ones in the Dock* (1982), *A State of Our Own* (1986) and *Conduct Unbecoming* (1993), investigate the hybridity of indigenous and western cultures. Whilst outlining the positive and negative aspects of both cultures, there is nevertheless strong support for the preservation of African customs and traditions. He has also written an autobiography, *My Years of Service* (1994).

M. Laurence, *Long Drums and Cannons* (1968).

Amadi, Elechi (1934–) Born in Aluu, Nigeria, he attended University College, Ibadan, graduating in physics and mathematics in 1959. He was associated with the military for many years as a soldier and administrator. He has published four novels – *The Concubine* (1966), *The Great Ponds* (1969), *The Slave* (1978) and *Estrangement* (1986) – as well as four plays, a memoir entitled *Sunset in Biafra* (1973), and a collection of essays entitled *Ethics in Nigerian Culture* (1982). Drawing upon the Nigerian rural environment for his fictional settings, he is well known for his depictions of closely knit postcolonial African communities, focusing upon romance, religions, beliefs, family arguments, and the collective values that characterised most African communities before colonial contact. However, his fiction shows ironic twists, hopes thwarted, and undermining forces at work, displaying a strong sense of disillusionment with humanity's antics and the organisation of power and authority.

E. Eko, *Elechi Amadi: The Man and his Work* (1991).

Amado, Jorge (1912–) Arguably the most famous Brazilian novelist, Jorge Fazenda Arucídia Amado was born in Ferradas, Brazil, and after graduating from the Federal University, Rio de Janeiro (1935), he worked as a reporter. A Communist deputy in the Brazilian parliament (1945–1948), he was forced into a series of exiles in the 1940s after the Communist Party was outlawed. He later became editor of the journal *Para Todos* in Rio de Janeiro in the 1950s. Hugely prolific, his many novels translated into English include the early 'proletarian' concerns in *Jubiabá* (1953, trans. 1984), which examines the African-Brazilian culture of Bahia and the developing political consciousness among the working classes, and further colourful stories idealising the struggles of the poor in *Sea of Death* (1936, trans. 1984), *Captains of the Sands* (1937, trans. 1988) and *The Golden Harvest* (1944, trans. 1992). Many consider *The Violent Land* (1943, trans. 1945) his most powerful novel, which documents the struggle of rival cocoa planters in south Bahia. A second phase in his fiction occurred with

Gabriela, Clove and Cinnamon (1959, trans. 1962), *Home Is the Sailor* (1961, trans. 1964) and *Donna Flor and Her Two Husbands* (1966, trans. 1969), which present colourful tales of regional life without the ideological orientation of his earlier work. Later novels include *Tieta, the Goat Girl* (1977, trans. 1979), *Showdown* (1984, trans. 1988) and *The War of the Saints* (1988, trans. 1993). Early social realism gave way to an increased use of popular culture and expression, and some have argued that his literary populism, regional exoticism and intense sentimentalism have compromised the quality of his writing.

B. Chamberlain, *Jorge Amado* (1990).

Ambler, Eric (1909–1998) A writer of espionage and crime fiction, born in London, England. He studied engineering at the University of London (1924–1927), and after working in advertising, turned to writing in 1937. His first successes were *The Dark Frontier* (1936), *Epitaph for a Spy* (1938), *Cause for Alarm* (1938), *The Mask of Dimitrios* (1939) and *Journey into Fear* (1940). During service with the British army during the Second World War, he became an army film director, and went on to write and produce films for the Rank Organisation after the war, his most famous screenplay being *The Cruel Sea* (1953). His thrillers are often written from a left-wing perspective in distinction from those of the more conservative, establishment works of people like John BUCHAN. His post-war novels were more varied in their style, and include *Judgment on Deltchev* (1951), set in the Balkans and based on Ambler's own knowledge of Europe, *The Schirmer Inheritance* (1953), *The Night-Comers* (1956), about a revolution in South-East Asia, *Passage to Arms* (1960) and *The Light of Day* (1962). There followed *The Levanter* (1972), *Doctor Frigo* (1974), set in the French Antilles, *Send No More Roses* (1977) and *The Care of Time*

(1981). His short stories are collected in *Waiting for Orders* (1990), and in 1985 he published *Here Lies: An Autobiography*. Several of his novels were made into films. He made his name as the first to conceive of realistic stories about intelligence operations, remoulding the genre conventions to create gritty, credible worlds with few patriotic idealists.

Amis, Kingsley (1922–1995) An English writer, born in London and educated at Oxford University (BA 1949), after which he taught at various universities. His first novel, *Lucky Jim* (1954), remains his most popular work, and is about a new, young, accident-prone lecturer, Jim Dixon, at a red-brick university, and satirises the self-importance and selfishness of the incumbent academics. As a result, Amis was associated with the social discontent of the 'angry young men' like John Osborne, Alan SILLITOE and Stan BARSTOW. Many of his later books were similarly bitingly satirical about middle-class British life and its mores, and include *That Uncertain Feeling* (1955), *I Like It Here* (1958), *Take a Girl Like You* (1960), *One Fat Englishman* (1963), about an English academic on sabbatical in America, *Ending Up* (1974), *Jake's Thing* (1976), a farce about male impotence, *Stanley and the Women* (1984), *That Uncertain Feeling* (1985), *The Old Devils* (1986, Booker Prize), a humorous look at middle-class Welsh people, *Difficulties with Girls* (1988), *The Folks That Live on the Hill* (1990), a satirical portrayal of middle age, *The Russian Girl* (1992), a comedy of manners, and *The Biographer's Moustache* (1995). He experimented with a number of different styles and genres during his career, and he also wrote several mystery stories, including *The Green Man* (1969), *The Riverside Villas Murder* (1973) and *The Darkwater Hall Mystery* (1978). As a poet, Amis was a representative member of a group known as 'The Movement', which produced direct, strictly metrical

and erudite verse. He was knighted in 1990 and his *Memoirs* were published in 1991. Known for his curmudgeonly manner, his fiction was always irreverent, iconoclastic and witty, yet often criticised by feminists for his antagonistic representations of women.

R. Bradford, *Kingsley Amis* (1989).

Amis, Martin (1949–) Martin Louis Amis was born in Oxford, England, the son of the novelist Kingsley AMIS. He went to Oxford University (BA 1971), and then worked as an editor and journalist with the *Times Literary Supplement* and *New Statesman*, before eventually turning to writing full-time in 1980. His first novel *The Rachel Papers* (1973, filmed 1989) was published at the age of 24, and proved controversial for its candid view of teenage sex in the swinging Britain of the early 1970s. *Dead Babies* (1975) continued the focus on the bizarre and decadent, while *Success* (1978) examined a family rivalry between brothers and their mixed fortunes. Further novels include *Other People* (1981), a mystery story with a profusion of doubles and complicated plots, *Money: A Suicide Note* (1984), depicting a culture obsessed with money and addiction, *London Fields* (1989), celebrated for its style and about a 1999 post-Thatcherite Britain and a bizarre sexual triangle of two men and a woman, and *Time's Arrow* (1991), in which time runs backwards. After *The Information* (1995), a satire about the publishing world and how the careers of two middle-aged friends who are writers affect each other, his most recent novel is *Night Train* (1997), a detective fiction about an apparently pointless murder. *Experience* (2000) is a candid memoir, recording the changing literary scene both in the UK and in the US, with many anecdotes and pen-portraits. Essays are collected in *The Moranic Inferno* (1986), *Einstein's Monsters* (1987) and *Visiting Mrs Nabokov* (1993), while short stories occur in *Heavy Water* (1998). Although he has developed a reputation as the 'bad boy' of British literature, he is nevertheless one of the leading contemporary British writers, recently made famous for commanding huge publisher's advances. His self-conscious fictional works are filled with wordplay, displaying a satirical and contemptuous attitude to what is perceived of as the depraved popular culture of contemporary Britain. His subsequent move to the US has caused a flurry of debate in the British media.

J. Diedrick, *Understanding Martin Amis* (1995).

Anand, Mulk Raj (1905–) A widely honoured writer who, together with Raja RAO and R.K. NARAYAN, is internationally recognised as one the most distinguished Anglo-Indian novelists of the twentieth century. Born in Peshawar, India, he was educated at Punjab University (BA 1924) and the University of London (Ph.D. 1929), and held various university posts between 1930 and 1966. He has been a director of Kutab Publishers in Bombay since 1946. His first novel was *Untouchable* (1935), one of his best known works, about a day in the life of Bakha, a young Indian 'untouchable', and the abuses and humiliations of the caste system. A prolific writer, he has written many novels, among which are *Coolie* (1936), about a lowly worker in pre-Second World War India, and *Two Leaves and a Bud* (1937), about exploitation on a tea plantation in Assam. A trilogy, consisting of *The Village* (1939), *Across the Black Waters* (1940) and *The Sword and the Sickle* (1942), involves the unsuccessful attempts by a Punjabi peasant to achieve justice in an inhospitable world, and was followed by *The Big Heart* (1945) and *The Road* (1961). A new direction after the war was marked by *The Private Life of an Indian Prince* (1953), a much respected, semi-autobiographical novel, which focused upon inner struggles rather than public political ones, and was continued with

The Old Woman and the Cow (1960), *Death of a Hero* (1963), *Morning Face* (1968), *Confession of a Lover* (1976) and *The Bubble* (1984). A writer of many short stories, collections include *The Lost Child* (1934), *The Barber's Trade Union* (1944), *The Power of Darkness* (1958), *Lajwanti* (1966) and *Tales Told by an Idiot* (1999). In addition to a vast amount of social commentary and art criticism, he also wrote a memoir entitled *Seven Summers* (1951), and his letters were edited in *Anand to Alma* (1994). A cosmopolitan writer enacting a dialogue between East and West, his grittily realist fiction is intensely political. Mahatma Ghandi proved to be a significant influence in shaping his political and social ideas, and his explorations of exploitation, colonisation and the Indian caste system are also strongly indebted to western socialism.

R. Dhawan, ed., *The Novels of Mulk Raj Anand* (1992).

Anaya, Rudolfo A. (1937–) Born in Pastura, New Mexico, Rudolfo Alfonso Anaya completed a degree at the University of New Mexico and taught at schools in Albuquerque and then at the University. His first novel, *Bless Me, Ultima* (1972), established him in the first rank of Chicano writers, introducing types and characters innovative to Chicano fiction. In Antonio Marez's first person narrative of his childhood and maturity, Anaya uses magic realism to create a new identity out of Spanish, Indian and Anglo elements. *Heart of Aztlan* (1976) and *Tortuga* (1979) completed the trilogy for which he became best known. His fiction continued to focus on racial identities in novels like *Lord of the Dawn* (1987), and *Alburquerque* (the original Spanish spelling, 1992), an adventure and political satire, wherein a ruthless real-estate developer seeks to turn the city into a desert Venice by diverting the Rio Grande. *Zia Summer* (1995) and *Jalamonta: A Message from the Desert* (1996) weave the historical with the mythical in an exploration of the variety of Chicano culture. A collection of his poetry is published in *The Adventures of Juan Chicaspatas* (1985), and short stories occur in *The Silence of Llano* (1982). He has edited a variety of anthologies, among which is *Voces: An Anthology of Nuevo Mexicano Writers* (1987), and has written several plays, travel narratives and children's stories. His most recent novel is *Shaman Winter* (1999), which entwines legend, dreams, mythical characters and the mysterious disappearance of young girls.

Anderson, Barbara (1926–) Born in New Zealand, she was educated at the University of Otago (BA 1946), and Victoria University in Wellington, where she has occasionally taught. Beginning with short stories in *The Peacocks* (1985) and *I Think We Should Go Into the Jungle* (1989), she turned to fiction late in her career. Her first novel, *Girls High* (1990), set in a school, was not a major success, but she continued with *We Could Celebrate* (1991) and established herself as a novelist with *Portrait of the Artist's Wife* (1992). Her most acclaimed novel is *All the Nice Girls* (1993), about an adulterous affair set in New Zealand in 1962. Other novels include *The House Guest* (1995), *Proud Garments* (1996) and *Long Hot Summer* (1999), all of which demonstrate her combination of wit and stylish prose. Her essays are collected in *Beginnings* (1998).

Anderson, Jessica (1923–) Born in Brisbane, Australia, she went to Europe when she was 21 years old, but returned to Sydney, where she has lived since 1946. Her best fiction occurs in the novels *The Commandant* (1975), a historical fiction about the processes of colonisation and focused upon a penal settlement on Brisbane River in the 1830s; *Tirra Lirra by the River* (1978), about Nora, the protagonist, whose spiritual progression from

the colonial periphery to the metropolis of London occurs in her journey back to the motherland England; and *The Impersonators* (1980, published in the UK as *The Only Daughter*, 1985), which explores expatriation and a family's acceptance of Australia as home in the 1970s. Other novels include *An Ordinary Lunacy* (1963), which explores obsessive passion in Sydney society, *The Last Man's Head* (1970), which is a psychological and moral crime novel, *Taking Shelter* (1990) and *One of the Wattle Birds* (1994). Short fiction occurs in *Stories from the Warm Zone and Sydney Stories* (1987), in which she contrasts the different regions of subtropical Brisbane and urban Sydney and explores the intersections of colonialism and gender. Her compressed style and delicate irony reflect the influence of Henry James; while her postcolonial concerns manifest themselves in the contrast between Europe and Australia, and an ambivalence about place and the journey.

Anderson, Sherwood (1876–1941) Born in Camden, Ohio, US, into an itinerant poor white family, he served in the Spanish-American War and held a variety of jobs before abandoning his family and children to move to Chicago in 1912 to become a full-time writer, under the guidance of Carl Sandburg, Theodor DREISER and Floyd Dell. His first novels, *Windy McPherson's Son* (1916) and *Marching Men* (1917), both concerned the claustrophobia and politics of small-town life. However, it was *Winesburg, Ohio* (1919) which brought him widespread attention and projected him into the front rank of the Chicago literary renaissance. Its depiction of a small town's distrust of mechanisation and its celebration of the primeval instincts of human nature set the tone for much of what followed in *Poor White* (1920), *Dark Laughter* (1925), heavily indebted to the self-consciously naïve style of Gertrude STEIN, *Beyond Desire* (1932) and *Kit Brandon* (1936). These novels depict the frustrations, bafflements and maladjustments of typical American folk trying to come to terms with the encroachment of modernisation. He also wrote poetry and social philosophy, possibly the most pertinent to contemporary readers being *Perhaps Women* (1931). His short stories are collected in *The Triumph of the Egg* (1921), *Horses and Men* (1923) and *Death in the Woods* (1933). His autobiographical writings include *Tar: A Midwest Childhood* (1925), *The Story Teller's Story* (1924), *Memoirs* (1942) and the posthumous *Letters* (1953). He exerted particular influence over HEMINGWAY and FAULKNER, both of whom owe their first publications to his efforts.

K. Townsend, *Sherwood Anderson* (1987).

Andrić, Ivo (1892–1975) A Serbian novelist, born in Travnik, Bosnia, he was imprisoned during the First World War for his struggle against the Austro-Hungarian empire. He studied literature and history at the universities of Zagreb, Vienna, Cracow and Graz (Ph.D. 1923), after which he served in the diplomatic service until the Second World War. He built his literary reputation during the 1920s and 1930s, writing short stories about Bosnians, their yearning for happiness and inability to achieve it, the driving impetus of love and passion, and the need for inter-ethnic understanding in Bosnia. Emerging as the leading Yugoslav writer in the late 1940s, he developed these themes in his principal novels, such as the epic *The Bridge on the Drina* (1945, trans. 1959), which focuses upon a symbolic bridge that becomes a metaphor for the link between races, nationalities and religions, *The Woman from Sarajevo* (1945, trans. 1965), which is a psychological novel set in the inter-war period, *The Days of the Consuls* (1945, trans. 1996), which is another epic set during the Napoleonic era and focusing upon the survival of Bosnians as foreign interests vie for power in the Balkans, and *The Vizier's Elephant* (1948, trans. 1962).

Short stories occur in *The Damned Yard* (1954, trans. 1992) and *Pasha's Concubine* (1963, trans. 1968). Many more works from his prolific career remain untranslated into English. He became a member of the Yugoslav parliament (1949–1955) and was awarded the Nobel Prize for Literature in 1961.

E. Hawkesworth, *Ivo Andrić: Bridge Between East and West* (1984).

Angelou, Maya (1928–) Born Maya Marguerite Annie Johnson Angelou, in St. Louis, Missouri, US, and raised after her parents' divorce by her grandmother in Stamps, Arkansas, she attended school in Arkansas and California and became a singer, dancer (studying with dancer/choreographer Martha Graham), composer and actress. In the 1950s and 1960s, she became involved in black political activism in the US. After a short time as an actor, she lived in Ghana between 1963 and 1966, and wrote for the *Ghanaian Times*, edited the *African Review* (1964–1966), and then began television work in 1968 with *Black, Blues, Black*. Best known for her frank and warm-hearted multi-volume autobiography, the first volume *I Know Why the Caged Bird Sings* (1969) was a major success. It tells of the rape that left her mute for years, and she becomes a symbolic character of a young black girl growing up in America in the 1930s. Later volumes include *Gather Together in My Name* (1974), *Sing'in and Swing'in and Gettin' Merry Like Christmas* (1976), *The Heart of a Woman* (1981) about her work with Martin Luther King and Malcolm X and her arrival in Africa, and *All God's Children Need Travelling Shoes* (1986), about her experiences in Ghana. Mixing many comic, angry and dignified voices, volumes of poetry include *Just Give Me a Cool Drink of Water 'Fore I Diiie* (1971), *And Still I Rise* (1978), *I Shall Not Be Moved* (1990) and *The Complete Collected Poems of Maya Angelou* (1994). Since 1966, she has taught American Studies at Wake Forest University in North Carolina, and was recently made a Professor. She has written several screenplays, plays and a television documentary about African-Americans, a memoir concerning spirituality, sensuality and healing entitled *Wouldn't Take Nothing For My Journey Now* (1993) and personal essays in *Even the Stars Look Lonesome* (1998). A crowning moment came when she read a poem at Bill Clinton's presidential inauguration on 20 January 1993.

D. McPherson, *Order Out of Chaos* (1991).

Anthony, Michael (1930–) Born in Mayaro, Trinidad, he became a mechanic and then emigrated to London in 1954 where he worked as a journalist. In 1968, he took up the post of cultural officer at the Trinidad Embassy in Rio de Janeiro, Brazil. Returning to Trinidad in 1970, he joined the ministry of education and then became a broadcaster (1975–1989). His novels, short stories and historical works all draw upon his personal experiences. The first phase of his writing career produced his major fiction, which included *The Games Were Coming* (1963), *The Year in San Fernando* (1965) and *Green Days by the River* (1967), all about young people maturing. Other novels include *Streets of Conflict* (1976), *All That Glitters* (1981), *Bright Road to El Dorado* (1982) and *In the Heat of the Day* (1996). His second phase resulted predominantly in historical and cultural writings, among which are *Profile Trinidad* (1975), a historical survey from discovery to 1900, *The Making of Port of Spain, 1757–1939* (1978), *Heroes of the People of Trinidad and Tobago* (1986) and *Historical Dictionary of Trinidad and Tobago* (1997). Both writing periods celebrate the physical, cultural and historical landscape of Trinidad, highlighting everyday life and the disturbing implications of colonial issues. Short stories appear in *Cricket in the Road* (1973), *Sandra Street* (1973),

Folk Tales and Fantasies (1976) and *The Chieftain's Carnival* (1993).

K. Ramchand, *The West Indian Novel and its Background* (1970).

Anzaldúa, Gloria (1942–) A Chicana-American writer, critic and poet, Gloria Evangelina Anzaldúa, was born in Hargill, Texas, and educated at the University of Texas at Austin and the University of California at Santa Cruz. She has taught Chicano lesbian studies, feminist studies and creative writing at several universities. She writes about her childhood growing up on the Texas-Mexico border, and her experiences as a *mestiza* (a woman of mixed Indian and Spanish ancestry). She is best known for her poetry and prose collection, *Borderlands/La Frontera: The New Mestiza* (1987), which traces the migration of pre-Aztec Indians from what is now the US south-west to central Mexico. She weaves stories of ancient gods and goddesses, blood sacrifices, dangerous journeys undertaken by illegal Mexican immigrants to the US and the Aztec War of Flowers, as well as articulating her vision of a positive *mestiza* consciousness and artistic practice. Anzaldúa is also well known for the seminal co-edited collection, with Cherríe Moraga, *This Bridge Called My Back: Writings by Radical Women of Color* (1981), winner of the Before Columbus Foundation American Book Award. *Making Face, Making Soul/Haciendo Caras: Creative and Critical Perspectives by Women of Color* (1990) continues her commitment to the writings of women of colour and feminist politics. In addition to her children's stories, there is also an edition of *Interviews/Entrevistas* (2000).

Aragon, Louis (1897–1982) Born in Paris, France, he entered the army as a medical aide in 1917, where he met André Breton and SOUPAULT, with whom he co-founded *Littérature*, a review devoted to avant-garde poetry, Dadaism and Surrealism. He began writing poetry, incorporating the ideas of Freud, particularly the notion of love conceived of as opening the way to a synthesis of the real and the marvellous. His growing left-wing commitment in the 1930s brought disillusionment with Surrealism, and he made several journeys to the USSR, eventually marrying the Russian poet Mayakovsky's sister-in-law. From 1932, his writing turned to more specifically political ends and in 1937 he was co-editor of the communist newspaper *Ce Soir*. His novels include *The Adventures of Telemachus* (1922, trans. 1966) and *Holy Week* (1958, trans. 1962), although his main novels are a series dealing with 'le monde réel', depicting the class struggle from 1880 to 1930. This tetralogy consists of *Bells of Basel* (1934, trans. 1936), *Residential Quarter* (1936, trans. 1938), *The Century Was Young* (1942, trans. 1942) and *Aurélien* (1944, trans. 1947), all of which mix history and fiction, depicting the corruption of Parisian bourgeois life from a Marxist perspective, and often characterising ideas as people. The cycle increasingly moved from fiction to interpolate personal interjections, with flashbacks and flash-forwards. An easy and prolific writer, many of his texts remain untranslated into English, although his non-fiction includes *A History of the USSR from Lenin to Kruschev* (1962, trans. 1964). In 1939 he served in the medical brigade, and during the German Occupation of France epitomised the spirit of the Resistance. After the Second World War he devoted himself to the communist cause, although he spoke out against Soviet actions in eastern Europe. In later life, several honours were bestowed upon him, and he will be remembered for his association with Dadaism, Surrealism and as the leading communist of the Resistance.

D. Caute, *Communism and the French Intellectuals* (1964).

Archer, Jeffrey (1940–) An English novelist, born near Weston-super-Mare, Somerset, Jeffrey Howard Archer attended Oxford University (1963–1966), and at the age of 29, became the youngest MP for the British Conservative Party (1969–1974). Having earned an early fortune, he was bankrupted as a victim of fraud in 1974, causing his political demise. He turned to writing to support himself, and his first novel, *Not a Penny More, Not a Penny Less* (1976), is based on his own experiences, a fictional account of investment, fraud and revenge, and was an instant bestseller in the US. He went on to write *Shall We Tell the President?* (1977), a controversial novel set in the early 1980s about a plan to assassinate President Edward Kennedy, which caused outrage from American reviewers who accused him of callousness. He continued to write bestsellers, including *Kane and Abel* (1980), based upon the hatred of a banker and a hotelier, to which *The Prodigal Daughter* (1982) was a sequel. Other novels include *First Among Equals* (1984), *A Matter of Honour* (1986), *As the Crow Flies* (1991), *Honour Among Thieves* (1993), *The Fourth Estate* (1996) and *The Eleventh Commandment* (1998). Short stories occur in *A Quiver Full of Arrows* (1982), *A Twist in the Tale* (1989), *Twelve Red Herrings* (1994), *The Collected Short Stories* (1997) and *To Cut a Long Story Short* (2000), and he has also written plays. Both the fiction and the man have attracted much public attention and controversy, and as Deputy Chairman of the Conservative Party (1985–1986), an unproven sex scandal in 1986–1987 led to his political demise once again, and more recently has continued to dog his attempt to stand for Mayor of London.

Arenas, Reinaldo (1943–1990) Born in Holguín, Cuba, he was an autodidact and became a library researcher (1963–1968) and editor of *La Graceta de Cuba* (1968–1974). A rebellious character, he ran into trouble with the government and was imprisoned in Havana (1974–1976) and not allowed to publish. He left Cuba in 1980 and held various academic positions in the US. His novels include *Ill-Fated Peregrinations of Fray Servando* (1969, trans. 1987), which is based upon the memoirs of a Mexican friar and concerns humanity's need for liberty. A pentagony about Cuban life from the perspective of marginalised characters in the Batista regime, who are reborn and reappear in the next novel, includes *Singing from the Wall* (1967, trans. 1987), *The Palace of the White Skunks* (1980, trans. 1990) and *Farewell to the Sea* (1982, trans. 1986), the other two remaining untranslated into English. Other novels include *Graveyard of the Angels* (trans. 1987), *The Doorman* (1989, trans. 1991) and *The Assault* (1991, trans. 1994). Novellas appear in *Old Rosa* (1980, trans. 1989), whilst non-fiction includes *El Central: A Cuban Sugar Mill* (1981, trans. 1984) and *Before Night Falls* (1992, trans. 1993). A cry for freedom, his writing was noted for its processes of re-writing and the characteristics of postmodernism, manifesting his central preoccupations of homosexuality, sexuality, eroticism, violence, death and the sea.

D. Foster, ed., *Reinaldo Arenas/Francisco Soto* (1998).

Armah, Ayi Kwei (1939–) Born to Fante-speaking parents in Takoradi, Ghana, he was educated at the universities of Ghana, Accra and Harvard. He has worked variously as a translator, teacher, lecturer and journalist, travelling widely throughout Africa and Europe. He writes passionately about Africa's continuing oppression and entrapment in a cycle of neo-colonial dependency, cultures caught in the trance of whiteness and fixated on material aggrandisement. The unrelenting scatological imagery of *The Beautyful Ones Are Not Yet Born* (1968) works as a hard-hitting allegory of social mess and waste,

and together with *Fragments* (1970), stresses the sterility, corruption and economic stagnation of a sluggish, ruling bourgeoisie. *Why Are We So Blest?* (1972) explores the manner in which white, western culture continues to infiltrate and confuse the fabric of African identity. *Two Thousand Seasons* (1973) and *The Healers* (1978) experiment with peculiar and absorbing literary forms, with myth, historical realism and racial memory, while *Osiris Rising: A Novel of Africa Past, Present and Future* (1995) is his latest work. Seeking to reaffirm the value of indigenous African forms and traditional cultural attributes, his fiction acts as a pursuit of an African aesthetics and the racial retrieval of an authentic ethnic world view.

D. Wright, *Ayi Kwei Armah's Africa* (1989).

Asimov, Isaac (1920–1992) A successful and widely honoured writer of science fiction and non-fiction, he was born in Petrovichi, USSR, emigrated to the US with his family in 1923 and was naturalised in 1928. Educated at Columbia University (Ph.D. 1948), he taught biochemistry at Boston University School of Medicine, while writing prolifically on science for the layperson and science fiction, amounting to approximately 500 volumes. He contributed science fiction stories to magazines in 1939, published his first science fiction novel, *Pebble in the Sky*, in 1950, and co-wrote his first science text, *Biochemistry and Human Metabolism*, with colleagues in 1952. His most famous, award-winning science fiction work is the *Foundation* trilogy – *Foundation* (1951), *Foundation and Empire* (1952) and *Second Foundation* (1953) – a narrative about the degeneration and rebirth of a vast futuristic interstellar empire. His writing ranges across science fiction, mysteries, science fact, histories, science compendia and miscellaneous science writings, explaining nuclear fusion to number theory. His novels *The Caves of Steel* (1954) and *The*

Naked Sun (1957), and the short story collections *I, Robot* (1950), *The Stars, Like Dust* (1951) and *The Rest of the Robots* (1964), are among the most notable of his other early science fiction works. He has been credited with introducing several innovative concepts into the genre, such as robotics and the so-called 'Three Laws of Robotics' – from his famous story 'Nightfall' (1941) – a set of ethics which prohibits robots from harming human beings, and his work has had a wide influence over the fictional representation of robots. Such novels as *The Gods Themselves* (1972), *Foundation's Edge* (1982), a sequel to the trilogy, and *The Robots of Dawn* (1983) are often considered archetypal and among the best science fiction writing. Later works include *Foundation and Earth* (1986), *Prelude to Foundation* (1988) and *Forward the Foundation* (1992). Among his major science books are the *Biographical Encyclopaedia of Science and Technology* (1964) and his widely acclaimed *Asimov's New Guide to Science* (1984). In addition to the collection in two volumes, *The Complete Stories* (1990, 1992), his autobiographical volumes are *Memory Yet Green* (1979), *In Joy Still Felt* (1980) and *Yours, Isaac Asimov: A Lifetime in Letters* (1995). Written in a lucid fashion, his science fiction was based on a highly informed scientific understanding and he did much to advance the form as a respectable literary genre.

M. White, *The Unauthorised Life* (1994).

Astley, Thea (1925–) Born in Brisbane, Australia, she grew up in Queensland and was educated at the University of Queensland. She taught English at Queensland country schools and then for a period at Macquarie University in Sydney (1968–1980). Her fiction has won several prizes and tends to depict small-town life, its prejudices and perspectives, and her complex and ambivalent relationship with Queensland and Catholicism. Her first

novel, *Girl With a Monkey* (1958), was followed by *A Descant for Gossips* (1960), *The Well Dressed Explorer* (1962), *The Slow Natives* (1965), *A Boat Load of Home Folk* (1968), *The Acolyte* (1972), *A Kindness Cup* (1974) and *An Item from the Late News* (1982). This early fiction attacks complacent social attitudes with a comic vision and ironic wit, often in a verbally complicated style. *Beachmasters* (1985), set against a Pacific island's struggle for independence, was followed by *It's Raining in Mango* (1987), which examines the exploitative acts of white history in Australia, *Reaching Tin River* (1990), about a woman in search of herself, the two novellas of *Vanishing Points* (1992), and the study of old age in *Coda* (1994). Recent fiction includes *The Multiple Effects of Rainshadow* (1996) and *Drylands: A Book for the World's Last Reader* (1999). Critical of egotism, hypocrisy, pretension, and institutionalised masculine attitudes, she nevertheless keeps a distance from feminism. In addition to short stories in *Hunting the Wild Pineapple* (1979) and *Collected Stories* (1997), she has written the critical study *Three Australian Writers* (1979).

P. Gilbert, *Coming Out from Under: Contemporary Australian Women Writers* (1988).

Asturias, Miguel Ángel (1899–1974) Born in Guatemala City, Guatemala, he studied law at San Carlos University (1917–1923) and anthropology at the Sorbonne, University of Paris (1923–1928). After travelling, he returned to Guatemala in 1933, and worked as a radio broadcaster and journalist (1933–1942), and held diplomatic posts before going into exile in Argentina in 1954. He wrote novels, poetry and plays, many of which have been translated into English. *The President* (1946, trans. 1963) established his reputation, depicting a society maimed by evil and corruption, and is one of South America's most notable dictator novels. His major work is 'The Banana Trilogy', consisting of *The Cyclone* (1949, trans. 1967), *The Green Pope* (1954, trans. 1971) and *The Eyes of the Interred* (1960, trans. 1973), which amounts to a powerful criticism of the degree and manner of US control and intervention in the Guatemalan economy and its affairs. Other works include *Men of Maize* (1949, trans. 1988), which depicts the Guatemalan landscape and natural phenomena in terms of a mythical analogue, the novella *The Bejewelled Boy* (1961, trans. 1971), and *Mulatta* (1963, trans. 1967), which is analogous to the Faust legend. His deep and abiding interest in the beliefs and culture of Central American indigenous peoples is evident in his study, *Guatemalan Sociology: The Social Problem of the Indian* (1923, trans. 1977). His fiction manifests a strong Jungian element in its use of mythical archetypes, and is also characterised by aspects of surrealism and the mode of magical realism, in its unsubtle presentation of political corruption and foreign economic exploitation in Central America. He was awarded the Nobel Prize for Literature in 1967.

R. Prieto, *Miguel Ángel Asturias's Archaeology of Return* (1990).

Atwood, Margaret (1939–) A widely acclaimed and honoured Canadian novelist and poet, Margaret Eleanor Atwood was born in Ottawa, and later moved to Toronto with her family. Educated at the universities of Toronto (BA 1961) and Harvard (MA 1962), she has taught at several universities, worked as an editor, and been writer-in-residence at the University of Toronto (1972–1973). Having established herself early on as one of Canada's most prominent poets with several volumes of highly acclaimed poetry, she has continued poetry throughout her career, much of which is collected in *Poems 1976–1986* (1992) and *Eating Fire* (1998). Her first novel, *The Edible Woman* (1969), which explored the menaces and tensions of sexual politics, announced her feminist concerns with the sexual imperialism of men in her fiction. Her lifelong preoccupation with the Canadian wilderness was signalled in *Survival* (1972) and continued in *Surfacing* (1972), in which the narrator searches for her botanist father in the Canadian wilderness and confronts issues of primitive nature; while *Lady Oracle* (1976) depicts the attempts of a woman to escape the oppressions in her life by faking her death. A larger scale to her fiction came in *Life Before Man* (1979), about a love triangle in WASP Toronto, and *Bodily Harm* (1981), about an escape from a constricting relationship onto a Caribbean island. These preceded *The Handmaid's Tale* (1985), regarded by many as one of her best novels, which explores identity and survival in a society where women are completely subjugated by the masculine state. More recently, *Cat's Eye* (1988), a loosely autobiographical book about an artist returning to Toronto, was followed by *The Robber Bride* (1993), about three women's self-exploration and empowerment, and *Alias Grace* (1996), about the nineteenth-century murderess Grace Marks. Her latest novel is *The Blind Assassin* (2000, Booker Prize), combining two interlaced stories – one about a woman looking back on her life, and the other a science fiction novel by her sister before her untimely death. In addition to short stories collected in *Dancing Girls* (1977), *Bluebeard's Egg* (1983), *Murder in the Dark* (1983), in which writing itself becomes the subject, and *Wilderness Tips* (1993), she has written children's books, and criticism in *Second Words* (1982) and *Good Bones* (1992). Witty and colloquial in style, her fiction can be demanding in terms of its formal concerns; while the characters tend to be alienated or without a sense of fixed identity and place, searching for a fresh beginning.

A. and C. Davidson, eds, *The Art of Margaret Atwood* (1981).

Auchincloss, Louis (1917–) Born in Lawrence, New York, US, Louis Stanton Auchincloss attended Yale University (1935–1938) and the University of Virginia Law School (1941). He practised law for the rest of his working life, and had a brief spell in the US Naval Reserve (1941–1945). From his first novel *The Indifferent Children* (1947), written under the pseudonym Andrew Lee, about a dilettante during the Second World War, to *The Lady of Situations* (1991), about a woman who struggles to regain her social standing after losing her money in the Depression, his vast output charts the fading powers of WASP culture, often producing comedies of manners and morals, money and marriages, centred upon the New York family élites. *Life, Law and Letters* (1979) collects essays and sketches, while several volumes of short stories are focused on specific themes – for example, tales of Manhattan in *The Injustice Collectors* (1950) and *Skinny Island* (1987) – while recent short stories occur in *Tales of Yesteryear* (1994) and *The Anniversary* (1999). Recent novels include *The Rector of Justin* (1999) and *Her Infinite Variety* (2000). He has also written studies of Edith WHARTON, Shakespeare, Henry James, the Vanderbilts, Woodrow Wilson (2000), and more recently, literary criticism in *La Gloire: The Roman Empire of Corneille and Racine* (1996).

V. Piket, *Louis Auchincloss: The Growth of a Novelist* (1989).

Auster, Paul (1947–) Born in Newark, New Jersey, US, after graduating from Columbia University (MA 1970) he moved to France, during which time he was busily engaged in translation work, and essay and poetry writing, much of which is published in *Disappearances: Selected Poems* (1989) and *Ground Work* (1990). Upon his return to New York (1974), he worked in a variety of jobs before publishing his first novel under the pseudonym Paul Benjamin, *Squeeze Play* (1982), a detective story centred on baseball. There followed *The Invention of Solitude* (1982), a partly autobiographical meditation on paternity, solitude, writing and chance. Major success came with *The New York Trilogy* (1987), comprising *City of Glass* (1985), *Ghosts* (1986) and *The Locked Room* (1987), which is a set of postmodern detective stories with metaphysical twists. The trilogy self-reflexively explores the relationship between author and plot, and is filled with narrative coincidences, doublings and mysteries. Set in an apocalyptic urban environment, *In the Country of Last Things* (1987) is about Anna Blume's search for her missing brother, exploring the way knowledge is shaped by place, while *Moon Palace* (1989) extends this quest for natural language, fathers, authority and history. *The Music of Chance* (1990) continues the themes of fate, solitude and history, while *Leviathan* (1992) explores the life and work of a writer within the context of a response to contemporary politics. *Mr Vertigo* (1994) is set in the 1920s, and blends magic realism with actuality in its tale of a little boy who learns to fly after joining a travelling fair. His latest novel is *Timbuktu* (1999), about a search for an old schoolteacher seen from the perspective of a dog called Mr. Bones. Auster has recently written film scripts for his short stories, published in *Smoke and Blue in the Face* (1995) and *Lulu on the Bridge* (1998). *The Art of Hunger* (1991) collects his essays, and *Hand to Mouth: A Chronicle of Early Failure* (1997) ponders the writer's difficulties in remaining financially secure. He has edited *The Random House Book of Twentieth-Century French Poetry* (1984) and translated Pierre Clastres' encounter with a Paraguayan tribe, entitled *Chronicle of the Guayaki Indians* (1998). Auster's postmodern fiction frequently turns on questions about language, knowledge and personal emancipation, engaging with paradoxes of identity, vanishing narrators and authorial control of the text.

D. Barone, ed., *Beyond the Red Notebook* (1995).

Awoonor, Kofi (1935–) Born at Wheta, in the Volta region of Ghana, and formerly known as George Awoonor-Williams, he studied at the University of Ghana (BA 1960), London University (MA 1968) and SUNY at Stony Brook, New York (Ph.D. 1972). He was an editor of the literary magazine *Okyeame* and Chair of the Ghana Film Corporation (1964–1967), and also taught at Stony Brook (1968–1975), before becoming Professor at the University of Cape Coast, Ghana in 1976. Since 1983, he has been a diplomat in Brazil, Argentina, Venezuela, and Ghana's ambassador to the United Nations. His novel *This Earth, My Brother* (1971) describes a man's struggle to adjust his western education to his corrupt indigenous culture, and more recently, in *Comes the Voyager at Last* (1992), he examines slavery in the New World and a return to Africa. His major poetry collections include *Rediscovery* (1964, under Awoonor-Williams), *Night of My Blood* (1971), *Ride Me, Memory* (1973), *The House by the Sea* (1978) and *Guardians of the Sacred Word: Ewe Poetry* (1974), translations of the oral verse of his Ewe tribe. Much of his work draws upon folklore and folksong, repudiating the cultural influence of western civilisation with a clear satiric edge. Non-fiction occurs in *The Breast of the Earth: A Survey of the History, Culture and Literature of Africa South of the Sahara* (1975), which examines the contributions to poetics of former and contemporary African authors, and *Africa, the Marginalized Continent* (1994).

Ayala, Francisco (1906–) Born in Granada, Spain, he gained his doctorate in law at the University of Madrid (1931), where he became a Professor (1932–1935). He was forced into exile in Argentina (1939–1950), during which time he travelled widely in the Americas until 1973. Among his works translated into English are the four novelettes of *The Lamb's Head* (1949, trans. 1971), which explore human shortcomings against the background of the Spanish Civil War, *Usurpers* (1949, trans. 1987), ten tales of usurpation of power set against Medieval and Renaissance backdrops, and *Death as a Way of Life* (1958, trans. 1964), which looks at tyranny, demagoguery and existential alienation. Much of his fiction focuses on contemporary humanity falling short of existential authenticity as it examines the complex issues of politics and sociology in a largely philosophical fashion. With a reputation as an essayist, Hispanicist and literary critic, most of his prolific output remains untranslated into English.

E. Irizarry, *Francisco Ayala* (1977).

Aymé, Marcel (1902–1967) Marcel André Aymé was born in Joigny, France. Among other jobs, he worked as a bank clerk, accountant, crime reporter and salesman. His novels include *The Hollow Field* (1929, trans. 1933), *The Green Mare* (1933, trans. 1955), which was one of his most popular novels, a satire of the hypocrisy and mock heroism between two feuding families told by an observing horse, *The Secret Stream* (1936, trans. 1953) and *The Second Face* (1941, trans. 1951). Other novels include *The Fable and the Flesh* (1943, trans. 1965), about divisive village politics told by a forest divinity, *The Miraculous Barber* (1943, trans. 1950), satirising the cinema during the Popular Front era, *The Bar Keep of Blemont* (1948, trans. 1950), a critique of French society shortly after the German Occupation, laying bare the hypocrisy of the right and the left, and *The Conscience of Love* (1960, trans. 1962). In addition to short stories in *The Walker Through Walls* (1943, trans. 1972), his later works were mainly plays, screenplays and children's books. Shunning public honours, he was a prolific writer and much of his work remains untranslated into English. Many of his stories are set in the country, but in his later work acerbic stories of the Paris bourgeoisie emerge.

D. Brodin, *The Comic World of Marcel Aymé* (1964).

B

Bâ, Mariama (1929–1981) Born in Dakar, Senegal, of Muslim parentage, she was brought up by strict grandparents after the death of her mother. Educated at the École Normale at Rufisque, Senegal, she began work as a secretary and a schoolteacher, before developing as a francophone novelist. Actively committed to several women's organisations, she spoke and wrote on feminist issues such as clitoridectomy, women's rights in marriage, child custody and polygamy, and these became major subjects in her fiction. *So Long a Letter* (1980) is an epistolary novel that acts as a testimony to the silent suffering of women in Africa, and was judged the best novel in a French territory, receiving the first Noma prize. *Scarlet Song* (1981), published posthumously, also deals with the subject of polygamy and mixed marriage in a Senegalese family setting.

E. Jones, ed., *Women in African Literature Today* (1987).

Bagley, Desmond (1923–1983) A prolific writer of popular adventure stories and thrillers, Bagley was born in Kendal, England. After travelling across Africa, he worked as a journalist in South Africa, and turned to novel writing in 1963. His first book, *The Golden Keel* (1963), involves a search for Mussolini's personal (looted) gold, lost in the Mediterranean during wartime. Among his other stories are *High Citadel* (1965), about a plane forced down in the Andes by hijackers, *Wyatt's Hurricane* (1966), *Landslide* (1967), *The Spoilers* (1969), *Running Blind* (1970), set in Iceland, *The Tightrope Men* (1973), with a Finnish setting, *The Snow Tiger* (1975), about an avalanche in New Zealand, *Flyaway* (1978), *Bahama Crisis* (1980), *Windfall* (1982), set in Kenya, *Night of Error* (1983) and *Juggernaut* (1984), published posthumously. A thoroughly professional writer with tight and engaging plots set all around the world, the backgrounds to his stories were always well researched and authentic.

Bail, Murray (1941–) An Australian writer born in Adelaide, he has lived in a variety of countries, including India (1968–1970), England and Europe (1970–1974), where he contributed to the *Times Literary Supplement* and other journals in London. *Contemporary Portraits* (1975, republished as *The Drover's Wife*, 1986), was a collection of short fiction varying between the experimental and conventional, dominated by the surreal absurdity of contemporary life. His first novel, *Homesickness* (1980), is a comic satire of thirteen Australians on an international package tour, which is pervaded by a sense of loss and the absence of 'home', while *Holden's Performance*

(1987) is concerned with Australian identity, place and consciousness. His most recent novel is *Eucalyptus* (1998), a fable about a girl who is only allowed to marry a man who can name all the species of eucalypt. He has also written a monograph on the Australian painter Ian Fairweather (1981), *Longhand: A Writer's Notebook* (1989), which is a memoir of his life abroad, and he has edited *The Faber Book of Contemporary Australian Short Stories* (1988). His short stories demonstrate a concern with linguistic self-reflexivity and artifice.

Bainbridge, Beryl (1933–) A prolific English novelist, Beryl Margaret Bainbridge was born in Liverpool, and became an actress on radio, television and in the theatre (1943–1972), before turning to writing as a second career. Her first novels were *A Weekend with Claud* (1967), *Another Part of the Wood* (1968), *Harriet Said* (1972), and perhaps her best known early novel of psychological realism, *The Dressmaker* (1973), which was set in Liverpool during the Second World War and concerns the painful and claustrophobic existence of a young girl living with two unmarried aunts. There followed *The Bottle Factory Outing* (1974), *Sweet William* (1975), *A Quiet Life* (1976), *Injury Time* (1977) and *Young Adolf* (1978), about a family reunion in Liverpool between the 16-year-old Adolf Hitler and his half-brother Alois. Other novels include *Winter Garden* (1980), a satirical tale of a group of artists who are invited to visit the USSR, *Watson's Apology* (1984), which is based upon a notorious Victorian murder, *Filthy Lucre* (1986) and *An Awfully Big Adventure* (1989, filmed 1995), about a local repertory theatre in Liverpool and the interaction of the cast during a production of *Peter Pan*. *The Birthday Boys* (1993) is based on Robert Scott's South Pole expedition in 1911, *Every Man For Himself* (1996) is an account of the Titanic disaster, and *Master Georgie* (1998) is set in Victorian

England and concerns an adventure in the Crimean War. Her latest novel is *According to Queenie* (2000). Short stories are collected in *Mum and Mr. Armitage* (1985) and *Collected Stories* (1994), and personal essays in *Something Happened Yesterday* (1993). Examining the lives and neuroses of the English middle classes, the love and lack of love between partners and families, and often surreally juxtaposing horror and dark subject matter with comic precision, she has earned critical acclaim and a wide readership for her subtly ironic fiction.

Ba Jin (1904–) The pseudonym of Li Feigan, he was born in Chengdu, Sichuan, China, and graduated from the Southeastern University, Nanjing (1925). After pursuing postgraduate study in France (1927–1928), he then worked as an editor in a wide range of jobs. One of China's most famous and influential writers, familiar throughout China, he began to write in the 1920s. His best known novel is *The Family* (1931, trans. 1972), which chronicles the decline and division of a large family in China when the tide of social reform reached inland China and the old system collapsed. Enormously influential in the 1930s, it portrayed young people struggling against authoritarianism. Among numerous other works in Chinese, the few translated into English include *Cold Nights* (1947, trans. 1978) and *Random Thoughts* (1981, trans. 1984), short stories in *Short Stories by Ba Jin* (1941) and *Autumn in Spring* (1981), and a *Selected Works* (1988). After the Communist Revolution in 1949, he tried to adapt his work to proletarian requirements and produced blandly positive pictures of the new socialist system. After enduring persistent persecution during the Cultural Revolution (1966–1976), he began writing again in the late 1970s, although his more recent work remains untranslated into English.

N. Mao, *Ba Jin* (1978).

Baker, Nicholson (1957–) Born in New York, he was educated at Haverford College, Pennsylvania, and then worked variously as an oil analyst, a word processor and technical writer, before becoming a full-time writer in 1987. His first novel, *The Mezzanine* (1989), is a humorous celebration of the trivia of everyday life, cramming a fascination with the minutiae of products and designs into the lunch-hour of Howie, its odd protagonist. Mike, the central figure of *Room Temperature* (1990), muses, ruminates and meditates upon his marriage and other issues in his life while feeding his baby a bottle for twenty minutes. *U and I* (1991) is a tribute to the influence of John UPDIKE on Baker, while *Vox* (1992) and *The Fermata* (1994) freeze moments of erotic observation and voyeurism, in comic and parodic explorations of sex and the excesses of pornography. *The Size of Thoughts* (1996) is a collection of essays, and his latest work, *The Everlasting Story of Nory* (1998), is an occasionally comic yet plotless stream-of-consciousness account of a 9-year-old American girl's thoughts while at a school in England.

Baldwin, James (1924–1987) Born James Arthur Baldwin, in Harlem, New York, US, where he preached for a short time, he left home at the age of 17, and his subsequent travels included a long sojourn in France. His first novel *Go Tell It on the Mountain* (1953), based on his childhood, is about a day in the life of various members of a Harlem church and their forebears. It established him as the major African-American writer since Richard WRIGHT, and has since become a classic of American fiction. There followed *Giovanni's Room* (1956), set in Paris and concerning the love torments of a homosexual man, and *Another Country* (1962), a tale of complex relationships between races and sexes. His later fiction becomes increasingly polemical, including *Tell Me How Long the Train's Been Gone* (1968), *If Beale Street Could Talk* (1974), and

Just Above My Head (1979), a novel about a Harlem gospel singer's search for identity and salvation. He earned an equally influential reputation as an essayist for his observations on African-American writers and culture, reminiscences of Harlem, race relations and the bleakness of African-American social life, collected in *Notes of a Native Son* (1955), *Nobody Knows My Name* (1961), *The Fire Next Time* (1963) and *The Devil Finds Work* (1976). He also wrote several well-known plays, including *Blues for Mr. Charlie* (1964) and *The Amen Corner* (1964), about race antagonism, evangelism and jazz. *Going to Meet the Man* (1965) is a collection of short stories and *Jimmie's Blues* (1983) is his selected poems.

D. Leeming, *James Baldwin: A Biography* (1994).

Ballard, J.G. (1930–) Full name James Graham Ballard, he is an English writer of fantasy and science fiction. Born in Shanghai, China, he studied medicine at Cambridge University (1949–1951). He often writes about the way in which humans cope with natural catastrophes or alterations in their environment to which they have unwittingly contributed. His earliest novel is *The Wind from Nowhere* (1962), about high winds around the Earth, and this was followed by one of his best works, *The Drowned World* (1962), about the melting ice caps. With these early books, he became a leading spokesman for 'New Wave' science fiction and the need for experimental literary techniques to represent a sophisticated subject matter. Often depicting obsessive characters searching for something beyond normal life in a surreal fusion of environment and the unconscious, other novels include *The Crystal World* (1966), *Crash* (1973), about a man's sexual fantasies attached to his obsession with dying in a car crash (which was made into a controversial film by David Cronenberg in 1996), *Concrete*

Island (1974), *The Day of Creation* (1988) and *Cocaine Nights* (1998). Short story collections include *The Four-Dimensional Nightmare* (1963), *Terminal Beach* (1964), the influential related collection entitled *The Atrocity Exhibition* (1970), which depicts a grim series of psychodramas, juxtaposing sex and violence in non-linear fashion, *Vermilion Sands* (1971), *The Venus Hunter* (1980), *Memories of the Space Age* (1988) and *War Fever* (1990). He has also written a much acclaimed semi-autobiographical novel, *The Empire of the Sun* (1984, filmed 1987), about the internment of an English boy in a Japanese civilian camp near Shanghai during the Second World War. Apart from its sequel, *The Kindness of Women* (1991), which brings his autobiography up to the 1970s, recent novels include the *Day of Creation* (1987), *Running Wild* (1989) and *Rushing to Paradise* (1995), about a women's utopia and the obsessive side of the female protagonist. His latest novel is *Super-Cannes* (2000), which deals with the executive super-capitalist dreams of utopia and explores how we might yet escape that dark and violent cul-de-sac. *A User's Guide to the Millennium* (1996) is a collection of his journalism. Repeatedly using a series of symbols such as crashed cars, abandoned buildings and beaches, his science fiction narratives replace the orthodox space operas with journeys into convoluted and tortured psyches.

Bambara, Toni Cade (1931–1995) Born in New York City, she graduated from Queen's College (BA 1959) and CUNY (MA 1964), before becoming a director and adviser for the Theatre of Black Experience between 1965 and 1969 and a well-known civil rights activist. Her many jobs included work as a social worker, professor, women's studies co-ordinator and writing instructor. She described herself as a 'Pan-Africanist-socialist-feminist' and her writing is infused with her politics. Her collections of stories, *Gorilla, My Love* (1972) and *The Sea Birds are*

Still Alive (1972), tell of growing up in a world of racial, sexual and economic inequalities, and political conflicts within black communities. Her complex, dense novel *The Salt Eaters* (1980) examines the individual's relationship with communities in the context of post-Vietnam America. *The Bones Are Not My Child* (1999) is the novel she had been working on for twelve years at the time of her death, while *Deep Sightings and Rescue Missions* (1996) is a collection of essays, fiction and interviews with her. She also wrote film scripts and edited important anthologies, such as *The Black Woman* (1970), *Tales and Stories for Black Folks* (1971) and *Southern Black Utterances Today* (1975).

S. Willis, *Specifying: Black Women Writing the American Experience* (1987).

Banks, Iain M. (1954–) Born in Fife, Scotland, and educated at the University of Stirling (BA 1975), Iain Menzies Banks is a writer whose work blends science fiction, fantasy and mystery, although he is best known for his macabre tales of horror. This was evident in his first novel, the black comedy *The Wasp Factory* (1984), a tale of odd obsessions with a ghastly revelation in its conclusion. Other novels include *Walking on Glass* (1985), *The Bridge* (1986), about an amnesiac's fantasy life, *Espedair Street* (1987), *Cleaning Up* (1987), which is a brilliant interweaving of three tales, *Canal Dreams* (1991), which is a semi-surreal revenge and terrorist thriller set in the Panama Canal, *Complicity* (1995), *Whit* (1995), *The Crow Road* (1996), which is a rites-of-passage story about a young Scot, including a mystery element (later adapted for television), *A Song of Stone* (1998) and *The Business* (1999). His science fiction, written under the name Iain M. Banks, has rewritten the genre, with bold experiments in style and narrative, for example the phonetic language of the protagonist in *Feersum Endjinn* (1995), and the talking spaceships in *Excession*

(1996). Other science fiction works include *Consider Phlebas* (1987), *The Player of Games* (1988), *The Use of Weapons* (1992), *Against a Dark Background* (1993), *Inversions* (1998) and *Look to Windward* (2000). Banks has also written short stories, entitled *The State of the Art* (1991).

Banks, Lynne Reid (1929–) Born in London, and trained at the Royal Academy of Dramatic Art (1947–1949), she was a professional actress, a television journalist and an English teacher in an Israeli kibbutz, before becoming a professional writer in 1971. Her first and best known novel was *The L-Shaped Room* (1960), about Jane Graham, a young woman pregnant with an illegitimate child, living in a London bedsit, and filmed with great success in 1962. Her other adult books are *An End to Running* (1962), *Children at the Gate* (1968), *The Backward Shadow* (1970) and *Two Is Lovely* (1974), both sequels to *The L-Shaped Room* and following Jane Graham's life and development, *Defy the Wilderness* (1981), inspired by her time in Israel, *The Warning Bell* (1984), *Casualties* (1986) and *Fair Exchange* (1998). She has written two fictional studies of the Brontës in *Dark Quartet* (1976) and *Path to the Silent Country* (1977). Despite her adult fiction, she was perhaps best known in the 1970s for her children's fiction, with such novels as *One More River* (1973), set during the Six-Day War in Israel of 1967, *The Adventures of King Midas* (1976) and *The Indian in the Cupboard* (1980), many of which feature magic and mystery.

Banks, Russell (1940–) An American novelist, born in Newton, Massachusetts, and educated at Colgate University and the University of North Carolina at Chapel Hill. His prolific writing career began with *Family Life* (1974), a satiric fable set in an imaginary land. Other novels tend to demonstrate the characteristics of postmodernism, such as *Hamilton Stark*

(1978), *The Book of Jamaica* (1980) and *The Relation of My Imprisonment* (1983), which is about religious heresy. He gained great success with *Continental Drift* (1985), which depicted the interlinked relationships of an American family with an impoverished Haitian refugee and mother. Other novels include *Affliction* (1989), *The Sweet Hereafter* (1991), *Rule of the Bone* (1995), and the highly successful realist novel *Cloudsplitter* (1999), which tackles racial politics in its portrayal of Owen, the son of John Brown, the man who led the raid on Harper's Ferry which ignited the American Civil War. Short stories occur in *Searching for Survivors* (1975), *Trailerpark* (1981), *Success Stories* (1986) and *Angel on the Roof: The Stories of Russell Banks* (2000).

Banville, John (1945–) A widely honoured writer, born in Wexford, Ireland and educated at St. Peter's College, Wexford. After a period in journalism and editing an Irish press, he became literary editor of the *Irish Times* in 1989. His first work was a volume of short stories entitled *Long Lankin* (1970), which examined Irish life from the perspective of several characters. His first novels were *Nightspawn* (1971), an existentialist thriller set in Greece in the 1960s, and *Birchwood* (1973), set in nineteenth-century rural Ireland, exploring the 'big house' theme in Irish literature. His next novels all explored scientists of genius, in *Doctor Copernicus* (1976), *Kepler* (1981), *The Newton Letter* (1982) and *Mefisto* (1987). *The Book of Evidence* (1989) is a confessional account of a man's murder of a young girl during a blundered art theft, and its sequel, *Ghosts* (1993), explores the theme of guilt as the murderer is wracked by his actions in remote exile. This trilogy is completed in *Athena* (1995), in which the murderer is sucked into his personal hell and continues Banville's exploration of art and the imagination, truth and fraud. *The Untouchable*

(1997) is about the lives of the Cambridge spies, especially Anthony Blunt, and explores the darker realms of the twentieth century. His most recent novel is *Eclipse* (2000), which tells the story of an actor, Alexander Cleave, who has performed his way through life, until at the peak of his career, he suddenly leaves. He begins to unravel his own past in his childhood home, where memory of the past fuses with details of his present. Science is an important preoccupation of his fiction, especially the paradoxes between systems and the chaos that lies outside them. His literary craftsmanship has been praised for its modernist self-conscious aesthetic quality and its attempts to capture epiphanic revelations.

J. McMinn, *John Banville: A Critical Study* (1990).

Barfoot, Joan (1946–) A Canadian novelist born in Owen Sound, Ontario, who became a journalist and writer after graduating from the University of Western Ontario (BA 1969). Her first novel was *Abra* (178), about a young mother who deserts her family to live as a recluse in the Canadian wilderness. There followed *Dancing in the Dark* (1982), about a woman living out her life in a journal after being judged criminally insane for the murder of her husband, *Duet for Three* (1985), *Family News* (1989), *Plain Jane* (1992), which is a dark comedy about a librarian's fantasies of suburban love, and *Charlotte and Claudia Keeping in Touch* (1994), about love, sexuality, ageing and female friendship. More recent works are *Some Things About Flying* (1997) and *Getting Over Edgar* (1999). Most of her novels explore female madness, women's domestic experiences and their desire for new freedoms, and the emotional scars inflicted by families.

Barker, A.L. (1918–) Full name Audrey Lillian Barker, born in Kent, England, she worked as a secretary and then as a sub-

editor for the BBC (1949–1978). Concentrating on the short story, her often complex fiction explores the social and psychological worlds of social outcasts and misfits. Her short story collections include *The Innocents* (1947), *Novelette with Other Stories* (1951), *Lost Upon the Roundabouts* (1964), *Femina Real* (1971), which offers nine studies of female characters, the autobiographical *Life Stories* (1981), *No Word of Love* (1985), and the ghost stories in *Elements of Doubt* (1992). Her novels include *The Joy Ride and After* (1963), *Apology for a Hero* (1950), *A Case Examined* (1965), a story of psychological unease in *John Brown's Body* (1969), a domestic satire in *A Source of Embarrassment* (1974), *Relative Successes* (1984), *The Gooseboy* (1987), *The Woman Who Talked to Herself* (1989), *Zeph* (1992) and *The Haunt* (1999). Frequently existing in extreme situations, her characters manifest her concern with the collision of innocence and experience, the ambivalence of love and the dangers of egoism in her carefully woven, tragi-comic tales.

Barker, Pat (1943–) Born in Thornaby-on-Tees, England, she graduated from the London School of Economics (1965), and was a teacher until 1970. She is among the most acclaimed British novelists to emerge in the 1980s, with a direct, spare prose in her depictions of the English working class. Her first novel, *Union Street* (1982, filmed 1989 as *Stanley and Iris*), was followed by *Blow Your House Down* (1984) and *Century's Daughter* (1986), and drew upon her memories of working-class women in the trying and unrewarding conditions of her mother's and grandmother's generations in the industrial north. Her next novel was *The Man Who Wasn't There* (1989), about the male psyche, and a fatherless teenager's fantasies about his absent parent. Anxious about being typecast, she changed direction radically with *Regeneration* (1991), the first novel in an acclaimed trilogy about mentally ill soldiers in the Great War and the therapist who struggles with his own moral values while treating them. The novel presents a fictional account of the English poet Siegfried Sassoon's treatment for shell-shock in Edinburgh in 1917, treated by Dr. Rivers. *The Eye in the Door* (1993) continues the story of Dr. Rivers and his patients, focusing on the bisexual lieutenant Billy Prior. The third in the trilogy, *The Ghost Road* (1995, Booker Prize), continues the focus on Rivers as he goes to a hospital in London, and Prior who goes back to the front. Her latest novel is *Another World* (1998), which is a narrative of a modern family, their demons and the Great War.

Barnes, Djuna (1892–1982) Born in Cornwall-on-Hudson, New York, US, she was educated at the Pratt Institute, Brooklyn (1911–1912) and the Arts Students' League (1915). She began as a journalist working in Brooklyn and was also a member of the Suffrage Movement, but left for Paris in 1920 to join the artistic expatriate community. Her first major work was *A Book* (1923), consisting of short plays and stories, which was later reissued as *A Night Among the Horses* (1929) with three new stories. *Ryder* (1928) was a satirical novel written in a stream-of-consciousness style, concerned with a man's relations with his wife, mother and mistress. Highly praised by T.S. Eliot, *Nightwood* (1936) became a cult book, depicting the relationships of five psychopathic people. She returned to New York in 1937, and among her other publications are the blank verse play *The Antiphon* (1958), her 1915 poems and drawings in *The Book of Repulsive Women* (1948), *Vagaries Malicieux* (1975), her juvenilia in *Smoke* (1982), and *Interviews* (1985), gathering her journalistic conversations with such people as James JOYCE and Jack Dempsey. *New York* (1989) collects from newspaper journalism her impressions of Coney Island and other local areas in 1913–1919. Always

concerned with female exploitation or suffering under heterosexual patriarchy, her explicit and often bawdy treatment of sexual desire offended many people.

M. Broe, ed., *Silence and Power: A Reevaluation of Djuna Barnes* (1991).

Barnes, Julian (1946–) A highly regarded and prolific writer, born in Leicester, England, Julian Patrick Barnes was educated at Oxford University (BA 1968). He has worked as a freelance writer from 1972, concurrently writing cultural journalism for the *New Statesman*, the *Sunday Times* and the *Observer*. His first novel was *Metroland* (1980), about a young man's decadent activities, followed by *Before She Met Me* (1982), about the darker side of obsessive fascination. His first major success came with *Flaubert's Parrot* (1984), a novel of ideas about a writer's obsession with the stuffed parrot Flaubert kept on his desk, exploring the interconnection between art and life, the impact of death and the consolation of literature, in a blend of different styles. There followed *Question and Answer* (1986) and the triptych *Staring at the Sun* (1987), before his next big success, *A History of the World in 10½ Chapters* (1989), a postmodern anti-novel in which a series of stories are linked by the primary metaphor of sea travel, and are based on debunking religion and history in a world where everything is subtly related to everything else via metaphor and analogy. *Talking It Over* (1991) was followed by *The Porcupine* (1992), a short novel set in an eastern European country in the post-communist era, *Letters from London* (1995), *Cross Channel* (1996), which is a series of stories set in France, and *England, England* (1998), a viciously funny attack on the myths and nostalgia that go towards making up England. His latest novel, *Love, etc.* (2000), a sequel to *Talking It Over*, revisits Stuart, Gillian and Oliver, using the same technique of allowing the characters to speak directly to the reader, to whisper their secrets, and to argue for their version of the truth. He has written a series of crime novels under the pseudonym Dan Kavanagh, entitled *Duffy* (1980), *Fiddle City* (1981), *Putting the Boot In* (1985), and *Going to the Dogs* (1987), in which a bisexual policeman, Duffy, investigates the seamier side of London. Along with his literary experiments, his comic, metaphorical and controlled prose has given him the reputation of being one of the most celebrated contemporary British postmodern novelists.

M. Moseley, *Understanding Julian Barnes* (1996).

Barstow, Stan (1928–) Born Stanley Barstow, in Horbury, Yorkshire, he worked in engineering until 1962, before turning to writing full-time. Emerging at the time of the politically and socially charged 'angry young men' of post-war Britain, like John BRAINE and Alan SILLITOE, his famous first novel, *A Kind of Loving* (1960), was an immediate best-seller and was written in office worker Vic Brown's first person, present tense narrative, depicting his harassed and trapped life in Cressley, a fictional amalgam of northern English towns. Vic Brown's struggles against the odds in a tough, no-nonsense world continued in two sequels, *The Watchers on the Shore* (1966) and *The Right True End* (1976), later released as *A Kind of Loving: The Vic Brown Trilogy* (1981). Presenting the tragic lives of people, other novels of this period were *Ask Me Tomorrow* (1962), *Joby* (1964), written from the perspective of a young boy, *A Raging Calm* (1968) and *A Brother's Tale* (1980), and continued similar themes of loneliness and marital difficulties in difficult social environments. *Just You Wait and See* (1986), *Give Us This Day* (1989) and *Next of Kin* (1991), comprise his next trilogy, set in the fictional Yorkshire town of 'Daker', about the Palmer family caught up in the maelstrom of the Second World War. In addition to the novel *B-*

Movie (1987), his short stories are collected in *The Desperadoes* (1961), *The Season with Eros* (1971) and *The Glad Eye* (1984). He has also written for the theatre, television and cinema, and much of his work explores working-class issues. His fiction has been a major contribution to the development of the English regional novel and the depiction of northern English working-class culture.

Barth, John (1930–) Born in Cambridge, Maryland, John Simmons Barth pursued a music career at the Julliard School of Music before taking a literature Masters at John Hopkins University (1952). He has worked at a variety of universities and is currently Professor of English and Creative Writing at Johns Hopkins University. One of the most significant post-Second World War American novelists, his experiments in postmodern writing demonstrate an innovative grasp of fictional technique. His early novels *The Floating Opera* (1956) and *The End of the Road* (1958) were realist in style, but already showed signs of the abstract, metaphysical problems and his skill at humorous satire that would characterise his later work. There followed the novel many consider his greatest, *The Sot-Weed Factor* (1960), which is a lively pastiche of seventeenth-century English prose that centres upon the activities of the poet Ebenezer Cooke in the New World. Another epic novel, *Giles Goat-Boy* (1966), is an allegory of Cold War politics, philosophy, Christianity and religion, fatherhood, writing and education, based upon the concept of the world divided into 'East' and 'West' campuses, each controlled by their own massive computers. Following *Chimera* (1972) and *Todd Andrews to the Author* (1979), he wrote *Letters* (1979), an epistolary novel with a convoluted plot of correspondence, followed by *Sabbatical* (1982) and *The Tidewater Tales* (1988), which draw upon the folklore of Chesapeake Bay, and the CIA, and are written in a style less experimental than his earlier fiction. *The Last Voyage of Somebody the Sailor* (1991) is his latest novel, while his short stories are collected in *Lost in the Funhouse* (1969) and *On with the Story* (1996). He has also written influential analytical essays on the transition from modernist to postmodernist fiction, in *The Literature of Exhaustion, and The Literature of Replenishment* (1982), as well as *The Friday Book* (1984) and *Further Fridays* (1996). Often blurring the worlds of fiction and reality, characters and authors, history and artifice, he has been in the vanguard of extending the forms of American fiction in the twentieth century.

C. Harris, *Passionate Virtuosity: The Fiction of John Barth* (1983).

Barthelme, Donald (1931–1989) An American novelist, born in Philadelphia, Pennsylvania, he was the brother of Frederick BARTHELME. After working as a reporter, he turned to writing, focusing on the bizarre. A prodigious writer of short stories in *Come Back, Dr. Caligari* (1964), *Unspeakable Practices, Unnatural Acts* (1968), *City Life* (1970), *Sadness* (1972), *Guilty Pleasures* (1974), *Amateurs* (1976), *Great Days* (1979) and *Overnight to Many Distant Cities* (1984), they are characterised by a remarkable wit in their non-ironic presentation of absurdly grotesque, illogical and meaningless matters, as if to indicate their irrationality. *Snow White* (1967), an oblique, incongruous version of the fairy-tale in episodic form, was followed by the bizarre *The Dead Father* (1975), the fantasy novel *Paradise* (1986), and *The King* (1990), a fanciful narrative of King Arthur and his Roundtable transposed to the Blitz in wartime England. *The Teaching of Don B.* (1992) collects previously unpublished stories, fables and plays, while *Not-Knowing* (1999) collects his essays and interviews. Frequently described as an 'anti-novelist' or 'metafictionalist' and compared to BARTH, BORGES, COOVER, GADDIS, PYNCHON

and VONNEGUT, his stories explore the potentials and limitations of reader, writer and text in contemporary fiction, an experimentation which also structures his novels through the foregrounding of language and pattern.

P. Maltby, *Dissident Postmodernists* (1991).

Barthelme, Frederick (1943–) Born in Houston, Texas, the brother of Donald BARTHELME, he was educated at several universities, including Tulane in New Orleans and Johns Hopkins at Baltimore. He has worked as an architectural draughtsman, an advertising technical writer and a university professor. His early fiction, such as *Rangoon* (1970) and *War and War* (1971), was self-consciously experimental. He established his own style and identity in the seventeen stories of *Moon Deluxe* (1983). This was a highly detailed style, with stories transmitting a strong sense of mystery and expectation, often set in the Sun Belt states on the Gulf Coast and focusing on middle-aged single men. The comedy of morals and manners in *Second Marriage* (1984) is continued in *Tracer* (1985), exploring the displacements and disconnections in his characters' lives. *Two Against One* (1988) again centres upon aimless and confused heroes, yearning for answers and making tentative steps towards finding them. *Natural Selection* (1990) is a darker novel, in which the comic surface is broken by the sudden impact of a fatal accident. In recent years, he has published further novels, including *The Brothers* (1993), its sequel *Painted Desert* (1995), and *Bob the Gambler* (1997), all of which are tinged with a combination of satirical observation and meditation on the mundane details and social absurdities of everyday life. Short stories occur in *Chroma* (1996), while *Double Down* (1999) written with his brother Steven, reflects upon their addictive experiences with and recovery from organised gambling.

Bassani, Giorgio (1916–2000) Born in Bologna, Italy, he graduated from the University of Bologna, and became an instructor in the history of theatre (1957–1968), as well as working for Italian radio and television. Although he has published poetry, he is best known for his fiction, which began with the short stories in *A Prospect of Ferrara* (1956, trans. 1962), set in the 1920s and 1930s, about the Ferrara people in the Po Valley, the setting for most of his fiction. His novels include *The Gold-Rimmed Spectacles* (1958, trans. 1960), *The Garden of the Finzi-Continis* (1962, trans. 1965), about an Italian adolescent struggling with identity in a world outside the protection of the family, *Behind the Door* (1964, trans. 1972), and *The Heron* (1968, trans. 1970), set in the post-war period, about the last day of a Holocaust survivor who cannot cope with his existential anguish. In addition to *Five Stories from Ferrara* (1969, trans. 1971), short stories occur in *The Smell of Hay* (1972, trans. 1975), and he edited the journal *Botteghe Oscure* since its founding in 1948 to 1960. His early fiction explores disappointment and renunciation, reserving all aspects of judgement. Frequently concerned with the gap between historical consciousness and what is about to happen, his writing also investigates the bleak themes of loneliness, exclusion and death.

D. Radcliff-Umstead, *The Exile into Eternity* (1987).

Bates, H.E. (1905–1974) One of the most prolific English writers, he was born Herbert Ernest Bates, in Rushden, Northamptonshire. He became known for his depictions of English rural and agricultural life, exemplified in his novels *The Poacher* (1935), *A House of Women* (1936) and *My Uncle Silas* (1940), and marked by a Rabelaisian humour. During the Second World War, as 'Flying Officer X', he gained great popularity and success writing stories about wartime flying, such as *The Greatest People in the World* (1942) and *How Sleep the Brave* (1943). He also wrote *Fair Stood the Wind for France* (1944), about a British bomber crew forced down in enemy territory, and *The Cruise of 'The Breadwinner'* (1946). Two novels set in Burma during the Japanese invasion, *The Purple Plain* (1946) and *The Jacaranda Tree* (1948), followed, in addition to *The Nature of Love* (1954), *The Sleepless Moon* (1956), *The Darling Buds of May* (1958) (about the Larkins, a loveable farming family in Kent, and which was adapted into a popular BBC television series in the 1990s), *The Distant Horns of Summer* (1967) and *The Triple Echo* (1970). Among his many short story collections are *The Flying Goat* (1939), *The Beauty of the Dead* (1941) and *Colonel Julian* (1951), and the posthumous *The Yellow Meads of Asphodel* (1976). Autobiographical works occur in *The Vanished World* (1969) and *The Blossoming World* (1971).

D. Baldwin, *H.E. Bates: A Literary Life* (1987).

Bawden, Nina (1925–) Born Nina Mary, in London, England, and educated at Oxford University (MA 1951), she has become well known for her incisive psychological explorations of family relationships in the educated middle class. Her first novel was *Eyes of Green* (1953), and her many subsequent novels include *The Birds on the Trees* (1970), about the domestic affairs of a middle-class family, *Anna Apparent* (1972) and *Afternoon of a Good Woman* (1976). Later novels tend to be social comedies about moral beings, such as *Walking Naked* (1981), about people unable to come to grips with their world, *The Ice House* (1983), about two women finding their marriages to be unhappy and unstable, *Circles of Deceit* (1987), about a tangled group of relationships, *Family Money* (1991) and *A Nice Change* (1997). Developing many of the issues evident in her adult fiction, she is also famous for her children's fiction, particularly *Carrie's War* (1973), about the evacuation of young children to a Welsh mining town during the Second World War, *The Peppermint Pig* (1975), and *Keeping Henry* (1988), again set in Wales during the War. *In My Own Time* (1994) is an autobiography. Examining the tensions and undercurrents of apparently calm and humdrum characters, she creates a psychological depth of humorous moods and self-deceptions.

Bear, Greg (1951–) Born Gregory Dale Bear, in San Diego, US, he was educated at San Diego State University (1969), after which he worked in bookstores, at a planetarium, as a freelance journalist and as a freelance teacher in San Diego. He has published numerous science fiction novels, including *Hegira* (1979), *Beyond River's Hell* (1980), *Psychlove* (1979), *Blood Music* (1985), a novel which made his name and deals with nanotechnology and the results of a biological experiment, *The Forge of God* (1987) and *Queen of Angels* (1990). *Eon* (1986), and its sequels *Eternity* (1988) and *Legacy* (1995), are set in a post-Holocaust scenario. His more recent novels include *Slant* (1997), *Dinosaur Summer* (1998), *Foundation and Chaos* (1998) and *Darwin's Radio* (1999), which is a scientific thriller focusing upon mysterious behaviour in families and an epidemic of stillbirths. *Tangents* (1989) collects short stories and *Heads* (1990) is a novella. He has also produced science fiction artwork, founding the ASFA (Association of Science Fiction Artists). Although not afraid to experiment (he has been tangentially associated with Bruce STERLING and cyberpunk), he is principally regarded as the emergent heir to 'hard' science fiction writers such as Larry NIVEN and Arthur C. CLARKE.

Beauvoir, Simone de (1908–1986) Born Simone Lucie Ernestine Marie Bertrand de Beauvoir, in Paris, France, she graduated in philosophy at the Sorbonne, University of Paris (1929), and worked as a teacher in France (1931–1943). In 1944, she founded and co-edited *Les Temps Modernes* with her lifelong partner Jean-Paul SARTRE. A widely honoured and influential writer and philosopher, her novels include *She Came to Stay* (1943, trans. 1949), based on her anguished three-way relationship with Sartre and his mistress, *The Blood of Others* (1946, trans. 1948), set during the Second World War and focusing upon the consequences of one's actions, and *All Men Are Mortal* (1946, trans. 1955), about the problems of immortality and death. *The Mandarins* (1954, Prix Goncourt, trans. 1956) is perhaps her most famous novel, portraying the euphoria of the Liberation and the subsequent disillusionment of French intellectuals, and is dedicated to her American lover Nelson ALGREN. Other novels include *Les Belles Images* (1966, trans. 1968) and *The Woman Who Destroyed* (1967, trans. 1969), both of which are about women coming to terms with their lives. She wrote several volumes of autobiography, detailing her intellectual, social and emotional life and relationships, including *America Day by Day* (1948, trans. 1952), *Memoirs of a Dutiful Daughter* (1958, trans. 1959), *The Prime of Life* (1960, trans. 1962), *The Force of Circumstance* (1963, trans. 1965), *A Very Easy Death* (1964, trans. 1966), *All Said and Done* (1972, trans. 1974), and a tribute in *Adieux: A Farewell to Sartre* (1981, trans. 1984). Short stories occur in *When Things of the Spirit Come First* (1979, trans. 1982). Her philosophy includes *The Ethics of Ambiguity* (1947, trans. 1948), about existentialism and the tensions of mortality, and perhaps her best known work, *The Second Sex* (1949, trans. 1953), which initially shocked readers but has since become a feminist classic for her frank discussion of women's conditions. Moral and ethical issues dominate her writing, and she is regarded by feminists as a major motivating force, opening horizons and moulding ideas with her keen philosophic mind.

M. Evans, *Simone de Beauvoir: A Feminist Mandarin* (1985); T. Moi, *Simone de Beauvoir: The Making of an Intellectual Woman* (1994).

Beckett, Samuel (1906–1989) Samuel Barclay Beckett was born in Foxrock, Co. Dublin. He was educated at Trinity College, Dublin, and then taught French in Belfast and Paris (1928–1930). He met James JOYCE in Paris, for whom he wrote the essay 'Dante...Bruno...Vico... Joyce' for *Our Exagmination Round the Factification for Incamination of Work in Progress* (1929), a collection of essays he edited on *Finnegans Wake*. Poems appeared in *Whoroscope* (1930), and he lectured at Trinity College (1930–1931) while writing his study, *Proust* (1931), in which he examined the breakdown of the traditional relations between subject and object, which prefigured his own later work. Between 1932 and 1937, he travelled in Germany, France, England and Ireland, producing the short stories in *More Pricks Than Kicks* (1934), about college life in Dublin, the poems in *Echo's Bones and Other Precipitates* (1935) and the *Dream of Fair to Middling Women* (written in the 1930s, unpublished until 1992). He settled in Paris in 1937, in hostile reaction to the nationalism of post-Independence Ireland, dismissing the Irish literary revival. He wrote his first novel *Murphy* (1938) and upon the occupation of France, joined the French Resistance in Paris (1941–1942). He escaped to Roussillon and wrote *Watt* (1953), his last novel to be written in English, which pushes the referential dimension of language to its limits. He was awarded the Croix de Guerre in 1945, and decided to write in French to purge his style of unwanted literariness. There followed *Mercier et Camier* (1946, published 1970) and *Premier Amour* (1970, translated as *First Love*, 1973), and his grimly humorous trilogy *Molloy* (1951), *Malone Dies* (1951) and *The Unnameable* (1953). This explores personal identity in fragmented narratives and enacts the breakdown of the perceiving mind and reality. He moved into experiments with dramatic form with his famous play *Waiting for Godot* (1949), with its despairing existential angst in a dialogue between two beggars, mixing futility, slapstick comedy and theological debate. Other plays include *Endgame* (1957), *All That Fall* (1957), *Krapp's Last Tape* (1958), *Happy Days* (1961) and *Not I* (1972) among others, establishing him as a leading figure in the Theatre of the Absurd. These plays offer images of the exhausted male ego of the twentieth century, and the spiritual and moral aridity of modern society. Other fiction includes *How It Is* (1961), *Imagination Dead, Imagine* (1965), *Ping* (1966), *Lessness* (1972), *The Lost Ones* (1972), *For to End Yet Again and Other Fizzles* (1976), *Company* (1980), *Ill Seen Ill Said* (1981), *Worstword Ho* (1983) and *Stirrings Still* (1988). This fiction frequently explores tensions of movement and fixity, as well as between speech and silence. Characters search in vain for meaning and identity and his rigorous, concentrated writing focuses on many of the difficult metaphysical questions of western philosophy. *The Collected Works of Samuel Beckett* (1970) was published in nineteen volumes, followed by the *Collected Poems in English and French* (1977) and *Disjecta* (1983), which collects various critical pieces. One of the most significant figures in twentieth-century literature, he was awarded the Nobel Prize for Literature in 1969.

D. Bair, *Samuel Beckett: A Biography* (1978); L. Hill, *Beckett's Fiction: In Different Words* (1990).

Bell, Madison Smartt (1957–) Born on a farm in Nashville, Tennessee, US, he was educated at Princeton (BA 1979) and Hollins College (MA 1981). He has had a variety of jobs, including working with an artists' co-operative and, recently, as writer-in-residence at Goucher College in Towson, Madison. He usually writes about society's misfits – petty criminals, drifters and lost souls – and his novels include *The Washington Square Ensemble* (1983), *The Year of Silence* (1987), *Soldier's Joy* (1989) and *Save Me, Joe Louis* (1993). Arguably his most ambitious novel to date, the epic *All Souls' Rising* (1995) is about a complex set of relationships at the time of the 1802 Haiti uprising, in which the countless atrocities are described. *Master of the Crossroads* (2000) continues his projected Haitian trilogy about Touissant l'Ouverture. The novel *Ten Indians* was published in 1996, and the non-fiction, *Narrative Design*, in 1997. Employing various genres, such as the thriller, he usually focuses on American environments in a laconic and often ironic style.

Bellow, Saul (1915–) An American novelist, born in Lachine, Canada, of Russian immigrant parents, and brought up in Montreal and, later, in Chicago. He was educated at the University of Chicago and Northwestern University, and has since taught at the University of Minnesota, Princeton and New York University, but has primarily been a realist writer articulating a humanist perspective. His Kafkaesque first novel, *Dangling Man* (1944), a psychological story about living in limbo while waiting to be inducted into the army, was followed by *The Victim* (1947), about an agonising and strained relationship between a Jew and Gentile. His first big success came with *The Adventures of Augie March* (1953), a naturalistic tale of the picaresque escapades of a young Chicago Jew. After laying out his humanist ideology in *Seize the Day* (1956), he wrote *Henderson the Rain King* (1959), and then his prototypical novel set in a Jewish intellectual environment about the difficulties and dilemmas posed by cultural assimilation into western Christian life in *Herzog*

(1964). A series of plays, collected in *Under the Weather* (1966), was followed by short stories in *Mosby's Memoirs* (1968), and *Mr Sammler's Planet* (1969), a fictive critique of modern society seen through the eyes of a Nazi concentration camp survivor living in New York. *Humboldt's Gift* (1975, Pulitzer Prize) was followed by an account of his trip to Israel in *To Jerusalem and Back* (1976), and *The Dean's December* (1982). There followed an increasingly pessimistic series of works about the demise of the individual's freedoms in *Him with His Foot in His Mouth* (1984), *More Die of Heart Break* (1987), *Theft* (1988), and *The Bellarosa Connection* (1989), about the uneasy yet successful lives of immigrant American Jews. *Something to Remember Me By* (1991) collects three stories and *It All Adds Up* (1994) is a collection of essays and memoirs. His recent novels are *The Actual* (1997), about the culmination of forty years of hidden love, and *Ravelstein* (2000), about a writer who writes about the death of culture and learning. Internationally recognised with the Nobel Prize for Literature in 1976, he has had wide acclaim for a style which mixes street dialogue with intellectual investigation, as he has explored the protagonists' aims for self-understanding and their travails in modernity.

E. Pifer, *Saul Bellow: Against the Grain* (1990); P. Hyland, *Saul Bellow* (1992).

Bely, Andrei (1880–1934) Born Boris Nikolayevich Bugayev in Moscow, Russia, he attended the University of Moscow before turning to writing. The most original and influential of the Russian symbolist movement, his masterpiece is *Petersburg* (1913, trans. 1959), an attempt at expressing the depths of spiritual life and communicating states beyond consciousness, and creating a prose which makes use of acoustic effects, rhythmic power and impressions of chaos in a symbolic prophecy of impending doom in Russia. Other fiction includes *The Silver Dove* (1909, trans. 1974), a study of a young intellectual's flirtation with and destruction by the mystical forces guiding a revolutionary sect in provincial Russia, *Kotik Letaev* (1922, trans. 1971), an autobiographical novel which is absorbed in the anthrosophical ideas of Rudolf Steiner, and *The Christened Chinaman* (1991, trans. 1927). *Selected Essays* (trans. 1985) and *Complete Short Stories* (trans. 1979) have also been published. His verbal artistry, stylistic innovations and explorations of form and language served as the first step towards the modernist revolution in Russian verse, as he sought spiritual meaning within the social and literary turmoil of pre-Soviet Russia.

K. Mochulsky, *Andrei Bely: His Life and Works* (1977).

Bennett, Arnold (1867–1931) Born Enoch Arnold Bennett, in Stoke-on-Trent, Staffordshire, England, he began a career in law, then moved into editorial work and journalism in the 1890s. His first novel was the somewhat gloomy realist novel *A Man from the North* (1898). He wrote a large number of stories set in the semi-fictional five towns Pottery district of the Midlands, beginning with the novel *Anna of the Five Towns* (1902), in an unrestrained realistic style, exploring the narrow materialism of characters' lives. Others include the short story collections *Tales of the Five Towns* (1905), *The Grim Smile of the Five Towns* (1907) and *The Matador of the Five Towns* (1912). Further novels of note were *Leonora* (1903), about a married man's love affair, *Sacred and Profane Love* (1905), which was an ambitious and sexually daring narrative, *Hugo* (1906), *The Old Wives' Tale* (1908), which is one of his masterpieces, about the lives of Constance and Sophie Scales in the Potteries, *The Statue* (1908) and *The Card* (1911). His novels about the Clayhanger family were another success, with *Clayhanger* (1910), *Hilda Less-*

ways (1911), *These Twain* (1915) and *The Roll Call* (1918). He also had success with *Riceyman Steps* (1923), one of his finest later novels, among others that include *Lord Raingo* (1926), a dark, political novel, and *Imperial Palace* (1930). He did not disdain commercial writing, and in addition to many successful plays and a variety of non-fiction, he wrote populist practical guides to journalism and popular information books. *Over There* (1915) described scenes from the Western Front in the First World War. He also published journalism, articles and diaries, and his letters were posthumously published in three volumes (1966–1970). His novels were masterpieces of realism and he epitomised the versatility of the traditional British man of letters, although he was scorned by modernists like Ezra Pound and Virginia WOOLF for his external realist-materialism that did not investigate the inner psychological lives of characters. Despite many admirers, his work has never recovered the wide popularity it had during his lifetime.

F. Swinnerton, *Arnold Bennett: A Last Word* (1978).

Berger, John (1926–) Born in London, England, John Peter Berger was educated at the Central School of Art and the Chelsea School of Art, and became a painter and teacher of drawing, and has had several exhibitions. Volumes of his art criticism include *Permanent Red: Essays in Seeing* (1960), *The Success and Failure of Picasso* (1965), *The Moment of Cubism* (1969), *Ways of Seeing* (1972), based on a highly regarded television series, *About Looking* (1980) and *Keeping a Rendezvous* (1991). His art criticism maintains his dedication to Marxist philosophies and issues of aesthetics and politics. His fiction tends to be eclectic, yet has nevertheless met with wide acclaim. His first novel was *A Painter of Our Time* (1958), followed by *The Foot of Clive* (1962), *Corker's Freedom* (1964), about the adventures in a day in the life of a 64-year-old man, who leaves the home he has shared with an invalid sister, and *G.* (1972, Booker Prize), an experimental work about a modern Don Juan and the impact of social structures on the individual character 'G'. Berger moved to a French village in the 1970s and began his best work, a trilogy entitled *Into Their Labours* (1991), consisting of *Pig Earth* (1979), *Once in Europa* (1987) and *Lilac and Flag: An Old Wives' Tale of a City* (1990). This concerns the French peasant class, and the modern world's intrusion into centuries old traditions, with the concomitant collapse and degradation of village life. As well as *To the Wedding* (1995), about two young lovers in an HIV-positive relationship, which culminates in their marriage, he has published his artwork in *Pages of the Wound* (1996), short stories in *Photocopies* (1996), and *King: A Street Story* (1999). Additional work includes essays on photography and screenplays.

G. Dyer, *Ways of Telling: The Work of John Berger* (1986).

Berger, Thomas (1924–) Born in Cincinnati, Ohio, he attended the University of Ohio and Columbia University. *Crazy in Berlin* (1958) was his first novel, which was the beginning of a comic saga about Carlo Rheinhart, a happy GI in occupied Germany at the end of the Second World War. This curious picaresque adventure of an anti-hero and survivor was continued in *Rheinhart in Love* (1961) and concluded in *Vital Parts* (1970). He wrote *Little Big Man* (1964), a fanciful parody of the myth of the Old West culminating in Custer's Last Stand, seen through the eyes of the mock-heroic Jack Crabb, made famous by the movie starring Dustin Hoffman (1970). This has recently been continued in *The Return of Little Big Man* (1999). He explored sanity, madness, crime and legality through a tale of a mass murderer in *Killing Time* (1967),

and picked up the story of Rheinhart, now in his fifties, in *Rheinhart's Women* (1981). Other works include a contemporary version of *Robinson Crusoe* in *Robert Crews* (1994), about isolation after an aeroplane crash in a lake, updates of literary classics like *The Oresteia* and the legend of King Arthur, and the novel *Suspects* (1996). Short stories occur in *Granted Wishes* (1984), and he has written a play entitled *Other People* (1970). A satirist and comic social commentator, he is a prolific novelist with nineteen works to his name.

D. Madden, ed., *Critical Essays on Thomas Berger* (1995).

Bernhard, Thomas (1931–1989) An Austrian novelist born in Heerland, The Netherlands, he graduated from the Mozarteum, Salzburg (1957). A novelist, poet, dramatist and journalist, he has been widely honoured with numerous prizes. His early novels include *Gargoyles* (1967, trans. 1970), which depicts his belief in the hopelessness of the human condition, *The Lime Works* (1970, trans. 1973), which is narrated by a salesman who weaves the story from a rumour about a farmer who blows his wife's head off, *Correction* (1975, trans. 1979), *Yes* (1978, trans. 1992), *Concrete* (1983, trans. 1984) and *The Loser* (1983, trans. 1991). His later fiction includes *Wittgenstein's Nephew* (1983, trans. 1989), *The Woodcutters* (1984, trans. 1988), in which the narrator deflates the pretentiousness of local artists, *Extinction* (1986, trans. 1995), *On the Mountain* (trans. 1991) and *Old Masters* (trans. 1992). The five volumes of his memoir, *Gathering Evidence* (1975–1983, trans. 1986), consist of *An Indication of the Cause*, *The Cellar: An Escape*, *Breath: A Decision*, *In the Cold* and *A Child*, and record his life troubled by illness. Much of his work remains untranslated into English. Noted for his pessimistic and melancholy views, his grim meditations on death, futility, madness and disease, and presenting his culture in a critical light, he gained a reputation for stylistic virtuosity in books which embody musical values of counterpoint and fugal structures. In uncompromising fashion, his will specified that none of his novels or plays were to be performed or published in Austria for the seventy years of copyright.

S. Dowden, *Understanding Thomas Bernhard* (1991).

Billing, Graham (1936–) Born in Dunedin, New Zealand, Graham John Billing attended Otago University (1953–1958) and studied for the Presbyterian ministry. He worked for a shipping company, then as a journalist, and after a spell with the New Zealand Antarctica Survey (1962–1964), he became a lecturer in English and a freelance writer. His first novel was *Forbush and the Penguins* (1965), about an ornithologist in Antarctica studying penguins and reflecting upon the cycles of birth and death. There followed *The Alpha Trip* (1969), *Statues* (1971), about a character employed to create a sculpture garden for an eccentric aristocrat, *The Slipway* (1973), about two days in the life of a protagonist, *The Primal Therapy of Tom Purslane* (1980), *The Chambered Nautilus* (1993), and *The Lifeboat* (1997), a psychological novel about psychiatric hospital patients. Many of his novels tend to be semi-autobiographical, involving protagonists who struggle over the profound questions of existence in situations fraught with symbolism and hidden meanings. Other works include *South: Man and Nature in Antarctica* (1964), *New Zealand: The Sunlit Land* (1966) and a volume of poetry, *Changing Countries* (1980).

Billington, Rachel (1942–) Born in Oxford, England, and educated at London University (BA 1963), Rachel Mary Billington is a novelist and playwright. Raised in the large and distinguished

Packenham family, of Labour peers, politicians, and writers like Antonia Fraser, her novels reflect the world of her upbringing in the prosperous English gentry. Her first novel, *All Things Nice* (1969), is about an English aristocratic heroine in New York City who becomes involved in the shady world of drug-dealing. This was followed by many others, including *The Big Dipper* (1970), *Lilacs Out of the Dead Land* (1971), *Cock Robin* (1973), *Beautiful* (1974), *A Painted Devil* (1975), *A Woman's Age* (1979), which is an ambitious novel about the life of the heroine from 1905 to 1975, charting the forces of the twentieth century on a woman's life, *Occasion of Sin* (1982), about an affair that ruins a woman's marriage, *The Garish Day* (1985), about two generations of diplomats during the British Raj, *Loving Attitudes* (1988), *Theo and Matilda* (1990), *The Family Year* (1992), *Bodily Harm* (1992), about the relationship between a woman and her attacker, and *Magic and Fate* (1996). Latest works are *Perfect Happiness* (1996), which is a sequel to Jane Austen's *Emma*, and *Tiger Sky* (1998). She has been accused of depicting the petty predicaments of the idle class, yet her characterisation is not unreflective, and many characters reveal empty and tense lives beneath the veneer of the privileged upper class.

Binchy, Maeve (1940–) Born in Dublin, Ireland, and educated at University College, Dublin (BA 1960), she has worked as a teacher and then as a journalist in the late 1960s, subsequently publishing selections from her columns in the *Irish Times*. Collections of short stories are linked by place and travel, as in *Central Line* (1977), *Victoria Line* (1980), *Dublin 4* (1982), *The Lilac Bus* (1984) and *The Return Journey* (1998). A romantic novelist, her first novel was *Light a Penny Candle* (1982), which became a bestseller, depicting the evacuation of a girl from London to a small Irish village during the Second World War. There followed *Echoes* (1985), *Firefly Summer* (1987), *Silver Wedding* (1988), *Circle of Friends* (1990, filmed 1995), *The Copper Beech* (1992) and *The Glass Lake* (1994), the latter two looking at small-town loves and jealousies and the search for freedom from religious and cultural oppression. Recent titles include *This Year it Will Be Different* (1995), *Evening Class* (1996) and *Tara Road* (1998). Her latest novel is *Scarlet Feather* (2000). She has also written plays, including one for television, *Deeply Regretted By* (1979). An immensely popular author, her novels are tinged with nostalgia for the Ireland of the 1950s and 1960s, with ordinary, sympathetic, tolerant characters in Irish family life.

Bissoondath, Neil (1955–) Born Neil (Devindra) Bissoondath, in Arima, Trinidad, the nephew of V.S. NAIPAUL, he emigrated to Canada in 1973, and was educated at York University (BA 1977) in Toronto. He then taught English and French in Toronto (1977–1985), before publishing his first book, a collection of short stories, *Digging Up the Mountains* (1985), which explored exile, estrangement, dislocation and domestic upheaval. His first novel was *A Casual Brutality* (1988), about social upheaval in the Caribbean islands as Raj Ramsingh returns from Canada to find political corruption and violence at home. Further short stories appeared in *On the Eve of Uncertain Tomorrows* (1990), again about cultural alienation and restlessness. Recent novels are *The Innocence of Age* (1992), which looks at the alienation of a white Canadian within the increasingly materialist Toronto culture, and *The Worlds within Her* (1998), the story of a woman who returns to her Indian community on the West Indian island of her birth, which creates new understandings for her before her return to Canada. He has also written the non-fiction study *Selling Illusions: The Cult of Multiculturalism in Canada* (1994). An

up-and-coming writer, he has won great acclaim for his fiction to date.

Blixen, Karen (1885–1962) Born Christenze Dinesen in Rungsted, Denmark, she studied English at Oxford University (1904) and painting in Copenhagen and Rome. Between 1913 and 1921, she managed a coffee plantation in Kenya with her husband, although the farm collapsed. She met Denys Finch Hatton, who became her lover and companion. She turned to writing in 1934 under the pen-name Isak Dinesen, and since she was bilingual, wrote in English and translated her own works into Danish. After the decadent nineteenth-century motifs in *Seven Gothic Tales* (1934), she wrote her widely acclaimed *Out of Africa* (1937, filmed 1985), which depicted her life in Africa in the form of a memoir and pastoral romance. There followed *Winter's Tales* (1942), little masterpieces derived from Shakespeare's plays, *Last Tales* (1957), about one's control over destiny, and *Anecdotes of Destiny* (1958), which included the story 'Babette's Feast' which was made into an acclaimed film (1987). Poor health accounts for the sparseness of publication in the 1940s and 1950s, although she did produce *Shadows on the Grass* (1961), four sentimental and anecdotal short stories set in Africa before her death. Posthumous publications include *Carnival* (1977), *Letters from Africa, 1914–1931* (1981), which revealed her patrician and snobbish outlook while in Africa, recollections of Hitler's Germany in *Daguerrotypes* (1979), images, reminiscences and descriptions collected in *Isak Dinesen's Africa* (1985), and *On Modern Marriage* (1986). She also wrote a thriller called *The Angelic Avengers* (1944, trans. 1946) under the pseudonym Pierre Andrezel. Twice nominated for the Nobel Prize for Literature, she is one of Denmark's most widely acclaimed writers, composing exotic and archaic tales set apart from the literary traditions of her day.

S. Aiken, *Isak Dinesen and the Engendering of Narrative* (1990).

Blythe, Ronald (1922–) Born in Acton, Suffolk, England, Ronald George Blythe was a librarian in Colchester who turned to writing in 1960. He has written a novel entitled *A Treasonable Growth* (1960), edited the anthology *Each Returning Day* (1989), and short stories occur in *Immediate Possession* (1961) and *The Stories of Ronald Blythe* (1985). However, his reputation rests upon his non-fiction, in particular two 'oral histories'. In 1967, he interviewed various people about their lives, edited the material, gave them fictional names, and placed them in his fictional rural village in East Anglia. This acclaimed imaginary portrait of an English village was *Akenfield* (1969), and the technique was repeated for another social history in *The View in Winter* (1979), this time an enquiry into old age and the social mores that surround it. More recently, he has written similar literary-historical books in *Word from Wormingford: A Parish Year* (1997) and *Out of the Valley: More Words from Wormingford* (2000), which depict the cycle of seasons in the life of a parish. His other non-fiction includes *The Age of Illusion* (1963), *From the Headlands* (1982), the travelogue *Divine Landscapes* (1986), *Private Words: Letters and Diaries from the Second World War* (1991), and *First Friends* (1997), which discusses the letters of the English artist Paul Nash. His skill occurs in his capacity for absorbing others' stories and imaginatively recasting them, and his eye for acute detail.

Bolger, Dermot (1959–) An Irish novelist and playwright, born in Dublin, who began writing as a poet, with *The Habit of Flesh* (1979). His first novel was *Night Shift* (1985), based upon his experience as a factory worker, and concerning a young man who copes with his girlfriend's pregnancy by a rushed marriage, and his subsequent unhappiness. Other novels include *The Woman's Daughter* (1987), which examines the physical and sexual abuse of a woman, *The Journey Home* (1990), a thriller that attacks political corruption, and *Emily's Shoes* (1992), which concerns an obsession and a man's unhappiness. *A Second Life* (1994) is about the search for his mother by a man who was adopted as a child, and was followed by *Father's Music* (1997). His novels frequently deal with the deprived people of Dublin, and invert the traditional depictions of the Irish people as exiles, instead showing them to be 'internal exiles', politically and economically severed from their own country. He has also written several plays including *The Lament for Arthur Cleary* (1989), *The Passion of Jerome* (1999) and *In High Germany* (1999), as well as many further volumes of poetry. He edited the important anthology of contemporary poetry written in Irish, *The Bright Wave/An Tonn Gheal* (1986) and *The Picador Book of Irish Contemporary Fiction* (1993). Recently, he has devised and edited *Finbar's Hotel* (1997) and *Ladies' Night at Finbar's Hotel* (1999), in which a set of tales are written by a number of authors each responsible for one chapter, although the reader is left to decide who wrote which chapter from the listed authors. His writing is committed to demystifying the present through reinterpretations of history.

Böll, Heinrich (1917–1985) Born Heinrich Theodor Böll, in Cologne, Germany, he loathed the Nazis and successfully resisted joining the Hitler Youth. After a brief period as a bookseller, a labourer and studying at university, he fought for the *Wehrmacht* in the Crimea and in France, before being captured by American forces in 1945. After his release, he became a writer, joining Gruppe 47, a group of young critical writers dedicated to salvaging German literature from post-war chaos. After the early novels *The Train Was on Time* (1949, trans. 1956) and *Traveller, If You Come to Spa* (1950, trans. 1956), he established his reputation with *Adam, Where Art Thou?* (1951, trans. 1955), a novel where he considers the final phase of German resistance in 1945, which became known as 'trummer-literatur' ('rubble literature'), set in the agonies of prostrate post-war Germany. The gloom and deep solemnity of 'trummer-literatur' gave way in the 1950s, 1960s and 1970s – the years of the German 'Economic Miracle' – to brilliant ironic treatments of post-war hypocrisy, of the Germans' ways of insulating themselves against the inconvenient past. The themes of remembering and forgetting energise four extraordinary later works: *Billiards at Half-Past Nine* (1959, trans. 1961), regarded by some as his greatest novel, marks a stylistic departure from the conventional novel and recounts within the space of twenty-four hours the key historical events and conflicts of the twentieth century as reflected in the lives of three generations of a family of architects; *The Clown* (1963, trans. 1965), looks at the effects of the Roman Catholic church; an amusing, sharp attack on relentless authoritarianism and bureaucracy occurs in *The End of a Mission* (1966, trans. 1967); and the cleverly structured satirical novel *Group Portrait with Lady* (1971, trans. 1973), is rich in incident and with a wealth of characters. His writing attacked Germany's fascist political past and the materialism of its contemporary society. In later years, Böll's growing alarm at the power of institutions and government over individuals moved him further to the left politically, and this is clearly reflected in his literary work. For example, *The Lost Honour of Katharina Blüm* (1974, trans. 1975) is a denunciation of the methods of character assassination employed by sections of the press. Later novels include *The Safety Net* (1979, trans. 1982), *A Soldier's Legacy*

(1982, trans. 1985), *The Casualty* (1983, trans. 1986) and *Woman in a River Landscape* (1985, trans. 1988). Perhaps the most outstanding German novelist of his generation, he also wrote a play, essays, articles, and a memoir in *What's to Become of the Boy?* (1981, trans. 1984). *The Silent Angel*, a previously lost early novel from the 1950s, was published in 1992. Documenting the development of the Federal Republic of Germany from its inception, he is noted for his stylistic polish, characterisation, plots, pitch-perfect irony and deep seriousness, in provocative works driven by a left-wing humanism tinged with anti-clerical Catholicism. He was awarded the Nobel Prize for Literature in 1972.

M. Butler, *Heinrich Böll and the Challenge of Literature* (1988).

Borges, Jorge Luis (1899–1986) Born in Buenos Aires, Argentina, he went to the Collège de Genève, Switzerland during the First World War, and returned to Argentina in 1921. He co-founded various journals, and worked as a columnist and librarian (1939–1946). After working as a poultry inspector, he went blind in 1955, although was appointed as the Director of the National Library (1955–1973) and was a Professor at the University of Buenos Aires (1955–1970). Widely honoured, he is arguably the most significant and influential Latin American writer, exerting a particular influence upon the development of postmodernist literature. His early fiction includes *A Universal History of Infamy* (1935, trans. 1971), in which stories about cruelty, violence and evil are purportedly based upon fact, and *Six Problems for Don Isidro Parodi* (1942, trans. 1981), written under the pseudonym H. Bustos Domecq with Adolfo Casares. His two mature fictional works are the short stories in *Fictions* (1944, trans. 1965) and *The Aleph* (1949, trans. 1970), which are modernist and postmodernist fables exploring a world of chance without certainties or ultimate meaning, in which language does not express or explore reality and his favourite symbol is the labyrinth. The most famous stories are 'Tlön, Uqbar, Orbis Tertius', 'The Aleph', 'Pierre Menard, Author of *Don Quixote*' and 'The Library of Babel', which break with the style of realism and engage with abstract questions and the problems of writing. There followed *Chronicles of Bustos Domecq* (1967, trans. 1982), *Dr Brodie's Report* (1970, trans. 1974), *The Congress* (1970, trans. 1974), and *The Book of Sand* (1975, trans. 1977). His volumes of poetry include *Dreamtigers* (1960, trans. 1964) and *In Praise of Darkness* (1969, trans. 1975), which show the influence of the European avant-garde. Essays and other works include *Other Inquisitions 1937–1952* (1952, trans. 1964) and *The Book of Imaginary Beings* (1957, trans. 1969), and recently compiled anthologies of his work are *Labyrinths* (1970) and *Selected Poems* (1972). With his existential preoccupations continually blurring the distinction between the imaginary and the real, no South American writer escapes his influence.

E. Monegal, *Jorge Luis Borges: A Literary Biography* (1978); S. Molloy, *Signs of Borges* (1994).

Bosman, Herman Charles (1905–1951) Born at Kuils River, near Cape Town, South Africa, he graduated from the University of Witwatersrand and Normal College, where he gained a teaching diploma in 1925. He then taught in a remote area of northern Transvaal, the setting for his 'Oom Schalk Louwrens' short stories, featuring an old raconteur with his anecdotes of generally wily Boer farmers and sharply realistic depictions of rural Afrikaner life, which were first collected in *Mafeking Road* (1947). Although an Afrikaner, he wrote almost exclusively in English, and his other short story collections include *Unto Dust*

(1963), *Jurie Steyn's Post Office* (1971), *Makapan's Cave* (1987) and *Romoutsa Road* (1990). He recounts his four years spent in prison for killing his brother in a family brawl in *Cold Stone Jug* (1949). On his release, he edited literary journals, lived in Europe for a time, and upon returning to South Africa in 1939, he continued with journalism and selling advertising. His first novel, *Jacaranda in the Night* (1947), was not a success and his fame was slow to spread. His best known work, *Willemsdorp* (1977), which was posthumously published, recollects the rise to power of an underprivileged Afrikaner after the 1948 elections. In addition to three volumes of poetry in the 1930s published under the pseudonym Herman Malan, other stories, later sketches and plays appear in two volumes of *The Collected Works of Herman Charles Bosman* (1981). *Uncollected Essays* also appeared in 1981.

S. Gray, ed., *Herman Charles Bosman* (1986).

Bowen, Elizabeth (1899–1973) Born Elizabeth Dorothea, in Dublin, Ireland, her early years were spent divided between Dublin, Bowen Court, her family ancestral house (which she inherited in 1930 and which she described in *Bowen's Court*, 1942), and south England resorts. After a brief time spent as an art student in London, she began writing novels, such as *The Hotel* (1927) and *The Last September* (1929), which are set in Ireland and portray youthful, romantic but short-lived engagements. There followed *Friends and Relations* (1931), about a battle for power in English middle-class life, *The North* (1932), about passions underlying social façades, and *The House in Paris* (1935). Her finest work is usually considered to be *The Death of the Heart* (1938) and *The Heat of the Day* (1949), the latter drawing upon her experiences of the ARP during the London Blitz. Later novels include *A World of Love* (1955), which is a romantic love story set in

Ireland, *The Little Girls* (1964) and *Eva Trout* (1969). A prolific writer of short stories, these include the volumes *Encounters* (1923), *Ann Lee's* (1926), *The Cat Jumps* (1934), *The Demon Lover* (1945) and *A Day in the Dark* (1965). Her *Collected Stories* were published in 1980. She also wrote criticism, history and travel works, such as *English Novelists* (1942), *Collected Impressions* (1950) and *A Time in Rome* (1960). Much of her fiction concerns innocence, manipulation, betrayal, fidelity, seeking security in relationships, and the fears and fantasies that lie beneath a veneer of respectability, be it in the 'Big House' in Ireland or the seasonal resorts of south England. Along with writers like her friends L.P. HARTLEY, Henry GREEN and Ivy COMPTON-BURNETT, her psychological and psychic narratives in a witty and mannered style are being reassessed as significant portrayals of the inter-war and post-Second World War years.

P. Lassner, *Elizabeth Bowen* (1990).

Bowen, John (1924–) Born in Calcutta, India, John Griffith Bowen attended Oxford University (MA 1952), worked in publishing from 1953 to 1960, and thereafter in drama and television. He began by writing novels, his first being *The Truth Will Not Help Us* (1956), about a historical event of piracy in 1705 in Britain, in terms which echo the McCarthyite atmosphere of 1950s America. Often containing sharp and memorable scenes, his fiction addresses the issues of form and varies across a wide range of styles: *After the Rain* (1959) is science fiction, *The Centre of the Green* (1959) is naturalistic, *Storyboard* (1960) is about an advertising agency, *The Birdcage* (1961) is in the form of a nineteenth-century essay on commercial television, written from an objectively detached perspective, *A World Elsewhere* (1966) is about a politician writing a parallel story of Philoctetes, *Squeak* (1983) is told from the perspective

of a racing pigeon, while *The McGuffin* (1984) is a first person narrative. Other novels include *The Girls* (1986), *The Precious Gift* (1992) and *No Retreat* (1994). *Hetty Wainthrop Investigates* (1995) and *Hetty Wainthrop: Woman of the Year* (1996) have been adapted with David Cook from the television series. In the mid-1960s, he turned to writing plays for stage and television, such as *After the Rain* (1967) and *Little Boxes* (1968), and more recently, *Cold Salmon* (1998).

Bowles, Jane (1917–1973) Born in New York City, she frequented the Greenwich Village bars and salons in the 1930s, where she met many members of the artistic community. She married author Paul BOWLES in 1930, and on their travels, she wrote *Two Serious Ladies* (1943), which established her reputation among the avant-garde. Mixing fantasy and autobiographical material of life on Staten Island, it depicts the relationship between two women, one rich and prosperous and one sinful and sensuous. Although she remained married to Paul until her death, her emotional relationships centred on women and, as her fiction reveals, her interest lay in the female psyche and consciousness. In the 1940s, she wrote several short stories (most significantly, 'Camp Cataract' in 1949) and a play, *In the Summer House* (1954). After a period in Morocco, she was partially stricken by a stroke in 1957. She spent the remainder of her life in and out of hospitals, and suffered serious writer's block during the 1960s. However, with Paul's editorial aid, she published a collection of short stories, *Plain Pleasures* (1966), and *The Collected Works* (1966). Her final five years were spent hospitalised in Malaga, Spain. An enlarged edition of her collected work was published as *My Sister's Hand in Mine* (1978), and *Feminine Wiles* (1976) collected her stories, sketches and letters. In a highly associative writing style exploring bisexuality and pictures of indecision and isolation, her humour, surprise and precision of fiction has gained her a cult following.

M. Dillon, *A Little Original Sin* (1981).

Bowles, Paul (1910–1986) An American novelist, born in New York City, he was educated at the University of Virginia at Charlottesville, which he left in 1929 to go to France. He studied music with Aaron Copland and Virgil Thomson, and during the 1930s and 1940s, he lived in New York and gained a reputation as a composer, writing scores for ballets, films, and an opera – *The Wind Remains* (1943). He married Jane (née Auer) BOWLES in 1938, beginning a tense and unconventional relationship until her death in 1973. In 1945 he began to write short stories, and sailed to Morocco to work on his first novel, *The Sheltering Sky* (1949, filmed in 1991 by Bertolucci), about alienated American emigrés travelling in North Africa and their existential crises in the face of Arabic culture. After this critical and commercial success, he settled in Tangier where he received a string of literary friends including Truman CAPOTE, William BURROUGHS and Allen Ginsberg, and continued writing about westerners in an Arab world. The themes of isolation, loneliness, loss of tradition, alienation and rootlessness structure *Let It Come Down* (1952) and *The Spider's House* (1955), while *Up Above the World* (1966) is about a couple in Central America. Short story collections include *A Little Stone* (1950), *Collected Stories* (1979), *A Delicate Episode* (1988) and *Unwelcome Words* (1989), while volumes of poetry include *The Thicket of Spring* (1972) and *Next to Nothing* (1981). He also published travel writings, a series of 'translations', which are the purported edited words from recordings of a young Moroccan servant with whom Bowles had a relationship, and include *Love with a Few Hairs* (1967), *M'Hashish* (1969) and *The Beach Café and the Voice* (1976); an

autobiography entitled *Without Stopping* (1972); and a collection of letters appeared in 1994. Long regarded as a central figure of the literary counter-culture, he has concerned himself with drug-induced visions, displaced and alienated westerners, French existentialism, and the quest for selfhood.

C.S. Laucanno, *An Invisible Spectator* (1989).

Boyd, Martin (1893–1972) Born in Lucerne, Switzerland, he came from a distinguished family in the arts in Europe and Australia, and spent his early years in Victoria, Australia. He went to theological college, but withdrew before he took orders, and practised architecture in Melbourne until the First World War, when he joined the British army in France, developing the disgust for militarism that pervades much of his fiction. His first work was *Retrospect* (1920), a volume of poems about post-war alienation, followed by three early novels written under the pseudonym Martin Mills, *Love Gods* (1925), *Brangane: A Memoir* (1926) and *The Montforts* (1928). Other novels include *The Lemon Farm* (1935), *The Painted Princess* (1936), *Night of the Party* (1938), *Nuns in Jeopardy* (1940), *Lucinda Brayford* (1946) and *Such Pleasure* (1949). His best known work was the Langton tetralogy, consisting of *The Cardboard Crown* (1952), *A Difficult Young Man* (1955), *Outbreak of Love* (1957) and *When Blackbirds Sing* (1962). The sequence dealt with Australian material influenced by the Graeco-Christian tradition, showing the dying aristocratic system by tracing an 80-year family history. Volumes of autobiography are entitled *A Single Flame* (1939) and *Day of My Delight* (1965), and after settling in Rome, he wrote the travel book *Much Else in Italy* (1958). His fiction shows the aristocracy and art embattled with modern forces of commerce, science and materialism, although his narrowness of social range has been the cause for some criticism.

B. Niall, *Martin Boyd* (1977).

Boyd, William (1952–) Born William Andrew Murray Boyd, in Accra, Ghana, he went to the University of Glasgow (MA 1975) and undertook some postgraduate study at Oxford University (1975–1980), since when he has been a novelist, screenwriter and newspaper journalist. His first novel, *A Good Man in Africa* (1981), was about the comic misadventures of a junior diplomat in postcolonial West Africa, followed by *An Ice-Cream War* (1982), a serio-comic tale set in East Africa during the First World War, in which six characters are swept up in the conflict and the senselessness of war. *Stars and Bars* (1985) is about a hapless Englishman abroad in Manhattan, struggling to understand a foreign culture and its mores, and *The New Confessions* (1988), inspired by Rousseau's *Confessions*, is about a Scottish film-maker looking back over his life. *Brazzaville Beach* (1990) returns to Africa and a naturalist's work with chimpanzee behaviour, *The Blue Afternoon* (1993) depicts a relationship when a woman architect meets an enigmatic man who claims to be her father, and his most recent novel is *Armadillo* (1998). He wrote *Nat Tate: An American Artist 1928–1960* (1998), which is a biography of an artist who was revealed to be a fictional character in a *New York Times* article in April 1998. Short stories are collected in *On the Yankee Station* (1981), *The Destiny of Nathalie 'X'* (1994) and *Killing Lizards* (1995). In addition to various screenplays, including Evelyn WAUGH's *Scoop* for television (1986), he has developed a wide reputation for his consistently darkly humorous and biting satirical fiction which is often set in the past and deals with memory.

Boyle, T. Coraghessan (1948–) Full name Thomas Coraghessan Boyle, he is an American novelist, born in Peekshill, New York, and is a descendant of Irish immigrants. He was educated at the State University of New York and the University of Iowa. His first novel was *Water Music* (1981), set in 1795 and interweaving scenes from London and the explorer Mungo Park's adventures in the Sahara. Subsequent novels are *Budding Prospects* (1984), about a marijuana cultivator, *World's End* (1987), *East Is East* (1990), which depicts a Japanese man's negotiation of western culture in America, *The Road to Wellville* (1993), which focuses upon the life of John Kellogg, the inventor of the cornflake, *Tortilla Curtain* (1995), which is a moving description of the difficult lives of immigrant and illegal Mexicans in California and white middle-class values, *Riven Rock* (1998), which explores misogyny, mental illness and the shadowy side of love, and *Friend of the Earth* (2000). Short stories occur in *Descent of Man* (1981), *Greasy Lake* (1985), *If the River Was Whiskey* (1989), *Without a Hero* (1995) and *The Collected Stories of T.C. Boyle* (1998). His style combines an anarchic and surreal humour, with a zeal for off-beat historical and cultural narratives.

Bradbury, Malcolm (1932–2000) An English writer, born Malcolm Stanley Bradbury, in Sheffield, Yorkshire, and educated at the universities of Leicester, London and Manchester. After travelling in the US, from 1959 he lectured at the universities of Hull, Birmingham and then East Anglia, where he became Professor of American Studies and ran a highly successful creative writing programme with such graduates as Ian MCEWAN and Kazuo ISHIGURO. His first novel was *Eating People Is Wrong* (1959), a satirical work about the provincial red-brick academic world in which he established his career. His next novel, *Stepping Westward* (1965), was based upon his American academic experiences. More innovative in style, *The History Man* (1975, adapted for television by Bradbury) gained him wide recognition and was about a manipulative lecturer at the 'plate-glass' university of Watermouth. This was followed by *Rates of Exchange* (1983), about a linguist in a fictional eastern European country, *Why Come to Slaka?* (1986), a guidebook to that fictional country, *Cuts* (1987) about Thatcherite Britain, and *Doctor Criminale* (1992), about modern history and eastern Europe. His other work includes many works of literary criticism including *Saul Bellow* (1982), *Ten Great Writers* (1989), *The Modern American Novel* (1993), *Dangerous Pilgrimages: Trans-Atlantic Mythologies and the Novel* (1995) and *Diderot at the Hermitage* (2000), an imaginary collection of humorous letters in *Unsent Letters* (1988), and several plays collected in *The After Dinner Game* (1982) and *Inside Trading* (1997). Often writing novels of ideas, he satirises British academic life and jargon in comic parodies.

Bradbury, Ray (1920–) Born Ray Douglas Bradbury, in Waukegan, Illinois, US, he was a writer of fantasy and science fiction, published initially in pulp magazines, but gradually becoming known as a serious author by 1945. His numerous novels include the famous *Fahrenheit 451* (1953, filmed 1966), a moral fable about a future totalitarian state and its prohibition on books – the title refers to the temperature at which book paper catches fire – *Dandelion Wine* (1957), *Something Wicked This Way Comes* (1962) and *A Graveyard for Lunatics* (1990). His voluminous short stories are collected in *Dark Carnival* (1947), *The Martian Chronicles* (1950), *The Illustrated Man* (1951), in which a man's tattoos eerily come to life as fantastic tales, *The Golden Apples of the Sun* (1953), *October Country* (1955), *A Meditation for Melancholy* (1959), *R Is for Robot, S Is for Space* (1962), *The*

Machineries of Joy (1964), *Twice Twenty-Two* (1966), *I Sing the Body Electric* (1969), *Quicker Than the Eye* (1996) and *Driving Blind* (1997). Bradbury has also written many plays and film scripts, and volumes of poems in *When Elephants Last in the Doorway Bloomed* (1977), *When Robot Men and Robot Women Run Round in Robot Towns* (1977), and *With Cat for Comforter* (1997). *Green Shadows, White Whale* (1992) is an account of his time working in Ireland in the 1950s as a scriptwriter on John Huston's film of *Moby Dick*, while essays are collected in *Yestermorrow* (1991) and *Journey to Far Metaphor* (1994).

Bradford, Barbara Taylor (1933–) Born in Leeds, Yorkshire, she worked as a journalist for magazines and newspapers between 1949 and 1964, and after her marriage and move to the US, became a columnist for American newspapers. She has written a variety of fashion, home design and decorating books, but has become one of the defining novelists of the popular, best-selling romance. Her first novel was *A Woman of Substance* (1979), which broke paperback records, and concerned Emma Harte, a Yorkshire woman who rises from obscurity to found a retail empire and exact revenge on her nobleman seducer. Similar plots of wealth, love, often illicit affairs and romance, intrigue and strong heroines, form the staple of her many subsequent novels, among which are *Voice of the Heart* (1983), *Hold the Dream* (1985), *Act of Will* (1986), *To Be the Best* (1988), *The Woman in His Life* (1990), *Angel* (1993), *Everything to Gain* (1994), *Love in Another Town* (1995), *Her Own Rules* (1996), *A Secret Affair* (1996), *Power of a Woman* (1997), *A Sudden Change of Heart* (1999) and *Where You Belong* (2000). Many of her books have been adapted for television mini-series.

Bragg, Melvyn (1939–) Born in Carlisle, England, he graduated from Oxford

University (MA 1961) in modern history, and has since become well known as a media personality in British television and radio. He has published over fifteen novels, many examining traditional life in the English countryside in Cumberland. His first novels *For Want of a Nail* (1965) and *The Second Inheritance* (1966) were about wasted human potential, yet his reputation was established with *Without a City Wall* (1968), about a sexual struggle set in Cumberland. There followed *The Hired Man* (1969), the first novel of what was later published as *The Cumbrian Trilogy* (1984), also consisting of *A Place in England* (1970) and *Kingdom Come* (1980). The trilogy centres upon the Tallentire family, exploring class and region in Cumberland from the Victorian period to the present. Among his other novels set in Cumberland are *Josh Lawton* (1972), *Autumn Manoeuvres* (1978), *The Maid of Buttermere* (1987), an historical narrative of 1802, and *A Time to Dance* (1990), the latter two set in the Lake District. Other novels include *The Nerve* (1971), *The Hunt* (1972), *The Silken Net* (1974), *Love and Glory* (1983), *Crystal Rooms* (1992) and *The Soldier's Return* (1999). In addition to screenplays, he has written biographies of the actors Laurence Olivier (1984) and Richard Burton (1988), as well as *Speak for England* (1976), the results of a series of interviews with people about their lives in his hometown of Wigton, Cumberland. Always exploring the connections between place and environment and characters' psychologies, fortunes and developments, he has made an understated yet significant contribution to the English regional novel.

Braine, John (1922–1986) An English writer, born John Gerard Braine, in Bradford, Yorkshire, and educated at the Leeds School of Librarianship. He became identified with the so-called 'angry young men', a term used to describe the alienated and abrasive northern English wri-ters of the 1950s, like Stan BARSTOW, Alan SILLITOE and the playwright John Osborne. They rejected what they saw to be the avant-garde devices and artistic élitism of modernism, espousing an ethic of individualism and rebellious, amoral youth. His best-known novel is the gritty, realist *Room at the Top* (1957, filmed 1958), which epitomised an age, and concerned Joe Lampton, a cynical working-class man who is trapped in an unhappy marriage with the daughter of a wealthy businessman as he makes his way to the top. *Life at the Top* (1962) was a sequel, about Lampton's disillusionment with the bourgeois society to which he had aspired. Subsequently abandoning his angry left-wing stance, other books are *The Vodi* (1959), *The Jealous God* (1964), *The Crying Game* (1968), *Stay with Me Till Morning* (1970), a thriller in *The Pious Agent* (1975), *Finger of Fire* (1977) and *One and Last Love* (1981). In addition to the autobiographical novel *These Golden Days* (1985), he also wrote a biography of J.B. PRIESTLEY (1978).

Brautigan, Richard (1935–1984) Born in Tacoma, Washington, he came to prominence in the 1960s as a San Francisco novelist who loosely conceived short 'novels' composed of cosmic, whimsical and surreal sketches of the Beat way of life. His fiction includes such well-known works as *A Confederate General from Big Sur* (1964), the hugely successful *Trout Fishing in America* (1967), about a parodic search for the perfect fishing spot, *In Watermelon Sugar* (1967), a description of commune life, *The Abortion: An Historical Romance* (1971), *The Hawkline Monster: A Gothic Western* (1974), *Sombrero Fallout* (1976) and *The Tokyo-Montana Express* (1980). Critical of the ideology of the American Dream, his writing frequently mixes humour with sadness, and yet looks optimistically to nature as a constant, which linked him to the nineteenth-century American Transcendentalists like Thoreau and Emerson.

His short stories were published as *Revenge of the Lawn* (1971), and he also released a number of poetry collections about uninhibited sexuality and personal encounters. He became one of the primary writers of the 'new fiction', and a guru of the 1960s hippy counter-culture. In the early 1980s, he left San Francisco and became an instructor at Montana State University. He committed suicide by shooting himself in California.

T. Malley, *Richard Brautigan: Writers for the Seventies* (1972).

Brink, André (1935–) Full name André Philippus Brink, he was born in Vrede, South Africa, into a conservative Afrikaner family who supported nationalism and apartheid. He was educated at the ultra-conservative University of Potchefstroom, Transvaal (BA 1955, MA 1959), and then at the Sorbonne, University of Paris (1959–1961), where he repudiated South Africa's racial policies. On returning to South Africa, he became a lecturer at Rhodes University and is currently Professor of English at the University of Cape Town. His name became associated with a group of young Afrikaner writers called the 'Sestigers' ('Sixtyers', i.e. of the 1960s), whose aim was to try to subvert the traditional parochial and conformist limits of Afrikaner writing. This meant writing frankly about sexual, moral and political issues, and developing an Afrikaans which was not solely identified with oppression, which inevitably antagonised the Afrikaner establishment. His first two novels, *The Price of Living* (trans. 1962) and *The Ambassador* (1963, trans. 1985), were not political books. However, his later work was highly critical of apartheid policy and its corrosive effect on the lives of all South Africans. *Looking on Darkness* (1973, trans. 1974) was the first Afrikaans-language work to be banned by the South African government. Depicting a 'Cape coloured' protagonist who has murdered his white lover awaiting execution on death row, it explores Afrikaner persecution and the torture of political prisoners in South African jails, and became something of an anti-apartheid handbook in 1976 during the Soweto riots. From then on, he wrote all his novels in both languages and translated them himself. Other books are *Rumours of Rain* (1978), set on the eve of the Soweto riots, *An Instant in the Wind* (1975, trans. 1976), about a love affair between a black man and a white woman, *A Dry White Season* (1979, filmed 1989), about a black man who dies in detention and his white friend who finds the state machinery turned against him when he seeks to find out what happened, and *A Chain of Voices* (1982), often considered his best novel, with multiple narrators exploring the forces of oppression and suffering against the background of a slave revolt in the Cape Colony in 1825. Later books include *The Wall of the Plague* (1984), *States of Emergency* (1988), *An Act of Terror* (1991), *On the Contrary* (1993), *The First Life of Adamastor* (1993), *Imaginings of Sand* (1993), and most recently, *Devil's Valley* (1998), which is a Dantesque descent into Devil's Valley during a crime reporter's search for information about an acquaintance. His recent fiction has adopted metafictional techniques, self-consciously foregrounding the act of writing and narration, in his explorations of the relationships between history, politics and fiction. As a literary critic, his essays have appeared in *Mapmakers: Writing in a State of Siege* (1983), *Reinventing a Continent* (1996), *Reinventions* (1996) and *The Novel* (1998), as well as studies and plays in Afrikaans. He has also edited, with J.M. COETZEE, *A Land Apart* (1986), an anthology of contemporary South African writing.

R. Jolly, *Colonisation, Violence, and Narration in White South African Writing* (1995).

Broch, Hermann (1886–1951) Born in Vienna, Austria, he was trained as a weaver and worked as a factory manager from 1907 to 1927. He gave up a distinguished business career and went to the University of Vienna (1926–1930), after which he became a writer. He moved to London after the Nazi *Anschluss* and became an American citizen in 1944. He is best known for the trilogy *The Sleep-walkers* (1931–1932, trans. 1932), which consists of *Pasenow; or the Romantic*, *Esch; or the Anarchist*, and *Hugenau; or the Realist*. Set in Germany between 1880 and 1918, they depict a society in crisis with the political orders breaking up and traditions being challenged, and people likened to sleepwalkers without moral guidance. Containing complex fictional structures, these novels began to experiment with new modes of narration. Other novels include *The Unknown Quantity* (1933, trans. 1935), *The Death of Virgil* (trans. 1945), an inner monologue of Virgil's visions and dreams during the final hours before his death, *The Guiltless* (1950, trans. 1974) and *The Spell* (1976, trans. 1987). A prolific essayist, he wrote plays and non-fiction, including a study of the Austrian dramatist and poet Hugo von Hofmannstahl (trans. 1978). Believing that art should set ethical standards for human conduct, his main theme is a plea for the re-consideration of moral values without which he thought society would decay.

S. Dowden, *Broch: Literature, Philosophy, Politics* (1988).

Brodkey, Harold (1930–1996) Born Harold Roy Brodkey, in Alton, Illinois, US. After graduating from Harvard University (1952), he made a considerable reputation for himself as a writer of short stories, which were frequently published in *The New Yorker*, for which he became a staff writer from 1987. The stories handle such subjects as adolescence, college life, marriage and parenthood, and many take the form of autobiographical narratives. Several collections were published: *First Love and Other Sorrows* (1957), *Women and Angels* (1985), *Stories in an Almost Classical Mode* (1988), and *Profane Friendship* (1994), about a homosexual relationship. After many years of preparation, 1991 saw the eventual publication of his eagerly awaited novel *The Runaway Soul*, which focused upon Wiley Silenowicz, an adopted 14-year-old boy, tormented by his half-sister. A prodigious work with Proustian and Joycean echoes, it is an exploration of memory and Wiley's maturing identity, and is a postmodern exploration of consciousness to rival Thomas PYNCHON's work. Considered an elusive writer, his writing is characterised by minute attention to details.

Brooke-Rose, Christine (1926–) Born in Geneva, Switzerland, after wartime service with the British intelligence, she gained degrees from Oxford University (BA 1949, MA 1953) and the University of London (Ph.D. 1954). She worked as a freelance literary journalist (1956–1968), and then living in France, became an academic at the University of Paris VIII in English and American literature. Known for her experimental fiction with a fascination for language games and playful poststructuralist aims and methods, her first works were the conventional novels *The Languages of Love* (1957) and *The Sycamore Tree* (1958). Her third novel, *The Dear Deceit* (1960), signalled her narrative experiments, reversing a man's life from death to birth. Her major experimental novels were *Out* (1964), *Such* (1965), *Between* (1968), *Thru* (1975) and *Amalgamemnon* (1984), often with verbal puns, typographical ruses and exposing fiction's fictionality. The much praised *Xorandor* (1986), and the sequel *Verbivore* (1990), use science fiction and experimental literary techniques to explore the perils of nuclear proliferation and informational technology, while recent works are *Textermination* (1992), *Remake* (1996), which is an autobiographical narrative in the third person, *Next* (1998) and *Subscript* (1999). Short stories occur in *Go When You See the Green Man Walking* (1969), and literary criticism and essays occur in *A Grammar of Metaphor* (1958), *A ZBC of Ezra Pound* (1971), *A Rhetoric of the Unreal* (1981) and *Stories, Theories and Things* (1991). Influenced by science fiction and the French 'New Novel', she abandoned linearity and constantly deconstructs the traditional novel by underlining the artifice of texts.

S. Birch, *Christine Brooke-Rose and Contemporary Fiction* (1994).

Brookner, Anita (1928–) An English art historian and writer, born in London and educated at the University of London and the Cortauld Institute of Art, London (Ph.D. 1952). Her first novel was *A Start in Life* (1981), and she has written virtually one a year since then. Perhaps her best-known book is *Hotel du Lac* (1984, Booker Prize), about an intelligent but lonely writer of romances, Edith Hope, who is in search of romantic love, a plot which characterises many of her novels. Frequently highly cultured, her female protagonists seem to be alienated and drawn into misalliances. Other novels include *Providence* (1982), *Look At Me* (1983), *Family and Friends* (1985), *The Misalliance* (1986), *A Friend from England* (1987), *Lewis Percy* (1989), *Brief Lives* (1990), *A Closed Eye* (1991), *Fraud* (1992), *Family Romance* (1993), *A Private View* (1995), *Incidents in the Rue Laugier* (1995), *Altered States* (1996) *Visitors* (1997), *Falling Shadow* (1998) and *Undue Influence* (1999). An admirer of the fiction of Edith WHARTON and holding a reasoned suspicion of feminism, her writing exudes an old-fashioned atmosphere, which has led to charges of conservatism, sentimentality and élitism. An expert on eighteenth-century painting,

she has also written several books of art criticism, notably *Watteau* (1967), *Greuze* (1972), *Jacques-Louis David* (1981) and *Soundings* (1997).

Brophy, Brigid (1929–1995) Born Brigid Antonia Susan, in London, England, she attended Oxford University (1947–1948) and was expelled for sexual offences. An *enfant terrible*, she was precocious as a child writer and outspoken in her adult life on a number of social, political, antivivisectionist, gender and environmental issues. Her first novel was *Hackenfeller's Ape* (1953), about a London zoologist who sets free an ape when he learns that it is to be used for space research. It was followed by *The King of a Rainy Country* (1956), *Flesh* (1962), about the courtship and romance of two young Jews, *The Finishing Touch* (1963), which is a lesbian love fantasy, a comedy of middle-class manners in *The Snow Ball* (1964), *In Transit: An Heroicycle Novel* (1969), which is an avant-garde work, about a girl's struggle for identity in an airport terminal, and *Palace without Chairs* (1978), an allegory about democracy. Her short stories occur in *The Crown Princess* (1953) and *The Adventures of God in His Search for the Black Girl* (1973). Critical works include an attack on realism and naturalism in *Black Ship to Hell* (1962), biographies of Mozart (1964), Aubrey Beardsley (1968) and Ronald FIRBANK (1973), and the literary and cultural essays in *Baroque 'n' Roll* (1987), which features an essay about her multiple sclerosis, and *Reads* (1989). The later years of her life were spent organising the Public Lending Rights Law of 1979, a fee paid to authors for the loan of library books.

Brown, George Mackay (1921–1996) A Scottish poet and novelist, he was born in Stromness, Orkney. After his education, which involved encouragement by the poet Edwin Muir, he published his first substantial collection of poetry entitled

The Storm (1954), followed by *Loaves and Fishes* (1959). This was succeeded by numerous collections of poetry, including *Fisherman with Ploughs* (1971), an historical sequence of the Orkney locality, and often regarded as his finest work. Among a varied writing career, he has published short stories celebrating the elements and Scottish island lives in *A Calendar of Love* (1967), *A Time to Keep* (1969) and *The Sun's Net* (1976), various plays, children's books, and musical compositions, including a collaboration with the composer Peter Maxwell Davies on *The Martyrdom of St. Magnus* (1976) and an opera libretto for *The Two Fiddlers* (1978). His novels include *Greenvoe* (1972), praised for its seamless quality and its evocative descriptions of the Orkneys, *Vinland* (1992), about the Viking era, and *Beside the Ocean of Time* (1994), which was shortlisted for the Booker Prize. His writings emphasised ancestral myths and folklore, Scottish scenery and ancient and modern religious themes, and he was considered one of the writers responsible for the flowering of the Scottish Renaissance in the 1960s.

Buchan, John (1875–1940) A Scottish writer of adventure stories, born in Perth, Perthshire, and educated at the universities of Glasgow and Oxford (MA 1899). In a colourful career, the magnitude of his writing was matched only by its diversity. He read for the Bar and then worked with the British High Commission staff in South Africa (1901–1903), forming a lifelong dedication to the British Empire. He returned to England, and published his first book, *Prester John* (1910), a prophetic adventure story of an African uprising. After the First World War, he became director of information for the British government, and later an MP (1927–1935), before being appointed Governor-General of Canada (1935–1940). The first of his secret service thrillers featuring the British secret agent Richard Hannay, *The Thirty-Nine Steps* (1915), was later made

into a classic film (1935) by Alfred Hitchcock, and was followed by several sequels, such as *Greenmantle* (1932), *The Three Hostages* (1924) and *The Island of Sheep* (1936). He also wrote several historical novels, among them *The Path of the King* (1921), *Midwinter* (1923) and *Witch Wood* (1927). His last novel, published posthumously, was *Sick Heart River* (1941), set in Canada. Short story collections include *The Watcher by the Threshold* (1902) and *The Gap in the Curtain* (1932), and he also wrote several biographical studies of historical persons, including *Sir Walter Raleigh* (1897), *Montrose* (1928), *Sir Walter Scott* (1932) and *Julius Caesar* (1932). In addition to his autobiographical *Memory Hold-the-Door* (1940), was a mammoth twenty-four volume history of the First World War.

J. Smith, *John Buchan and His World* (1979).

Buck, Pearl S. (1892–1973) Born Pearl Sydenstricker Buck, in Hillsboro, West Virginia, US, she was a widely honoured and prolific writer who was awarded the Nobel Prize for Literature in 1938. The daughter of Presbyterian missionary parents, she lived in China until she moved to the US for her education. She went to Randolph-Macon Women's College (BA 1914) and Cornell University (MA 1926), before returning to Nanjing, China, as a missionary and university teacher in 1921. Her first work, *East Wind, West Wind* (1930), was followed by her best-known novel *The Good Earth* (1931, Pulitzer Prize 1932), which became a best-seller and is the first volume of a Chinese peasant family saga describing their struggle to gain land and position. The trilogy was completed by *Sons* (1932) and *A House Divided* (1935). She returned to the US in 1935, where she continued to publish a series of novels set in China, including *The Mother* (1934) and *Dragon Seed* (1942), which are the two novels considered to be her greatest achievement, *Far and Near* (1947), a study of the Chinese Empress Tzu Hsi in *Imperial Women* (1956), *The Three Daughters of Madame Lian* (1969) and *The Good Deed* (1969). American settings featured in *Portrait of a Marriage* (1945), *Voices in the House* (1953), the autobiographical *The Time Is Noon* (1967), and *The Goddess Abides* (1972). Her other writings include the much praised biographies of her parents, *Fighting Angel* (1936) and *The Exile* (1936), and an autobiography, *My Several Worlds* (1954). She was heavily involved in East–West humanitarian projects and children's welfare causes.

P. Doyle, *Pearl S. Buck* (1980).

Bulgakov, Mikhail (1891–1940) Born in Kiev, Russia, Mikhail Afanas'evich Bulgakov graduated in medicine from the University of Kiev (1916) and practised as a physician until 1919. He then turned to writing and drama and worked as a journalist until 1925, before becoming a producer at the Moscow Art Theatre (1930–1936). His novels include *The White Guard* (1925, trans. 1971), about the life of the Turbin family in Kiev in the late 1910s, which was a fictional reworking of his much loved play, *Days of the Turbins* (1926), the unfinished *Black Snow* (1965, trans. 1967), and *The Heart of a Dog* (trans. 1968). *The Master and Margarita* (1967, trans. 1967) is his masterpiece and is widely regarded as one of the greatest twentieth-century Russian novels. Blending satire, realism and fantasy, the three-stranded narrative explores the philosophical basis of good and evil in what is partly a Christian allegory. His short stories occur in *Diaboliad* (1925, trans. 1972), *A Country Doctor's Notebooks* (1963, trans. 1975) and *Notes on the Cuff* (trans. 1992), and he wrote a biography in *The Life of Monsieur de Molière* (1962, trans. 1970). One of the foremost satirists of post-revolutionary Russia, his fiction concerns the adjustment of Russian intellectual life under

communist rule. Censorship prevented his manuscripts from being published until after his death.

L. Weeks, ed., *The Master and Margarita: A Critical Companion* (1996).

Burgess, Anthony (1917–1993) A prolific novelist who published under the name Anthony Burgess, he was born John Wilson, in Manchester, England, and was educated at Manchester University (BA 1940). After serving in the British army in the 1940s, he worked as a teacher, and then served as an educator in the Colonial Service in Malaya and Borneo. His literary career began in the mid-1950s, with *Time for a Tiger* (1956), *The Enemy in the Blanket* (1958) and *Beds in the East* (1959), novels written as a result of his colonial experiences, and later published as *The Malayan Trilogy* (1972). He has subsequently written approximately sixty books, including novels, film scripts, plays, essays and translations. He is perhaps best known for *A Clockwork Orange* (1962), a bleak novel set in a drug-laden future society, and centring upon the brutally violent and sexually promiscuous activities of Alex, a gang leader. The novel examines conformity and freedom and behavioural reform methods as a cure for social delinquency. Stanley Kubrick's film version (1971) stirred up huge censure and was withdrawn from cinematic distribution in the UK by the director in the wake of press and public criticism. Also of note was the 'Enderby' series, the first of which is *Inside Mr Enderby* (1963, published under the pseudonym Joseph Kell), which introduced the adventures of F.X. Enderby, a middle-aged poet who often acted as a mouthpiece for Burgess himself concerning the situation of the artist. The series was continued with *Enderby Outside* (1968), *The Clockwork Testament, or Enderby's End* (1974), in which Enderby dies, only to be resurrected by popular appeal in *Enderby's Dark Lady, or No End to Enderby*

(1984), as a 'lost chapter' in Enderby's life. Among a huge number of other significant novels are *One Hand Clapping* (1961, as Joseph Kell), *Napoleon Symphony* (1974), about Beethoven, *Nineteen-Eighty Five* (1978), *Earthly Powers* (1980), often considered to be his masterpiece, about religious belief as the protagonist, Kenneth Toomey, a famous homosexual playwright and novelist, decides to record his memoirs, *The Kingdom of the Wicked* (1985), *The Pianoplayers* (1986), *Any Old Iron* (1989), and *A Dead Man in Deptford* (1993), a mystery novel focusing on the murder of the sixteenth-century English playwright Christopher Marlowe. In addition to a vast array of critical works, including books on James JOYCE like *Joysprick* (1973) and language like *Language Made Plain* (1964), he wrote two volumes of autobiography in *Little Wilson and Big God* (1987) and *You've Had Your Time* (1990), and the screenplay for Franco Zeffirelli's film, *Jesus of Nazareth* (1977). A prodigious writer, he contributed much to the world of post-war British literature.

C. Dix, *Anthony Burgess* (1971).

Burke, James Lee (1936–) An American writer, born in Houston, Texas, US, and educated at the universities of Southwestern Louisiana, Missouri and Columbia. His earliest novels were *Half of Paradise* (1965), *To the Bright and Shining Sun* (1970), *Lay Down My Sword and Shield* (1971), and his first big critical success, *The Lost Get-Back Boogie* (1986). He then turned to writing crime fiction, with the Cajun detective Dave Robichaux as his protagonist, the setting being the steamy oppressiveness of the bayou country of southern Louisiana, which is vividly conveyed in Burke's descriptive passages of the area. The Robichaux stories include *The Neon Rain* (1987), *Heaven's Prisoners* (1988), *Black Cherry Blues* (1988), *A Morning for Flamingoes* (1990), *In the Electric Mist with the Confederate Dead*

(1993) and *Dixie City Jam* (1994). Recent titles include *Cimarron Rose* (1997), *Heartwood* (1999) and *Purple Cane Road* (2000), while short stories are collected in *The Convict* (1985).

Burroughs, Edgar Rice (1875–1950) An American author born in Chicago, Illinois, US, and educated at Andover and Michigan Military Academy. A prolific writer, he is chiefly remembered for his character Tarzan, an English aristocrat, Lord Greystoke, who from the age of 1 is raised in a feral state by great apes in an African forest. *Tarzan of the Apes* (1914) was the first of a sequence of many novels about Tarzan, then his son, and eventually his grandson. The Tarzan character formed the basis for a large number of popular Hollywood films. Burroughs also wrote a large amount of science fiction, including *A Princess of Mars* (1917), *Gods of Mars* (1918) and *The Warlords of Mars* (1919).

Burroughs, William S. (1914–1997) Born in St. Louis, Missouri, and educated at Harvard University (BA 1936), William Seward Burroughs inherited the vast fortune of his grandfather who invented the typewriter. He began somewhat aimlessly, drifting through jobs in the 1930s and 1940s, before moving to Mexico City. In 1951, he tragically shot his wife in an accident, partly depicted in *Queer* (1986), which recounted the homosexual and drug-addicted environment in Mexico City. There followed trips to South America and Morocco, where his first novel *Junkie* (1953) was finished under the pseudonym of William Lee. This relates the painful experiences of the drug addict's involvement with the underworld, but also offers an analysis of society from the addict's perspective. Drawing on his period in Tangier (1953–1958), he wrote *The Naked Lunch* (1959, filmed 1991), his most famous book, which made use of experimental techniques like the 'cut-up' and 'fold-in' methods of collage writing.

The book scrutinised the drug addict's experiences on heroin, but also analysed totalitarianism. *The Naked Lunch*, and other novels from this period which used similar techniques – for example, *The Soft Machine* (1961), whose writing refers to the human brain, *The Ticket that Exploded* (1962) and *Nova Express* (1964) – form a tetralogy which explores the activities of the Nova Mob in a science fiction world. Further works include *The Exterminator* (1960), *Minutes to Go: Poems* (1960, written in collaboration with the American poet Gregory Corso), *Dead Fingers Talk* (1963), and *The Yage Letters* (1963), written with Allen Ginsberg. The 1970s saw the publication of *Speed* (1970), *The Wild Boys* (1971), about a group of hashish smokers who travel through time and space beyond social structures, and *Port of Saints* (1973). A late resurgence in his writing brought a trilogy in *Cities of the Red Night* (1981), which resurrected characters from *The Wild Boys*, *The Place of Dead Roads* (1983), set in the 1890s features Will Seward Hall, a writer of Westerns, and *The Western Lands* (1985). He produced his first record in 1990, the novella *Ghost of Chance* (1991), and in 1995 wrote *My Education: A Book of Dreams*, which paid homage to influences on his life, like Brion Gysin. There have been editions of *The Letters of William S. Burroughs 1945–1959* (1993) and *Last Words: The Final Journals of William S. Burroughs* (2000). Burroughs continues to inspire a cult following, and has exerted a huge influence as an experimental writer, an avant-garde theorist and a figure of the counter-culture.

T. Morgan, *Literary Outlaw: The Life and Times of William S. Burroughs* (1988); J. Skerl and R. Lydenberg, *William S. Burroughs at the Front* (1991).

Butler, Octavia E. (1947–) Born in Los Angeles, US, Octavia Estelle Butler was educated at Pasadena City College and California State University at Los Angeles. She has emerged as a significant and widely regarded science fiction writer who combines African mythology, urban realism and spiritualism into stories about aliens, genetic mutation and telepathy. Her narratives challenge conventional representations of sci-fi heroes, with her strong and intelligent African and African-American women and their efforts to secure a better and more tolerant society. Among her prolific novels are the 'Patternist' series, including *Patternmaster* (1976), *Mind of My Mind* (1977) and *Wild Seed* (1980), which focus upon a telepathic community and the way in which genetic mutation, gender and race affect the society, and the 'Xenogenesis' series, including *Dawn* (1987), *Adulthood Rites* (1988) and *Imago* (1989), which imagine the effects of cross-breeding between an alien race and humans in a post-nuclear holocaust environment. More recent novels include *Parable of the Sower* (1993), *Parable of the Talents* (1998) and *Lilith's Blood* (2000), with short stories in *Bloodchild* (1995).

Butler, Robert Olen (1945–) An American novelist born in Granite City, Illinois. He was educated at Northwestern University and the University of Iowa, and then spent a year (1971) in Vietnam as a linguist for US army intelligence. His first novel, *The Alleys of Eden* (1981), dealt with sexual obsession, and the cultural problems and legacy of the Vietnam War, themes which figure in many of his subsequent novels. There followed *Sun Dogs* (1982), *On Distant Ground* (1985), *Wabash* (1987), and he had significant success with *A Good Scent from a Strange Mountain* (1992, Pulitzer Prize 1993), which is a series of interlaced stories about South Vietnamese people seeking to integrate themselves into American culture. Sexual obsession returns in *They Whisper* (1994), which extends the territory of his first novel with an even more intimate style, while more recent novels are *The Deep Green Sea* (1997), which explores the lingering wounds of the Vietnam War, and *Mr Spaceman* (2000), a metaphysical comedy set in 2000 presenting an extraterrestrial's perspective of earth. Short stories occur in *Tabloid Dreams* (1996). He subsequently became a Professor at McNeese State University in Louisiana.

Butor, Michel (1926–) Born Michel Marie François Butor, in Mons-en-Baroeul, France, he graduated from the Sorbonne, University of Paris (1946), and during the 1950s and 1960s, taught variously in France, Egypt, Britain, Greece and Switzerland. He began by writing poetry, but turned to fiction and gradually became interested in more experimental writing. His fiction demands the reader's participation by disrupting orthodox fictional conventions, such as typography and characterisation. His novels include *Passing Time* (1956, trans. 1960), a complex reflection on the problems with writing fiction, and the relationship between the real and the fictional, *Second Thoughts* (1957, trans. 1958, also *Change of Heart*, trans. 1959), about a protagonist's decisions between his wife and mistress, *Degrees* (1960, trans. 1961), which is a series of polyphonic perspectives of a class in a Paris lycée, and *Niagara* (1965, trans. 1969). He has written a considerable number of novels, plays, verse, travel books and literary essays, most of which have not been translated into English. In the vanguard of the twentieth-century French 'New Novel', along with such writers as ROBBE-GRILLET, SARRAUTE and SIMON, his books became increasingly open-ended, attracted to juxtaposition and assemblage, as he used the novel to challenge its very being.

J. Sturrock, *The French New Novel: Claude Simon, Butor, Alain Robbe-Grillet* (1969).

Byatt, A.S. (1936–) Full name Antonia Susan Byatt, born in Sheffield, England, she is the sister of the novelist Margaret DRABBLE. She went to Cambridge University (BA 1957), and after some postgraduate study at Bryn Mawr College and Oxford University, she worked as an academic at the University of London, becoming a full-time writer in 1983. Her first novel was *The Shadow of the Sun* (1964), about an author's difficulties in combining a marriage and career, while *The Game* (1967) fictionalised childhood and student days. *The Virgin in the Garden* (1979) and *Still Life* (1987) are part of a tetralogy which is still in progress, about the symbolic events of the Potter family, which has a complex alternating time scheme treating the 1950s as a second 'Elizabethan Age'. There followed her most famous novel, the intricately worked romance *Possession* (1990, Booker Prize), about two literary scholars whose passionate affair is mirrored in the two Victorian poets who are the central figures of their research. Using a series of literary devices with great precision, the book was widely praised for Byatt's re-creation of Victorian letters, diaries and poetry. Subsequent works are *Angels and Insects* (1992), set in the Victorian era and exploring free-will, determinism, rationalism and mysticism, *The Djinn in the Nightingale's Eye* (1995), *The Matisse Stories* (1994), which all refer to the French Impressionist painter, *Babel Tower* (1996), *Elementals* (1998) and *The Biographer's Tale* (2000). Short stories feature in *Sugar* (1987) and *Five Fairy Stories* (1995). Her non-fiction includes two studies of Iris MURDOCH, *Wordsworth and Coleridge in Their Time* (1970), *Passions of the Mind* (1991), and numerous other editions and literary essays. A discriminating and intellectual writer, her fiction usually demonstrates great knowledge and often combines her roles as critic and novelist.

C

Cabrera Infante, G. (1929–) Born Guillermo Cabrera Infante, in Gibara, Cuba, he graduated from the University of Havana in 1956. He edited *Lunes*, the literary supplement of the Cuban paper *Revolucion* (1959–1961), worked as a Professor of English (1960–1961), and then emigrated to England in 1966, where he worked as a scriptwriter until 1972. He became a British citizen, and currently lives in London. His fiction includes *Three Trapped Tigers* (1965, trans. 1971), a prize-winning novel about three friends participating in pre-Castro Havana's nightlife, a multi-perspectival narrative which established his reputation as an innovative writer. Other novels include *A View of Dawn in the Tropics* (1974, trans. 1978) and *Infante's Inferno* (1979, trans. 1984), which incorporates various linguistic jokes and puns. He wrote the screenplays for *Wonderwall* (1968) and *Vanishing Point* (1970), and edited the collection of Cuban writings in *Mea Cuba* (1992, trans. 1994). Other works include a study of the cigar and its representation in films in *Holy Smoke* (1985) and a collection of his film reviews in *A Twentieth Century Job* (1963, trans. 1991). With his emphasis on spoken rather than written language, playing with words is an important part of his fiction.

R. Souza, *Gabriel Cabrera Infante: Two Islands, Many Worlds* (1996).

Cain, James M. (1892–1977) An American writer of 'hard-boiled' crime fiction, he was born James Mallahan Cain, in Annapolis, Maryland, and went to Washington College, Maryland. His first novel, *The Postman Always Rings Twice* (1934), established the darker side of crime writing, in which a drifter plots with his employer's wife to murder her husband, the owner of a diner. It was a great success and has been made into a film twice (1946 and 1981). Other books include *Serenade* (1937, filmed 1956), *Mildred Pierce* (1941), *Love's Lovely Counterfeit* (1942), *Three of a Kind* (1943), which is a book of three novellas (*Sinful Woman, Double Indemnity, The Embezzler*), *The Butterfly* (1947), *Jealous Woman* (1955), *The Moth* (1948), *The Root of His Evil* (1954), *Mignon* (1963) and *Rainbow's End* (1975). *Double Indemnity* and *Mildred Pierce* were also made into well-known films, in 1944 and 1945 respectively. Cain's short stories are collected in *Career in C Major* (1943).

W. Marling, *The American Roman Noir* (1995).

Caldwell, Erskine (1903–1987) Born Erskine Preston Caldwell, in White Oak, Georgia, US, into a Presbyterian family, he was educated at the University of Virginia. Major acclaim came for *Tobacco Road* (1932), about the Lester family, poor white farmers desperately trying to make a living in the Deep South. Following *God's Little Acre* (1933), a narrative about the Walden family, their jealousies and adventures, he developed a focus on social, racial and regional values in the Deep South, which characterised many of his subsequent novels, such as *Journeyman* (1935), an exploration of religious excesses in the South, *Trouble in July* (1940), *Tragic Ground* (1944) and *House in the Uplands* (1946). A prolific writer, other novels include *The Sure Hand of God* (1947), *This Very Earth* (1948), *A Place Called Estherville* (1949), *Gretta* (1955), *Summertime Island* (1966) and *Annette* (1973). Often considered to be best as a writer of short stories, volumes include *We Are the Living* (1933), *Jackpot* (1940), *The Courting of Susie Brown* (1952) and *When You Think of Me* (1959). After early praise, reception for his work has been varied over the years despite his enormous output. He also produced non-fiction, such as the portraits of American life in *Some American People* (1935), a memoir about war experiences in *All Out on the Road to Smolensk* (1942), an autobiography entitled *Call It Experience* (1951), and a collaborative work on Southern sharecroppers during the Depression entitled *You Have Seen Their Faces* (1937).

D. Miller, *Erskine Caldwell: A Biography* (1995).

Callaghan, Morley (1903–1990) A widely honoured Canadian novelist and short story writer, Morley Edward Callaghan was born in Toronto, and lived there all his life. He graduated from the University of Toronto (1925) with legal training, but never practised law. He was encouraged by Ernest HEMINGWAY to publish stories after working with him on Toronto's *Daily Star*, and was later aided by F. Scott FITZGERALD. He published a series of collections of short stories at this time, including *A Native Argosy* (1929) and

Now That April's Here (1936), both collected in *Morley Callaghan's Stories* (1959). He went to Paris in 1929, and became friendly with American literary exiles such as Fitzgerald, recounted in *That Summer in Paris* (1963). His first novel *Strange Fugitive* (1928) was set in Toronto's Prohibition period, and was followed in short succession by *It's Never Over* (1931), *A Broken Journey* (1932), *Such Is My Beloved* (1934), *They Shall Inherit the Earth* (1935) and *More Joy in Heaven* (1937). There followed a long interval until *The Loved and the Lost* (1951) and the more ambitious formal structures of *The Many Colored Coat* (1960) and *A Passion in Rome* (1961), interfused with a Christian humanism. His other novels include *A Fine and Private Place* (1975), *Close to the Sun Again* (1977), *A Time for Judas* (1983), an unusual rewriting of the Passion, and *A Wild One on the Road* (1988). Significant for breaking the literary mould in Canada, in a paradoxical career, he sought to develop a non-European style and form but refused to support nationalist movements.

D. Staines, ed., *The Callaghan Symposium* (1981).

Callow, Philip Kenneth (1924–) Born in Birmingham, England, he was educated at St. Luke's College, Exeter (1968–1970). He became a full-time novelist in 1966, although several early novels, including *The Hosanna Man* (1956), *Common People* (1958) and *Clipped Wings* (1965), acted as prototypes and experiments in voice for his later work. His trilogy consists of *Going to the Moon* (1968), *The Bliss Body* (1969) and *Flesh of Morning* (1972), and centres upon the anti-hero Colin Patten's adventures and experiences of factory work and working-class life. *Yours* (1972) was an extended letter by a girl to her ex-lover, *The Story of My Desire* (1976) extends the trilogy with Colin's marital problems, and was followed by several other novels, including *Janine* (1977), *The Subway to New York* (1979), *The Painter's Confessions* (1989), *Some Love* (1991), about an underprivileged boy, and *The Magnolia* (1994). Other works include volumes of poetry, short stories in *Native Ground* (1959), an autobiography entitled *In My Own Land* (1965), and biographies of D.H. LAWRENCE (1975), Van Gogh (1990), Walt Whitman (1992), Cézanne (1995) and Chekov (1998). He frequently utilises his autobiographical insights and information to structure his fiction.

Calvino, Italo (1923–1985) Born in Santiago de Las Vagas, Cuba, he grew up in San Remo, Italy. He graduated from the University of Turin (1947), and worked on the editorial staff of Einaudi publishers until 1983. A much respected novelist, he is regarded as one of the world's best fabulists, and is frequently compared to BORGES and MARQUEZ. Early works include *The Path to the Nest of Spiders* (1947, trans. 1956), *The Baron in the Trees* (1957, trans. 1959) and *Time and the Hunter* (1967, trans. 1970). The short stories of *Cosmicomics* (trans. 1968) are about the adventures of the strange, chameleon-like creature called 'Qfwfq', while *Invisible Cities* (1972, trans. 1974) presents an imaginary conversation between Marco Polo and Kubla Khan. His most experimental and widely known novel is *If on a Winter's Night a Traveller* (1979, trans. 1981), which has a novel-within-a-novel format. Other notable novels include *The Castle of Crossed Destinies* (1973, trans. 1976), *The Seasons in the City* (1973, trans. 1983), *Mr. Palomar* (1983, trans. 1985) and *Under the Jaguar Sun* (1986, trans. 1988). Short stories occur in *Adam, One Afternoon* (trans. 1957), *The Watcher* (trans. 1971), *Difficult Loves* (trans. 1984) and *Numbers in the Dark* (trans. 1995). He has also published essays in *The Uses of Literature* (1980, trans. 1986), *Six Memos for the Next Millennium* (trans. 1988)

and *The Road to San Giovanni* (trans. 1993), and a collection of *Italian Folk Tales* (1972, trans. 1975). The use of fable is central to his fictional style, which often utilises tensions between character, environment and youthful narrators, injecting fantasy into realist worlds and transforming the mundane into the marvellous. His work acquired a science fiction quality in the 1960s and 1970s, as he left the tenets of neo-realism and opened up vertiginous possibilities for fiction. As a careful student of semiotics and narratology, his writing explored patterns, sequences, diagrams and forms with a structural fascination. Regarded as one of the pre-eminent Italian writers of the twentieth century, he has gained an international reputation for his fiction which initiated many of the features of literary postmodernism.

L. Re, *Calvino and the Age of Neorealism: Fables of Estrangement* (1990).

Camus, Albert (1913–1960) Born in Mondovi, Algeria, into extreme poverty, he attended the University of Algiers (1936), after which he worked variously as a meteorologist, stockbroker, civil servant, a journalist with the anti-colonialist newspaper *Alger-Republicain* (in 1938), and a teacher in Oran (1940–1942). His detailed newspaper reports on the condition of poor Arabs in the Kabyles region were later published in abridged form in *Actuelles III* (1958). An editor of the Resistance newspaper *Combat* during the war, he later became a reader for Editions Gallimard (1943–1960). His editorials, both before and after the Liberation, showed a deep desire to combine political action with strict adherence to moral principles. During the war, Camus published the main works associated with his doctrine of the absurd – his view that human life is rendered ultimately meaningless by the fact of death and that the individual cannot make rational sense of his or her experience. These works include the novel *The Stranger* (1942, trans. 1946), perhaps his finest work of fiction, which memorably embodies the twentieth-century theme of the alienated stranger or outsider; a long essay on the absurd, *The Myth of Sisyphus* (1942, trans. 1955); and two plays, *Cross Purpose* (1944, trans. 1948) and *Caligula* (1944, trans. 1948). These works explored contemporary nihilism, but his own attitude toward the 'absurd' remained ambivalent, since Camus found that neither his own temperament nor his experiences in occupied France allowed him to be satisfied with the total moral neutrality demanded by philosophical absurdism. The growth of his ideas on moral responsibility is partly sketched in the essays collected in *Resistance, Rebellion, and Death* (1960, trans. 1961). Henceforth, Camus was concerned mainly with exploring avenues of rebellion against the absurd as he strove to create something like a humane stoicism. *The Plague* (1947, trans. 1948) is a symbolic novel in which the important achievement of those who fight bubonic plague in Oran lies not in the little success they have but in their assertion of human dignity and endurance. In his controversial essay *The Rebel* (1951, trans. 1954), he criticised what he regarded as the deceptive doctrines of 'absolutist' philosophies like Christianity and Marxism. He argued in favour of Mediterranean humanism, advocating nature and moderation rather than historicism and violence, which subsequently led him into a bitter controversy with Jean-Paul SARTRE over these issues. He wrote two overtly political plays, the satirical *State of Siege* (1948, trans. 1958) and *The Just Assassins* (1950, trans. 1958), although arguably he scored his major theatrical success with stage adaptations of such novels as William FAULKNER's *Requiem for a Nun* (1956) and Dostoevsky's *The Possessed* (1959). Other works include a third novel, *The Fall* (1956, trans. 1957), which some critics read as a flirtation with Christian ideas, and a collection of

short stories noteworthy for their technical virtuosity, *Exile and the Kingdom* (1957, trans. 1958). Posthumous publications include two sets of *Notebooks* covering the period 1935–1951, an early novel, *A Happy Death* (1971, trans. 1973), and a collection of essays, *Youthful Writings* (1973, trans. 1976 and 1977). Capturing the moral climate of the mid-twentieth century, he was one of the first major writers to emerge from North Africa. He was awarded the Nobel Prize for Literature in 1957.

J. Cruickshank, *Albert Camus and the Literature of Revolt* (1960).

Capek, Karel (1890–1938) Born in Male Svatonovice, Bohemia (now Czechoslovakia), he gained a doctorate from Charles University (1915). After working as a newspaper journalist in Prague, he became a writer, playwright and novelist. His novels include *The Absolute at Large* (1922, trans. 1927), *Krakatit* (1924, trans. 1925) and *President Masaryk Tells His Story* (1928, trans. 1934). The science fiction trilogy consisting of *Hordubal* (trans. 1933), *Meteor* (1934, trans. 1935) and *An Ordinary Life* (1934, trans. 1936), probes philosophical problems of the relativity of truth and reality, and the virtues of democracy. Later fiction continues his concern with philosophical questions and includes *The War with the Newts* (1936, trans. 1937), a satire of the Nazis, in which intelligent salamanders are enslaved by humans, but later they revolt and take over the world, *The First Rescue Party* (1937, trans. 1939), and the unfinished novel *The Cheat* (1939, trans. 1941). Short stories appear in *Money* (1921, trans. 1929), *Apocryphal Stories* (1932, trans. 1939) and *Fairy Tales* (1932, trans. 1934). He also published several travel books, including *Letters* from various European countries, and a collection of essays *In Praise of Newspapers* (1931, trans. 1950). As well as his fiction writing, he is perhaps best remembered for his play

R.U.R.: Rossum's Universal Robots (1920, trans. 1921), which introduced the symbol of robots.

W. Harkins, *Karel Capek* (1962).

Capote, Truman (1924–1984) An American writer and playwright, born Truman Streckfus Persons in New Orleans, Louisiana. His first novel was *Other Voices, Other Rooms* (1948), and is about a Southern boy's search for his father and the recognition of his own homosexuality. Short stories written at about this time are collected in *A Tree of Night* (1949). He also wrote *The Grass Harp* (1951), *The Muses are Heard* (1956) and *Breakfast at Tiffany's* (1958, filmed 1961), which focuses upon a spontaneous young woman, Holly Golightly. *In Cold Blood* (1966) is a semi-fictive account of a real multiple murder committed in Kansas by two young psychopaths, an early example of 'faction', which was also filmed (1967). Capote also wrote screenplays for the films *Beat the Devil* (1953) and *The Innocents* (1961, based on Henry James' story *The Turn of the Screw*), and with the composer Harold Arlen, a musical entitled *The House of Flowers* (1954). He earned some notoriety in his early years for fiction which championed characters normally deemed socially immoral or amoral, or who were seeking to escape the restrictions of society.

G. Clarke, *Capote: A Biography* (1988).

Cardinal, Marie (1929–) Born in Algiers, Algeria, she went to the University of Algeria, and then taught French in Greece, Portugal and Austria in the late 1950s and early 1960s. She later moved to Canada, where she became a teacher in Montreal. The author of a dozen bestsellers, many of an autobiographical inspiration, she has become a noted figure in feminist circles, with often honest and uncomfortable attempts to integrate disparate experiences. Her writing examines the problems of couples, of motherhood,

and writing. Her novels include *The Words to Say It*, (1975, trans. 1984), a fictional treatment of a long and painful period of psychoanalysis which brought her to fame, *In Other Words* (1977, trans. 1995), which follows similar issues but is situated in a firmly feminist perspective, *Country* (trans. 1980), which explores her feelings about Algeria, and *Devotion and Disorder* (1987, trans. 1991), looking at the problems of heroin addiction within the framework of a mother and daughter relationship.

Carew, Jan (1925–) Born in Agricola, Guyana, Jan Rynveld Carew went to Howard University, Case Western Reserve University, Charles University in Prague and the Sorbonne, University of Paris (MSc 1952). He has worked as a customs officer in Guyana, an artist, an actor, and a Professor of African-American studies at Northwestern University, Illinois (1972–1987). In addition to many volumes of poetry, plays and juvenile fiction, his novels include *Black Midas* (1958), *The Wild Coast* (1958), *The Last Barbarian* (1960), set in Harlem, *Moscow Is Not My Mecca* (1964), set in the USSR, *University of Hunger* (1966) and *The Third Gift* (1975). *Fulcrums of Change* (1987) is a collection of essays. His fiction is largely about colonisation, exile and rootlessness in Caribbean culture, and presents vivid depictions of the Guyanese landscape. Non-fiction includes *The Origins of Racism and Resistance in the Americas* (1976), *Rape of the Sun-People* (1976), *Grenada* (1985), *The Rape of Paradise: Columbus and the Birth of Racism in the Americas* (1994), and a biography of Malcolm X in *Ghosts in Our Blood* (1994).

Carey, Peter (1943–) An Australian novelist born in Bacchus Marsh, Victoria, he was educated at Monash University, where he studied science but became interested in writing. He worked for advertising agencies in Melbourne and

London, before returning to Sydney in 1974, and now divides his time between writing and running his own agency. His first three novels remain unpublished, but short stories appearing in the 1960s and 1970s have been subsequently collected in the critically acclaimed *The Fat Man in History* (1974) and *War Crimes* (1979). His first published novel was *Bliss* (1982), a schematically conceived work which dealt with the three lives of a male protagonist, resurrected to new hellish or heavenly experiences, while its futuristic vision offers a satirical account of the advertising world. *Illywacker* (1985) was a magic realist critique of the Americanisation of Australian culture, while *Oscar and Lucinda* (1988, Booker Prize, filmed 1997) was an ebullient narrative combining pastiche and magic realism as a couple attempt to build a glass church in the Australian outback. *The Tax Inspector* (1991) is a surreal black comedy about the Catchprice family, *The Unusual Life of Tristan Smith* (1994) focuses on imaginary countries and folklore, and *Jack Maggs* (1997) depicts the return of a deported Victorian criminal in a variation on Charles Dickens' *Great Expectations*. His *Collected Short Stories* were published in 1995. Many of his fictional worlds blend fantasy and realism, absurd paradoxes and the contradictions of the contemporary world, and his metafictional focus on storytelling parallels that of novelists like Donald BARTHELME and Jorge Luis BORGES. Several of his stories have been made into films.

H. Daniel, *Australian New Novelists* (1988).

Carpentier, Alejo (1904–1980) A celebrated novelist, Carpentier was born in Havana, Cuba, of European parentage. He studied architecture for one year at the University of Havana, but in the 1920s turned to journalism and magazine editing. He was imprisoned in 1928 for his political activities against the Machado regime, and moved to France, although

he returned to Cuba as a musicologist in 1939. Thereafter, he was an itinerant, spending time in Caracas as a broadcaster, working as a publishing director in Cuba in the 1960s, and eventually dying in Paris. Widely educated and one of the most significant Latin American writers of the twentieth century, his architecture and musical education is always present in his fiction. His first novel was *The Kingdom of This World* (1949, trans. 1957), set during Haiti's wars of independence at the end of the eighteenth century. This was followed by *The Lost Steps* (1953, trans. 1956), describing the new realities of the Orinoco and Amazon basins, *The Chase* (1956, trans. 1989), *Explosion in a Cathedral* (1962, trans. 1963), *Baroque Concerto* (1974, trans. 1991), *Reasons of State* (1974, trans. 1976) and *The Harp and the Shadow* (1979, trans. 1990). Short stories appear in *War on Time* (1958, trans. 1970). Like other writers of the 'Boom' period, such as MARQUEZ and CORTÁZAR, and their search for a form particular to the multifaceted Latin American experience, he is best known for the 'marvellous in the real', the New World reality perceived on a whole new series of levels and contexts which defy European imagination. Abandoning traditional linear narratives for a simultaneous plane, his later works became increasingly Marxist.

R. Ganzález Echevarría, *Alejo Carpentier: The Pilgrim at Home* (1977).

Carter, Angela (1940–1992) Born in Eastbourne, Sussex, England, Angela Olive Carter was educated at the University of Bristol (BA 1965), and worked as a journalist (1958–1961) before turning to creative writing full-time. Carter achieved wide recognition and honours as a novelist and short story writer for her blend of myth, fairy tale and legend. Her first novel, *Shadow Dance* (1966), introduced themes that were to become her trademarks: a focus upon performance, sex, eroticism and an interrogation of reality. These themes were continued in *The Magic Toyshop* (1967), in which a toy-maker and patriarch manipulates the sexualities of an adolescent girl and her chosen 'suitor'. There followed *Several Perceptions* (1968), *Heroes and Villains* (1969), which ventures further into the realm of dark sexuality and explores rape as a means of controlling women, and *Love* (1971), which extends her exploration of sexual fixation and control, focusing upon a sexually violent love triangle. *The Infernal Desire Machines of Doctor Hoffman* (1972) marks a departure from these earlier preoccupations, as the eponymous Doctor Hoffman seeks to destroy all structures of reason and to liberate the world from the chains of reality, through his new (infernal) technologies which use erotic energy in order to make the dreams and fantasies of individuals 'real'. Owing to its concerns with the nature of 'reality', desire, identity, marginality and subversion, it attracted critical attention as a postmodern novel. These concerns also featured prominently in her next novel, the critically acclaimed *The Passion of New Eve* (1977), in which the male narrator, Evelyn, is remade in a Frankenstein-style manner as a woman called Eve. Carter described this novel as an 'anti-mythic novel', working against the myths of the creation of Eve and against Mary Shelley's novel. It is set in a quasi-apocalyptic landscape of an urban America on the verge of meltdown, with an unnamed desert peopled by an impotent tyrant, Zero, his harem and a sect of feminist guerrilla fighters. Carter's later novels include *Nights at the Circus* (1984), a love story set in the theatrical world of the circus, *Black Venus* (1985), and *Wise Children* (1991), a tribute to Shakespearean comedies. Adept at combining a transformative imagination and literary allusion in her short stories, these appear in *Fireworks* (1974) and *The Bloody Chamber* (1979). Uncollected stories were posthumously published in *Ghosts and*

Old World Wonders (1993) and *Burning Your Boats* (1995). Her other writings include cultural criticism in *The Sadeian Woman* (1979), a screenplay of *The Bloody Chamber*, with Neil Jordan, entitled *The Company of Wolves* (1984), edited collections in *The Virago Book of Fairy Tales* (1990) and *Wayward Girls and Wicked Women* (1986), and occasional writings and reviews collected in *Nothing Sacred* (1982) and *Expletives Deleted* (1992). She also wrote radio plays, poetry and children's stories. She has been championed by feminist critics in recent years for her uninhibited exploration of sexual politics and gender stereotypes. A significant influence in moving British fiction away from its concern with parochial social realism, her fiction insists upon textual pluralism and eclectic reading.

L. Sage, ed., *Flesh and the Mirror* (1994).

Cartland, Barbara (1901–2000) Barbara Hamilton Cartland was born in England, and is known as the 'Queen of Romance' and the 'High Priestess of Love'. Beginning with her first novel, *Jigsaw* (1925), she wrote approximately 690 romance novels, making her a household name. Described as a 'one woman fantasy factory', her escapist stories are characteristically class-ridden and anti-feminist. Typically, they involve a chaste and beautiful young woman meeting a rich and handsome (but lovably rakish) man in an exotic place, usually set sometime in the nineteenth century. They fall in love and after overcoming various obstacles, the heroine finally marries the man, and the couple's emotions are allowed free rein. Cartland uses stereotypical gender characters, and even if the locations differ, the plots are interchangeable and are deliberately simplified – lacking in any real subplots – so as to eliminate complications and diversions for the reader. She also published under her married name of Barbara McCorquodale. She was step-grandmother to the late Diana, Princess of Wales, and her several autobiographical volumes include *The Isthmus Years* (1943), *I Search for Rainbows* (1967) and *I Seek the Miraculous* (1978).

G. Robyns, *Barbara Cartland: An Authorised Biography* (1984).

Carver, Raymond (1938–1988) Born in Oregon in the US, and educated at Chico State College and Humboldt State College, he also attended the Iowa Writers' Workshop. An early volume of short stories, *Put Yourself in My Shoes* (1974), was followed by *Will You Please Be Quiet, Please?* (1976), *Furious Seasons* (1977) and *What We Talk About When We Talk About Love* (1981). Drawing upon his own experiences, he writes largely about the intimate lives of working-class families, focusing upon such characters as travelling salesmen, waitresses and office workers who are caught up in broken marriages, drunkenness and domestic violence as the result of communication breakdowns. His stories are often presented as monologues, and are notable for their stylistic efficiency with compressed and minimal descriptive detail. Often upheld as a master of American realism, his short fiction has had wide influence. The stories of *Cathedral* (1983) and the miscellaneous prose and verse in *Fires* (1983), together with the short stories in *Elephant* (1988), form his last publications. *No Heroics, Please* (1992) was a posthumous edition of his uncollected writings.

R. Runyon, *Reading Raymond Carver* (1992).

Cary, Joyce (1888–1957) A prolific English novelist, born Arthur Joyce Lunel Cary, in Londonderry, Ireland, he was a graduate of Oxford University (1912), and worked for the Nigerian Political Service until 1920. His early novels, *Aissa Saved* (1932), *An American Visitor* (1932), *The African Witch* (1936) and his well known *Mister Johnson* (1939), were based on his experiences in Africa, and explored the clash between European and African cultures resulting from the exploitation and modernisation of British colonialism. He is also known for two trilogies, the first of which comprises the sequence *Herself Surprised* (1941), *To Be a Pilgrim* (1942) and *The Horse's Mouth* (1944). An examination of the struggle between freedom and authority, all three novels are narrated in the first person and offer different angles on each character. This narrative mode was repeated in the second trilogy, consisting of *Prisoner of Grace* (1952), *Except the Lord* (1953) and *Not Honour More* (1955), which deals with a complex world of politics with tense and desperate characters. Other novels include the widely praised *The House of Children* (1941), based on his childhood, *The Moonlight* (1946) and *A Fearful Joy* (1949). *Art and Reality* (1958) and *Selected Essays* (1976) were published posthumously. Frequently exploring creation and the established order, after some neglect, he was re-evaluated in the 1960s as a significant English novelist. Although traditional in form, his novels are innovative in their first person, present tense narratives which bring something like the modernist stream-of-consciousness and immediacy to his fiction.

M. Foster, *Joyce Cary: A Biography* (1968).

Cassola, Carlo (1917–1987) Born in Rome, Italy, he graduated from the University of Rome (LLB 1939), and became a teacher (1942–1961) and a highly regarded writer. *Fausto and Anna* (1952, trans. 1960) is based on his experiences as a partisan and follows the disillusionment of Fausto with middle-class life, his joining of the Italian Communist resistance, and his horrified reactions to war. Other novels include *Bebo's Girl* (1960, trans. 1962), a bitter-sweet love story, which depicts events following the war in Italy, *An Arid Heart* (1961, trans. 1964), another love story which depicts a woman's ruin, and *Portrait of Helena* (1973, trans. 1975). His early fiction depicts characters on the fringes of society, and much of his writing is a poetic rendering of the day-to-day, eschewing political and ethical questions. A prolific writer, much of his fiction remains untranslated into English.

P. Pedroni, *Existence as Theme in Carlo Cassola's Fiction* (1985).

Castillo, Ana (1953–) A Chicana-American poet and novelist, born in Chicago, Illinois. She was educated at Northern Illinois University (BA 1975), the University of Chicago (MA 1979) and the University of Bremen (Ph.D. 1991), since when she has held various university positions. Her first novel was *The Mixquiahuala Letters* (1986), which uses the device of letters written over a ten-year period, exploring the changing role of Hispanic women in the US and Mexico in the 1970s and 1980s. *Sapogonia* (1990) looks at a man's obsession with a woman he is unable to conquer, and *So Far from God* (1993) is a magic realist narrative about a Latina woman and her four daughters. Her latest novel, *Peel My Love Like an Onion* (1999), concerns the life of a once renowned flamenco dancer, Carmen Santos, and her dreams of economic and emotional freedom. In addition to the short stories in *Loverboys* (1996), her poetry collections include *Zero Makes Me Hungry* (1975), *i close my eyes (to see)* (1976), *The Invitation* (1979), *Women Are Not Roses* (1984) and *My Father Was a Toltec* (1988). She has also edited two influential collections of feminist essays, entitled *This Bridge Called My Back* (1988) with Cherrie Moraga, and *Massacre of the Dreamers: Reflections on Xicanisma* (1994), which expresses feminist concerns and the social implications of Chicana feminism. She currently divides her time between Albuquerque, New Mexico and Gainesville, Florida. A highly respected Chicana poet and writer, although her work is based upon established oral traditions, she is nevertheless regarded as one of the most daring, innovative and experimental of Latino novelists.

A. Horno-Delgado, ed., *Breaking Boundaries: Latina Writings and Critical Readings* (1989).

Cather, Willa (1873–1947) Born Willa Sibert Cather, into a small farming community in the Shenandoah Valley in Virginia, US, her parents moved to the widely mixed immigrant state of Nebraska in 1883, whose lives are documented in much of her fiction. After graduating from Nebraska University (1896), she worked for a decade as a journalist and a teacher, during which time she published stories in national magazines such as *McClure's* and *Scribner's*, a collection of poems entitled *April Twilights* (1903) and short stories in *The Troll Garden* (1905). She moved to New York City and eventually became managing editor of *McClure's* between 1906–1912. Her first novel, *Alexander's Bridge* (1912), was about an engineer torn between two loves, but it was with *O Pioneers!* (1913) that she made her name, about an immigrant girl's frontier life and strength in the face of adversity. She left journalism for literary success, and published a string of novels, which include *The Song of the Lark* (1915), *My Ántonia* (1918), again about the pioneer spirit of endurance as the Bohemian Shimerdas family struggle to carve out a life in Nebraska, *Youth and the Bright Medusa* (1920), *One of Ours* (1922, Pulitzer Prize), *A Lost Lady* (1923) and *Obscure Destinies* (1932). *Not Under Forty* (1936) was essays presenting a theory of fiction, and short stories in *The Old Beauty* (1948) were published posthumously. Her first novels were considered to have brought a breath of fresh air to American fiction, and she won high praise and enjoyed a wide readership. Writing against the forces of banality, materialism and mortality, she celebrates the human desire and ability to make life through art, family and narratives.

E. Brown and L. Edel, *Willa Cather: A Critical Biography* (1987).

Caute, David (1936–) Born John David Caute, in Alexandria, Egypt, he was educated at Oxford University (BA 1959, D.Phil. 1963), and since 1959 has been a lecturer at various British universities. A playwright, novelist and historian, he has consistently dealt with the subjects of socialism, communism and the relationships between First World and Third World countries. *At Fever Pitch* (1959) was based on his experiences as an infantryman in the Gold Coast before it became independent Ghana, and explores the sexual psychology of militarism. It was followed by *Comrade Jacob* (1961), about Gerard Winstanley in the seventeenth century, and *The Decline of the West* (1966), set in the fictional African country of Coppernica, about post-revolutionary turmoil. *The Confrontation* (1971) is a trilogy – consisting of a play entitled *The Demonstration*, an essay in *The Occupation*, and a novel entitled *The Illusion* – concerning a left-wing academic called Steven Bright and exploring the gap between people's public and personal lives. Other novels are *The K-Factor* (1983), a fictional account of Zimbabwe and its racial stratification, *News from Nowhere* (1986), about the adventures of an academic in Rhodesia, *Veronica or the Two Nations* (1989), a dramatic presentation of Britain's social ills, *The Women's Hour* (1991), a satirical exploration of the implications of dogmatic feminism and postmodern ideology in a British university in the 1980s, *Dr Orwell and Mr Blair* (1994) and *Fatima's Scarf* (1998). In addition to radio and screenplays, his non-fiction includes studies of Frantz Fanon (1970), the collapse of white Rhodesia in *Under the Skin* (1983), the filmmaker Joseph Losey (1994), and several

works on European socialism, with essays and reviews in *Collisions* (1974).

Cela, Camilo José (1916–) Born in La Coruña, Spain, he attended the University of Madrid in the 1930s, and also served in General Franco's army during the Spanish Civil War. His career and literary interests were deeply affected by his early acceptance and later rejection of Franco's dictatorial rule. He later held university posts in Europe and the US. His first novel was *The Family of Pascual Duarte* (1942, trans. 1946), about a convicted murderer awaiting execution, showing how his killing was a response to poverty and frustration. After *Rest Home* (1943, trans. 1961), he wrote arguably his greatest work, *The Hive* (1951, trans. 1953), which has a cinematographic style similar to that of *Manhattan Transfer* by John DOS PASSOS, and depicts the atmosphere of Madrid in the years after the Second World War. The experimental anti-novel, *Mrs. Caldwell Speaks to Her Son* (1953, trans. 1968), de-emphasised plot and is structured as 212 chapters over about 200 pages. In 1956, Cela founded the influential Spanish literary magazine *Papeles de Son Armadáns* and served thereafter as its editor. He wrote several travel books, among them *Journey to the Alcarría* (1948, trans. 1964) and *Avila* (1952, trans. 1956). Other works include *San Camilo, 1936* (1969, trans. 1991) and *Mazurka for Two Dead Men* (1983, trans. 1992). Many further novels, short stories and travelogues in Spanish remain untranslated into English. Although not widely known outside Spain, he has played a pivotal role in the literature of the twentieth-century Hispanic world. His style of brutal realism, known as the 'tremendismo' literary movement, dwells on the darker side of life, the grotesque, vulgar and distasteful, in defiance of Spanish traditionalist moral codes. Synonymous with the rebirth of the Spanish novel, his wide honours include the Nobel Prize for Literature in 1989.

D. Foster, *Forms in the Work of Camilo José Cela* (1967).

Céline, Louis-Ferdinand (1894–1961) The pseudonym of Louis-Ferdinand Destouches, he was born in Courbevoie, France, and worked at various jobs, before going to London in 1915 after injury in the First World War. He qualified as a doctor at the University of Rennes (1924), and worked in private practice in Paris from 1928. He began writing with *Journey to the End of the Night* (1932, trans. 1934), which was an immediate success, but criticised for its obscenity. A heavily fictionalised autobiography, it narrates the protagonist Bardamu's attempts to escape death and life's futility. Other works include *Death on the Installment Plan* (1936, trans. 1938), which is a fictionalised account of Céline's early life and considered by some as his greatest novel, *Guignol's Band* (1944, trans. 1950), a light-hearted, blithe narrative in the present tense, and *Conversations with Professor Y* (1955, trans. 1986). His outspoken anti-Semitism and pro-fascism during the 1930s and the German Occupation, caused him enormous trouble, and he fled to Denmark after the Second World War where he was imprisoned for one year. In 1951, he was granted a pardon by France, although he experienced cold hostility to his writings, and he practised quietly as a doctor. A trilogy consisting of *Castle to Castle* (1957, trans. 1968), *North* (1960, trans. 1972) and *Rigadoon* (1969, trans. 1974), recounts his period in Germany in 1944 before going to Denmark, a work which has divided critical opinion. Non-fiction includes an anti-Soviet treatise in *Mea Culpa and the Life and Work of Semmelweis* (1936, trans. 1937). His political views appear to have compromised his literary judgements and his early novels are regarded as his best work. Much of

his fiction considers death and the erotic, and focuses upon physical gestures in scabrous hallucinating passages.

M. Thomas, *Céline* (1979).

Cendrars, Blaise (1887–1961) Born Frederic Sauser-Hall, in La Chaux-de-Fonds, Switzerland, he attended the University of Berne (1907–1909). After travelling to Paris in 1912, he served with the French Foreign Legion during the First World War, and later worked at various jobs, including journalism. An adventurous personality with a renowned bohemian lifestyle, he began as a poet influenced by the Surrealists, before turning to fiction, much of which is picaresque tales combining fantasy and personal experiences. Under his pseudonym, his prolific works include *Panama: Or the Adventures of My Seven Uncles* (1918, trans. 1931), *Gold: Being the Marvellous History of General John Augustus Sutter* (1925, trans. 1984), which is his most successful novel, and is a fictionalised account of a Swiss immigrant to the US who sees his Californian agriculture empire destroyed when gold is discovered on his land, *Moravagine* (1926, trans. 1968), which follows a misogynist anarchist who murders for pleasure, *Dan Yack* (1927, trans. 1987) and *The Confessions of Dan Yack* (1929, trans. 1990), both about a man and his self-fulfilment in life and love. Later writing includes a series of autobiographical novels such as *The Astonished Man* (1945, trans. 1970), *Lice* (1946, trans. 1973), *To the End of the World* (1956, trans. 1967) and *Night in the Forest* (1929, trans. 1985), which although based upon his life experiences are also dressed up in mythology. Memoirs include *Hollywood* (1936, trans. 1995), *Sky* (trans. 1992), and essays occur in *Modernities and Other Writings* (trans. 1992).

J. Bochner, *Blaise Cendrars: Discovery and Recreation* (1978).

Chamoiseau, Patrick (1953–) Born in Fort de France, Martinique, in the French West Indies, he went to the University of Sceaux, France. He is a leading member of the 'creolite' movement, which has flourished in the French Caribbean since the 1980s, advancing the Creole language and literature, and extending the ideas of Aimé Cesaire. His novel writing began with *Solibo Magnificent* (1988, trans. 1998), about an investigation into a mysterious death which leads to torture and murder. *Texaco* (1992, Prix Goncourt, trans. 1997) was highly acclaimed, and concerns a stranger arriving in a makeshift village called Texaco which has grown up under the shadow of the petroleum installation, and interwoven with the saving of the shantytown is a riotous and ribald history of Martinique and the Caribbean. Other works include *Creole Folktales* (trans. 1994), a memoir in *School Days* (1994, trans. 1997), and several autobiographies. An influential theorist and literary historian of the Caribbean region, his fiction deals with problems concerning the morals, identity and ethics of the area.

Chandler, Raymond (1888–1959) An American crime and mystery writer, born Raymond Thornton Chandler, in Chicago, Illinois, he had a chequered career before finding his métier as a crime novelist. His family emigrated to England in 1900, and he studied in France and Germany, before returning to London in 1907 and, with misgivings, joining the Civil Service. After this, he worked for a time as a reporter and book reviewer. He returned to the US in 1912 and made his home in California. He served in the Canadian Army during the First World War, and then entered business and became an executive in an oil company. With the onset of the Great Depression of the 1930s, Chandler returned to writing. With his tough, cynical private detective Philip Marlowe, the star of many of his books, he is regarded as the originator of the 'hard-boiled' crime novel. Most of his stories are set in and around a sleazy and violent Los Angeles, and are definitive examples of American *noir* detective fiction. His novels comprise *The Big Sleep* (1939), *Farewell My Lovely* (1940), *The High Window* (1942), *The Lady in the Lake* (1943), *The Little Sister* (1949) and *The Long Goodbye* (1954). Almost all of his Marlowe novels have been made into well-known films. Chandler also worked as a scriptwriter for movies, including *Double Indemnity* (1944) and *Strangers on a Train* (1951).

F. MacShane, *The Life of Raymond Chandler* (1976).

Charteris, Leslie (1907–1993) An American writer, born Leslie Charles Bowyer Lin in Singapore, he was educated at the University of Cambridge. From 1935 he lived in the US, working as a Hollywood scriptwriter, and was naturalised in 1946. He will chiefly be remembered as the creator of the dapper Simon Templar, or The Saint, a devil-may-care, contemporary Robin Hood who forcibly takes on villains to help the deserving (needless to say, often a maiden in distress). He wrote a large number of novels about The Saint, the first being *X Esquire* (1927), with *The Saint in New York* (1935), *The Saint in Miami* (1940) and *Vendetta for The Saint* (1964) among the many to follow. There are also many volumes of short stories featuring The Saint, such as *The Brighter Buccaneer* (1938), *The Saint at Large* (1943) and *The Saint on the Spanish Main* (1955). Charteris also wrote plays and a non-fiction book called *Spanish for Fun* (1964).

Chase, James Hadley (1906–1985) A *nom de plume* for René Brabazon Raymond, a prolific English writer of 'hard-boiled' crime fiction, who was born in London, England. He also wrote under the pseudonym Raymond Marshall, among others. Like Peter Cheyney, he used American locales, characters and vernacular speech, but with far greater verisimilitude. Chase paid only two desultory visits to the US, and his knowledge of America came from a diligent study of books. His first novel was *No Orchids for Miss Blandish* (1939, filmed 1948), and among many others, are *Miss Callaghan Comes to Grief* (1941), *More Deadly Than the Male* (1946), *Lay Her Among the Lilies* (1950), *The Guilty Are Afraid* (1957), *Come Easy, Go Easy* (1960), *A Coffin from Hong Kong* (1962), *Cade* (1966), *My Laugh Comes Last* (1977) and *Get a Load of This* (1984). His complex, intricate plots are peopled with gaudy, explosive characters, and his private eyes include men like Vic Mallory, Mark Girland, Dave Fenner, an ex-reporter turned private eye, Brick-Top Corrigan, and Don Mickelson, a millionaire playboy.

Chatwin, Bruce (1940–1989) Born Charles Bruce Chatwin, in Sheffield, England, he joined Sotheby's in 1958 and gained an instant and rapid rise to become a director in 1965, although he left to study anthropology at Edinburgh University. He became an art consultant, a journalist for the *Sunday Times Magazine* and an author, developing a reputation for his distinctive travel books such as *In Patagonia* (1977), recording impressions of the desolate region of South America, and *Songlines* (1987), a travel book linking his autobiography into an innovative narrative of Australian Aboriginal myth. His first novel was *The Viceroy of Ouidah* (1980), an historically based account of the life of a monstrous Brazilian slave trader, set in Africa in the 1800s, followed by the widely acclaimed *On the Black Hill* (1982, filmed 1988), examining the bleak existence of farming twin brothers in the isolated regions of rural Wales, and *Utz* (1988, filmed 1992), about the moral and personal ambiguities of a collector of Meissen porcelain and set in post-Second World War Europe. Essays and journalism are collected in *What Am I Doing Here?* (1989), and the posthumous *Photographs and Notebooks* (1993), collected from his

travels in Africa and Asia. He died from what was thought to be a rare bone marrow wasting disease contracted in China, although it has subsequently been speculated that he was a victim of AIDS.

Cheever, John (1912–1982) Born in Quincy, Massachusetts, he is widely considered one of the finest American writers of short stories. He was expelled from Thayer Academy, which became the subject of his first story in 1930. A regular contributor to *The New Yorker*, his satiric stories tend to focus on the rich suburban communities of Westchester and Connecticut, in which upwardly mobile American lives show a lack of purpose and direction. Bored in jobs, trapped in lifestyles of loneliness and moral decay, the values of the white American middle classes are dissected in tales of despair and nostalgia. Perhaps his most famous story is 'The Swimmer', made into a film starring Burt Lancaster (1968). His collections of short stories include *The Way Some People Live* (1943), *The Housebreaker of Shady Hill* (1958), *Some People, Places and Things That Will Not Appear in My Next Novel* (1961), *The Brigadier and the Golf Widow* (1964), *Homage to Shakespeare* (1965), *The World of Apples* (1973) and *The Stories of John Cheever* (1978, Pulitzer Prize 1979). Often episodic in structure, the stories lend themselves to the sketch and an acute observationist stance. Although less widely regarded as a novelist, he has published *The Wapshot Chronicle* (1957) and *The Wapshot Scandal* (1964), an episodic sequence which depicts the decline of a once wealthy family in a New England town, *Falconer* (1977) about an academic's attempt to order his life, and *Oh, What a Paradise It Seems* (1982), among others. In 1988, both *Uncollected Stories* and his controversial *Letters* were published.

J. Aldridge, *Time to Murder and Create* (1966).

Chesterton, G.K. (1874–1936) An English novelist, essayist, poet and journalist, born Gilbert Keith Chesterton, in London, and educated at the Slade School of Art. He worked for the *Daily News*, *The Bookman* and the *Illustrated London News*, as well as several other papers. Fervent and outspoken, along with Hilaire Belloc, he criticised British imperialism and capitalism. His first novel *The Napoleon of Notting Hill* (1904), is a romance set in the future, and *The Man Who Was Thursday* (1908) examines anarchist politics. Among his vast output, other novels include *The Ball and the Cross* (1910), *Manalive* (1912) and *The Return of Don Quixote* (1927). He is perhaps best known for his short stories, particularly those about Father Brown, the East Anglian Catholic priest as master detective, which combine moral theology and detection. Collections of these stories include *The Innocence of Father Brown* (1911), *The Wisdom of Father Brown* (1914), *The Incredulity of Father Brown* (1926), *The Secret of Father Brown* (1927) and *The Scandal of Father Brown* (1935). A large amount of critical works include *The Victorian Age in Literature* (1913), *Robert Browning* (1903), *Charles Dickens* (1906), *George Bernard Shaw* (1910) and *Chaucer* (1932). His conversion to Roman Catholicism in 1922 is recorded in *The Everlasting Man* (1925), and his other writings include volumes of verse, history, plays, essays and an *Autobiography* (1936).

D. Conlon, ed., *G.K. Chesterton: A Half Century of Views* (1987).

Ch'ien, Chung-Shu (1910–) Born in Wuhsi, Kiangsu province, China, he was educated at Qinghua University (1929–1933), Oxford University (BA 1937), and undertook further study in Paris (1937–1938). He turned to writing in 1932, but also worked as a teacher at various schools and universities in China, and became a fellow of the Chinese Academy of Social Sciences. His novel *Fortress Besieged* (1947, trans. 1979) is regarded as one of the greatest Chinese literary works of the twentieth century. The title is a metaphor for marriage derived from a French proverb, and it is set mainly in Japanese-occupied China during 1937–1939. Describing the protagonist hero who becomes involved in a love triangle, it comically satirises the westernised pseudo-intellectuals as it investigates the confrontation between old and new worlds and the moral dissolution of society from within. Other works include essays in *Limited Views* (trans. 1998), but mostly a large body of essays, stories, edited anthologies of Chinese poetry, and critical works on Chinese literature are untranslated into English. He played a significant role in the post-Cultural Revolution resurgence of interest in Chinese poetry. In addition, he edited the English-language journal *Philobiblion*, and his writing is represented in such anthologies as *Modern Chinese Stories and Novellas, 1919–1949* (1949). Largely unknown in the West, he is one of the most distinguished literary figures in China and retains an honoured position among Chinese intellectuals.

T. Huters, *Qian Zhongshu* (1982).

Chinodya, Shimmer (1957–) A Zimbabwean novelist and poet, born in Gweru, he attended the University of Zimbabwe and the University of Iowa, and then worked in the Ministry of Education in Harare. He has published a number of textbooks for children under the pseudonym B.S. Chiraska. He has written three novels: *Dew in the Morning* (1982), which focuses on the rural physical and cultural landscape in post-Independence Zimbabwe; *Farai's Girls* (1984), about personal development and an insight into love; and *Harvest of Thorns* (1989), depicting the psychology of a maturing consciousness and the effects of the Zimbabwean war of liberation on teenage combatants. Shorts stories occur in *Can*

We Talk (1998) and his poetry has appeared in various magazines. The relationship between the past and present, and the depiction of rural life, are recurrent interests in his fiction, which displays technical competence and conceptual breadth.

Christie, Agatha (1891–1976) An English murder mystery writer, born Agatha Mary Clarissa Miller, in Torquay, Devon. She is a hugely popular writer with a vast output, and her books have been translated into forty languages. After her first marriage to Archie Christie (divorced 1928), she married archaeologist Max Mallowan, whom she would accompany on his digs in the Middle East, and used her experiences there to write *Murder in Mesopotamia* (1930), *Death on the Nile* (1937) and *Appointment with Death* (1938). She is best remembered for her two very different detectives: Hercule Poirot, the dapper Belgian who solves mysteries by application of what he terms his 'little grey cells', and Miss Jane Marple, an elderly English spinster who unravels murders through her inquisitiveness about human nature. Poirot is the hero of, for example, her first novel *The Mysterious Affair at Styles* (1920), *The Murder of Roger Ackroyd* (1926), *Murder on the Orient Express* (1934) and *Mrs McGinty's Dead* (1952); and Marple of *A Murder Is Announced* (1950) and *They Do It with Mirrors* (1952). Both these characters have served as the basis for several popular television series and films. Other novels featuring neither detective, are *Ten Little Niggers* (1939) and *Endless Night* (1967). Her plays include *The Mousetrap*, which set a record in London by running uninterruptedly for thirty years, from 1952. She also wrote two works of non-fiction, *Come, Tell Me How You Live* (1946), describing the archaeological expeditions she shared with Mallowan, and *Agatha Christie: An Autobiography* (1977). Although her style is undistinguished and her characterisation somewhat utilitarian, her fame comes largely for her extremely ingenious plots.

C. Osborne, *The Life and Crimes of Agatha Christie* (1982).

Cisneros, Sandra (1954–) Born in Chicago, Illinois, US, she was educated at Loyola University (BA 1976) and the University of Iowa Writer's Workshop (MFA 1978). She taught in a Latina school until 1980, and then became a guest lecturer at various American universities. She began by writing volumes of poetry, including *Bad Boys* (1980), *My Wicked, Wicked Ways* (1987) and *Loose Woman* (1994). However, she is best known for the novel *The House on Mango Street* (1984), a series of vignettes and stories centred upon Esperanza, a Latina adolescent, and her problems. Short stories occur in *Woman Hollering Creek* (1991), which are set near San Antonio, Texas, and are a series of interior monologues about the difficulties of assimilation into American culture. Despite her relatively small body of writing, she has generated huge critical acclaim and popular success. She draws heavily upon her childhood experiences, her ethnic heritage of Chicana background, and the Latino dialect. Addressing such issues as poverty, cultural suppression, self-identity and gender roles in her books, her vivid Latina/o characters are usually shown as marginalised and alienated from US mainstream culture.

Clancy, Jr. Tom (1947–) Born Thomas Clancy, Jr., in Baltimore, Maryland, US, he graduated from Loyola College, Baltimore (1969), and worked successfully in insurance until 1980. A hugely popular writer of detailed novels about espionage, military operations and military technology, he has achieved best-seller status for his techno-thrillers. His prolific novels include *The Hunt for Red October* (1984, filmed 1990), about a race between the US and the USSR to capture a defecting state-of-the-art Russian submarine, and

Red Storm Rising (1986) about a non-nuclear World War Three. *Patriot Games* (1987, filmed 1992), about an IRA terrorist attack on the British royal family, focuses upon Jack Ryan, an ex-Marine Officer with CIA and FBI links, who is the central protagonist in several subsequent novels including *The Cardinal of the Kremlin* (1988), about the 'Star Wars' defence technology, *Clear and Present Danger* (1989, filmed 1994), about drug enforcement in South America, *The Sum of All Fears* (1991), about Middle East politics, *Debt of Honour* (1994) and *Executive Orders* (1996). In addition to several non-fiction works on military matters, he has published a series of military adventure novels under the titles of *Tom Clancy's Op-Center*, while his most recent novel is *The Bear and Dragon* (2000). With his use of taut suspense and rousing plots, his fiction specialises in a remarkable knowledge of contemporary military technology.

Clarke, Arthur C. (1917–) Born in Minehead, Somerset, England, Arthur Charles Clarke worked for the British Civil Service (1936–1941) before joining the RAF as a radar instructor during the Second World War. He graduated from London University (BSc 1948), and became a prolific freelance writer in 1951, continuing with underwater exploration, television and radio commentary. He is most famous for his science fiction, beginning with *The Sands of Mars* (1951). Other novels include *Islands in the Sky* (1952), *Childhood's End* (1953), now regarded as a science fiction classic, about the appearance of the Overlords and their gradual control over the human race and its evolution, *The City and the Stars* (1956), *The Deep Range* (1957), *A Fall of Moondust* (1961), *A Rendezvous with Rama* (1973), another science fiction classic, with its study of an artificial, mysterious object in space called Rama, *Imperial Earth* (1975), *The Fountains of Paradise* (1979), and *The Songs of Distant Earth*

(1986), which is set on the ocean world of Thalassa. He is also famous for his long and complex screenplay, *2001: A Space Odyssey* (1968), filmed by Stanley Kubrick to wide acclaim for its landmark visual effects, and the sequel *2010: Odyssey Two* (1982, filmed 1984). Short story collections include *Expedition to Earth* (1953) and *Reach for Tomorrow* (1956). Equally renowned for his first-rate scientific and technical writing covering themes of space exploration, undersea exploration and works on the future and the mysterious, they include *The Exploration of Space* (1951), a scientific exposition for laymen, *Arthur C. Clarke's Mysterious World* (1980), and the two memoirs *The View from Serendip* (1977) and *Astounding Days* (1989). A dominant figure in the genre of science fiction and futurist writing, he currently lives in Sri Lanka.

J. Hollow, *Against the Night, the Stars: The Science Fiction of Arthur C. Clarke* (1983).

Clarke, Austin C. (1934–) Born Austin Chesterfield Clarke, in St. James, Barbados, he studied economics and politics at the University of Toronto (1955). He worked as a teacher, reporter, broadcaster and freelance journalist in Canada, and has subsequently held various visiting professorships in the 1970s and 1980s. His early novels were set in Barbados and explore colonial self-hatred and Caribbean poverty, such as his first novel *The Survivors of the Crossing* (1964), about the race conflict when workers attempt to strike at a sugar plantation, and *Amongst Thistles and Thorns* (1965), about the alienation of a 9-year-old child. *The Prime Minister* (1977) attacks political corruption in Barbados, *Proud Empires* (1986) examines political corruption in the 1950s, and *The Origin of Waves* (1997) deals with the chance reunion of two old friends and their reminiscences and the lives of immigrants to Canada. His most significant work is 'The Toronto Trilogy', consisting of *The Meeting Point*

(1967), *Storm of Fortune* (1973) and *The Bigger Light* (1975), which details the lives of Barbadians who emigrate to Toronto hoping to improve their lives, describing the problems of integration, cultural dislocation and the role of the cultural outsider. A prolific writer of short stories, collections include *When Women Rule* (1985), *Nine Men Who Laughed* (1986), *In This City* (1992) and *There Are No Elders* (1993). Other works include a memoir in *Growing Up Stupid Under the Union Jack* (1980), a reminiscence of Sam SELVON in *A Passage Back Home* (1994), and *Pigtails 'n' Breadfruit: The Rituals of Slave Food* (1999). The basis for his fiction is the experiences of colonial Barbados and the cultural contradictions of black immigrants to Canada struggling for success in a predominantly white society.

S. Algoo-Baksch, *Austin C. Clarke: A Biography* (1994).

Clavell, James (1925–1994) Born James duMaresq Clavell, in Australia, he went to the US in 1953 and was naturalised in 1963. He served with the British Royal Artillery during the Second World War, and after being captured by the Japanese, spent three-and-a-half years in the notorious Changi prisoner-of-war camp. He attended Birmingham University in England (1946–1947), and then worked as a screenwriter, director, producer and novelist until his death in 1994. *King Rat* (1962) was set in Changi, depicting the survival of an English prisoner, and marked the beginning of his best-selling sagas of the Far East, Hong Kong and Japan, exploring the gulf between Asian and Occidental views of the world. *Tai-Pan* (1966) and *Noble House* (1981) are historical accounts of the fictional Noble House trading company in Hong Kong, under the management of the Struan family; while *Shogun* (1975) is about an Englishman becoming a samurai warrior in the 1600s. On the back of such success,

publishers marketed his subsequent novels with his name: *James Clavell's 'Whirlwind'* (1986), *James Clavell's 'Thrump-o-moto'* (1986), and *James Clavell's 'Gai-Jin'* (1993), continuing the Noble House saga set in Japan in the 1860s. Keenly researched, set against exotic backgrounds and dealing with war, power, giant corporations and espionage, many of his action-packed novels have been produced as films. His list of screenplays is also impressive, including *The Fly* (1958), *Watsui* (1959), *The Great Escape* (1963), *633 Squadron* (1964) and *The Satan Bug* (1965).

Cleary, Jon (1917–) Born in Sydney, Australia, he left school at the age of 15, and undertook various occupations before joining the Australian Army to fight in the Middle East and Pacific between 1940 and 1945. Turning to full-time writing in 1945, he lived extensively in the US, UK and Europe. He travelled widely to research his novels, which have had wide international audiences, and several of his works have been produced as films. A prolific writer of thirty-nine novels, the first was *You Can't See Round Corners* (1947), followed by, among others, *Just Let Me Be* (1950), *The Sundowners* (1952, filmed 1960), about an itinerant outback Australian family, *Justin Bayard* (1955), *The High Commissioner* (1966, filmed 1968), *Peter's Pence* (1974), *High Road to China* (1977), *Spearfield's Daughter* (1982), *Dragons at the Party* (1987) and *Murder Song* (1990). He uses various settings for his fiction, and is best known as a crime fiction writer, especially for the Scobie Malone novels, about a Sydney detective. These came in two bursts in 1966 to 1973 and 1987 onwards, and are popular adventures with gripping action of psychological and moral complexities, evident in recent titles like *Endpeace* (1996), *Five Ring Circus* (1998) and *Dilemma* (1999). Short story collections include *These Small Glories* (1946) and *Pillar of Salt* (1963), and he has written scripts for radio, television and film.

Cloete, Stuart (1897–1976) Born in Paris, France, his life followed three distinct paths: after serving with the Coldstream Guards during the First World War, he became a rancher in South Africa (1926–1935), before turning to writing. His first novel was *The Turning Wheels* (1937), which began a trilogy about the Afrikaners. Others include *Watch for the Dawn* (1939), about the Great Trek, and *Rags of Glory* (1963), which tells of their defeat in the Anglo-Boer War (1899–1902). Many other novels are either set in Africa or involve African affairs, such as *The Hill of Doves* (1941, filmed 1969), *Christmas in Matabeleland* (1942), *Mamba* (1956), *Gazella* (1958), *The Fiercest Heat* (1960, filmed 1969), *How Young They Died* (1969) and *The Abductors* (1970), which looks at white slavery. Collections of short stories include *The Soldier's Peach* (1959), *The Silver Trumpet* (1961) and *Canary Pie* (1976), and in addition to poems, travelogues and biographies of Cecil Rhodes and Paul Kruger, he wrote two autobiographies in *A Victorian Son* (1972) and *The Gambler* (1973). His novels were not well received in South Africa owing to his themes of interracial love and religious disillusionment, and many of his books were banned in the apartheid era.

Cocteau, Jean (1889–1963) Born Jean Maurice Eugene Clement Cocteau, in Maisons-Lafitte, Yvelines, France, he was a highly respected poet, playwright and novelist. His plays include, among others, *Antigone* (1922, trans. 1961), *Orphée* (1927, trans. 1954), *The Human Voice* (1930, trans. 1951) and *The Infernal Machine* (1934, trans. 1936). He wrote several film scripts, including *The Blood of a Poet* (1932, trans. 1949), about immortality and art, and *Beauty and the Beast* (1945, trans. 1970), and produced a seminal work in modern ballet in collaboration with Pablo Picasso, Erik Satie and Jean-Paul SARTRE entitled *Parade* (1917). His fiction includes the novels *The Grand Écart* (1923, trans. 1925), about the associations of pain with beauty as a result of childhood psychological patterns, *The Impostor* (1923, trans. 1954), about a 16-year-old boy searching for stability in his life in the army, and *Enfants Terribles* (1929, trans. 1930), perhaps his most famous work, centred upon rebellious siblings Paul and Elizabeth, in a study of adolescent alienation. A large amount of non-fiction remains untranslated into English. A leading figure in the Parisian avant-garde in the early decades of the twentieth century, he was full of provocative aphorisms.

F. Steegmuller, *Cocteau: A Biography* (1970).

Coe, Jonathan (1961–) Born in Birmingham, England, he gained degrees at the universities of Cambridge (BA 1983) and Warwick (MA 1984, Ph.D. 1986), before becoming a freelance writer and journalist in 1988. His first novel was *The Accidental Woman* (1987), about a female protagonist's attempt to order her life which is interrupted by random occurrences, and in which the author continually intrudes and comments on the course of the narrative and plot. This was followed by *A Touch of Love* (1989), about a protagonist immersed in political affairs and the confusion of his own life, and *The Dwarves of Death* (1990), another novel about a protagonist disheartened by events around him, told as a series of misadventures set in London. After publishing biographies about the screen actors Humphrey Bogart (1991) and James Stewart (1994), he wrote *What a Carve Up!* (1994), a savage, comic satire of Thatcherite Britain, in which a man investigates a murder in an aristocratic family. His most recent novel, *The House of Sleep* (1997), solidifies his reputation for his humorous and brooding comic style, with a comedy about the powers we acquire and relinquish when we fall asleep.

Coetzee, J.M. (1940–) A highly regarded writer, John Michael Coetzee was born in Cape Town, South Africa, and was educated at the University of Cape Town (BA 1960, MA 1963) and the University of Texas, Austin (Ph.D. 1969). After working as a computer programmer in England (1962–1965), he has since worked as a lecturer in universities, including SUNY Buffalo, and the University of Cape Town, where he is currently Professor. His first work was *Dusklands* (1974), two novellas presenting the parallel stories of 'The Vietnam Project' and 'The Narrative of Jacobus Coetzee', which explore state and individual violence within a context wider than South Africa. *In the Heart of the Country* (1977) explores racial conflict and mental deterioration as a farm girl tells her story of loneliness, anger and despair at her father's affair with an African workman's wife. *Waiting for the Barbarians* (1980) is a bleak tale about a mythical land and tough decisions in the face of a 'barbarian' invasion, and was followed by *The Life and Times of Michael K* (1983, Booker Prize 1984), a Kafkaesque narrative which follows a man's struggle to protect himself during a time of civil war in South Africa, while *Foe* (1987) rewrites *Robinson Crusoe* to explore issues of racism and colonialism. *Age of Iron* (1990) directly addresses the realities of apartheid in South Africa in a Cape Town setting, while *The Master of Petersburg* (1994) is a fictional treatment of Dostoevsky and the processes of creation. In addition to *Boyhood: Scenes from a Provincial Life* (1997), he has written a chilling and uncompromising view of post-apartheid society in *Disgrace* (1999, Booker Prize), making him the first author to win the Booker Prize twice. With a high reputation as an academic, his essays have appeared in *White Writing* (1988), *Doubling the Point* (1992) and *Giving Offense* (1996), and he edited the

anthology of contemporary South African writing *A Land Apart* (1987) with André BRINK. He is also the translator of numerous texts from Dutch, German, French and Afrikaans. Exploring the implications of oppressive societies on the lives of their inhabitants, he has developed a symbolic and allegorical mode of fiction which seeks to explore the psycho-pathological underpinnings of the sociological, locating the archetypal in the particular, partly to assuage the South African censors.

D. Atwell, *J. M. Coetzee: South Africa and the Politics of Writing* (1993).

Cohen, Leonard (1934–) A Canadian poet, novelist and singer/songwriter, Leonard Norman Cohen was born in Montreal, and attended McGill University. By the age of 30, he had published three volumes of poetry, *Let Us Compare Mythologies* (1956), *The Spice-Box of Earth* (1961) and *Flowers for Hitler* (1964), and a novel *The Favourite Game* (1963). His second novel, *Beautiful Losers* (1966), was a controversial book, a religious meditation and sexual fantasy based upon the life of a seventeenth-century Iroquois saint. Additional poetry volumes include *Parasites of Heaven* (1966), *Selected Poems, 1956–1968* (1968) and *Book of Mercy* (1984). In 1968, he recorded his first album, *Songs of Leonard Cohen*. Widely praised, this marked a shift from poet to singer and his subsequent albums include *Songs from a Room* (1969), *Various Positions* (1985) and *The Future* (1992). Drawing heavily on mythologies and romanticism, he has been perceived as somewhat escapist in his poetry. However, his preoccupations are erotic, spiritual and political, often in the form of a personal religious quest depicting the life of the artist.

L. Hutcheon, *The Canadian Postmodern* (1988).

Colegate, Isabel (1931–) Born Isabel Diana, in Lincolnshire, England, her writing has explored the English obsession with aristocracy and the nuances of class, particularly in the light of the changes brought about by the social upheavals of the twentieth century. Her first novels, *The Blackmailer* (1958), *The Man of Power* (1960) and *The Great Occasion* (1962), were set against the background of global post-Second World War unrest, depicting aristocratic alliances with new sources of wealth and their inability to understand the welfare state in Britain. Later work roots these social changes before and in the First World War. After *Statues in the Garden* (1964), there came *Orlando King* (1968), which together with *Orlando at the Brazen Threshold* (1971) and *Agatha* (1973), comprised *The Orlando Trilogy* (1984). Restructuring the Oedipus myth, this charts the rise and fall of the politician Orlando King, between 1930 and 1956. Following *News from the City of the Sun* (1979), came her best novel, *The Shooting Party* (1980, filmed 1985). Set in 1913, and using the allegory of a shooting party on an estate and an accidental killing, it reveals the vulnerability and demise of the aristocracy on the eve of its destruction. Later works include the short stories in *A Glimpse of Sion's Glory* (1985), and the novels, *Deceits of Time* (1988), *The Summer of the Royal Visit* (1991) and *Winter Journey* (1995). With characters struggling to maintain desired positions in society, her fiction traces the permanent transformations of the aristocracy wrought during the twentieth century.

Colette (1873–1954) Born Sidonie-Gabrielle Colette, in Burgundy, France, she worked as a music hall dancer and mime (1906–1911), before turning to writing in earnest. Driven by her first husband, and under the pseudonym of Willy, she wrote the 'Claudine' novels, consisting of *Claudine at School* (1900, trans. 1930), *Young Lady of Paris* (1901, trans. 1931), *The Indulgent Husband* (1902, trans. 1935),

The Innocent Wife (1903, trans. 1935) and *Retreat from Love* (1907, trans. 1974), which follow a young woman growing up through her obsessions, bisexual and lesbian adventures, and gaining her independence. A second cycle based upon her music hall years and set in the world of travelling singers, consists of *The Vagabond* (1910, trans. 1954), *The Captive* (1913, trans. 1970) and *Mitsou* (1919, trans. 1930). *Chéri* (1920, trans. 1930, filmed 1949 and 1958) depicted some of her most memorable characters in an ageing courtesan and Chéri, the younger son of a friend, while *My Mother's House* (1922, trans. 1953) evoked the lost world of childhood. Other major works of the 1920s, such as *Ripening Seed* (1923, trans. 1955), *The Other Woman* (1924, trans. 1971), *The Last of Chéri* (1926, trans. 1932) and *Break of Day* (1928, trans. 1961), depict young men caught between generations of women. Later fiction includes *Sido* (1929, trans. 1953), *The Pure and the Impure* (1932, trans. 1933), which is perhaps her most explicit work about homosexuality, *Looking Backwards* (trans. 1941), *Gigi* (1944, trans. 1952; filmed in France in 1948, and remade by Vincente Minnelli for Hollywood in 1958), perhaps her best-known post-war novel which is part romance and part analysis of women's social lives, *The Evening Star* (1946, trans. 1973) and *The Blue Lantern* (1949, trans. 1963). Short stories appear in *The Tender Shoot* (trans. 1959) and *The Collected Stories of Colette* (trans. 1983), while autobiography occurs in *My Apprenticeships* (1936, trans. 1957) and *Letters from Colette* (trans. 1980). An important figure in French twentieth-century literature, her fiction deals principally with love and betrayal, nostalgic reminiscences of childhood, descriptions of nature, and sexual adventures among women which displaces the male-centred perspective. With a flair for the theatrical, she developed an evocative and sensual style.

J. Thurman, *Secrets of the Flesh: A Life of Colette* (1999).

Collins, Jackie (1941–) Born in London, Collins is an English novelist who moved to Hollywood. Her first novel, *The World Is Full of Married Men* (1968), was followed by *The Stud* (1969) and *The Bitch* (1979), both raunchy romances set in glamorous worlds, which were subsequently filmed starring her older sister, the actress Joan Collins. Since then, she has published a series of successful novels (she has sold in excess of 170 million copies), including *Hollywood Wives* (1983), *Hollywood Husbands* (1996), *Hollywood Kids* (1995), and the 'Lucky Santangelo' novels, including *Chances* (1981), *Sinners* (1984), *Lucky* (1985), *Rock Star* (1988), *Lady Boss* (1990) and *Dangerous Kiss: A Lucky Santangelo Novel* (1999). Her latest novel is *Lethal Seduction* (2000). Many of these later novels have been made into films. Set in the sex-drenched world of celebrities, the rich and the ambitious, her best-selling novels tend to focus on Hollywood, the music business, or the illegal world of gangsters, and offer a mix of power, fame, sex, obsession and revenge.

Collins, Merle (1955–) Born in Aruba, Grenada, in the West Indies, she worked as a researcher in Latin American Affairs (1979–1983), before moving to Britain after the US invasion. She was a member of a performance group and wrote poetry committed to political liberation and the feminist movement in Grenada and elsewhere. Her poetry appears in *Because the Dawn Breaks* (1985) and *Rotten Pomerack* (1992), which make much use of the Creole dialect. Her first novel was *Angel* (1987), which portrays the lives of three generations of Grenadian women in their confrontations and negotiations with colonialism and postcolonial politics. There

followed *The Colour of Forgetting* (1995), a lyrical and passionate homage to the Caribbean in her depiction of several generations of an ordinary family. Short stories about Grenada occur in *Rain Darling* (1990), and she has also edited *Watchers and Seekers: Creative Writing by Black Women in Britain* (1987).

Compton-Burnett, Ivy (1884–1969) Born in Pinner, Middlesex, England, she graduated from the University of London. The year 1920 proved to be a watershed in her life. She had acted as governess to her siblings after their mother's death in 1911, and had adopted the fierce authority of her mother. However, several brothers and sisters died or tragically committed suicide, and she entered a period of mental breakdown in the early 1920s. Although her first novel was *Dolores* (1911), she disowned this as a false start. Her first mature work was *Pastors and Masters* (1925), and there were about eighteen subsequent novels, including *Brothers and Sisters* (1929), about incest and claustrophobia in a family, *Men and Wives* (1931), *More Women Than Men* (1944), *Daughters and Sons* (1937), *Parents and Children* (1941), *Elders and Betters* (1944) and *The Last and the First* (1969). Her fiction was generally narrated entirely through dialogue with an epigrammatic quality, often depicting domestic and parental tyranny and conflicts over power and property in Victorian and Edwardian upper-class households, as explored in her best-known novels *A House and Its Head* (1935), *A Family and a Fortune* (1939) and *Manservant and Maidservant* (1947), the latter reflecting power and authority at all levels of domestic hierarchy. With plots that were often melodramatic and perfunctory, settings in country houses of the Victorian gentry, pages of dialogue, and formulaic titles, her work is not usually considered part of literary modernism, although her fiction has been likened to Cubism and post-Impressionism in the visual arts.

H. Spurling, *Secrets of a Woman's Heart* (1984).

Condon, Richard (1915–1996) An American novelist, he was born Richard Thomas Condon, in New York City, and worked in advertising between 1936 and 1957. In a vision both cynical and satirical, he wrote extravagant fantasies of 'alternate worlds' about the American Dream, which resulted in political thrillers and satires. He is perhaps best known for *The Manchurian Candidate* (1959, filmed 1962), which concerns a superior kind of brainwashing, and incorporates elements of the political thriller in a story of an attempted assassination of the US president. Other novels include *An Infinity of Mirrors* (1964), which scrutinised Nazi Germany, *Any God Will Do* (1966), *The Ecstasy Business* (1967), which is about Hollywood, *Mile High* (1969) about the American Prohibition era, *The Vertical Smile* (1971), *Winter Kills* (1974), another story about an assassination of the US president, *Death of a Politician* (1975), *The Whisper of the Axe* (1976), *The Emperor of America* (1990), which presages a successful overturning of the US government, *Money Is Love* (1975), a rococo fantasy, and *The Final Addiction* (1991). He is also well known for the Prizzi trilogy: *Prizzi's Honour* (1982, filmed 1985 by John Huston), *Prizzi's Family* (1986) and *Prizzi's Glory* (1983), a sequence which mocked the American obsession with organised crime.

Conrad, Joseph (1857–1924) The Anglicised name of Józef Teodor Konrad Nalecz Korzeniowski, he was born in Berdyczów, in Russian-annexed Polish-Ukraine. His early upbringing was amidst fervent political and literary activity in an environment of cultural internationalism and political revolution. In 1874, Conrad left for France and began twenty years as

a sailor in the Mediterranean, the West Indies and South America. He joined the British Merchant Navy in 1878, becoming a naturalised subject in 1886, and spent until 1894 plying the sea routes to Africa, India, the Far East and Australia. These experiences provided the locations, as well as the themes of fear, endurance, isolation, betrayal, idealism and disillusionment, that were the basis for many of his subsequent novels. Counting Ford Madox Hueffer (FORD), H.G. WELLS, Henry James, Arthur Symons and, later, Bertrand Russell in his circle of literary friends, Conrad settled in Kent, England. His first novels were *Almayer's Folly* (1895) and *An Outcast of the Islands* (1896), both set in the Malay archipelago, and displaying his characteristic elliptical narratives, the interlacing of the political with the personal, and the ambiguous treatment of gender and racial stereotypes. The period of his major work began with *Nigger of the 'Narcissus'* (1897), with a symbolic power beneath its realistic narrative of power, anxiety and mutiny onboard a ship, and whose famous 'Preface' became a central statement for modernist aesthetics, with its stress on art making one *see*. *Lord Jim* (1900), *Heart of Darkness* (1902) and 'Youth' (appearing with 'The End of the Tether' in 1902), feature the sceptical sea captain narrator Marlow, who becomes the moral guide in the narratives, although he should not be confused with Conrad's own viewpoint. The novels of this period experimented with narrative complexities, delayed chronological sequences, ironic distancing and ambiguities of identity. Conrad continued with *Typhoon and Other Stories* (1903), followed by perhaps his most complex and challenging historical novel, *Nostromo* (1904), which deals with revolutionary politics in South America. There followed *The Secret Agent* (1907), focusing upon an anarchist in Victorian London, *Under Western Eyes* (1911), and the popular novels *Chance* (1911) and *Victory* (1913). Later novels include *The Shadow-Line* (1917), *The Arrow of Gold* (1919), *The Rescue* (1920), *The Rover* (1923), and the post-humously published and unfinished *Suspense* (1925). Short stories occurred in *A Set of Six* (1908), *'Twixt Land and Sea* (1912), which included 'The Secret Sharer', and *Within the Tides* (1915), while late autobiographical pieces occur in *Notes on Life and Letters* (1921) and *Last Essays* (1926). Collections of his letters have also been published. Upon his death, Conrad was regarded as one of the principal modernist writers, whose writing was championed by F.R. Leavis, although his reputation received criticism in recent years for his treatment of women and non-European races.

J. Baines, *Joseph Conrad: A Critical Biography* (1960); F. Karl, *Joseph Conrad: The Three Lives* (1979).

Conran, Shirley (1932–) Born in London, England, Shirley Ida Conran attended the Southern College of Art in Portsmouth, and married designer and restaurateur Terence Conran (divorced 1962). She worked in the design world over the years, and wrote a variety of design and domestic management books, called the *Superwoman* books, which she recanted in *Down with Superwoman* (1990). She turned to fiction with the publication of her first novel *Lace* (1982), a best-seller and made into a television mini-series, which was set in the glamorous capitals of the world, and concerns power and sex in the milieu of satin sheets, lingerie, champagne and caviar. Her other novels include *The Magic Garden* (1983), the sequel *Lace II* (1985), *The Legend* (1985), *Savages* (1987), *The Amazing Umbrella Shop* (1990), *Crimson* (1992), *Tiger Eyes* (1994) and *The Revenge of Mimi Quinn* (1998). With their sexual versions and perversions, her novels are the definitive 'schlock' novels of the 1980s.

Conroy, Frank (1936–) Born in New York City, and educated at Haverford College, he has contributed to periodicals and magazines such as *The New Yorker* and *Harper's*. His reputation rests principally upon his hugely successful debut, *Stop-Time* (1967), an autobiographical memoir which described a metamorphosis from childhood to adolescence, within the context of American urban social circumstances. Eighteen years passed before *Midair* (1985), a collection of short stories, and the publication of his second novel, *Body and Soul* (1993), which deals with the transformation of a child prodigy into a master pianist and composer.

Conroy, Pat (1945–) Born Donald Patrick Conroy, in Atlanta, Georgia, US, he was educated at The Citadel (BA 1967), South Carolina's Military Academy. After a short stint as a teacher, his first novel, *The Water Is Wide* (1972), was a semi-autobiographical account of these early years teaching at a school for African-American children on the coast of South Carolina. Much of his fiction is considered autobiographical, and his second work, *The Great Santini* (1976), was a blend of lurid reality and fantastic comedy in a story of a boy's initiation into manhood, based upon his own upbringing with his soldier father. It was followed by *The Lords of Discipline* (1980), a bleak portrayal of the military institutionalisation of The Citadel and the conflict between the loyalty to individuals and to groups; *The Prince of Tides* (1986, filmed 1991), about a relationship between twins and their family history; and *Beach Music* (1995), set in South Carolina, and about family, betrayal and place as the past comes into the present. Several of his novels have been adapted for Hollywood films, and his descriptions of relationships with father-figures and jarring yet humorous views of life in contemporary South Carolina, have made him a best-selling author.

Cookson, Catherine (1906–1998) Born in Tyne Dock, South Shields, in northern England, Catherine Anne Cookson was a prolific writer of historical novels, romances and family sagas, and frequently appeared on the best-seller lists, beginning with her first novel, *Kate Hennigan* (1950), and continuing with her late work, *Tinker's Girl* (1995). Her upbringing among the working class on Tyneside provided her with material for her novels, depicting northern English settings, the British class structure and the portrayal of appealing female characters. Her protagonists tend to be solid, hard-working people, while the plots are usually formulaic, often narrating the meeting of a man and a woman, who, despite little initial affection or attraction, gradually fall in love. Her 'Mary Ann' series consists of eight novels about the heroine Mary Ann Shaughnessy, collected in *The Mary Ann Omnibus* (1981), while the 'Mallen' novels focus on an aristocratic dynasty. Her last Tyneside romances were the posthumous publications *The Blind Years* (1998) and *A House Divided* (2000). In addition to the juvenile stories under the pseudonym Catherine Marchant, she has written autobiographies in *Our Kate* (1969) and *Catherine Cookson Country* (1986), collected essays, poetry and paintings in *Let Me Make Myself Plain* (1988), and published two volumes of *Selected Works* (1978 and 1980).

Cooper, Jilly (1937–) An English novelist and humorous non-fiction writer, born in Hornchurch. Among many other jobs, she worked as a reporter (1957–1959), and wrote for the *Sunday Times* (1969–1982). Her first book was *How to Stay Married* (1969), followed by *Jolly Super* (1971) and *Men and Super Men* (1972). She also wrote a series of romantic novels during her early writing career, including *Emily* (1975) and *Prudence* (1978), where the titles are the names of their romantically inclined but gutsy, earthy and occasionally anarchic heroines. Her first major best-seller was *Riders* (1985), an epic romp through the show-jumping world, from English county gymkhanas to the Los Angeles Olympics. She followed this with a series of other blockbusters, including *Rivals* (1988), about the world of television, *Polo* (1991), set in the world of horse polo, *The Man Who Made Husbands Jealous* (1993), set in fictional Rutshire, *Araminta's Wedding* (1993), *Appassionata* (1996), and her latest, *Score!* (1999). Combining cut-throat ambition and boardroom exploits with romance, many of these novels have been made into successful television adaptations.

Coover, Robert (1932–) Born Robert Lowell Coover, in Charles City, Iowa, US, he was educated at a variety of universities. Coover has consistently written fiction in a distinctively experimental manner, often described as postmodern, in which 'reality' and history are linguistically constructed and regarded as narrative fabrications. *The Origin of the Bruinists* (1965) typically fuses realism, satire and fantasy in a narrative about a mystic cult. *The Universal Baseball Association, Inc., J. Henry Waugh, Prop.* (1968) is another fantasy which tells of a lonely accountant and his imaginary baseball league, in a social allegory about the United States. *Pricksongs and Descants* (1969) is a series of short fictional pieces juxtaposing famous legends with Coover's own reworkings, while *The Public Burning* (1976) is a surreal blend of fantasy with the Rosenbergs' trial and execution, to produce a provocative and satirical condemnation of the McCarthy years. Later works include *A Political Fable* (1982), a novella about politics, *Spanking the Maid* (1982), which satirises the use of sadism in fiction, and *Gerald's Party* (1986), about human chaos. His overtly self-reflexive style was continued in *Whatever Happened to Gloomy Gus of the Chicago Bears?* (1987), about an athlete's success during the Depression years, *A Night at the Movies* (1987), *Pinnochio in*

Venice (1991), *Briar Rose* (1996), which is a series of changes wrought on 'Sleeping Beauty', *John's Wife* (1996), a scathing picture of suburbanised mid-West America, and *Ghost Town* (1998), a parody of the Western genre. Other short story collections include *Hair o' the Chine* (1979), *After Lazarus: A Filmscript* (1980), *Charlie in the House of Rue* (1980) and *The Convention* (1982). In addition, he has written several plays collected in *A Theological Position* (1972) and *In Bed One Night and Other Brief Encounters* (1983).

Cope, Jack (1913–1991) Christened Robert Knox Cope, on a farm near Mooi River, Natal, South Africa, he began his writing career as a journalist in Durban and London. Returning to the farm in 1940, he concentrated on creative writing. As editor of the English and Afrikaans literary magazine *Contrast* (1960–1979), he was a powerful influence on South African writing in the 1960s and 1970s, encouraging younger writers of different races and popularising local literatures through anthologies. He published eight novels, including *The Fair House* (1955), *The Golden Oriole* (1958), which explores the collective psyche of black people through individual characterisation, *The Road to Ysterberg* (1959), *Albino* (1964), *The Rain-Maker* (1971), which is a partial reconstruction of Zulu tribal customs, and *My Son Max* (1978). Central to his novels is a critique of the destruction of the black cultures in South Africa perpetrated by apartheid, and the ways in which black South Africans seek to regain their identity. His short stories appear in *The Tame Ox* (1960), *The Man Who Doubted* (1967), *Alley Cat* (1973), and *Selected Stories* (1986), which are generally regarded as his finest talent. As well as a few volumes of poetry and plays, he wrote *The Adversary Within: Dissident Writers in Afrikaans* (1982) in England.

Cornwell, Bernard (1944–) The pseudonym of Bernard Wiggins, he was born in London, England, attended the University of London (BA 1967), and then worked in current affairs and production for the BBC until 1979. He is most famous for his series of novels based upon Richard Sharpe, a fictional British army rifleman, which were adapted to popular acclaim for British television in the 1990s. Beginning with *Sharpe's Eagle* (1981) and concluding with *Sharpe's Battle* (1995), twelve novels recount the picaresque adventures of Sharpe during the course of the Peninsular War against Napoleon to the final defeat at Waterloo. This series has been recently extended with additional Sharpe adventures in *Sharpe's Tiger* (1997), *Sharpe's Triumph* (1999) and *Sharpe's Fortress* (2000), about his service in India. Other novels include *Redcoat* (1987), about the American War of Independence seen through the eyes of a disillusioned British soldier, *Wildtrack* (1988), *Sea Lord* (1989), *Killer's Wake* (1989), *Stormchild* (1991) and *Scoundrel* (1992). *The Winter King* (1995), *Enemy of God* (1996) and *Excalibur* (1997) form a sequence about King Arthur, while *Rebel* (1993), *Copperhead* (1993), *Battle Flag* (1995) and *The Bloody Ground* (1996) form a sequence about the American Civil War. He has also written novels under the pseudonym Susannah Kell, including *A Crowning Mercy* (1983), *The Fallen Angels* (1984) and *Coat of Arms* (1986). Most recently, he has written *Stonehenge: A Novel about 2000 BC* (1999), and *Harlequin* (2000), set during the Hundred Years War between France and England. Ranked alongside the historical novels of C.S. FORESTER and Alexander Kent, Cornwell's work is marked by exciting narratives, painstaking research and authentic detail.

Cortázar, Julio (1914–1984) Born in Brussels, Belgium, his family moved to Argentina in 1918. He was educated at the

University of Buenos Aires (1936–1937), after which he became a schoolteacher and translator, before going to Paris as a Péronist exile in 1951, where he naturalised. A relentlessly experimental writer, he delights in doubles and fantastic parallels and the improvisation of jazz. Following his first novel, *The Winners* (1960, trans. 1965), was the experimental *Hopscotch* (1963, trans. 1966), often regarded as one of the greatest Latin American works of the twentieth century. The game of hopscotch symbolises the searches of various characters, but also the challenge facing the reader, to whom the narrative is offered in two ways: either as a linear narrative, or as a process of jumping about the novel. *62: A Model Kit* (1968, trans. 1972) provides the elements for a reader to build the narrative, while *A Manual for Manuel* (1973, trans. 1978) seeks to reconcile aesthetic and political concerns in a collage style. Short stories and science fiction occur in *Cronopios and Famas* (1962, trans. 1978), *All Fires the Fire* (1966, trans. 1973), *A Certain Lucas* (1979, trans. 1984) and *We Love Glenda So Much* (1981, trans. 1983), while anthologies of his stories occur in *End of the Game* (1967) and *A Change of Light* (1980). Essays appear in *Around the Day in Eighty Worlds* (1967, trans. 1986), *Paris: The Essence of an Image* (trans. 1981) and *Nicaraguan Sketches* (1983, trans. 1989). One of the most influential and famous writers of the Latin American 'Boom' period of the 1960s, with MARQUEZ and CARPENTIER, much of his work can be read as political allegory.

S. Boldy, *The Novels of Julio Cortázar* (1980).

Coupland, Douglas (1961–) A Canadian writer, born at a military base in Baden-Soellingen, Germany, he went to study art and design in Vancouver in 1984. His first novel was a best-seller entitled *Generation X: Tales for an Accelerated Culture* (1991), about twenty-somethings in Palm Springs, California, and which originated the term 'Generation X' to describe Americans born between the 1960s and early 1970s and their defining concerns and preoccupations. This was followed by *Shampoo Planet* (1992) about the contemporary age of information and video stimulation, and *Life After God* (1994). His next major novel was *Microserfs* (1995), which is about young computer programmers, introspective, observant people who are hyperactively engaged in realising the future computer vision of Bill Gates, followed by *Girlfriend in a Coma* (1998), about a girl who goes into a coma in 1979 and wakes up in the late 1990s, allowing a disjunctive perspective on the millennium, and *Miss Wyoming* (1999), a romance about thirty-something Hollywood burn-outs searching for meaning. *Polaroids from the Dead* (1996) collects essays and short fiction. Regarded as a spokesperson for his generation, he sprinkles his work with neologisms, cartoons, slogans and pop culture, as his witty, quirky fiction seeks to register the buzz of 1990s society.

Cozzens, James Gould (1903–1978) Born in Chicago, and reared on Staten Island in New York, he was educated at Harvard (1924) where he completed his first novel *Confusion* (1924), about an aristocratic, rebellious French girl. Further early novels include *The Son of Perdition* (1929), and *S.S. San Pedro: A Tale of the Sea* (1931), set in the US merchant navy. In a detached style of disenchantment, his novels are frequently concerned with the clash of social values. *Men and Brethren* (1936) explores homosexuality within the Church, while *The Just and the Unjust* (1942) is concerned with society's legal system and its stand against anarchy. *Guard of Honour* (1948, Pulitzer Prize), explored the issues of command, duty and responsibility within the military setting of an airbase in Florida during the Second World War. *By Love Possessed* (1957) was highly acclaimed for its social observations about small-town America, and his last novel was *Morning Noon and Night* (1968). Short stories occur in *Children and Others* (1964) and *A Flower in Her Hair* (1974). Cozzens earned a reputation for conservatism during the age of Eisenhower for his preoccupation with law, custom and tradition, although more serious attention to his work has begun in recent decades.

D. Maxwell, *Cozzens* (1964).

Crace, Jim (1946–) Born James Crace, in Lemsford, Hertfordshire, England, he attended Birmingham College of Commerce and graduated with an external degree from the University of London (BA 1968). After working in Africa, in 1970 he turned to freelance journalism, and fiction in 1986. His first book was the loosely connected short story collection *Continent* (1986), which was set on an imaginary continent and examined how new developments impinge on Old World ways and exploit the native inhabitants. This was followed by the novel *The Gift of Stones* (1988), about a prehistoric community whose livelihood rests on stone-crafting skills, exploring themes of art and technological progress. Subsequent work includes the novels *Arcadia* (1992), an urban futuristic tale of the late twentieth century, *Signals of Distress* (1995), set in an English fishing village in 1836, about an incident concerning a freed slave from an American ship, and *Quarantine* (1997), which was shortlisted for the Booker Prize, and is set in the Judean Desert at the time of Christ. His most recent novel, *Being Dead* (1999), logs the death of two natural scientists from an appropriately physical perspective. His fiction usually explores human social and political problems, often examining communal behaviour in unique settings. In a dispassionate prose, he merges the real with the concocted, the mundane and the bizarre, with a clarity of narrative structure.

Crichton, Michael (1942–) Born John Michael Crichton, in Chicago, Illinois, US, he was educated at Harvard University (BA 1964) and Harvard Medical School (MD 1969). A successful commercial writer, he has adapted many of his exciting, thrilling and suspenseful novels for film. His first novel, *A Case of Need* (1968), was written under the pseudonym Jeffrey Hudson, and he has written several other novels under the pseudonyms of Michael Douglas and John Lange. His other novels under his own name include *The Andromeda Strain* (1969), about a dangerous bacteria, *The Terminal Man* (1972), *Westworld* (1974, filmed 1973), about a futuristic fantasy world, and *The Great Train Robbery* (1975), a historical fiction set in Victorian England. Other blockbuster novels are *Congo* (1980), about industrial espionage, *Sphere* (1987), *Jurassic Park* (1990, filmed 1993), about a theme park on a remote island on which reside dinosaurs cloned from genetic residue, and the sequel *The Lost World* (1995, filmed 1997), *Rising Sun* (1992), about a mystery in a Japanese corporation, *Disclosure* (1994, filmed 1994), which is about sexual ethics and corporate corruption, *Airframe* (1996) and *Timeline* (1999). His plots often pit the benefits of modern technology against the destruction of everyday life, and he 'documents' his stories with a disarming array of facts and fictional sources, for example chaos theory in *Jurassic Park* and virtual reality in *Disclosure*. Apart from these well-known plot-driven narratives, lesser known works include a study of the painter Jasper Johns (1977) and non-fiction in *Travels* (1988), as well as a collection of essays.

Cronin, A.J. (1896–1981) Full name Archibald Joseph Cronin, born in Cardross, Dunbartonshire, he was a Scottish doctor and writer, who studied medicine at the University of Glasgow. After serving as a surgeon in the Royal Navy during the First World War, he practised medicine in

Glasgow and London. His first novel, *Hatter's Castle* (1931), the story of a hatmaker's obsession about the possibility of his noble birth, established him as a popular realist novelist of some repute. Leaving medicine, he wrote a string of best-sellers, of which the most famous is *The Citadel* (1937), about how a private physician's avarice can distort good medical ethics. Other much-admired works include *The Stars Look Down* (1941), about various social injustices in a north England mining community, and *The Keys of the Kingdom* (1942), about a Roman Catholic missionary in China. Later works, such as *The Green Years* (1944), *Shannon's Way* (1948), *The Judas Tree* (1961) and *A Song of Sixpence* (1964), received criticism for their sentimentalism. His strength lay in combining acute observation with graphic description and many of his novels were made into films, with the long-running television series *Dr. Finlay's Casebook* based on one of his characters. He died in Switzerland, a tax exile.

Cross, Amanda (1926–) The pseudonym of Carolyn Gold Heilbrun, an American born in East Orange, New Jersey, and educated at Wellesley College and Columbia University (Ph.D. 1959), where she has been Professor of English since 1972. She is the author of several critical studies on English literature, as well as the writer of several detective stories, usually set in an academic environment and written from a feminist perspective. Kate Fansler, the protagonist, is a Professor of English at an unspecified New York university, who brings the methods of literary criticism to bear on crimes. *The Last Analysis* (1964) was the first novel and uses Freud to solve the mystery. Thereafter, other titles include *The James Joyce Murder* (1967), which hides solutions in embedded texts, *The Theban Mysteries* (1971), *Death in a Tenured Position* (1981), about misogyny at Harvard, *A Trap for Fools* (1989), *The Players Come*

Again (1990) and *The Puzzle Heart* (1998). Her novels construct an imaginative reinvention of womanhood and are invariably learned, literary and political in their orientation.

Crowley, John (1942–) An American novelist, born John William Crowley, in Presque Isle, Maine, he was educated at the University of Indiana. Beginning as a photographer and artist, he then turned to freelance writing for film and television, before full-time fiction writing in 1967. He writes finely wrought works of science fiction, fantasy or magic realism, often mixing the genres with folktales. His first novel, *The Deep* (1975), is an allegorical battle between the Reds and the Blacks on a far-off planet, which was followed by *Beasts* (1976), *Engine Summer* (1979), *Little, Big* (1981), about an American family's entanglement with the supernatural, and *Aegypt* (1987), which centres upon the protagonist's desire to find the meaning of life through a study of mythical and hermetic arcane knowledge. *Love and Sleep* (1994) is a second novel in a projected sequence, *Daemonomania* (2000) is his most recent novel, while his short stories are collected in *Novelty* (1989) and *Antiquities: Seven Stories* (1993).

Cussler, Clive (1931–) Born in Aurora, Illinois, US, Clive Eric Cussler attended Pasadena City College (1949–1950), and then worked in advertising, leaving the business with the success of his fiction. His early underwater adventure novels feature Dirk Pitt, a witty, handsome, devil-may-care character, who dives and searches ships and collects cars. His action-packed novels began with *The Mediterranean Caper* (1973), and include, among many others, *Iceberg* (1975), *Raise the Titanic* (1976), *Vixen 03* (1978), *Night Probe* (1981), *Pacific Vortex!* (1983), *Deep Six* (1984), *Cyclops* (1986), *Treasure* (1988), *Dragon* (1990), *Sahara* (1992), *Inca Gold* (1994), *Shock Wave* (1996), *Flood Tide* (1997), *Atlantis*

Found (1999) and *Serpent* (1999). Often escapist adventures with improbable, incredible 'what if?' plots, the narratives of derring-do represent fast-paced, modern pulp fiction.

D

Danticat, Edwidge (1969–) Born in Port-au-Prince, Haiti, she emigrated to the US in 1981 to join her parents. She was educated at Barnard College and Brown University (MFA 1993), and became a freelance writer in 1994. Her novel *Breath, Eyes, Memory* (1994), about Sophie Caco's early years in Haiti and her move to the US to be with her mother, incorporates thinly veiled autobiographical references. *Krik? Krak!* (1995) is a volume of short stories that focus on human relations, and whose title derives from the Haitian practice of storytelling, in which the narrator asks 'Krik?' ('are you ready?') and the audience respond with 'Krak!' ('yes we are!'). In her latest novel, *The Farming of Bones* (1998), Danticat's subject is the 1937 massacre by Dominican islanders of Haitians living within their borders, on the order of Dominican dictator Trujillo – experienced, and then remembered many years afterward, by the story's narrator, Haitian maidservant Amabelle Desir. An up-and-coming American novelist, she has gained a significant reputation as the voice of Haitian-Americans.

Dark, Eleanor (1901–1985) A widely honoured Australian novelist, she was born and grew up in Sydney, before moving to the Blue Mountains in 1923. The daughter of writer Dowell O'Reilly, she began writing novels early in life, including *Slow Dancing* (1932), *Prelude to Christopher* (1934), *Return to Coolami* (1936) and *Waterway* (1938). These earlier works were meditative, with long passages of exposition and often set in small country towns. Her best-known fiction is the historical trilogy, comprising *The Timeless Land* (1941), *Storm of Time* (1948) and *No Barrier* (1953), which traces the settlement of white Australia in the eighteenth and nineteenth centuries. Through extensive research and a broad narrative sweep, the trilogy subjects the origins of white Australia to comprehensive examination, and demonstrates a respect for the Aborigines and their attitudes to the land. Published in one volume as *The Timeless Land* (1963), it is widely regarded as a seminal text in Australian national literature for its realistic portrayal of the emergent nation. With its psychological focus and temporal shifts, her style was clearly influenced by modernist writers, and was preoccupied with the representation of inward experiences of reality and feminist interests.

A. Grove Day, *Eleanor Dark* (1976).

De Bernières, Louis (1954–) Born in London, England, Louis (Henry Piers) De Bernières was educated at the University of Manchester (BA 1977) and London University (MA 1985). A sometime landscape gardener, mechanic and teacher in

Colombia, he has emerged as a very successful contemporary British novelist. Mixing humour and magic to make serious points, his fiction frequently focuses on freedom, power and ideology in Latin America, as in his early novels *The War of Don Emmanuel's Nether Parts* (1990), *Señor Vivo and the Coca Lord* (1991), about the cocaine trade, and *The Troublesome Offspring of Cardinal Guzman* (1992), about a latter-day Inquisition in a small town. His very successful novel *Captain Corelli's Mandolin* (1994, filmed 2000) is a romance set on the Greek island of Cephalonia during the Second World War, between a mandolin-playing Italian officer and a Greek doctor's daughter, charting the Greek way of life under the Italian occupation of the islands.

De Botton, Alain (1969–) Born in Zurich, Switzerland, he attended Cambridge University, and became a journalist. He emerged as a much discussed contemporary novelist with his first work, *Essays in Love* (1993), plotted with deliberate simplicity about a love affair begun on an aeroplane, and surrounded by the apparatus of commentary, proving to be an erudite and witty treatise on love. This was followed by *The Romantic Movement: Sex, Shopping and the Novel* (1994), another love affair accompanied by a philosophical commentary, and *Kiss and Tell* (1995), a playful and adroit novel presented as a biography of a woman named Isabel. The quirky *How Proust Can Change Your Life: Not a Novel* (1997), comments on PROUST's major work, *Remembrance of Things Past*, and suggests that the epic modernist novel can be used as a self-help book. A humorous and parodic fiction writer, his most recent work is *Consolations of Philosophy* (2000), a witty book of solace and humour taken from the history of philosophy.

De La Roche, Mazo (1879–1961) A Canadian novelist, born in Toronto, and among Canada's most popular and prolific writers during the first half of the twentieth century. Two early novels, entitled *Possession* (1923) and *Delight* (1926), explored the constrictions of life in rural slums. Her popularity began in 1927 with the publication of *Jalna*, the first in a fifteen novel historical sequence about the Whiteoak family, spanning from 1852 to 1952, and centring upon Jalna, the family estate in southern Ontario, named after a military station in India where the family ancestors were once located. Her novels depict an anxiety about technological advances, the threats to individualism and the erosion of social order brought about by a burgeoning modernism. However, while championing liberty, the novels are not unaware of the destructive effects of uncontrolled individualism, and her fiction stresses continuity, hierarchy and the persistence of tradition. A sort of conservative literary soap opera set in the Ontario landscape, the narratives often seem to result from adolescent fantasies, but they were widely read and hugely influential.

D. Duffy, *Gardens, Covenants, Exiles* (1982).

De Vries, Peter (1910–1993) An American author, born in Chicago, Illinois, who graduated from Calvin College (AB 1931), and became a writer and editor of *Poetry* magazine. He joined *The New Yorker* and generally became a prolific novelist and story writer. He disowned his first three novels, which were *But Who Wakes the Bugler?* (1940), *The Handsome Heart* (1943) and *Angels Can't Do Better* (1944). He regarded *The Tunnel of Love* (1954) as his first main novel, and subsequent novels include *Comfort Me with Apples* (1956) and its sequel *The Tents of Wickedness* (1959), *The Mackerel Plaza* (1958) and *Through the Fields of Clover* (1961). *The Blood of the Lamb* (1962) marks something of a departure, since it is a combination of comedy and tragedy, about a father who wrestles with questions of religion while coming to terms with the death of his child, and was followed by such novels as *Reuben, Reuben* (1964), *The Vale of Laughter* (1967), *Mrs. Wallop* (1970), *I Hear American Singing* (1976), *Sauce for the Goose* (1981), *Slouching Towards Kalamazoo* (1983) and *Peckham's Marbles* (1986). His fiction in the 1970s explored feminism, gender identity and sexual freedom, although most of his novels are comic satires of society's shortcomings with wit, irony and pun-addicted wordplay. Recurrent themes are love, lust, marriage and its alternatives, religion, and the release of the repressed individual from social institutions.

J. Bowden, *Peter De Vries* (1983).

Deighton, Len (1929–) Born Leonard Cyril Deighton, in London, England, he graduated from the Royal College of Art, before working in a variety of jobs. His early novels established him in the first rank of espionage novelists, along with Ian FLEMING, John LE CARRÉ, and Graham GREENE. *The Ipcress File* (1962) introduced the nameless British Intelligence officer, who was a reluctant spy, a working-class cynic who disliked and distrusted authority. Given the name Harry Palmer in the film adaptations starring Michael Caine, they are clipped, elliptical, episodic Cold War sagas. Other titles include *Horse Under Water* (1963), *Funeral in Berlin* (1964), *The Billion Dollar Brain* (1966) and *XPD* (1981). His most significant later works are three trilogies: the first is *Berlin Game* (1983), *Mexico Set* (1985) and *London Match* (1985); the second is *Spy Hook* (1988), *Spy Line* (1989) and *Spy Sinker* (1990); and the latest is *Faith* (1995), *Hope* (1995) and *Charity* (1996), dealing with moles, defections and betrayals in the spy business. Other historical fiction includes several Second World War narratives in *SS-GB: Nazi Occupied Britain, 1941*

(1978), *Goodbye, Mickey Mouse* (1982), *Winter* (1988) and *City of Gold* (1992). Non-fiction includes a variety of books on the Second World War and on cookery, and several screenplays, including *Oh What A Lovely War!* (1969). Writing realist fiction with a light ironic touch, his hallmark is attention to accuracy in espionage and military details.

Delafield, E.M. (1890–1943) The pseudonym of Edmee Elizabeth Monica de la Pasture Dashwood, she was born in Sussex, England, and was a prolific writer of fiction during the 1920s and 1930s. Her first novel was *Zella Sees Herself* (1917), and among many others, were *The War Workers* (1918), the well-known *Messalina of the Suburbs* (1924), which was a fictionalised account of a famous 1922 murder case in London, *What Is Love?* (1928) and *Now No-one Will Know* (1941). She became best known for her semi-autobiographical series of novels that followed the daily concerns of the Provincial Lady, such as the *Diary of a Provincial Lady* (1930), *The Provincial Lady Goes Further* (1930) and *The Provincial Lady in Wartime* (1932). First appearing in humorous vignettes in *Time and Tide*, the Provincial Lady was a member of the nobility but full of concerns that endear her to those who are not, and the novels, marked by convincing realistic backgrounds, explicit detail and natural patterns of conversation, follow the frugal domestic management of her country home, her development as a writer, her journeys to the US and USSR, and her patriotic war effort work. A pillar of the Women's Institute, Delafield also wrote three plays.

V. Powell, *The Life of a Provincial Lady: A Study of E.M. Delafield and Her Works* (1988).

Delany, Samuel R. (1942–) Full name Samuel Ray Delany, an American novelist and critic, influential in science fiction genres, he was born and raised in Harlem, New York City, and educated at the City College. He has subsequently taught at several universities and was made Professor of Comparative Literature at the University of Massachusetts in 1988. He became famous early for his first novel, *The Jewels of Aptor* (1962), followed by *The Fall of Towers* trilogy: *Captives of the Flame* (1963), *The Towers of Toran* (1964) and *City of a Thousand Suns* (1965). His early novels are structured as quests with physically and psychologically damaged heroes, and show an interest in mythology as well as the problems of communication and linguistics. These structural linguistic interests were intensified in *Empire Star* (1966) and *Babel-17* (1966), which stress the manner in which the perception of reality is partly formed by our language. He was widely praised for the dystopian *Dhalgren* (1975), a long and ambitious work, about urban culture in the violent near-future Bellona City, in which the opening sentence completes the last sentence in an enigmatic cyclical structure. Other novels include the cryptic *tour de force*, *The Einstein Intersection* (1967), the space opera *Nova* (1968), *Triton* (1976), which posits interesting ideas about sexuality and the freedom of choice, *Stars in My Pocket Like Grains of Sand* (1984), and the *Nevèryön* sequence (1979–1987), which is a fantasy adventure series playing with the reader's expectations, and exploring ideas of the erotic to the economic in a self-reflexive, allusive style. Recent fiction includes *The Mad Man* (1994) and *Times Square Red, Times Square Blue* (1999). His critical works include *The Jewel-Hinged Jaw* (1977), *The American Shore* (1978), *Starboard Wine* (1984), *The Straits of Messina* (1989), *Longer Views* (1996) and *Shorter Views* (1999), which are frequently structuralist and postmodernist in focus, seeking to define science fiction's protocols. *Driftglass* (1971) and *Atlantis* (1995) collect stories, while *The Motion of Light in Water* (1988) illuminates his ambiguous sexuality and the science fiction he wrote in the 1960s, with its concerns about the cultural and social mechanisms of eroticism and love, and *Bread and Wine* (1998) is an autobiographical work of his life in New York.

S. McEvoy, *Samuel R. Delany* (1985).

Delderfield, R.F. (1912–1972) Born Ronald Federick Delderfield, in London, England, he worked as a reporter, editor and journalist, serving with the RAF during the Second World War. He began writing after the war, and wrote several generational family sagas punctuated by strong romantic impulses, offering panoramic descriptions of the life and times of his characters. After a successful play called *Worm's Eye View* (1948), his early novels were often set during the period of the Napoleonic Wars, like *Seven Men in Gascony* (1949), and other novels include *Farewell the Tranquil* (1950), *Diana* (1960), about a cockney orphan and a wealthy heroine, *The Unjust Skies* (1962), *Too Few for Drums* (1964), *The Green Gauntlet* (1968), *Theirs Was the Kingdom* (1971) and *The Avenue Story* (1964). His best-known novels are *A Horseman Riding By* (1966), about a meeting on the Western Front during the First World War between a once-married couple, in which the ex-wife instils a new understanding to the man's present marriage, *God Is An Englishman* (1970), about a marriage in late Victorian England, and *To Serve Them All My Days* (1972), set in a boarding school. Autobiographies include *Bird's Eye View* (1954), *For My Own Amusement* (1968) and *Overture for Beginners* (1970). Often writing about middle-aged or elderly romances, his fiction stressed married love and mutuality on all levels of experience.

S. Sternlicht, *R.F. Delderfield* (1988).

Deledda, Grazia (1875?–1936) Born in Nuovo, Sardinia, Italy, Grazia Cosima

Deledda was a prolific and popular writer who started writing early in her life, albeit scorned by the Sardinian community. She set numerous novels in the primitive world of her Sardinian homeland, depicting its traditions and values in such works as *After the Divorce* (1902, trans. 1905), *Ashes* (1904, trans. 1908), *Nostalgia* (trans. 1905) and *The Woman and the Priest* (1920, trans. 1922). Extensive details of the island and its culture emerge in naturalist narratives which usually hinge upon the transgression of some ancient law and the ensuing conflicts, seen from the perspective of a young girl. She was awarded the Nobel Prize for Literature in 1926, only the second woman to have been awarded the honour at the time.

C. Balducci, *A Self-made Woman* (1975).

Delibes Setien, Miguel (1920–) Born in Valladolid, Spain, he was educated at the University of Valladolid, and received a doctorate in law in 1944. He became a lecturer in mercantile law at the University of Valladolid, serving in the Spanish Navy in 1938–1939. Writing under the name Miguel Delibes, his fiction includes *The Path* (1950, trans. 1961), *Five Hours with Mario* (1966, trans. 1989), which is regarded as his masterpiece and looks at the human fight for liberty, *The Hedge* (1969, trans. 1983), about a fearful clerk who degenerates into doing almost anything to maintain his material security in an Orwellian world, and *Smoke on the Ground* (trans. 1972), which is characterised by a harsh, nineteenth-century bleakness. Other works include *The Wars of Our Ancestors* (1975, trans. 1992) and *The Stuff of Heroes* (1987, trans. 1990), while many other novels and non-fiction remain untranslated into English. Considered one of Spain's most important novelists, his starkly realist depiction of well-developed characters manifests his recurrent theme of the ways in which technical and social changes of the twen-

tieth century lead to the alienation and repression of the individual.

J. Díaz, *Delibes* (1971).

DeLillo, Don (1936–) A prolific American novelist, he was born in New York City and educated at Fordham University. Since his first novel, *Americana* (1971), about a television executive who outgrows his business and moves into the unreal world of film, he has established a reputation as a satirist of the 'American Dream', whose novels often include devastating and disturbing vignettes of the absurdities and violence in American life. *End Zone* (1972) is an existential comedy, in which American football is treated as a metaphor for both alienation and atomic war; *Ratner's Star* (1976) is a grim, surreal, futurist novel about a child prodigy in mathematics whose job it is to decode a message from a star; *Players* (1977) is about rich New York people caught up in terrorism; while *Running Dog* (1978) and *The Names* (1982) continue the theme of violence in contemporary western societies. *Great Jones Street* (1983) deals with pop art, consumerism and American junk culture, defined by the co-ordinates of drugs and rock 'n' roll music, while *White Noise* (1985), widely regarded as a comic masterpiece exploring postmodern society, deals with problems of communication and representation in contemporary American society. There followed *Libra* (1988), a fictional-historical investigation of the assassination of J.F. Kennedy and contemporary paranoia about government plots, and *Mao II* (1991) concerning a reclusive writer who suffers from writer's block and his involvement in terrorism. Recently, he has published the epic *Underworld* (1997) to great acclaim, which is a black comedy looking at the Cold War and US culture during the past fifty years. He has also published two plays, entitled *The Day Room* (1987) and *Valparaiso* (1999), a mock-heroic journey towards identity and transcendence. Much of his fiction examines the cult of the charismatic hero, the role of media spectacles in tacitly promoting and normalising violence, and the impact of popular culture in contemporary society. A significant writer in contemporary America, he explores popular culture, the politics of representation, violence and family relationships, crowds and charismatic characters, consumerism and the new media.

F. Lentricchia, *Introducing Don DeLillo* (1991).

Desai, Anita (1937–) Born in Mussoorie, India, of half Indian and half German parentage, she grew up in Delhi, and went to the University of Delhi (BA 1957). She has taught at various universities and since 1993, has been teaching creative writing at the Massachusetts Institute of Technology in the US. Her first novel was *Cry, the Peacock* (1963), about a woman trying to assert her individuality, and she has since written many works. Other novels include *Voices of the City* (1965), *Bye-Bye, Blackbird* (1968), about the East–West cultural clash, *Where Shall We Go This Summer?* (1975), *Fire on the Mountain* (1977), about generational differences, *Clear Light of Day* (1980), *In Custody* (1984), *Baumgartner's Bombay* (1989), about exile and displacement as German Jews flee Nazi Germany for India, *Journey to Ithaca* (1995) and *Feasting, Fasting* (1999). *Diamond Dust* (2000) is a collection of stories. Many of her novels are situated in north India, depicting the personal struggles of Indian characters coping with the social and cultural changes since Independence. Often centring upon family members and women's problems, her novels are usually short but highly detailed, presenting the local colour of India. With little recourse to native story-telling traditions, her fiction is regarded as that of a Europeanised sensibility by some, with its significant use of imagery and its focus on the private lives and interior psychological landscapes

of her characters. Short stories appear in *Games at Twilight* (1978).

I. Sivanna, *Anita Desai as an Artist* (1994).

Desani, G.V. (1909–) Born Govindas Vishnoodas Desani, in Nairobi, Kenya, he emigrated to the US in 1970 and was naturalised in 1979. He went to England in 1926, returning to India in 1952, where he worked mainly as a journalist, a broadcaster for the BBC and a lecturer on Indian affairs. He studied Buddhism, philosophy and mysticism, wrote for the *Illustrated Weekly of India* (1960–1967), and then became Professor of Philosophy at the University of Texas, Austin (1969–1979). His only novel is *All About H Hatterr, a Gesture* (1948), an influential work which he has revised and expanded since its first publication and republished as *All About H Hatterr* (1951). An avant-garde text that demonstrates versatile humour, crazy comedy, absurdism, a mix of idioms and forms, jokes and gestures, it describes the hilarious misadventures of Mr Hatterr. Making use of popular culture and linguistic trickery, this episodic, picaresque novel explores illusion and reality, and its multiple reprints indicate its endurability. His miscellaneous sketches, parodies, short stories and essays are collected with his only other work of note, the poetic drama *Hali* (1951), in *Hali and Collected Stories* (1990).

M. Ramanujan, *G.V. Desani: Writer and Worldview* (1984).

Deshpande, Shashi (1938–) Born in Dharwar, India, she was educated at Elphinstone College (BA 1956) and Mysore University (MA 1984). She began writing in the 1970s, and has published over seventy short stories, five novels and several children's books. Often described as a feminist writer, she focuses upon well-educated women and their conflicts with the demands of post-Independence Indian society. Early novels, such as *The Dark Holds No Terrors* (1980), *If I Die*

Today (1982) and *Roots and Shadows* (1983), show women breaking out of the stranglehold of the family and then an inexplicable need to return to their roots. Other novels include *Come Up and Be Dead* (1983), *That Long Silence* (1988), which some regard as her most accomplished work, *The Binding Vine* (1993) and *A Matter of Time* (1996), which depict women's relationships tugging at them after having striven for independence and autonomy. Her short stories are also women centred, and appear in *The Legacy* (1978), *It Was Dark* (1986), *The Miracle* (1986), *It Was the Nightingale* (1986) and *The Intrusion* (1994). At odds with the traditional Indian ethical and emotional values going back to Vedic times, her female characters straddle western literary representations and the archetypes of Indian mythology, although they resist the total surrender of self to children and husbands.

S. Sandhu, *The Novels of Shashi Deshpande* (1991).

Dexter, Pete (1943–) Born in Pontiac, Michigan, US, he graduated from the University of South Dakota (1970). He worked as a journalist until 1985, when he turned to full-time writing. He began with three highly acclaimed novels that explored the effects of violence and murder on communities: *God's Pocket* (1984) turns on the death of an abrasive construction worker in Philadelphia; *Deadwood* (1986) is about the assassination of 'Wild Bill' Hickok in a western gold-rush town; and *Paris Trout* (1988), set in Georgia, US, in the 1950s, tells of a brutal, abusive shopkeeper and moneylender, who, after committing the murder of a young black girl, slides into insanity. *Brotherly Love* (1991) is set in Philadelphia and concerns a young Irish boxer caught up in gang warfare between Italian mobsters and Irish labour bosses, while *The Paperboy* (1995), set in the northern

Florida swamps, concerns an intrusive investigation by two brothers, one a reporter, into the killing of a sheriff. Mixing violence with humour, he has a sharp ear for dialogue and a good eye for detail.

Dick, Philip K. (1928–1982) An American science fiction writer, born Philip Kindred Dick, in Chicago, Illinois, he attended the University of California, Berkeley. Apart from writing, his other principal interest was music: he ran a record shop for a time and also a classical music programme for a local radio station. A prolific writer, his best-known novels include *Solar Lottery* (1955), *Eye in the Sky* (1957), *Time Out of Joint* (1959), *The Man in the High Castle* (1962), an alternative history in which World War Two is won by the Nazis, *The Three Stigmata of Palmer Eldritch* (1964), which depicts a society controlled by drug-induced fantasy and television, *The Crack in Space* (1966), *Ubik* (1969), about time dislocation, time travel and telepathy, *Martian Time-Slip* (1976), *A Scanner Darkly* (1977) and *The Man Whose Teeth Were All Exactly Alike* (1984). His book *Do Androids Dream of Electric Sheep?* (1968), set in a twenty-first century dominated by information technology, was the basis for the cult Hollywood movie *Blade Runner* (1982). He has also written three curiously wooden novels that do not belong in the science fiction category, expressing an acerbic view of modern society: *Confessions of a Crap Artist* (1975), *In Milton Lumky Territory* (1985) and *Humpty Dumpty in Oakland* (1986), the last two published posthumously. Numerous collections of science fiction short stories occur in *A Handful of Darkness* (1955), *The Preserving Machine* (1969) and *The Golden Man* (1981), and a five-volume *Collected Short Stories* (1990–1991). A significant influence on the 'New Wave' in science fiction, he has also proved to be something of a forerunner for contemporary cyberpunk writers.

S. Umland, *Philip K. Dick: Contemporary Critical Interpretations* (1995).

Dickens, Monica (1915–1992) Born Monica Enid Dickens, in London, England, the great-granddaughter of Charles Dickens, her writing reflected a wide range of interests and independent concerns. She rebelled against the social trappings of her upper-middle-class upbringing, and worked in various public and domestic jobs, experiences which often provided her with fuel for her fiction. For example, *Thursday Afternoons* (1945) and *The Happy Prisoner* (1946) reflected her work as a nurse during the Second World War, and *The Fancy* (1943) reflected her life as a mechanic in an aeroplane repair factory. Many of her early works were semi-autobiographical, with *One Pair of Hands* (1939) narrating her life as a cook and maid, *One Pair of Feet* (1942) depicting her wartime nursing, *My Turn to Make the Tea* (1951) her time as a reporter and journalist, and *No More Meadows* (1953) and *Man Overboard* (1958) drawing upon her marriage to an American naval officer. Her later works turned to social issues such as poverty, child abuse and suicide, as in *The Heart of London* (1961), *Kate and Emma* (1964) and *The Listeners* (1970). Impressed with the work of the Samaritans while researching the latter book, she founded the Samaritans of the US in Boston. Her last novels were *Closed at Dusk* (1990), *Scarred* (1991) and *One of the Family* (1993). *An Open Book* (1978) is her final autobiographical work.

Didion, Joan (1934–) An American novelist, born in Sacramento, California, and educated at the University of California at Berkeley (BA 1956). After working for *Vogue* in Paris, she gradually established herself as a freelance writer, with her first novel *Run River* (1963) about a collapsing Sacramento family. Other novels include *Play It As It Lays* (1970), about a woman caught in the transience of southern Californian life, *A Book of Common Prayer* (1977), about alienated and separated yet growing self-awareness, and a self-reflexive novel in *Democracy* (1984). Her most recent novel is *The Last Thing He Wanted* (1996). Despite these novels, she is principally known for her essays and 'new journalism', the blending of literary technique with journalist fact, such as her work on the 1960s and 1970s in *Slouching Towards Bethlehem* (1968), which collects information on the fragmentation of Californian lifestyles and includes her well-known essay on hippy culture and Haight Ashbury, and in *The White Album* (1979). Other journalist works include *Salvador* (1983), about her personal experiences in the civil war; *Miami* (1987), a non-fictional examination of Cuban immigrants; *After Henry* (1992), a collection of essays about people in New York, Washington DC, and Los Angeles; and *Joan Didion: Essays and Conversations* (1984) and *Sentimental Journeys* (1993). Writing in a spare, terse style, she frequently shows a nostalgia for a lost America. She is married to John Gregory DUNNE.

K. Henderson, *Joan Didion* (1981).

Disch, Thomas M. (1940–) Born in Des Moines, Iowa, US, and educated at New York University, Thomas Michael Disch worked in advertising and in a bank before turning to full-time writing in the mid-1960s, and has since been a visiting professor at a range of universities. Part of the 'New Wave' of science fiction writers of the 1960s who sought to challenge conventional expectations of the genre, his first novel, *The Genocides* (1965), offers an alien perspective of humanity. After *Mankind Under the Leash* (1966), *102 H-Bombs* (1966) and *Black Alice* (1968), came his high point, *Camp Concentration* (1968), which takes the form of a journal and is about an inmate in a near-future US concentration camp, and is an allegory of the Vietnam War. Further novels include *On Wings of Song* (1979), about a near-future New York, and *The Priest: A Gothic Romance* (1995), part of his preoccupation with the Catholic Church. Short stories are collected in *Under Compulsion* (1968), *Getting Into Death* (1973), and *334* (1972), a series of linked stories which pivot upon the urban lives of the inhabitants of 334 East 11th Street in the Manhattan of AD 2025. Recent writing includes *The Castle of Indolence* (1995), *The Dreams Our Stuff Is Made Of* (1998) and *The Sub: A Study of Witchcraft* (1999).

S. Delany, *The American Shore* (1978).

Diski, Jenny (1947–) Born in London, England, she spent her early life in psychiatric care, and lived for four years with the novelist Doris LESSING. She taught for five years before attending London University (1982–1984), and then turned to writing. *Nothing Natural* (1986) was her daring first novel, a blunt narrative about a sadomasochistic relationship of obsession and self-destructive sexual practices. This was followed by *Rainforest* (1987), about an environmentalist gaining self-knowledge in the Borneo forests, *Like Mother* (1988), about the birth of a disabled child, with an imaginative twist to the narrative perspective, *Then Again* (1990), about reincarnation, madness and questions of existence, and *Happily Ever After* (1991), a black comedy about sexual relationships in a claustrophobic situation. Recent works include *Monkey's Uncle* (1994), *The Vanishing Princess* (1995), *The Dream Mistress* (1996), *Skating to Antarctica* (1997), *Don't* (1998), which is a collection of essays demythologising a wide range of late twentieth-century saints, and *Only Human* (2000). Known for her quirky, sometimes shocking black humour about modern life, her fiction frequently explores the boundaries of rationality and insanity, and the inner recesses of the human psyche.

Döblin, Alfred (1878–1957) Born in Stettin, Germany, he studied medicine at Berlin and Freiberg universities (1900–1905), and became a medical officer during the Second World War. He practised as a physician in Berlin (1911–1914), after which he became a writer and reviewer. He went to France in 1933 to escape the Nazis, then to the US, and returned to Germany in 1945. His greatest novel is *Berlin Alexanderplatz* (1929, trans. 1931), a work which depicts the modern metropolis and the cultural ferment of the city, experimenting with narrative methods by combining documentary realism and lyrical passages while narrating the life of a furniture removal man over a period of eighteen months. Filmed by Rainer Werner Fassbinder in a mammoth fifteen-hour version in 1980, the novel pushes language to its limits. Other works include *The Three Leaps of Wong-lun* (1915, trans. 1991), set in eighteenth-century China, about passive resistance against imperialist authorities, *Men without Mercy* (1935, trans. 1937) and *A People Betrayed* (1949, trans. 1983), both of which deal with the revolutionary and fascist tendencies in post-First World War Germany. His autobiography is *Destiny's Journey* (1949, trans. 1992), and much else remains untranslated into English. Versatile yet enigmatic, he had a formative influence on Bertolt Brecht and constantly explored social injustice and hypocrisy. After his return to Germany, he was largely forgotten until Fassbinder's film renewed critical interest in his fiction, which has established him as a key figure in European modernism.

W. Kort, *Alfred Döblin* (1974).

Doctorow, E.L. (1931–) An American novelist of wide repute, born Edgar Laurence Doctorow, in New York, and educated at Kenyon College and Columbia University. After working in the film industry, he became a professor at Sarah Lawrence College (1971–1978), and is now at New York University. His first novel, *Welcome to Hard Times* (1960), which depicted the devastation of a Dakota frontier town by an evil outsider, was followed by a science fiction satire entitled *Big As Life* (1966). He then wrote *The Book of Daniel* (1971), a fictional treatment of the Rosenberg trial and an examination of the United States from the McCarthyite epoch to the 1960s. The critically acclaimed *Ragtime* (1975) explored the relationship of the past and the present in a jazzy rewriting of the American 1920s, which fuses the tale of Coalhouse Walker with the lives of such historical figures as Henry Ford, Scott Joplin, Emma Goldman and Houdini. Similar explorations occurred in *Loon Lake* (1980), a novel about the American Depression, *World's Fair* (1985), *Billy Bathgate* (1989), about a Bronx boy who drifts into gangsterism, and *The Waterworks* (1994), which evokes New York in the 1870s in a fantastic detective story. His most recent novel is *City of God* (2000), a mystery set in 1999 which metafictively explores the varieties of religious experience. His other works include the play *Drinks Before Dinner* (1979), *Essays and Conversations* (1983), *Lives of the Poets* (1984) and *Poets and Presidents: Selected Essays 1977–1992* (1994). Known for his philosophical probings, and the subtlety and variety of his prose, he has always been concerned with the representation and reconstruction of history and its dependency on current assumptions.

Dodge, Jim (1945–) Born in the US, he was educated at Humboldt State University (BA 1967) and the University of Iowa (MFA 1969). He was a teacher at an Iowa college (1970–1971), and held other various jobs before turning to writing. His first novel was *Fup* (1983), about two

bachelors and Fup, a mallard duck, who mystically changes the lives of the eccentric bachelors. The title of *Not Fade Away* (1987) was taken from a Buddy Holly song, and recounts the journey of a truck driver to honour the singer's death. *Stone Junction* (1990) is about the life of a child and its mother hitching a ride out West and their connection to the Alliance of Magicians and Outlaws. Connecting the marvellous and ordinary, it is an adventure-cum-fairy tale, as the child is apprenticed to the group. He has also written various poetry chapbooks.

Donaldson, Stephen R. (1947–) An American novelist, born Stephen Reader Donaldson, in Cleveland, Ohio, and educated at the College of Wooster, Ohio (BA 1968) and Kent State University (MA 1971). After working for a time as a teacher, at a hospital and in publishing, in 1977 he published the first novels in *The Chronicles of Thomas Covenant* series: *Lord Foul's Bane*, *The Illearth War* and *The Power That Preserves*. This series was an epic fantasy that mixed the marvellous with the mundane, in which the leper Thomas Covenant is translocated into The Land, a fantasy world ravaged by social problems, and his quest for a personal cure parallels his role as the saviour of The Land. Ironically, Donaldson laboured long and hard on this series and was rejected by forty-seven publishers before enjoying immense success upon publication and a cult following similar to Tolkien's fantasy. The sequence concluded with *The Wounded Land* (1981), *The One Tree* (1982) and *White Gold Wielder* (1983). Two separate fantasy novellas entitled *Golden Fire* (1981) and *Daughter of Regals* (1984) also appeared at this time. Another series entitled *Mordaunt's Need*, centring upon a female protagonist called Terisa Morgan, only resulted in *The Mirror of Her Dreams* (1986) and *A Man Rides Through* (1987). He has also published several pseudonymous detective mystery stories (as Reed

Stephens) called *The Man Who Killed His Brother* (1980), *The Man Who Risked His Partner* (1984) and *The Man Who Tried to Get Away* (1990). More recently, from 1991 to 1996, he has been engaged in writing the *Gap* series, a science fiction sequence centring upon a female character, Morn Hyland. Short stories have appeared in *Reave the Just* (1999).

K. Fonstad, *The Atlas of The Land* (1985).

Donleavy, J.P. (1926–) Full name James Patrick Donleavy, he was born in Brooklyn, New York City, of Irish parents. After the Second World War he studied at Trinity College, Dublin. His best-selling first novel, *The Ginger Man* (1955), upon which his reputation largely rests, depicts the racy adventures of seduction and high jinks in bohemian Dublin, in which the sponging philanderer Sebastian Dangerfield extricates himself from numerous scrapes. The book's sexually frank prose and descriptions of Dublin caused comparisons with James JOYCE and Flann O'BRIEN. A stage version was mounted in London in 1961, and other plays also followed. He naturalised in Ireland in 1967, and wrote increasingly facetious works, including *A Singular Man* (1961), *The Saddest Summer of Samuel S* (1966), *The Onion Eaters* (1971), *Shultz* (1980), *Are You Listening Rabbi Low?* (1987) and *That Darcy, That Dancer, That Gentleman* (1991). *The Lady Who Liked Clean Rest Rooms* (1995) and *Wrong Information Is Being Given Out at Princeton* (1998) are chronicles of strangeness set in New York. Indeed, many of his works are set in the US, though *The Beastly Beatitudes of Balthazar B* (1968) returns to Ireland. Shorter pieces appear in *Meet My Maker, the Mad Molecule* (1964) and *The Author and His Image* (1997), and other works include *A Singular Country* (1989), which contains personal impressions, and an autobiography in *The History of the Ginger Man* (1994).

Donoso, José (1924–1996) Born in Santiago, Chile, he went to Princeton University (AB 1951), and has worked as a shepherd, teacher, journalist, literary critic and an academic. After his first novel *Coronation* (1957, trans. 1965), there followed *Hell Has No Limits* (1966, trans. 1972), which provides searching questions about sexual identity, and *This Sunday* (1966, trans. 1967). In *The Obscene Bird of Night* (1970, trans. 1973), he turned from realism to reflexive interrogation, providing critical reflections on writing and authorship. There followed *Sacred Families* (1973, trans. 1977), an incisive evaluation of modern bourgeois culture, *A House in the Country* (1978, trans. 1984), which is a political allegory about the Allende government, the meditations on exile in *The Garden Next Door* (1981, trans. 1992), *Curfew* (1986, trans. 1988), and two novellas in *Taratuta* (1990, trans. 1993). Short stories occur in *Charlestown* (1960, trans. 1977), and essays in *The 'Boom' in Spanish American Literatures* (1971, trans. 1977). One of the pre-eminent authors of the 'Boom' period of influential Latin American fiction in the 1960s, along with CORTÁZAR, FUENTES, MÁRQUEZ and VARGAS LLOSA, his fiction examines the social and cultural realities of Chile and South America. Interrogating questions of national identity and language, his novels engage with modern literary theory and criticism.

F. Gonzalez Mandri, *José Donoso's House of Fiction* (1995).

Doolittle, Hilda (1886–1961) A poet, novelist and autobiographer, she was born in Bethlehem, Pennsylvania, US. Educated at Bryn Mawr College, and in her youth closely associated with Ezra Pound, Marianne Moore and William Carlos Williams, she is perhaps best known as 'H.D.', after Pound wrote 'H.D. Imagiste' on one of her poetry manuscripts. Her reworkings of Judaeo-Christian religion and Hellenic cults, especially *Helen in*

Egypt (1961) and the major long poems written during the Second World War, later collected as *Trilogy* (1973), are significant achievements. After marrying Richard ALDINGTON in 1913, her marriage collapsed in 1919, and she became attached to Bryher (Winnifred Ellerman). Early prose works include autobiographical attempts in *Paint It Today* (1921, reprinted 1992), *Asphodel* (1921–22, reprinted 1992), *Hedylus* (1928), *Palimpsest* (1929) and *The Hedgehog* (1936). She also wrote *End to Torment* (written 1958, published 1979), much of it about her brief engagement to Pound. Between 1933 and 1934, she underwent a period of analysis with Freud in Vienna, which greatly influenced her writing. *Tribute to Freud* (1954) describes their collaborative research into occult phenomena and matriarchal prehistory, and indeed, many of these earlier autobiographical attempts, the most successful of which was *The Gift* (1969), sought self-analysis through dream interpretation, childhood reminiscences, recollections and free association. *Bid Me to Live* (1960) is a stream-of-consciousness account of Bloomsbury life in 1917, while *Hermione* (1981), which collects stories about the strains of lesbianism and heterosexual attraction, and *Hermetic Definition* (1972) were both published posthumously. With a style that is often notable for its concision and clarity, she has emerged as a significant poet in recent years as feminist literary critics have re-evaluated her work.

B. Guest, *Herself Defined* (1984).

Dorfman, Ariel (1942–) Born in Buenos Aires, Argentina, he went to Chile in 1954, naturalising in 1967. He graduated from the University of Chile, Santiago (1967), and held various academic posts in Chile and the US. Exiled by Pinochet in 1973, and after a period in Europe during the 1970s, he went to the US to work as an academic. His first novel was *Hard Rain* (1973, trans. 1990), a fictional

collage of the Allende Marxist experiment of socio-economic reforms, and the experimental approach to language owes much to CORTÁZAR. There followed *My House Is On Fire* (1979, trans. 1990), *Widows* (1981, trans. 1983), set in a Greek village under Nazi occupation, *The Last Song of Manuel Sandero* (1982, trans. 1987), a formally experimental novel about exile, dictatorship and the abuse of power, and *Mascara* (trans. 1988), a further study of dictatorial power. More recently, his works include *Konfidenz* (1994, trans. 1995), *Heading South, Looking North: A Bilingual Journey* (trans. 1998), *The Resistance Trilogy* (trans. 1998), which collects earlier works, and *The Nanny and the Iceberg* (trans. 1999). The formal and thematic complexity of his fiction forces the reader to participate in the creative reading process. In addition to poetry, he has written several plays, including the provocative prize-winning play *Death and the Maiden* (trans. 1991), and his writings on popular culture appear in *How to Read Donald Duck* (1971, trans. 1975), a sociological study of Disney comics and imperialism, and *Some Write to the Future* (1984, trans. 1991).

Dos Passos, John (1896–1970) Born in Chicago, and educated at Harvard University, John (Roderigo) Dos Passos emerged as one of the most significant American modernist novelists and a champion of the left in the 1920s and 1930s. Despite his father's efforts to direct him into architecture, he joined the famous Norton-Harjes ambulance unit and served in Italy and France during the First World War. These experiences formed the basis of his first novel, *One Man's Initiation – 1917* (1920, later published as *First Encounter*, 1945), as they did for his second work, *Three Soldiers* (1921), which described the impact of warfare on the lives of three men. After the war, he turned to journalism and travel, writing poetry (*A Pushcart at the Curb*, 1922), and critical essays on Spanish culture in *Rosinante to the Road Again* (1922). After *Streets of Night* (1923), he wrote *Manhattan Transfer* (1925), the novel that marked his maturity, with its collective portrait of fictional episodes of diverse life in New York City. He became increasingly political during the 1930s, writing a tract against the Sacco and Vanzetti Trial of 1927 in *Facing the Chair* (1927), and joining the board of the socialist journal *New Masses* in 1926. He began to write several plays with an acute political consciousness, some of which are in *Three Plays* (1934), examining corporate business, trade disputes and the machinations of capitalism. However, much of his effort went into writing his major trilogy, *U.S.A.* (1938), which comprised *The 42nd Parallel* (1930), *1919* (1932) and *The Big Money* (1936), which tells the story of the first three decades of twentieth-century America, and the degradation of people's lives in a decaying commercialised civilisation. It employs a wide range of fictional devices, including 'newsreel' panoramic backgrounds, impressionistic stream-of-consciousness passages, all of which depict the corruption, futility, frustration and defeat of American life. Thereafter, the trilogy *District of Columbia* (1952) explored the politics of the New Deal and the Second World War, in which his gradual disillusionment with the left began to be evident. Other works include *The Prospect Before Us* (1950), *Chosen Country* (1951), *Most Likely to Succeed* (1954), *The Great Days* (1958), and *Midcentury* (1961), which demonstrates a firmly conservative perspective. He has also produced a large body of reportage, including *The Villages Are the Heart of Spain* (1937), *Journeys Between Wars* (1938), *Tour of Duty* (1946) and *Brazil on the Move* (1963). His later works of the 1950s and 1960s were his historical and political analyses of American democracy, such as the autobiographical *The Ground We Stand On* (1941), *Prospects of a Golden Age* (1959), *Mr*

Wilson's War (1963), and his book about Jeffersonian democracy, *The Shackles of Power* (1966). Travel writings appeared in *Orient Express* (1927) and *In All Countries* (1934), and selections of letters and diaries have been published as *The Fourteenth Chronicle* (1973).

T. Ludington, *John Dos Passos* (1980).

Douglas, Ellen (1921–) The pseudonym of Josephine Ayres Haxton, she was born in Natchez, Mississippi. She graduated from the University of Mississippi (BA 1942), and has subsequently worked as a writer and lectured at various American universities. Her novels consist of *A Family's Affairs* (1962), *Where the Dreams Cross* (1968), *Apostles of Light* (1973), *The Rock Cried Out* (1979), about an ex-hippie who returns to his homeland and gets embroiled in problems of miscegenation, hatred, revenge and murder, *A Lifetime Burning* (1982), which is in the form of a diary as a 62-year-old woman tries to make sense of her life, and *Can't Quit You Baby* (1988), about the relationship between a white middle-class woman and her black female servant. *Black Cloud, White Cloud* (1963) collects novellas, *The Magic Carpet* (1987) collects her reworkings of fairy tales, and four stories appear in *Truth* (1998). Like William FAULKNER, she created a fictional Mississippi county, called Homochito County, in which she sets most of her fiction, examining racial relations and the position of women, and relating these to wider issues in the US.

Doyle, Arthur Conan (1859–1930) Born in Edinburgh, Scotland, he studied medicine at Edinburgh University and then practised in Plymouth and Southsea, before serving in the Boer War as an army physician. *A Study in Scarlet* (1888) introduced probably the most famous detective in literature, Sherlock Holmes, who solves mysteries with his deductive powers, and his friend Dr. Watson, the narrator of many of the stories, who resides with him at 221B Baker Street in London. Other Sherlock Holmes novels are *The Sign of Four* (1890), *The Hound of the Baskervilles* (1902) and *The Valley of Fear* (1914). However, Doyle's real popularity derives from the Holmes short stories, appearing principally in the *Strand Magazine*, beginning with 'A Scandal in Bohemia' (1891). Although he tried to kill off Holmes in 1893, popular demand forced a resurrection in 1903. These stories are collected in *The Adventures of Sherlock Holmes* (1892), *The Memoirs of Sherlock Holmes* (1894), *The Return of Sherlock Holmes* (1905), *His Last Bow: Some Reminiscences of Sherlock Holmes* (1917) and *The Case-Book of Sherlock Holmes* (1927). Many of these stories have been filmed, the best known being those starring Basil Rathbone in the 1940s. His other fiction includes many historical novels, for example *The White Company* (1891), *Rodney Stone* (1896), the adventures of a French Napoleonic officer in *The Exploits of Brigadier Gerard* (1896), *Sir Nigel* (1906) and *The Lost World* (1912). Many volumes of non-fiction include a history of the First World War, *The Great Boer War* (1900) and *History of Spiritualism* (1926).

O. Edwards, *The Quest for Sherlock Holmes: A Biography of Sir Arthur Conan Doyle* (1983).

Doyle, Roddy (1958–) Born in Dublin, Ireland, he was educated at University College, Dublin, and he initially worked as a schoolteacher in Kilbarrack, a rundown suburb of Dublin, which became the 'Barrytown' of his novels. Concerned with the people who live on the north Dublin housing estates, his novels manifest a vibrant, irrepressible humour and dynamic characters. His first book, *Your Granny's a Hunger Striker* (1982), showed his talent for comedy. The hilarious trilogy, comprising *The Commitments* (1987, filmed 1991), *The Snapper* (1990) and *The Van* (1991, filmed 1996), and published as *The Barrytown Trilogy*

(1992), follows the fortunes and adventures of various members of the feckless but closely-knit Rabbitte family. His best-selling novel *Paddy Clarke Ha Ha Ha* (1993, Booker Prize), gives a picture of life as seen through the bewildered eyes of 10-year-old Patrick Clarke and his perception of his parents' sinking marriage. *The Woman Who Walked into Doors* (1996) is more serious, and describes the life of a woman after the death of her abusive husband, *A Star Called Henry* (1999) marks a new turn in his fiction with a historical novel about Henry Smart growing up in the slums of Dublin in 1902, while *The Giggler Treatment* (2000) is his latest work. Doyle also works as a screenwriter and playwright, and his plays include *Brownbread* (1987) and *War* (1989).

Drabble, Margaret (1939–) Born in Sheffield, England, she is the sister of A.S. BYATT, and graduated from Cambridge University (BA 1960). Her first novels, *A Summer Bird-Cage* (1963), *The Garrick Year* (1964) and *The Millstone* (1965), gave her a reputation for portraying the modern 1960s woman – young, talented, articulate and attractive. Her fiction frequently deals with the dilemmas of educated young women caught in a complex web of maternity, sexuality, intellectual and economic aspiration. Subsequent novels are *Jerusalem the Golden* (1967), about a working-class girl who goes to London University and confronts the class structures, and *The Waterfall* (1969), which explores stylistic experiments. Her biggest novels emerged in the 1970s with *The Needle's Eye* (1972), exploring personal morality, and *The Realms of Gold* (1975), about the possibilities of individual development despite social limitations. There followed *The Ice Age* (1977) and *The Middle Ground* (1980), before a trilogy consisting of *The Radiant Way* (1987), *A Natural Curiosity* (1989) and *The Gates of Ivory* (1991), which depicted the progress of three Cambridge university friends from the 1950s into the changing social and political environment of Britain in the 1980s. Her most recent novel is *The Witch of Exmoor* (1996). She has also written various television plays and screenplays, biographies of the novelists Arnold BENNETT (1974) and Angus WILSON (1995), and edited several books. Exploring women's alienation from the system and the attempts to forge female self-definition, her typically realist fiction depicts protagonists struggling to survive and to maintain an identity in the face of a disintegrating social order.

J. Creighton, *Margaret Drabble* (1985).

Dreiser, Theodore (1871–1945) An American author, born Theodore Herman Albert Dreiser, in Terre Haute, Indiana, and educated at Indiana University. He began work as a journalist, and frequently drew upon the prevalent social and economic circumstances for his early novels and earned a certain notoriety in his day for his frank handling of sexual themes. His first book was *Sister Carrie* (1900), about a young country girl's passage, via Chicago, to a New York stage career. Public denunciations of the novel caused him to work as a magazine editor before he completed his second novel, *Jennie Gerhardt* (1911), which received similarly reproving reviews. Other novels are the trilogy consisting of *The Financier* (1914), *The Titan* (1914), and completed by the posthumously published *The Stoic* (1947), about ruthless American businessmen and the powerful interests vested in extreme wealth, *The Genius* (1915), *Twelve Men* (1919), *A Gallery of Women* (1929) and *The Bulwark* (1946). However, Dreiser is best known for *An American Tragedy* (1925), based on a true event, concerning a young man of humble origins who murders his pregnant girlfriend when he meets a girl from a wealthy background whom he considers will better aid him in furthering his ambitions. Dreiser also wrote plays, verse and non-fiction, the latter including *Life, Art and America*

(1917), *Tragic America* (1931) and *America Is Worth Saving* (1941). In addition to a three-volume selection of *The Letters of Theodore Dreiser* (1959), he wrote a range of memoirs and social criticism. Deriving significant influence from Zola, Balzac and Tolstoy, much of his writing depicts his belief in the power of society to shape individuals and their influence on the world in turn.

D. Pizer, *The Novels of Dreiser: A Critical Study* (1976).

Du Maurier, Daphne (1907–1989) Born in London, England, she turned to writing in 1931, becoming one of the more famous British Gothic fiction writers, and displaying a fondness for romance and intrigue. Her first novel, *The Loving Spirit* (1931), was a romantic family chronicle. Her first popular novel was *Jamaica Inn* (1936), a story about shipwreckers, followed by *Rebecca* (1938), which tells of the arrival of a second wife in a new husband's home, combining mystery, suspense and violence. Both novels were turned into films by Alfred Hitchcock (in 1939 and 1940, respectively), and he also adapted her story 'The Birds' in 1963. Other novels include *Frenchman's Creek* (1941, filmed 1944) *Hungry Hill* (1943), *The King's General* (1946), *My Cousin Rachel* (1951, filmed 1952) and *The Scapegoat* (1957), while short story collections include *Come Wind, Come Weather* (1940), *The Apple Tree* (1952), *The Breaking Point* (1959), *Early Stories* (1959) and *Don't Look Now* (1971, filmed 1973). In addition to her autobiography *Myself When Young* (1977), she wrote an account of her actor-father Gerald du Maurier and several other biographies. With archetypally and stereotypically gendered characters, her fiction was devoted to Cornwall and demonstrated a particular sense of the macabre.

M. Forster, *Daphne du Maurier: The Secret Life of the Renowned Storyteller* (1993).

Duckworth, Marilyn (1935–) A widely honoured New Zealand author, born in South Auckland, New Zealand, she is the younger sister of the well-known poet Fleur Adcock, and was educated in England and Wellington. After spending the war years in England, she returned to New Zealand in 1947. Her first novel was *A Gap in the Spectrum* (1959), a science fiction novel about dislocation and the problems of independence. There followed, among others, *The Matchbox House* (1960), *A Barbarous Tongue* (1963), *Over the Fence Is Out* (1969), *Disorderly Conduct* (1984), which is perhaps her most successful novel, set during the 1981 Springbok rugby tour protests, and about a heroine embroiled in family and domestic complexities, *Rest of the Wicked* (1986), *Married Alive* (1985), an analysis of marriage set in the near future, *Pulling Faces* (1987), *A Message from Harpo* (1989) and *Unlawful Entry* (1992). More recent novels include *Seeing Red* (1993), *Fooling* (1994), *Leather Wings* (1995) and *Studmuffin* (1997). Short stories occur in *Explosions on the Sun* (1989), poems in *Other Lovers' Children* (1975) and a memoir in *Camping on the Faultline* (2000). Primarily a realist, her fiction includes elements of fantasy in her investigations of the social restrictions placed upon women.

Duff, Alan (1950–) A Maori, born in Rotorua, New Zealand, he has worked as a syndicated newspaper columnist since 1974. His novels include *Once Were Warriors* (1994, filmed 1994), about the violent and alcohol-drenched lives of an urban Maori underclass which stunned New Zealand and broke box-office records, and its sequel, *One Night Out Stealing* (1995), which continues this focus by concentrating on two thieves and a burglary that changes their lives. He has also written the non-fiction study *Maori: The Crisis and the Challenge* (1993). More recently, he has written *What Becomes of the Brokenhearted?* (1996),

Both Sides of the Moon (1998) and *Out of the Mist and Steam: A Memoir* (1999). His writing explores the relationships between Maori and Pakeha (white New Zealand) culture, and the contemporary politics of assimilation, separatism and cultural identity in New Zealand.

Duffy, Maureen (1933–) Born in Worthing, Sussex, England, Maureen Patricia Duffy graduated from London University (BA 1956), and taught adult classes and creative writing. A prolific novelist, playwright, poet and historian, her first novel was *That's How It Was* (1962), a moving autobiographical account of her childhood and her relationship with her mother, followed by *The Single Eye* (1964), *The Microcosm* (1966), *The Paradox Players* (1967), exploring voluntary isolation on a houseboat in the Thames in the 1960s, *Wounds* (1969), and the complex, fantasy-based *Love-Child* (1971). With inventive plots, deft and vivid characterisation, her protagonists are often displaced, marginal to society, or frustrated in their ambitions, such as in *Capital* (1975), *Londoners* (1983) and *Illuminations* (1991). Other novels include *Housespy* (1978), *Gor Saga* (1981), about her concerns with animal rights, *Change* (1987), the thriller *Occam's Razor* (1993), which oscillates backwards and forwards in history, comparing Irish terrorism with the Italian mafiosi, and *Restitution* (1998). Her plays include *The Lay-Off* (1961), while there are several volumes of poetry, including a *Collected Poems* (1985). Other volumes include some social histories, biographies of Aphra Behn (1977) and Henry Purcell (1994), and a Freudian study in *The Erotic World of Faery* (1972). A versatile writer who often deals frankly with homosexuality, she has developed a reputation as an idiosyncratic stylist who combines realism with fantasy. She worked vigorously with Brigid BROPHY for Public Lending Rights between 1972 and 1982, and has been active in various writers' professional organisations.

Duhamel, Georges (1884–1966) Born in Paris, France, he studied medicine at the University of Paris (MD 1907), and became a physician during the First World War, finding time to write the war stories in *The New Book of Martyrs* (1917, trans. 1918) and *Civilisation 1914–1917* (1917, Prix Goncourt, trans. 1918), which depicted the anguish and suffering in military hospitals. He directed the literary magazine *Mercure de France* (1935–1937), and became a director of French Radio during the Second World War. Although now largely forgotten, he was principally famous for two post-First World War novel cycles. The first consists of the five novels of the 'Salavin' series, which are now literary classics, depicting a mediocre yet introspective man who fails at most of his endeavours despite his aspirations. Praised for their psychological portrayal, the novels represent Salavin as the prototype of the ordinary twentieth-century man, a precursor of CAMUS' and SARTRE's existential anti-heroes. The second cycle is the 'Pasquier' series, which gives a broad picture of French middle-class life from the 1880s to the First World War. Collected in *The Pasquier Chronicles* (trans. 1937) and *Cecile Among the Pasquiers* (trans. 1940), it is a family saga which attacked materialism and defended the rights of individuals. In addition to plays, he wrote the memoir *Light of My Days* (trans. 1948) and collected essays in *The Heart's Domain* (trans. 1919). Responsible for founding the artists' colony L'Abbaye with Jules ROMAINS, the painter Albert Gleizes and others in 1906–1907, he shared Romains' philosophy of spiritual Unanimism.

Dunmore, Helen (1952–) Born in Beverley, Yorkshire, England, and educated at York University (BA 1973), she worked as a nursery teacher, and first established herself as a poet. With her first volume *The Apple Fall* (1983) to her most recent volumes *Bestiary* (1997) and *Bouncing Boy* (1999), her poetry has displayed rhythmical confidence. Subsequently moving into fiction, her first novel *Going to Egypt* (1992), was followed by *Zennor in Darkness* (1993), in which two perspectives on the First World War are presented, *Burning Bright* (1994), about a young girl's gradual decline into crime, and *A Spell of Winter* (1995), about an incestuous relationship between a brother and sister. Recent fiction includes *Talking to the Dead* (1996), which focuses upon the relationships of two sisters, *Your Blue-eyed Boy* (1998), which deals with a woman's handling of a difficult present and a past about to catch up with her, and *With Your Crooked Heart* (1999), which is an exploration of adult self-delusion and the emotional relativity of relationships as siblings battle out their relationship. Short stories occur in *Love of Fat Men* (1997) and *Ice Cream* (1999).

Dunne, John Gregory (1932–) Born in Hartford, Connecticut, US, of Irish-American descent, he graduated from Princeton University (BA 1954). After a period working as a journalist, he turned to writing fiction with his first novel *Vegas: A Memoir of a Dark Season* (1974), about three characters in Las Vegas. This was followed by a best-seller, *True Confessions* (1977), loosely patterned on the Los Angeles Black Dahlia murder case in 1947, although the focus of the book falls on the relationship between two Irish Catholic brothers. The Irish-American experience became his main focus in much of his fiction, and *Dutch Shea Jr.* (1982) pursues this in an exploration of corruption in an Irish-American milieu, as does *The Red White and Blue* (1987), which follows the protagonist Jack Broderick from the Vietnam War to the present, and his jobs as reporter and film writer. His most recent novel is *Playland* (1994), which scrutinises Hollywood and the film industry. In addition to screenplays with his wife Joan DIDION, he has produced studies of the film business in *The Studio* (1967) and *Monster: Living Off the Big Screen* (1997), essays in *Quintana and Friends* (1978), literary journalism in *Crooning* (1990), and a semi-autobiography in *Harp* (1989). A versatile writer, he examines many of the traditional figures of Irish-American life, literature and cinema – the policeman, priest and politician.

Dunnett, Dorothy (1923–) Born in Dunfermline, Scotland, she has gained a reputation as a writer of historical fiction and thrillers. After working for the British Civil Service, she became a successful portrait painter. *The Game of Kings* (1961) began the six-volume 'Lymond Saga', which concluded with *Checkmate* (1975), which deals with power struggles in sixteenth-century Scotland, focusing on the mysterious background and adventures in European exile of Francis Crawford of Lymond. She also wrote about half a dozen books of suspense under the name Dorothy Halliday, about the bifocal-wearing American portrait painter Johnson Johnson and his boat 'The Dolly', which were later re-titled and published under her own name. Her second historical sequence was the 'House of Niccolo' series, set in a fifteenth-century Mediterranean world and focused on the character of Claes, who ascends the ranks of social class through various adventures. Beginning with *Niccolo Rising* (1986), the most recent novels are *To Lie with Lions* (1996), *Caprice and Rondo* (1998) and *Gemini* (2000). In addition to *King Hereafter* (1982), about Macbeth in eleventh-century Scotland, reset in an Old Norse context, she has written several books about the Scottish Highlands.

E. Morrison, *The Dorothy Dunnett Companion* (1994).

Duras, Marguerite (1914–1996) Born Marguerite Donnadieu in Giadinh, Indochina (now Vietnam), at 17 she left for Paris and studied at the Sorbonne, University of Paris. A secretary at the French Ministry of Colonies (1935–1941), she joined the Resistance during the German Occupation, about which she wrote in *The War: A Memoir* (1985, trans. 1986). A widely honoured novelist, playwright and screenwriter, she has written prolifically since the 1950s. Her first novel was *The Sea Wall* (1950, trans. 1952, filmed 1958), an autobiographical story based upon her mother's failed attempts to save the family's rice plantation in Vietnam by building a sea wall. Her novels of the 1950s, such as *The Sailor from Gibraltar* (1952, trans. 1966), *The Square* (1955, trans. 1959) and *Moderato Cantabile* (1958, trans. 1960), experiment with some of the techniques of the French 'New Novel', such as pared down narrative, minimal plot, silences and ambivalences. She began to add cinematic techniques to her fiction, evident in works like *The Ravishing of Lol Stein* (1964, trans. 1966), *The Vice-consul* (1966, trans. 1968), *L'Amante Anglaise* (1967, trans. 1968), *Destroy, She Said* (1969, trans. 1970), which deals with the social changes of 1968, pitting desire against conventional attitudes towards sexuality, and *The Malady of Death* (1982, trans. 1986). Later novels include the famous *The Lover* (1984, Prix Goncourt, trans. 1985, filmed 1992), which returns to autobiographical terrain in its depiction of a love affair between a woman and a wealthy Chinese planter, focusing upon memory of the past and sexual initiation, *Blue Eyes, Black Hair* (1986, trans. 1988), *Emily L* (1987, trans. 1989), *Green Eyes* (trans. 1990), *The North China Lover* (1991) and *Yann Andrea Steiner* (trans. 1994), which transforms her real-life partner into a fictional character. She has also written the landmark screenplays of *Hiroshima, mon amour* (filmed by Alain Resnais in 1959) and *India Song* (filmed 1973). Drawing heavily upon the details of her own life for much of her fiction, it has pushed at formal constraints and defies easy classification.

L. Hill, *Marguerite Duras: Apocalyptic Desires* (1994).

Durrell, Lawrence (1912–1990) Born Lawrence George Durrell, in Jalundur, India, he worked at various jobs, travelled widely in Greece and Egypt, served in the British Diplomatic Corps (1944–1952), and after moving to France, became a prolific full-time writer in 1957. He dismissed his first novel, *Pied Piper of Lovers* (1935), as an apprentice work, and the first work to receive literary notoriety was *The Black Book* (1938), about sickness, sex, death and decay as a writer composes his autobiography on a Greek island. After the satirical *Cefalû* (1947) and the adventure *White Eagles Over Serbia* (1957), he began *The Alexandria Quartet* (1961) which achieved international fame: *Justine* (1957), *Balthazar* (1958), *Mountolive* (1958) and *Clea* (1960). Narrated by a young man on a quest for self-knowledge, the tetralogy was an experiment in form which shifts perspective in each novel, and central to the prose-poem set in the city of Alexandria, are new ideas of Einsteinian spacetime. The tetralogy was succeeded by *The Revolt of Aphrodite* (1974), consisting of *Tunc* (1968) and *Nunquam* (1970), set in a futuristic world of big business and computers, and exploring freedom in an increasingly mechanised life. His other major work was the 'Avignon Quintet', consisting of five novels designed after the medieval quincunx garden pattern of five trees, and involving a search for the treasure of the Knights Templar after the Second World War: *Monsieur* (1974), *Livia* (1978), *Constance* (1982), *Sebastian* (1983) and *Quinx* (1985). Considered a good poet, he wrote many volumes of poetry, including a *Collected Poems, 1931–1974* (1980), as well as a series of satirical short story collections about the bumbling Antrobus in the British diplo-

matic service, including *Esprit de Corps* (1957), *Stiff Upper Lip* (1958), *Sauve Qui Peut* (1966) and *Antrobus Complete* (1985). In addition to plays and selections of letters to Henry MILLER (1988), he wrote several travel books on Greece, including *Prospero's Cell* (1945), *Reflections on a Marine Venus* (1953) and *Bitter Lemons* (1957). An experimentalist who caused contention for his characterisation and layering of ideas, his fictional techniques chart a movement from a modern to postmodern consciousness.

A. Friedman, *Critical Essays on Lawrence Durrell* (1987).

Dutton, Geoffrey (1922–) Born in Kapunda, South Australia, he was educated at the University of Adelaide, and joined the RAAF as an instructor (1941). In the 1940s, he was associated with the 'angry Penguins', a group of self-consciously modernist Australian writers and artists including Sidney Nolan, Harry Roskolenko and Max Harris. After study at Oxford University (1946–1949), he travelled extensively in the 1950s and then lectured in English at the University of Adelaide from 1955, before turning to a career in publishing in 1962. He founded Sun Books in 1965 and worked extensively as an editor and organiser of Australian journals and magazines. He has written several novels, including *The Mortal and the Marble* (1950), which is a study of Anglo-Australian cultural differences, *Andy* (1968), a picaresque tale of a wartime flying instructor, *Tamara* (1970) which is a love story set in Russia, *Queen Emma of the South Seas* (1976), based upon the life of a Pacific island woman, and *Flying Low* (1990). A versatile writer, he has also written several collections of verse, much of it collected in *Findings and Keepings* (1970), short stories in *The Wedge-Tailed Eagle* (1980), critical studies of Patrick WHITE (1961) and Walt Whitman (1961), three historical biographies in *Founder of a City* (1960), *The*

Hero as Murderer (1967) and *Australia's Last Explorer: Ernest Giles* (1970). In addition to volumes of art appreciation, travel, children's fiction and popular books on Australia, he has edited anthologies of verse and edited essays in *The Literature of Australia* (1964), and written autobiography in *Out in the Open* (1994). His earlier modernist and experimental writing gave way in his later work to a more reflective lyricism.

E

Eastlake, William (1917–1997) An American novelist, born William Derry Eastlake, in New York City. After army service and residence in Paris, France, in the 1950s he moved to a New Mexico ranch. A first batch of novels chronicle the American South West, such as *Go in Beauty* (1956), *Bronc People* (1958), set in New Mexico, which is about a contrast between brothers, *Portrait of an Artist with Twenty-Six Horses* (1963), which is a fantasy and suspense involving a white man about to die and his Navajo friend, and *Dancers in the Scalp House* (1975), which is concerned with the Navajo's fight against a dam project in New Mexico. These novels register an increasing concern with the plight of the Native-Americans and the impact of an ephemeral American society on their culture. A second set of novels engages with war, such as *Castle Keep* (1965), about American soldiers seizing a castle in the Second World War, *Bamboo Bed* (1969), about a love affair during the Vietnam War, and *The Long, Naked Descent into Boston* (1977), a comic treatment of the American Revolutionary War. *Jack Armstrong in Tangier and Other Escapes* (1984) is a collection of short stories.

D. Phelps, *Covering Ground* (1969).

Eco, Umberto (1932–) Born in Alessandria, Italy, he graduated from the University of Turin (Ph.D. 1954), and began by working in Italian radio (1954–1959). He became an academic in semiotics (the science of signs) at various Italian universities, including Milan, Florence, Bologna, and a renowned visitor to prestigious American universities. He has an international reputation as a scholar of European medieval culture and semiotics, with such seminal texts as *A Theory of Semiotics* (trans. 1976), *The Role of the Reader* (trans. 1979), *Semiotics and the Philosophy of Language* (trans. 1984) and *The Search for the Perfect Language* (1993, trans. 1994). His other literary studies include *The Aesthetics of Thomas Aquinas* (1956, trans. 1988), *The Open Work* (1962, trans. 1989), *Misreadings* (1963, trans. 1993), *Art and Beauty in the Middle Ages* (trans. 1986), *Travels in Hyperreality* (trans. 1986), *The Aesthetics of Chaosmos* (trans. 1989) and *Apocalypse Postponed* (trans. 1994). However, he is perhaps most widely known for his fiction, beginning with *The Name of the Rose* (1980, Prix Medicis, 1982, trans. 1983), which became a surprise international best-seller, and a film starring Sean Connery (1986). A long philosophical novel, it is a murder mystery set in a northern Italian monastery in 1327, amidst the rivalry between factions of the Franciscan order. William of Baskerville, with his assistant Adso, sent to unravel the series of murders, become involved in a Sherlock Holmesian detective story, which combines theological digressions, the worlds of semiotic codes, writing and signs, a labyrinthine library, a power struggle between Church and State, and philosophical issues about order and disorder in the universe. This was followed by the equally complex best-seller, *Foucault's Pendulum* (1988, trans. 1989), another semiotic murder mystery wrapped up in layers of meaning. Dealing with the occult, the Knights Templars, and Foucault's pendulum in Paris, it is a grand orchestration of a variety of textual allusions, knowledge and characters, probing the issue of text as reality and reality as text. His most recent novel is *The Island of the Day Before* (1994, trans. 1995), which excavates truth by sifting language and meaning. Set in the early seventeenth century, it tells of an Italian castaway, marooned alone on a ship in the South Pacific, and his driftings back to his past in his imagination. Another pyrotechnic display of literary allusion and linguistic knowledge, it has confirmed Eco as a pre-eminent postmodern novelist who manages to produce fiction with a broad range of social, historical, philosophical reference while testing the boundaries of language and representation.

T. Inge, ed., *Naming the Rose: Essays on Eco's 'The Name of the Rose'* (1988).

Ekwensi, Cyprian (1921–) Born in Minna, northern Nigeria, he trained in forestry and pharmacy in Nigeria and London, and also received some training with the BBC. He has written film scripts, novels, novellas, short stories and collections of folk tales. By his own admission, he has aimed at being a populist writer, and his first novella, *When Love Whispers* (1948), which looks at generational conflict through a romance plot, inaugurated the tradition later labelled the Onitsha Market Literature (a pulp fiction which flourished in Onitsha between 1940 and 1960). Other

popular fiction followed with the adventure thrillers *Yaba Roundabout Murder* (1962), *Samankwe and the Highway Robbers* (1979) and *Masquerade Time* (1991). More serious social criticism emerged in *People of the City* (1954) and *Jagua Nana* (1961), and its sequel, *Jagua Nana's Daughter* (1986), which explored the problems of urbanisation, political violence and corruption, foreshadowing much of the postcolonial disillusionment. Other novels include the pan-Africanist *Beautiful Feathers* (1963), *Iska* (1966), which explored ethnic tensions, *Survive the Peace* (1976) and *Divided We Stand* (1980), both of which focus on the Nigerian Civil War, and *King For Ever* (1992), which was a bitter political allegory. Although often technically conservative, his style is accessible and deliberately aimed at a mass readership, dovetailing social criticism with thriller and romance plots and elements of the marvellous (as with *Burning Cross*, 1962). Many have argued that his fiction suffers from looseness, a lack of tight control and inconsistent characterisation; yet one might also perceive this as spontaneity, a love of snapshots, topicality and sensationalism. In recent years, he has published *For a Roll of Parchment* (1986) and a children's book *Gone to Mecca* (1991).

E. Emenyonou, *Cyprian Ekwensi* (1974).

Elkin, Stanley (1930–1995) An American novelist, born in New York City, and educated at the University of Illinois (Ph.D. 1961), Stanley Laurence Elkin was a Professor at Washington University, St. Louis from 1959. Considered by many to be a major contemporary Jewish writer, his fiction satirises contemporary American life and is marked by a piercing black humour. His first novel, *Boswell* (1964), is a comic depiction of a young man who attaches himself to prominent people, while *A Bad Man* (1967) is a meditation on morality depicting a department store owner who ends up in prison. *The Dick*

Gibson Show (1971) narrates the adventures of an early radio announcer, but real fame accompanied the series of novellas in *Searches and Seizures* (1973). Further novels include *The Franchiser* (1976), *George Mills* (1982), *The Magic Kingdom* (1984), *The Rabbi of Lud* (1987) and *MacGuffin* (1991). *The Living End* (1979) contains three long stories satirising religion, while *Criers and Kibitzers, Kibitzers and Criers* (1966) and *Early Elkin* (1985) collects his short stories. Many of these manifest the linguistic vitality and comic inventiveness characteristic of much of his writing, as he invites readers to laugh at the absurdities, frustrations and disappointments of life.

D. Bargen, *The Fiction of Stanley Elkin* (1980).

Elliott, Janice (1931–) Born in Derby, England, she graduated from Oxford University (BA 1953), before becoming a journalist and novelist. Her early novels were *Cave with Echoes* (1962), *The Somnambulists* (1964) and *The Godmother* (1966), before her 'England Trilogy', which explores the vicissitudes of an upper-middle-class family in the immediate aftermath of the Second World War: *A State of Peace* (1971), *Private Life* (1972) and *Heaven on Earth* (1975). There followed *Summer People* (1980), a novel of social criticism with a futuristic setting, and her best-seller, *Secret Places* (1982), a comic story set in wartime Nottingham, about a German refugee girl in an English boarding school. Among numerous other novels are *Magic* (1983), *Dr. Gruber's Daughter* (1986), about Adolf Hitler's daughter by a niece, *The Sadness of Witches* (1987), *Life on the Nile* (1989), *Necessary Rites* (1990), about Thatcherite Britain, *City of Gates* (1992) and *Figures in the Sand* (1994). Short stories occur in *The Noise from the Zoo* (1991), and there is also various children's fiction. With an economical use of language and image, she has received consistent critical acclaim for her authentic re-creations of the past.

Ellis, Alice Thomas (1932–) Pseudonym of Alice Haycraft, born in Liverpool (although she grew up on the North Wales coast), England. She attended Liverpool Art College, and is now the fiction editor for Duckworth's. Her first novel was *The Sin Eater* (1977), set in Wales about relationships within a family called Ellis, as the father draws near to death. As the centre of a literary clique in the 1980s, comprising Beryl BAINBRIDGE, Caroline Blackwood and Patrice Chaplin, their writing has become known as the 'Duckworth style', which is short novels, written by women featuring women, set in contemporary Britain, with plots focusing on domestic and marital strife and in which traditional expository techniques are underplayed. Subsequent novels include *The Birds of the Air* (1980), *The Twenty-Seventh Kingdom* (1982), which is a fantasy set in 1950s Chelsea, London, *The Other Side of the Fire* (1983) and *Unexplained Laughter* (1985). A much praised trilogy consists of *The Clothes in the Wardrobe* (1987), *The Skeleton in the Cupboard* (1988) and *The Fly in the Ointment* (1989). Recent novels include *The Inn at the Edge of the World* (1990), *Pillars of Gold* (1992) and *Fairy Tale* (1996), while *A Welsh Childhood* (1990) is autobiographical and *Serpent on the Rock* (1994) is a study of the Catholic Church. She has collected her columns for the *Spectator* in *Home Life* (1986) and other volumes, published short stories in *The Evening of Adam* (1994), co-authored several books on child psychiatry, and edited *Wales: An Anthology* (1989). Praised for her short, tense comedies about human failure in the face of some ultimate good, she frequently represents Welsh culture as mysterious, 'primitive' and ancient. Satirical representations of family life are lifted out of realism by elements of the supernatural and Christian mysticism, as Catholicism and feminism provide constant themes.

Ellis, Bret Easton (1964–) An American novelist born in Los Angeles, he attended Bennington College (BA 1986). His first novel, *Less Than Zero* (1985, filmed 1988), catapulted him to success; it offered vignettes of the ennui of wealthy Los Angeles adolescent life, as the protagonists indulged in sex, drugs, expensive possessions and the video culture. *Rules of Attraction* (1987) continued in the same vein, depicting the parties, petty crime and traumas of disaffected youth in a New England university. *American Psycho* (1991, filmed 2000) provoked uproar for its representation of violence towards women, in its portrayal of Patrick Bateman, a wealthy young Wall Street executive who is a brutal serial killer. *The Informers* (1994) focuses on vampirism, random violence and murder among the beautiful college children in Los Angeles, while his latest novel, *Glamorama* (1999), depicts a model and hipster who finds himself involved in international terrorism. Associated with other 'brat pack' writers like Tama JANOWITZ and Jay MCINERNEY, he has charted the collapse of morality and ethical values within the US postmodern materialist culture.

Ellison, Harlan (1934–) A short story writer, born Harlan Jay Ellison, in Cleveland, Ohio, US, most of his work is science fiction or fantasy. He attended Ohio State University before being expelled, and has adopted a host of pseudonyms over the years, such as Cordwainer Bird and Jay Charby. A controversial writer, he has been associated with American 'New Wave' science fiction writing since he moved to New York in the 1950s and met Robert Silverberg. *Rumble* (1958) depicted the vigour and violence of urban life and the complexities of an American city, and his early works, such as *The Deadly Streets* (1958), *The Juvies* (1961), *Gentleman Junkie ...* (1961) and

Rockabilly (1961), regularly flouted the distinctions between science fiction and other genres of writing. His stories have been published in a number of volumes, including *Paingod* (1965), *I Have No Mouth and I Must Scream* (1967), *Over the Edge* (1970), *Shatterday* (1980), *Angry Candy* (1988), *Mind Fields* (1994) and *Slippage* (1997). These stories often depict the horrors within humans, using aggressive, violent rhetoric and raw thrusts of emotion. He edited the famous 'New Wave' anthologies *Dangerous Visions* (1967–1972), has written numerous television plays and screenplays, and collected essays in *Memos from Purgatory* (1961) and *The Glass Teat* (1970).

G. Slusser, *Harlan Ellison* (1977).

Ellison, Ralph (1914–1994) A novelist, short story writer and essayist, Ralph Waldo Ellison is recognised as one of the most prominent African-American literary figures. He was born in Oklahoma City, and educated in a segregated school system in Oklahoma, winning a scholarship to Tuskagee Institute in Alabama, so that the State did not have to integrate him into the white Oklahoma college or university system. Displaying a wide range of accomplishments as a sculptor and musician, he went to New York City in 1936 where he met Langston Hughes and Richard WRIGHT. Supported by the New York Federal Writers' Project, he recorded folk material in the African-American community, which became the experience for his famous and influential novel, *Invisible Man* (1952). Narrated by a nameless protagonist, it traces the development of an African-American who learns to assert himself within the complexities of racial politics in an urban environment. In addition, he edited *The Negro Quarterly* in 1942, and several sections from an unpublished novel on religion and politics, begun in 1958, and short stories, have subsequently been published. His essays on jazz, literature and

African-American social issues appear in *Shadow and Act* (1964), and in *Going to the Territory* (1986) he writes about the racist society of the Deep South. A posthumous edition of short stories occurs in *Flying Home* (1996), while the novel *Juneteenth* (1999) has been spliced together from notes and manuscripts left behind after his death, and deals with the complex relationship between a bigoted white racist senator and a black Baptist minister.

M. Busby, *Ralph Ellison* (1991).

Ellroy, James (1948–) A prolific American crime novelist, born in Los Angeles, he led a youth of petty crime and alcoholism, and worked in a variety of jobs until 1984, when he turned to writing full-time. Writing in the 'hard-boiled' style, his fiction vividly portrays the seamier side of Los Angeles, often depicting in an uncompromising fashion a world of pent-up sexual desires and endemic criminality. His early fiction includes *Brown's Requiem* (1981), which launched him, *Clandestine* (1982), *Suicide Hill* (1986) and *Silent Terror* (1986). His best fiction to date is his *LA Quartet*, which tours the obscene, violent, gritty, obsessive and darkly sexual world of the Los Angeles underbelly in the 1940s and 1950s. This sequence consists of *The Black Dahlia* (1987), based on a famous unsolved Los Angeles murder case of 1947, *The Big Nowhere* (1988), about McCarthyism and Hollywood, *LA Confidential* (1990, filmed 1997), about prostitution rackets in Hollywood's film business, and *White Jazz* (1992), which is a complex set of murders and motivations. Widely held to be a grippingly literate detective story writer, he began a new series with *American Tabloid* (1995). Other works include a memoir about his mother's mysterious murder in California in *My Dark Places* (1996), and a collection of reportage about Los Angeles in *Crime Wave* (1999).

Emecheta, Buchi (1944–) Born of Ibuza parentage near Lagos in Nigeria, Florence Onye Buchi Emecheta was educated at the Methodist Girls' High School in Lagos. After moving to England with her student husband in 1962, she worked as a library officer in the British Museum (1965–1969), graduated from the University of London (BSc 1972) in sociology, and worked as a sociologist for the Inner London Education Authority (1969–1976), and as a community worker (1976–1978). After becoming a writer in 1972, she has also held various university positions. She now lives in London with her five children. She is the author of the novels *In the Ditch* (1972), *Second Class Citizen* (1974), *The Bride Price* (1976), *The Slave Girl* (1977), *The Joys of Motherhood* (1979), *Destination Biafra* (1981), *Double Yoke* (1982), *The Rape of Shavi* (1983), *Gwendolen* (1989), *The Family* (1990) and *Kehinde* (1994). She has also written an autobiography, *Head Above Water* (1986), and several children's books. Her novels explore the pain of racism and the experience of emigration, focusing particularly upon women's experiences of patriarchy and discrimination. Many are historical novels set in Nigeria, both before and after Independence, in which she comments on the clash of cultures and the impact of western values upon agrarian traditions and customs. Strongly autobiographical in her focus, she was selected as one of 1983's Best Young British Writers and is the winner of several literary prizes.

Engel, Marian (1933–1985) A Canadian writer, born in Toronto and educated at McMaster (BA 1955) and McGill (MA 1957) universities, who subsequently lived and worked in London and Cyprus. Her first novel, *No Cloud's of Glory!* (1968), later reissued as *Sarah Bastard's Notebook*, concerned a woman academic who challenges men. There followed *The Honeymoon Festival* (1970), *Monodromos* (1973, reissued as *One Way Street*,

1974), about a woman expatriate's experiences in Cyprus, and *Joanne* (1975). The search for female identity continues in the fantasy *Bear* (1976), an infamous novel about an erotic relationship between a woman and a bear, set in the environment of the Great Lakes. In addition to the novels *The Glassy Sea* (1978) and *Lunatic Villas* (1981), there are also two collections of short stories, entitled *Inside the Easter Egg* (1975) and *The Tattooed Woman* (1985), and several children's books. Her stories use an economic structure and style, combined with biting irony, and the characters appear to be constantly striving to define themselves against the Ontario background, often by appeals to European sophistication. Her analysis of the position of women results in marriage being depicted as a battleground on which women seem to lose.

C. Howells, *Private and Fictional Words* (1987).

Erdrich, Louise (1954–) An American novelist, short story writer and poet, born in Little Falls, Minnesota, of mixed Chippewa, French and German descent. She grew up in North Dakota, where her work is frequently set, and was educated at Dartmouth College (BA 1976) and Johns Hopkins University (MA 1979). She is best known for her tetralogy of novels focusing upon the lives of two Native-American families across three generations: the widely acclaimed *Love Medicine* (1984), which spans from 1934 to 1984, and heralded a new departure in Native-American fiction, *The Beet Queen* (1986), which covered much the same period as the first, *Tracks* (1988), which is something of a research novel and an adventure story, and *The Bingo Palace* (1994), which continued the narrative of the families' lives interlinked with Native-American history. *Tales of Burning Love* (1996) returns to the life of the husband of June Kapshaw (the female protagonist of *Love Medicine*) and his five ex-wives. She has also written collections of poetry,

including *Jacklight* (1984), *Baptism of Desire* (1989), and a fictional study of the impact of Columbus on Native-American culture (co-written with her husband, Michael Dorris), *The Crown of Columbus* (1991). One of the most influential Native-American literary voices, her stories are preoccupied with ethnic and female identity, and display a breadth of knowledge about Native-American culture and folklore. The novel *The Antelope Wife* was published in 1998, and her forthcoming novel is entitled *Last Report on the Miracles at Little No Horse* (2000).

Erickson, Steve (1950–) Born in Santa Monica, California, US, he attended the University of California at Los Angeles. He wrote the 'Guerrilla Pop' column for the *Los Angeles Reader* for several years, and subsequently contributed to various magazines, including *Esquire* and *Rolling Stone*, as a freelance journalist. His first novel, *Days Between Stations* (1985), about a search for identity within a bleak futuristic environment, established his shifting, surrealistic and cinematic style. Similar blends of science fiction, political fable and fantastic romance occur in *Rubicon Beach* (1986), *Tours of the Black Clock* (1989), and *Arc d'X* (1993), a historical fantasy about Thomas Jefferson's involvement with his slave Sally Hemings. The slippage of names and scenes often imparts a dreamlike narrative shape, as in the novel, *Amnesiascope* (1996), which is a nightmarish depiction of a futuristic Los Angeles underworld. He has also written two accounts of US presidential campaigns: *Leap Year* (1989), about the 1988 campaign, and, more recently, about the 1996 campaign trail, *American Nomad* (1997), for which he was fired by *Rolling Stone* for his increasingly bizarre dispatches. His latest novel is *The Sea Came in at Midnight* (1999), a haunting exploration of memory, desire and redemption in a landscape of dreamlike logic. With its displaced identities, temporal slippages, and hybrid versions of fantasy and history, Erickson's fiction has often been acclaimed by writers like Thomas PYNCHON as a paradigm of postmodern fiction.

Esquivel, Laura (1950–) Born in Mexico City, Mexico, she has been a teacher and written film scripts and children's books. Along with Isabel ALLENDE, she is perhaps one of the best-known Latin American women novelists. Her novel *Like Water for Chocolate* (1989, trans. 1993) was a best-seller in Mexico, and subsequently an international film success (1991). It portrays a romantic rural past in the face of urbanisation, as Tita's and Pedro's love affair is punctuated by recipes and culinary metaphors for Tita's plight. She has subsequently published *The Law of Love* (1995, trans. 1996). Despite her magic realist style, her depiction of traditional notions of femininity and the authenticities of Mexican culture root her novels in conventional and conservative ideologies.

Evans, Caradoc (1878–1945) Born David Caradoc Evans, in Carmarthenshire, Wales, he went to work as a draper at the age of 14, and gradually worked his way to London departmental stores. In 1899, he turned to journalism which culminated in co-editing *T.P.'s Weekly*. He burst on to the literary scene during the First World War with *My People* (1915), a short story collection attacking the Welsh establishment in rural Wales, for which he was pilloried by the Welsh, although it was to become a seminal text of modern Anglo-Welsh literature. He suffered further obloquy for his famous novel *Nothing to Pay* (1930), about a miserly Welsh draper clawing his way eastward from Nonconformist Wales to London. His other fiction includes the novels *This Way to Heaven* (1934), *Wasps* (1935) and *Mother's Marvel* (1949); the short story collections *Capel Sion* (1916), *My Neighbours* (1920), *The Earth Gives All and Takes All* (1942) and *Pilgrim in a Foreign Land* (1942); and the play *Taffy* (1923), which was also excoriated by the Welsh and attended by riots at the performances. Despite the hate engendered by his savage satires, he returned to spend the last years of his life in Wales, at Aberystwyth.

F

Fairbairns, Zoë (1948–) A British novelist, born in Tunbridge Wells, Kent, Zöe Ann Fairbairns graduated with a degree in history from St. Andrews University, Scotland (MA 1972). She has written on feminist issues and the Campaign for Nuclear Disarmament, and her fiction frequently reworks popular genres from a feminist perspective. She has published several novels, including *Live as Family* (1968), *Down: An Exploration* (1969), *Benefits* (1979), a futuristic novel of sexual politics and patriarchal oppression, *Stand We At Last* (1983), a historical family saga, set in 1855, which explores women's emancipation, *Here Today* (1984), a crime thriller set in the world of office secretaries, *Closing* (1987), *Daddy's Girl* (1991), which examines three teenagers through history, and *Other Names* (1998). Short stories appear in several anthologies, including *Tales I Tell My Mother* (1978), which was edited with Sara MAITLAND, Valerie Miner, Michèle Roberts and Micheline Wandor, *More Tales I Tell My Mother* (1987), and *Cinderella on the Ball* (1991), an edited collection of feminist fairy tales. She also regularly teaches creative writing workshops. Her fiction set out to document and inform as she dramatises social existence and anatomises social structures.

Fante, John (1911–1983) An American novelist, John Thomas Fante was born in Denver, Colorado, and attended Long Beach City College. Most of his fiction is set in California, where he lived, and his early stories appeared in H.L. Mencken's *American Mercury* magazine. His first novels, *Wait Until Spring, Bandini* (1938) and *Ask the Dust* (1939), are about Arturo Bandini, a young poet moving to professional maturity, and needing to transcend his troubled family life. *Dago Red* (1940, later republished as *The Wine of Youth*, 1984), is about an Italian-American family in Colorado, and *Full of Life* (1952) concerns the adjustment of a husband to his wife's pregnancy. Despite going blind in 1978, he continued to write, and his later novels include *The Brotherhood of the Grape* (1977) and *Dreams from Bunker Hill* (1982). *The Road to Los Angeles* (1985), *1933 Was a Bad Year* (1985) and *West of Rome: Two Novellas* (1986) were published posthumously. He became a screenwriter in later life, and his scripts include *Jeanne Eagles* (1957) and *Walk on the Wild Side* (1962). His initial lack of commercial success was rectified by Black Sparrow's reprinting of his novels, which brought a wider readership in the later 1970s. His *Selected Letters 1932–1981* were published in 1991.

S. Cooper, *Full of Life: A Biography of John Fante* (2000).

Farah, Nuruddin (1945–) Born in Baidoa, Somalia, he was educated at Mogadishu, and at the universities of Essex and London in Britain, and Chandigarh in India. His principal preoccupation throughout his writing career has been the oppression of Somalia by General Siyad Barre. In particular, his novels depict the negative collusions of family, state authoritarianism and of tribalism, and feature pioneering studies of the patriarchal subjection of women in the Horn of Africa. *Crooked Rib* (1970), set in the colonial 1950s, focuses on Elba, a Somali woman determined to escape bartered marriages, and *Sardines* (1981) explores similar predicaments of women in a male world. *A Naked Needle* (1976) is set during the period of Barre's Soviet-backed military coup, and the onset of totalitarian dictatorship is further explored in *Sweet and Sour Milk* (1979). This was the first in a trilogy, which included *Sardines* and *Close Sesame* (1983), which presents a deranged and dystopian world of political corruption, as domestic violence mirrors state violence. Writing with stylistic verve and ideological conviction, his next novel, *Maps* (1986), ventures into postmodern territory with an indeterminacy between the literal and allegorical, reality and illusion, maintaining that the novelist's duty is to redraw the colonial maps of his or her world. *Gifts* (1992) examines the complex psychology of donorship and aid, and its binding ties and dependencies in the contemporary world, while *Secrets* (1998) is about the Somali rebellion of Xasan. *Yesterday, Tomorrow: Voices from the Somali Diaspora* (1999), discusses literature, culture and identity.

P. Alden, *Nuruddin Farah* (1999).

Farmer, Beverley (1941–) An Australian writer, born in Melbourne, and educated at the University of Melbourne. Known principally for her short stories, they concentrate upon human issues and are characterised by a plain style. She married a Greek man, and many of her stories provide insights into the Greek culture in Greece and Australia. These are collected in such volumes as the highly acclaimed *Milk* (1983), *Hometime* (1985), *Place of Birth* (1990), which collects stories from the two earlier volumes, and *A Body of Water* (1990), a diary that incorporates short stories in an interlocking structure. Other works include the early novel *Alone* (1980), about the lesbian relationship of a young woman, and *The Seal Woman* (1992), based upon a Scandinavian myth of undying love, written from the consciousness of a Danish woman. Along with her *Collected Short Stories* (1996), her most recent novel is *The House in the Light* (1995), which examines the emotions unleashed by a woman's return to her marital family in Greece. Occasionally modernist in her writing style, place and autobiography frequently feature as strong elements within the fiction.

Farrell, J.G. (1935–1979) Full name James Gordon Farrell, born in Liverpool, England, he was educated at Oxford University, where he contracted poliomyelitis. His first novel was *A Man from Elsewhere* (1963), set in France where he spent several years as a teacher, followed by *The Lung* (1965), which describes the experiences of a polio victim, and *A Girl in the Head* (1967), set in an English seaside resort. His reputation rests upon three novels which explore Britain's imperial past: *Troubles* (1970) is about the sojourn of a British officer at a decaying but once grand hotel in Ireland immediately after the First World War, and is set against Sinn Fein violence, yet it contains several scenes of hilarious eccentricity; *The Siege of Krishnapur* (1973, Booker Prize) concerns the Indian Mutiny and the absurdities behind the façade of British civilisation; and *The Singapore Grip* (1978) involves the fall of Singapore to the Japanese during the Second World

War. Often depicting characters caught up in the collapse of imperialism with sympathy and compassion, Farrell's major works combine pathos, comedy and acute observation. *The Hill Station* (1981) set in India, is unfinished owing to his death by drowning when swept off the rocks while fishing off the Irish coast.

R. Crane, *Troubled Pleasures: The Fiction of J.G. Farrell* (1997).

Farrell, James T. (1904–1979) An American novelist in the naturalist tradition, born James Thomas Farrell, on the South Side of Chicago, and educated at the University of Chicago. He worked in several jobs – as a clerk, a salesman and a newspaper reporter – and moved to New York in 1931. He was immediately successful with *Studs Lonigan: A Trilogy* (1935), comprising *Young Lonigan* (1932), which records the protagonist's youth on Chicago's downbeat South Side in a stream-of-consciousness style; *The Young Manhood of Studs Lonigan* (1934), which develops his moral collapse after becoming involved in Chicago's underworld; and *Judgment Day* (1935), which narrates his decline and death. Depicting the social and economic inequalities of American life, Farrell keenly felt the need for a new style for distinctive speech patterns of the city. His literary credo is primarily set out in *A Note on Literary Criticism* (1936), describing his views as a Marxist, but not of the 'crass' sort, but also described in *The League of Frightened Philistines* (1945) and *Literature and Morality* (1947). He keeps to his naturalist style in his later five-volume series about Danny O'Neill, in *A World I Never Made* (1936), *No Star Is Lost* (1938), *Father and Son* (1940), *My Days of Anger* (1943) and *The Face of Time* (1953); and in a three-volume series, *Bernard Clare* (1946) and its sequels, centring on a disillusioned communist New York writer in the 1920s. In the 1920s, he began an unfinished tetralogy

about a Chicago University student, with a first volume entitled *The Silence of History* (1963). However, he wrote many other novels apart from these cycles, including *Gas-House McGinty* (1933), *Ellen Rogers* (1941), *This Man and This Woman* (1951) and *What Time Collects* (1964). Volumes of short stories include *Calico Shoes* (1934), *An American Dream Girl* (1950) and *Dangerous Women* (1957). He wrote a few other occasional books, including his observations on a visit to Israel in *It Has Come to Pass* (1958), and his *Collected Poems* (1965).

E. Branch, *Studs Lonigan's Neighborhood and the Making of James T. Farrell* (1996).

Fast, Howard M. (1914–) A prolific American novelist, he was born Howard Melvin Fast, in New York City, and worked doing odd jobs until 1932, when he turned to writing. His first fiction was historical, in *Two Valleys* (1933), *Conceived in Liberty* (1939) and *The Unvanquished* (1942), all set in the American Revolution. He later returned to this historical setting in *Citizen Tom Paine* (1943) and *The Proud and the Free* (1950). Many of these novels were used as sites to explore American freedom and the struggle for a classless society, being an avowed communist in his early years. Although he later renounced communism in the face of Stalinism, his books were very successful behind the Iron Curtain, which helped him win the International Peace Prize for fiction in 1954, despite running into trouble with McCarthyism. His socialist affiliations are narrated in his memoirs *The Naked God* (1958) and *Being Red* (1990). Other novels include *The Last Frontier* (1941), *Freedom Road* (1944), *Silas Timberman* (1954), all set in America, while *Spartacus* (1951, filmed 1960), *Moses, Prince of Egypt* (1958) and *Agrippa's Daughter* (1964) were set in ancient times. *The Outsider* (1984) and *Immigrant's Daughter* (1985) explore the forgotten history of immigrants, while other novels include *The Bridge Builder's Story* (1995), *An Independent Woman* (1997), a suspense set in San Francisco, *The Crossing* (1999), about the Battle of Trenton in 1776, and *Greenwich* (2000). Under the pseudonym E.V. Cunningham, he has also written a number of detective novels featuring a fictional Japanese-American detective, Masao Masuto, in Los Angeles.

A. Macdonald, *Howard Fast: A Critical Companion* (1996).

Faulkner, William (1897–1962) Widely regarded as one of the greatest American writers, he was born in New Albany, Mississippi, into a patrician southern family and raised in the nearby town of Oxford. He attended the University of Mississippi after the First World War, but abandoned formal education without completing his degree. After travelling through Europe in the 1920s, he wrote his first novel, *Soldier's Pay* (1926), about the homecoming of a dying soldier, which was followed by a minor work, *Mosquitoes* (1927). Faulkner then set about creating for his literary purposes the imaginary Yoknapatawpha County (based on his home region, Lafayette County, Mississippi). His style often results in long, stream-of-consciousness sentence constructions with little punctuation, which some have criticised as exaggerated and inflated rhetoric, and he sometimes employs abrupt disjunctions in time and unannounced switches of narrator. Nevertheless, a reader's perseverance is hugely repaid by encountering the rich variety of the Yoknapatawpha characters and Faulkner's understanding of human motives. A good introduction to his work is through the trilogy *The Hamlet* (1940), *The Town* (1957) and *The Mansion* (1959), which chronicle the rise to fortune of the poor white Snopes family through their insatiable acquisitiveness and native cunning. Other books, *Sartoris* (1929), *The Sound and the Fury* (1929) and *Absalom, Absalom!* (1936), describe the decline in the fortunes and aspirations of the patrician Sartoris, Compson, Benbow, McCaslin and Sutpen families. *As I Lay Dying* (1930) is a story about the gathering of a family to bury their mother. *Sanctuary* (1931) was republished as *Light in August* (1932). *The Unvanquished* (1938) concerns the Sartoris family during the American Civil War, and *The Wild Palms* (1939) is about the effects of a Mississippi flood on the lives of several people. *Go Down Moses* (1942) is a collection of Yoknapatawpha short stories, and *Intruder in the Dust* (1948) concerns the defence by a white lawyer of a black man accused of killing a white man. There followed *Requiem for a Nun* (1951), *A Fable* (1954), set in France, and *The Reivers* (1962), an amusing account of a boy's misadventures with disreputable older friends in the early 1900s. For the latter two books Faulkner twice won the Pulitzer Prize, in 1955 and 1963. He was awarded the Nobel Prize for Literature in 1950. His fiction charts the gradual transition of the South from an aristocratic-agrarian society into a modern industrial and suburban society, and combines tragedy, comedy and a diverse range of characters.

M. Millgate, *The Achievement of William Faulkner* (1966); F. Karl, *William Faulkner: American Writer* (1989).

Faulks, Sebastian (1953–) Born in Newbury, England, he went to Cambridge University (BA 1974), and began work as a teacher before turning to journalism and radio broadcasting in 1979. His first novel, *A Trick of the Light* (1989), was followed by *The Girl at the Lion d'Or* (1989) and *A Fool's Alphabet* (1992), which is organised as twenty-six alphabetical chapters, from Anzio to Zanica, the place names reflecting an importance in the life of the protagonist which is explored at a leisurely pace. *Birdsong* (1993) brought critical acclaim, about the life of a British soldier during the First World War, alternating between the battlefields and London in 1978, as the war diaries are discovered and read by his granddaughter. His reputation for innovative novels that explore the lives and histories of ordinary people continued in *The Fatal Englishman* (1996), a triple biography about three lives tragically cut short in the 1920s, during the Second World War and in the Cold War, and in the recent *Charlotte Gray* (1998), about a young Scottish woman who goes to France in 1942 on a special operations mission to find her lover. He recently edited the *Vintage Book of War Stories* (1999).

Federman, Raymond (1928–) An American novelist born in Paris, France, of eastern European Jewish descent, whose father was murdered at Auschwitz. He emigrated to the US in 1947, worked on a factory-line for Chrysler in Detroit, and later moved to New York as a factory worker. After serving in the Korean War, he went to Columbia University on the G.I. Bill (BA 1957, MA 1959) and then completed a Ph.D. in French at UCLA (1963). He has subsequently taught at a variety of universities and received many honours and fellowships. As a central figure in postmodern writing, he coined the word 'surfiction' to describe his experimental, radically non-linear fiction that challenges realist styles of narration. His first novel, *Double or Nothing* (1971), is about a man writing a story about another man who is locked in a room in New York City for one year to write a novel about a third man, and such formal games like this infinite regression in narrative are typical of his fiction. There followed *Take It or Leave It* (1976), *The Voice in the Closet* (1979 in French, 1985 in English), *The Twofold Vibration* (1982), which plays with names like the reversal of his name in Namredef and the French pun in Moinous (I/we), and *Smiles on Washington Square* (1985). Recent work includes the prose-poem *The*

Worm (1996) and *The Line* (1997). His critical works include studies of Samuel BECKETT, and the influential edited collections of essays *Surfiction* (1976) and *Critifiction* (1993). Assuming an irrational, chaotic universe in which truth and reality are fictions that we create, his iconoclastic style constantly challenges conventional narrative typography, punctuation and syntax, while constructing characters who are unstable and unnamable.

J. Kutnik, *Novel as Performance* (1986).

Feinstein, Elaine (1930–) Born in Bootle, England, and brought up in Leicester, she went to Cambridge University (MA 1955), and subsequently worked as a publishing editor and a lecturer until 1971, when she turned to full-time writing. A playwright, novelist, and translator of Russian, she made her early reputation as a poet, with volumes including *In a Green Eye* (1966), *Selected Poems* (1994), *Daylight* (1997) and *Gold* (2000). Her early novels, such as *The Circle* (1970) and *The Amberstone Exit* (1972), involve women who are mired in domestic responsibility searching for their identities. Later fiction is preoccupied with the persistence of the past in characters' lives, and includes *The Shadow Master* (1977), *The Survivors* (1982), which is a multigenerational saga of a Russian Jewish family fleeing Odessa for Liverpool, *The Border* (1984), *Loving Brecht* (1992), *Dreamers* (1994), about mid-nineteenth-century Vienna and the Jewish contributions to society and culture of Central Europe, and *Lady Chatterley's Confession* (1995), a sequel to D.H. LAWRENCE's novel. In addition to the short stories in *Matters of Chance* (1972) and *The Silent Areas* (1980), there are plays and radio plays, and biographies of Bessie Smith (1986), Marina Tsvetaeva (1987), D.H. Lawrence in *Lawrence's Women* (1980), and Pushkin (1999). Her fascination with her east European forebears, Jewish background and origins in Tsarist Russia is reflected in her fiction, which often deals with exile, suffering and loss in a prose released from provincial limitations.

Fell, Alison (1944–) Born in Dumfries, Scotland, and educated at Edinburgh College of Art (Diploma 1967), she co-founded the Welfare State Theatre in Leeds in 1970, before working with the women's movement as an underground press journalist and an editor for the magazine *Spare Rib*. Her fiction includes a work for children in *The Grey Dancer* (1981), *Every Move You Make* (1984), which is her first adult novel in the realist mode, and *The Bad Box* (1987), about the maturity of a Scottish teenager and her sexual fantasies. *Mer de Glace* (1991) combines male and female perspectives in a passionate love triangle, while *The Pillow Boy of the Lady Onogoro* (1994) deals with a variety of tales within tales, and *The Mistress of Lilliput, or, The Pursuit* (1999) looks at male and female relationships. Volumes of poetry occur in *Kisses for Mayakovsky* (1984), *The Crystal Owl* (1988) and *Dreams, Like Heretics* (1997), and she has written various contributions for edited collections and adaptations for BBC radio. A versatile writer with a preoccupation with myths, dreams and desires, Fell has become a significant feminist novelist in the late 1980s alongside such writers as Marina WARNER and Michèle Roberts.

Ferber, Edna (1887–1968) An American writer, born in Kalamazoo, Michigan. Her first novel, *Dawn O'Hara* (1911), was followed by three volumes of short stories, *Roast Beef, Medium* (1913), *Personality Plus* (1914) and *Emma McChesney and Co* (1915), the latter about a business woman. Among her novels are *Fanny Herself* (1917), about anti-Semitism, *The Girls* (1921), and *So Big* (1924, Pulitzer Prize 1925), a family drama, set on a farm, about a woman gardener. Thereafter came *Showboat* (1926), which

served as the basis for the successful musical about racism and miscegenation, *Cimarron* (1930), *American Beauty* (1931), about Polish immigrants, and *Come and Get It* (1935), concerning the logging industry. Other novels include *Saratoga Trunk* (1941), *Great Son* (1945), about a Seattle family, *Giant* (1950), about a Texas rancher, and *Ice Palace* (1958), set in Alaska. Many of her books have been made into films. Ferber also wrote plays, and two volumes of autobiography entitled *A Peculiar Treasure* (1929) and *A Kind of Magic* (1963). Often regarded as sentimental and too overtly didactic, her stories nevertheless also garnered praise for her socio-historical research.

Findley, Timothy (1930–) A Canadian novelist, born in Toronto, he travelled widely in his first career as an actor, then worked in radio, television and theatre in Canada. In 1962, he turned to writing full-time, although continued to write television and radio scripts, among which are *The National Dream* (1974), *Dieppe 1942* (1979) and some of the scripts for *The Whiteoaks of Jalna* (for CBC 1971–1972). His first novel, *The Last of the Crazy People* (1967), which focused on a family and its spiritual emptiness, was followed by *The Butterfly Plague* (1969), about morality in the film industry and Nazi Germany. This focus on violence and power informed his 'counter-history', *The Wars* (1977, filmed 1982), set during the First World War, and based on diaries and oral histories. *Famous Last Words* (1981) offered a fictional story of Hugh Selwyn Mauberley, adapted from a character in Ezra Pound's poetry, and records the relationship between aestheticism and fascism. This was followed by a humorous rewriting of the Biblical story of the flood in *Not Wanted on the Voyage* (1984), *The Telling of Lies: A Mystery* (1986), which explores the collusion of contemporary society in the perpetuation of mistaken histories, *Headhunter* (1993), *The Piano Man's Daughter* (1995) and *Pilgrim* (2000). Self-consciously writing out of and against colonialism and American imperialism, his versatile and self-reflexive narratives search out the tensions between public and personal histories. Short stories occur in *Dinner Along the Amazon* (1984), *Stones* (1988) and *Dust to Dust* (1997), a play in *The Stillborn Lover* (1993), while autobiography has appeared in *Inside Memory* (1990) and *From Stone Orchard* (1998).

A. Bailey, *Timothy Findley and the Aesthetics of Fascism* (1998).

Finlayson, Roderick (1904–1992) Born in Auckland, New Zealand, where he lived all his life, he became close to several Maori families in his youth. His first stories are on Maori themes, in which the Maori characters are neither comic nor romanticised, in contrast to the prevailing tendency in New Zealand literature. Presenting a bleak view of the effects on Maori society of landlessness, tribal disintegration and urban migration, his collections of short stories in *Brown Man's Burden* (1938) and *Sweet Beulah Land* (1942) set the New Zealand short story on a new track. Other short story collections and novellas include *Other Lovers* (1976) and *In Georgina's Shady Garden* (1988), while his two novels are *Tidal Creek* (1948) and *The Schooner Came to Atia* (1952). He also considered industrial capitalism as an impoverishment of Pakeha (white New Zealand) life and the natural environment, as expressed in the essays in *Our Life in This Land* (1940). He has also written a novel for children, *The Springing Fern* (1965).

Firbank, Ronald (1886–1926) An English writer, born Arthur Annesley Ronald Firbank, in London, he attended Cambridge University (1906–1909), leaving without a degree but as a converted Catholic. Regarded as the first impressionist writer,

and a modernist like JOYCE and LAWRENCE, he was a well-to-do dandy and dilettante who travelled widely before settling in isolation in Oxford during the war years. Here he wrote *Vainglory* (1915), *Inclinations* (1916) and *Caprice* (1917). *Valmouth* (1917) was followed by a play *The Princess Zoubaroff* (1920), before he travelled again. There followed *Santal* (1921), and his mature novels, *The Flower Beneath the Foot* (1923), which is set in an imaginary Vienna and depicts a sour portrait of English literary society, *Prancing Nigger* (1924), which is set on a Caribbean island and depicts the social ambitions of a family moving from a village to the city, and *Concerning the Eccentricities of Cardinal Pirelli* (1926), about the moral and social unorthodoxy of a Spanish clergyman. His style is delicate and epigrammatic, witty and satiric, although there is little in the way of plot development. Often exploring the dilemma of the hypersensitive young man isolated in a depraved world, he left parts of a new novel on his death entitled *The New Rythum* (1962), set in New York City. Under-appreciated during his lifetime, he nevertheless influenced Evelyn WAUGH and Anthony POWELL.

M. Benkowitz, *Ronald Firbank* (1969).

Fitzgerald, F. Scott (1896–1940) An American writer, born Francis Scott Key Fitzgerald, in Saint Paul, Minnesota, and a chronicler of the 1920s, or the 'Jazz Age' as it came to be called. He studied at Princeton University but never graduated. His first novel, *This Side of Paradise* (1920), about the emptiness of the lives of the post-Great War generation, won him fame and wealth, and he married Zelda Sayre, the daughter of an Alabama judge. The marriage was to prove a pivotal point in his life, both because of its later unhappiness and because their lives together formed a strong autobiographical element in his later fiction. His second book, *The Beautiful and Damned*

(1922), is about a bright, rich young couple who expect and await an inheritance which, when it eventually materialises, is too late to save them from themselves. During this time, Fitzgerald was producing a multitude of popular, highly-paid short stories for magazines which enabled himself and Zelda to lead an expensive, near profligate, lifestyle. Some of these stories appear in *Flappers and Philosophers* (1920), *Tales of the Jazz Age* (1922), *All the Sad Young Men* (1926) and *Taps at Reveille* (1935). In 1924, the Fitzgeralds moved to France, where they mixed with such figures as Gertrude STEIN, Ernest HEMINGWAY and Ezra Pound. Here, he completed his most famous novel, *The Great Gatsby* (1925), which is a farcical and tragic rags-to-riches story narrated by the naïve Nick Carraway as he becomes involved with the old and new money of Long Island society. Around this time, Zelda began to suffer bouts of mental illness and eventually entered a sanitorium, and Fitzgerald himself had become a chronic alcoholic. His next novel, *Tender Is the Night* (1934, filmed 1961), is about a doctor who treats a mentally unstable young woman, and is based upon his life with Zelda. He recovered enough from his alcoholism to become a Hollywood screenwriter in 1937, an experience which informed his last, unfinished novel *The Last Tycoon* (1941, filmed 1976), published posthumously, concerning the life of a Hollywood director. During this period he also wrote *The Pat Hobby Stories* (1962), short stories about a Hollywood writer down on his luck, while the *Letters of F. Scott Fitzgerald* were published in 1968.

A. Mizener, *The Far Side of Paradise* (1965); J. Meyers, *Scott Fitzgerald: A Biography* (1994).

Fitzgerald, Penelope (1916–2000) Born in Lincoln, England, she went to Oxford University (BA 1939), and then worked for the BBC (1939–1953) and in a book-shop. She then became a writer, living on the Thames in a barge. She published her first novel, *The Golden Child* (1977), at the age of 59, and her early works were loosely based upon her life experiences. *The Bookshop* (1978) is about a courageous female bookshop entrepreneur defying the stuffy prejudices of her town in East Suffolk, while her acclaimed *Offshore* (1979, Booker Prize) is about a community of eccentric characters who live on a Thames barge in Battersea Reach. Other novels include *Human Voices* (1980), about wartime work at the BBC, *At Freddie's* (1982), *Innocence* (1986), set in Florence during the post-war era, *The Beginning of Spring* (1988), a comedy of manners set in Moscow in 1913, *The Gate of Angels* (1990), which focuses upon an academic community, and *The Blue Flower* (1995). In addition, she wrote several biographies, including *Edward Burne-Jones* (1975), *The Knox Brothers* (1977), about her father and brothers and their distinctive contributions to English culture, and *Charlotte Mew and Her Friends* (1984). She established a firm reputation for her ironic, compressed and comic fiction, depicting patterns of stoical human relationships and people's interactions.

Flanagan, Mary (1943–) Born in Rochester, New Hampshire, US, and educated at Brandeis University (BA 1965), she emigrated to England in 1969, where she now lives. Her initial work was a collection of short stories entitled *Bad Girls* (1984), which explores the morally 'bad' behaviour of women who are victims of their own illusions. She followed this with the large novel *Trust* (1987), a moral tale about a quest for elusive trust, and *Rose Reason* (1991), an equally wide-ranging novel about a young woman who changes her identity and fights for her independence. Further light and sometimes surreal short stories emerged in *The Blue Woman* (1994), before her latest novel, *Adèle* (1996), a sex-crime thriller about a woman who is rescued by a doctor from death at the hands of vicious villagers, and who becomes embroiled in a mystery about clitoridectomy. Her fiction tends to depict desire opposing ethics, and people striving against social conditioning.

Fleming, Ian (1908–1964) An English author of racy spy fiction, Ian Lancaster Fleming was born in London. He is known as the creator of the high-living James Bond, British secret agent 007. Fleming's career before becoming a novelist embraced journalism, banking, stockbroking and British intelligence during the Second World War. His first Bond novel was *Casino Royale* (1953), which sold 18 million copies in eleven languages. Bond, with his chauvinistic liking for beautiful women, fast cars and expensive whisky, was pitted against bizarre arch-enemies in exotic locations, and featured in twelve other books: *Live and Let Die* (1954), *Moonraker* (1955), *Diamonds are Forever* (1956), *From Russia with Love* (1957), *Dr No* (1958), *Goldfinger* (1959), *For Your Eyes Only* (1960), *Thunderball* (1961), *The Spy who Loved Me* (1962), *On Her Majesty's Secret Service* (1963), *You Only Live Twice* (1964) and *The Man with the Golden Gun* (1965, issued posthumously). All the Bond books have been filmed – although often taking liberties with the original plots, they established Bond as a defining figure in the popular imagination about international spy-cultures. Fleming also wrote a popular book for children, *Chitty Chitty Bang Bang* (1964, filmed 1968), essays in *Thrilling Cities* (1963), and an obscure early novel, *The Diamond Smugglers* (1957).

D. McCormick, *The Life of Ian Fleming* (1993).

Ford, Ford Madox (1873–1939) Born Ford Hermann Hueffer in Surrey, England, he was influenced in his early life by the Pre-Raphaelite artists and writers, about which he wrote in *The Pre-Raphaelite Brotherhood* (1907). His service and injury in the First World War provided the impetus for much of his poetry from 1918 onwards. He was particularly significant in the development of English modernist techniques, collaborating with CONRAD on his three novels *The Inheritors* (1901), *Romance* (1903) and *The Nature of a Crime* (1924), developing a fictional style derived from Impressionism. His major work was *The Good Soldier* (1915), which is the best example of this impressionistic style in an exploration of the darker forces of humanity. In a prolific career, he published a wide-range of novels, from historical romances to comedies of manners, including such works as *The Fifth Queen Trilogy*, consisting of *The Fifth Queen* (1906), *Privy Seal* (1907) and *The Fifth Queen Crowned* (1908), which depicts the life of Catherine Howard, the fifth wife of Henry VIII. His other major sequence is the 'Tietjens Tetralogy', which consists of *Some Do Not* (1924), *No More Parades* (1925), *A Man Could Stand Up* (1926) and *The Last Post* (1928), following the life of Christopher Tietjens. Non-fiction includes autobiography in *Return to Yesterday* (1931) and *It Was the Nightingale* (1933), as well as criticism in *The March of Literature* (1938). He was a leading figure in the English avant-garde who supported emergent writers like D.H. LAWRENCE, Ezra Pound and Wyndham LEWIS, while his editorship of two influential journals, *The English Review* and *The Transatlantic Review*, published and influenced European and American writers like Eudora WELTY and William Carlos Williams.

M. Saunders, *Ford Madox Ford: A Dual Life* (1996).

Ford, Richard (1944–) Born in Jackson, Mississippi, US, and educated at Michigan State University (BA 1966) and the University of California at Irvine (MFA 1970), he is associated with writers who have emerged from the Midwest. After working as a university lecturer, he is now a full-time writer. *A Piece of My Heart* (1976), set on the Arkansas and Mississippi border region, invoking the environment of the South, concerns the quests of two people, while *The Ultimate Good Luck* (1981) is about US citizens caught up in the drug business of Mexico. He was acclaimed for *The Sportswriter* (1986), about Frank Bascombe's exploration of his unhappy suburban life in the town of Princeton, and continued in the sequel, *Independence Day* (1995), in which Bascombe is now a real estate salesman in his mid-forties. Other works include the stories of *Rock Springs* (1988), *Wild Life* (1990), about the collapse of a Montana family seen through the eyes of a 16-year-old, and more recently, *Women with Men: Three Stories* (1997). He has edited the *Granta Book of the American Short Story* (1992) and the *Essential Tales of Chekov* (1998). Associated with the 'dirty realist' writers like Raymond CARVER and Tobias WOLFF, his fiction offers a laconic humour and a detached style of observation.

H. Guagliardo, *Perspectives on Richard Ford* (2000).

Forester, C.S. (1899–1966) Cecil Scott Forester, the pseudonym of Cecil Lewis Troughton Smith, was born in Cairo, Egypt, but grew up in the suburbs of London, England. He studied medicine at Guy's Hospital, London, although did not qualify. His major creation was a nineteenth-century British naval officer called Horatio Hornblower, a character who has captured the public imagination over the years through a series of books, newspaper serialisations, a film and television adaptations. From *The Happy Return* (1937) to *Hornblower and the Crisis* (1967), the eleven-novel saga of Hornblower, from a 17-year-old recruit through various commands, promotions and adventures, depicts in great detail the historical naval milieu during the Napoleonic Wars in vivid, episodic and strongly

characterised stories. The stories were collected in *The Hornblower Companion* (1964). Other fiction includes historical novels about the Peninsular War in *Death to the French* (1932) and *The Gun* (1933), as well as a host of other novels, including *The African Queen* (1935, filmed by John Huston in 1951), *The Ship* (1943) and *The Sky and the Forest* (1948), short stories and numerous non-fiction works on nineteenth-century naval and Napoleonic history. Although he won few prizes, his books sold in large numbers, and his obituary made the front page of the *New York Times*.

S. Sternlicht, *C.S. Forester* (1981).

Forster, E.(dward) M.(organ) (1879–1970) An English writer born in Stevenage, he went to Cambridge University, where he was elected to the Apostles, an élite group which included such intellectuals as Bertrand Russell, Lytton Strachey and Leonard Woolf, all of whom were influential in the Bloomsbury group. After travelling abroad for a few years, his literary work began in 1903, and his first novel was *Where Angels Fear to Tread* (1905), which depicts the relationships of a group of young English people in Italy. There followed *The Longest Journey* (1907), *A Room with a View* (1908), about another group of English people in Italy, and the novel which secured his reputation, *Howards End* (1910), which analyses English class relationships by focusing upon the intellectual Schlegel sisters and their friendship with the Wilcox and Bast families. Utilising the realist mode, these novels examine the tensions between languid disinterest and naïve honesty, and articulate the modernist desire to 'only connect' instead of flailing around in fragmentation. After a trip to India in 1912, he returned to England to write *Maurice* in 1913, his novel about homosexual love, which was only published posthumously in 1971. After service as a fire-watcher in the First World

War, he went to Egypt, which led to his *Alexandria: A History and Guide* (1922). Upon his return to Britain (1919), he worked as editor of the left-wing paper the *Daily Herald*. After several fresh journeys to India, he wrote his last novel *A Passage to India* (1924), a treatment of British colonial rule during the Raj and dealing with the overwhelming cultural impact of the country upon a young woman who travels out to meet her fiancé. Thereafter he turned to criticism and journalism, with essays and lectures collected in *Aspects of the Novel* (1927), *Abinger Harvest* (1936), *Two Cheers for Democracy* (1951) and *The Hill of Devi* (1953), while short stories occur in *The Celestial Omnibus* (1911), *The Eternal Moment* (1928), and the posthumous volume, *The Life to Come* (1972), and a biography of his aunt *Marianne Thornton* (1956). Celebrated as a champion of many liberal causes, much attention has been paid to the ways his fiction sought to create symbolic unities and connections in order to counteract the pernicious influences of an alienating modern world. However, more recent critical attention has focused upon the disunities and fractures in the texts, partly due to his difficulty in articulating his homosexuality and the restrictive form of realism. Many of his novels have been adapted for the screen.

P. Furbank, *E.M. Forster: A Life* (1977–1978); N. Beauman, *Morgan* (1993).

Foster, David (1944–) An Australian writer born in Sydney, he was educated at the University of Sydney and the Australian National University, Canberra. After working as a research scientist in the US and Australia, he turned to full-time writing in 1972. His novels include *The Pure Land* (1974), about three stages in an Australian photographer's life, and *The Empathy Experiment* (1977), an unsuccessful science fiction novel co-written with D.K. Lyall. His reputation was secured with *Moonlite* (1981), the picaresque adventures of a nineteenth-century Scotsman, which gradually focuses upon Australia and becomes an allegorical account of Australian immigration. There followed *Plumbum* (1983), about a group of Canberra musicians, *Dog Rock* (1984), a parody of the detective quest, and *The Pale Blue Crochet Coathanger Cover* (1987). Novellas include *North South West* (1973), *The Adventures of Christian Rosy Cross* (1986), set in the Middle Ages, and the pastiche *Testostero* (1987). Other fictional works include *Hitting the Wall* (1989), *Mates of Mars* (1991), *A Slab of Fosters* (1994), *Glade within the Grove* (1996) and the *Ballad of Erinungarah* (1997). Short stories occur in *Escape to Reality* (1977), poetry in *The Fleeing Atalanta* (1975), while an account of two centuries of explorers and travellers in Australia occurs in *Crossing the Blue Mountains* (1997). His scientific interests are made clear in his choice of subjects, for example entropy, and in his eclectic vocabulary, and his play with language, parodic modes and bizarre, surreal wit, recalls the postmodern fiction of writers like Thomas PYNCHON.

Fowles, John (1926–) Born in Leigh-on-Sea, Essex, England, he went to Edinburgh and Oxford universities (BA 1950), and then taught in France, Greece and London (1951–1963). His best-selling first novel, *The Collector* (1963), which explores the issue of freedom in a narrative about the abduction and captivity of a woman, was followed by *The Magus* (1966), about a teacher on a Greek island who becomes mixed up with an enigmatic millionaire and a series of mysterious events. His most famous and successful novel, *The French Lieutenant's Woman* (1969, filmed 1981), examines Victorian England at the dawn of a new age in the 1860s. Its clever pastiche of Victorian romantic fiction focuses on a love triangle, notoriously offering alternative endings to the reader, as the novel maintains a dialogue between modern and Victorian England. There followed *Daniel Martin* (1977), in the high modernist realist style of psychological reality or stream-of-consciousness, *Mantissa* (1982), an erotic allegory about creative processes set inside a skull, and *A Maggot* (1985), a historical mystery story about the disappearance of a duke's son. *Wormholes* (1998) collects essays and occasional writings, and short stories occur in *The Ebony Tower* (1974). In addition to three photo compilations in *Islands* (1978), *Shipwreck* (1975) and *The Tree and the Nature of Nature* (1995), he has written several plays, verse, and various books about his home landscape of Lyme Regis, Dorset. Despite his avowedly left-wing affiliations, the non-fictional *The Aristos: A Self Portrait in Ideas* (1964) sought to explore philosophies such as existentialism and Jung's thought. Exploring the freedom of the individual, and the eruptions of the irrational and the mystical into human life, he has frequently been preoccupied with the question of whether there is human agency beyond the determining forces of the psychological and social pressures of the environment.

S. Loveday, *The Romances of John Fowles* (1985).

Frame, Janet (1924–) Born in Dunedin, New Zealand, she grew up in the Otago region of the South Island. In 1956, she spent a period abroad in England and the US, before returning to New Zealand. Characteristically described as a writer of intense visions, she is regarded as the foremost New Zealand writer. Early short stories in *The Lagoon* (1951) were published while she was incarcerated in a New Zealand mental institution, and her first novel was *Owls Do Cry* (1957), about a dysfunctional family in a small-town New Zealand setting. Subsequent novels include *Faces in the Water* (1961), *The Edge of the Alphabet* (1962), which explores the West during the Cold War

years, *Scented Gardens for the Blind* (1963), *The Adaptable Man* (1965), *A State of Siege* (1966), *The Rainbirds* (1968), *Intensive Care* (1970), *Living in Maniototo* (1979), *You Are Now Entering the Human Heart* (1983), *The Carpathians* (1988), which deals in a metafictional manner with narrative and reality, and *The Reservoir* (1996). Her first volume of autobiography, *To the Is-land* (1982), tells of her childhood, which was marked by poverty and alienation, while the subsequent volumes, *An Angel at My Table* (1984) and *The Envoy from Mirror City* (1985), continue her story of female artistic development. Widely acclaimed, they were printed as one volume, entitled *Autobiography* (1989). Preoccupied with history, change, the inevitability of death and people's inability to communicate, her fiction focuses self-reflexively upon the writing activity and the role of the artist's need to create meaningful patterns of identity. Her poetry occurs in *The Pocket Mirror* (1967), while her life was dramatised in the Jane Campion film, *An Angel at My Table* (1990).

M. Dalziel, *Janet Frame* (1980).

France, Anatole (1844–1924) The pseudonym of Jacques Anatole François Thibault, he was born in Paris, France, and worked as an editorial assistant for a Parisian publisher in the mid-1860s, a schoolteacher, publisher, and librarian (1876–1889). A prolific writer, his early novels include the comic satire *Jocasta and the Famished Cat* (1879, trans. 1912), *The Crime of Sylvestre Bonnard* (1881, trans. 1890), a tale of the Franco-Prussian war in *The Aspirations of Jean Servien* (1882, trans. 1912), and *Thais* (1890, trans. 1891), an exotic tale of a courtesan turned saint. His best fiction began with *The Romance of Queen Pedanque* (1893, trans. 1950), and four novels about contemporary history, in *The Elm-Tree on the Mall* (1897, trans. 1910), *The Wicker Work Woman* (1897, trans. 1910), *The Amethyst Ring* (1899, trans. 1919) and *Monsieur Bergeret in Paris* (1901, trans. 1921). These novels offer intensely realistic situations based upon observation, and act as microcosms of French society in the 1890s, becoming increasingly socialist in perspective. Later novels include *The Penguin Island* (1908, trans. 1909), *The Gods Will Have Blood* (1912, trans. 1979), which is a study of revolutionary fanaticism and corruption, *The Revolt of the Angels* (1913, trans. 1914), a playful but subversive satire of Christianity, and a barely fictionalised novel evoking his childhood in *The Bloom of Life* (1922, trans. 1923). Short story collections include *Balthasar* (1889, trans. 1909), *Mother of Pearl* (1892, trans. 1908) and *The Well of St. Claire* (1895, trans. 1909). A large number of short stories, plays, poetry, articles, collections of letters and other works remain untranslated into English. He was awarded the Nobel Prize for Literature in 1921.

R. Virtanen, *Anatole France* (1968).

Frank, Waldo (1889–1967) An American novelist, literary and social critic, Waldo David Frank was born in Long Branch, New Jersey, and went to Yale University. He began as a freelance journalist for New York papers, and was a co-founder in 1916 of the influential arts magazine *The Seven Arts*. Among his early novels are *The Unwelcome Man* (1917), *The Dark Mother* (1920), *Rahab* (1922), *City Block* (1922), *Holiday* (1923) and *Chalk Face* (1924). A prominent literary radical during the 1920s and 1930s who was influenced by Freud and Marxism, he was associated with such writers as John Reed, Max Eastman, H.L. Mencken and Van Wyck Brooks. As editor of *The Masses* and *New Republic* in the 1930s, he was at the centre of controversial debates about politics and aesthetics. Later novels, such as *The Death and Birth of David Markand* (1934), *The Bridegroom Cometh* (1938), *Summer Never Ends*

(1941), *Island in the Atlantic* (1946) and *The Invaders* (1948), reflected his left-wing politics by directly addressing social problems. He also wrote extensively about Hispanic culture in such volumes as *Our America* (1919), *America Hispaña* (1931) and *South American Journey* (1943). Other works include *The Jew in Our Day* (1944), *Bridgehead* (1957), *The Prophetic Island* (1961) and his *Memoirs* (1973). His fiction is a blend of Marxism and a romantic concept of cosmic mysticism, albeit directing itself to social problems.

M. Orgorzaly, *Waldo Frank: Prophet of Hispanic Regeneration* (1994).

Franklin, Miles (1879–1954) An Australian novelist, born in Talbingo, New South Wales, Miles Stella Marie Sarah Franklin descended from a convict on the First Fleet and from Irish immigrants. Her early years were spent at the family farm at Brindabella, New South Wales, later described in her posthumously published autobiographical volume, *Childhood at Brindabella* (1963), before moving to Sydney in 1914. Her celebrated first novel, *My Brilliant Career* (1901, filmed 1979), concerns a woman's struggle against the constrictions on female life in Australian bush society, although it also rhapsodises about the beauty of the outback. Franklin worked briefly as a nurse, housemaid and freelance journalist, and became involved in the Australian feminist movement. She left for the US in 1909, where she did secretarial and editorial work, then worked in town planning in London, before finally returning to Sydney in 1932. She began a series of novels chronicling Australian pioneer life and nationalism under the pseudonym 'Brent of Bin Bin', consisting of *Up the Country* (1928), *Ten Creeks Run* (1930), *Back to Bool Bool* (1931), *Prelude to Waking* (1950), *Cockatoos* (1954) and *Gentlemen at Gyang Gyang* (1956), which were widely broadcast in Australia. Other novels include *Some Everyday Folk and Dawn* (1909), about the drabness of small-town Australian life, *Old Blastus of Bandicoot* (1931), *Bring the Monkey* (1933), *All That Swagger* (1936), recounting her family saga of immigration to Australia, and *My Career Goes Bung* (1946), a sequel to the earlier novel. Written with Dymphna Cusack, *Pioneers on Parade* (1939) was a satirical attack on established Australian society, and she co-wrote *Joseph Furphy* (1944) with Kate Baker. Lectures were published in *Laughter, Not for a Cage* (1956), and the novel *On Dearborn Street*, set in Chicago in 1914, was posthumously published in 1981. Her writing frequently defied the ultra-conservative values of late Victorian Australian society, challenging established gender roles and rejecting patriarchy. A committed feminist, socialist and pacifist, she bequeathed her estate in 1948 to establish the Australian annual literary prize, the Miles Franklin Award.

M. Barnard, *Miles Franklin* (1967); V. Coleman, *Her Unknown Brilliant Career* (1981).

Fraser, George MacDonald (1925–) Born in Carlisle, England, he worked as a journalist and newspaper editor from 1947 to 1969. He is principally famous for his creation of the nineteenth-century rogue, Harry Flashman, the eponymous bully from *Tom Brown's Schooldays*, who made his first appearance in *Flashman: From the Flashman Papers, 1839–1842* (1969), a purportedly true account of the adventures of a young British captain in imperial India. A best-seller, it was followed by a series of additional entertaining narratives of his adventures around the world, such as *Royal Flash* (1970), *Flashman at the Charge* (1973), *Flashman and the Redskins* (1982), *Flashman and the Angel of the Lord* (1990) and *Flashman and the Tiger* (1999). Although never with the same popularity, another rogue – a rough Scottish soldier – was created in *The General Danced at Dawn* (1970)

McAuslan in the Rough (1974) and *The Sheikh and the Dustbin* (1988), released as *The Complete McAuslan* (2000). *Black Ajax* (1997) depicted social life and boxing in the nineteenth century. He has written numerous film scripts, including *The Three Musketeers* (1973), *The Four Musketeers* (1975), the James Bond fantasy *Octopussy* (1983), and *Red Sonja* (1985). Other works include a memoir of his experiences with the British army in Burma during the Second World War in *Quartered Safe Out Here* (1992), and a history of the Anglo-Scottish Border Reivers, entitled *The Steel Bonnets* (1971).

Freeling, Nicholas (1927–) Born in London, England, he was a professional cook in European hotels between 1948 and 1960, recounted in his autobiography *The Kitchen* (1970). He turned to fiction in 1960, inaugurating his career as a prolific writer of detective fiction with *Love in Amsterdam* (1961). He created three detective characters, who have appeared in some twenty novels: the Dutch policeman Piet van der Valk, whom he killed off in *A Long Silence* (1971); a series of investigations centred upon his wife, Arlette van der Valk; followed by the French detective Henri Castang, in a French provincial setting, in such works as *Wolfnight* (1982), *You Who Know* (1994), and the latest in the series, *Dwarf Kingdom* (1996). Internal monologues give a nervous, oblique style to Freeling's fiction, which has achieved wide popularity over the years. He has also written a collection of essays on the art of detective writing in *Criminal Convictions* (1994).

French, Marilyn (1929–) Born in New York City, US, and educated at Hofstra University (BA 1951, MA 1964) and Harvard University (Ph.D. 1972), she began work as a teacher and literary critic before turning to fiction. Her studies include *The Book as World: James Joyce's 'Ulysses'* (1976) and *Shakespeare's Division of Experience* (1981), which explores tragedy and comedy in terms of gender principles. She is best known for her explosive and provocative first novel, *The Women's Room* (1977), which was a best-seller and established her as an important voice of the American women's movement. It narrates the story of Mira, a submissive and repressed young woman, whose conventional upbringing prepares her for marriage and motherhood, which is ended suddenly by divorce leaving her liberated but alone. She followed this with *The Bleeding Heart* (1980), *Her Mother's Daughter* (1987), *Our Father* (1995) and *My Summer with George* (1997). An American feminist scholar, whose fictional works have a strong and cogent feminist theme, her non-fiction includes polemical essays in *Beyond Power: On Women, Men, and Morals* (1985), and *The War Against Women* (1992), with a memoir in *Season in Hell* (1998), which depicts her struggle against cancer in later life. Much of her work explores the ethics of sex antagonism, feminism and the socially conditioned roles of women.

Freud, Esther (1963–) Born in London, England, she is the daughter of the painter Lucien Freud and the great-granddaughter of the psychoanalyst Sigmund Freud. She was the co-founder of the Norfolk Broads, a women's theatre company, and has subsequently achieved critical acclaim for her first two novels. The semi-autobiographical *Hideous Kinky* (1992, filmed 1998) narrates her childhood experiences in Morocco with her mother and sister, as they search for adventure and freedom in the 1960s. Her second novel, *Peerless Flats* (1993), is a bleak tale of the effects and manifestations of a break-up in family life. Set in 1970s London, it depicts the life of Lisa, who lives in an abandoned building called Peerless Flats with her mother and brother. *Gaglow* (1997) interweaves the story of Sarah, a pregnant actress, with that of her ancestors in Germany during the First World War, as the long confiscated estate Gaglow, which

is about to be returned, may bring the generations together across the decades. Her most recent novel, *The Wild* (2000), presents a view of the baffling world of adults from a child's perspective.

Fuentes, Carlos (1928–) Born in Panama City, he travelled all over the Americas as a child, and at the age of 16 went to Mexico. He was educated at university in Mexico City (LLB 1948), and did several governmental jobs in the 1950s, eventually rising to become the Mexican ambassador to France (1974–1977), after which he held academic posts at several prestigious universities in the US. A prolific and widely honoured novelist, his first novel was *Where the Air Is Clear* (1958, trans. 1960), a complex, modernist collage of Mexico City in the 1940s and 1950s. There followed *The Good Conscience* (1959, trans. 1961), *The Death of Artemio Cruz* (1962, trans. 1964), which is his best-known novel and traces the paths of families from Mexican independence in three alternating voices, *Aura* (1962, trans. 1965), *Holy Place* (1967, trans. 1972) and *A Change of Skin* (1967, trans. 1968), both carnivalesque, irreverent, mockingly self-referential texts. Other novels include *Terra Nostra* (1975, trans. 1976), a vast, ambitious epic history from the age of Christ to Paris in 1999, *The Hydra Head* (trans. 1978), a spy thriller about the Arabs and Israelis and Mexican oil reserves, *Distant Relations* (1980, trans. 1982), *The Old Gringo* (trans. 1985), *Christopher Unborn* (1987, trans. 1989), *The Campaign* (1990, trans. 1991) and *Diana, The Goddess Who Hunts Alone* (1994, trans. 1995). His recent work includes *The Crystal Frontier* (1996, trans. 1998), which is a network of nine stories, explaining Mexicans and Americans to each other, and *The Years with Laura Diaz* (trans. 2000), an epic which follows one woman through twentieth-century Mexico. Short stories appear in *Burnt Water* (trans. 1981), *Constancia* (1989, trans. 1990) and *The Orange Tree*

(1993, trans. 1994), and he has edited *The Picador Book of Latin American Stories* (1998). In addition to plays and poetry, non-fiction includes *The Argument of Latin America* (trans. 1963), *The Buried Mirror* (trans. 1992) and *A New Time for Mexico* (1994, trans. 1996), while essays occur in *Selected Literary Essays* (trans. 1986) and *My Self with Others* (trans. 1988). Along with Juan RULFO, he is the most significant twentieth-century Mexican author, and his cosmopolitan exploration of literary modernity and Mexican identity emerges as a dialogue with other traditions and styles. Frequently reshaping ancient Mexican mythology, his fiction at times parades artifice in an openly postmodern manner.

W. Faris, *Carlos Fuentes* (1983).

Fuller, John (1937–) Born Leopold John Fuller, in Ashford, Kent, England, the son of the British poet Roy Fuller, he was educated at Oxford University (MA 1964, B.Litt. 1965), and has subsequently been a lecturer at Manchester University (1963–1966) and Oxford University. Initially developing a reputation as a poet with works like *Fairground Music* (1961), *The Illusionist* (1980) and *Selected Poems* (1985), he has also edited several poetry collections, written children's books and a critical work on W.H. Auden. He received considerable acclaim and attention for his brief novel *Flying to Nowhere* (1983, Booker Prize), a religious mystery story

set in sixteenth-century Wales. Other fiction includes the short stories in *The Adventures of Speedfall* (1985), and the novels *Tell It Me Again* (1988), *The Burning Boys* (1989), set on the coast of Lancashire during the Second World War and telling two parallel stories, *Look Twice* (1991) and *The Worm and the Star* (1993). Recent works include his *Collected Poems* (1996) and *A Skin Diary* (1998).

Furst, Alan (1941–) Born in New York City, US, he was educated at Oberlin College (AB 1962) and Pennsylvania State University (MA 1967). His novels include *Your Day in the Barrel* (1976), *The Paris Drop* (1980), *The Caribbean Account* (1981), *Shadow Trade* (1983), *Night Soldiers* (1988), about KGB and communist spies in the 1930s and 1940s, *Dark Star* (1991), *The Polish Officer* (1995), *The World at Night* (1996), *Red Gold* (1998), about underground movements in France, and *The Prince of Shadows* (2000). His fiction explores the complex and morally questionable techniques of the spy world of the European Intelligence services in the 1930s and during the Second World War. Usually set on a historically and factually accurate stage, he examines the birth of modern espionage, which occurs well before the advent of the Cold War espionage novels of John LE CARRÉ and Ian FLEMING.

G

Gadda, Carlo Emilio (1893–1973) Born in Milan, Italy, he attended the Milan Polytechnic Institute, and became an engineer, working in Argentina, France, Germany and Italy between 1920 and 1935, after which he turned to writing. Much of his writing remains untranslated into English. His masterpiece is *That Awful Mess on Via Merulana* (1957, trans. 1965), about a philosopher-detective who investigates two murders in Rome. A subtle, psychological study of characters, it uses a linguistically rich concoction of dialects and vernaculars. Allusive, loaded with puns, satire and word tricks, his passion for language has established him as an experimental modernist. A further novel, *Acquainted with Grief* (1963, trans. 1969), depicts tormented family relationships. In a characteristically bleak and disenchanted outlook, his fiction explores the failures of the mind.

R. Dombroski and M. Bertone, *Carlo Emilio Gadda: Contemporary Perspectives* (1997).

Gaddis, William (1922–1998) Born in New York City, US, he attended Harvard College (1941–1945) before travelling abroad for a period of time and turning to freelance writing. Although highly regarded, he is little known to the wider reading public, mainly because his writing involves long, complex narratives. His first novel, *The Recognitions* (1955), is about Wyatt Gwyon, who solves his social disintegration by turning to the forgery of Old Masters, and becomes mixed up in a world of counterfeits in which the 'recognitions' of authenticity are nearly impossible. This was followed by a satire of corporate America in *J.R.* (1975), in which J.R. Vansant, a clever 11-year-old, transforms small stocks and shares into a massive paper empire. The book is written entirely in dialogue which requires a keen and active engagement by the reader. *Carpenter's Gothic* (1985), a shorter book, probes the ambiguous nature of reality and is also a critique of religion, the plot of which is set in a 'carpenter gothic' house in the Hudson River valley. His last novel was *A Frolic of His Own* (1994), a devastating satire of the justice system, which charts a labyrinthine set of legal suits and counter-suits. He was completing *Agape Agape* on his death, which he descibed as a 'secret history of the player piano'. Centring upon displaced, disoriented characters, with his hallmark narrative style of disconnected, unpunctuated dialogue, Gaddis' novels are often allusive and densely woven critical visions of America failing to fulfil its potential.

G. Comnes, *The Ethics of Indeterminacy in the Novels of William Gaddis* (1994).

Gaines, Ernest J. (1933–) A widely honoured African-American novelist, Ernest James Gaines was born in Oscar, Louisiana, on a plantation, before he moved to California at the age of 15. He was educated at San Francisco State (BA 1957) and Stanford universities, and later became Professor of English at the University of Southwestern Louisiana at Lafayette. His work is set in Louisiana, in the fictional Bayonne area, whose multicultural mix and conflicts are central to his novels in their social realist style. Often depicting a search for identity within a society wracked by racism, his first two novels, *Catherine Carmier* (1964) and *Of Love and Dust* (1967), deal with love thwarted by racial boundaries and barriers and the destructiveness of the South's racial codes. *Bloodline* (1968) was a collection of five first person narratives, and was followed by a critique of racial prejudice in his most acclaimed novel, *The Autobiography of Miss Jane Pittman* (1971), which focused upon a 110-year-old narrator's account of African-American life from slavery to Martin Luther King, and asserted the political need for social change. Other novels include *In My Father's House* (1978), *A Gathering of Old Men* (1983), set in the 1970s with different narrators challenging the racist history of the region, and *A Lesson Before Dying* (1993), exploring the effects of institutional racism in 1948. A significant figure within African-American literature, he adopted the style of the speaking voice for most of his wide array of characters, symbolically giving vent to the long-silenced voice of African-Americans in his dissections of the dehumanising and destructive effects of racism.

V. Babb, *Ernest Gaines* (1991).

Gaite, Carmen Martín (1925–) Born in Salamanca, Spain, she graduated from the University of Salamanca (1949) and received her doctorate from the University of Madrid (1972). Most of her fiction, much of which remains untranslated into English, treats feminist themes centring upon entrapped female characters and their enforced non-participatory social and political roles. The preoccupations of the domestic enclosure and social imprisonment of women are depicted in the long realist novel *Behind the Curtains* (1958, trans. 1990), about a girl growing up in provincial post-war Spain, and in her last major novel to date, *The Back Room* (1978, trans. 1983), which is about a girl growing up under the repressive Spanish fascist regime. Moving from the realist mode in the 1950s to a more experimental linguistic style in the 1970s, the latter novel is a meta-literary text with intertextual references and allusions to critical theory. Fourteen years of silence was broken by *Variable Cloud* (1992, trans. 1995), which deals with female friendships expressed in an exhaustive exchange of letters, while *The Farewell Angel* (1994, trans. 1999) was widely honoured and is a psychodrama of the exploration of the past of the protagonist's parents. Her non-fiction also focuses on gender relations in *Love Customs in Eighteenth-Century Spain* (1972, trans. 1991).

L. Chown, *Narrative Authority and Homeostasis in the Novels of Doris Lessing and Carmen Martín Gaite* (1990).

Gaitskill, Mary (1954–) Born in Lexington, Kentucky, US, she went to the University of Michigan (BA 1981), and has developed a reputation for writing novels which are populated by sexual eccentrics with their pathologies. *Bad Behaviour* (1988), a collection of short stories, depicts the seamier side of New York City and its troubled characters, who abuse drugs, others and themselves. *Two Girls, Fat and Thin* (1991), a novel about the relationship between Justine Sade and Dorothy Never, charts the difficult attraction of two women who are opposites. *Because They Wanted To* (1997), another collection of short stories, has a cast of depressed and depraved characters, and like *Bad Behaviour*, charts their sexual relationships and games. The stories generally centre upon the abuse given or suffered by characters' warped sexualities and actions, as they create inner worlds and fantasies as a consequence of their unhappy, disconnected lives and pathetic solitude.

Gale, Patrick (1962–) Born on the Isle of Wight, England, he went to Oxford University (BA 1983). His first novel, *The Aerodynamics of Pork* (1985), about love and lust in modern life and its insecurities, anxieties and crises, was followed by *Ease* (1985), about a successful English playwright whose search for experience beyond her privileged lifestyle leads to tragedy. Subsequent novels include *Kansas in August* (1987), about unorthodox sexual relations, *Facing the Tank* (1987), *Little Bits of Baby* (1989), *The Cat's Sanctuary* (1990), depicting the relationship between two sisters, *The Facts of Life* (1995), which follows three generations of a Jewish family through and after the Second World War, and the psychological narrative of *Tree Surgery for Beginners* (1997). He has edited short stories in *Dangerous Pleasures* (1996), recently written a biography of Armistead MAUPIN (1999), and his new novel, *Rough Music*, is forthcoming in 2000. An aspiring young British novelist, his spare, disengaged style focuses on human foibles in an ironic, comic and dramatic fashion.

Gallant, Mavis (1922–) A Canadian writer, born in Montreal, who worked for the Canadian National Film Board and in journalism before moving in the 1950s to Europe and Paris, the setting for much of her fiction. She has written many stories for *The New Yorker*, collected in *The Other Paris* (1956), *My Heart Is Broken* (1964), *The Pegnitz Junction* (1973), *The End of the World* (1973) and *From the Fifteenth District* (1973). *Home Truths* (1981), the faintly autobiographical stor-

ies about a woman's struggle for personal and intellectual independence, was followed with the collections *Overhead in a Balloon* (1985) and *In Transit* (1988). Her work often focuses on the lives of the dispossessed and deracinated, such as her two novels *Green Water, Green Sky* (1959), an episodic novel about the destruction of a girl by her protective mother, and *A Fairly Good Time* (1970), about a marriage failure. Identifying herself as a Canadian abroad, her stories repeatedly recount the lives and states of mind of Canadian expatriates and exiles. *Paris Notebooks* (1986) contains political observations, while her recent collections of stories are *The Moslem Wife* (1993), *Across the Bridge* (1993) and *The Selected Stories of Mavis Gallant* (1996).

N. Besner, *The Light of Imagination* (1988).

Galloway, Janice (1956–) Born in Kilwinning, Scotland, she went to Glasgow University (MA 1978), and has worked as a Welfare Rights worker (1976–1977) and a teacher (1980–1990). The short stories in *Blood* (1991) articulated a series of repressed narratives, and was followed by a novel, *The Trick Is to Keep Breathing* (1991), about a woman's slow descent into madness. There followed *Foreign Parts* (1995), which focuses upon two Scottish women on holiday in France, and the short stories in *Where You Find It* (1996), as well as several collections of Scottish writing. A widely praised contemporary Scottish writer, distinguished by wit, idiosyncratic female protagonists, graphic imagery and unconventional typography, her fiction contains a Gothic sensibility and a black humour with a strong ear for dialogue and innovation.

Galsworthy, John (1867–1933) Born in Kingston-upon-Thames, England, he went to Oxford University (BA 1889), and became a widely honoured and successful novelist and playwright. Initially practising as a barrister, he travelled extensively, making a firm friendship with Joseph CONRAD in 1892. His writing career began under the pseudonym John Sinjohn with the short stories in *From the Four Winds* (1897). There followed *Jocelyn* (1898), *Villa Rubein* (1900) and *A Man of Devon* (1901), before his first novel under his own name, *The Island Pharisees* (1904), a satirical portrait of Edwardian society. *The Man of Property* (1906) launched his success as a writer, with the Edwardian family chronicle about the Forsytes, the narratives for which he is most famous. This series was continued in many novels, including *In Chancery* (1920), *To Let* (1921), *Swan Song* (1928), *Maid in Waiting* (1931) and *Flowering Wilderness* (1932). Many of his other novels addressed various social ills, such as *Strife* (1909) which dealt with the sufferings of families during a strike, and *Loyalties* (1922), which attacked anti-Semitism. Despite becoming one of the most successful and prolific British writers of the first third of the century, he was regarded as the last great Victorian novelist for his traditional, conventional, albeit somewhat verbose style. Famously dismissed along with the likes of Arnold BENNETT by Virginia WOOLF, his reputation was nevertheless restored by the immensely popular BBC television serialisation of *The Forsyte Saga* on the centenary of his birth in 1966–1967. He also wrote a number of successful plays, in which he confronted thorny social problems, including *The Silver Box* (1906), about the disparities of economic wealth, and *Justice* (1910), which contributed to prison reform. An extremely generous man, he signed over royalties to charities and the war effort, and upon being awarded the Nobel Prize for Literature in 1932, gave this to the Author's Society, P.E.N., which he founded. Volumes of his letters, collected essays, and literary criticism have also been published.

C. Dupre, *John Galsworthy: A Biography* (1976).

Gardner, Erle Stanley (1889–1970) An American writer, born in Malden, Massachusetts, he was an attorney for twenty years, which acted as a source of inspiration when he came to write detective fiction. His earliest mystery, *The Case of the Velvet Claws* (1933), was the first of over eighty books featuring the lawyer-sleuth Perry Mason. Others include *The Case of the Spurious Spinster* (1961) and *The Case of the Amorous Aunt* (1963). These stories are highly formulaic: Mason accepts as a client someone accused of murder, an investigation ensues, followed by a courtroom dénouement, where Mason ingeniously acquits his client. The Perry Mason character served as the basis for a popular television series and had a defining role in establishing the courtroom sleuth in American film and cinema. Gardner also wrote a series of novels featuring Doug Selby, district attorney, as protagonist; and under the *nom de plume* A.A. Fair, a series featuring detective Bertha Cool and lawyer Donald Lam. His books have sold around 135 million copies in the US.

Garner, Helen (1942–) An Australian novelist born in Geelong, Victoria, who graduated from Melbourne University (1965). She was a high school teacher until 1972, when she was controversially dismissed for discussing sexual matters frankly with the pupils. She then worked as a journalist and writer, publishing her first novel, *Monkey Grip*, in 1977. A controversial prize-winner, upsetting conservative readers with its explicit depiction of inner-city, counter-cultural lifestyles, drug-taking and sexual freedom, it has been since widely acclaimed as a definitive description of urban Australia in the 1970s. After a sojourn in Paris (1978–1979), she wrote *Honour and Other People's Children* (1980), two novellas depicting the tensions and emotions of everyday life. Her economic and concentrated style is developed in *The Children's Bach* (1984), a novella about the external pressures on a family, *Cosmo Cosmolino* (1992), a novella and two interlinked stories in a less naturalistic style, and *The First Stone* (1995), which explores issues of sex and power. Short stories occur in *Postcards from Surfers* (1985), again concerning the details of the everyday life of families, and *My Hard Heart: Selected Fiction* (1998).

P. Gilbert, *Coming Out from Under: Contemporary Australian Women Writers* (1988).

Garner, Hugh (1913–1979) A Canadian writer, born in Batley, Yorkshire, England, he went to Canada with his family in 1919. He spent most of his life in Toronto, which he represented in mostly autobiographical novels. His first novel, *Storm Below* (1949), drew on his naval wartime experiences, while *Cabbagetown* (1950, reprinted 1968), a largely autobiographical work and acclaimed as one of Canada's finest social novels, offers depictions of working-class life which are echoed in his later work *The Silence on the Shore* (1962), and many of his short stories. These latter titles are collected in such volumes as *The Yellow Sweater* (1952), *Hugh Garner's Best Stories* (1963), *Men and Women* (1966), *Violation of the Virgins* (1971), which depict sympathy for the downtrodden and dispossessed. Other novels include *A Nice Place to Visit* (1970) and *The Intruder* (1975), and the police novels set in Toronto, *The Sin Sniper* (1970), *Death in Don Mills* (1975) and *Murder Has Your Number* (1978). His non-fiction includes the autobiography *One Damn Thing After Another* (1973), and magazine journalism in *Author! Author!* (1964). Suffering from posthumous neglect, he was nevertheless one of Canada's best practitioners of realist fiction and a champion of the 'common man'.

P. Stuewe, *The Storms Below* (1988).

Gass, William H. (1924–) Born William Howard Gass, in Fargo, North Dakota,

US, he was educated at Kenyon College (BA 1947) and Cornell University (Ph.D. 1954). He has since taught philosophy at a variety of universities and was made Professor of Philosophy at Washington University, St. Louis (1979). He has developed a reputation for anti-realist literary inquiries in his examination of the nature of fiction-making and technical experimentation. His highly praised first novel, *Omensetter's Luck* (1966), was about a man who settles in an Ohio River town, and was followed by the five novellas of *In the Heart of the Heart of the Country* (1968, revised 1981), which examines small-town life in the Midwest in a variety of rhetorical styles. *Willie Master's Lonesome Wife* (1970) is a novella about a stripteaser's activities, which also acts as a comment on art in general. His expansive novel *The Tunnel* (1995) explores issues of representation, autobiography and history using the metaphor of tunnelling and excavation, and his most recent fiction is *Cartesian Sonata and Other Novellas* (1998). His essays on contemporary fiction and novelists appear in *Fiction and the Figures of Life* (1970), *The World Within the Word* (1978), *On Being Blue: A Philosophical Inquiry* (1976), a fantasy meditation on the colour blue, *Habitations of the Word* (1985), which collects literary essays, *Finding a Form* (1996) and *Reading Rilke* (1999). In their self-referential integrity, many of his texts focus on the operations and workings of language in a postmodernist manner, although this is generally a term he has resisted.

W. Holloway, *William Gass* (1990).

Gee, Maggie (1948–) Born in Poole, England, Maggie Mary Gee went to Oxford University (MA 1970, M.Litt. 1973) and Wolverhampton Polytechnic (Ph.D. 1980). She has worked as an editor in publishing (1972–1974) and as a research assistant (1975–1979), since when she has worked as a writer. Her first novel was *Dying, in Other Words* (1981), a murder mystery set in Oxford with eccentric characters, while *The Burning Book* (1983) is an apocalyptic novel which explores the nuclear threat by following four generations of a family through both world wars. *Light Years* (1985) is a humorous romance about a couple who separate and eventually come together again, and was followed by *Grace* (1989), an allegorical treatment of Thatcherite Britain, *Where Are the Snows* (1991), *Lost Children* (1994) and *The Ice People* (1998), which speculates about love and life in a frozen, future twenty-first century. Widely acclaimed as a technically adept experimentalist, her fiction is introspective, dark and wryly humorous, with vivid character portraits in often difficult books involving sinister themes and a surreal edge.

Gee, Maurice (1931–) Born in Whakatane, New Zealand, he was raised in Henderson, and educated at the University of Auckland. From 1955 he worked as a schoolteacher and a labourer, and in 1961 he spent a year in England. His first novel was *The Big Season* (1962), about an individual's struggle against the pressures of community. There followed *A Special Flower* (1965), which presents the multiple perspectives of a brother and sister, *In My Father's Den* (1972), which explores the individual's capacity for revolt in post-provincial New Zealand, and *Games of Choice* (1976), which focuses upon the break-up of a suburban family. *The Plumb Trilogy* (1994) consists of *Plumb* (1978), *Meg* (1981) and *Sole Survivor* (1983), and traces the Plumb family, using an overlapping narrative method similar to that developed by Joyce CARY. An excellent example of New Zealand realism, it is full of images of the country's life. Other novels include *Prowlers* (1987), *The Burning Boy* (1990), *Going West* (1992), *Crime Story* (1994), which deals with the criminal world, politics and high finance, *Loving Ways*

(1996), set in New Zealand's South Island, about a son visiting his dying father, *Orchard Street* (1998), and *Live Bodies* (1998), about the alienation of Austrian Jews in New Zealand in the 1940s. Early short stories occur in *A Glorious Morning, Comrade* (1975), republished in *Collected Stories* (1986). Manifesting a variety of styles of narration and narrative perspective, his fiction deals with processes of remembrance and perception.

B. Manhire, *Maurice Gee* (1986).

Gellhorn, Martha (1908–1998) Born in St. Louis, Missouri, US, she attended Bryn Mawr College, before taking up journalism (1929). After working as a freelance reporter in Europe, she returned to the US (1935), where she became outraged by living conditions in the South and New England, reporting her views to President Franklin D. Roosevelt and documenting them in *The Trouble I've Seen* (1936). She reported on the Spanish Civil War for *Collier's* magazine after meeting Ernest HEMINGWAY, whom she married in 1940, and her stories occur in *The Heart of Another* (1941). She reported on conflicts in Cuba, Finland, China and Europe, and after her divorce in 1945, has continued to cover wars in Java, Vietnam, the Middle East and Central America. Her journalism is collected in *The Face of War* (1954) and *The View from the Ground* (1988), with an autobiography in *Travels with Myself and Another* (1983). Her fiction shows an acute and penetrating eye for detail, and includes such novels as *What Mad Pursuit* (1934), *A Stricken Field* (1940), set in Prague on the eve of the Second World War, *Liana* (1944), *His Own Man* (1961), *The Lowest Trees Have Tops* (1967) and *The Point of No Return* (1989); and six short story collections, including *The Honeyed Peace* (1954), and *The Weather in Africa* (1978), about the effects of poverty. Recent publications include *The Short Novels of Martha Gellhorn* (1991), *The Novellas* of *Martha Gellhorn* (1991), and most recently, the co-written play *Love Goes to Press* (1995). Always espousing the conviction that wars are futile, her reporting career has spanned nearly all the twentieth-century's major conflicts.

C. Rollyson, *Nothing Ever Happens to the Brave* (1990).

Genet, Jean (1910–1986) Born in Paris, France, he joined the French Foreign Legion and later deserted, becoming a beggar, thief and homosexual prostitute before being imprisoned. He began writing his first novels in prison between 1942 and 1948, with *Our Lady of the Flowers* (1942, trans. 1949) and the prose-poem *Miracle of the Rose* (1943, trans. 1965), both of which are prison cell fantasies woven around celebrated Parisian murderers. There followed *Querelle of Brest* (1947, trans. 1966), *Funeral Rites* (1947, trans. 1969) and *The Thief's Journal* (1949, trans. 1954), which challenge the reader with their scandal and complicity. Disregarding conventional psychology, lacking careful transitions, confusing chronology, and without coherent plot structures, his fiction combines aesthetics and pornographic content, inspiring a deep reaction in most readers. In later life, he wrote prolifically for the theatre, including the well-known plays *The Maids* (1947, trans. 1954), *Deathwatch* (1949, trans. 1954) and *The Balcony* (trans. 1958), demonstrating a concern with drama as ritual and ceremony, and there is also a volume of *The Complete Poems* (trans. 1980). He published little after 1961 owing to ill-health, although he was a fervent supporter of social causes like the Black Panthers and the PLO. He was ardently defended by COC- TEAU and SARTRE, the latter presenting him as an existential hero in his portrayal *Saint Genet* (1952), which elevated him to

cult status and around whom many myths and legends emerged.

J-P. Sartre, *Saint Genet: Actor and Martyr* (1952, trans. 1963).

Ghose, Zulfikar (1935–) A Pakistani-American writer, born in Sialkot, Pakistan, he travelled to England in 1952 and went to Keele University (BA 1959). He taught in London between 1963 and 1969, and worked as a cricket correspondent between 1960 and 1965. In 1969, he moved permanently to the US and became a lecturer at the University of Texas, Austin. His early work reflects rural displacement and cultural conflict in pre-Independence India, in *The Contradictions* (1966) and *The Murder of Aziz Khan* (1967). Beginning with *Hulme's Investigations Into the Bogart Script* (1981), his fiction began to undermine its apparent mimetic function, and his interest in metafictional and magic realist modes and techniques continued in *A New History of Torments* (1982), *Don Bueno* (1983), *Figures of Enchantment* (1986), *The Triple Mirror of the Self* (1991) and *Veronica and the Góngora Passion* (1998). In addition, he has written 'The Incredible Brazilian' trilogy – *The Native* (1972), *The Beautiful Empire* (1975) and *A Different World* (1978) – about the character, Gregorio, in a series of incarnations, and confronting ethical, historical and mythological ideas of Brazil spanning 400 years of history. Other works include short stories in *Statement Against Corpses* (1964) with B.S. JOHN- SON, autobiography in *Confessions of a Native-Alien* (1965), and several volumes of poetry including a *Selected Poems* (1991). Literary studies occur in *The Fiction of Reality* (1983), *The Art of Creating Fiction* (1991) and *Shakespeare's Moral Knowledge* (1993). Confronting the metaphysics of life and death, ideals and practicalities, his self-reflexive fiction foregrounds artifice and the adventures of the psyche.

C. Kanaganayakam, *The Writings of Zulfikar Ghose* (1993).

Ghosh, Amitav (1956–) Born in Calcutta, India, he was educated at Delhi University (BA 1976, MA 1978) and Oxford University (Ph.D. 1982). He returned to lecture in sociology at Delhi University in 1983. He has emerged as one of the new generation of Anglo-Indian writers, and his first two novels have been compared with those of Salman RUSHDIE. *The Circle of Reason* (1986) was his first English-language novel, a complex narrative partly inspired by *Moby Dick*, about an Indian boy's adventures at home and abroad. There followed *The Shadow Lives* (1988), which juxtaposes two lives, one Indian and one English, and questions and examines the blurred lines between nations and families, and *In an Antique Land* (1992), which is loosely based upon his time in Egypt, adjusting to rural life, analysing the convergence of ancient and modern Arabic, Jewish and Hindu cultures. His most recent works include *The Calcutta Chromosome* (1995), a science fiction adventure about the transmigration of souls, and *Countdown* (1999), a transcript of discussions held with people on the sub-continent about the nuclear tests by India and Pakistan in 1998. He draws heavily upon the contradictions and traditions of India, although the characters and themes extend beyond the national boundaries to the Middle East and Britain, as he exposes cross-cultural links.

Gibbon, Lewis Grassic (1901–1935) The pseudonym of James Leslie Mitchell, an Anglo-Scottish writer born in Auchterless, Scotland. He pursued a career in journalism in Glasgow, and served in the armed forces in the Middle East and Central America. He adhered to the fashionable 'diffusionist theory' of civilisation, which blamed the corruption of people's essential goodness on the 'accidental' diffusion of civilisation. Consequently, his characters are constantly struggling to retain a purity and simplicity of life which is threatened by industrialisation. His main work is the trilogy *A Scot's Quair* (1946), comprising *Sunset Song* (1932), *Cloud Howe* (1933) and *Only Granite* (1934), a lyrical realistic account of a Scottish community and the novel's heroine Christine Guthrie, which became an unprecedented success for capturing the Scots idiom in dialogue and narrative. Other titles include *Spartacus* (1933) and *Niger: The Life of Mungo Park* (1934). Work written under the name James Leslie Mitchell includes *Stained Radiance* (1930), *The Thirteenth Disciple* (1931), *The Gay Hunter* (1934), and the historical works *Hanno* (1928) and *The Conquest of Maya* (1934). He is regarded as a key figure in the Scottish Renaissance, the revival in consciousness and culture of Scotland between the world wars.

Gibbons, Stella (1902–1989) Born in London, England, Stella Dorothea Gibbons attended London University, and then worked for the United British Press, and later as a journalist for the *Evening Standard* and *The Lady*. She is best known for her first novel *Cold Comfort Farm* (1932), about a city woman who visits her gloomy country relatives, and a parody of the somewhat clichéd conventions and absurdities of contemporary regional novelists like D.H. LAWRENCE and T.F. POWYS. Among her other works are twenty-five novels, including *Ticky* (1943), a satire of army life, *Enbury Heath* (1935), *Here Be Dragons* (1956), *The Charmers* (1965), *The Snow Woman* (1969) and *The Woods in Winter* (1970), and several short story collections including *Roaring Tower* (1937) *Christmas at Cold Comfort Farm* (1940) and *Conference at Cold Comfort Farm* (1949), the latter two an attempt to revive her earlier success. She published her *Collected*

Poems in 1950. Much of her fiction focuses on social manners in the domestic settings of literary, middle-class London suburbs like Hampstead or Highgate, although this fiction has largely been obscured by her initial success.

Gibson, Graeme (1934–) A Canadian novelist, born in London, Ontario, he studied at the University of Western Ontario. A significant figure in cultural politics since the early 1970s, he has travelled widely and has lived in Toronto with Margaret ATWOOD since 1973. His first novel, *Five Legs* (1969), appeared to be an iconoclastic new force in Canadian fiction, with an oblique stream-of-consciousness style and literary allusions to JOYCE, Eliot and others. Its sequel, *Communion* (1971), continued the theme of resistance to social conformity, and both were reprinted as one volume in 1983. *Perpetual Motion* (1982), a more accessible novel set in rural Ontario in the nineteenth century, is an allegory about ecological exploitation, while *Gentleman Death* (1995) is his latest work.

Gibson, William (1948–) Born in the United States, William Ford Gibson later moved to Canada, and has lived in Vancouver since 1968. He graduated from the University of British Columbia (BA 1977), and began writing short stories from then until 1983, much of this work being collected in *Burning Chrome* (1986), including the story 'Johnny Mnemonic' which was made into a film starring Keanu Reeves in 1995. He is primarily associated with cyberpunk science fiction, works set in dystopian, computer-driven, high-tech, near-future cities, whose inhabitants are streetwise and socially disconnected. The publication of *Neuromancer* (1984) stunned readers with its introduction of cyberspace and rapidly produced a cult following. This was followed with the sequels *Count Zero* (1986) and *Mona Lisa Overdrive* (1988). These novels are con-scious hybrids of popular and 'high' culture, blending the styles of film noir, the California thrillers by Raymond CHANDLER, punk youth drug culture, Japanese corporate capitalism, and contemporary computer technology. Their bleak vision centres upon worlds which seem unable to be understood, displaced individuals who experience a loss of self, and who hack into computer cyberspace as a way of escaping the flesh for the cerebral substitute of the virtual reality world within the computer matrix. Gibson has subsequently published *The Difference Engine* (1990) with Bruce Sterling, a 'steampunk' novel in which Victorian culture is dominated by Charles Babbage's computer in a wholly totalitarian and rationalised society. This was followed by a trilogy, consisting of *Virtual Light* (1993), *Idoru* (1996), and most recently, *All Tomorrow's Parties* (1999), which although abandoning cyberspace, nevertheless is still set in the dystopian, high-tech cultural scenarios of California and Japan.

D. Kellner, *Media Culture* (1995); G. Slusser and T. Shippey, eds, *Fiction 2000* (1992).

Gide, André (1869–1951) Born André-Paul-Guillaume Gide, in Paris, France, he was the co-founder of *La Nouvelle Revue Française* in 1909, and worked in various government capacities, including the Colonial Ministry in Africa (1925–1926). He travelled extensively and became a major force in French twentieth-century intellectual life. His fiction includes the early *Urien's Voyage* (1893, trans. 1964), although *The Immoralist* (1902, trans. 1930) is his first major narrative work. It is narrated by Michel, whose 'immorality' consists of his attempts to free himself from restrictions imposed upon him by his education and society, in a gratification of his instincts. *Strait Is the Gate* (1909, trans. 1924) examines self-denial, Christian renunciation and mysticism, while *Two Symphonies: Isabelle and The Pastoral*

Symphony (trans. 1931) tells of a Swiss pastor who falls in love with a blind girl he adopts. *The Counterfeiters* (1926, trans. 1927) is an elaborate set of modernist self-reflective structures concerning the conflict between the real world and its representations, narrated in first person *récits*. Other works include reflections on literature and modernity in *Pretexts* (1903, trans. 1959), autobiography, journals and correspondence in *Imaginary Interviews* (1942, trans. 1944), *If It Die* (1920, trans. 1935), and an account of the writing of the novel in *Journal of 'The Counterfeiters'* (1926, trans. 1951). His *Journals of André Gide* (trans. 1956) constitute a major landmark in French literature for his self-examination of his life. A master of prose narrative, his intensely patterned works sought to break the hold of realism. A wide-ranging man of letters in twentieth-century France, he was awarded the Nobel Prize for Literature in 1947.

D. Walker, *André Gide* (1990).

Gilchrist, Ellen (1935–) Born in Vicksburg, Mississippi, US, she studied philosophy at Millsaps College (BA 1967), and began her professional career at the age of 40, when she started writing for newspapers in New Orleans. Turning to poetry at first, she has published several volumes including *The Land Surveyor's Daughter* (1979) and *Riding Out the Tropical Depression* (1986). Yet it was with the collection *In the Land of Dreamy Dreams* (1981), a series of stories set in New Orleans about young people's struggles with their dreams and aspirations, that she attracted significant interest. Other short story collections include *Light Can Be Both Wave and Particle* (1982), *Drunk with Love* (1986), *Rhoda: A Life in Stories* (1995), *The Courts of Love* (1996), *Flights of Angels* (1999) and *The Cabal* (2000). Her first novel was *The Annunciation* (1983), capturing class consciousness, racism and restrictive gender

roles in a realist style. *Victory Over Japan* (1984), a gathering of stories about women, was followed by *Falling Through Space, The Author's Journals* (1987), *The Anna Papers* (1988), and *Not of Jewels* (1992), about a young girl's growth. Recent novels include *Starcarbon* (1994), charting the adventures of a North Carolina family, *Anabasis* (1994), set in ancient Greece, and is about an orphaned slave girl and her adventures, and *Sarah Conley* (1997), about the life of a journalist forced to choose between career and love. Her feisty characters frequently return in her fiction, and their idiosyncratic and pitiable situations have caused Gilchrist to be compared with such writers as Carson MCCULLERS and Flannery O'CONNOR.

Gilman, Charlotte Perkins (1860–1935) Born in Hartford, Connecticut, US, and largely self-educated, Charlotte Anna Perkins Gilman was a reformist from an early age and became a prominent American feminist intellectual at the turn of the twentieth century. After years of intense relationships with several women, she married in 1882, and following the birth of her daughter in 1885, suffered from depression. Dr. S. Weir Mitchell diagnosed 'female hysteria' and prescribed a 'rest cure'. This experience resulted in her famous short story 'The Yellow Wall-Paper' (1892), which was a severe indictment of the sexual politics of marriage and patriarchal ideologies of women. She moved to California in 1888, where she lectured on her utopian socialist views and feminism after her divorce (1894), establishing the feminist magazine *The Forerunner*. *In This Our World* (1903) includes political poems on the women's movement, and in addition to a number of other social studies of the politics of domestic life, her major work was *Women and Economics* (1898), in which she criticised the androcentric nature of the socio-economic world. In a witty and ebullient style, often addressing issues of feminist politics and gender roles, she wrote several novels, including *The Crux* (1911), *What Diantha Did* (1912), *Moving the Mountain* (1912), *Benigna Machiavelli* (1914), and *Herland* (1915), her famous utopian vision of a community of women without men. An autobiography was posthumously published as *The Living of Charlotte Perkins Gilman* (1935).

A. Lane, *To 'Herland' and Beyond* (1990).

Ginzberg, Natalia (1916–1991) Born in Palermo, Italy, Natalia Levi Ginzberg worked for Einaudi publishers in Turin, and was a member of the Italian parliament. Owing to her Jewish background, she was confined to a small village between 1940 and 1943. One of the best-known post-war Italian novelists, her fiction includes the two novellas in *The Road to the City* (1942, trans. 1949), *The Dry Heart* (trans. 1949), *Dead Yesterdays* (1952, trans. 1956), which is presented through the eyes of an adolescent, *Sagittarius* (1957, trans. 1975), *Voices in the Evening* (1961, trans. 1963), *Family Sayings* (1963, trans. 1967), a family saga which develops into a masterpiece analysing wider events, *Never Must You Ask Me* (1970, trans. 1973), *Dear Michael* (1973, trans. 1975), about a young revolutionary living in an apartment, *Family* (1977, trans. 1988), *The City and the House* (1984, trans. 1987), *All Our Yesterdays* (trans. 1985) and *The Manzoni Family* (trans. 1987). She was also a playwright and an essayist, and her cool, controlled style, with a keen eye for characterisation, portrays traditional values and captures the detail of provincial life.

Giraudoux, Jean (1882–1944) Born Hippolyte Jean Giraudoux, in Bellac, France, he had a career as a French diplomat (1910–1940). Although known primarily for his dramatic works, such as *Tiger at the Gates* (1935, trans. 1955) and *Ondine* (1939, trans. 1954), he was also a prolific short story writer and novelist. His novels include *Suzanne and the Pacific* (1921,

trans. 1923), about a heroine who abandons a Paradise of her own free will, and *Bella* (trans. 1926), a witty political satire woven into the Romeo and Juliet story. His fiction deals with types, and is recognised for its humour, whimsy, highly ornate rhetoric and fantasy. Much of his work remains untranslated into English.

R. Cohen, *Giraudoux: Three Faces of Destiny* (1968).

Glaspell, Susan Keating (1876–1948) Born in Davenport, Iowa, US, Susan Keating Glaspell was a graduate of Drake University (1899), and became a reporter for newspapers in Des Moines before becoming a full-time writer in 1901. Her first, rather sentimental novel was *The Glory of the Conquered* (1909), followed by *The Visioning* (1911), about a young woman learning the harsh realities of life. Her other novels include *Fidelity* (1915), regarded by some as her finest novel, *Brook Evans* (1928), *Fugitive's Return* (1929), *The Morning Is Near Us* (1939), *Cherished and Shared of Old* (1940), *Norma Ashe* (1942) and *Judd Rankin's Daughter* (1945). These last four are set in the Midwest, and focus on women's struggles to retain their idealism. In 1915, she founded The Provincetown Players with her husband George Cook, aiming to revolutionise American drama, with plays by Djuna BARNES, Edna FERBER, and their major discovery, Eugene O'Neill. She wrote many plays herself, including *The Verge* (1921), an experimental psychological study of a woman, and *Alison's House* (1930, Pulitzer Prize) about Emily Dickinson. In addition, she wrote a biography of Cook entitled *The Road to the Temple* (1926), and short stories are collected in *Lifted Masks* (1912). Her explorations of women's social circumstances repeatedly resulted in representations of marital and sexual restrictions, as she sought to find new modes for female lives.

Gold, Michael (1893–1967) Born Irving Granich in New York City, US, and educated at New York and Harvard universities, he emerged as a proletarian writer before the Second World War, criticising the US government and capitalism, alongside writers like John STEINBECK, James T. FARRELL, Upton SINCLAIR and Theodor DREISER, and espousing a Marxist-socialist politics of radical change. After *The Life of John Brown* (1924), he wrote *The Damned Agitator and Other Stories* (1926), and *120 Million* (1929), which is sketches of the oppressed life of the American labourer. Written after *Charlie Chaplin's Parade* (1930), his most widely acclaimed work was *Jews Without Money* (1930), a semi-autobiographical depiction of ghetto life on New York's East Side, with its poverty, crowds, prostitution and disease. *Change the World!* (1937) is a collection of his journalism from his columns and editorial work for the *Daily Worker* and *New Masses*, while *The Hollow Men* (1941) contains critical articles on literature. In addition to several plays and his association with the innovations of The Provincetown Players, his work is anthologised in *The Mike Gold Reader* (1954) and *Mike Gold: A Literary Anthology* (1972). As one of the foremost writers and intellectuals of the left during the 1920s, 1930s and 1940s, he advocated a neo-Stalinist literary practice, coining the term 'proletarian realism' to describe the bitter and revealing style of proletarian novels, and was embroiled in a major controversy for his attack on the 'genteel' style of Thorton Wilder.

J. Pyros, *Gold: Dean of American Proletarian Writers* (1979).

Golding, William (1911–1993) A widely honoured British novelist, William Gerald Golding was born in St. Columb Minor, Cornwall, and went to Oxford University (BA 1935). He worked as a settlement house worker after graduating, and then served as a schoolmaster in Wiltshire from 1930 to 1961. During the war, he commanded a rocket ship in the Royal Navy, and began writing in earnest after the war. His first novel was the widely acclaimed *Lord of the Flies* (1954), which powerfully describes the gradual collapse of the social values of a group of boys stranded on an island. It emerged as a cynical allegory about the veneer of civilised attitudes and characterised human history as moral regression rather than progress. There followed *The Inheritors* (1955), about the doom of the Neanderthal age in the face of the evolution of *Homo sapiens*, while *Pincher Martin* (1955) is about a naval officer who drifts aimlessly in the Atlantic and latches on to a barren rock, reliving his past in rambling form, only to be concluded with a trick ending. These novels set the style of his allegorical preoccupation with humanity's constant struggle between the civilised self and a darker nature. *Sometime, Never* (1956), three tales written with John WYNDHAM and Mervyn PEAKE, was followed by *Free Fall* (1959), which depicts the flashbacks of an artist while in a Nazi prison, and *The Spire* (1964), about the obsession of a fourteenth-century clergyman in building a 400-foot spire above his church, in an allegory about overweening pride and the Fall. The novellas in *The Pyramid* (1967) and *The Scorpion God* (1971) were followed by yet another exploration of morality in *Darkness Visible* (1979). His maritime trilogy 'To the Ends of the Earth' consists of *Rites of Passage* (1980, Booker Prize), *Close Quarters* (1987) and *Fire Down Below* (1989), and is an allegory of the British nation depicted in the emotions and high drama of an early nineteenth-century ship on its way to Australia. Other works include the novel *The Paper Men* (1984), about an ageing novelist's conflicts with his publisher, the draft novel *The Double Tongue* (1995), which was published posthumously, volumes of poetry, and a play entitled *The Brass Butterfly* (1958). Occasional essays are collected in *The*

Hot Gates (1965) and *A Moving Target* (1982), while *An Egyptian Journal* (1985) is a travelogue. Many of his books have been adapted for film. He was knighted in 1988, and was the most recent English writer to have been awarded the Nobel Prize for Literature in 1983.

L. Friedman, *William Golding* (1993).

Gombrowicz, Witold (1904–1969) Born in Warsaw, Poland, he graduated in law from the University of Warsaw (1926), and emigrated to Buenos Aires, Argentina, where he worked as a bank employee until 1962. He then lived in Berlin, and finally settled in France in 1964. One of the leading Polish novelists of the twentieth century, who has exerted a great influence on modernity in Polish fiction, his novels include *Ferdydurke* (1937, trans. 1961), the adventures of a 30-year-old man transformed into a schoolboy by an intimidating teacher, *Trans-Atlantyk* (1953, trans. 1994), which is set in Buenos Aires at the beginning of the Second World War, *Pornografia* (1960, trans. 1966), which is set in Poland during the Second World War, and which denounces traditional approaches to love and moral values, and inverts traditional novelistic stereotypes, *Cosmos* (1965, trans. 1966), which depicts a frustrating effort to find patterns in a world of confusing 'clues', and the thriller *Possessed: Or, the Secret of Myslotch* (1973, trans. 1980). Other works include *A Kind of Testament* (1968, trans. 1973), *Three Plays* (trans. 1998), and his *Diary* (trans. 1988), which spans the years 1953 to 1956. Blending fiction and non-fiction, literary games and personal content, his writing is highly intellectual and is offset by Rabelaisian clowning and carnivalesque, a style which anticipates postmodernism in his oscillations between destruction and construction. Parodying long-established genres with metafictional commentary, structure, form and pattern are the key to his fiction.

E. Thompson, *Witold Gombrowicz* (1979).

Gordimer, Nadine (1923–) A highly regarded writer, born in Springs, South Africa, she attended the University of Witwatersrand for one year. She began writing early, with her first story published in 1939, when she was still a teenager. Her first novel was *The Lying Days* (1953), in which the protagonist Helen rebels against the bigotry of her parents' world, as the novel explores impotence of white middle-class liberalism in the face of apartheid. This became a consistent theme in her fiction, which has consistently opposed racial injustice over a period of fifty years. Subsequent novels include *A World of Strangers* (1958), *Occasion for Loving* (1963), *The Late Bourgeois World* (1966), often regarded as one of her best works and banned for its explicit condemnation of South African society. There followed *Guest of Honour* (1971), a somewhat pessimistic book about a post-apartheid future, *The Conservationist* (1974, joint winner Booker Prize), about an Afrikaner industrialist's struggle to reclaim the wilderness and unsuccessfully trying to defend it from black squatters, *Burger's Daughter* (1979), which depicts the political and cultural impasses faced by the daughter of well-known Marxist parents in South Africa, and *July's People* (1981), which again looks to a possible post-apartheid future. *A Sport of Nature* (1987) was succeeded by *My Son's Story* (1990), which explored interracial relations as the son of a black activist falls in love with a white woman, *None to Accompany Me* (1994), which examines two families, one black and one white, as they move into the post-apartheid era, and most recently, *The House Gun* (1998), an examination of the social issues facing South Africa in the aftermath of the transition to majority rule. Her short story collections include *Face to Face* (1949), *Six Feet of the Country* (1956), *Friday's Footprint* (1960), *Livingstone's Companions* (1971), *A Soldier's Embrace* (1980), *Something Out There* (1984), *Jump* (1991) and *Why Haven't You Written?* (1993). Her critical studies include *The Black Interpreters* (1973), *The Essential Gesture: Writing, Politics and Places* (1988), and other non-fiction includes *Lifetimes: Under Apartheid* (1986), *Crimes of Conscience* (1991) and *Living in Hope and History* (1999), which is notes on the twentieth century. She has written several documentaries, collaborating with her son Hugh Cassirer on the television film *Choosing for Justice: Allan Boesak*. She was awarded the Nobel Prize for Literature in 1991. An active campaigner against censorship and apartheid, she taught in various American universities during the 1960s and 1970s.

J. Newman, *Nadine Gordimer* (1988); D. Head, *Nadine Gordimer* (1994).

Gordon, Mary (1949–) Born on Long Island, New York in the US, Mary Catherine Gordon attended Barnard College (BA 1971) and Syracuse University (MA 1973), and has taught at Poughkeepsie and Amherst colleges. Writing fiction which often reflects her Catholicism and interest in feminism, her first novel, *Final Payments* (1978), is about a young girl's attempt to remake her life after caring for her terminally ill father for eleven years and her sense of self-sacrifice. *The Company of Women* (1980) studies a conservative priest's influence on the lives of several women, while *Men and Angels* (1985) concerns the relationships forged between women and men. *The Other Side* (1989), about Irish immigrants travelling to the US, is a generational story of self-sacrifice and the limitations of love, told within the structure of a single day. Considered some of her finest writing,

The Rest of Life (1993) is three novellas about women's relationships; while more recently, she has written the memoir of her father's shadowy past in *The Shadow Man* (1996), a novel in *Spending* (1998), about the values we place on money, sex and art, and reflections on place and identity in *Seeing Through Places* (2000). In addition to the short story collection *Temporary Shelter* (1987), she has published essays in *Good Boys and Dead Girls* (1992) and a biography of Joan of Arc (2000).

Gorky, Maxim (1868–1936) Born Alexei Maximovich Peshkov, in Nizhny-Novgorod, Russia, he is one of the most prominent Russian writers of the early twentieth century. In the early 1900s, he established one of the first Bolshevik newspapers, and went into exile in 1905, travelling and settling in Italy until 1913. During the Russian Revolution, he wrote political articles and eventually returned to the USSR in 1931. His novels include *Foma Gordeiev* (trans. 1901), *Mother* (trans. 1907), *A Confession* (1908, trans. 1910), *The Artamonov Business* (1925, trans. 1948), a series of novels written between 1927 and 1936 in *Bystander* (trans. 1930), *The Magnet* (trans. 1931), *Other Fires* (trans. 1933) and *The Specter* (trans. 1938), and *Orphan Paul* (trans. 1946). In addition to short stories in *Twenty-Six Men and a Girl* (1902, trans. 1928), *Creatures That Once Were Men* (trans. 1905) and *Chelkash* (trans. 1915), he also wrote several plays and the acclaimed autobiographical works of *My Childhood* (1915, trans. 1928) and *The Autobiography of Maxim Gorky* (trans. 1949). One of the earliest practitioners of socialist realism, he presents sympathetic portrayals of proletarian heroes with the emphasis on the physical difficulties in their lives. His later works defended the Soviet system, and he became so famous that his hometown was renamed Gorky

by the Soviet authorities. He was presumed murdered in a puzzling death.

F. Borras, *Maxim Gorky the Writer* (1967).

Goudge, Elizabeth (1900–1984) Born in
Wells, England, she attended Reading
University Art School for two years, and
then taught design and applied art between 1922 and 1932, before becoming a
writer in 1938. After her first novel *Island
Magic* (1934), she published a large number of novels, plays and short stories,
including *A City of Bells* (1936), *Gentian
Hill* (1949), and a trilogy set in Devon in
The Bird in the Tree (1940), *The Herb of
Grace* (1948) and *The Heart of the
Family* (1953), which describes the lives
of the Eliot family of Damerosehay. Her
most famous work was *Green Dolphin
Country* (1944, filmed 1947), about a
female character who chafes against the
restrictions of gender, in a narrative focusing upon three interwoven life stories. In
fifteen novels with historical settings, her
popular fiction describes an underlying
peace and certainty as sensitivity and
moral heroism redeem all sorrows of love
or marriage in quiet dependable narratives. In addition to several children's
books, *The Joy of Snow* (1974) was an
autobiography, which manifests her
strongly held Christianity.

Goytisolo, Juan (1931–) Born in Barcelona, Spain, he went to the universities of
Madrid and Barcelona (1948–1952),
where he was a leading member of the
Turia literary group, along with writers
like MATUTE. He emigrated to France,
where he became the editor of Editions
Gaillimard in Paris (1958–1968). One of
the best-known novelists of his generation
outside Spain, his first book to gain wide
recognition was *The Young Assassins*
(1954, trans. 1959), focusing on delin-
quent children from well-to-do families.
There followed *Children of Chaos* (1955,
trans. 1958), a study of youthful innocence destroyed in the Spanish Civil War,

Fiestas (1958, trans. 1960), *Island of
Women* (1961, trans. 1962) and *The
Party's Over* (1962, trans. 1966). Alvaro
Mendiola is the protagonist in a trilogy –
Marks of Identity (1966, trans. 1988),
Count Julian (1970, trans. 1990) and
Juan the Landless (1975, trans. 1990) –
all three novels characterised by linguistic
experimentation and an attack on the
Franco regime. Other novels include *Mak-
bara* (1980, trans. 1981), *Landscapes
After the Battle* (1982, trans. 1987), *The
Virtues of the Solitary Bird* (1988, trans.
1991), the latter a complex novel, combining Christianity, mysticism and sensuality, *Quarantine* (1991, trans. 1994),
and *The Marx Family Saga* (1993, trans.
1996), a surreal, witty handling of Marx's
family life. Other works include the autobiographies *Forbidden Territory* (1985,
trans. 1989) and *Realms of Strife* (1986,
trans. 1990), in which he acknowledges
his homosexuality and discusses creative
processes, selected literary essays in *Saracen Chronicles* (trans. 1992) and the
Marrakesh Tales (2000). Haunted by the
Spanish Civil War, his cryptic postmodern
fiction contrasts the world of make-
believe with reality, although he disavowed his earlier social realist style for
more structuralist and formalist doctrines
in the early 1960s.

A. Six, *Juan Goytisolo: The Case for Chaos*
(1990).

Grace, Patricia (1937–) A Maori author,
born in Wellington, New Zealand, she
descends from the Ngati Toa and Te Ati
Awa tribes. After training, she worked as
a schoolteacher in the King Country,
North Island, and since the 1970s, has
lived on ancestral lands as a teacher. Her
short stories appeared in the 1960s and
1970s in such magazines as *Landfall*,
Islands and *Te Ao Hou*, many of which
have been collected in *Waiariki* (1975),
which was the first collection by a Maori
woman, *Dream Sleepers* (1980), *Electric
City* (1987), *Selected Stories* (1991), *The*

Sky People (1994) and *Collected Stories* (1994). Her first novel was *Mutuwhenua: The Moon Sleeps* (1978), which looks at the effects on Maori lives of tensions between Maori and Pakeha (white New Zealand) lifestyles. It depicts the social and cultural dislocation of a young woman before she receives help from her extended family. Other novels are *Potiki* (1986), which depicts the regeneration of a Maori community and the history and culture of the Maoris, *Cousins* (1992) and *Baby No-Eyes* (1998). She has written a pictorial representation of women from Maori mythology in *Wahine Toa: Women from Maori Myth* (1984) for young adults, and several children's books. Charting the rhythms of Maori speech, she has gradually moved to a position where Maori language and objects take a central position in New Zealand culture.

P. Beatson, *The Healing Tongue* (1989).

Graham, Winston (1909–) Born Winston Mawdsley Graham, in Manchester, England, he began freelance writing in 1934, and has published prolifically, from his first novel *The House with the Stained-Glass Window* (1934) to his most recent *The Ugly Sister* (1998). Many of his novels are set in coastal Cornwall and include such titles as *Take My Life* (1947), *Night Without Stars* (1950), *Fortune Is a Woman* (1950) and *The Sleeping Partner* (1955). *Marnie* (1960, filmed in 1964 by Alfred Hitchcock) is about an unconventional heroine protagonist trying to break out of her past life of theft and embezzlement, and recently, in *Tremor*, (1995) he examines the effects of an earthquake on holidaymakers in Morocco. He is perhaps most famous for his series of novels about the Poldark and Warleggan families, beginning with *Ross Poldark* (1945), set in eighteenth-century Cornwall, and made into a popular BBC television series in 1975, and continuing with such novels as *The Twisted Sword* (1990), *The Loving Cup* (1996) and

Warleggan (1996). Short stories occur in *The Japanese Girl* (1971), and history in *The Spanish Armada* (1972) and *Poldark's Cornwall* (1983). A writer who is adept at handling atmosphere and suspense, his fiction depicts an interest in character psychology in works which cover mystery, suspense, historical novels and non-fiction.

Grass, Günter (1927–) Born Günter Wilhelm Grass, in Danzig, Germany (now Gdansk, Poland), after war service, he trained as an artist and sculptor at the State Academy of Fine Arts, Berlin (1953–1955). He has worked at a variety of jobs, but has become an internationally acclaimed and honoured novelist. He established his reputation with the volumes of *The Danzig Trilogy* (1980, trans. 1987), which consists of *The Tin Drum* (1959, trans. 1962, filmed 1979), *Cat and Mouse* (1961, trans. 1963) and *Dog Years* (1963, trans. 1965). Set in Danzig, the city becomes the prism through which he conveys his vision of the world, as he investigates the crimes of the Nazis, the complicity of the citizens, the suppression of guilt, economic reconstruction and the loss of moral values in the contemporary post-war reality. There followed *Local Anaesthetic* (trans. 1969), an examination of contemporary politics in the Vietnam War and radical student protests, *From the Diary of a Snail* (1972, trans. 1973), which charts his involvement in the election campaign of his friend Willy Brandt as Chancellor in 1969, and his masterpiece, *The Flounder* (1977, trans. 1978), which embraces the whole sweep of twentieth-century German social and political history, feminism and oppression. Other fiction includes *The Meeting at Telgte* (1979, trans. 1981), *Headbirths: Or, the Germans Are Dying Out* (1980, trans. 1982), about the problems facing the industrial world, *The Rat* (1986, trans. 1988), depicting a dystopian, post-nuclear apocalyptic world, where humans are superseded by rats, and *The Call of the*

Toad (trans. 1992), a historical novel which returns to Danzig to re-enact the fraught relations between Germany and Poland in previous years. His plays are collected in *Four Plays* (trans. 1967), verse in *In the Egg* (trans. 1977), and other non-fiction includes his political speeches, commentaries and open letters in *Speak Out!* (1968, trans. 1969), *Etchings and Words 1972–1982* (1984, trans. 1985), *On Writing and Politics, 1967–1983* (trans. 1985), and *My Century* (1999), in which one hundred short chapters review events from the last millennium. One of the new generation of critical realists, like BÖLL and Martin WALSER, he reminded fellow countrymen of their guilty acquiescence with Nazi Germany. Advocating reform rather than revolution, he has been critical of German re-unification in recent years, and was awarded the Nobel Prize for Literature in 1999.

P. O'Neill, ed., *Critical Essays on Günter Grass* (1987).

Graves, Robert (1895–1985) Born Robert von Ranke Graves, in Wimbledon, London, England, his father was an Anglo-Irish poet and his mother descended from the famous German historian, Leopold von Ranke. Wounded at the Battle of the Somme (1916), he became associated with the war poets Siegfried Sassoon and Wilfred Owen through his volumes of poetry. After the war, he went to Oxford University (B.Litt. 1925), and wrote his famous autobiographical work, *Goodbye to All That* (1929), which looked back at his life at school, at the Front and as a struggling writer. He became Professor of English at the University of Cairo in 1926, where he lived an unconventional domestic relationship with his wife and the American poet Laura Riding, with whom he wrote *A Survey of Modernist Poetry* (1928), a critical work on poetic ambiguity. He separated from his wife and went to live in Majorca (where he

mainly lived for the rest of his life) with Riding, until their separation in 1939. He was hugely prolific after the Second World War, writing around 140 volumes of poetry, short stories, drama and essays. His *Collected Poems* (1986) contain love poetry and witty allegories of modern life. As Professor of Poetry at Oxford University (1961–1966), he also wrote several critical studies of poetry, including *Poetic Craft and Principle* (1967) and *On Poetry* (1969). His novels began with *My Head! My Head!* (1925), but he is most famous for *I Claudius* (1934) and *Claudius the God* (1934), which rank as excellent novels about the Roman period. Among his other novels are *Count Belisarius* (1938), *Sergeant Lamb of the Ninth* (1940), *Proceed, Sergeant Lamb* (1941) *The Golden Fleece* (1944), *King Jesus* (1946) and *Homer's Daughter* (1955). His interest in mythology resulted in the influential *The White Goddess* (1948, rev. 1966), in which he ascribes the poet's impulse to the ancient matriarchal presence, his two volume study of *The Greek Myths* (1955), and *Mammon and the Black Goddess* (1965). In addition to his *Collected Short Stories* (1971), there is a biography of T.E. Lawrence, and he is the translator of many works.

M. Seymour, *Robert Graves* (1995).

Gray, Alisdair (1934–). Born in Glasgow, Scotland, Alasdair James Gray was educated at the Glasgow School of Art (1957), and became a part-time art teacher in the Glasgow region (1958–1962). From 1963, he became a freelance writer, playwright and painter, and rose to literary prominence in the Scottish literary renaissance of the 1980s, with his most acclaimed work, *Lanark: A Life in Four Parts* (1981). A fantasy comedy set in Unthank, an ugly declining city, it depicts the life of Lanark, a lonely man unable to tell his past, and is set in parallel to that of Duncan Thaew in twentieth-century Glasgow. Other novels include *1982*

Janine (1984), which records the sordid fantasies and thoughts of the protagonist during a long night of heavy drinking, *The Fall of Kevin Walker* (1985), *McGrotty and Ludmilla* (1989), *Something Leather* (1990), which was generally poorly received owing to its pornographic passages, and *Poor Things* (1992), which was in better form, and combines eccentric humour with a pastiche of the Victorian novel, in a tale of medical experiments and sexual satire set in Glasgow in the 1880s. His most recent novel is *The History Maker* (1995), a science fiction novel set in the twenty-third century, about war between the Scots and the English. In addition to his collection *An Anthology of Prefaces* (2000), short stories occur in *Unlikely Stories, Mostly* (1983), *Lean Tales* (1985), with James KELMAN, *Ten Tales Tall and True* (1993) and *Five Letters from an Eastern Empire* (1995). His fiction is a mixture of realistic social commentary and vivid fantasy, often accompanied by evocative illustrations by Gray himself. With a reputation as an experimentalist, he draws upon a contemporary Scottish background, albeit one in which Scotland appears in gradual decline.

R. Crawford and T. Nairn, eds, *The Arts of Alasdair Gray* (1991).

Green, Henry (1905–1973) The pseudonym of Henry Vincent Yorke, he was born near Tewkesbury, England, and went to Oxford University without taking a degree. He wrote his first novel *Blindness* (1926) while still at university, about a boy who accidentally loses his sight. He then became a shop-floor worker in a Birmingham engineering factory, writing *Living* (1929) about factory life and developing an impressionistic style of writing with the omission of orthodox grammar. There followed *Party Going* (1939), a comedy of class manners set in a railway station, and the autobiography *Pack My Bag* (1940). During the Second World War, he served in the London Fire

Service, and used his experiences there as the background to *Caught* (1943). He returned to engineering as a manager, but continued to write fiction, including *Loving* (1945), his most successful novel, set in an Irish castle during the war, *Back* (1946), about an injured solider looking for his lost lover upon returning from the war, and *Concluding* (1948), set in a girls' college. He finished with two novels which were attempts to write entirely in dialogue, *Nothing* (1950) and *Doting* (1952). *Surviving* (1992) was a posthumous edition of his uncollected writing. Regarded as a potentially major English novelist of the mid-twentieth century for his explorations of the English working and middle classes and a genuinely innovative style, he became quintessentially English and reclusive in his old age.

R. Mengham, *The Idiom of the Time* (1982).

Greene, Graham (1904–1991) Born Henry Graham Greene, in Berkhamsted, England, he studied history at Oxford University (1922–1925), where he published his only book of poetry, *Babbling April* (1925), and then went into journalism in Nottingham, followed by a job on *The Times* (1926–1930). He converted to Roman Catholicism in 1927 in order to marry, although he remained a doubtful Catholic during his life, evident in many of the later novels regarded as his supreme achievements, like *Brighton Rock* (1938), *The Power and the Glory* (1940), *The Heart of the Matter* (1948) and *The End of the Affair* (1951). His first novel, *The Man Within* (1929), about smuggling in the nineteenth century, was followed by two novels which were later suppressed, *The Name of Action* (1930) and *Rumour at Nightfall* (1931). There followed *Stamboul Train* (1932), which survived a libel action and became very popular, ushering in his distinctive environment of a realistic, seedy arena of disappointed hopes. A prolific writer, he often courted the controversy of libel and censure. Flirting briefly with the socialism of the 1930s, he wrote the satire of industrialism in *England Made Me* (1935), a sympathetic portrayal of Republican Spain in *The Confidential Agent* (1939), and critiques of capitalist economic systems in *It's a Battlefield* (1934) and *A Gun for Sale* (1936). He ran the distinguished literary journal *Night and Day* in 1937, became literary editor of *The Spectator* (1937–1940), and was a director of Bodley Head publishers (1958–1968). He settled in France in 1966. An inveterate traveller, he travelled widely during the 1930s in dangerous and politically unstable parts of the world, which resulted in many travel books, including *Journey Without Maps* (1936) and *The Lawless Roads* (1939). Africa, Mexico, Vietnam, then as an MI6 agent in Sierre Leone during the Second World War, the Far East, Asia and Latin America in the 1950s and 1960s, provided the variety of locations for his novels, such as *The Quiet American* (1955), *Our Man in Havana* (1958), *The Comedians* (1966), set in Haiti, and *The Honorary Consul* (1973), set in Argentina. Other novels include *A Burnt-Out Case* (1961), *Travels with My Aunt* (1969), *The Human Factor* (1978), *Doctor Fischer of Geneva* (1980), *Monsieur Quixote* (1982), and his last published novel, *The Captain and the Enemy* (1988). In addition to autobiography in *A Sort of Life* (1971) and *Ways of Escape* (1980), he also wrote screenplays, most famously *The Third Man* (1950), and essays and articles in *Reflections* (1990). Volumes of *Collected Essays* (1969), *Collected Stories* (1972) and *Collected Plays* (1985) have also appeared. Dealing with the inner psychological stresses and spiritual anxieties of his characters, nearly all his novels have been filmed, which is testimony to his huge popularity and his astute ability to write economic and visually evocative prose.

N. Sherry, *The Life of Graham Greene*, 2 vols (1989 and 1994).

Greenwood, Walter (1903–1974) Born in Salford, England, he did various menial and poorly paid work before writing his first and most famous work, *Love on the Dole* (1933). An overwhelming success, its narrative about unemployment, inhuman factory conditions and the social security benefit system known as the 'dole', helped to instigate social reforms in Parliament. Dramatised in 1934 and filmed in 1941, its achievement as a robust evocation of working-class life was never quite repeated, despite numerous other novels and short stories, including such titles as *His Worship the Mayor* (1934), *Only Mugs Work* (1938), *So Brief the Spring* (1952) and *Saturday Night as the Crown* (1959). In addition to various plays, his autobiography is entitled *There Was a Time* (1967). His novels depicting harsh social conditions, established him as one of the leading British 'proletarian' novelists, foreshadowing the 'angry young men' of the 1950s like John BRAINE and Alan SILLITOE.

Grey, Zane (1872–1939) An American author and the originator of the 'Western' genre, he was born Pearl Grey in Zanesville, Ohio. At first he trained as a dentist, but on successfully publishing *Betty Zane* (1904), based on the diaries of a forebear, he turned to writing. He is most famous for *Riders of the Purple Sage* (1912), a Western romance about rustlers and outlaws set in the canyons of Utah, and exploring the social and religious tensions between the Mormons and others. He wrote over eighty books, most of them Westerns, and other novels include *The Spirit of the Border* (1905), *The Last of the Plainsmen* (1908), *The Heritage of the Desert* (1910), *The Lone Star Ranger* (1915), *The U.P. Trail* (1918), *Call of the Canyon* (1924), *The Thundering Herd* (1925), *Code of the West* (1934) and *West of the Pecos* (1935). Among his non-fiction is *Tales of Fishing* (1925). He established the formula Western as one of America's most popular genres.

S. May, *Zane Grey: Romancing the West* (1997).

Grisham, John (1955–) Born in Jonesboro, Arkansas, US, he gained degrees from Mississippi State University and the University of Mississippi, practised as a lawyer (1981–1990), and was elected to the Mississippi House of Representatives (1984–1990). One of the best-selling novelists in the US, his works are generally legal thrillers written to the formula of innocence caught up in corruption, and many have been turned into successful films. His first novel, *A Time to Kill* (1989), had limited success at first, but was followed by the highly popular *The Firm* (1991), about a Memphis-based law firm and organised crime discovered by new Harvard law graduate Mitchell McDeere. *The Pelican Brief* (1992) focuses on a young female law student's investigation into a conspiracy, and *The Client* (1994) is a legal thriller involving the Mob and the FBI. *The Chamber* (1994) is a less formulaic story about a Ku Klux Klan member on death row being defended by his grandson. He has written a novel a year, and others include *The Rainmaker* (1995), *The Runaway Jury* (1996), *The Partner* (1997), *The Street Lawyer* (1998), *The Testament* (1999), and his most recent, *The Brethren* (2000), which weaves two narratives about ex-judges with an elaborate blackmail scheme and the rise of a presidential candidate.

J. Pringle, *John Grisham* (1997).

Guterson, David (1956–) An American writer, born in Seattle, Washington, and educated at the University of Washington (BA 1978, MA 1982). He was a schoolteacher on Bainbridge Island between 1984 and 1994, and his first book was *The Country Ahead of Us, The Country Behind* (1989), a collection of coming-of-age short stories which met with little success. However, his novel *Like Snow Falling on Cedars* (1995) was widely acclaimed. Set on an island in the northern part of Puget Sound, it is both a love story and a mystery, against a backdrop of racial tensions between Japanese-American farmers and fishermen and their white compatriots. His most recent novel, *East of the Mountains* (1999), concerns the life of a recently widowed heart surgeon, whose spreading cancer spurs him to face death on conditions of his own design.

H

Hagedorn, Jessica T. (1949–) Born in the Philippines, Jessica Tarahata Hagedorn immigrated to the US in the 1960s, where she naturalised. In the 1970s, she worked in New York City as a performance artist. She has published several volumes of poetry, entitled *Dangerous Music* (1975), *Pet Food and Tropical Apparitions* (1981) and *Danger and Beauty* (1993). Her first novel was *Dogeaters* (1989), a collage-like, humorous novel, which presents an unflinching depiction of the contrasts between slum life in the Philippines with the splendour of the dictator President Marcos. A second novel, *The Gangster of Love* (1996), takes the reader from the Philippines to San Francisco and New York City, as a family of immigrants experience the highs and lows of US culture. She co-wrote a play, with Ntozake Shange and T. Nkabinda, called *Where the Mississippi Meets the Amazon* (1977), a screenplay entitled *Fresh Kill* (1994) and *Two Stories* (1992). She has also edited the influential and ambitious anthology of contemporary Asian-American fiction, *Charlie Chan Is Dead* (1993). Known for her graphic poetry and prose, her fiction focuses upon disturbing issues like drug abuse, murder, physical abuse and madness. Generally depicting the lives of outcasts, prostitutes, drag queens and Asians cut off from their culture, her writing shows the influence of the Beats and the postcolonial consciousness of a Filipino woman.

Haley, Alex (1921–1992) Born Alexander Murray Palmer Haley, in Ithaca, New York, he grew up in Tennessee, and joined the US Coast Guard in 1939, for which he worked for twenty years, before becoming a freelance writer in 1959. He began writing sketches of his coastguard work in the 1940s, but it was with a series of interviews with such people as Miles Davis, Martin Luther King, Malcolm X and Muhammad Ali for *Playboy* magazine in the 1960s that he made his name. In 1965, his collaborative efforts resulted in *The Autobiography of Malcolm X*, one of the most influential African-American autobiographies of the twentieth century. His research into his family background emerged in *Roots* (1976, Pulitzer Prize), a seven-generation family chronicle charting the movement from Africa to America as slaves and then gradual freedom. Two major television adaptations made the novel a massive success in the 1970s, and although it was criticised for historical inaccuracy and a lack of originality, it had a huge cultural rather than literary significance, provoking a national discussion about slavery and the legacy of racism in the US. He continued writing short pieces in the 1980s, and wrote *A Different Kind of Christmas* (1988), a historical novel about a slave-owner's son who becomes an abolitionist. *Alex Haley's Queen* (1993) was published posthumously.

Hall, Radclyffe (1886–1943) Born Marguerite Radclyffe Hall, in Bournemouth, England, she attended London University, before turning to writing. Reared as a boy by her parents, she became the companion of Lady Mabel Batten and later, of Batten's niece, Una Troubridge, and wrote numerous volumes of accomplished poetry. She is best known for her partially autobiographical novel *The Well of Loneliness* (1928), one of the first modern fictional works on lesbian relationships. It narrates the story of a young girl called Stephen who is brought up as a boy, detailing her lesbian relationships and her service in the First World War. Condemned and banned upon publication, it is nevertheless regarded as one of the premier lesbian works, opening the door for the acceptance of later writers. Other novels evince the same preoccupations, but were overshadowed by *The Well of Loneliness*. After her early novel *The Forge* (1924), *The Unlit Lamp* (1924) was a thematic precursor in its handling of a same-sex relationship. Other works include *A Saturday Life* (1925), *Adam's Breed* (1926), about a young man's anxiety over the excesses of material consumption in contemporary society and the plight of animals, *The Master of the House* (1932), about a man whose life paralleled that of Jesus Christ, *The Sixth Beatitude* (1936), about a poor woman's unconventional life, and the short stories in *Miss Ogilvy Finds Herself* (1934).

U. Troubridge, *The Life of Radclyffe Hall* (1973).

Hall, Rodney (1935–) A widely honoured Australian novelist, born in Solihull, England, who emigrated to Australia in 1948, where he graduated from the University of Queensland (1971). He worked for the Australian Council for the Arts, and was poetry editor of *The Australian*

(1967–1978). He edited several collections of verse, including *The Collins Book of Australian Poetry* (1981), the first to include a significant amount of Aboriginal writing. He has been a prolific poet, and his verse can be sampled in his *Selected Poems* (1975). His contribution to fiction rests on several novels, the first being *The Ship on the Coin* (1972), a satiric allegory of bourgeois society. There followed *A Place Among People* (1975), which was a suggestive, open-ended, 'imagistic' work, *Just Relations* (1982), a key Australian novel of the 1980s, describing a web of relations between past, present and future, *Kisses of the Enemy* (1987), about a political take-over of Australia by the US, and more recently, *The Island of the Mind* (1996). His much praised *The Yandilli Trilogy* (1994) consists of *Captivity Captive* (1988), about an Irish pioneer family and a triple murder, *Second Bridegroom* (1991) and *The Grisly Wife* (1993). Other works include a portrait of the artist Andrew Sibley (1968), and the text of photography collections of Australia in 1983 and 1988. With a quizzical, almost confrontational stance in his writing, his fiction challenges expectations and displays virtuoso formal techniques.

Hammett, Dashiell (1894–1961) An American writer of 'hard-boiled' crime and detective fiction, born Samuel Dashiell Hammett, in Saint Mary's County, Maryland. He worked as a private detective for Pinkerton's Detective Agency, which later stood him in good stead as a crime writer. He subsequently worked as a scriptwriter for Hollywood, where he met his life-long companion, the playwright and author Lillian Hellman. His first two novels, *Red Harvest* (1929) and *The Dain Curse* (1929) were immensely successful, as was *The Maltese Falcon* (1930, filmed 1941), which introduced his most famous character, Sam Spade. These were followed by his masterpiece, *The Glass Key* (1931), about political corruption in an American city, and *The*

Thin Man (1934), a book in a lighter vein, featuring husband-and-wife detectives Nick and Nora Charles, and which inspired a series of Hollywood films. He also wrote *$106,000 Blood Money* (1943) and a plethora of short stories, many of which were compiled and edited by Ellery Queen. Hammett ran foul of the McCarthyist anti-communist witch-hunts and was briefly imprisoned in 1951. He has emerged as one of the leading American private-eye novelists of the twentieth century, rivalled only by CHANDLER and CAIN.

P. Woolfe, *Beams Falling: The Art of Dashiell Hammett* (1980).

Hamsun, Knut (1859–1952) Born Knut Pedersen, in Lorn, Norway, he worked at a variety of jobs both in Norway and the US, before becoming a farmer in Norway (1918–1952). Considered by many to be the greatest novelist Scandinavia has produced, he was one of the pioneers of psychological literature, developing a stream-of-consciousness style well before the more famous modernists, James JOYCE and Virginia WOOLF. Writing under his pseudonym, his early fiction was adept at portraying the isolated individual from the inside out, using the technique of interior monologue. His four great novels all depict gifted outsiders – isolated, self-destructive and having difficulty in integrating themselves socially. These include *Hunger* (1890, trans. 1920), his first and most famous major work, which attacked naturalistic fiction with its autobiographical depiction of suffering in Oslo and Copenhagen, *Mysteries* (1892, trans. 1927), *Pan, from Lieutenant Thomas Glahn's Papers* (1894, trans. 1955) and *Victoria* (1898, trans. 1923). In a prolific writing career, subsequent novels began to turn attention to the outside world rather than inner consciousness, and include *Look Back on Happiness* (1912, trans. 1940), *Children of the Age* (1913, trans. 1924) and its sequel *Segelfoss Town* (1915,

trans. 1925), *The Woman at the Pump* (1920, trans. 1928), the famous 'August Trilogy', made up of *Wayfarers* (1927, trans. 1980, first trans. as *Vagabonds*, 1930), *August* (1930, trans. 1931) and *The Road Leads On* (1933, trans. 1934), and *The Ring Is Closed* (1936, trans. 1937), about corruption in modern life. Non-fiction includes *The Intellectual Life of Modern America* (1889, trans. 1969), essays depicting the US as a philistine country, memoirs in *On Overgrown Paths* (1949, trans. 1967), and volume one of *Selected Letters* (1990). His later novels tended to be shorter, 'social' works, set in the environment of northern Norway, and concerned with spiritual emptiness, illness, and death as a result of industrialisation. Celebrated with the award of the Nobel Prize for Literature in 1920, his sympathy for Nazi Germany cast a pall over his later life.

H. Naess, *Knut Hamsun* (1984).

Hanrahan, Barbara (1939–1991) Born in Adelaide, Australia, after three years at art college, she taught briefly, before continuing her art studies in London in 1963. After an expatriate existence in London, she settled in Adelaide, where she developed an international reputation as a painter and printmaker. Her vivid evocation of her childhood in the memoir *The Scent of Eucalyptus* (1973) was followed by the sequel *Kewpie Doll* (1984). Among her novels are *Sea Green* (1974), about a young Adelaide artist who travels to London, *The Albatross, Muff* (1977), *Where the Queens All Strayed* (1978), about Edwardian Adelaide, *The Peach Groves* (1979), about Adelaide and New Zealand in the 1880s, *The Frangipani Gardens* (1980), about the seething horrors of Adelaide in the 1920s, *Annie Magdalene* (1985), detailing the obscure life of a woman in an Adelaide suburb, and *Flawless Jude* (1989). Short stories are collected in *Dream People* (1987), while the novel *Good Night,*

Mr. Moon (1992), and the autobiographical works *Iris in Her Garden* (1992) and *Michael and Me and the Sun* (1992) were published posthumously. A nostalgia for early Australia pervades her early novels, which are concerned with the issues of 'centre' and 'periphery', 'home' and 'exile'. A plain but suggestive prose style depicts the seamier sides of Adelaide society, as dark emotions and fantastic impulses lurk below its genteel exterior.

Hardy, Frank (1917–1994) Born in Bacchus Marsh, Victoria, Australia. After 1937, he lived in Melbourne, Sydney and France, and later recorded his experiences of rural work, unemployment and Depression poverty in *The Man from Clinkapella* (1951) and *Legends from Benson's Valley* (1963). He joined the Communist Party in 1939, and the Realist Writers' group, and his humorous stories with anti-authoritarian Australian characters often reveal his socialist commitments. His first and best-known novel was *Power Without Glory* (1950), which instigated a criminal libel charge, for which he was acquitted after nine months. Upon a broad social canvas, it was a semi-fictional account of the millionaire John Wren, and blurred documentary and fictional genres in its exploration of corruption. Socialist realism structures his early stories and *Journey into the Future* (1952) recounts a trip to the USSR, while multiple narrators emerge in *The Four-Legged Lottery* (1958) and *But the Dead Are Many* (1975), a study of Marxist intellectuals. Later work returns obsessively to the writing of his first novel and the trial, in *The Hard Way* (1961) and *Who Shot George Kirkland?* (1980), exploring the relation of truth, fiction, history and artistic motivation. Other works include *The Unlucky Australians* (1968), *The Outcasts of Foolgarah* (1971), *The Obsession of Oscar Oswald* (1983) and *The Loser Now Will Be Later to Win* (1985). He is also known for his

collections of light yarns by Billy Borker, a bar dweller and folksy humorist (1965 and 1967). *A Frank Hardy Swag* (1982) is a collection of his controversial articles.

P. Admas, *The Stranger from Melbourne, Frank Hardy: A Literary Biography* (1999).

Harris, Wilson (1921–) Born Theodore Wilson Harris, in New Amsterdam, British Guiana (now Guyana), he emigrated to Britain in 1959. After studying surveying and geomorphology, he worked as a government surveyor in Guyana and became a full-time writer in 1959. His best-known work is the 'Guiana Quartet', and consists of *Palace of the Peacock* (1960), *The Far Journey of Oudin* (1961), *The Whole Armour* (1962) and *The Secret Ladder* (1963), and which features the landscape of the Guyanese interior and the history of the country's successive conquests by foreigners. A prolific writer, his other novels include *Heartland* (1964), *The Eye of the Scarecrow* (1965), *Tumatamuri* (1968), *The Tree of the Sun* (1978), and 'The Carnival Trilogy', which consists of *Carnival* (1985), *The Infinite Rehearsal* (1987) and *The Four Banks of the River of Space* (1990). Recent novels include *Resurrection at Sorrow Hill* (1993), and *Jonestown* (1996), which interweaves Latin American history with the story of a fictional survivor of the mass suicide in Jonestown, Guyana, in 1978. Short stories occur in *The Sleepers of Roraima* (1970) and *The Age of the Rainmakers* (1971). In addition to volumes of poetry, his nonfiction includes the essays in *Tradition, the Writer, and Society* (1967), *The Womb of Space* (1983), *The Radical Imagination* (1992) and *The Selected Essays of Wilson Harris: The Unfinished Genesis of the Imagination* (1999). His fiction breaks the boundaries between dreams, hallucinations, psychic experiences and history, and blends complex symbolism and metaphors to create new visions of reality. Operating at a high level of abstraction, he envisages a new world of cultural heterogeneity.

H. Maes-Jelineck, *Wilson Harris* (1982).

Harrison, Jim (1937–) Born James Thomas Harrison, in Grayling, Michigan, US, he was educated at Michigan State University (BA 1960, MA 1964), and has developed a reputation as both a novelist and poet, publishing several volumes of poetry, including *Plain Song* (1965) and *Selected and New Poems, 1961–1981* (1982). He has published many novels: his early works include *Wolf: A False Memoir* (1971), about rejecting civilisation for life in the rural outback of Michigan; a Vietnam story in *A Good Day to Die* (1973); and *Farmer* (1976). He is perhaps best known for his three novellas *Legends of the Fall* (1979), which reached a wider audience with the film (1994), about redemption and revenge, in violent portraits of men and their exposure to fate and their obsessions in a rural setting. Other novels include *Warlock* (1981), *Sundog* (1984), set in the wilds of Michigan as a dam-builder narrates his life, *Dalva* (1988), about a part-Sioux businesswoman and the treatment of the Native-Americans, and *The Road Home* (1998), which continues the story of Dalva and her ancestry on the Midwestern prairies. Novellas occur in *The Woman Lit by Fireflies* (1990) and *Julip* (1994), which are built on myths of masculinity, while *Just Before Dark* (1991) collects non-fiction. Often making environmental statements in his fiction, his generally allusive and eclectic work is about people's struggles in the natural world.

E. Reilly, *Jim Harrison* (1996).

Hartley, L.P. (1895–1972) Full name Leslie Poles Hartley, an English author, born in Whittlesey, Cambridgeshire, and educated at Oxford University. His first book was a collection of short stories, *Night Fears* (1924), followed by other stories in *The Killing Bottle* (1932). He spent much of his adult life in Venice, which formed the setting for his novella *Simonetta Perkins* (1925). His major work was a trilogy about a brother and sister: *The Shrimp and the Anemone* (1944), *The Sixth Heaven* (1946) and *Eustace and Hilda* (1947). *The Boat* (1949) is about a recluse and loner who tries to avoid the English ethic of 'togetherness' during the Second World War. His most critically successful novel, *The Go-Between* (1953, filmed 1970), is about a boy who conveys messages between two lovers, and whose relationship he inadvertently destroys. Other books include *A Perfect Woman* (1957), *Poor Clare* (1963), *The Brickfield* (1964), *My Sister's Keeper* (1970), which again explores a brother and sister relationship, *The Harness Room* (1971), and the posthumously published *The Will and the Way* (1973). Much of his fiction nostalgically evokes childhood in the Norfolk landscape, and as a writer, he is preoccupied with Freud's teachings on the formation of identity, British moral values and class interaction. A collection of his essays occurs in *The Novelist's Responsibility* (1968).

Hasek, Jaroslav (1883–1923) Jaroslav Matej Frantisek Hasek was born in Prague, Czechoslovakia, and graduated from the Czechoslavonic Commercial Academy (1902). He became a writer in 1901, but also worked as a clerk, editor and cabaret performer. He served in the Austrian army during the First World War, was captured by the Russians in 1915, and took the opportunity to join the Free Czech Legion against the Austro-Hungarian empire. An internationally famous Czech author who wrote over 1,200 stories, his reputation rests entirely upon the four-volume incomplete novel *The Good Soldier Svejk and His Fortunes in the World War* (1920–1923, trans. 1973). A cynical and satiric treatment of all forms of ideology, it depicts the picaresque wanderings and adventures of the idiot-hero Svejk. An anti-establishment satirist and representative of the counter-culture to the Austro-Hungarian Germanic minority, Hasek was concerned with unmasking the reality hidden behind the pretence and rhetoric of the State. Other works include the short story collections of *The Tourist Guide* (1913, trans. 1961) and *The Red Commissar* (trans. 1981), which depict life in central and eastern Europe with gentle irony ranging to vicious satire.

C. Parrott, *Jaroslav Hasek: A Study of 'Svejk' and the Short Stories* (1982).

Hasluck, Nicholas (1942–) An Australian novelist, born in Canberra, he graduated from the universities of Western Australia (1963) and Oxford (1966). A lawyer and versatile writer, he began with several volumes of verse. His novels include *Quarantine* (1978), a suspense-thriller and satire about a group of passengers detained in the Suez Canal, *The Blue Guitar* (1980), about entrepreneurial double-dealing, *The Hand That Feeds You* (1982), a satire about contemporary Australian social preoccupations like cricket and tax evasion, and *The Bellarmine Jug* (1984), arguably his best novel, dealing with the 1629 mutiny and massacre perpetrated by a group from a Dutch vessel. Further novels are *Truant State* (1987), *The Country Without Music* (1990), *The Blosseville File* (1992) and *A Grain of Truth* (1994). Short stories are collected in *The Hat on the Letter 'O'* (1978), and other works include the prose writings in *A Chinese Journey* (1985), with C.J. KOCH, *Collage: Recollections of the Universe of Western Australia* (1987), and autobiographical writings from his distinguished legal career in *Offcuts from a Legal Literary Life* (1993).

Hau'ofa, Epeli (1939–) Born in Salamo, Papua New Guinea, of Tongan missionary parents, he trained as a social anthropologist at McGill University, Canada, and at the Australian National University, Can-

berra (Ph.D.), and started as a tutor in anthropology at the University of the South Pacific, Fiji. He became a secretary to the King of Tonga (1978), and in 1981 returned to academia at the University of the South Pacific, where he became a Professor of Sociology (1983). His early writing was non-fictional, with sociological studies in *Our Crowded Islands* (1977), *Corned Beef and Tapioca* (1979), and *Mekes* (1981), about the inequalities of village life. His fiction writing started with *Tales of the Tikongs* (1983), which were stories linked by issues of racism, poverty and corruption, and *Kisses in the Nederends* (1987), the bizarre adventures of the protagonist Bamboki, which allegorises the pain in the South Pacific caused by the accelerated changes brought about by colonialism and neo-colonialism. His perspective is pan-Pacific and international, and like Albert WENDT, he employs both oral and literary modes in a style which is exuberant and humorous.

Hawkes, John (1925–1998) Born John Clendennin Burne Jr. Hawkes, in Stanford, Connecticut, US, and educated at Harvard University (BA 1949), he was Professor of English at Brown University until 1958. Often characterised as an avant-garde writer whose work reflects upon the status of fiction, his first novel, *The Cannibal* (1949), was a surrealistic work containing two related stories about devastation in post-Second World War Germany. Other novels include *The Beetle Leg* (1951), *The Lime Twig* (1961), about the psychopathic effects on a man during and after the London Blitz, *Second Skin* (1964), *The Frog* (1964), about a young French boy who swallows a frog who becomes a permanent resident named Armand, *The Blood Oranges* (1971), *Travesty* (1976), which is about erotic pleasure derived from driving and speed, *Owl* (1977), *Universal Fears* (1978), *The Passion Artist* (1979), *Virginie, Her Two Lives* (1982), which alludes to de Sade's work, and *Whistlejacket* (1997). His most recent fiction is *An Irish Eye* (1997), about a young foundling girl. Four plays occur in *The Innocent Party* (1966), early fiction is collected in *Lunar Landscapes* (1969), and a 'fictional autobiography' occurs in *Adventures in the Alaskan Skin Trade* (1985). His unconventional narrative methods construe structure as the most significant aspect of fiction to the exclusion of plot, character, theme and setting, and his narratives contain a dreamlike pace and feel. Often admiringly compared to other postmodern writers, his oblique and highly idiosyncratic novels depict a world of fragmentation, self-destruction and absurdity.

R. Ferrari, *Innocence, Power, and the Novels of John Hawkes* (1996).

Head, Bessie (1937–1986) Born in Pietermaritzburg, South Africa, of racially mixed parentage, Bessie Amelia Head trained as a primary schoolteacher and taught for four years in South Africa and Botswana. She also spent two years as a journalist at *Drum* publications in Johannesburg. Exiled from South Africa, in 1963 she moved to Botswana, where she remained until her death. Her adopted country formed the subject matter of much of her writing, and her first novel, *When Rain Clouds Gather* (1969), is a vivid account of Botswana village life, and the relationship between an Englishman and an embittered black South African. *Maru* (1971) is also about a Botswana village, and the problems caused by the arrival of a new teacher with whom two chiefs fall in love, while *A Question of Power* (1973) concerns a young woman experiencing mental breakdown, exploring madness, sexuality and guilt in an attack on the indignities perpetrated by apartheid. Short stories occur in *The Collector of Treasures* (1977), which explores the position of women in African life. *Serowe: Village of the Rainwind* (1981) and *A Bewitched Crossroad* (1984) are historical accounts and interviews combined with regional folklore, spanning a period from 1875 to 1959. An early novel and stories were posthumously published in *The Cardinal* (1993), autobiographical writings in *A Woman Alone* (1990), and biographical writings in *A Gesture of Belonging* (1991). Her work is deeply personal, and her abiding concern is with discrimination in all its forms.

G. Eilersen, *Bessie Head, Realist and Drummer: Her Life and Writings* (1994).

Hearne, John (1926–) Born in Montreal, Canada, of Jamaican parents, John Edgar Caulwell Hearne was brought up in Jamaica and attended Jamaica College and Edinburgh University (BA 1950). After gaining a teaching diploma, he taught at schools in London (1950–1959) before becoming a lecturer at the University of the West Indies in Kingston, Jamaica, in 1962. His first novel was *Voices Under the Window* (1955). He then wrote a series of novels which took place on Cayuna, a mythical exotic counterpart to Jamaica, which included *Stranger at the Gate* (1956), *The Faces of Love* (1957), *The Autumn Equinox* (1959) and *Land of the Living* (1961). With Morris Cargill, he wrote *Fever Grass* (1969) and *The Candywine Development* (1970), under the joint pseudonym of John Morris. Under his own name, he wrote *The Sure Salvation* (1981), set on a sailing ship in the South Atlantic, chronicling the slave trade. His short stories have appeared in numerous anthologies, and his other works include *Our Heritage* (1963), an anthology of Caribbean fiction in *Carifesta Forum* (1976), and a selection of the speeches of Jamaican Prime Minister Michael Manley in *Search for Solutions* (1976). Composing vivid depictions of life among the West Indies and its people, his focus falls mainly on Jamaica and its complex moral and social problems and inequities.

L. James, ed., *The Islands in Between* (1968).

Heath, Roy A.K. (1926–) Full name Roy Aubrey Kelvin Heath, born in Georgetown, Guyana, he worked as a civil servant in Guyana (1942–1950), and then at various clerical jobs in London (1951–1958). After graduating from London University (BA 1956), although he was called to the Bar in 1964, he became a schoolteacher of French and German. His early novels were *A Man Came Home* (1974), about the 'yard society' of Georgetown, and *The Murderer* (1978), about the mental turmoil of the protagonist leading to a murder. There followed *The Armstrong Trilogy* (1994) – *From the Heat of the Day* (1979), *One Generation* (1980) and *Genetha* (1981) – which is set in Guyanese culture of the 1920s to the 1950s, and centres upon the Armstrong family and upon the paranoid men and the women they destroy in their madness. Other novels include *Kwaku: Or, the Man Who Could Not Keep His Mouth Shut* (1982), which is a trickster narrative about a shoemaker in a Guyanese village, *Orealla* (1984), about class and racial prejudice in Guyanese society, *The Shadow Bride* (1988), about East Indians living in Guyana, and *Ministry of Hope, or, the Metamorphosis of Kwaku* (1996), about getting ahead in political corruption in Guyana. Other works include lectures in *Art and History* (1983) and a memoir in *Shadows Round the Moon* (1990). Offering detailed descriptions of the city of Georgetown, Guyana, he has chronicled twentieth-century Guyana through a complex web of psychological characterisations, myths, dreams, customs and prejudices, while evoking a deep compassion for the land of his birth.

Heinesen, William (1900–1991) Born in Tórshavn, in the Faroe Islands, he went to the Copenhagen School of Commerce (1916–1919), and worked as a journalist until 1932. One of the outstanding writers of twentieth-century Scandinavia, although he began writing poetry (much of which is untranslated into English), he is chiefly known for his prose, and later in life, his short stories. Although he wrote in Danish rather than Faroese, he is an intensely Faroese writer, and, uniquely, presents the Faroe Islands as a microcosm intelligible to all outsiders. His major novels include *The Black Cauldron* (1949, trans. 1992), *The Lost Musicians* (1950, trans. 1971), *The Kingdom of the Earth* (1952, trans. 1971), his masterpiece *The Good Hope* (1964, trans. 1981), which is an historical novel and an allegory about a fascist dictatorship, *The Tower at the Edge of the World* (1976, trans. 1981) and *Laterna Magica* (1985, trans. 1987). His short stories are in *The Winged Darkness* (1985, trans. 1987). With stylistic and linguistic brilliance, his fiction moves into the realms of fantasy and imagination, reflecting humanity's place in the universe, confronting life and death, and the mystery of the human psyche.

H. Brønner, *Three Faroese Novelists* (1973).

Heinlein, Robert A. (1907–1988) A widely praised American science fiction writer, he was born Robert Anson Heinlein, in Butler, Missouri, and educated at the University of Missouri at Columbia, the US Naval Academy at Annapolis, and the University of California at Los Angeles. He began writing professionally in 1939, with short stories for the magazine *Astounding Science*, and his first books, *Rocket Ship Galileo* (1947) and *Space Cadet* (1948), were both for children. He continued to publish a large number of stories and novels for adults and children, including the collections *The Man Who Sold the Moon* (1950), *Assignment in Eternity* (1953), *Destination Moon* (1979) and *Expanded Universe* (1980), although after the 1940s he largely avoided shorter fiction. His best-known novel is *Stranger in a Strange Land* (1961), which concerns a human raised by Martians, who, upon returning to Earth, becomes the centre of a new religion. Other novels include the successful *Starship Troopers* (1959), about a war between insects and humans on alien worlds, which was made into a spoof science fiction film (1997), *Beyond This Horizon* (1948), *The Puppet Masters* (1951), *Double Star* (1956), *Citizen of the Galaxy* (1957), *Methuselah's Children* (1958) and *Glory Road* (1963). *The Moon Is a Harsh Mistress* (1966) is an account of a revolt of moon colonists against Earth's government; and in *I Will Fear No Evil* (1970), a dying man's brain is transplanted into a woman's body. Later fiction includes *Friday* (1982) and *Job* (1984), while the travel memoir *Tramp Royale* (1992) and *Fantasies of Robert Heinlein* (1999) have been published posthumously. Exploring the impact of changes in technology and science on society, especially the effects of space travel, he is known for his convincing creation of future worlds with strong heroes who exploit and domesticate the universe.

Heller, Joseph (1923–) Heller was born in Brooklyn, New York. After serving with the USAAF in the Second World War, he went to New York University (BA 1948) and Columbia University (MA 1949). He has worked subsequently as a journalist and a university teacher. His most famous first novel, *Catch-22* (1961, filmed 1970), the title of which became a byword for being caught in frustrating circumstances, was published during the Vietnam War and immediately became a significant anti-war statement and part of the 1960s counter-culture. Drawing upon his own experiences in the Second World War, it shows how military bureaucracy and regulations are designed to keep soldiers at war indefinitely by staying one step ahead. In the book, Yossarian, a pilot in the airforce, pleads to be grounded for his madness, but catch-22 states that anyone rational enough to want to be grounded could not possibly be insane, and therefore must return to duties. This was followed by *Something Happened* (1974),

which depicts the psychological alienation of Bob Slocum's life caused by the world of business and capitalism. Controversial for its depiction of Jewish-Americans, *Good as Gold* (1979) portrays the absurd workings of politics and government in Washington DC, in which Gold opportunistically pursues his political ambitions. *God Knows* (1984) is a satiric novel about the Bible in which the narrator is a cocky Old Testament hero, David; while *Picture This* (1988) is a reflection on such historical figures as Rembrandt, Socrates, Plato and various American presidents and political institutions. More recently, he has written a sequel to *Catch-22* in *Closing Time* (1994), which depicts Yossarian and some of the other characters in the 1990s, and *Now and Then* (1998), a memoir of growing up on Coney Island. His latest novel, *Portrait of an Artist, as an Old Man* (2000), is about a writer seeking inspiration for his next novel. Apart from numerous screenplays and two plays, there is also the non-fictional *No Laughing Matter* (1986), written with his friend Speed Vogel, who aided him through a convalescence from a nerve disease.

T. Tanner, *City of Words* (1971).

Helprin, Mark (1947–) Born in New York City, US, and raised in the West Indies, he was educated at Harvard University (BA 1969, MA 1972), and has served in the Israeli Defence Forces. Defined by its large, elaborate style, his first work was a collection of short stories, *A Dove of the East* (1975), and along with one other collection, *Ellis Island* (1981), showed his ability to mix realism and fantasy. His first novel, *Refiner's Fire: The Life and Adventures of Marshall Pearl, a Foundling* (1977), was a picaresque tale, which was followed by *Winter's Tale* (1983), a mythic story of New York City trying to free itself from crime and poverty, and *Swan Lake* (1989). Two further novels followed: the wide-ranging *A Soldier of the Great War* (1991), set in the First

World War on the Austrian-Italian front, depicting the meaninglessness of war with the loss of youth and age; and *Memoir from Antproof Case* (1995), a memoir of an elderly narrator, written in a document kept in an ant-proof case. He has recently written two children's books, *A City in Winter* (1996) and *The Veil of Sorrows* (1997).

Helwig, David (1938–) A Canadian novelist and poet, he was born and raised in Toronto, but has been associated with Kingston, Ontario for most of his life. He completed degrees at the universities of Toronto (BA 1960) and Liverpool, England (MA 1962), and then taught at Queen's University in Kingston for nearly twenty years, although he has been a professional, full-time writer since 1980. With fiction that is often low-key and intimate, and associated with small presses, he has not become well-known despite being prolific. *After the Day Before Tomorrow* (1971), about a diplomat turned spy, he produced a tetralogy set in Kingston: *The Glass Knight* (1976), *Jennifer* (1979), *It Is Always Summer* (1982) and *A Sound Like Laughter* (1983). Other novels include *The King's Evil* (1981), which juxtaposes contemporary life with historical events, *The Bishop* (1986), *The Only Son* (1984), *A Postcard from Rome* (1988), *Old Wars* (1989), *Of Desire* (1990), *A Random Gospel* (1996), *The Child of Someone* (1997) and *The Time of Her Life* (2000). He has edited several collections of essays on Canadian culture in *The Human Elements* (1978), *The Human Elements II* (1981) and *Love and Money* (1980), and short stories occur in *The Streets of Summer* (1969). In addition to radio plays, volumes of poetry include *Figures in the Landscape* (1967), the narrative poem *Atlantic Crossing* (1974), *The Hundred Old Names* (1988) and *The Beloved* (1992).

Hemingway, Ernest (1899–1961) An American writer, born Ernest Miller

Hemingway, in Oak Park, Illinois. His style is direct and the subject matter is intensely masculine, reflecting his love of hunting, fishing and bullfighting, his physical courage and his fascination with war. After early work as a journalist, he was a combatant in the First World War, and then acted as a war correspondent during both the Spanish Civil War and the Second World War. After serving with distinction in the First World War, he returned home and worked in Chicago, writing and doing odd jobs. He then went to Paris where he mixed with a number of expatriate writers, like Scott FITZGERALD, Ford Madox FORD and Ezra Pound, whom Gertrude STEIN dubbed 'the lost generation'. His earliest work was *Three Stories and Ten Poems* (1923). *In Our Time* (1925), a book of short stories, followed, and then the novel *The Sun Also Rises* (1926, published as *Fiesta* in Britain), about a group of amoral American and British expatriates living in France and Spain after the Great War. More short stories occurred in *Men Without Women* (1927) and *Winner Take Nothing* (1933). Hemingway's second important novel is *A Farewell to Arms* (1929), a poignant story of a young American officer serving in Italy during the Great War who falls in love with an English nurse. Two works of non-fiction followed with *Death in the Afternoon* (1932), about bullfighting, and a book about big-game hunting in Tanganyika, *The Green Hills of Africa* (1935). *To Have and Have Not* (1937) is set in Key West, Florida during the Great Depression, while *The Fifth Column and the First Forty-nine Stories* (1938) contains further short stories, including the well-known 'The Snows of Kilimanjaro'. His next major novel, *For Whom the Bell Tolls* (1940), drew on his experiences in the Spanish Civil War, and is the story of an American who joins a Republican guerrilla group behind Nationalist lines. *Across the River and Into the Trees* (1950) received little acclaim, but *The*

Old Man and the Sea (1952; Pulitzer Prize 1953), a story about an old Cuban fisherman, was widely esteemed. Other posthumous works include *A Moveable Feast* (1964), which is a collection of anecdotes of his apprentice years in Paris, the novels *Islands in the Stream* (1970) and *The Garden of Eden* (1987), another bullfighting work in *The Dangerous Summer* (1985), and a 'fictional memoir' completed by his son, entitled *True at First Light* (1999). Many of his novels and stories were made into films and he received the Nobel Prize for Literature in 1954. In 1960, Hemingway was treated for depression and mental illness, but a year later he took his life.

C. Baker, *Ernest Hemingway: A Life Story* (1969); W. Williams, *The Tragic Art of Ernest Hemingway* (1981).

Henry, O. (1862–1910) The pseudonym of William Sidney Porter, he was born in Greensboro, North Carolina, US, and after a variety of jobs, began a humorous and satirical newspaper called *The Rolling Stone* in 1894. The newspaper collapsed, and he was tried for embezzlement, but he skipped jail and went into exile in Honduras. Upon his return to the US, he was sentenced to five years in 1897. While in prison in Ohio, he began writing short stories under a variety of pen-names until he settled upon O. Henry. After serving his time, he moved to New York City, where his stories appeared in well-known magazines. His first book was *Cabbages and Kings* (1904), short stories about Honduras, which was followed by stories about New York in *The Four Million* (1906). Having established himself, he wrote prolifically, and among his collections are *Heart of the West* (1907), *The Gentle Grafter* (1908), *The Voice of the City* (1908), *Options* (1909), *Roads of Destiny* (1909), *Strictly Business* (1910), *Whirligig* (1910), *Sixes and Sevens* (1911), *Stones* (1912), *Waifs and Strays* (1917) and *O.*

Henryana (1920). Although his stories frequently suffer from contrived conclusions and sentimentality, this is partially mitigated by his powers of observation and support for the underdog. Posthumous publications include *Postscripts* (1923), *The Complete Works of O. Henry* (1953) and *The Collected Stories of O. Henry* (1979). The annual short story prize in the United States is awarded in his name.

D. Stuart, *O. Henry: A Biography of William Sidney Porter* (1990).

Herbert, Frank (1920–1986) Born in Tacoma, Washington, US, Frank Patrick Herbert attended the University of Washington, Seattle between 1946 and 1947. A West Coast journalist between 1939 and 1969, he was also a successful writer of science fiction, and was most famous for his large 'Dune' trilogy, filmed in 1984 by David Lynch. Consisting of *Dune* (1965), *Dune Messiah* (1970) and *Children of Dune* (1976), it is a narrative of good versus evil, as different political forces vie for control of the desert planet Arrakis, or Dune, with its time-travelling agent known as 'spice', in a complex and wide-ranging exploration of ecological, economic, social and imperial politics. A brilliant creation of imagined worlds, this is one of the most ambitious attempts at a self-consistent, logical alien world, complete with its own languages, ecologies, histories and cultures. He later extended the best-selling trilogy, with *God Emperor of Dune* (1981), *Heretics of Dune* (1984) and *Chapterhouse: Dune* (1985). Other science fiction novels include *The Dragon in the Sea* (1956), *The Eyes of Heisenberg* (1966), *The Green Brain* (1966), *The Heaven Makers* (1968), *Hellstrom's Hive* (1973), *The Dosadi Experiment* (1977), *Direct Descent* (1980) and *The White Plague* (1982). Collections of short stories occur in *The Priests of Psi* (1980) and *The Best of Frank Herbert* (1974).

T. O'Reilly, *Frank Herbert* (1981).

Herbert, James (1943–) Born in London, England, and educated at the Hornesy College of Art, he worked as a typographer, and then as an art director in advertising until 1977, when he turned to full-time writing. His first novel, *The Rats* (1974), was a gory chiller about a man battling against animals, followed by *The Fog* (1975), a disaster story about a gas released into the atmosphere. *The Survivor* (1976) introduced his increasing interest in the supernatural, from when he has published almost a novel a year, all involving the supernatural, occult, horror and mysterious circumstances. Other titles include *Lair* (1979), *Shrine* (1983), *Sepulchre* (1987), *Creed* (1990), *'48* (1996) and *Others* (1999). Many of his novels have been made into films. A popular and prolific writer, he is able to keep the reader guessing with unconventional science fiction plots and strange, mysterious, often specifically English, settings and idioms.

Herbert, Xavier (1901–1984) Born in Port Hedland, western Australia, he left school at 14, qualified as a pharmacist, and began to write short stories and newspaper articles. He periodically took up a variety of other vocations before going to London in 1930, where he wrote *Capricornia*, which was rejected by publishers. Returning to Australia in 1932, he revised the novel and it was published in 1938, and it became a savage and satirical bestseller, examining miscegenation and life in the Northern Territory. After war service in northern Australia, he wrote the novella *Seven Emus* (1959), and his next novel *Soldier's Women* (1961), an urban story about women's love-lust in the social pressures of the Second World War. His *magnum opus* was his hefty third novel, *Poor Fellow My Country* (1975), which depicted the life of northern Australia during the 1930s and 1940s. Short stories are collected in *Larger Than Life* (1963) and *South of Capricornia* (1991), with an autobiography in *Disturbing Element* (1963). A legendary figure in Australian literature, he venerated the outback and scorned urbanism, and his stories tell of the corruption of an Australian Eden by foreign immigrants. Attacking colonialism, he manifested a strong chauvinism against all non-Australians.

L. Clancy, *Xavier Herbert* (1981).

Herbst, Josephine (1892–1969) Born in Sioux City, Iowa, US, Josephine Frey Herbst was educated at Berkeley (BA 1918), and then moved to Europe via New York, where she began writing. Her first published novel, *Nothing Is Sacred* (1928), was quickly followed by *Money For Love* (1929), both of which were experimental early works, partly autobiographical, and well received. She is best known for her social realist Depression-era trilogy, consisting of *Pity Is Not Enough* (1933), *The Executioner Waits* (1934) and *Rope of Gold* (1939). This was an ambitious set of panoramic novels which explored the disintegrating effects of capitalism on a middle-class family and their relationships, from the Civil War to the 1930s. An increasingly significant figure on the American literary left in the 1930s and 1940s, she wrote a considerable amount of political journalism for the *New Masses* and *Scribner's*, about the European communist and fascist struggles. Later novels include *Satan's Sergeants* (1941), *Somewhere the Tempest Fell* (1947), and the non-fiction study *New Green World* (1954), a celebration of the pre-revolutionary naturalists John and William Bartram. Later years saw some short memoirs of her life in the 1930s and 1940s and a well-received novella, *Hunter of Doves* (1954).

E. Langer, *Josephine Herbst* (1984).

Herriot, James (1916–1995) The pseudonym of James Alfred Wright, born in Sunderland, England, who graduated as a veterinary surgeon from Glasgow Veterinary College in 1938. He then established a practice in Yorkshire, and turned to writing in 1966. His extremely popular stories based on his autobiographical experiences as a simple, unpretentious, rural Yorkshire vet began with *All Creatures Great and Small* (1972), which was made into a film in 1974. This was followed by *All Things Bright and Beautiful* (1974), *All Things Wise and Wonderful* (1977), *The Lord God Made Them All* (1981) and *Every Living Thing* (1992). Many of his stories were adapted for the television and screen. In the late 1980s, he also wrote a series of children's books about animals.

Hesse, Hermann (1877–1962) A Swiss writer born in Calw, Germany. He detested conventional schooling and left to work as an apprentice clock-maker, and then as a bookdealer in Basle (1899–1903), and editor and writer. His first novel was *Peter Camenzind* (1904, trans. 1961), about a dissolute writer, while his experience of formal schooling is reflected in *Beneath the Wheel* (1906, trans. 1968). There followed *Gertrude* (1910, trans. 1935) and *Rosshalde* (1914, trans. 1970). During the First World War, he moved to Switzerland and in 1923 took Swiss citizenship. Personal problems led him to Jungian psychoanalysis, and Jungian thought influenced his later writing, as in his first major work *Demian* (1919, trans. 1923), which is one of the earliest texts to deal sympathetically with adolescence, as the protagonist puts bourgeois society behind him to follow the amoral, unconventional destiny of his soul, and in *Journey to the East* (1932, trans. 1956). He also developed an interest in Eastern mysticism, and wrote *Siddhartha* (1922, trans. 1951), based on the youth of Buddha and depicting a search for the self in which one learns to stop thinking 'exclusively'. Arguably his best known novel, *Steppenwolf* (1927, trans. 1963), is a semi-autobiographical exploration of the double nature, human and lupine, of

the artist. *Narcissus and Goldmund* (1930, trans. 1968), set in medieval times, is an allegorical narrative about the inescapable responsibility of individual self-discovery. Other novels include *Knulp* (1915, trans. 1971), *Klingsor's Last Summer* (1920, trans. 1970), and *The Glass Bead Game* (1943, trans. 1969), which is set in a utopian future and concerns the theme of personal multiplicity and a grandiose scheme for harmonising all knowledge, while raising questions about stasis and progress, culture and barbarism. Short stories occur in *Strange News from Another Star* (1946, trans. 1972), *Stories of Five Decades* (trans. 1972) and *Pictor's Metamorphoses* (trans. 1982). In addition to the publication of volumes of essays, notebooks, autobiography and letters to Thomas MANN (trans. 1975), some of his poetry was set to music by Richard Strauss (*The Four Last Songs*). With roots in German romanticism, Eastern religious thought, Nietzschean philosophy, and Jungian theory, his writing places a recurrent stress on transgression and the individual's need for emancipation. His euphonic flowing prose is generally regarded as an exemplary stylistic mastery of the German language. He was a widely honoured writer and was awarded the Nobel Prize for Literature in 1946.

R. Freedman, *Hermann Hesse: Pilgrim of Crisis: A Biography* (1979).

Heyer, Georgette (1902–1974) Born in Wimbledon, England, she lived in Africa and Yugoslavia for short periods, and wrote a large number of historical romances and mystery novels. From her first novel *The Black Moth* (1921), written when she was 17, to *My Lord John* (1975), she held a huge and devoted readership for more than fifty years. Many of her novels were set in the Regency period of England, with expertly detailed accounts of the customs, clothes and manners of the time, and she constructed authenticity with sprinkles of

Regency slang. Although peopled with stock characters and structured by somewhat predictable plots, the novels are witty, tongue-in-cheek portrayals of early nineteenth-century manners, producing a lively and entertaining escapist literature with such popular titles as *Devil's Cub* (1934), *Regency Buck* (1935), *Royal Escape* (1938), *Venetia* (1958) and *Lady of Quality* (1972). Her series of twelve mystery novels, centred on two detectives, Inspector Hemingway and Superintendent Hannasyde, never quite reached the same popularity, although *Penhallow* (1942) is perhaps the best.

J. Aiken Hodge, *The Private World of Georgette Heyer* (1984).

Heym, Stefan (1913–) Born in Chemnitz, Germany, he attended the universities of Berlin and Chicago (MA 1935), and became a writer, editing an anti-Nazi weekly in New York in the 1930s and fighting for the US army during the Second World War. He naturalised in 1943, but returned to East Berlin in 1952. He wrote all his books in English until the 1970s. His first novel was *Hostages* (1942, reprinted as *The Glasenapp Case*, 1962), a detective story of the resistance movement in Prague, followed by *Of Smiling Peace* (1944), *The Crusaders* (1948), which is a panoramic Second World War narrative about the US advance through Europe, *The Eyes of Reason* (1951), *Goldsborough* (1953), *Uncertain Friend* (1969), *The King David Report* (1972), which is a reconsideration of the biblical stories in the books of *Samuel* and *Kings*, *Five Days in June* (1974), *Collin* (1979, trans. 1980), which is a study of the Stalinist elements in the German Democratic Republic, and *The Wandering Jew* (trans. 1984), an historical and theological satire of reformation Germany. Short stories appear in *The Cannibals* (1958) and *Queen Against Defoe* (1974), while non-fiction appears in *Nazis in the USA* (1938). His una-

shamed realist fiction owes much to his wide-ranging experience as a highly successful journalist, and he repeatedly isolates the struggling intellectual as a focus for broad questions of truth, influence of power, and death.

Hiaasen, Carl (1953–) Born in Fort Lauderdale, Florida, US, he attended Emory University and the University of Florida (BS 1974), before becoming an award-winning investigative journalist in Florida. His comic yet caustic thrillers reflect his exposure to Miami's social ills, and he combines a sense of the absurd with the macabre in his fast-paced narratives. To wide acclaim, he co-authored *Powder Burn* (1981), *Trap Line* (1982) and *A Death in China* (1984) with William Montalbano, before writing his first solo novel, *Tourist Season* (1986), a tongue-in-cheek narrative about a bizarre terrorist crime. There followed *Double Whammy* (1987), about skulduggery on the bass-fishing circuit, *Skin Tight* (1989), a satire and thriller about plastic surgery, *Native Tongue* (1991), about ecological guerrilla warfare in Florida Keys, *Strip Tease* (1993, filmed in 1996), about a woman who subjects herself to nude dancing to continue her fight for custody of her daughter, *Stormy Weather* (1995), about post-hurricane greed and corruption, *Naked Came the Manatee* (1996), *Lucky You* (1997), about a lottery winner and race relations, and *Sick Puppy* (1999), a surreal revenge story. *Kick Ass* (1999) is a selection of his newspaper columns. Often attacking the exploitation and destruction of the environment, he is emerging as a widely acclaimed thriller writer.

Higgins, Aidan (1927–) Born in Celbridge, Co. Kildare, Ireland, and brought up in Dalkey and Dun Laoghaire, Aidan Charles Higgins travelled widely after school, spending time in South Africa, Germany, London and Spain. These travels influenced his writing, such as the short stories in *Felo de Se* (1960, republished as

Asylum, 1971), whose setting in these countries provides a sophisticated resistance to the provincial realism of Sean O'FAOLAIN and Frank O'CONNOR. His best-known work is his first novel *Langrishe, Go Down* (1966), an avant-garde experiment which deals with the 'Big House' in Ireland and a doomed love affair in sterile times. There followed his most ambitious novel, *Balcony of Europe* (1972), which experiments with narrative techniques in its analyses of late twentieth-century tedium from a first person perspective, while the characters appear again in *Scenes from a Receding Past* (1977). Later novels include *Bornholm Night-Ferry* (1983), which depicts an affair between an Irish novelist and his Danish mistress in the form of a diary and correspondence, and *Lions of the Grünewald* (1993), which revisits cosmopolitan settings in Berlin in the late 1980s. Short stories appear in *Helsingør Station and Other Departures* (1989), and travel writing occurs in *Images of Africa* (1971) – an impressionistic account of his sojourn in South Africa – and *Ronda Gorge and Other Precipices* (1989). *Donkeys' Years* (1995) is an autobiographical memoir, to which *Dog Days* (1998) is a sequel about two years in Co. Wicklow, and *Flotsam and Jetsam* (1996) is a selection of prose. His work deals with varieties of stasis and decay and explores estrangement and futility in innovative forms.

Higgins, George V. (1939–1999) An American novelist, born George Vincent Higgins, in Brockton, Massachusetts, and educated at Boston College and Stanford University. He worked as an attorney and a newspaper columnist, and held a professorship at Boston University. Higgins' literary milieu is mainly Boston and its environs, and it is peopled by politicians (often corrupt), lawyers, policemen and minor gangsters. He has an acute ear for vernacular speech, and his dialogue is often racily funny. Among some forty books are *The Friends of Eddie Coyle*

(1972), *Cogan's Trade* (1974), *The Rat on Fire* (1981), *A Choice of Enemies* (1984), *Imposters* (1986), *Wonderful Years* (1988), *Defending Billy Ryan* (1992), *Bomber's Law* (1993), and more recently *The Agent* (1998), *A Change of Gravity* (1999) and *At End of Day* (2000). He is regarded as one of the principal innovators in American crime fiction, along with CHANDLER and HAMMETT.

Highsmith, Patricia (1921–1995) Born Mary Patricia Highsmith, in Fort Worth, Texas, US, she was educated at Barnard College (BA 1942), and from 1963 lived in France and England, where she has enjoyed a wider critical success than in the US. She built her reputation as a top-notch mystery writer with the instant success of her first novel, *Strangers on a Train* (1950, filmed in 1951 by Alfred Hitchcock), in which the chance meeting of two unknown men on a train leads to the hatching of a murder plot. This set the style for her inverted mystery plots, which frequently show good men capable of murder and evil men innocent of technical criminality. More concerned with the nature of justice, guilt and motive than with crime, in many ways she transcended the limits of the mystery and detective genre, exploring the moral values and psychopathologies of her unpleasant protagonists. Some of her best mysteries feature the detective Mr Tom Ripley, an opportunistic and amoral man incapable of feeling guilt, collected in *The Mysterious Mr Ripley* (1985; *The Talented Mr Ripley* was filmed in 2000). Some of her other fiction includes the novels *The Blunderer* (1954), *The Tremor of Forgery* (1969), *Found in the Street* (1986) and *Small g: A Summer Idyll* (1995). Writing in many cases under the pseudonym Clare Morgan, she also wrote many collections of short stories, such as *Slowly, Slowly in the Wind* (1979) and *The Black House* (1981).

B. Brophy, *Don't Never Forget* (1966).

Hijuelos, Oscar (1951–) Born in New York City, US, he was educated at the City University of New York. One of his main concerns is expatriate Cubans who make new lives for themselves in New York City. His first novel, *Our House in the Last World* (1983), concerns a Cuban family who move to the US in the 1940s. This was followed by *The Mambo Kings Play Songs of Love* (1989, Pulitzer Prize 1990), an exuberant story about two Cuban brothers, musicians originally from Havana, who play in New York's mambo clubs, and which was adapted for the screen as *The Mambo Kings* (1992). He has also written *The Fourteen Sisters of Emilio Montez O'Brien* (1993), about the complex Montez O'Brien family's relationships in small-town Pennsylvania, *Mr Ives' Christmas* (1995), and *Empress of the Splendid Season* (1999), in which the trials and difficulties of the protagonist manifest the collision of Cuban dreams with the harsh realities of America.

Hill, Susan (1942–) Born in Scarborough, England, Susan Elizabeth Hill went to the University of London (BA 1963), and became a novelist, playwright and critic from 1960 onwards. Her first novel, *The Enclosure* (1961), was published when she was 19, and has been followed by a prolific variety of fiction, including *Do Me a Favour* (1963), *Gentlemen and Ladies* (1968), *A Change for the Better* (1969), *I'm the King of the Castle* (1970), which is a tragic story about a relationship between two boys, *Strange Meeting* (1972), about a relationship between two officers during the First World War, the title taken from Wilfred Owen's celebrated poem, and *In the Springtime of the Year* (1974). *The Woman in Black* (1983) was a ghost story which was adapted into a long-running stage play, and was followed by another ghost story in *The Mist in the Mirror* (1992). *Mrs de Winter* (1993) was her much publicised sequel to DU MAURIER's *Rebecca*, followed by *Air and Angels* (1994) and *The Service*

of the Clouds (1998), in which split narratives tell about a mother and her son. Hill's novels tend to involve characters living outside mainstream lifestyles, and are rooted in dialogue and in English (albeit far from cosy) settings. Short stories occur in *The Albatross* (1971), *The Custodian* (1972) and *A Bit of Singing and Dancing* (1973), and she has written many radio plays. She has also produced many edited works, and her non-fiction includes a trilogy of books loosely based on her life in the Oxfordshire countryside. She is married to the Shakespearean scholar Stanley Wells.

Hillerman, Tony (1925–) An American murder mystery writer, born Anthony Hillerman, in Sacred Heart, Oklahoma, and educated at Oklahoma State University. After serving with the US Army during the Second World War, he became a journalist, and later taught at the University of New Mexico. Hillerman's sleuths, Joe Leaphorn and Jim Chee, are Navajo tribal policemen whose domain is the graphically depicted landscape of canyons and mesas of north-eastern Arizona, where the tribal reserves of the Native-American Pueblo and Navajo peoples are situated. Hillerman's knowledge of Navajo customs forms an integral part of each story and his Navajo detectives' solutions to the crimes with which they are confronted depends largely upon their intimate understanding of the lore and customs of their tribe. His books include *The Blessing Way* (1970), *Dance Hall of the Dead* (1973), *Listening Woman* (1977), *The Dark Wind* (1981), *The Ghostway* (1984), *Skinwalkers* (1987), *A Thief of Time* (1988), *Talking God* (1989), *Coyote Waits* (1990), *Sacred Clowns* (1993), *The Fallen Man* (1996), *Finding Moon* (1996), *The First Eagle* (1999) and *Hunting Bridge* (2000). His novels usually pitch the oblique Native-American traditions and customs against the more uncompromising demands of contemporary existence.

Hilliard, Noel (1929–) Born in Napier, New Zealand, and educated at the University of Wellington, he has published several works of non-fiction. He is best known for his fiction, particularly the Netta Samuel–Paul Bennett tetralogy, consisting of *Maori Girl* (1960), *Power of Joy* (1965), *Maori Woman* (1974) and *The Glory and the Dream* (1978). The first New Zealand novelist to concentrate upon the plight of urban Maori life, the tetralogy examines the difficulties of racism and interracial courtship and marriage. Other fiction includes the novel *A Night at Green River* (1969), about race relations, and the short story collections *A Piece of Land* (1963), *Send Somebody Nice* (1976) and *Selected Stories* (1977). Despite his topical political subject matter, his fiction has lacked popularity owing to his somewhat unfashionable proletarian social realist style.

Himes, Chester (1909–1984) Born in Jefferson City, Missouri, US, Chester Bomar Himes attended Ohio State University before being expelled in 1928. At the age of 19, he was convicted of armed robbery of $53,000, and was sentenced to twenty years in Ohio State Penitentiary. During his time in prison, he began writing, and on his release in 1935, he worked for the Federal Writers' Project, as a journalist and an odd-job worker. His first novel, *If He Hollers, Let Him Go* (1945), described five days of mounting tension in the life of Bob Jones, a black foreman in a shipyard, and was followed by *Lonely Crusade* (1947). There followed several classics of black protest literature: the largely autobiographical *Cast the First Stone* (1952), a classic prison novel, *The Third Generation* (1954), about racism in a black family, and *The Primitive* (1955), about a violent relationship between a white woman and a black man. In 1956, he went to Paris, where he was commissioned to write a series of Harlem crime thrillers in the 'Serie Noir', which led to the successful *For Love of Imabelle*

(1957) and a further nine titles for the series. His formula was a violent crime touching off extreme reactions in Harlem, which was then investigated by his two detectives Jones and Johnson, who try to bring order to the scene, often by illegal means. With irony and mordant humour, he managed to blend social protest with popular crime thrillers, all focused on the tangled oppressions, problems and pressures of racism. *The Autobiography of Chester Himes* was published in two volumes in 1972 and 1977, while *Black on Black* (1973) collects his short stories. He died in Spain, where he spent the last fifteen years of his life.

S. Milliken, *Chester Himes: A Critical Appraisal* (1976).

Hines, Barry (1939–) Born Barry Melvin Hines, in Barnsley, England, he was good at football as a boy and attended Loughborough College of Education, and worked as a sports teacher until 1972, when he turned to writing. His first novel, *The Blinder* (1966), was about football as a means of escape from working-class life, but it was with *A Kestrel for a Knave* (1968) that he established his name, in a story about a boy who emerges from his shell when he adopts and trains a kestrel. Made into the widely acclaimed film *Kes* (1970) by Ken Loach, the book was subsequently reissued under this title. Although less well known, other novels include *First Signs* (1972), *The Gamekeeper* (1975), about a year in the life of an urban protagonist on a large rural estate, *The Price of Coal* (1979), about the British miners' strike in the 1970s, *Looks and Smiles* (1981), about a school leaver looking for work, *Unfinished Business* (1983), a comment on poverty during the Thatcher years, *The Heart of It* (1994) and *Elvis Over England* (1998). In addition, he has written various film and television scripts. Often compared with the work of working-class writers like Alan SILLITOE and David STOREY in his exploration of class boundaries and loyalties, he is a prominent figure in the second wave of social realist writers depicting life in northern England.

Hoban, Russell (1925–) An American writer, born in Lonsdale, Pennsylvania, Russell Conwell Hoban moved to England in 1969. Largely self-educated, he was formerly an artist and illustrator, and later became an author, publishing stories for adults and children. He is perhaps best known for the critically acclaimed *Riddley Walker* (1980), a science fiction novel about a post-nuclear holocaust world and civilisation. Set in southern England, it is narrated in a fragmented, phonetical English by a 12-year-old boy struggling to comprehend the past. Other novels include *The Lion of Boaz-Jachin and Jachin-Boaz* (1973); *Kleinzeit* (1974) and *Turtle Diary* (1976), both about worlds displaced by language; *Pilgermann* (1983), about an eleventh-century protagonist inhabiting various cultures from the Crusades; *The Medusa Frequency* (1987), about a writer plagued by mythic narratives; *Fremder* (1996), a science fiction novel, set in a near-future Earth amid the gang cultures of materialism; *Mr Rinyo-Clackton's Offer* (1998), a Faustian narrative about death, power and the complexity of human relations; and a portrait of male sexuality in *Angelica's Grotto* (1999). Short stories and essays occur in *The Moment Under the Moment* (1992), while *A Russell Hoban Omnibus* (1999) collects various novels and previously uncollected writings.

Hodgins, Jack (1938–) A Canadian writer, who grew up in the rural settlement of Merville on Vancouver Island, he studied creative writing at the University of British Columbia (B.Ed. 1961). After teaching and travelling, he became a professor at the University of Ottawa. His style is influenced by magic realism, and northern Vancouver Island is the setting for much of his work, in such novels as *The Invention of the World* (1977), *The Resurrection of Joseph Bourne* (1980), which together with the short story collection *The Barclay Family Theatre* (1981), concentrates upon the characters of the Barclay family and their locale. Concerned with the interaction between self and place, other novels include *The Honorary Patron* (1987), *Left Behind in Squabble Bay* (1988), *Innocent Cities* (1990), which is about linguistic dislocation and cultural displacement, *The MacKen Charm* (1996) and *Broken Ground* (1998). Short stories are collected in *Spit Delaney's Island* (1976), which features eccentric characters in a fusion of realism and parable. Other writing includes the travel observations in *Over Forty in Broken Hill* (1992), and *A Passion for Narrative* (1994), a work on fiction techniques.

D. Jeffrey, *Jack Hodgins and His Works* (1989).

Høeg, Peter (1957–) Born in Denmark, he worked variously as an actor, dancer, teacher and sailor before becoming a writer in 1983. An emerging Danish writer of great international acclaim, he is widely known for his best-seller, *Miss Smilla's Feeling for Snow* (1992, trans. 1993), a thriller about a Danish-Inuit glaciologist, who lives in Copenhagen and becomes involved in a search for a mysterious object in Greenland. His other novels include *The History of Danish Dreams* (1988, trans. 1995), a series of dreams which narrates a generational saga over four centuries about four families meshing into one family, *Borderliners* (1990, trans. 1994), about the survival of three children at a Danish boarding school as they subvert the school's social experiment, *The Woman and the Ape* (trans. 1996), which depicts a thinking, talking ape named Erasmus who runs amok in London and seduces the wife of an eminent zoologist, and the short stories in *Tales of the Night* (1990, trans. 1998).

Hoffman, Alice (1952–) Born in New York City, US, she was educated at Adelphi University (BA 1973) and Stanford University (MA 1975), after which she turned to full-time writing. Portraying a near-Gothic strangeness and enchantment on the edges of everyday experiences, she has published with remarkable consistency over the last twenty-five years. Writing various stories for *American Review* and *Playgirl*, her first novel was *Property Of* (1977), which was a gritty romance set in an urban gang environment. She has currently written ten more novels, including *The Drowning Season* (1979), *Angel Landing* (1980), which is a romance set near a nuclear power plant, *White Horses* (1982), about a young girl's incestuous obsession with her older brother, *Fortune's Daughter* (1985), *Illumination Night* (1987), *At Risk* (1988), *Seventh Heaven* (1990), *Turtle Moon* (1993), *Second Nature* (1994), *Practical Magic* (1995, filmed 1997), about magic and the relationship between two sisters in small-town America, *Here on Earth* (1997), and *The River King* (2000), about how a split community is forced together by a mysterious death. *Local Girls* (1999) is a collection of short stories centred upon Gretel Samuelson, a young girl growing up in small-town America. Her characters tend to be rebels, eccentrics or outsiders, and her fiction is preoccupied by a fusion of magic and reality in the daily domestic domain, as the characters struggle in their search for identity and continuity.

Hogan, Desmond (1950–) Born in Ballinasloe, Co. Galway, Ireland, he went to University College, Dublin, and began his writing career with two plays, entitled *A Short Walk to the Sea* (1975) and *Sanctified Distances* (1976). His atmospheric first novel, *The Ikon Maker* (1976), is about a young writer who returns to Ireland from England and rediscovers an intimacy with his mother, who in turn recognises his homosexuality. *The Leaves on Grey* (1980) and *A Curious Street* (1984) are complex narratives of manifold stories which explore personal consciousness, and national and communal histories. There followed *A New Shirt* (1986) and *A Link with the River* (1989), which yoke history and personal experience, and anatomise the fictional world of the western midlands of Ireland. Short stories appear in *The Diamonds at the Bottom of the Sea* (1979), *The Mourning Thief* (1987) and *Lebanon Lodge* (1988), while *The Edge of the City* (1993) is a collection of travel essays. *A Farewell to Prague* (1995) is an odyssey of exploration into personal, sexual and cultural histories. Many of his writings explore themes of exile, loss and memory.

Hollinghurst, Alan (1954–) Born in Stroud, England, he went to Oxford University (M.Litt. 1979), and worked as a lecturer at Oxford until 1981. He then went to London and worked as an editor for the *Times Literary Supplement* until 1990, since when he has worked part-time. He received acclaim for his early collection of poetry, *Confidential Chats with Boys* (1982), before writing his first novel, *The Swimming Pool Library* (1988), which brought explosive and controversial fame for its narrative about the sexual exploits of a handsome and arrogant aristocrat in pre-AIDS gay London. *The Folding Star* (1994) was set in Bruges, Belgium, about the numerous conquests of a gay man, and was shortlisted for the Booker Prize. In addition to his most recent novel, *The Spell* (1998), about the gay culture of four men in London and Dorset, he has also translated Racine's tragedy *Bajazet* (1991). With a casual prose style, his fiction examines the complex and delicate balance between lust and love in homosexual relationships.

Hood, Hugh (1928–) A prolific Canadian writer, born in Toronto, and educated at the University of Toronto (Ph.D. 1955), he has subsequently taught at universities in Connecticut and Montreal. His fiction is characterised by a humanist-Catholic perspective and the relation of the Canadian past to wider histories. He has laid out what he calls his aesthetics of 'superrealism' (which is the manifestation of the transcendent essence of things) in *The Governor's Bridge Is Closed* (1973) and *Trusting the Tale* (1983). His short story collections include *Around the Mountain* (1967), *Flying a Red Kite* (1962), *The Fruit Man, the Meat Man and the Manager* (1971), *Dark Glasses* (1976), *None Genuine Without This Signature* (1980), *August Nights* (1985) and *You'll Catch Your Death* (1992). His novels include *White Figure, White Ground* (1964) and *The Camera Always Lies* (1967), both of which focus on deception and betrayal, *A Game of Touch* (1970), *You Can't Get There from Here* (1972), *Black and White Keys* (1982) and *Dead Men's Watches* (1995). More recently, he has written the 'New Age' cycle, a twelve-novel sequence due to conclude in 2000, which began with *The Swing in the Garden* (1975) and includes *Property and Value* (1990), *Be Sure to Close Your Eyes* (1993) and *Great Realizations* (1997). Focusing on Matthew Goderich, this series is a documentary fantasy or social mythology of Canada in the twentieth century, mixing novel and allegory, and is imbued with his Christian perspective of redemption and atonement. A collection of his essays has appeared in *Unsupported Assertions* (1991).

Hope, Christopher (1944–) Born Christopher David Tolley Hope, in Johannesburg, South Africa, he was educated at the University of Witwatersrand (BA 1965, MA 1971) and the University of Natal (BA 1970). He worked in insurance, journalism and copywriting, before becoming a teacher in Halesowen in England in 1972. After writing poetry, he turned to fiction with his first novel *A Separate Development* (1980) – the phrase being the official euphemism for

apartheid – which was banned in South Africa. It told of a white boy who leaves his white suburb to live in a black township, 'passing' as a 'coloured', and encountering apartheid from the other side. There followed *Kruger's Alp* (1984), an allegorical narrative about a white boy coming to terms with his South African heritage, *Black Swan* (1987), *The Hottentot Room* (1986), which is a tale about a London pub where South African exiles meet to remember the past, *The Chocolate Redeemer* (1989), *Serenity House* (1992), which is a black satire set in London, the comic *The Love Songs of Nathan J. Swirsky* (1993), and *Darkest England* (1996), a satirical attack on contemporary England. Recent works are *Me, the Moon and Elvis Presley* (1997), about the characters and concerns of a small South African town on the veldt, and *Signs of the Heart* (1999), about country life in southern France. In addition to plays and juvenile stories, short stories occur in *Private Parts* (1981) and his non-fiction includes the acclaimed *White Boy Running* (1988), a memoir about his return trip to South Africa in 1987 after exile, and the travel book *Moscow! Moscow!* (1990). Although he has lived in England since 1972, the wrenching discriminatory politics of apartheid has been the subject of his writing, often depicting the absurdities of the racial system.

Hornby, Nick (1957–) A freelance journalist, novelist and teacher, he made a big impact with his book *Fever Pitch* (1992), a memoir of growing up as an ardent Arsenal football fan, depicting how life revolved around this fixation, masculinity and class, and which captured the voice of a generation about football and the obsessions of fans. *High Fidelity* (1995, filmed 2000) depicts Rob and his obsessive construction of 'top-five' music lists, exploring the loneliness and childishness of adult life. More recently, *About a Boy* (1998) tells of the relationship between an adult, Will, who helps an adolescent called Marcus with his social and psychological troubles. He has edited *Contemporary American Fiction* (1992), essays on the 'dirty realist school', and a collection of football writings in *My Favourite Year* (1993), and his writing generally displays a down-to-earth manner and a sense of humour.

Hospital, Janette Turner (1942–) An Australian novelist, born in Melbourne and educated in Brisbane, she moved to the US in 1965, and has also lived in India and England. Since 1971, she has been a full-time writer, living in Canada. After an early novel *The Ivory Swing* (1982), her first major novel was *The Tiger in the Tiger Pit* (1983), which was about a mother's attempts to yoke her family together, followed by *Borderline* (1985), *Charades* (1988), which suggests the power of female storytelling, *The Last Magician* (1992), a complex work about the structures of corruption in contemporary Sydney, and *Oyster* (1996), a surreal Gothic narrative about a bleak fictional town in the outback, as the frontier Australians deal with the arrival of a mysterious stranger called Oyster. Short stories are collected in *Dislocations* (1986), *Isobars* (1990) and *Collected Stories* (1995). Often set in foreign places, her fiction involves expatriate Australian experience, the exile's perspective, political questions and postmodern philosophies. Investigating the illusory nature of reality through multiple temporal perspectives, her fiction also examines guilt and redemption and feminist politics.

Howard, Elizabeth Jane (1923–) Born in London, England, she trained as an actress and has since had a varied career as a broadcaster for the BBC, a secretary, a publishing editor and a writer. From 1965, she had a reputedly tempestuous marriage to the British novelist Kingsley AMIS, until their divorce in 1983. Her early fiction focused on sympathetic female characters in satirical set-pieces, such as her first novel, *The Beautiful Visit* (1950), which was an award-winning account of a girl's coming-of-age. *The Long View* (1956) traces a marriage backward in time to the couple's first meeting, *The Sea Change* (1959) is an alternating narrative by four protagonists, and *After Julius* (1965) is an acclaimed comedy of manners. Subsequent novels continued her focus on the nuances of human relationships, sometimes in comical situations, for example *Something in Disguise* (1969), *Odd Girl Out* (1972), and *Getting It Right* (1982), about a sexual encounter. Her recent novels form the 'Cazalet Chronicle': *The Light Years* (1982), *Marking Time* (1991), *Confusion* (1993) and *Casting Off* (1995). This quartet follows the trials and tribulations of the wealthy Cazalet family and its servants over a period of three generations, from 1937 onwards. *Falling* (1999) is a tense psychological study about the drama of relationships. In addition to screenplays and radio plays, short stories occur in *We Are for the Dark* (1951) and *Mr Wrong* (1976), and her non-fiction includes a biography of Betting von Arnim (1957) and several books on food and gardening.

Hoyle, Fred (1915–) An English astronomer, cosmologist, science writer and science fiction author, born in Bingley, Yorkshire, and educated at Cambridge University. His science fiction novels include *Ossian's Ride* (1959), *Fifth Planet* (1963), *Into Deep Space* (1974), *The Black Cloud* (1957), *The Westminster Disaster* (1978) and *Comet Halley* (1985), and short stories occur in *Element 79* (1967). *Home Is Where the Wind Blows* (1994) is an autobiography, and he has written many non-science fiction works on space, astronomy and cosmology. His fiction is written with a commanding authority, and his themes concern experiments with time travel and metaphysical and political fantasies.

Hughes, David (1930–) Born in Alton, Hampshire, England, David John Hughes was educated at Oxford University (BA 1953), and from 1961 he worked as an editor and freelance writer. His early novels were *A Feeling in the Air* (1957), *The Horsehair Sofa* (1961), and *The Major* (1964), which is a satirical view of military life that received significant critical acclaim. His most successful novel was *The Pork Butcher* (1984), about a German officer finding redemption by returning to the scenes of his wartime crimes in occupied France. Other novels include *The Man Who Invented Tomorrow* (1968), which is another humorous satire directed at the role of television in contemporary life, *Memories of Dying* (1976), *A Genoese Fancy* (1979), *The Imperial German Dinner Service* (1983), *But for Bunter* (1985), which is a set of variations on the well-known schoolboy character by Frank Richards, and more recently, *The Little Book* (1996), a compelling semi-autobiographical and surreal novel. While his fiction has not always been widely received, he has also written non-fiction, including the travel book *The Road to Stockholm and Lapland* (1964), *The Seven Ages of England* (1968), *The Rosewater Revolution* (1971), *Himself and Other Animals* (1997), edited several series of short stories and written a critical biography of J.B. PRIESTLEY (1958). He was married to the Swedish actress and director Mai Zetterling until their divorce in 1976.

Hughes, Langston (1902–1967) Born James Mercer Langston Hughes, in Joplin, Missouri, US, he grew up mainly in Lawrence, Kansas. Despite leaving Columbia University in 1922 for menial work, he emerged in the mid-1920s as a gifted African-American poet, with such volumes as *The Weary Blues* (1926) and *Fine Clothes to the Jew* (1927). He became a major force in the Harlem Renaissance with his 1926 manifesto essay 'The Negro Artist and the Racial Mountain' in the *Nation*, which proclaimed race pride and artistic independence. Graduating from the traditionally black Lincoln University in Pennsylvania in 1929, he wrote his first novel, *Not Without Laughter* (1930), about a sensitive, black mid-Western boy and his struggling family. He spent a year in the USSR in 1932, which marked a firm turn to the political left. A well-known collection of short stories in *The Ways of White Folks* (1934), whose sardonic realism indicated a pessimism about race relations, was followed by several plays, for example *Mulatto* (1935), about miscegenation and parental rejection, *Little Ham* (1936) and *Emperor of Haiti* (1936), amidst the founding of the Harlem Suitcase Theatre in the late 1930s. He wrote two volumes of autobiography: *The Big Sea* (1940), which is episodic and lightly comic, and *I Wonder as I Wander* (1956), which recounts his time in the Soviet Union. *Tambourines to Glory* (1958) was his second novel, before his launch into journalism in the 1940s for the *Chicago Defender*, with satirical sketches of his celebrated fictional creation, the Harlem resident Jesse B. Semple, also known as Simple, which focused on race and racism. These were collected in five volumes, such as *Simple Speaks His Mind* (1950), and eventually inspired a musical, *Simply Heaven* (1957). McCarthyism was a source of some trouble due to his left-wing politics, but he continued to write, among which were the lyrics for Elmer Rice and Kurt Weill's musical *Street Scene* (1947), a gospel inspired dramatisation of *Tambourines to Glory* (1963), as well as the Christmas musical *Black Nativity* (1961). Later volumes of poetry include *One Way Ticket* (1949), *Montage of a Dream Deferred* (1951) and *The Panther and the Lash* (1967). In addition to several books for children, he illustrated histories of African-American and Harlem life, wrote a history of the NAACP, called *Fight for Freedom* (1962), and edited numerous anthologies of African-American writing. His prolific, diverse and flexible output bears testimony to his command over the nuances of black urban and cultural life, and an art that was firmly rooted in race pride and the cherished freedom of a nationalist and cosmopolitan democratic artist.

A. Rampersad, *The Life of Langston Hughes*, 2 vols (1986–1988).

Hulme, Keri (1947–) Born in Christchurch, New Zealand, of Maori, Scottish and English ancestry. She abandoned a law degree at the University of Canterbury and worked at various labouring jobs, while writing in her spare time. Her first book was a collection of poetry, *The Silences Between: Moeraki Conversations* (1982), which explored her Maori identity and culture. Further poetry was published in *Strands* (1992). Her first novel, *The Bone People* (1983, Booker Prize), achieved international fame. It resisted affiliation with a European literary tradition, and presented positive images of Maori women as models for racial reconciliation, raising a controversy about her identification with the Maoris and her status as a Maori writer. Short stories appeared in *Te Kaihau: The Windeater* (1986). Much of her writing looks at Maori myths and images and the experiences of cultural alienation. She has also written *Homeplaces* (1989), essays about New Zealand's South Island, her present place of residence.

Humphreys, Emyr Owen (1919–) Born in Prestatyn, Wales, he was educated at the University of Wales, Aberystwyth, and worked variously as a teacher, a radio and television producer for BBC Wales, a university lecturer, and a prolific writer. As a conscientious objector during the Second World War, he worked as a farmer and a war relief worker (1940–1946). An ardent Welsh nationalist and concerned with the issues of Christianity and Wales, his first novel was *The Little Kingdom*

(1947), which made a strong case for Welsh nationalism and pacifism as a means to solving political problems. Subsequent novels include *The Voice of a Stranger* (1949), *A Change of Heart* (1951), *Hear and Forgive* (1953), *Outside the House of Baal* (1965), *Jones* (1984), about a man's irresponsible relations and his torments, *An Absolute Hero* (1986), *Open Secrets* (1988), *The Triple Net* (1988), *Bonds of Attachment* (1990), *Outside Time* (1991), *Unconditional Surrender* (1996) and *The Gift of a Daughter* (1998). 'The Land of the Living' sequence consisted of *Flesh and Blood* (1974), *The Best of Friends* (1978) and *Salt of the Earth* (1985). *The Taliesin Tradition* (1983) is an exploration of the Welsh character over the years, and his *Collected Poems* appeared in 1999. In stories, novels, and poetry, he is one of the most distinguished Welsh novelists writing about Wales, whose traditional themes are nevertheless countered by experimental techniques and styles.

I. Williams, *Emyr Humphreys* (1980).

Hurston, Zora Neale (1903–1960) Born in Eatonville, Florida, she is considered one of the leading African-American writers and folklorists of the twentieth century, writing about the rural American South. She worked for a touring troupe, but then went to Howard University and Barnard College (BA 1928). After publishing short stories in her twenties, she attracted the attention of the leading Harlem Renaissance writers. She established the short-lived literary magazine *Fire!* with Langston HUGHES and later collaborated with Hughes on a play, *Mule Bone* (1931). She studied anthropology with Franz Boas at Columbia University in the 1920s and 1930s, and wrote *Mules and Men* (1935), an anthropological study of black American folklore, which was followed by *Tell My Horse* (1938), a similar study of Caribbean folklore. Her first novel, *Jonah's Gourd Vine* (1934), was followed by her best-known work, *Their Eyes Were Watching God* (1937), which has received increasingly wide critical acclaim for its assertion of the integrity of selfhood of African-American women. She also published *Moses, Man of the Mountain* (1939), which explores black mythological treatments of the figure of Moses, *Seraph on the Suwanee* (1948), and a factually questionable 'autobiography', entitled *Dust Tracks on a Road* (1942). Withdrawing from public life in the 1950s, she later died in poverty after many years of ill-health. Posthumous publications include *The Complete Stories* (1994), *Novels and Stories* (1995) and *Folk-lore, Memoirs, and Other Writings* (1995).

C. Wall, *Women of the Harlem Renaissance* (1995).

Huxley, Aldous (1894–1963) Born Aldous Leonard Huxley, in Godalming, England, into a family of distinguished scientists and writers, he went to Oxford University (BA 1916), and became a prodigious writer with views on all aspects of modern society. His early novels were carnivalesque in style and owe a debt to his associations with the intelligentsia circles of Lady Ottoline Morrell at Garsington Manor. His first novel was *Crome Yellow* (1921), followed by *Antic Hay* (1923) and *Those Barren Leaves* (1925). *Point Counter Point* (1928) was a more ambitious and complex work, a novel of ideas set on a cruise ship and concerned with the interaction of its passengers, attempting to explore the multifaceted nature of humanity. This was followed by arguably his most famous novel, *Brave New World* (1932), a satiric science fiction novel about the misuse of technology and the conditioning of people for social roles in a dystopian world state. Thereafter, his novels explored the ramifications of humanity's scientific and social progress, although his later works never achieved the same degree of popularity. Novels such as *Eyeless in Gaza* (1936), *After Many a Summer (Dies the Swan)* (1939), *Time Must Have a Stop* (1944), *Ape and Essence* (1948), *The Genius and the Goddess* (1955) and *Island* (1962), tended to be mystical apologues and literary propaganda about the salvation of humanity from wars and ecological disaster. He wrote a considerable amount of nonfiction, covering such diverse topics as philosophy, art, language, religion, ecology and science, and his experiments with hallucinogenic drugs, including mescaline and LSD, are recounted in *The Doors of Perception* (1954) and *Heaven and Hell* (1956). In addition to writing plays, volumes of short stories, such as the *Collected Short Stories* (1957), and several volumes of poetry, collected in 1971, he was a skilful essayist and his prolific writing always demonstrated breadth, style and vision. Although many critics regard his later work to be less defined and incisive, he is nevertheless held up as one of the major intellectuals and satirists of the early twentieth century.

P. Bowering, *Aldous Huxley: A Study of the Major Works* (1968).

I

Ibuse, Masuji (1898–1993) Born in Hiroshima, Japan, he attended Waseda University, and became a widely acclaimed writer who drew extensively from Japanese culture, and was the recipient of some of Japan's highest literary honours. His fiction includes *Waves* (1930–1938, trans. 1986), two short novellas set in the late twelfth century which examine the power of warlords and nobles, *John Manjiro, the Castaway, His Life and Adventures* (1938, trans. 1941), and the two novellas in *No Consultations Today and A Far-Worshipping Commander* (trans. 1964). Short stories occur in *Two Stories* (trans. 1970) and *Salamander* (trans. 1981), ranging from petty crime to human foibles, in which an earthiness and humour is dominant. *Black Rain* (1966, trans. 1969) is regarded as his masterpiece, and for which he is best known in the west. A densely patterned documentary novel, it is an elegy for the city and population of Hiroshima, weaving together documents, eye-witness accounts and the effects of the A-bomb in 1945. Numerous short stories, essays, novels and poems have made him a major figure in Japanese literature and given him an international reputation.

Ihimaera, Witi (1944–) Born in Gisborne, New Zealand of Maori descent, Witi Tame Ihimaera was educated at the universities of Auckland and Victoria, and then worked as a journalist, a civil servant and as New Zealand consul to the US. His *Pounamu, Pounamu* (1972) was the first volume of short stories to be published by a Maori writer, and addressed issues of cultural difference. His novel *Tangi* (1973) was the first to be published by a Maori as well, and focused upon Tama Mahana's response to his father's death, followed by *Whanau* (1974), about village life. Further short stories appeared in *The New Net Goes Fishing* (1977), and *Dear Miss Mansfield* (1989), which were specific Maori variations on some of Katherine MANSFIELD's work. *The Matriarch* (1986) is his most complex and critically controversial novel, a postcolonial epic and history of the violence of colonisation. With textual fragmentation and intertextual references to Maori cosmology, mythology and other texts, the narrative focuses upon Artemis, a woman who fought for Maori rights. His other work includes a collection of Maori writing, entitled *Into the World of Light* (1982), an opera called *Waituhi* (1984), *The Whale Rider* (1987), an edition of contemporary Maori writing in *Te Ao Marama* (1992), and *Bulibasha: King of the Gypsies* (1994). Recent works are short stories in *Kingfisher Come Home* (1995) and the novel *The Dream Swimmer* (1997). Sharing characters and places among his fictions, he writes about Maori people and contexts, redressing what he perceives as a lack of familiarity in New Zealand with Maori culture. His later books are increasingly polemical in their contrast of Pakeha (white New Zealand) and Maori values, as he explores the importance of history and genealogy to contemporary Maori culture.

U. Ojinmah, *Witi Ihimaera: A Changing Vision* (1993).

Ireland, David (1927–) An Australian novelist born in Lakemba, New South Wales, he held a variety of jobs before becoming a full-time writer in 1973. One of Australia's most controversial novelists, he is overtly political, savagely attacking the alienating and dehumanising aspects of capitalist society. He began his career as a playwright, and then went on to write his first novel, *The Chantic Bird* (1968), a bleak naturalistic account of adolescence. His best-known work is *The Unknown Industrial Prisoner* (1971), an angry critique of capitalist exploitation, similar in content to *The Flesheaters* (1972). *A Woman of the Future* (1978) is a surreal narrative about a young girl growing up in a near-future Australia who is transformed into a leopard, while *Burn* (1974) is a day in the life of an Aboriginal family, and *The Glass Canoe* (1976) explores the masculinity of Australian culture. Other works include *City of Women* (1981), a macabre and surreal allegory which polarised the feminist movement, *Archimedes and the Seagle* (1984), a dog narrator's view of his family owners, *Bloodfather* (1987) and *The Chosen* (1997). Often experimenting with different styles, his innovative and non-representational fiction is frequently a bitter indictment of the futility of contemporary industrialised existence.

H. Daniel, *Double Agent* (1982).

Iroh, Eddie (1946–) Born in Nigeria, he has worked variously as a clerk, columnist, correspondent, publisher, producer and writer. During the Nigerian Civil War, he worked for the Biafran War Information Bureau, before moving to Reuters and then into publishing. He produced features and documentaries for Nigerian television in Enugu, and then went to London to work as a journalist on Nigerian affairs. Arguably best known for his first novel, *Forty-Eight Guns for the General* (1976), this focuses on a group of ruthless mercenaries who are flown in to help Biafra during the civil war, with the ensuing problems of foreign intervention in an indigenous struggle. There followed his trilogy of historical fiction on the civil war: *Toads of War* (1979), which places a love story within the context of the social crises and corruption that derive from war and civil unrest, *Without a Silver Spoon* (1981) and *The Siren in the Night* (1982). Situated within action-packed, popular fictional genres similar to thrillers and spy stories, his plots are characterised by careful, detailed research which lend them the semblance of insider knowledge.

Irving, John (1942–) Born in Exeter, New Hampshire, US, John Winslow Irving was educated at the universities of New Hampshire (BA 1965) and Iowa (MFA 1967), since when he has been a novelist and an occasional university lecturer in English. *Setting Free the Bears* (1969), about two men's motorcycling adventures in Austria, *The Water-Method Man* (1972), about an Iowa graduate's fantastic misadventures, and *The 158-Pound Marriage* (1974), about two couples engaged in mate-swapping, are collected in *Three by John Irving* (1980). Critical acclaim and success came with *The World According to Garp* (1978), filmed in 1982 and starring Robin Williams, which is about a writer who is killed for ideological reasons, and explores the violent side of life – rape, assassination and suicide – but always infused with comedy. This style is continued in *The Hotel New-Hampshire* (1981, filmed 1984), which explores issues of incest and terrorism in a family saga of four generations of the Berry family. *The Cider House Rules* (1985, filmed 2000) is a statement on abortion, set in an orphanage in Maine, while *A Prayer for Owen Meany* (1989) examines good and evil with a Christ-like hero who has the gift of prophecy and thinks he is God's instrument. Other works include the stories in *Trying to Save Peggy Sneed* (1993), while *A Son of the Circus* (1994) is a tale of a Hindu film star and the collision of various characters in India. In addition to the memoirs *The Imaginary Girlfriend* (1996) and *My Movie Business* (1999), his latest novel, *A Widow For One Year* (1998), is a farce-tragedy about writers. Producing intricate self-referential narratives with a sense of humour, he has written many novels which blend the madcap, macabre and mundane, in a nineteenth-century mixture of character and sentiments, which has earned him a reputation as a postmodernist.

Isherwood, Christopher (1904–1986) An English writer, born Christopher William Bradshaw Isherwood, in Disley, Cheshire, and educated at the University of Cambridge. He worked in Berlin as a private tutor between 1928 and 1933, and wrote two novels, *All the Conspirators* (1928) and *The Memorial* (1932). He also drew on his experiences in Berlin to write two books of short stories, *The Last of Mr Norris* (1935) and *Goodbye to Berlin* (1939), based on the lives of his faintly louche companions and acquaintances, either oblivious of, or simply trying to ignore, the ominous rise to power of the Nazis. These stories were later adapted as a play, *I Am a Camera* (1951), and as a musical, *Cabaret*, which was also made into a successful film (1972). Isherwood wrote three plays in collaboration with W.H. Auden, entitled *The Dog Beneath the Skin* (1935), *The Ascent of F6* (1936) and *On the Frontier* (1938). His book *Lions and Shadows* (1938) is semi-auto-

biographical and based on his schooldays and his time at university. In 1939, he moved to the US, eventually settling in California. Here, he wrote several books: *The Condor and the Cows* (1949), about a visit to South America, *The World in the Evening* (1954), *Prater Violet* (1945), which is a novel about the film industry, *Down There on a Visit* (1962), *A Single Man* (1964) and *A Meeting by the River* (1967). He developed an interest in Hindu thought and wrote *The Essentials of the Vedanta* (1969). Isherwood also wrote *Kathleen and Frank* (1972), a biography of his parents, and *Christopher and His Kind* (1976), a frank account of his homosexuality and its effect on his life and writing.

J. Fryer, *Isherwood: A Biography* (1977).

Ishiguro, Kazuo (1954–) Born in Nagasaki, Japan, in 1960 he moved to England with his family, where he has remained. He was educated at the universities of Kent and of East Anglia, where he was one of Malcolm BRADBURY's creative writing graduates. Widely honoured as a writer, he has written several novels: *A Pale View of Hills* (1981), about a Japanese woman living in England and her memories of and interactions with her children; *An Artist of the Floating World* (1986), set in post-war Japan, about the life of a once-famous Japanese painter; *The Remains of the Day* (1989, Booker Prize), about a butler who suppresses every aspect of his own life in serving his master, and filmed in 1993; and the widely acclaimed *The Unconsoled* (1995), a somewhat Kafkaesque novel set in an unnamed eastern European city. His latest novel is *When We Were Orphans* (2000), set in 1930s England and exploring the mysterious disappearance of the protagonist's parents in Shanghai as a child. His fiction often deals with self-deception, evasions and the effects of narrow-minded perspectives. He has also written short stories and television plays.

Iyayi, Festus (1947–) Born in Benin City, he was educated in Nigeria, Kiev in the USSR, and gained a doctorate from the University of Bradford, England. He subsequently lectured for many years in business administration at the University of Benin, until his radical politics caused his dismissal in 1988. Firmly committed to the belief that literature ought to be utilised for the liberation of the oppressed, novels like *Violence* (1979), *The Contract* (1982) and *Heroes* (1986) examine the nature of class conflict within the neo-colonial context of contemporary Nigeria. *Heroes* – winner of the Commonwealth Writers Prize (1988) – suggests that the oppressive structures on both sides of the struggle in the Nigerian Civil War were the ruling élites. His most recent novel is *Awaiting Court Martial* (1996). Usually portraying a naïve protagonist's education into sympathy with the oppressed, his fiction explores the violence of a social structure founded upon injustice and exploitation.

J

Jacobson, Dan (1929–) A highly regarded novelist, he was born in Johannesburg, South Africa, and educated at the University of Witwatersrand (BA 1949). After various administrative jobs, he moved to London in 1954, where he took up writing and later became a lecturer at the University of London (1974–1994). In a hugely prolific writing career, his first novel was *The Trap* (1955), about corruption, violence and betrayal on a South African farm. Other early novels also have a strong focus on South Africa: these include *A Dance in the Sun* (1956), *The Price of Diamonds* (1957), *The Zulu and the Zeide* (1959), *The Evidence of Love* (1960), which was about 'passing' in a society riven by racial segregation, *No Further West* (1961), and *The Beginners* (1966), an autobiographical novel about a Jewish South African family. Further novels include *The Rape of Tamar* (1970), which is a modern retelling of the biblical story, *The Wonder-Worker* (1973), *The Confessions of Joseph Baisz* (1979), and *Her Story* (1987), which is set in England, retelling biblical stories about mothers and sons. More recent works include *Hidden in the Heart* (1991), *The God-Fearer* (1992), *The Electronic Elephant* (1994), about a return trip to post-apartheid South Africa, and *Heshel's Kingdom* (1998), a memoir about his grandfather and the escape to South Africa of his Lithuanian Jewish family. Short stories appear in *Beggar My Neighbour* (1964), *Through the Wilderness* (1968) and *Inklings* (1973), while essays occur in *Time of Arrival* (1963) and *Adult Pleasures* (1989). His non-fiction includes *The Story of Stories* (1982) about the Old Testament Bible, and autobiographical essays in *Time and Time Again* (1985). Much of his fiction is preoccupied with the struggles in apartheid South Africa, race relations, class consciousness and morality.

S. Roberts, *Dan Jacobson* (1984).

Jacobson, Howard (1942–) Born in Manchester, England, Howard Eric Jacobson was educated at Cambridge University (BA 1964), and was a university lecturer for fifteen years. He left academia, and made a name as an urbane, and somewhat acerbic, television commentator and journalist. Heavily reliant on some aspect of autobiography in his fiction, *Coming from Behind* (1983) is a downmarket university campus satire in the vein of David LODGE and Tom SHARPE, while *Peeping Tom* (1984) is a comic satire which charts a character's progress from writing into voyeurism and necrophilia. *Redback* (1986) draws upon his experiences of life in Australia, *The Very Model of a Man* (1992) looks at the Jewish experience in the light of stories of Adam and Eve, and Cain and Abel, *No More Mr Nice Guy* (1998) deals with a marriage separation and the man's future, while his most recent novel is *The Mighty Walzer* (1999), about the art and life of an ace ping-pong player in Jewish north Manchester in the 1950s. Non-fiction includes *Shakespeare's Magnanimity* (1978), and travel books about Australia in *In the Land of Oz* (1987) and Israel in *Roots Shmoots* (1993).

James, P.D. (1920–) The pseudonym of Phyllis Dorothy James White, she was born in Oxford, England. She worked as an administrator in a hospital, and then for the British Home Office Criminal Policy Department until 1979, at which time she turned to writing full-time. Now an establishment figure, she has won numerous awards for her crime fiction and has emerged in recent years as the doyenne of British murder writing, acclaimed for her combination of psychologically credible characters and complex and puzzling plots, particularly in her novels featuring Commander Adam Dalgliesh of Scotland Yard. Her many books include *Cover Her Face* (1962), *A Mind to Murder* (1963), *Unnatural Causes* (1967), *Shroud for a Nightingale* (1971), *An Unsuitable Job for a Woman* (1972), which features a woman detective Cordelia Gray, *The Black Tower* (1975), *Death of an Expert Witness* (1977), *Innocent Blood* (1980), about an adopted girl's search for her real parents, *Devices and Desires* (1989), *The Children of Man* (1992), which is a futuristic dystopian tale, *Original Sin* (1995) and *A Certain Justice* (1997). Many of her novels have been adapted as television mini-series. In addition to several omnibus collections, she has also written *The Maul and the Pear Tree* (1971), a non-fictional study of a gruesome murder in London in 1811. *Time to be in Earnest* (1999) is part autobiography and part diary. Although there is an old-fashioned quality to her mystery novels about middle-class England in a realist style, she nevertheless pushes at the boundaries of the genre.

Janowitz, Tama (1957–) An American novelist associated with the 'brat pack' writers, like Bret Easton ELLIS and Jay MCINERNEY, she was born in San Francisco, and educated at Barnard College (BA 1977) and Hollins College (MA 1979). In addition to her writing, she has worked as an art director and a model. Her first novel, *American Dad* (1981), is a coming-of-age story as Earl Przepasniak indulges in chasing women and bohemian pleasures. *Slaves of New York* (1986, filmed 1989), a series of loosely connected stories, depicts the arty characters of downtown Manhattan and their sophisticated monotony and quirky outlooks on life. *A Cannibal in Manhattan* (1987) is the fictional diary of Mgungu from a South Sea Island who takes up with an American heiress, while *The Male Cross-Dresser Support Group* (1992) explores sexual identity in a relationship between a middle-aged woman and a 9-year-old boy. Recent works are *By the Shores of Gitchee Gumee* (1996), which is inspired by Longfellow's poem 'Song of Hiawatha', and is a parody of trailer life, and *A Certain Age* (1999), about Manhattan and Hampton life in the 1990s, as a single woman looks for a husband in a parody of Edith WHARTON's fiction. Focusing upon lethargic East Coast artists and intellectuals, Janowitz has become well known for blending the mundane with the outlandish, in her representations of strained, postmodern metropolitan life.

Jen, Gish (1956–) A Chinese-American novelist, who grew up in Scarsdale, New York, Gish Lillian Jen was educated at Harvard University (BA 1977), and after attending Stanford, went to the University of Iowa (MFA 1983). Her work has appeared in *The Atlantic Monthly*, *The New Yorker* and *Best American Short Stories* of 1988 and 1995, and many of her stories have been anthologised. She is the author of several critically and commercially successful novels, the first of which was *Typical American* (1991), following a trio of young Chinese immigrants to the US and their slow transformation into 'typical Americans'. *Mona in the Promised Land* (1996), set in American suburbia, is about a young girl who is Asian-American by birth but chooses to be Jewish. Both novels are set in the 1950s and 1960s, and depict the Chinese-American Chang family, focusing with wry humour upon ethnic identity and the American Dream. Her most recent work is *Who's Irish?* (1999), containing eight stories which examine the life of foreigners and cross-immigrant experiences and marriage between Chinese-American and Irish-American families. An up-and-coming novelist, she has been widely praised for her exploration of American hybrid identities.

Jhabvala, Ruth Prawer (1927–) A German-born novelist and screenwriter of Polish parents, born Ruth Prawer in Cologne, her parents went to England as refugees in 1939. She graduated from London University in 1951, married an Indian architect and moved to India until 1975, when she moved to New York City. Her early fiction gained recognition for her comic transcultural portrayals of manners and the residual legacies of colonialism on contemporary Indian society. These include *To Whom She Will* (1955), *The Nature of Passion* (1956), *Esmond in India* (1958), *The Householder* (1960), *Get Ready For Battle* (1962), *A Backward Place* (1965) and *A New Dominion* (1972). *Heat and Dust* (1975, Booker Prize), perhaps her best novel, is about the experiences of a young Englishwoman in modern India set in parallel with an ancestor's affair with an Indian prince in the 1920s. This was adapted for the screen under the production of Ismail Merchant and James Ivory, with whom she established a highly successful working relationship, producing the screenplays for *Shakespeare Wallah* (1965), *The Guru* (1965), adapting E.M. FORSTER's novels, *A Passage to India*

(filmed 1973), *A Room with a View* (filmed 1986) and *Howard's End* (filmed 1992), and Henry James' *The Bostonians* (filmed 1984). Additional novels include *In Search of Love and Beauty* (1983), *Three Continents* (1987), about the clash between the easternised West and the westernised East, *Poet and Dancer* (1993) and *Shards of Memory* (1995), and short stories occur in *Like Birds, Like Fishes* (1963), *A Stranger Climate* (1968), *Out of India* (1986) and *East into Upper East* (1998). Tracing the interaction of westerners and Indians in postcolonial India, her fiction contrasts different types of morality, ethics and culture, and more recently, has moved to linking up these experiences with life in America.

L. Sucher, *The Fiction of Ruth Prawer Jhabvala: The Politics of Passion* (1989).

Johnson, B.S. (1933–1973) Full name Bryon Stanley William Johnson, born in London, England, he went to the University of London (BA 1959), and became a writer, and a film and television director and producer. Generally regarded as an experimental writer, his early novels were *Travelling People* (1963), which employed many different styles and techniques to transform the novelistic medium, *Albert Angelo* (1964), and *Trawl* (1966), an interior monologue which seeks to represent the inside of a mind. *The Unfortunates* (1969) is among the best-known of British avant-garde novels, in which Johnson's sense of the randomness of human experience led him to issue the book held together by removable wrapping paper in a box, so that the book could be read in any order. *House Mother Normal* (1971), an attempt to present the experience of nine people as nearly as possible, was followed by *Consequences* (1972), written with Margaret DRABBLE, *Christie Malry's Own Double Entry* (1973), in which the author intrudes into the life of a bank clerk who bears a grudge against society and who evaluates his life in the form of a double-entry accounts ledger, *A Dublin Unicorn* (1973) and *Everybody Knows Somebody Who's Dead* (1973). Concluded just before his suicide, *See The Old Lady Decently* (1975) was the first of a projected 'Matrix' trilogy and continued his fictional experimentation. With many television plays to his credit, he also wrote a few volumes of poetry, a collection of short stories with Zulfikar GHOSE, entitled *Statement Against Corpses* (1964), and *The Evacuees* (1968), a series of personal narratives. Setting himself against illusionistic storytelling with metafictional devices and probing the structure of the novel with innovative forms in prose, he regarded James JOYCE and Samuel BECKETT as his literary forebears. He always shifted the frontiers of the novel, keeping the relationship of the writer to his material in the foreground of his fiction.

Johnson, Charles R. (1948–) Born Charles Richard Johnson, in Evanston, Illinois, US, he first manifested his talents in cartoons and drawings as a graphic artist, publishing two collections of work in *Black Humor* (1970) and *Half-Past Nation Time* (1972). He was an undergraduate at Southern Illinois University at Carbondale, going on to do graduate study in philosophy at SUNY-Stony Brook (Ph.D. 1976). His first novel, *Faith and the Good Thing* (1974), was an amalgamation of folk wisdom and philosophical enquiry, in Faith's search for meaning. Adopting a philosophical approach in much of his fiction, his next work was *Oxherding Tale* (1982), followed by his highly praised novel about the slave trade, *Middle Passage* (1990). Both novels are profound explorations of the concept of freedom, as they examine nineteenth-century America from the perspective of contemporary philosophy, depicting African-American men seeking liberation from various sorts of bondage. His latest novel is *Dreamer* (1998), about the Civil Rights movement, and Martin Luther

King and his relationship with a look-alike. He has written various screenplays, and a collection of short stories, entitled *The Sorcerer's Apprentice* (1986). Essays and criticism occur in *Being and Race* (1988) and the forthcoming *Black Philosophical Fiction*, while selected writings occur in *I Call Myself an Artist* (1999). Acknowledging the influence of Ralph ELLISON and James BALDWIN, his work often explores the postmodern connection between history and chronology, in a style which blends fiction and philosophy. He is currently Professor at Emory University.

Johnson, Eyvind (1900–1976) Born Eyvind Olof Verner Johnson, in Saltsjobaden, Sweden, he was self-educated. After working in a number of menial jobs, he became a newspaper correspondent in Germany in 1921, and worked for UNESCO in the late 1940s. Relatively unknown outside Sweden, much of his writing remains untranslated into English, particularly his major allegorical *Krilon* trilogy of the 1940s. *1914* (1934, trans. 1963), or 'The Novel About Olof' is the first of a tetralogy, and is regarded as a Swedish classic for its tale of an adolescent who comes of age before the First World War, reflecting his own life in experimental techniques and a personal vision. *Return to Ithaca* (1946, trans. 1952) is a novelistic interpretation of Homer's *Odyssey*, and other works include *The Days of Grace* (1960, trans. 1968) and *Dreams of Roses and Fire* (1974, trans. 1984). His themes range from socialist reform to Swedish culture, and he was fervently anti-Nazi, speaking out against evil in his later historical novels. He was co-winner of the Nobel Prize for Literature in 1974 with Harry MARTINSON, although the Swedish Academy was strongly criticised for honouring them owing to their relative lack of international standing.

Johnston, Jennifer (1930–) Born in Dublin, Ireland, and educated at Trinity

College, Dublin, Jennifer Prudence Johnston settled near Derry in the 1970s. The
novels *The Captains and the Kings* (1972)
and *The Gates* (1973) established her as a
leading Irish writer, focusing upon political, social and religious issues, and the
friendships, loyalties and tensions among
the Anglo-Irish gentry. There followed
How Many Miles to Babylon? (1974),
which examines the friendship between
an officer and soldier from different
classes in the First World War trenches,
Shadows on Our Skin (1977), about a
tragic relationship between a Catholic
schoolboy and a Protestant teacher in
contemporary working-class Derry, *The
Old Jest* (1979), about an Anglo-Irish
girl's quest for personal integrity told in
diary form, and *The Christmas Tree*
(1981), the story of a dying woman's love
for a Holocaust survivor. Other novels
include *The Railway Station Man* (1984),
Fool's Sanctuary (1987), both about private worlds destroyed through violence,
The Invisible Worm (1991), about a girl's
relationship with a priest, *The Illusionist*
(1995), a love story partly set in London,
and *Two Moons* (1998), about a family
disturbed by the arrival of a daughter and
her new boyfriend. Her dramatic pieces
are gathered in *The Nightingale Not the
Lark* (1988), and other fiction in *The
Essential Jennifer Johnston* (1999). Her
novels are carefully crafted in a simple,
exact and sensitive style.

R. Imhof, ed., *Contemporary Irish Novelists*
(1990).

Jolley, Elizabeth (1923–) Born in Birmingham, England, she trained as a nurse and
emigrated to Australia in 1959. Alongside
her career as a writer, she has worked at a
variety of jobs, and now teaches creative
writing at Fremantle Arts Centre and
Curtin University of Technology. After
early radio drama, she wrote short fiction
in *Five Acre Virgin* (1976), *The Travelling
Entertainer* (1979), *Woman in a Lamp-
shade* (1983) and *Fellow Passengers*

(1997). Her first novel was *Palomino*
(1980), followed by, among others, *The
Newspaper of Claremont Street* (1981),
about an eccentric cleaning woman, *Mr
Scobie's Riddle* (1982), *Miss Peabody's
Inheritance* (1983), *Milk and Honey*
(1983), *Foxybaby* (1985), *The Well*
(1986), *My Father's Moon* (1989) and
Cabin Fever (1990). Recent novels include
The Georges' Wife (1993), *The Orchard
Thieves* (1995), *Lovesong* (1997), about
single men in an Australian boarding-
house, *An Accommodating Spouse* (1999),
and *News from Claremont* (2000), about
an old cleaning woman and her dreams of
escape. With an unerring eye for the
absurd, she contrasts English and Australian values, with characters often represented as exiles, lost and dislocated.
Recycling her material in her work, characters, motifs and images often reappear
as she teases readers with self-reflexive
metafictional narrative modes.

P. Gilbert, *Coming Out from Under: Contemporary Australian Women Writers* (1988).

Jones, Gayl (1949–) An American writer
of short stories, novels, plays and poetry,
Gayl Amanda Jones was born in Lexington, Kentucky, and educated at Connecticut College (BA 1971) and Brown
University, Rhode Island (MA 1973, DA
1975). Between 1975 and 1983, she
taught English at the University of Michigan, Ann Arbor. Her best-known work is
the novel *Corregidora* (1975), which has
become a classic of African-American
fiction, detailing the life of Ursa Corregidora, a blues singer from Kentucky, and
her battles against racism and sexism.
Like her second novel, *Eva's Man* (1976),
it explores the psychological effects of
slavery and sexual abuse of women
caught up in turbulent relationships and
subjected to a double oppression through
race and gender. Her next novel, after a
twenty year gap, was *The Healing* (1998),
a stream-of-consciousness tale about a life
made out of popular culture, followed by

Mosquito (1999), a huge novel in African-American vernacular about Chicana characters on the US–Mexican border. She has also written a play, entitled *Chile Woman* (1975), short stories in *White Rat* (1977), and two poetry collections in *Song for Anninho* (1981) and *The Hermit-Woman* (1983). In addition to her fictional work, she has written a study of African-American literature in *Liberating Voices: Oral Tradition in African-American Literature* (1991), and this focus is reflected in her fiction, where her language often deliberately imitates the oral patterns and rhythms of black speech.

Jones, Glyn (1905–1995) Born Glyn Morgan Jones, in Merthyr Tydfil, Wales, he was a teacher and schoolmaster in Cardiff, and worked as a reviewer, interviewer and translator (from Welsh) for radio. His numerous works include the novels *The Valley, the City, the Village* (1956), which is largely autobiographical, about a young painter aware of his vocation, *The Learning Lark* (1960), which satirises the state of education in a corrupt mining valley, and *The Island of Apples* (1965), which evokes a vanishing youth in its exploration of the adolescence of a boy named Dewi. His short stories occur in *The Blue Bed* (1937), *The Water Music* (1944), *Selected Short Stories* (1971) and *Welsh Heirs* (1977). In addition to essays on Anglo-Welsh writers collected in *The Dragon Has Two Tongues* (1968), he has published numerous collections of poetry in *Poems* (1939), *Selected Poems* (1975) and *The Story of Heledd* (1994), and edited *The Oxford Book of Welsh Verse in English* (1977). The illuminating quality of his exuberant prose is his love of people.

Jones, Gwyn (1907–1999) Born in Blackwood, Monmouthshire, he was educated at the University of Wales, Cardiff (MA 1929), and was then a teacher until 1935, when he became a lecturer at the University of Wales until 1965. Manifesting a dual emphasis on history and literature in his work, he is a noted Welsh scholar, who has published editions of Welsh, English and Norse literature. His histories of Norse and Viking cultures occur in *The Norse Atlantic Saga* (1964) and *A History of the Vikings* (1968). His fiction tends to be based on Welsh and English history, such as *Richard Savage* (1935), which centres upon the English eighteenth-century poet, *Garland of Boys* (1938), portraying the Elizabethan writer Robert Greene, and *The Flowers Beneath the Scythe* (1952), about the life of a young Welsh heiress during the two world wars. Active in promoting Anglo-Welsh literature and culture, other works include the novel *Walk Home* (1963), his *Selected Short Stories* (1974), an edited anthology of *Classic Welsh Short Stories* (1971), and a translation with Thomas Jones of the Welsh legend, *The Mabinogion* (1974).

C. Price, *Gwyn Jones* (1976).

Jong, Erica (1942–) Born in New York City, US, and educated at Barnard College (BA 1963) and Columbia University (MA 1965), Erica Mann Jong has taught English at various universities over the years. Her writing is informed by feminist politics, and she has shocked some readers by her graphic portrayal of female sexuality. She is best known for her novel *Fear of Flying* (1973), which depicts Isidora Wing's search for the ideal sexual experience, and the novel's sexual frankness made it infamous and a huge success. It was followed by a lesser-known sequel, *How to Save Your Own Life* (1977); but the bawdy eighteenth-century pastiche *Fanny* (1980) achieved a degree of infamy. Other novels include *Serenissima, A Novel of Venice* (1987), which is a comic novel about Shakespearean drama, and she continued to explore female sexuality and politics in *Parachutes and Kisses* (1984), which continued Isidora's life as a single mother in the 1980s, *Megan's Book of Divorce* (1984), a frivolous children's book for adults, and *Any Woman's Blues* (1990), which focused on the Reagan era in the 1980s. A mid-life memoir is *Fear of Fifty* (1994), and *The Devil at Large* (1993) is a biographical study of Henry MILLER. Volumes of poetry include *Fruit and Vegetables* (1971) and *Becoming Light* (1991), and collections of essays and poems occur in *Witches* (1981) and *What Do Women Want?* (1998).

Jose, F. Sionil (1924–) Born Francisco Sionil Jose, in Rosales, Philippines, he was educated at the University of Santo Tomas (B.Litt. 1949). While working as a journalist in Manila, he moonlighted writing short stories and novels. In 1965, he started his own publishing house, Solidardad, and one year later he began publishing *Solidarity*, a journal of current affairs, ideas and arts, which is still going strong today. Writing in English rather than in his national language Tagalog, his major work is the epic five-volume 'Rosales' series. The series depicts Filipino history from 1872 to 1972, and consists of *The Pretenders* (1962), *Tree* (1978), which explores the tensions between wealthy and poor Filipinos, *My Brother, My Executioner* (1979), *Mass* (1982) and *Po-on* (1985, published later as *Dusk*, 1998), some of which have been collected in *Don Vincente* (1999). Other novels include *The Chief Mourner* (1953), *The Balete Tree* (1956), *Ermita* (1988), which is a story about a prostitute which symbolically explores the rape and exploitation of the Philippines by its conquerors, *Gagamba, the Spiderman* (1991), *Viajero* (1993), *Sin* (1994), which ruminates upon the sins visited by the Filipino élite on the people, and *Sins* (1996). Short stories appear in *The God Stealer* (1968), *Waywaya* (1980), *Platinum* (1983) and *Olvidon* (1988), while he has edited an anthology of new Filipino writing in *Equinox I* (1965), and *In Search of the Word* (1998) collects essays. A well-known writer in the Philippines, his fiction concerns the search for identity and integrity in the face of the effects of urbanisation, and the exploration of the colonial history of the Philippines. Although his novels tend to focus on political issues, this does not occur at the expense of the illuminating prose.

A. Morales, ed., *F. Sionil Jose and his Fiction* (1989).

Joshi, Arun (1939–) Born in India, and educated in India and the US, he has emerged as a highly distinguished Anglo-Indian novelist. His first novel was *The Foreigner* (1968), about a young man who languishes in India after having fallen in love. This was followed by *The Strange Case of Billy Biswas* (1971), about a wealthy youth who vanishes in India's hinterlands to be later discovered living with a tribe, *The Apprentice* (1975), about an apathetic civil servant, *The Last Labyrinth* (1981), which depicts a businessman's journey to the holy city of Benares, and *The City and the River* (1990), a complex, socio-political novel that extols the virtues of effort over achievement. Short stories occur in *The Survivor* (1975). He has also written a biography of the innovative Indian industrialist *Shri Ram* (1968), and a study of his business methods in *Laila Shri Ram* (1975).

R. Dhawan, *The Fictional World of Arun Joshi* (1986).

Joyce, James (1882–1941) Born James Augustine Aloysius Joyce, in Rathgar, Dublin, Ireland, he had a Jesuit education at Clongowes Wood (1888–1892) and Belvedere College, although he rejected a religious vocation. In 1895, he went to University College, Dublin to study modern languages, but he strayed into literature, and began collecting prose sketches of epiphanies and moments of heightened perception, which formed the basis of his subsequent fiction. Joyce attacked the Irish literary revival for its increasingly nationalistic politics, and left for Paris in 1902 after graduation, although he returned to write for the Dublin *Daily Express* in 1903. His first publication was the poetry collection *Chamber Music* (1907). He also began writing an auto-biographical-based novel of spiritual growth in psychological realism as an antidote to the idealistic folk-art of the revival, which was his first prose work, *Stephen Hero* (posthumously published in 1944). This became the draft for his first published novel, *A Portrait of the Artist as a Young Man* (1916). An elaborate, mythical allegory that experimented with new forms of prose, which sought to remove authorial intrusion, *Portrait* explored the development of the artistic consciousness in the protagonist Stephen Dedalus as he tries to escape Irish social and political snares. Joyce met Nora Barnacle and their first day of courtship was 16 June 1904, a day which was to remain sacred, although they only married in 1932. He left for Trieste in 1904, where he remained for the next ten years working as a teacher. He was aided by Ezra Pound in 1913, who provided financial support as well as securing a publisher for *Portrait*, which first appeared in New York. Pound also saw Joyce's short story collection, entitled *Dubliners* (1914), into print, which had been written in 1906, but had experienced censorship difficulties. The stories detail the moribund lives of mostly lower-middle-class Dubliners, showing the crippling effects of family, religion and nationalism, themes which were amplified in *Stephen Hero* and *Portrait*. Joyce began *Ulysses* in 1914, and it was written during his movements to Zurich during the war, to Trieste and then Paris in 1920, where he became the centre of the expatriate community, which included Gertrude STEIN, HEMINGWAY, Pound and Wyndham LEWIS. *Ulysses* (1922), modelled on Homer's *Odyssey*, is a remarkable manipulation of different styles and a deliberate resistance to authorial intrusion. It is extensively experimental in form, and depicts one day (16 June 1904, commonly memorialised

as 'Bloomsday') in the life of the central characters, Leopold and Molly Bloom and Stephen Dedalus, and their Dublin friends. It remains one of the most highly regarded novels of the twentieth century. There followed an unsuccessful play, *Exiles* (1919), which is a study of jealousy, and a poetry volume, *Poems Penyeach* (1927). Meanwhile, Joyce worked on notes for a new book, known before publication as 'Work in Progress', and after taking seventeen years, it was finally published as *Finnegans Wake* (1939). Written in a highly innovative yet uncompromising dream language, with multilingual puns and a stream-of-consciousness technique, the central figures are Humphrey Earwicker, his wife Anna Livia Plurabelle, and their sons and daughter, Shem, Sham and Issy. The first words are a continuation of the last words, since the narrative is shaped and structured in cyclical form.

A vast critical machinery has emerged for the study of Joyce's writing, and there are three volumes of *The Letters of James Joyce* (1957; 1966), and *The James Joyce Archive* (1977–1979), a massive sixty-three volume edition of the totality of his notebooks manuscripts, typescripts and galleys. Joyce is celebrated as one of the most significant authors of the twentieth century and his influence on his peers like WOOLF and BECKETT, as well as writers as diverse as Saul BELLOW, John UPDIKE and Thomas PYNCHON, has been enormous.

R. Ellmann, *James Joyce* (1959, rev. 1982); D. Attridge and D. Ferrer, eds, *Poststructuralist Joyce* (1984); B.K. Scott, *James Joyce* (1987); D. Attridge, *The Cambridge Companion to James Joyce* (1990).

Jünger, Ernst (1895–1998) Born in Heidelberg, Germany, he studied biology at Naples and Leipzig (1923–1926), and served in the German army from 1914 until 1923. A contributor to radical right-wing journals (1925–1931), he became a prolific freelance writer in 1927. Early novels include *The Storm of Steel* (1920, trans. 1929) and *Copse 125* (1925, trans. 1930), both based upon his war experiences, and which established his reputation with their description of the plight and glory of modern warfare. After *African Diversions* (1936, trans. 1954), he wrote *On the Marble Cliffs* (1939, trans. 1947), a somewhat surrealistic novel in a timeless setting with futuristic and mythic features, and with thinly veiled references to the power struggles in Germany during the 1920s and 1930s. He became an example of the 'inner emigration' in Germany, which was a loose body of writers, remaining in Nazi Germany, who criticised the regime in symbolic and allegorical forms. Other novels include *The Glass Bees* (1957, trans. 1961) and *Aladdin's Problems* (1983, trans. 1993). One of the most controversial twentieth-century German writers, his proto-fascism did much harm to his later reception. He began as an innovator, went through mid-career isolation without completely eschewing his Nazi sympathies, and finished with writing a mass of essays and non-fiction, including *The Peace* (1945, trans. 1948). Combining the soldier-warrior with intellectual pursuits, he was a neo-Romantic at heart, probing the innermost regions of consciousness.

M. Bullock, *Ernst Jünger's Visions and Revisions on the European Right* (1992).

K

Kadare, Ismail (1936–) Born in Giroka-
ster, Albania, he gained a teaching diploma at the University of Tirana (1956),
and carried out advanced study at the
Gorky Institute, Moscow (1956–1961). A
prominent east European writer, he is a
prolific novelist, and one of the few
Albanian writers to be translated. *The
General of the Dead Army* (1963, trans.
1971) was the first Albanian novel to be
published in the US, and is about a
foreign general sent to recover the remains of an army killed in the Second
World War in Albania. An anti-war novel,
it was endorsed by the Albanian government as a powerful nationalist portrait
depicting the Albanians as a strong, moral
people. There followed *The Wedding*
(1968, trans. 1972), *Chronicle in Stone*
(1971, trans. 1987), which is a semi-
autobiographical work about a boy's experiences during the Second World War,
considered by many to be one of his best
works, and *The Castle* (1970, trans.
1980). *The Three-Arched Bridge* (1978,
trans. 1995) is set in medieval Albania,
examining the political and social tensions
of the Albanians and the Turks. Other
novels include *Doruntine* (1980, trans.
1988), *Broken April* (1980, trans. 1990),
set in twentieth-century Albania and focusing on traditional codes of honour, and
which was censored by the Albanian
government, *The Palace of Dreams*
(1980, trans. 1993), *The File on H*

(1980, trans. 1998), *The Concert* (1988,
trans. 1994), which parodied Albania's
relationship with Maoist China, and *The
Pyramid* (1992, trans. 1996). In addition,
he has written a wide range of poetry,
short stories, criticism and essays, much
of it in French. During the 1970s, as a
member of the People's Assembly, he had
the unique privilege of travelling outside
Albania, although he experienced censorship trouble in 1975, and was sent into
internal exile. His fiction stands out for
resisting the pressures of socialist realism
and Marxist ideology, ranging from historical and contemporary tales of Albanian people to scathing parodies of
totalitarian rule. Recently, *Elegy for Ko-
sovo* (1998, trans. 2000) compares current problems in the Balkans with a
legendary battle in 1389 against the
Turks, and explores the roots of ethnic
cleansing by the Serbians. Regarded as
something of a living legend by Albanians, in 1990 he received political asylum
in France, where he now lives.

Kadohata, Cynthia (1956–) A Japanese-
American novelist, born in Chicago, Illinois, who lives in Los Angeles. She gained
a degree from the University of Southern
California, and carried out postgraduate
work at the universities of Pittsburgh and
Columbia. She worked as a department
store clerk and waitress, before turning to
writing full-time. Her short stories have

appeared in *The New Yorker* and *Grand Street*. She is the author of two novels: the highly acclaimed *The Floating World* (1989), which tells the story of a Japanese-American family drifting through the 'ukiyo' or floating world of America in the 1950s, from the perspective of a young girl; and a futuristic dystopian novel, *In the Heart of the Valley of Love* (1992), which depicts America in 2052 as an ecological and spiritual wasteland, from the viewpoint of a 19-year-old Japanese-American girl called Francie. Kadohata's work examines the dislocation of the immigration experience, as well as family relationships, from the perspective of Japanese-American women narrators. She is widely hailed as a new voice for Japanese-Americans.

Kafka, Franz (1883–1924) Born in Prague, Czechoslovakia (then the Austro-Hungarian empire), he graduated in law at Karl Ferdinand University, Prague (1907). He did unpaid work in law courts (1906–1907), and then worked for an insurance company (1907–1908) and the Workers Accident Insurance Institute (1908–1922). As a German Jew living in the Austro-Hungarian empire experiencing cultural homelessness, his fiction depicts the modern themes of alienation, displacement and isolation. *The Trial* (1925, trans. 1935) charts the directionless journey of Joseph K. as he is placed on trial for an unknown crime by an unidentifiable government organisation. The book depicts a life of existential anxiety, the bureaucratic anonymity of modern authority, and the inability of the modern individual to grasp the circumstances of his existence, in a narrative mode which blends a realistic style with the distortions and ambiguities of nightmare scenarios. *The Castle* (1926, trans. 1930) and *America* (1927, trans. 1928) continue the presentation of the conflicts and confusion between demands of the external world and an interior idiosyncratic mindscape, and has made 'Kafka-

esque' a contemporary adjective for the solitary individual facing an incomprehensible, labyrinthine and potentially malevolent universe. Acclaimed as a central figure in European modernism, other work includes *The Diaries of Franz Kafka* (trans. 1948–1949, 2 vols), and *The Complete Stories* (trans. 1971), among which is the famous allegorical tale 'The Metamorphosis', in which Gregor Samsa awakes one morning to find himself transformed into an enormous insect who faces animosity from his family.

E. Pawel, *The Nightmare of Reason* (1984).

Katz, Steve (1935–) An American novelist, born in the Bronx, New York, and educated at Cornell University (BA 1956) and the University of Oregon (MA 1959), since when he has worked in various universities as a professor of English and as a writer. *The Lestriad* (1962) was a metafictional parody of the heroic quest, and this was followed by collections of poems in *The Weight of Antony* (1964) and *Cheyenne River Wild Track* (1973). *The Exagggerations of Peter Prince* (1968) was his first novel. Collections of short stories have appeared in *Creamy and Delicious* (1970) and *Stolen Stories* (1984), while other novels include *Posh* (1971), written under the pseudonym Stephanie Garos, *Saw* (1972), *Moving Parts* (1977) and *Journalism* (1990). *Wier and Pouce* (1984), *Florry of Washington Heights* (1987) and *Swanny's Ways* (1995) form a surreal trilogy about the life and death of a Manhattan neighbourhood and its characters. Known for his metafictional experimentation, he constantly pushes at the boundaries of literary form.

J. Klinkowitz, *Life of Fiction* (1978).

Kawabata, Yasunari (1899–1972) Born in Osaka, Japan, he was educated at the Tokyo Imperial University (BA 1924), and became a widely honoured novelist, journalist and playwright. He came to literary prominence as a student in 1924, when he was the mouthpiece of the Neo-Sensualist movement, an avant-garde group which experimented with Cubism and Surrealism to capture pure sensations and feelings in life. His fiction includes *Snow Country* (1937, trans. 1957), *The Sound of the Mountain* (1952, trans. 1970), which is a self-analysis provoked by old age, *Thousand Cranes* (1952, trans. 1974), *The Master of Go* (1954, trans. 1972), which is arguably his most famous work to western readers, and charts the clash of old and new Japanese cultures, *The Lake* (1961, trans. 1974), and *Beauty to Sadness* (1965, trans. 1975), about a novelist and his relationships with his wife and mistress. His short stories collections include *The Izu Dancer and Others* (1925, trans. 1964) and *The House of the Sleeping Beauties* (trans. 1969), which capture many of his preoccupations, such as loneliness, alienation, love, guilt, transience and death. There are also a large number of novels, short story, editions and essays remaining untranslated into English. He translated *Aesop's Fables* (1968) into Japanese and his work is also represented in the edited anthologies *Modern Japanese Literature* (1956) and *Modern Japanese Stories* (1961). The first Japanese writer to be awarded the Nobel Prize for Literature (1968), his own suicide by gassing himself was clearly influenced by the public ritual suicide of his pupil Yukio MISHIMA. In a writing which is characterised by sadness, nostalgia, eroticism and melancholy, his precision and delicate images are allusive and difficult to translate into English.

Van C. Gessel, *Three Modern Novelists: Soseki, Tanizaki, Kawabata* (1993).

Kazantzákis, Nikos (1883–1957) Born in Iraklion on the island of Crete, Greece, he graduated from the University of Athens with a law degree (1906), and carried out further studies in Paris, Germany and Italy (1906–1910). He held various posts in the Greek government (1919–1946) and became a respected writer and wide traveller. Early novels include *Serpent and Lily* (1906, trans. 1980), *Toda Raba* (1934, trans. 1964) and *The Rock Garden* (1936, trans. 1963). He then wrote his most famous work, *Zorba the Greek* (1946, trans. 1952), which catapulted him to international fame, and was later filmed starring Anthony Quinn (1964). The novel concerns a friendship between a bookish intellectual and an unsophisticated peasant, and explores the split between a human's physical and intellectual natures. *Freedom and Death* (1953, trans. 1956) deals with the Cretans' fight for independence, and controversy was stirred up with *The Greek Passion* (1954), which depicts Christianity as a power-hungry, ineffectual institution. Controversy persisted with *The Last Temptation of Christ* (1955, trans. 1960; and filmed in 1980 by Martin Scorsese), which depicted an uncertain, emotionally troubled Christ, tempted to renounce his calling and live like an ordinary man. The novel caused a world-wide furore, angering the Greek Orthodox and Roman Catholic churches, who threatened Kazantzákis with excommunication. Later novels include *Saint Francis* (1956, trans. 1962), *The Fratricides* (1963, trans. 1964) and *Alexander the Great* (1979, trans. 1982). In addition to plays, history, criticism and travel books, he wrote an epic poem *Odysseia* (1938), based upon Homer's *Odyssey*. Regarded as the most important Greek writer of the twentieth century, he is widely translated. In a passionate style suffused with imagery, his philosophical fiction probes humanity's physical and intellectual natures, seeking to reconcile these dualities of flesh and spirit.

H. Kazantzákis, *Nikos Kazantzákis: A Biography Based on His Letters* (1968).

Keane, Molly (1904–1996) An Irish writer, born in Co. Kildare, Molly Mary

Nesta Keane wrote her first novel, *The Knight of the Cheerful Countenance* (1926), under the pseudonym M.J. Farrell to hide her literary activity from her society friends, and continued to use this name for her next ten novels. Her fiction is often set in the big houses of the Anglo-Irish ascendancy, following the traditional hunting and shooting pursuits of the Anglo-Irish country society and the tensions with the Irish people. Central characters tend to be young, romantic and in revolt against their parents, which is especially characteristic of *Young Entry* (1928), *Taking Chances* (1929) and *Mad Puppetstown* (1931). *Two Days in Aragon* (1941) is set against the Troubles of 1919–1921, while *Devoted Ladies* (1934) is set in bohemian London. She also wrote a number of successful plays, including *Spring Meeting* (1938), *Ducks and Drakes* (1941), *Guardian Angel* (1944) and *Treasure Hunt* (1949). A prolific author of psychologically exact writing with deliberate use of motif-phrases, other novels include *Full House* (1935) and *The Rising Tide* (1937), both of which look at generational conflicts, *Loving without Tears* (1951) and *Treasure Hunt* (1952). After an absence from writing for more than twenty years, she re-emerged with her first novel under her own name, the black comedy *Good Behaviour* (1981), which was adapted for television in 1983. Her later novels depict greater introspection and egoism in characters' behaviour and personalities, and include *Time After Time* (1983), *Loving and Giving* (1988) and *Queen Lear* (1989). *A Portrait of the Artist as a Young Girl* (1986) is an autobiographical essay. With story incidental to her novels, many of them explore the protected and selfish lives led by her characters in a narrow and sheltered society.

Keillor, Garrison (1942–) Born Garrison Gary Edward Keillor, in Anoka, Minnesota, US, and educated at the University of Minnesota (BA 1966), he became famous for his radio show, 'A Prairie Home Companion', broadcast on Minnesota Public Radio from 1974 until 1987. Always introduced by the line 'It has been a quiet day in Lake Wobegon, my hometown', the show incorporated music and focused on the values of small-town America. It became the basis for his successful novel, *Lake Wobegon Days* (1985), about the characters of second generation immigrant German and Norwegian families in the fictional semi-rural Minnesota town. Blending a sense of the absurd and ironic wit with a remarkably tender and sympathetic perspective, he has published a number of novels and short stories which deal with similar Minnesotan characters: *Happy to Be Here* (1982), *Leaving Home* (1987), *We Are Still Married* (1989), *A Radio Romance* (1991) and *Wobegon Boy* (1997); while *The Book of Guys* (1993) is a comic spin-off about male bonding, and *Me* (1999) is a political satire about a wrestler-turned-governor of Minnesota. In 1989, he began a new radio programme in New York City, and he has recently published several children's books.

P. Scholl, *Garrison Keillor* (1993).

Kelman, James (1946–) Born in Glasgow, Scotland, he worked at a number of manual jobs before attending the University of Strathclyde (1975–1978, 1981–1982), and has emerged as one of the finest and most provocative contemporary British writers. A working-class writer in the realist tradition, his first work was a collection of short stories entitled *Not Not While the Giro* (1983), which explored the social and economic aspects of the poor in London and Glasgow. Other collections of short stories occur in *Lean Tales* (1985), *Greyhound for Breakfast* (1987), *The Burn* (1991) and *The Good Times* (1998), many of which chart the dreary lives of his working-class characters. *The Busconductor Hines* (1984) was his first novel, and portrays a bus conductor who hates his job and is bored with his life, although it met with little critical appreciation. Similar themes are developed in *A Chancer* (1985), and *A Disaffection* (1989), about a week in the life of a Glaswegian schoolteacher, Patrick Doyle, depicting his frustrated, disenchanted and bored life. Yet it was with the much celebrated *How Late It Was, How Late* (1994, Booker Prize), about a drunken spree down Glasgow's meanest streets, and how the working class in Glasgow endures a bleak existence, urban decay and menial jobs, that Kelman's fiction met wide acclaim. With its black humour and raw language in Scottish dialect, the novel was criticised for its profusion of obscenities, although Kelman defended this as the living language of Glasgow. *Some Recent Attacks* (1993) collects essays and journalistic pieces on various social issues affecting Britain.

Kemal, Yaşar (Yaşar Kemal Gokceli) (1922–) A widely honoured Turkish novelist, he was born Yaşar Kemal Gokceli, in Hemite, Adana, Turkey, and worked at various manual jobs before becoming a journalist in 1952, and a full-time writer in 1963. A member of the Turkish Labour Party, he has been imprisoned periodically for his political views. He has written a wide variety of novels, and his first novel translated into English was *Memed, My Hawk* (1955, trans. 1961), made into a film by Peter Ustinov, about a brigand who becomes a folk hero by taking up arms to help the exploited. There followed what is widely regarded as his most enduring novel, *The Wind from the Plain* (1960, trans. 1963), followed by *Iron Earth, Copper Sky* (1963, trans. 1974) and *The Undying Grass* (1969, trans. 1977), these three novels forming part of Turkey's so-called 'village literature', which dealt with the plight of the peasants in a feudal system. Other translated novels include *Anatolian Tales* (1967, trans. 1968), a sequel to *Memed, My Hawk* in *They Burn the Thistles* (1969,

trans. 1973), *The Legend of Ararat* (1970, trans. 1975), *The Legend of the Thousand Bells* (1971, trans. 1976), *The Saga of a Seagull* (1976, trans. 1981), *The Birds Have Also Gone* (1978, trans. 1987), *The Sea-Crossed Fisherman* (1978, trans. 1985), *Salman the Solitary* (1995, trans. 1998), about Kurds in exile, and *Castle Gate* (trans. 1999). While his later fiction became less combative, he continued to explore economic exploitation and injustice, developing a stronger reliance on stream-of-consciousness techniques and a blend of realism and fantasy. Immensely popular in Turkey and with a strong affinity with Turkish oral traditions, his work has drawn praise, particularly in France, Scandinavia and socialist countries.

Keneally, Thomas (1935–) An internationally respected Australian novelist, born Thomas Michael Keneally, in Sydney, he commenced study for the Catholic priesthood at the age of 17, but abandoned it before ordination in 1960, and became a schoolteacher and clerk. His first novels, *The Place at Whitton* (1964), *The Fear* (1965, published as *By the Line*, 1969), and *Three Cheers for the Paraclete* (1968), all examine the significance of Roman Catholicism. *Bring Larks and Heroes* (1967), set in New South Wales, was his first major success, and was followed by *The Survivor* (1969), set in Antarctica (as was the later *A Victim of the Aurora*, 1977), and *A Dutiful Daughter* (1971), an analysis of contemporary Australia. *The Chant of Jimmie Blacksmith* (1972, filmed 1978), explored the sectarian and racial prejudice in European attitudes towards Aborigines, while *Blood Red, Sister Rose* (1974) was about Joan of Arc. Other novels include *Gossip from the Forest* (1975), about the Armistice talks at the end of the First World War, *Season in Purgatory* (1976), about the partisan war in Yugoslavia, *Passenger* (1979), *Confederates* (1979), about Stonewall Jackson in the American Civil War, and *The Cut-Rate Kingdom* (1980). Perhaps his most famous book is *Schindler's Ark* (1982, Booker Prize), about the Nazi Holocaust and Oskar Schindler's role in saving hundreds of Jews, and made into the acclaimed film *Schindler's List* (1994) by Steven Spielberg. Further novels include *A Family Madness* (1985), *The Playmaker* (1987), *Towards Asmara* (1989), about the war in contemporary Eritrea, *Flying Hero Class* (1991), *Women of the Inner Sea* (1992), *Jacko the Great Intruder* (1994), *A River Town* (1995), and two books about the Second World War, under the pseudonym William Coyle, entitled *Act of Grace* (1988) and *Chief of Staff* (1991). Travel books include *Outback* (1983), *Now and in Time to Be* (1992), about Ireland, and *The Place Where Souls Are Born* (1992), about the American Southwest desert regions. In addition, he has written stage-plays, and television and film adaptations of his fiction, as well as the autobiographical works *Memoirs from a Young Republic* (1993) and *Homebush Boy* (1995). *The Great Shame* (1998) is a non-fictional narrative about the Irish in the Old and New Worlds. A fluent writer, popular in Australia and abroad, his writing spans a wide range, from idiomatic and vernacular language to the symbolic and the rhetorical. His explorations of the connection between history and fiction have led to controversy, but his novels are not merely historical reconstructions. Set around the world, his fiction explores persecution, the predicaments of the individual and the resistance to political, racial or institutional authority.

P. Quartermaine, *Thomas Keneally* (1991).

Kennedy, A.L. (1965–) Full name Alison Louise Kennedy, born in Dundee, Scotland, and educated at Warwick University, she has emerged as a widely acclaimed contemporary Scottish writer. Her first work was a volume of short stories, entitled *Night Geometry and the Gars-*

cadden Trains (1990), set in Scotland, and focusing on silent female characters and their social and domestic problems. Her first novel followed, *Looking for the Possible Dance* (1993). Set in Scotland again, and looking at a community worker, it depicts the ugliness of city life with an appalling act of violence at the book's conclusion. There followed the novels *So I Am Glad* (1995), blending realism and magic elements in a study of disconnection and alienation in a fantasy about Cyrano de Bergerac in modern Glasgow, and *Everything You Need* (1999), about a novelist who seeks to redeem his relationship with his daughter. The short story collections *Now That You're Back* (1995), set in Paris, Britain and the US, and *Original Bliss* (1997), on the topics of love and sex, continue to demonstrate her careful prose and the presentation of the surreal in everyday life. Her latest book is about bullfighting in Spain (1999).

Kennedy, William (1928–) An Irish-American novelist, born in Albany, New York, William Joseph Kennedy was educated at Siena College (BA 1949). After a lengthy period as a respected and versatile journalist on various newspapers, he became a lecturer in English at SUNY-Albany in 1974, and Albany and journalists feature prominently in his fiction. His early fiction was ignored until his success with *Ironweed* (1983, Pulitzer Prize 1984), which depicts the down-and-out life of Francis Phelan, a drifter in Albany boarding-houses during the Depression, and his past and present personal relationships. Subsequently filmed starring Jack Nicholson (1987), for which Kennedy wrote the screenplay, it caused attention to be refocused on Kennedy's earlier fiction. His first novel, *The Ink Truck* (1969, reprinted 1984), deals with a newspaper strike in Albany; *Legs* (1975) is about a gangster, Jack 'Legs' Diamond; while *Billy Phelan's Greatest Game* (1978) recounts the story of Francis Phelan's son, and is set in the dives of Albany. All these novels are hard-hitting, unsentimental accounts of destitution and corruption in 1930s Albany. *Quinn's Book* (1988), set in pre-Civil War Albany, begins another cycle on the residents of Albany, continued in *Very Old Bones* (1992) and *Flaming Corsage* (1996), which oscillates between 1884 and 1912, and depicts the class and wealth in Albany. He also co-wrote the screenplay for *The Cotton Club* (1984), Francis Coppola's film of 1930s gangsterism. Other works include a book of articles on Albany in *Albany! An Urban Tapestry* (1983) and selected non-fiction in *Riding the Yellow Trolley Car* (1993).

Kerouac, Jack (1922–1969) An American writer, born Jean Louis Lebrid de Kerouac in Lowell, Massachusetts, of a French-Canadian background. He studied briefly at Columbia College as an undergraduate, but left to serve as a US merchant marine during the 1940s. Kerouac, with author Ken KESEY and poet Allen Ginsberg, is considered a leading light of the Beat generation: drop-outs who claimed to reject the materialism of mainstream society. His first novel was *The Town and the City* (1950), which adapted his personal experiences into a narrative about a man who leaves a city for adventures on the road. This links to his most famous novel, *On the Road* (1957), the story of a restless and aimless trip across America, which became a defining novel for the counter-culture in the 1960s. Other novels include *The Dharma Bums* (1958), which was another road story, *The Subterraneans* (1958), about the love affair between a Beat author and a black girl, *Doctor Sax* (1959), *Maggie Cassidy* (1959), and *Tristessa* (1960), about a drug-addicted Creole prostitute. He also wrote *Big Sur* (1962), *Visions of Gerard* (1963), *Vanity of Duluoz* (1968), and a non-fiction book, *Satori in Paris* (1966), about a trip Kerouac made to Paris to trace his French ancestry. *Lonesome Traveller* (1960) collects travel sketches,

while *Pic* (1971), published posthumously, is the story of the progress of a black jazz musician to Harlem from the American South. His poems occur in *Mexico City Blues* and *Scattered Poems* (1971). His best-known work makes use of an improvisational style, which he called 'spontaneous prose', an urgently paced and freely discursive idiom in the manner of jazz improvisation.

G. Nicosia, *Memory Babe* (1983).

Kesey, Ken (1935–) Ken Elton Kesey, an American author, was born in La Junta, Colorado, and educated at the University of Oregon and Stanford University. A member of the Beat generation, he was a friend of Jack KEROUAC. After undergoing volunteer tests on the drug LSD in the late 1950s, he continued working as a ward attendant at the hospital in California, which provided him with the basis for his most famous and critically acclaimed novel, *One Flew Over the Cuckoo's Nest* (1962). Set in a mental institution, where a new patient, Randall Patrick McMurphy, liberates the brow-beaten inmates from the tyranny of a despotic Nurse Ratched and a dehumanising institutional process, it became a significant text in the American counter-culture of the 1960s, and a famous film starring Jack Nicholson in 1975. *Sometimes a Great Notion* (1964), set in Oregon, is a long, panoramic and rambling book about concerns in the Northwest region, leaping backward and forward in time and making use of typographical intrusions. *Kesey's Garage Sale* (1973) presents interviews and articles, and he has also written a short story called *The Day Superman Died* (1980), the miscellaneous collection *Demon Box* (1986), written in the 1970s and 1980s about his psychedelic and other experiences of the counter-culture, *The Further Inquiry* (1990), and *Sailor Song* (1992), about a Hollywood film company who, on location in Alaska, encounter an Indian tribe who have had little contact with whites, and *Last Go Round* (1994), a dime-Western narrated by a seasoned rodeo veteran. He was associated with the hippie movement and was a member of The Merry Pranksters, a group which travelled around in a bus at the height of experimental drug use in the 1960s. His drug experiences and celebrated trend-setting, West Coast lifestyle is recorded in Tom WOLFE's *The Electric Kool-Aid Acid Test* (1968), and he embodies the arche-typal American social rebel who is constantly in search of heightened con-sciousness.

P. Gilbert, *The Art of Grit: Ken Kesey's Fiction* (1982).

Kiely, Benedict (1919–) Born in Dromore, Co. Tyrone, Ireland, he was educated by the Jesuits and went to University College, Dublin. He worked as a journalist in Dublin (1945–1964), taught at several American universities (1964–1968), and has since lectured at University College, Dublin. His earliest work was *Counties of Contention* (1945), which attacked the partitioning of Ireland, followed by *Poor Scholar* (1947), a study of William Carle-ton's writings, and *Modern Irish Fiction* (1950). His earliest novels dealt with small-town life, depicting personal rela-tionships against the turbulent political upheavals in Ireland. *Land without Stars* (1946) is about two brothers, one an IRA member and the other a bank robber, and their rivalry for the same woman, *In a Harbour Green* (1949) is a love triangle plot set in the west of Ireland, while *Call for a Miracle* (1950) is an urban novel about complex sexual relationships in Dublin. *The Cards of the Gambler* (1953), *The Captain with the Whiskers* (1960) and *Dogs Enjoy the Morning* (1968) all merge strands of fantasy with reality, and *There Was an Ancient House* (1955) is a disillusioned Jesuit noviciate's view of life. Other novels include the reproaches to extremist Protestant and Catholic violence in *Proxopera* (1977),

and *Nothing Happens in Carmincross* (1985), while essays occur in *A Raid into Dark Corners* (1999), and *The Waves Behind Us* (1999) is a memoir. Short stories appear in *A Journey to the Seven Streams* (1963), *A Ball of Malt and Madam Butterfly* (1973), *A Cow in the House* (1978) and *A Letter to Peachtree* (1987). His narratives often draw upon country story-telling modes, partly de-tailed in *Drink to the Bird* (1991), a memoir of local lore and nostalgia. He has also edited *The Penguin Book of Irish Short Stories* (1981), *The Small Oxford Book of Dublin* (1983), and an anthology of Irish songs in *As I Rode by Granard Moat* (1996).

G. Eckley, *Benedict Kiely* (1975).

Kincaid, Jamaica (1949–) Born Elaine Potter Richardson in St. Johns, Antigua, she was educated at Franconia College, New Hampshire, US, and now resides in Bennington, Vermont. She worked as a staff writer for *The New Yorker* from 1976 to 1995. She achieved wide acclaim for her first two works, a collection of short stories in *At the Bottom of the River* (1983), which details life's mundanities and daily chores, and the novel *Annie John* (1985), a series of interrelated stor-ies about a girl's coming-of-age in Anti-gua. Further novels include *Lucy* (1990), a first person narrative by the 19-year-old Lucy, struggling to adjust as an *au pair* in an American city and her separation from her homeland, and *Autobiography of My Mother* (1995), about the life of the elderly narrator Xuela. Essays have ap-peared in *A Small Place* (1988), a memoir in *My Brother* (1997), and gardening anecdotes in *My Garden Book* (1999). Much of her fiction is about the Carib-bean, written in a highly poetic style, and she has emerged as a significant voice in American fiction.

D. Simmons, *Jamaica Kincaid* (1994).

King, Stephen (1947–) Born in Portland, Maine, US, and educated at the state university at Orono, Stephen Edwin King is regarded as one of the most popular novelists of science fiction and horror. In a highly successful and prolific career, many of his novels have been made into films, such as his first novel *Carrie* (1973), and *The Shining* (1977), about evil supernatural forces. Widely credited with revivifying the macabre in fiction and film, his name has become synonymous with the genre of horror and the supernatural. At the rate of almost one a year, his huge output of novels includes *The Stand* (1978), *Pet Sematary* (1983), *Needful Things* (1991), *Dolores Claiborne* (1993), *Rose Madder* (1995), *Desperation* (1996) and *The Girl Who Loved Tom Gordon* (1999). *Bag of Bones* (1998) is partly inspired by Daphne DU MAURIER's *Rebecca*, while *Hearts in Atlantis* (1999) is five stories about children in the 1960s. He considers horror to be cathartic, and often instils it with elements of optimism. He has also written various screenplays and a series of novels under the pseudonym Richard Bachman. His recent 'e-book', *Riding the Bullet* (2000), clogged the Internet for three days when it was released on various bookseller websites.

Kingsolver, Barbara (1955–) Born in Annapolis, Maryland, US, she was educated at De Pauw University (BA 1977) and Arizona University (MS 1981). After working as a research assistant in physiology, she became a technical writer on arid land studies, and turned to freelance journalism and writing in the mid-1980s. Her first novel, *The Bean Trees* (1988), about the relationships between a group of women in Arizona, met an enthusiastic reception. There followed *Animal Dreams* (1990), about the growth of Codi Noline, as she returns to her hometown in Arizona after fourteen years' absence and finds a lack of stability, *Pigs in Heaven* (1993), a sequel to *The Bean Trees*, a tale of adoption and economic struggle in a journey of personal development, and *The Poisonwood Bible* (1998), which is about a missionary and his family in the Belgian Congo in 1959 and the problems they encounter. Her latest novel is *Prodigal Summer* (2000). Short stories appear in *Homeland* (1989), and other books include *Holding the Line* (1989), about women in the great Arizona mine strike of 1983, a volume of poetry in *Another America/Otra America* (1992), and essays in *High Tide in Tucson* (1996). In her comic and lyrical depictions of middle America, her stories often focus upon a strong sense of family relationships and community as people derive inspiration through communal bonding.

Kingston, Maxine Hong (1940–) A Chinese-American writer of novels, memoir, short stories and occasional writings, Maxine Ting Tong Hong Kingston was born and raised in Stockton, California. She was educated at the University of California, Berkeley (BA 1962), and has taught at the University of Hawaii, and at the University of California at Berkeley since 1990. Kingston's complex multi-genre text, *The Woman Warrior* (1976), was published to universal acclaim. Ostensibly a memoir, but incorporating features of fiction, biography, autobiography and myth, the novel explores themes of mother and daughter relationships, memory and history, and cross-cultural experiences and understanding. It has been widely anthologised and taught, and has paved the way for a host of similar writing, perhaps most notably the novels of fellow Chinese-American writer, Amy TAN. While *The Woman Warrior* recorded the experiences and stories of Kingston's female forebears, including her mother, its companion volume, *China Men* (1980), imaginatively recounts the histories of her male relatives and ancestors. It bears the same characteristics of mixed-genre prose as *The Woman Warrior*, although it has not been as successful. In 1987, she published a collection of occasional writings entitled *Hawaii One Summer*, and the novel *Tripmaster Monkey: His Fake Book*. A departure from her previous work, the novel is a manic, slightly off-kilter novel about 1960s hip poet, Wittman Ah Sing, and it alienated some readers, despite a generally positive critical reception. Married to the actor Earll Kingston, Kingston is currently completing her latest novel, which is due for publication in 2001.

K-K. Cheung, *Articulate Silences* (1993).

Kinsella, W.P. (1935–) A Canadian writer, born William Patrick Kinsella, in Edmonton, Alberta, he spent two years in business before studying creative writing at the University of Victoria (BA 1974) and at the Iowa Writers' Workshop (MFA 1978). He has since worked as a teacher of creative writing at the University of Calgary. His writing is characterised by a spontaneity, passion and anti-authoritarianism, such as his Indian stories in *Dance Me Outside* (1977), *Scars* (1978), *Born Indian* (1981), *The Moccasin Telegraph* (1983) and *The Fencepost Chronicles* (1986). Focusing on the perspective of an 18-year-old Native-Canadian named Silas Ermineskin, these stories imagine the reactions to various experiences, and incline towards satire and pathos. One of his short stories in the collection, *Shoeless Joe Jackson Comes to Iowa* (1980), which attacks vice and prejudice, was filmed as *Field of Dreams* (1989). Other books about baseball include *The Thrill of the Grass* (1984) and *The Iowa Baseball Confederacy* (1986), while his short stories are collected in *Red Wolf, Red Wolf* (1987), *The Alligator Report* (1985) and *Brother Frank's Gospel* (1996). Recent novels are *Box Socials* (1991), about life in a backwater town of Alberta in the 1940s, *The Winter Helen Dropped By* (1995), a coming-of-age story told by a young boy, and *Magic Time* (1998),

another baseball narrative set in small-town Iowa.

Kipling, Rudyard (1865–1936) An English writer and poet, he was born Joseph Rudyard Kipling, in Bombay, India. His ethos was one of unquestioning belief in the ideals of the British Empire and loyalty to King and Country. He spent an early, unhappy childhood at school in England, but returned to India in 1882, where he worked as a journalist. He published the satirical verses *Departmental Ditties* (1986) and a collection of short stories *Plain Tales from the Hills* (1887) and, between then and 1889, six further volumes of short stories, including *Soldiers Three* (1888), *The Phantom Rickshaw* (1888) and *Wee Willie Winkie* (1888), which firmly established his reputation as a writer. More verse followed, with experiments in popular forms and dramatic soldiers' vernacular voices in *Barrack-Room Ballads* (1892). His important novels are *The Light That Failed* (1891), about a blind artist; a sea story in *Captains Courageous* (1897); *Stalky & Co.* (1899), about three rebellious boys at a boarding school, based loosely on his own experience at a school in Westward Ho, Devon; and most notably, *Kim* (1901), a colourful story of street life in India. Further short story collections occur in *Life's Handicap* (1891), *Many Inventions* (1893), *The Day's Work* (1898), *Traffics and Discoveries* (1904), *Actions and Reactions* (1909), *Debits and Credits* (1926) and *Limits and Renewals* (1932). He was a versatile stylist, and in addition to these volumes, Kipling wrote a number of entertaining stories for children, including *The Jungle Book* (1894), *The Second Jungle Book* (1895), *Just So Stories for Little Children* (1902), *Puck of Pook's Hill* (1906) and *Rewards and Fairies* (1910). As well as his rather unrevealing autobiography, *Something of Myself* (1937), there are several travel books, including *From Sea to Sea* (1899). Despite being the first English recipient of the Nobel Prize for Literature, in 1907, his reputation has fluctuated over the decades, especially with the advent of the experimentalism of modernism and the continuing criticism of his apparent celebration of imperial supremacy.

J. Harrison, *Rudyard Kipling* (1982); M. Seymour-Smith, *Rudyard Kipling* (1990).

Kiš, Danilo (1935–1989) Born in Subotica, Yugoslavia, he was educated at the University of Belgrade (BA 1958), and after the Second World War, he lectured in universities in France, where he spent a large part of the remainder of his life, eventually dying in Paris. He was associated in the 1960s with a group of young writers who sought to introduce new trends into Serbian fiction, and his novel in Serbo-Croatian, *Mansarda* (1962, 'The Attic'), which depicts the pains of adolescence during the war, set the preoccupations of much of his later fiction, with its treatment of wartime racial and political persecution of the Jews. *Garden, Ashes* (1965, trans. 1978) and *Hourglass* (1972, trans. 1990) are about the Holocaust and war experiences, and are also monuments to the memory of his father who died in a pogrom and who left a deep impression upon his son. The short stories of *A Tomb for Boris Davidovič* (1976, trans. 1978) look at communist anti-Semitism and the Stalinist purges, while *The Encyclopaedia of the Dead* (1983, trans. 1989) contains stories about the disappearance of eastern European Jews. *Homo Poeticus* (1995) collects essays and interviews, and *Early Sorrows* (trans. 1998) is a biography of his childhood and youth during the Second World War. Many regard him as one of the most important Yugoslavian writers of the twentieth century, often presenting a peculiar perception of reality as a cross between the real and the fantastic, and between the comprehensible and the bizarre.

Kittredge, William (1932–) Born in Portland, Oregon, US, he attended Oregon State University (BS 1953) and the University of Iowa (MFA 1969). He was a cattle rancher between 1957 and 1967 in Montana, and in 1969 he began teaching at the University of Montana, at Missoula. His diverse works chronicling the American West began with *The Van Gogh Field* (1979) and *We Are Not in This Together* (1982), short stories about drink, guns and horses, in which life and death are the main focus. Under the joint pseudonym of Owen Rowntree, he wrote the 'Cord' series with Steven Krauzer between 1982 and 1986, nine adventure novels which explore the Western milieu. *Owning It All* (1987) and *Who Owns the West?* (1996) are collections of essays, and he has edited *Montana Spaces* (1988), a depiction of the wilder areas of the state, and *The Last Best Place* (1988), which is work by Montanans on their state. He has written a memoir seeking atonement and redemption in *Hole in the Sky* (1992) and *Taking Care: Thoughts on Storytelling and Belief* (1999).

Klíma, Ivan (1931–) Born in Prague, Czechoslovakia, he graduated from Charles University (MA 1956), and worked as an editor in publishing from 1959 to 1969, when he turned to writing full-time. He spent three years of his childhood in the Nazi concentration camp of Terezín, an experience which recurs in his fiction. His novels include *A Ship Named Hope* (1969, trans. 1970), which uses travel as an allegorical conceit, *A Summer Affair* (1973, trans. 1987), a depiction of a love affair, in which a scientist squanders his promise for the future, *My First Loves* (1985, trans. 1986), *Love and Garbage* (1986, trans. 1990), which has an autobiographical basis in the experience of Czech dissident writers, *Judge on Trial* (1986, trans. 1993), where a judge gradually realises that it is he who is on trial, *Waiting for the Dark, Waiting for the Light* (1993, trans. 1994), and *The Ultimate Intimacy* (1996, trans. 1997), an exploration of one crucial year in the life of a minister. Short stories occur in *Lovers for a Day* (trans. 1999), while *Between Security and Insecurity* (trans. 1999) is a study of social values and ethics at the turn of the millennium. His work was banned in 1968 after the Soviet invasion, but he chose not to emigrate along with exiles like SKVORECKÝ and KUNDERA; and since the 'Velvet Revolution' of 1989, he has been rehabilitated as a leading Czech intellectual and spokesperson after his significant involvement in the movement, along with the dissident writer Vaclav Havel. His fiction explores the possibilities of resistance, capturing the choking suffocation of oppression characteristic of the twenty years after 1968 in Czechoslovakia.

Koch, C.J. (1932–) Full name Christopher John Koch, an Australian author, born in Hobart, Tasmania, and educated at the University of Tasmania, he has lived in Europe and America, and travelled widely in Asia. After working as a producer for ABC, he turned to full-time writing in 1973, and currently lives near Sydney. In addition to poetry, radio plays and television scripts, his novels are *The Boys in the Island* (1958), about boyhood and adolescence in provincial Australia and the lure of the metropolitan; *Across the Sea Wall* (1965, rev. 1982), about the protagonist's experiences after his voyage 'home' to England is diverted to India; *The Year of Living Dangerously* (1978, filmed 1982), about journalists in the Indonesian coup of 1965 and examining postcolonial Australian identity; *The Doubleman* (1985), in which the postcolonial exploration continues in an Australian setting; and *Highways to a War* (1995), about the Vietnam War. His essays are collected in *Crossing the Gap: A Novelist's Essays* (1987). Shadows and doubles recur throughout his novels, as he explores postcolonial identities and the ironies of Anglo culture in vastly different colonial environments. He deploys Asian philoso-phies as mediating terms in the postcolonial construction of Australian identity.

Koestler, Arthur (1905–1983) Born in Budapest, Hungary, he attended the University of Vienna (1922–1926), and became a British subject after the Second World War. He carried out a range of jobs, including farming, journalism, editing and writing. After his first novel, *The Gladiators* (1939), he gained an international reputation for his fictionalised account of the Moscow Trials of 1938, entitled *Darkness at Noon* (1940), an indictment which exposed the reality behind the façade of justice as Bolshevik revolutionaries were put to death by the Soviet government. He viewed the Trials as an abandonment of the socialist ideals and his book grew out of his own gradual disillusionment with the Communist Party after seven years' membership. Subsequent fiction continued to explore political idealism and power, and the difficult transformation of ideals into practice. There followed *Arrival and Departure* (1943), about a young revolutionary who suffers a nervous breakdown, *Thieves in the Night* (1946), which concerns the settlement of Israel by the Jews, *The Age of Longing* (1951), about a nuclear future, and a satirical perspective of high-powered intellectuals in *The Call Girls* (1972). In the 1950s, he gave up political writing and his anti-communist polemics, and devoted his time to scientific and philosophical matters. A prolific writer of non-fiction, including history, sociology and psychology, he is most widely known for *The Act of Creation* (1964), a synthesis of a mass of material, in addition to *The Lotus and the Robot* (1960) and *The Ghost in the Machine* (1967). As well as essays in *The Yogi and the Commissar* (1945) and *The Heel of Achilles* (1974), he wrote various volumes of autobiography, including *Spanish Testament* (1937), about his arrest and liberation during the Spanish Civil War, *Scum of the Earth* (1941), which records his imprisonment in a French concentration camp in 1940, *Amour in the Blue* (1952) and *The Invisible Writing* (1954). Suffering from a terminal illness, he and his devoted third wife Cynthia Jefferies died in a suicide pact, their last days recorded in their jointly written *Stranger on the Square* (1984).

S. Pearson, *Arthur Koestler* (1978).

Konwicki, Tadeusz (1926–) Born in Nowa Wilejka, Poland, he attended the University of Warsaw and the Jagellonian University in Cracow (1945–1949). A novelist, screenwriter and film director, his novels include *A Dreambook for Our Time* (1963, trans. 1969), whose first English translation caused him to be compared to James JOYCE and Joseph CONRAD, and which painfully explored the guilt and memory in tormented survivors of the German Occupation, *The Polish Complex* (1977, trans. 1982), which contrasts Polish history of 1863 with pre-Solidarity Poland of the late 1970s in an ironic fashion, *A Minor Apocalypse* (1979, trans. 1983), a darkly humorous, surreal book about conditions in Warsaw and the grim conditions of communist society, *Moonrise, Moonset* (1982, trans. 1987), which depicts conditions in Poland in the 1980s with memories from Poland's past, and *Bohin Manor* (1987, trans. 1990), a romance set on a Lithuanian manor farm in 1875. His memoirs occur in *New World Avenue and Vicinity* (1986, trans. 1991), which revisits his history. One of Poland's leading novelists of the twentieth century, he presents comic yet despairing portraits of Polish society.

Koontz, Dean R. (1945–) An American writer, born Dean Ray Koontz, in Everett, Pennsylvania, who writes mainly macabre fantasy and horror fiction. His writing career began in about 1970, and he has become very popular and successful, writing over forty novels under his own name and many more under pseudonyms – for example, Brian Coffey, Deanna Dwyer, Leigh Nichols and Christopher Snow, among others. He originally wrote science fiction, but turned to suspense fiction, with tightly constructed plots and rich characters, combining horror, science fiction, suspense and romance. He dates his serious writing career from *Chase* (1972), about the effects of the Vietnam War on a veteran, and *Hanging On* (1973), a comic novel, although his big break in sales came with *Whispers* (1980), about a psychopathic madman who assaults women. Other novels include *Beastchild* (1970), *A Werewolf Among Us* (1973), *Darkfall* (1984), *The Mask* (1988), *The Bad Place* (1990), *Dragon Tears* (1993), *Shadow Fires* (1993), *Icebound* (1994), *Intensity* (1996), *Seize the Night* (1998), and *False Memory* (1999), a tense thriller about mind control and brainwashing. Several of his books have been made into films, including *Demon Seed* (1973), *Shattered* (1973), *Watchers* (1987) and *Hideaway* (1992). He has also written many short stories in the same vein, some of which are collected in *Soft Come the Dragons* (1970). Two works of non-fiction are *Writing Popular Fiction* (1973) and *How to Write Best-selling Fiction* (1981). Although his characters are often pitted against unspeakable evil and overwhelming odds, they nevertheless emerge victorious.

Kosinski, Jerzy (1933–1991) Born Nikodem Jerzy Kosinski, in Lodz, Poland, and educated at the University of Lodz (BA 1950), and later at Columbia University, he went to the US in 1957, and was naturalised in 1965. He is best known for his novel *The Painted Bird* (1965), a semi-autobiographical story about a child who is abandoned to wander through war-torn eastern Europe during the Nazi occupation of Poland. Almost always depressing and disturbing, his other novels include *Steps* (1968), *Being There* (1971, filmed 1979), which is a satire about American politics and television,

The Devil Tree (1973), *Cockpit* (1975), *Blind Date* (1977), *Passion Play* (1979), and *Pinball* (1982). These works often depict the individual's struggle against alienation and isolation within society and culture, and the workings of chance in the formation of selfhood. His later life was dogged by charges of plagiarism, which is thinly narrated in *The Hermit of 69th Street* (1988), and is a good example of the way in which he mingled art and life. Under the pseudonym of Joseph Novak, he wrote two works of non-fiction, entitled *The Future is Ours, Comrade* (1960) and *No Third Path* (1962), about totalitarian societies; while selected essays occur in *Passing By* (1992). He won several plaudits for his performance as Grigory Zinoviev in Warren Beatty's film *Reds* (1981). He committed suicide in New York City.

J. Klinkowitz, *Literary Disruptions* (1975).

Kotzwinkle, William (1938–) Born in Scranton, Pennsylvania, US, he attended Rider College and Penn State University. In addition to a large amount of children's fiction, he has written short stories, collected in *Elephant Bangs Train* (1971). His adult fiction includes the science fiction novels *Hermes 3000* (1972), and *Doctor Rat* (1976), an anti-vivisection story set in a cancer research laboratory, narrated from the animal's perspective. A versatile writer, he has also produced two cult classics, *The Fan Man* (1974) and *Fata Morgana* (1977), both of which contain intricate plots and blend fantasy and playful reality. His other novels include *Herr Nightingale and the Satin Woman* (1978), *Jack in the Box* (1980), *The Exile* (1987) which satirises Hollywood actors, *The Midnight Examiner* (1989), about a journalist who gets involved with the mafia, voodoo and other sorceries, and *The Hot Jazz Trio* (1989). Recent fiction includes *The Game of Thirty* (1994), a 'hard-boiled' crime novel based upon an ancient Egyptian game,

and a satire on the book publishing industry in *Bear Went Over the Mountain* (1996). He has produced two popular novelisations in *E.T. the Extra-Terrestrial* (1982), based on Steven Spielberg's film, and *Superman III* (1983). His fiction crosses boundaries with ease, passing from everyday realities into alternate fantastic or science fiction worlds, often deriving from his Buddhist conception of the universe.

Krantz, Judith (1927–) Born in New York City, US, she graduated from Wellesley College (BA 1948). After working as a fashion editor for *Good Housekeeping* magazine and as a journalist, she turned to fiction and wrote the best-seller *Scruples* (1978), the first novel about the staggeringly luxurious life of a Beverley Hills boutique and the people working in it. On the success of this, her next novel, *Princess Daisy*, (1980) broke all records for publisher's advances. Other novels include *Mistral's Daughter* (1982), *I'll Take Manhattan* (1986), *Till We Meet Again* (1988), *Dazzle* (1991), the sequel *Scruples II* (1992), *Lovers* (1994), *Spring Collection* (1996), and most recently, *The Jewels of Tessa Kent* (1998). Labelled the 'queen of glitz and glamour', her fiction is generally set against the backdrop of the Hollywood glitterati and includes copious quantities of sex, name-dropping and shopping. *Sex and Shopping: Confessions of a Nice Jewish Girl* (2000) is her memoir.

Kroetsch, Robert (1927–) A Canadian novelist of wide repute, born in Heisler, Alberta, and educated over a period of years at the University of Alberta (BA 1948), Middlebury College, Vermont (MA 1956) and the Iowa Writer's Workshop (Ph.D. 1961). He then taught at SUNY-Binghamton, before eventually becoming a professor at the University of Manitoba. His first novel, *But We Are Exiles* (1965), is based on his experience working on the MacKenzie River boats, and is in the realist style, although his interest in mythic and literary parallels to the narrative events is already apparent. He abandons realism for more surreal and fabulous events with his next series of interrelated novels which forms the 'Out West' trilogy, in *The Words of My Roaring* (1966), *The Studhorse Man* (1969) and *Gone Indian* (1973). Showing a strong interest in postmodernism, the mythic dominates the literal in these stories set in small-town Alberta in the 1930s, 1940s and 1970s. This preoccupation with formal innovation is continued in *Badlands* (1975), which focuses on a man's archaeological trip as a quest narrative, and *What the Crow Said* (1980), which investigates myth and seeks to 'deconstruct' the novel, as he explains in *The Crow Journals* (1980), an account of writing the novel. Apart from the novels *Alibi* (1983) and *Puppeteer* (1992), he largely turned to poetry in the 1970s, with various earlier collections ultimately being re-assembled in *Field Notes* (1981 and 1985), and finished with *Completed Field Notes* (1989). In addition, he has been a significant literary critic, and his essays have appeared in *The Lovely Treachery of Words* (1989). Recent work includes *A Likely Story: The Writing Life* (1995) and *The Man from the Creeks* (1998). Promoting the heterogeneity of Canadian writing, he has focused on formal and philosophical attention to discontinuity, fragmentation and dialectical construction.

P. Thomas, *Robert Kroetsch* (1980); S. Neuman and R. Wilson, eds, *Labyrinths of the Voice* (1982).

Kundera, Milan (1929–) Born in Brno, Czechoslovakia, he graduated from Charles University, Prague (1956), after which he worked as a labourer and jazz pianist. Emigrating to France in 1975, and naturalising in 1981, he worked as an academic in French universities and joined the staff of the École des hautes études en sciences

sociales, Paris, in 1980. His early novels include *The Joke* (1967, trans. 1969), about a joke which backfires and a warning about the dangers of being too serious in the world, *Life Is Elsewhere* (1973, Prix Medicis, trans. 1979) and *The Farewell Party* (1978, trans. 1979). *The Book of Laughter and Forgetting* (1979, trans. 1981) was an inquiry into laughter, the power of memory as a means of self-preservation, and the politics of fanaticism and scepticism. This was followed by *The Unbearable Lightness of Being* (trans. 1984, filmed 1988). Set in Czechoslovakia at the time of the Russian invasion, it examines the hardships and limitations which can result from commitment and the meaninglessness of life without such responsibility. Later novels are *Immortality* (trans. 1990), which is set in France and examines how the media manipulates popular culture and has developed into instruments of propaganda, *Slowness* (1996), about the failure of a speed-obsessed age to appreciate slowness, and *Identity* (1997, trans. 1998), about near-misses and mistaken identities as a man searches for a woman. Short stories occur in *Laughable Loves* (1970, trans. 1974), while essays with polemical fervour are collected in *The Art of the Novel* (1986, trans. 1988) and *Testaments Betrayed* (trans. 1995). His fiction provides a combination of abstraction, sensuality and wit, and deals with sex, love and death, all playfully mixed with history, fantasy and philosophy. A major literary figure in the Prague Spring of 1968, he was banned after the Russian invasion, although he has emerged as a widely honoured novelist in Europe in recent decades.

A. Aji, ed., *Milan Kundera and the Art of Fiction* (1992).

Kureishi, Hanif (1954–) A novelist, playwright, film director and screenwriter, born in Bromley, England, he graduated from London University, and has become an astute commentator on postcolonial experiences of Asian identity in the widest contexts of post-1960s Britain. An acclaimed writer, he began with such plays as *Soaking Up the Heat* (1976), *The Mother Country* (1980) and *The King and Me* (1980). However, he is best known for his screenplays, such as the controversial *My Beautiful Launderette* (1986), set within the British Asian community, about a young Asian manager of a laundromat and his gay white lover whom he employs, and *Sammie and Rosie Get Laid* (1987), about a racially mixed couple with an open marriage, set against the backdrop of the London race riots. His first novel was *The Buddha of Suburbia* (1990), a wry and comic novel set in the 1960s and 1970s, which explored the ironies of adolescence and the cultural flux of unstable British Asian identities, and which was adapted for television.

This was followed by *The Black Album* (1995), set during the Salman RUSHDIE affair, again exploring the polarities of essentialist Asian identity and western liberalism, *Love in a Blue Time* (1997), about the complications of middle-class London life in the 1970s to the 1990s, and most recently, *Intimacy* (1999), which is the thoughts and memories of a middle-aged writer as he is about to walk out of his marriage for a younger woman. He has also written short stories about the ins-and-outs of relationships in *Midnight All Day* (1999). His writing concerns social issues, including racism, sexual freedoms and class differences, in a conglomeration of influences derived from British youth culture, the British Asian experience, sexuality and experimentation, and politics and resistance.

L

La Guma, Alex (1925–1985) Born Justin Alexander La Guma, in Cape Town, South Africa, he was a correspondent student with the London School of Journalism (1964) and the Cape Technical College (1965). He worked as a journalist for the left-wing newspaper *New Age* in Cape Town (1955–1962), and then turned to freelance writing in 1962. A member of the Cape Town Communist Party, until it was banned in 1950, and a lifelong member of the African National Congress (ANC), he was arrested in the Treason Trial of 1956 to 1961, and constantly imprisoned or kept under house arrest for his political activities. He emigrated to London in 1966, and eventually died in Havana, where he was the ANC's representative to Cuba. His first work, the grimly realistic novelette *A Walk in the Night* (1962), centres upon a crime resulting from racism, and was followed by the novels *And a Threefold Cord* (1967), *The Stone Country* (1967) and *In the Fog of the Season's End* (1972), about a group of black South Africans' attempts to subvert the apartheid regime in Cape Town. *Time of the Butcherbird* (1979) is regarded as his best work, in which he describes a black man returning from prison for vengeance on an Afrikaner farmer who had murdered his brother, and the various tragic consequences involving white and black people. His fiction was banned in South Africa until 1990, much of it deal-ing with the lives and events of the District Six area of Cape Town, and displaying his active opposition to racism in a social realist style.

K. Balutansky, *The Novels of Alex la Guma* (1990)

Lagerkvist, Pär (1891–1974) Born in Växjö, Sweden, Pär Fabian Lagerkvist was educated at the University of Uppsala (1911–1912), and became a theatre critic and writer. One of Sweden's most influential twentieth-century writers, he was a leading expressionist dramatist in the 1930s and a literary innovator. His novels include *The Dwarf* (1944, trans. 1945), which is an analysis of evil, set in an Italian Renaissance court, and depicting the dwarf within us, *Barabbas* (1950, trans. 1951), about the biblical robber who is treated as an archetype of the lonely modern man, an existentialist figure searching for belief, *The Sibyl* (1953, trans. 1958), a symbolic work about humanity's relationship with God, and *Mariamne* (1967, trans. 1968), which deals with evil and Christian hope in the days of Herod and Jesus. A trilogy, entitled *The Pilgrim* (trans. 1966), consists of *The Death of Ahasuerus* (1960, trans. 1962), *Pilgrim at Sea* (1962, trans. 1964) and *The Holy Land* (1964, trans. 1966), and depicts the Wandering Jew finding reconciliation between God and humanity. In addition to short story collections in *The Eternal Smile* (trans. 1954), *Guest of Reality* (trans. 1989) and *The Marriage Feast* (trans. 1955), his essays are collected in *Literary Art and Pictorial Art* (1913, trans. 1991) and *Five Early Works* (trans. 1989). Exploring religious and theological issues, the careful architectural structure of his novels derives from his Cubist method. Widely honoured in his lifetime, he was awarded the Nobel Prize for Literature in 1951.

Lamming, George (1927–) George William Lamming was born in Carrington, Barbados, and after working as a teacher in Trinidad (1946–1950), emigrated to England where he became a factory worker. His first novel, *In the Castle of My Skin* (1953), was semi-autobiographical and universally acclaimed, and has become a 'classic' of West Indian fiction for its exploration of Caribbean cultural displacement and fragmentation. Along with other novels, such as *The Emigrants* (1954), *Of Age and Innocence* (1958) and *Season of Adventure* (1960), which invokes an African heritage, his early fiction explores the West Indian search for identity, which so often led to England and (for some) back to Caribbean roots. Other novels include *Water with Berries* (1972), which uses the plot of *The Tempest* to deal with West Indian postcolonial problems and the effects of history of the present, and *Natives of My Person* (1972), a complex allegorical work about the voyage of a sixteenth-century ship from England to America by way of Africa. Short stories occur in *David's World* (1948), *A Wedding in Spring* (1960), *Birthday Weather* (1966) and *Birds of a Feather* (1970), while essays appear in *The Pleasures of Exile* (1960). He has been widely acclaimed for his investigations of the psychic recesses of the West Indies, the effects on the present of its colonial past, and its search for

identity resulting from its colonial alienation.

S. Paquet, *The Novels of George Lamming* (1982).

L'Amour, Louis (1908–1988) Christened Louis Dearborn Lamoore, and born in Jamestown, North Dakota, he was a prolific American writer of Westerns (over one hundred books). He won no critical acclaim, but his work was always very popular with the public, and many of his novels of frontier life, with backgrounds that were always thoroughly researched, were made into films and television productions. His first novel was *Westward the Tide* (1950), and his first Western (written under the pen-name Tex Burns) was *Hopalong Cassidy and the Riders of the High Rock* (1951). *Hondo* (1953), which became a best-seller, followed shortly afterwards. Some of his other novels are *Heller with a Gun* (1954), *Kilkenny* (1956), *Guns of the Timberland* (1955), *The Burning Hills* (1956) and *How the West Was Won* (1963). His autobiography, published posthumously, is entitled *Education of a Wandering Man* (1989). One of the defining writers of the American pulp Western genre, he is rivalled only by Zane GREY.

Lampedusa, Giuseppe di (1896–1957) An Italian writer, born into a noble family from Palermo, Sicily, Giuseppe Tomasi di Lampedusa was educated at the Licco-Ginnasio Garibaldi in Palermo, and he served in the Italian army between 1914 and 1921. His complete *œuvre* is small, but he is nevertheless famous on account of his remarkable and absorbing novel *The Leopard* (1958, trans. 1960). It recounts the reactions of a Sicilian nobleman and his family to the political and social changes in the turbulent times of Garibaldi's annexation of Sicily, and for background draws heavily on the author's own family history. The book was made into an equally compelling film by Visconti, starring Charlton Heston (1963). He wrote two short stories, also concerned with the inevitability of change and death, entitled *Joy and the Law* and *The Siren*, published later with a fragment intended to be a sequel to *The Leopard*, in *Two Stories and a Memory* (1956, trans. 1961). All his fiction was written in the two years before his death.

D. Gilmour, *The Last Leopard: A Life of Giuseppe di Lampedusa* (1988).

Lardner, Ring W. (1885–1933) Born Ringold Wilmer Lardner, in Niles, Michigan, US, he was educated at the Armour Institute of Technology, Chicago, and he became a sportswriter and columnist in Chicago and New York City. Principally known for his short stories, his first collection was *You Know Me, Al: A Busher's Letter* (1916), written in the racy idiom of the baseball diamond about a rookie's early years in his career, recounted in letters to his hometown friend Al. His use of humorous vernacular to portray typical Americans continued in the satirical pieces of *Gullible's Travels* (1917), the humorous story sequence *The Big Town* (1921), which dissects American society in the post-First World War years, and the short story collections *The Real Dope* (1919), *How to Write Short Stories* (1924), *What of It?* (1925), *The Love Nest* (1926), *Round Up* (1929) and *First and Last* (1934). *June Moon* (1929) was a comedy written with George Kaufman, which satirised the songwriters of Tin Pan Alley, and *The Story of a Wonder Man* (1927) was a satirical autobiography. *The Best of Ring Lardner* (1984) is a collection of his writings.

D. Elder, *Ring Lardner: A Biography* (1956).

Laski, Marganhita (1915–1988) Born in London, England, she graduated from Oxford University (BA 1936), and became a writer, broadcaster and journalist, writing for *The Times* and *The Times*

Literary Supplement. Love on the Supertax (1944), *To Bed with Grand Music* (1946), which was published under the pseudonym Sarah Russell, and *Tory Heaven* (1948), all involve upper-class women and their class relations. *Little Boy Lost* (1949) is set against the bleak backdrop of post-Second World War France, followed by *The Village* (1952) and *The Victorian Chaise-Longue* (1953), which moves from satire to terror in a suspense-nightmare about the protagonist's metamorphosis into the body of a dying Victorian lady. Other works include studies and biographies of literary figures, two studies of religious and secular experiences in *Ecstasy* (1961) and *Everyday Ecstasy* (1980), and *Victorian Tales* (1947), which comments sympathetically on an outdated habit of idealisation, and an anti-nuclear play, *The Off-Shore Island* (1959).

Laurence, Margaret (1926–1987) A highly regarded Canadian novelist, born Jean Margaret Laurence, in Neepawa, Manitoba, and educated in Winnipeg. In 1949, she left Canada to travel widely through Europe and Africa, before finally returning permanently to Ontario in 1974. Her first work, *A Tree for Poverty* (1954), is a translation and re-telling of Somali poems and folk tales, and there followed several more works set in Africa concerning the disjunction between the 'old' and 'new' worlds, and oral cultures, such as *This Side Jordan* (1960), *The Tomorrow-Tamer* (1963), *The Prophet's Camel Bell* (1963), and *Long Drums and Canons* (1968), a critical work on Nigerian writers. In addition to this African-based work, she is best known for her novel sequence set in the fictional Manawaka, based on her hometown: *The Stone Angel* (1964), *A Jest of God* (1966), *The Fire-Dwellers* (1969) and *The Diviners* (1974). These are tightly structured works, and focus on the restrictions of small-town life on the personal and social freedoms of several women. Other publications include a volume of short stories, *A Bird in* the House (1970), her essays in *Heart of a Stranger* (1976), and a posthumous memoir *Dance on the Earth* (1989).

P. Morley, *Margaret Laurence: The Long Journey Home* (1991).

Lavin, Mary (1912–) Born in East Walpole, Massachusetts, US, of Irish parents, she moved to Ireland in 1922 and lived in Athenry, which is fictionalised as Castlerampart in many of her stories. She was educated at University College, Dublin (MA 1937), and her first stories in *Tales from Bective Bridge* (1943) were a critical success. Her numerous volumes include *The Long Ago* (1944), *The Becker Wives* (1946), *A Single Lady* (1951), *The Patriot Son* (1956), *A Likely Story* (1957), *The Second-Best Children in the World* (1972), *A Memory* (1972), *The Shrine* (1977), *A Family Likeness* (1985) and *In a Café* (1995). *The House in Clewe Street* (1945) describes the act of rebellion by a man who runs off with a servant girl, and *Mary O'Grady* (1950) focuses upon a Dublin family. Her *Collected Stories* appeared in three volumes between 1964 and 1985. Concentrating on epiphanic results, her narrative style has been commended for its artlessness.

A. Kelly, *Mary Lavin: Quiet Rebel* (1980).

Lawrence, D.H. (1885–1930) Born David Herbert Richards Lawrence, in Eastwood, Nottinghamshire, England, he was the son of a coal-miner and a schoolteacher. His mother encouraged his creative talents, and he trained as a teacher at the University of Nottingham. His early poems were sent to Ford Madox FORD and published in 1909. In 1908, he went to teach at a school in Croydon, although he resigned in 1912 due to recurrent illness. His first novel, *The White Peacock* (1912), was succeeded by *The Trespasser* (1912), although it was the autobiographical novel *Sons and Lovers* (1913) which established his reputation, narrating a skewed family history and based

upon his early sexual experiences and aspirations as an artist. He eloped with and married Frieda von Richthofen in 1914, who introduced him to a range of European thought, including the psychoanalytical ideas of Freud. Moving in the avant-garde literary circles of Lady Ottoline Morrell, which included E.M. FORSTER, Bertrand Russell and Katherine MANSFIELD, he then published the controversial novel *The Rainbow* (1915). Under suspicion as German sympathisers during the First World War, the couple lived under duress and surveillance, during which time Lawrence developed his anti-industrialism and his ideas about the sanctity of individual life. Leaving Britain after the war, the Lawrences lived an itinerant life, travelling first to Italy, where he underwent a particularly productive period, writing *The Lost Girl* (1920), *The Sea and Sardinia* (1921), *Women in Love* (1921), a sequel to *The Rainbow* which was a critical and pessimistic critique of social values, *Aaron's Rod* (1922), and several stories and novellas. Many of these manifested a preoccupation with renewal and the liberation from social and cultural restrictions, often explored in ambivalent depictions of complex sexual relationships. He then travelled to Sri Lanka and Australia (where he began his novel *Kangaroo*, 1923) and to New Mexico in the US, writing *St Mawr* (1925), *The Plumed Serpent* (1926) and *The Woman Who Rode Away* (1928), before settling in Taos. These works showed explicit political interests, leading to many criticisms for his affiliation with right-wing ideologies and the celebration of masculine authority. His final novel, the infamous *Lady Chatterley's Lover* (1928), focuses on the unhappy marriage of Sir Clifford Chatterley to Constance, and her explicit sexual affair with the gamekeeper Oliver Mellors. An unexpurgated version was not published in Britain until 1960 after a celebrated trial, which established Lawrence in the popular conception as simply an erotic novelist. After several illnesses, he returned to Europe to settle in Italy in the mid-1920s, and died in Vence, France. Now also recognised as an adept writer of short stories, many are collected in *The Prussian Officer* (1914), *England, My England* (1922) and *Love Among the Haystacks* (1933). In addition to his novels and stories, he wrote numerous poems (collected in 1964), several plays, travel books in *Twilight in Italy* (1916) and *Mornings in Mexico* (1927), and other non-fictional works, including the influential *Studies in Classic American Literature* (1923), *Fantasia of the Unconscious* (1923) and *Movements in European History* (1924). Lawrence wrote a passionate prose, often searching for a new lexicon for psychological and sexual experiences, although this led to vilification for his male-centredness by many feminists in their re-evaluation of his work in the 1960s.

J. Worthen, *D.H. Lawrence: The Early Years (1885–1912)* (1991); T. Pinkney, *D.H. Lawrence* (1990).

Laxness, Halldór (1902–1998) Halldór Kiljan Laxness was born Hallór Gudjonsson, in Reykjavik, Iceland. He was educated in Iceland and travelled to Europe in 1919, to the US in 1927 (where he turned to communism), and returned to Iceland in 1930. His literary breakthrough came in 1923 with the novel *The Great Weaver from Kashmir* (untranslated into English), which is about conversion to Roman Catholicism. Thereafter he published prolifically, including his major novel *Salka Valka* (1931–1932, trans. 1936), which deals with the establishment of a trade union in a fishing village and the effects upon the environment and Salka herself. Social novels include *Independent People* (1934–1935, trans. 1945), about freedom and exploitation, and *World Light* (1955, trans. 1969), written in the 1930s, about a visionary pauper persecuted by his peers.

The Atom Station (1948, trans. 1961) and *The Happy Warriors* (1952, trans. 1958) glorify the Icelandic character and contrast individual versus impersonal bureaucracy. Other novels include *The Fish Can Sing* (1957, trans. 1966), *Paradise Reclaimed* (1960, trans. 1962), which is a long epic about an Icelander tempted by Mormonism, *A Quire of Seven* (1964, trans. 1974), and *Christianity at the Glacier* (1968, trans. 1972), a philosophical work about religion. *The Bread of Life* (trans. 1987) is an autobiography. Much of his fiction examines Catholicism and communism, although he was ultimately attracted to Taoism, and explores the confrontation of the individual and monolithic authority, or individual conscience and the conformist pressure of the major ideologies. He was awarded the Nobel Prize for Literature in 1955.

Le Carré, John (1931–) Born in Poole, Dorset, England, Le Carré is the adopted pseudonym of David John Moore Cornwell, who, owing to his position in the British diplomatic service, was prevented from publishing under his own name. He attended Oxford University (BA 1956), worked for the British Army Intelligence Corps, and after a spell as a teacher, joined the British Foreign Office (1959–1963), where he began writing fiction. Widely honoured for his grubby realist depictions of the clandestine era of Cold War espionage – portrayed as a morally ambiguous world of treachery, betrayal and deceit – his first novel was *Call For the Dead* (1960), which introduced the improbable intelligence agent George Smiley, who featured in many of his later works. After *A Murder of Quality* (1962), came *The Spy Who Came in from the Cold* (1963), which attracted widespread acclaim and was an international bestseller. There followed *The Looking Glass War* (1965), *A Small Town in Germany* (1968), *The Naïve Sentimental Lover* (1971), and then a loosely connected trilogy, later published as *The Quest for*

Karla (1982): *Tinker, Tailor, Soldier, Spy* (1974), *The Honourable Schoolboy* (1977), and *Smiley's People* (1980, adapted for the BBC in 1982), which pits Smiley against the Russian spymaster 'Karla' in a plot of narrative twists and turns. *The Little Drummer Girl* (1983) was set in the different arena of the Palestinian refugee camps in the Middle East. His later works returned to Europe, reflecting the dissolution of the former USSR and the demise of the Cold War, while portraying characters still caught up in sinister and covert circumstances, as in *A Perfect Spy* (1986), *The Russia House* (1989), *The Secret Pilgrim* (1991), *The Night Manager* (1993), *Our Game* (1995), *The Tailor of Panama* (1996), a spy intrigue set against the backdrop of Central America, and *Single and Single* (1999). His latest novel is *The Constant Gardner* (2000). The inventor of slang terms like 'mole', and 'circus' for the British Secret Service, which have entered common parlance, his fiction revolutionised the spy novel and became a political statement of the moral confusion and bankruptcy of the Cold War.

D. Monaghan, *The Novels of John le Carré: The Art of Survival* (1985).

Le Guin, Ursula K. (1929–) An American science fiction writer, born Ursula Kroeber Le Guin, in Berkeley, California, the daughter of the anthropologist Alfred Kroeber. Educated at Radcliffe College (BA 1951) and Columbia University (MA 1952), her fiction has generally drawn on mythography, archaeology, psychology and theology to explore humanity's gropings towards connectedness and communication. Her first novels offered 'alternate world' scenarios, such as the Hainish universe in *Rocannon's World* (1966), *Planet of Exile* (1966) and *City of Illusions* (1967), all of which reflected an interest in anthropology and holistic ecology. *A Wizard of Earthsea* (1968) was the first in a young adult trilogy, about

adolescent self-awareness and sexuality, followed by *The Tombs of Atuan* (1971) and *The Farthest Shore* (1973). *The Left Hand of Darkness* (1969) is about gender politics, as an ethnologist visits a planet with a non-gendered environment; and was followed by her most significant novel, *The Dispossessed: An Ambiguous Utopia* (1974), about a male protagonist and his views on anarchism in a set of balanced worlds. Other novels include *Orsinian Tales* (1976), *Malafrena* (1979), *The Beginning Place* (1980), and *Tehanu* (1990), a sequel to 'The Earthsea Trilogy'. Poetry is collected in *In the Red Zone* (1983), and essays in *The Language of the Night* (1979) and *Dancing at the Edge of the World* (1989). A multimedia work of narration, poetry, music and illustration about post-ecological disaster Oregon, occurs in *Always Coming Home* (1985). Recent works are the four interconnected stories about her Hainish world in *Four Ways to Forgiveness* (1995) and *The Telling* (2000). Her various dystopian tales are invariably structured on quest motifs.

C. Spivak, *Ursula K. Le Guin* (1984).

Le Sueur, Meridel (1900–) An American writer, born in Murray, Iowa. In a long and controversial career, she worked as a factory worker in New York City, a journalist and labour reporter, and as an actress in the 1920s, before becoming a poet and novelist. Her first work was *Annunciation* (1935), recording her reactions to the execution of the anarchists Sacco and Vanzetti, followed by the well-received short stories in *Salute to Spring* (1940), about the Midwest during the Depression in the 1930s. *The Girl* (1939) was a novel portraying the hardships of women during the Depression, while *North Star Country* (1945) and *Crusaders* (1955) were based upon her Midwest childhood. The people, history and traditions of the Midwest were a large influence upon her work, giving it an edge of social awareness and protest. An active participant in proletarian movements, her work was banned under McCarthyism in the 1950s, resulting in twenty years of obscurity. She continued to write surreptitiously, and *Harvest and Song for My Time* (1977) depicts her struggles while blacklisted. However, with work frequently narrated from a woman's perspective and dealing with the lives and struggles of women, she found a new audience for her writing in the 1970s, particularly from feminists. Short stories appeared in *I Hear Men Talking* (1984), while non-fiction includes *Conquistadors* (1973), *The Mound Builders* (1974) and *Women on the Breadlines* (1977), and *Ripening* (1982) collects selected work from 1927 to 1980.

Lee, Harper (1926–) Born in Monroeville, Alabama, US, Nelle Harper Lee was educated at the universities of Alabama and Oxford, England. She worked for an airline company before turning to writing, but has become somewhat reclusive. Her reputation rests exclusively upon her only novel, *To Kill a Mockingbird* (1960, Pulitzer Prize 1961), which is the story of the defence by a small-town Alabama lawyer of a black man wrongly accused of raping a white woman. The narrative is told through the eyes of the defence-attorney's daughter, who, together with her brother, witness the sensational trial of the man, as the novel records the obsessed and scandalised reactions of the Deep South town's inhabitants. The novel was made into a highly praised film in 1962.

Lee, Laurie (1914–1997) Born near Stroud, Gloucestershire, England, he left his home village and walked to London as a teenager, where he worked as a clerk, labourer and publications editor, and wrote film scripts for the Ministry of Information during the Second World War. He began by writing poetry in the 1940s, much of which is represented in the two collections *Laurie Lee: Poems*

(1960) and *Selected Poems* (1983). He turned to fiction with *A Rose for Winter* (1955), which described his walking travels in Andalusia, in post-Civil War Spain, and around the eastern Mediterranean. This was followed by his best-known work, *Cider with Rosie* (1959), a lyrical and joyful autobiographical account of his boyhood in rural Gloucestershire, in his hometown of Slad in the Cotswolds. (Although, ironically, when he returned there to live in later life, he incurred the wrath of many of the villagers who were angry with his portrayal of them.) The sequels *As I Walked Out One Midsummer Morning* (1969) and *A Moment of War* (1991), continue to describe his early years of travelling, while *I Can't Stay Long* (1975) collects prose pieces. He published sparsely in later years, although other works include *Innocence in the Mirror* (1978) and the revision of an earlier work in *Two Women* (1983). A vivid prose writer, his writing brought him much acclaim and popularity for its freshness and clarity.

V. Grove, *Laurie Lee: The Well-Loved Stranger* (1999).

Lehmann, Rosamond (1901–1990) Born in Bourne End, Buckinghamshire, England, Rosamond Nina Lehmann attended Cambridge University (1919–1922), and was co-director of her brother John's publishing company (1946–1953). She had a long and happy relationship with the English poet Cecil Day Lewis. Along with such writers as Elizabeth BOWEN and Virginia WOOLF, she was perceived as the creator of the modern 'feminine' novel, which focused upon the 'woman's sensibility'. Her novels are *Dusty Answer* (1927), a delicate yet taboo-breaking treatment of adolescent lesbianism, *A Note in Music* (1930), *Invitation to the Waltz* (1932), and its sequel *The Weather in the Streets* (1936), *The Ballad and the Source* (1945), which, in an innovative style, reworks the myth of Demeter and

Persephone in its portrayal of the domineering Sybil Jardine, *The Echoing Grove* (1953), and *A Sea-Grape Tree* (1976), depicting a dream world in which past and present mingle. Short stories appear in *The Gipsy's Baby* (1946), and several volumes of her letters have also been published. *The Swan in the Evening* (1967) recounts her mystical experiences following the death of her daughter. In some senses, a romantic novelist, her fiction explores the inner lives of a wide range of restless heroines in a prose praised for its lyrical beauty. This psychological insight is often tinged with a nostalgia for lost youth.

D. LeStourgeon, *Rosamond Lehmann* (1965).

Lem, Stanislaw (1921–) Born in Lvov, Poland, he studied medicine at Lvov before and after the Second World War. Escaping internment in the Warsaw Ghetto, he worked as a garage mechanic during the war. He turned to writing full-time in 1949, becoming widely translated and best known for his science fiction. His early work depicts a world free of nuclear threat with one-world government in social realist form, and includes *The Star Diaries* (1957, trans. 1976), *Hospital of the Transfiguration* (1957, trans. 1988) and *Eden* (1959, trans. 1989). *Solaris* (1961, trans. 1970), filmed in 1971 by Andrei Tarkovsky, was the first of his novels to be translated into English, and explored humanity's inadequacies in an alien environment, showing humans' paranoia and fear when studying a huge, sentient ocean on Solaris. Humanity's confrontation with alien phenomena that cannot be comprehended recurs in *The Invincible* (1964, trans. 1973), while other novels include *His Master's Voice* (1968, trans. 1983), *The Futurological Congress* (1971, trans. 1974) and *Peace on Earth* (1987, trans. 1994). Short stories occur in *Pirx the Pilot* (1968, trans. 1979–1982), which uses strange beings to demonstrate humans' limitations, the Cy-

beriad cycle (1965, trans. 1974), *Perfect Vacuum* (1971, trans. 1978), *Imaginary Magnitude* (1973, trans. 1984), *Mortal Engines* (trans. 1973), *The Cosmic Carnival* (trans. 1981), *Fiasco* (1986, trans. 1987) and *One Human Minute* (trans. 1986). Essays are collected in *Microworlds* (trans. 1984), and a memoir occurs in *Highcastle* (1991, trans. 1997). Combining science fiction with philosophical enquiry, he is also concerned with the moral and ethical consequences of advancing technology. With dazzling formal virtuosity and an in-depth knowledge of medicine, cybernetics and engineering, he has been immensely popular in the former USSR.

R. Ziegfeld, *Stanislaw Lem* (1985).

Lenz, Siegfried (1926–) Born in Lyck, East Prussia (now Elk, Poland), he served in the navy during the Second World War, and was educated at the University of Hamburg (1945–1948). He became the literary editor of *Die Welt* (1950–1951), and then turned to freelance writing. An early novel, *The Survivor* (1963, trans. 1965), set in occupied Norway during the war, about overcoming the past, both individually and collectively, manifests the thematic kernel of his fiction. There followed *The German Lesson* (1968, trans. 1971), which is set in a corrective institution on the Elbe and shows an inmate searching for a true perspective on life against the backdrop of German history in the war, *An Exemplary Life* (1973, trans. 1976), *The Heritage* (1978, trans. 1981), *The Breakdown* (1981, trans. 1986), which deals with the loss of speech and communication, and *Training Ground* (1985, trans. 1991). Short stories appear in *The Lightship* (1960, trans. 1962), *Das Wrack* (trans. 1967) and *Selected Stories* (trans. 1989). A member of Gruppe 47, with Heinrich BÖLL, his fiction, which blends politics with writing, has turned increasingly to his native eastern Europe. Often featuring violence, and emotional and spiritual tension, his work has been widely honoured in Germany, and he has enjoyed success and popularity as one of the foremost twentieth-century German writers.

Leonard, Elmore (1925–) An American writer, born in New Orleans, Louisiana, he served in the US Navy during the Second World War, and after the war was educated at the University of Detroit. He turned to full-time writing, with Westerns (for example *Hombre*, 1961, and *Valdez Is Coming*, 1970) and crime novels, of which he is generally held to be probably the best living exponent. His world is one of amoral small-time hoodlums, drug-pushers, hustlers and ex-convicts. Leonard's forte is an unerring ear for speech patterns and the ability to transcribe street argot, often with grimly comical effect. Among some twenty crime novels are *52 Pickup* (1974), *Swag* (1976), *The Switch* (1979), *Cat Chaser* (1982), *Gold Coast* (1982), *Stick* (1983), *LaBrava* (1983), *Glitz* (1985), *Bandits* (1987), *Freaky Deaky* (1988), *Killshot* (1989) and *Get Shorty* (1990). More recent titles include *Rum Punch* (1992), *Out of Sight* (1996), *Cuba Libre* (1998), *Be Cool* (1999) and *Pagan Babies* (2000). Many of his books, of both genres, have been successfully adapted for the screen.

Lessing, Doris (1919–) A widely honoured writer, Doris May Lessing was born in Kermanshah, Persia (now Iran), and was brought up in Southern Rhodesia. She worked as a nursemaid, secretary, and Hansard typist until 1949, when she went to England and wrote her first novel, *The Grass Is Singing* (1950), about an affair between a white woman and an African servant, which ends in the woman's murder. This began an illustrious writing career and her fiction has explored many of the major issues of the twentieth century, such as imperialism, racism, world conflict, technological development and feminism. Her early works drew upon her African experiences, such as *This Was the Old Chief's Country* (1952) and *African Stories* (1964), and her other early novels include *Five: Short Novels* (1955) and *Retreat to Innocence* (1956). Her most significant and controversial novel, *The Golden Notebook* (1962), about political and sexual attitudes, freedoms and responsibilities, was championed by the women's movement. In a daring narrative experiment, it depicts the multiple selves of a contemporary woman trying to free herself from the chaos and hypocrisy afflicting her generation. The semi-autobiographical 'Children of Violence' sequence traced a woman's life against a twentieth-century backdrop of the politics of race and world conflict, consisting of *Martha Quest* (1952), *A Proper Marriage* (1954), *A Ripple from the Storm* (1958), *Landlocked* (1966) and *The Four-Gated City* (1969). Other short story collections occur in *Habit of Loving* (1958), *A Man and Two Women* (1963), *The Story of a Non-Marrying Man* (1972) and *The Real Thing* (1992), and other novels include *Briefing for a Descent into Hell* (1971), about her interest in the ideas of the psychiatrist R.D. Laing, *The Summer Before the Dark* (1973), and works written under the pseudonym Jane Somers in the late 1970s, about women, old age, identity and psychological conflict. There followed the *Canopus in Argos* (1992) sequence, a science fiction series about the destruction of life by catastrophe and tyranny, consisting of *Re: Colonised Planet V, Shikasta* (1979), *The Marriage Between Zones Three, Four and Five* (1980), *The Sirian Experiments* (1981), *The Making of the Representative for Planet 8* (1982) – later to become a libretto for an opera with Philip Glass – and *Documents Relating to the Sentimental Agents in the Volyen Empire* (1983). Later novels include *The Good Terrorist* (1985), a satire about romantic politics, *The Fifth Child* (1988), about a violent, anti-social child's effects on his society, *Writer in July* (1993), *Love, Again*

(1996), *Mara and Dann* (1999), and *Ben, in the World* (2000), a dystopian allegory in future 'Ifrik'. In addition to short stories in *Spies I Have Known* (1995), her non-fiction includes *Going Home* (1957), *In Pursuit of English* (1961), essays in *A Small Personal Voice* (1975), *Prisons We Choose to Live Inside* (1987), and *African Laughter* (1992), which is about her return visits to Zimbabwe. *Under My Skin* (1994) and *Walking in the Shade* (1997) are the first two in a proposed three-volume autobiography. Widely regarded as one of the most important post-Second World War twentieth-century writers, her fiction has remained innovative, engaging and critically acclaimed.

P. Schlueter, *The Novels of Doris Lessing* (1973).

Lette, Kathy (1958–) Born in Sydney, Australia, she began as a reporter for Australian television (1983–1987), and subsequently worked in Los Angeles, before moving to work for the BBC in London, England, where she now lives. A successful writer, her satirical fiction depicts the struggles of young women in misogynistic environments. *Puberty Blues* (1979) is a satire of the 1970s surf culture in Australia, while *Hit and Ms.* (1984) is a flippant guide to surviving in the 1980s. After the short stories of *Girls' Night Out* (1988), there followed the novels *The Llama Parlour* (1991), about a young Australian woman in Hollywood, the widely acclaimed *Foetal Attraction* (1993), a hilarious novel about a woman's experiences in love, London and childbirth, *Mad Cows* (1996), about the difficulties and chaos of parenting, and *Altar Ego* (1998), about the phobia of commitment in 1990s relationships. In what is described as 'new feminist humour', she has captured the social anxieties of professional twenty- and thirty-something women at the latter end of the twentieth century.

Levi, Primo (1919–1987) Levi was born in Turin, Italy, and studied chemistry at the University of Turin (BS 1941). As an Italian Jew, he joined the Resistance in 1943, and was arrested and imprisoned in Auschwitz concentration camp until 1945, where he survived by working as a chemist. Upon his release, he was interned in Belorussia, after which he returned, through a war-devastated Europe, to Italy, where he worked as a chemist from 1948 to 1977 for a chemical company. He is regarded as one of the premier chroniclers of the Holocaust and the conditions in the Nazi concentration camps. *If This Is a Man* (1947, trans. 1959) provides a moving account of his survival in Auschwitz, remarkable for its detached, almost objective narration rather than the stance of a victim. While he is always wholly condemnatory of the cruelty and inhumanity that he witnessed in the camps, his criticism is dispassionate, if not analytical. *The Truce* (1958, trans. 1965) narrates his return to Italy via the USSR after the Liberation, a story repeated to great effect in *If Not Now, When?* (1982, trans. 1985). Other fiction includes *The Periodic Table* (1975, trans. 1984), a fascinatingly poised set of stories based upon twenty-one of the chemical elements in the Periodic Table, which he uses, loosely, as metaphors for the attributes of people he encountered in the camps. Other fiction includes *The Wrench* (1978, trans. 1986), about the Holocaust and Piedmontese protagonists, *Moments of Reprieve* (1981, trans. 1986), *The Drowned and the Saved* (1986, trans. 1988), and the fantastical fables in *The Sixth Day* (trans. 1990). *The Mirror Maker* (trans. 1989) collects stories and newspaper articles, and essays appear in *Other People's Trades* (trans. 1989). His poetry appears in *The Collected Poems of Primo Levi* (trans. 1988). Above all, a moralist of profound insight, his novels, written in a crystalline prose, engage with the psychology of survival, and the difficulty and moral necessity of remembering. He gradually became despondent over what he considered to be the world's disregard for the Jewish Holocaust experiences, something which ultimately drove him to suicide.

N. Patruno, *Understanding Primo Levi* (1995).

Levine, Norman (1923–) A Canadian novelist and short story writer, born and raised in Ottawa. After serving in the RCAF during the Second World War, he went to McGill University, and then went back to England in the late 1940s, where he lived (mostly in St. Ives, Cornwall) until his return to Canada in 1980. His best-known work is an autobiographical account of a cross-country tour of Canada in the 1950s, entitled *Canada Made Me* (1958), which looked at the underside of Canada from the perspective of a down-and-out. His novels are *The Angled Road* (1952), a story about an RCAF pilot in England during the war, *From a Seaside Town* (1970), about a Canadian writer in England reckoning with the concerns of everyday life, and *She'll Only Drag You Down* (1975). A prolific writer of short stories, they are collected in *One-Way Ticket* (1961), *I Don't Want to Know Anyone Too Well* (1972), *Thin Ice* (1979), *Why Do You Live So Far Away?* (1984), *Champagne Barn* (1984), and *Something Happened Here* (1991). His short stories frequently focus on domestic life, writer's problems, and the need to come to terms with the past. Books of poetry include *Myssium* (1948), *The Tightrope Walker* (1950) and *I Walk by the Harbour* (1976).

Lewis, Sinclair (1885–1951) An American writer, born Harry Sinclair Lewis, in Sauk Center, Minnesota, and educated at Yale University, he worked as a newspaper reporter and literary editor from 1907 to 1916, during which time he wrote two minor novels, *Our Mr Wrenn* (1914) and *The Trail of the Hawk* (1915). This was followed by *The Innocents* (1917), although *The Job* (1917) is regarded as

his first important novel. His next books were *Main Street* (1920), which contrasts cosmopolitan city life with the sterility of Midwestern small-town culture, and *Babbitt* (1922), which satirises the conformity and complacency of the life of a small-town real-estate agent, George F. Babbitt (who yet occasionally has self-revelatory glimpses, however quickly stifled by his vacuous cronies, of the futility of his existence), and they are regarded as his best works. Other books which followed these successes were *Elmer Gantry* (1927), a story about a drunken, rabble-rousing evangelist, *The Man who Knew Coolidge* (1928), *Dodsworth* (1929), *Ann Vickes* (1933), *Work of Art* (1934), *It Couldn't Happen Here* (1935), *The Prodigal Parents* (1938), *Bethel Merriday* (1940), about a show-girl, *Gideon Planish* (1943), *Cass Timberlane* (1945), *Kingsblood Royal* (1947), a story about racism, *The God Seeker* (1949) and *World So Wide* (1951). Lewis was generally scornful of literary awards and turned down the Pulitzer Prize in 1926 for *Arrowsmith* (1925), although he accepted – as the first American winner – the Nobel Prize for Literature in 1930.

M. Schorer, *Sinclair Lewis: An American Life* (1961).

Lewis, Wyndham (1882?–1957) Born Percy Wyndham Lewis on a ship anchored off Nova Scotia, Canada, he emigrated to England in 1888, where he attended the Slade School of Art (1898–1901). A poet, painter, essayist and prolific novelist, he moved in the celebrated London art and literary circles in the early decades of the twentieth century, and became a leading proponent of vorticism in 1909, collaborating with Ezra Pound on the magazine *Blast* in 1914. After enlisting as a gunner during the First World War, his first novel, *Tarr* (1918), was set in the Paris bohemia, narrating the parallel lives of two English and German artists. Among the plethora of writing that followed, the most significant fiction includes *The Childermass* (1928), part of a proposed tetralogy called *The Human Age*, and offering views on metaphysics, politics and literature in a fantasy about judgement in heaven, *The Apes of God* (1930), a savage critique of his artistic peers in Bloomsbury for which he was never forgiven, and *Blasting and Bombardiering* (1937), a memoir about his wartime years and subsequent experiences. His non-fiction treatise *The Art of Being Ruled* (1926) articulated support for authoritarian structures of government, whilst his magnum opus, *Time and the Western Man* (1927), lambasted the cult of time he identified in the likes of James JOYCE and Ezra Pound. These, along with other writings in the 1930s which manifested a support for Hitler, fascism and anti-Semitism, caused him further social ostracism. He later reconsidered and recanted his political views on Germany in *The Jews, Are They Human* (1939), and after his self-imposed exile in Canada during the war, he became an art critic for *The Listener*. Later novels include *Monstre Gai* (1956), *Malign Fiesta* (1956), and *Self Condemned* (1954), which follows the trials of a couple in self-imposed exile and is considered by some to be his best novel. However, financial difficulties and his extreme and aggressively written views contributed to his isolation and social ostracism in later years.

F. Jameson, *Fables of Aggression* (1979).

Lispector, Clarice (1920–1977) Born in Tchetchelnik, Ukraine, her family moved to Brazil in 1926, where she studied at the National Faculty of Law, Rio de Janeiro (1944). Her husband's diplomatic postings took her to Europe in the 1940s and 1950s, although she returned to Rio de Janeiro in 1959. Her novels include *Near to the Wild Heart* (1944, trans. 1990), partly autobiographical and showing the use of innovative language, *The Apple in*

the Dark (1961, trans. 1967), her longest novel, in which the protagonist realises the world is like an apple that cannot be explained, *The Passion According to G.H.* (1964, trans. 1988), about a female protagonist in a confessional first person narrative with intertextual references to myths and biblical references, *An Apprenticeship, Or the Book of Delights* (1969, trans. 1986), *The Stream of Life* (1973, trans. 1989) and *The Flow of the Star* (1977, trans. 1986). Short stories appear in *Family Ties* (1960, trans. 1972) and *The Foreign Legion* (1964, trans. 1986), both of which demonstrate an innovative use of language in cinematic, slow-motion close-ups of the characters. Her newspaper articles occur in *Discovering the World* (1984, trans. 1992), and *Soulstorm* (trans. 1989) is an anthology. One of the major writers in Portuguese, her fiction embraces questions about existence, the nature of subjectivity, gender and writing, and in a stream-of-consciousness style, explores the feminine condition from a Latin American perspective. In recent years, the French feminist Hélène Cixous has argued that she is an exemplar of *écriture féminine*.

M. Peixoto, *Passionate Fictions* (1994).

Lively, Penelope (1933–) A widely honoured English writer of juvenile and adult fiction, Penelope Margaret Lively was born in Cairo, Egypt, and educated at Oxford University (BA 1956). After writing many children's books, in the late 1970s she turned to adult fiction, with her first novel *The Road to Lichfield* (1977), about a woman's childhood memories being suddenly changed by a discovery in adulthood. Her numerous novels often examine the past and its impact and effects upon the present, for example in such works as *Moon Tiger* (1987, Booker Prize), a widely praised novel about the transitory nature of life, as a historian contemplates her life from her deathbed in a complex series of flashbacks. More recent novels include *Passing On* (1989), exploring themes of mortality, sexuality, corruption and ecology, *City of the Mind* (1990), about an architect's recovery from a stressful divorce and his contemplation of the past and present of London, *Cleopatra's Sister* (1993), a marvellous love story set in a fictional African state, *Heat Wave* (1996), and *Spiderweb* (1999), which is about the adjustment of retirement and the reassessment of one's life. Short stories occur in *Pack of Cards* (1986) and *Beyond the Blue Mountains* (1997), while *Oleander, Jacaranda* (1994) is a memoir of her childhood in Egypt. With a certain degree of wry humour, her fiction dwells on the foibles of character, life's tragedies and offers some historical insights.

Lodge, David (1935–) Born in England, David John Lodge studied at London University (BA 1955, MA 1959) and the University of Birmingham (1967), where he has lectured since 1960. His academic writing includes books on the formalistic and stylistic developments in fiction and literary theory, such as *The Modes of Modern Writing* (1977), *Working with Structuralism* (1981), *After Bakhtin* (1990), and more recently, *The Art of Fiction* and *The Art of Writing* (1996). But he has gained his broader, popular reputation as the writer of comic satires of post-war British society. His first novel was *The Picturegoers* (1960), about a year's experiences of a group of Catholics living in a London suburb, and was followed by *Ginger, You're Barmy* (1962), which grew out of his service in the army, depicting the tensions between a committed soldier and an intellectual, *The British Museum Is Falling Down* (1965), which is a comic satire of Catholics struggling to live within the rigid Church doctrines, a theme picked up later in *How Far Can You Go?* (1980). After *Out of the Shelter* (1970), he had a wide-ranging popular success with *Changing Places*

(1975), which narrates the differing cultural experiences of Morris Zapp, a flamboyant American academic and Philip Swallow, an English academic, who swap their respective university campuses, lives and wives, on an academic exchange scheme. The two characters reappear in *Small World* (1984), which follows their adventures on a global conference jet-setting circuit. A further campus novel, *Nice Work* (1988), follows an academic and an industrialist who 'shadow' each other's jobs. More recent novels include *Paradise News* (1991), *Therapy* (1995), about a middle-aged writer and his mid-life crisis, and *Home Truths* (1999), a novella about middle-aged revenge, adapted from his play of the same name.

Lo-Johansson, Ivar (1901–1990) Born Karl Ivar Lo-Johansson, in Ösmo, Sweden, he was self-educated and worked as a stonecutter, farm-hand and journalist, before becoming a full-time writer in 1929. He is regarded as one of Sweden's foremost modern writers, but despite his international reputation, relatively little of his prolific writing has been translated into English. One of the so-called *statar-eskolan* in Swedish literature (writers depicting the lowest class of worker, tied to the estate and substandard living conditions), he is credited with opening the eyes of politicians and Swedes to the poverty of the *statare* through his fiction and improving their lot by breaking the system. *Breaking Free* (1933, trans. 1990) depicts a young man struggling for his freedom, in which a dream world is set in opposition to the oppressive existence on the estate, although *Only a Mother* (1939, trans. 1991) is better known, a study of entrapment within class and stereotype, depicting a woman branded as a fallen woman by her fellow estate workers. A keen eye for detail, he is also one of the foremost Swedish writers of desire, sex, the erotic and male sexuality, evident in *Bodies of Love* (1962, trans.

1971), while *Peddling My Wares* (1975, trans. 1995) is an autobiographical novel.

London, Jack (1876–1916) Born in San Francisco, US, Jack (John Griffith) London led a reckless youth, but joined a sealing ship to Japan in 1893. He travelled widely through America and Canada, and following a short period of education, he returned to the Oakland waterfront. After joining the Klondike Goldrush of 1897, he began writing about his experiences, publishing short stories about the Yukon in magazines like *Atlantic Monthly*. His first collection, *The Son of the Wolf*, appeared in 1900, portraying the harsh life in the far north of America. In 1902, he went to London and made a close study of the slum conditions for *The People of the Abyss* (1903). He was more successful in later life: he became a reporter for the Hearst papers, went on lecture tours and sailing trips, and wrote prolifically. Among these works were short story collections such as *Love of Life* (1907), *Lost Face* (1910), *South Sea Tales* (1911) and *On the Makaloa Mat* (1919). However, it is for books like *The Call of the Wild* (1903), about a dog leading a wolf pack in the far north, and *White Fang* (1906), in which a wild dog is domesticated, that London's real literary fame continues. His talent lay in his ability to represent primitive violence, and despite his sometimes contradictory strong beliefs in Marx and Nietzsche, he believed in collectivism as an inevitable next step in human evolution. The tensions between these social and political views are evident in *The Iron Heel* (1908), a work set in the American future, in which a fascist dictatorship is undermined by a socialist challenge. Other works which earned him considerable attention include *The Sea-Wolf* (1904) for its depiction of an uncompromising captain of a sealing ship, *The Game* (1905), about a boxer, *Before Adam* (1906), and *Martin Eden* (1909), a loosely autobiographical novel about a

writer. His *Letters* were published in three volumes in 1989.

R. O'Connor, *Jack London: A Biography* (1964).

Lovelace, Earl (1935–) Born in Toco, Trinidad, he attended the Eastern Caribbean Institute of Agriculture and Forestry (1961–1962), and later Howard (1966–1967) and Johns Hopkins (MA 1974) universities. He has worked as a proofreader, forest ranger (1956–1966), and more recently, at the University of the West Indies, Trinidad, as a lecturer in creative writing. His novels are generally set in Trinidad or the West Indies, and frequently written in local patois. They include *While Gods Are Falling* (1965), about a man's sense of imprisonment by identity and poverty, *The Schoolmaster* (1968), which is a folk fable about building a school in rural Trinidad, *The Dragon Can't Dance* (1979), about poor and dispossessed folk and their renewal in an annual carnival, and his best-known work, *The Wine of Astonishment* (1982), which deals with religious censorship and the clash between tradition and the modern. More recently, he has written *Salt* (1997), a story about racial integration and the reconciliation of history with the present. In addition to plays in *Jestina's Calypso and Other Plays* (1984), short stories occur in *A Brief Conversation* (1988). One of the Caribbean's most gifted writers, the individual and the community are the central foci of his fiction, which seeks for the human's view of himself, or the 'presented', his preferred term for 'identity'.

Lowry, Malcolm (1909–1957) An English writer, born Clarence Malcolm Lowry, in Birkenhead, Cheshire, he graduated from Cambridge University in 1932. He was an experimental writer, who produced a small but important body of writing, influenced by the modernist stream-of-consciousness style. He worked on a ship, and his first novel, *Ultramarine* (1933), concerned the psychological and social development of a young sailor journeying to the Far East. After travelling in North America, and eventually settling in Mexico, he wrote his crowning achievement, *Under the Volcano* (1947, filmed 1984). A complex novel, it recounts the mental and physical collapse of the final day of an alcoholic English consul in Mexico. Lowry was himself an incorrigible alcoholic, as are several of his fictional characters. *Lunar Caustic* (1968), a thinly veiled autobiographical novella about a patient in a psychiatric hospital, was published posthumously, along with short stories started in the 1940s in *Hear Us O Lord from Heaven Thy Dwelling Place* (1961), and the incomplete novels, *Dark as the Grave Wherein My Friend Is Laid* (1968) and *October Ferry to Gabriola* (1970). His *Collected Poetry* (1992) was followed by *Sursum Corda!* (1995), volume one of his collected letters.

D. Day, *Lowry: An Autobiography* (1973).

Ludlum, Robert (1927–) Born in New York City, US, he was educated at Wesleyan University (BA 1951), and became an actor on Broadway and in television (1952–1960), and then a producer (1960–1970). In a second career, he turned to full-time writing in 1971, and has become a prolific and popular writer of suspense thrillers, many of which have been filmed or made into television miniseries. His first novel, *The Scarlatti Inheritance* (1971), about financiers funding the Third Reich, involving espionage and corruption, set the pattern for his fiction. Among his other novels is the 'Bourne' spy trilogy, consisting of *The Bourne Identity* (1980), *The Bourne Supremacy* (1986) and *The Bourne Ultimatum* (1990), in which the eponymous spy tackles his arch-enemy, the Jackal. Recent novels include *The Scorpio Illusion* (1993), *The Matarese Countdown* (1997), *The Cry of the Halidon* (1997) and *The Hades Factor* (2000). Dealing with conspiracy, terrorism, international intrigue, mayhem and death, his tangled plots are often set against historical backgrounds.

Lurie, Alison (1926–) Born in Chicago and educated at Radcliffe College (BA 1947), she began teaching at Cornell University in 1969. She has written a considerable number of comic and satiric novels, showing an acute eye for detail, and often dealing with the eccentric lives of academics and authors. Her first novel, *Love and Friendship* (1962), showed her leanings towards an Austenesque comedy of manners, in its focus on the rivalries on a small New England campus. *The Nowhere City* (1965) is about assimilation into Californian lifestyles, *Imaginary Friends* (1967) deals with religious cults, and *Real People* (1969) looks at the artistic community. There followed *The War Between the Tates* (1974, filmed 1976), which made her name, about hostilities between the generations and sexes; *Only Children* (1979) which is wryly narrated from the perspective of children; *Foreign Affairs* (1984, Pulitzer Prize 1985), about sex in middle age; *The Truth About Lorin Jones* (1988), which is about a woman's difficulties in writing a biography; and *Last Resort* (1998), about an estranged relationship breaking down in Florida. *Women and Ghosts* (1994) is nine tales focusing on women haunted literally and metaphorically by spirits. *The Language of Clothes* (1981) is an incisive non-fictional exploration of fashion, and *Don't Tell the Grown-ups* (1990) is a study of children's fiction. She has also written stories for children.

M

McCarthy, Cormac (1933–) An American novelist with a distinguished reputation, he was born in Rhode Island, educated in Tennessee, and from 1976, has lived in El Paso. His first novel, *The Orchard Keeper* (1965), is a tale of murder and the grim lives of a community in the Great Smoky Mountains, while *Outer Dark* (1968) is a Gothic tale in a Southern setting, recording the wanderings of a woman searching for her son by her brother. *Child of God* (1974), about grotesque characters in a Kentucky backwoods, was followed by *Suttree* (1979), about a drop-out loner in the violent tenderloin district of Knoxville. The widely acclaimed *Blood Meridian* (1985) rewrote the Western genre, following the life of a runaway boy who hooks up with a band of bounty killers of Indians in their wide-ranging pillaging and murdering spree. His recent fiction has focused on the Mexican-American frontier territory in *The Border Trilogy* (1999), the first of which was *All the Pretty Horses* (1992), focusing on two boys and their dangerous adventures in mid-nineteenth-century Mexico. The second novel was *The Crossing* (1994), which narrates the adventures of a young boy taking a trapped wolf for release in the Mexican Sierra de la Madera mountains, and *Cities of the Plain* (1998) completes the cycle, depicting a young man working in Texas in the 1950s, and his determination to release and marry a young Mexican whore. In addition, he has written a play, *The Stonemason* (1994), about a multi-generational black family in Louisville in the 1970s.

McCarthy, Mary (1912–1989) A widely honoured American writer, Mary Therese McCarthy was born in Seattle, Washington, and educated at Vassar College (BA 1933). One of America's most prominent intellectuals, she was renowned for her outspokenness against hypocrisy. She rose to prominence in New York in the 1930s as part of an intellectual circle, which included Edmund Wilson, Philip Rahv and Lillian Hellman. An adept social critic, she wrote essays and reviews for such journals as the *Nation*, *New Republic* and *Partisan Review*. She began novel writing with *The Company She Keeps* (1942), set in Greenwich Village, about young New Yorkers searching for identity and truthfulness. There followed the satire of liberalism in *The Oasis* (1949), the campus novel *The Groves of Academe* (1952), *A Charmed Life* (1955), and her best-known novel, *The Group* (1963), made into a successful film in 1966, which was a frank exposé of her own and her peers' failings, depicting the lives of eight Vassar graduates over seven years. In the 1960s, she published anti-Vietnam War journalism, collected in *Vietnam* (1967), *Hanoi* (1968) and *Medina* (1972), and spoke out vociferously about the Watergate Scandal in the 1970s, in *The Mask of State* (1974) and *The Seventh Degree* (1975). Other works include short stories collected in *Cast a Cold Eye* (1950), a much praised memoir about her youth and abused childhood in *Memories of a Catholic Girlhood* (1957), a translation of Simone Weil's *The Iliad* (1947), and essays, travel writing, reportage, theatre reviews, and political journalism in *Sights and Spectacles* (1956) and *On the Contrary* (1961). Before her death, she completed the novels *Birds of America* (1971), about the fate of nature, and *Cannibals and Missionaries* (1978), a terrorist hijack story, and more volumes of autobiography in *How I Grew* (1987) and *Intellectual Mem-oirs* (1992). Attempting to cut through social and political mystification, she displayed an interest in the morality of politics and an intolerance of deception and distortion.

C. Gelderman, *Mary McCarthy: A Life* (1988).

McCullers, Carson (1917–1967) Carson Smith McCullers was born in Columbus, Georgia, US, and educated at Columbia University and New York University. She held a variety of jobs while writing her stories. Left partially paralysed at an early age by crippling strokes, and leading a hectic and torrid married life, she nevertheless published her first and most famous novel, *The Heart Is a Lonely Hunter* (1940) at the age of 23, which features outsiders and eccentrics, especially in the relationship between a musical and unloved adolescent girl and two deaf mutes. Writing of lonely, alienated, grotesque characters, which symbolise humanity's isolation and failure to communicate, *Reflections in a Golden Eye* (1941) is set in an army camp in the Deep South, and concerns festering human passions and eccentricities, while *The Member of the Wedding* (1946) deals with the symbolic loneliness of a young girl, and became one of two plays, the other being *The Square Root of Wonderful* (1958).

The stories in *The Ballad of the Sad Café* (1952) feature a hunchback and a once-powerful woman, while *Clock Without Hands* (1957) centres upon a premature death from leukaemia and the racial problems in the South. Despite becoming very ill from cancer in later life, she wrote some children's stories, and her uncollected writings were published posthumously as *The Mortgaged Heart* (1971). As evident from her *Collected Short Stories* (1952) and her other fiction, often with southern settings, her writing evinces a sympathy, passion and tenderness for the isolated figures searching for love and belonging.

H. Bloom, ed., *Carson McCullers* (1986).

McCullough, Colleen (1937–) Born in Wellington, New South Wales, Australia, of Irish Catholic background, she was educated at the University of Sydney. After stints as a schoolteacher, library assistant and journalist, she worked between 1967 and 1976 as a neurophysiologist in Australia, England and at the Yale School of Medicine. Her first novel, *Tim* (1974), depicts a couple's relationship, and received an unenthusiastic critical reception. However, *The Thorn Birds* (1977), a chronicle of several generations of the Cleary family on Drogheda station in northern New South Wales, became a best-seller, and a television series in 1983. There followed *An Indecent Obsession* (1981), about duty, which contained the best-selling ingredients of sex, romance, violence and paranoia, with a sensationalist plot. *The Ladies of Missalonghi* (1987) was dogged by allegations of the plagiarism of L.M. MONTGOMERY's *The Blue Castle*, although nothing has ever been proved. Recent novels form the 'Masters of Rome' series, including *First Man in Rome* (1990), *The Grass Crown* (1991), *Caesar's Women* (1996) and *Caesar, Let the Dice Fly* (1997), depicting the years of Roman ascendancy under Julius Caesar and the Gallic wars. A popular writer, McCullough is Australia's foremost romance author.

McElroy, Joseph (1930–) An American novelist, born in Brooklyn, New York, and educated at Williams College (BA 1951) and Columbia University (Ph.D. 1961). He has been Professor of English at Queens College, CUNY since 1964. His first novel, *A Smuggler's Bible* (1966), deals with the adventures of a young antiquarian bookseller, and was followed by *Hind's Kidnap* (1969), and *Ancient History* (1971), which was an exploration of spatial relationships, and indicates his continuing interest in epistemological studies of contemporary life. *Lookout Cartridge* (1974), about a filmmaker caught in sinister situations, and *Plus* (1977), a science fiction story about a brain's relationship to an engineer dying of radiation burns, are regarded by some as forerunners of the cyberpunk style. There followed *Ship Rock* (1980) and *Women and Men* (1987), the latter a lengthy treatment of the lives of a man and a woman unconnected except for the fact that they live in the same apartment block. *The Letter Left to Me* (1988) is an account of a boy whose father has just committed suicide and left him a note. His style of 'fabulation', often compared to that of Thomas PYNCHON, Don DELILLO and William GADDIS, has gained him a reputation for intellectually formidable novels.

McEwan, Ian (1948–) A widely honoured British novelist, Ian Russell McEwan was born in Aldershot, England. He went to Sussex University (BA 1970) and the University of East Anglia (MA 1971), and is perhaps the most famous protégé of Malcolm BRADBURY at UEA. His first work was the collection of sinister short stories, *First Love, Last Rites* (1975), which was submitted for his MA thesis. There followed *In Between the Sheets and Other Stories* (1978), and the novel *The Cement Garden* (1978), about four chil-

dren's regression into a feral state with chilling events. Other novels include *The Comfort of Strangers* (1981), about a sadomasochistic murder involving a couple on holiday in Venice, *The Child in Time* (1987), about parents' responsibilities and insecurities for their children, *The Innocent* (1990), exploring espionage in Cold War tensions, *Black Dogs* (1992), about a man trying to compile his memoir, *The Daydreamer* (1994), *The Short Stories* (1995), *Enduring Love* (1997), which analyses varieties of love, and *Amsterdam* (1998, Booker Prize), a cold satire of the world of politics and journalism in a novel about death and scandal. He has also written several plays, the film script *The Ploughman's Lunch* (filmed 1983, published 1985), adapted Timothy MO's *Sour Sweet* for screen (1989), and written the libretto for Michael Berkeley's opera *Or Shall We Die?* (1983). His fiction is haunted by perversity, adolescence and violence, power and aberrant sexuality and political authoritarianism, focusing increasingly on the manner in which social and political issues determine personal lives.

McGahern, John (1934–) Born in Dublin, Ireland, he grew up in Cootehill, Co. Cavan, and was educated at University College, Dublin. He became a schoolteacher in Dublin, and his first literary success came with the novel *The Barracks* (1963). This was followed by *The Dark* (1965), which was banned under the Censorship Act of 1929 for its uncompromising attitudes towards sex, and he was dismissed from his teaching position. Following a furious public controversy, he moved to London to work as a teacher and construction worker. After travelling, he returned to settle in Mohill, Co. Leitrim. Other novels include *The Leave-taking* (1974), *The Pornographer* (1979), and *Amongst Women* (1990), the study of an ageing farmer remembering his days as a republican veteran and exploring the repressive confines of Irish society. Short stories appear in *Nightlines* (1970), *Getting Through* (1978) and *High Ground* (1985), with a *Collected Stories* published in 1992. He has also written a play entitled, *The Power of Darkness* (1991). Mainly centred on the people who inhabit the Irish west midlands, his longer fiction depicts human characters in their harsh rural environment, and embraces religious doubt in a world of formal believers.

D. Sampson, *Outstanding Nature's Eye: The Fiction of John McGahern* (1993).

McGrath, Patrick (1950–) Born in London, England, he went to the University of London (BA 1971), and has subsequently worked as an editor of *Speech Technology* magazine, and worked at mental institutions in England and Canada. His first work, the short story collection *Blood and Water* (1988), established his penchant for neo-Gothic narratives, mixing the grotesque with the comic. His first novel was *The Grotesque* (1989, filmed 1995), and is a story about murder and machinations in a country house, told by an unreliable narrator. *Spider* (1990), a narrative told by schizophrenic Dennis 'Spider' Cleg, who returns to his childhood neighbourhood in London's East End and recalls his unpleasant childhood, was followed by *Dr. Haggard's Disease* (1993), about obsessive love and adultery, *Asylum* (1997), about irrational passion and its consequences when a doctor's wife has an affair with a criminally insane hospital inmate, and most recently, *Martha Peake* (2000), set in London and America during the revolutionary years of the 1770s. In addition to the short stories in *The Angel* (1995), he has edited *The New Gothic* (1992). His fiction frequently explores power, mental pathology, psychosis and obsession, and the dark and hidden aspects of human psyches.

McGuane, Thomas (1939–) Full name Thomas Francis III McGuane, he is an American novelist who was born in Wyandotte, Michigan, and educated at Michigan State University (BA 1962). In 1968, he turned to film directing and freelance writing, with his first novel *The Sporting Club* (1968), a satire about wealthy sportsmen and their forest club set in the northern Michigan woods. Much of his fiction pays close attention to the special atmosphere of regions. He moved to a setting in the Florida Keys with *The Bushwhacked Piano* (1971), *Ninety-two in the Shade* (1973) and *Panama* (1978), which all feature dropouts rejecting suburban culture in an encounter with alternate American models of life. *Nobody's Angel* (1982) had a Montana setting, which concerned the change and loss of isolated characters, while *Something to be Desired* (1984), *Keep the Change* (1989) and *Nothing But Blue Skies* (1992) are also about a return to ranch life in Montana. *To Skin a Cat* (1986) collects short stories about American manners in the West, while *An Outside Chance* (1980) is essays on sport, *Longest Silence* (1999) is essays on angling, and *Some Horses* (1999) is essays on horses. His many screenplays include *The Missouri Breaks* (1975) and *Tom Horn* (1980). Deriving much from HEMINGWAY in his focus on virile heroes and anti-heroes, his fiction explores the modern American male's retreat from the banality of middle-class life to live a more authentic and self-aware existence.

D. Westrum, *Thomas McGuane* (1991).

McIlvanney, William (1936–) William Angus McIlvanney was born in Kilmarnock, Scotland, educated at Glasgow University (MA 1959), and had a career as a schoolmaster and lecturer. His mainstream fiction, which often explores the economic hardships and working-class culture of mining communities, includes *Remedy Is None* (1966), *A Gift from Nessus* (1968), *Docherty* (1975), *The Big Man* (1985), which is arguably his most famous novel about social relations in the decaying mining industry, and *Strange Loyalties* (1991). His two most highly regarded novels, which recount specific murder mysteries and involve the wider concerns of truth, justice and integrity, are *Laidlaw* (1977) and *The Papers of Tony Veitch* (1983). *The Kiln* (1996) is set in the 1990s in an Edinburgh flat, as a man tries to make sense of his youth in a mining town in the 1950s. In addition to volumes of poetry and a screenplay, his short stories occur in *Walking Wounded* (1989) and a collection of journalism in *Surviving the Shipwreck* (1991). His novels often feature hard-bitten men who need to come to terms with their working-class inheritance, situating him in the company of novelists like James KELMAN.

McInerney, Jay (1955–) An American novelist, born in Hartford, Connecticut, who graduated from Williams College (BA 1976). After working in journalism and publishing, he became a full-time writer with the publication of his first novel *Bright Lights, Big City* (1984), which was a major success. It portrayed the 1980s New York club scene, as a disillusioned youth, trying to deal with several personal problems, goes from club to club in search of women and cocaine, in a life of pointless hedonism. *Ransom* (1985) continued the theme of a quest for meaning and direction, while *Story of My Life* (1988) is a hip narrative about a young woman caught in the shallowness and sexual liberalism of the 1980s. *Brightness Falls* (1992) looks at the club culture and drug-use of the New York yuppie at the time of the 1987 stock market crash, *The Last of the Savages* (1996) compares the lives and careers of two men from varying backgrounds, and *Model Behaviour* (1998) portrays the ennui and numbing effects of a journalist's Manhattan media career. Heralded as part of the 'literary brat pack', along with Tama JANOWITZ and Bret Easton ELLIS, by the press for his youthful success, self-

promotion and high royalty demands, his novels embrace the pop idiom catch-phrases in their satirical representation of the excesses of the 1980s yuppie generation.

Mackay, Shena (1944–) Born in Edinburgh, Scotland, she became a writer in 1959. She began with two novellas, *Dust Falls on Eugene Schlumberger* (1964) and *Toddler on the Run* (1964), and her first major novel was *Music Upstairs* (1965), which explored bisexual rites-of-passage in Earl's Court, London. There followed the bleak tale of an old woman in *Old Crow* (1967); *An Advent Calendar* (1971); *A Bowl of Cherries* (1984); *Redhill Rococo* (1986), which is a black comedy with the suburban domestic world described in ornate, almost surreal prose; and the huge and ambitious *Dunedin* (1992), which follows the progress of a Scottish family at the turn of the nineteenth century. Her most recent novel is *The Artist's Widow* (1998), set in London and depicting an artist's widow, a painter in her own right. She has also edited a volume of short stories by women on sisterhood in *Such Devoted Sisters* (1993) and edited literature on friendship in *Friendship* (1997). Her short stories occur in *Collected Short Stories* (1994), *The Laughing Academy* (1993) and *The World's Smallest Unicorn* (1999), many of which are set in Surrey, England, and like many of her novels, chronicle apparent ordinariness and explore hysteria, loneliness, revenge and the menace of everyday life. Offering a unique perspective, and technically accomplished, her short stories are widely broadcast on BBC radio.

MacLennan, Hugh (1907–1990) A widely honoured Canadian novelist, born John Hugh MacLennan, in Glace Bay, Nova Scotia, he was educated at Dalhousie University, Oxford University and Princeton University. He began as a part-time lecturer at McGill University, and was eventually made a professor there in 1968. Writing in the psychological realist style, he gained a reputation as a nationalist and an explorer of the effects of colonialism on the mental attitudes and self-images of individuals and nations. His first novel, *Barometer Rising* (1941), drew on his boyhood experiences, and with the critical success of *Two Solitudes* (1945) and *The Precipice* (1948), he turned to freelance writing, analysing social forces and the decline of western civilisation. Sometimes criticised for overt didacticism in his fiction, *The Watch That Ends the Night* (1959) recounts his wife's death, while other novels include *Each Man's Son* (1951), and *Return of the Sphinx* (1967), about the linguistic divisions in Canada. The science fiction novel *Voices in Time* (1980) is a scathing indictment of contemporary civilisation's exploitative activities. His highly acclaimed essays are collected in *Cross Country* (1949), *Thirty and Three* (1954) and *Scotchman's Return* (1960), while *The Rivers of Canada* (1974) offers a more regional focus.

T. MacLulich, *Hugh MacLennan* (1983).

McMillan, Terry (1951–) Born in Port Huron, Michigan, US, she graduated from the University of California, Berkeley (BA 1979) and Columbia University (MFA 1979), and then worked at the universities of Wyoming and Arizona until 1992. Her first novel was *Mama* (1987), about an African-American mother raising five children, followed by *Disappearing Acts* (1989), in which the narrative alternates between star-crossed lovers as it explores the difficulties of relationships in the modern world. Her highly successful *Waiting to Exhale* (1992, filmed 1996) examines the lives of four black professional women who have everything except the love of a man, while *How Stella Got Her Groove Back* (1996, filmed 1998) deals with a successful black businesswoman looking to shake up her boring

life by involving herself with a Jamaican man. She edited the anthology of African-American fiction, *Breaking Ice* (1990), to correct what she saw to be the neglect of black writers. Extremely popular, her fiction probes the modern difficulties facing the successful, independent-minded professional African-American women in terms of their relationships with men.

McMurtry, Larry (1936–) Born in Wichita Falls, Texas, US, Larry Jeff McMurtry was educated at North Texas State College (BA 1958) and Rice University (MA 1960). He has taught at various universities since 1961, and owned a bookstore in Washington DC and elsewhere. Set squarely within the mainstream of the realist novel, he has published widely, often nostalgically reconstructing the myths of the American West, cowboys, Indians, freedom and life in the undeveloped territories in such novels as *Horseman, Pass By* (1961) and *Buffalo Girls* (1990), which is a fictional rendering of the life of Calamity Jane and the hardships and violence of the West. His novel *Anything for Billy* (1988) demonstrates that his treatment of the West is not entirely romantic and idealistic, as he presents Billy the Kid as a foolish gunman caught in a web of pointless violence. And the West is again divested of myth with the portrayal of the hardships and difficulties of a trail-drive from Texas to Montana in 1876 in *Lonesome Dove* (1986, Pulitzer Prize) and its sequel *Streets of Laredo* (1993). Frequently depicting rootless people in the 1970s, in novels which focus on character and their development, other works include *The Last Picture Show* (1966, filmed 1971), about small-town America, and three friends moving from high school to adulthood, picked up twenty years later in *Texasville* (1987, filmed 1990), *Moving On* (1970), *All My Friends* (1972), *Terms of Endearment* (1975, filmed 1983), *Somebody's Darling* (1978), *Cadillac Jack* (1982), a humorous treatment of Washington DC, and *The Desert Rose* (1983), about a Las Vegas showgirl. More recent novels include *Evening Star* (1992), *Pretty Boy Floyd* (1994), *Dead Man's Walk* (1995), which is a prequel to *Lonesome Dove*, *Comanche Moon* (1997), *Duane's Depressed* (1999) and *Roads* (2000). *Crazy Horse* (1999) is a biography of the Native-American chief, while *Walter Benjamin at the Dairy Queen* (1999) is a memoir. Many of his books have been adapted for film, and his success can be traced to his persistent treatment of the West as a site of significant imaginative power that is still a large part of current consciousness of contemporary America.

C. Reynolds, ed., *Taking Stock* (1989).

Māhfuz, Naguīb (1911–) Naguīb Abdel Aziz al-Sabilgi Māhfuz was born in Cairo, Egypt. He was educated at the University of Cairo (BA 1934), and following postgraduate study, worked as a secretary, journalist, and civil servant, before retiring in 1971. A prolific and highly regarded writer, many of his works have been translated into English. His first book was published in 1939, but his better known work began with *Midaq Alley* (1947, trans. 1966), set in Cairo during the Second World War, about a woman's decision to be a prostitute or a wife. His masterpiece is the 'Cairo Trilogy' – *Palace Walk* (1956, trans. 1990), *Palace of Desire* (1957, trans. 1991) and *Sugar Street* (1957, trans. 1992) – concerning the emotional and intellectual development of the hero Kamal, the adventures of members of his family, and during which the characters act as mirrors for wider events in Egypt from 1917 to 1944. Among his many other novels are *The Thief and the Dogs* (1961, trans. 1984), which is a brief, grim account of a convicted felon who attempts to gain revenge on his betrayer, *Autumn Quail* (1962, trans. 1985), *The Search* (1964, trans. 1987), *Children of Gebelawi* (1967,

trans. 1981), which draws on Abrahamic religions for an allegory about mankind's search for spiritual values, and which was banned in Egypt, *Mirrors* (1972, trans. 1977), *Fountain and Tomb* (1975, trans. 1988), which uses Islamic mysticism as part of a framework for vignettes about back-street life, *The Journey of Ibn Fattouma* (1983, trans. 1992) and *Akhenaten: Dweller in Truth* (1985, trans. 2000). In addition to *Sketches of an Autobiography* (trans. 1997), short stories occur in *The Time and the Place* (trans. 1989). Considered one of the most important figures of twentieth-century Egyptian fiction, his work has been translated into an unprecedented number of languages for a modern Arabic author. Mostly set in contemporary Cairo, his fiction frequently depicts the different strata and aspects of Egyptian society, and the comic or pathetic attempts by humans to make sense of fleeting moments of consciousness. Noted for his psychological penetration, he has recently tended to abandon social realism, favouring experiments in rapid, minimal story-telling. He was awarded the Nobel Prize for Literature in 1988.

M. Beard and A. Hayden, *Naguīb Māhfuz: From Regional Fame to Global Recognition* (1993).

Mailer, Norman (1923–) Born Norman Kingsley Mailer, in Long Branch, New Jersey, and educated at Harvard University (B.Sc. 1943), he is a highly honoured American writer, who self-consciously plays with the categories of fiction and non-fiction, journalism and stories. His experiences in the US army in the Pacific during the Second World War were the basis for his first successful novel, *The Naked and the Dead* (1948), about a platoon fighting the Japanese. After *Barbary Shore* (1951) and *The Deer Park* (1955), the latter a satire of Hollywood's world of drugs, pimps and politics, he moved increasingly into journalism and essay-writing, especially to what became known as the 'new journalism' and its blurring of subjectivity and objectivity. His turbulent life after the war, his gradual attraction to a personal existential philosophy, his marriages and divorces, and his writing practices, are described in the material collected in *Advertisements For Myself* (1959), and other work of this period includes *The Presidential Papers* (1963), *Cannibals and Christians* (1966), the powerful pieces of polemic in *Why Are We in Vietnam?* (1967) and *The Armies of the Night: History as a Novel, the Novel as History* (1968, Pulitzer Prize 1969), his commentaries on America's involvement in Vietnam and the anti-Vietnam protests in 1967. Not without controversy, he has often adopted outspoken and confrontational standpoints in his writing, such as *The Executioner's Song* (1979, Pulitzer Prize 1980), about Gary Gilmore's criminal life, and his most infamous work, *An American Dream* (1965), about Stephen Rojack, a gruesome depiction of violence as he murders his wife and sexually abuses her maid. This latter work initiated a confrontation with leading feminists, notably Kate Millett, who criticised him for an egotistical masculine self-confidence and a misogynistic representation of women, an argument antagonised by his *The Prisoner of Sex* (1971), in which he attacks Millett and condemns feminism for its intellectual fragility. He unsuccessfully ran for Mayor of New York in 1969, but continued to write numerous books, including *A Fire on the Moon* (1970), about NASA's first moon flight; *Marilyn* (1973), a biography of the Hollywood actress; *The Fight* (1975), an account of the Foreman–Ali boxing match in Zaïre; and *Genius and Lust* (1976), an appreciation of the writings of Henry MILLER. Among numerous other collections of essays, memoirs, and occasional material on American culture and politics, are *Miami and the Siege of Chicago* (1968), *St. George and the God-*

father (1972), *Existential Errands* (1972), *Some Honorable Men* (1975) and *Pieces and Pontifications* (1982). Other works include *Ancient Evenings* (1983), a large historical novel set in Egypt; *Tough Guys Don't Dance* (1984); *Harlot's Ghost* (1991), another huge novel, about the CIA and its machinations in the arena of intelligence and counter-intelligence; *Oswald's Tale: An American Mystery* (1995); *Pablo and Fernande* (1995), a biography of Picasso; *The Time of Our Time* (1997), which chronicles the twentieth century and his life from excerpts from his writings; and *The Gospel According to the Son* (1997), a first person account of a human Jesus Christ. Often writing about public events which become personally significant and take on metaphorical status about contemporary America, power in all its forms – political, sexual, physical – is the central focus of Mailer's work, although his reputation has never entirely recovered from the feminists' critique.

K. Millett, *Sexual Politics* (1970); B. Morton, *Norman Mailer* (1991).

Maitland, Sara (1950–) Born in London, England, and educated at Oxford University, after marrying an Anglican priest, Sara Louise Maitland turned to freelance academic research and writing. Somewhat uniquely, her writing seeks to reconcile Christianity and feminism as she challenges the orthodoxy of patriarchal religious world views. She was associated with the feminist writers Zoë FAIRBAIRNS, Michèle Roberts and Michelene Wandor in the 1970s through the collection of short stories, *Tales I Tell My Mother* (1978). Her highly acclaimed first novel, *Daughter of Jerusalem* (1978), considers the dilemmas of feminism and the struggle for a first child, told within the context of biblical stories. This was followed by *Virgin Territory* (1984), about a rape of a nun and the rape of a people by the Spanish conquistadores, *A Book of Spells*

(1988), *Three Times Table* (1990), about three generations of women, each reflecting upon a crisis, *Home Truths* (1993), which explores the interrelations of a large family, *Hagiographies* (1996), and *Brittle Joys* (1999), about a woman trying to live up to people's perceptions of her. Her short stories encompass a rich variety of forms and occur in *Telling Tales* (1983), *Weddings and Funerals* (1984), *Arky Types* (1987), with Michelene Wandor, *Women Fly When Men Aren't Watching* (1993), *Angel and Me* (1995) and *Angel Maker* (1996), and a book of Greek myths in *Pandora's Box* (1995). Her non-fiction includes *A Map of the New Country: Women and Christianity* (1983), *Gender and Writing* (1983), the *Rushdie File* (1984), a biography of Vesta Tilley (1986), and *Big-Enough God* (1995), a feminist's search for theology.

Major, Clarence (1936–) A noteworthy African-American writer, born in Atlanta, Georgia, he was educated at SUNY, Albany, and the Union for Experimenting Colleges and Universities (Ph.D. 1978). He has had a largely academic career, lecturing at various US universities, and has been Professor of English at the University of California at Davis since 1989. At the forefront of American experimental prose and poetry, he published a large number of volumes of poetry between 1954 and 1992, which can be sampled in *Configurations: New and Selected Poems* (1998). Nevertheless, he is best known for his fiction, which began with *All-Night Visions* (1969), and continued with *NO* (1973), a literary detective story of sorts, *Reflex and Bone Structure* (1975), *Emergency Exit* (1979), *My Amputations* (1986), about a prisoner taking a writer hostage and then usurping his identity, *Such Was the Season* (1987), which focuses on an African-American middle-class female narrator in Atlanta, *Painted Turtle: Woman with Guitar* (1988) and *Dirty Bird Blues* (1996). His

non-fiction includes essays on African-American writers in *The Dark and Feeling* (1974), and short stories in *Fun and Games* (1990), which bend and twist social realism around experimental prose narratives. He has edited a wide range of work, including *Juba to Jive* (1994), a dictionary of African-American slang, and a selection of African-American poetry in *The Garden Thrives* (1996). Like Ishmael REED, he draws on his experience as an African-American from a small-town in the South to challenge white literary traditions. With a high level of violence in his work, he provides interesting explorations of sexual, literary, cultural and ethnic identities.

Malamud, Bernard (1914–1986) An American writer, born in Brooklyn, New York, and educated at the City College of New York and Columbia University. He taught English at Oregon State University (1949–1961), and at Bennington College, Vermont, from 1961 onwards. A Jew himself, many of his books are concerned with the Jewish experience, particularly in the US. His first novel, *The Natural* (1952), is a story that treats satirically a baseball player as the embodiment of the American mythical hero. This was followed by *The Assistant* (1957), a novel about impoverished Jewish life in Brooklyn, and *A New Life* (1961), a satire on the life of a Jewish professor in an Oregon college. Perhaps his most famous book is *The Fixer* (1967, Pulitzer Prize), a moving and harrowing story, set in Russia and based on a true-life incident that occurred in 1911, about a poor, ill-educated and defenceless Jewish odd-job man who is accused of the ritual murder of a gentile child. Later novels are *Pictures of Fidelman* (1969), about a Bronx man who optimistically goes to Italy in the hope of becoming an artist, *The Tenants* (1971) about the tensions and conflicts between two writers, one white and one black, who are neighbours in a run-down tenement, *Dubin's Lives* (1979) and *God's*

Grace (1982). Short stories are to be found in *The Magic Barrel* (1958), *Idiots First* (1963) and *Rembrandt's Hat* (1973).

L. Field and J. Field, *Bernard Malamud: A Collection of Critical Essays* (1975).

Mallet-Joris, Françoise (1930–) Born in Antwerp, Belgium, she later became a French citizen. She attended Bryn Mawr College and the Sorbonne, University of Paris, and worked for Editions Julliard (1960–1965), and Editions Grasset from 1965. A prolific novelist, her fiction includes *The Illusionist* (1951, trans. 1952), which was something of a *succès de scandale*, about the seduction of a 15-year-old girl by her father's mistress, *The Red Room* (1955, trans. 1956), novels about male delusions in *House of Lies* (1956, trans. 1957), *Café Celeste* (1958, trans. 1959) and *The Favourite* (1961, trans. 1962), and an historical novel about Marie Mancini, Louis XIV's lover, entitled *The Uncompromising Heart* (1964, trans. 1966). Other novels include *Signs and Wonders* (trans. 1966), which probes personal compromises caused during the French-Algerian War, *The Witches* (1968, trans. 1969), three tales of sorcery based upon three documented trials in the Renaissance, and *The Underground Game* (1973, trans. 1974). Her memoirs include *A Letter to Myself* (1963, trans. 1964) and *The Paper House* (1970, trans. 1971), which describe her path towards religion, and the conflicting demands this places on a writer. A devout convert to Catholicism, which is an important force in her work, she has a gift for historical imagination, exploring isolation, free-will and the hidden self.

Malouf, David (1934–) An Australian writer, born in Brisbane, he was educated at the University of Queensland, and spent the early 1960s in Europe, particularly in Birkenhead, England, as a schoolteacher. He returned to Australia in 1968 to lecture at the University of Sydney, and

became a full-time writer in 1977. He first established himself as a poet, collected in *New and Collected Poems* (1991). His first novel was the semi-autobiographical *Johnno* (1975), one of the most widely read Australian novels, set in Brisbane in the 1940s and 1950s, about the postcolonial problems of establishing a sense of place and identity. There followed *An Imaginary Life* (1978), which is a symbolic fable with a mythological function about incarceration and freedom, the metafictional *Child's Play* (1981), which explores how language constructs reality, *Fly Away Peter* (1982), which is about two Australians fighting in France during the First World War, *Harland's Half Acre* (1984), about a painter's contribution to Australia taking possession of its culture, *The Great World* (1990), which explores spatial and poetic history, *Remembering Babylon* (1993), a tale about cultural and racial readjustment, and *The Conversations at Curlow Creek* (1996), in which two men talk one night in a hut in New South Wales in 1827, moving between nature and justice. A prolific and diverse writer, he has published short stories in *Antipodes* (1985) and *Dream Stuff* (2000), essays in *12 Edmondstone Street* (1985), several opera librettos, including a version of Patrick WHITE's *Voss* (1986), as well as criticism and reviews. Like his poetry, his fiction blurs the boundaries between history and fiction, and deals with the tension between 'cultured' Europe and 'natural' Australia, and the ecological interdependence of humans and nature.

P. Neilson, *Imagined Lives: A Study of David Malouf* (1990).

Malraux, André (1901–1976) Born Georges-André Malraux, in Paris, France, he attended the Lyceé Condorcet and the École des Langues Orientales, where he studied archaeology and oriental art. He worked in Indochina as an archaeologist in the 1920s, and as art editor for Gallimard upon his return to France in

1927. Campaigning with anti-fascist organisations in the 1930s, he organised the Resistance in south-west France during the Occupation, and later became a government minister in Charles de Gaulle's cabinet. Combining philosophical thoughts with his fiction, his works include *The Temptation of the West* (1926, trans. 1961), which explores the western preoccupation with the individual, *The Conquerors* (1928, trans. 1929), which centres upon events in Indochina and the postcolonial uprising, while his best-known book is *Man's Estate* (1933, Prix Goncourt, trans. 1948), set in Shanghai in 1927, depicting events surrounding Chiang Kai-Shek and the communist revolutionaries, and exploring human alienation. Other novels include *Days of Wrath* (1935, trans. 1936) and *Man's Hope* (1937, trans. 1938), both written against fascism and Nazism, and *The Walnut Trees of Altenburg* (1943, trans. 1952), which affirms humanity's ability to find reconciliation in a hostile world. Art criticism occurs in the four volumes of *The Voices of Silence* (1951, trans. 1953), *The Metamorphosis of the Gods* (1957, trans. 1960) is about religion and philosophy in art, and his *Anti-Memoirs* (1967, trans. 1968), which was a best-seller in France, question the boundaries between fiction and non-fiction. A prolific writer and thinker, his belief in the 'death of God' often made him seem a forerunner to Jean-Paul SARTRE, Albert CAMUS and the existentialists.

A. Madsen, *Malraux: A Biography* (1976).

Mann, Heinrich (1871–1950) The brother of Thomas MANN, his full name was Luiz Heinrich Mann, and he was born in Lübeck, Germany. He worked in publishing, and then travelled around Europe, before becoming a lecturer and journalist in the 1920s. He naturalised as a Czech citizen in 1936, although he went to the US, along with Franz WERFEL, in 1940, and worked as a writer for the Hollywood studios until 1949. A prolific writer

of fiction, his novels include *In the Land of Cockaigne* (1900, trans. 1929), a satire of the way society is dominated by financiers and businessmen; *The Blue Angel* (1905, trans. 1931), arguably his best novel, and filmed in 1930 with Marlene Dietrich, about a professor's infatuation with a night-club singer, with the protagonist abandoning himself to anarchical impulses, thus bringing him into opposition with bourgeois society; *Man of Straw* (1918, trans. 1947), perhaps his weightiest novel, about the rise to power of a ruthless opportunist in Wilhelminian society; *Mother Mary* (1927, trans. 1928); *The Royal Woman* (1928, trans. 1930); and *The Hill of Lies* (1932, trans. 1934). He also wrote a quartet about Henry IV, set in sixteenth-century France, in which the search for greater humanity is embodied in the King, of which two volumes have been translated into English, *Young Henry of Navarre* (1935, trans. 1937) and *Henry, King of France* (1938, trans. 1939). In addition to plays, literary studies, and his correspondence with his brother, he wrote essays in defence of culture, which were increasingly hostile to the Nazis. Much of his work depicts his belief in the duality of *Geist* and *Macht*, although it met with mixed receptions in the West, criticised for its aesthetic unevenness. Despite living under the shadow of his brother, he is widely acclaimed in Germany.

D. Gross, *The Writer and Society* (1980).

Mann, Thomas (1875–1955) Born Paul Thomas Mann, in Lübeck, Germany, the brother of Heinrich MANN, he worked for an insurance company from 1894 to 1895, when he turned to writing. He went to Switzerland in the 1930s to avoid the Nazis, and then travelled to the US, remaining there until 1952, at which time he returned to Switzerland. One of the principal figures in European modernism, he wrote prolifically, and many of his novels are regarded as important literary works of the twentieth century. His early work *Buddenbrooks* (1900, trans. 1924), was followed by *Royal Highness* (1909, trans. 1916), and one of his most famous books, *Death in Venice* (1912, trans. 1925), which depicts the decline of Gustav Aschenbach, who from his highly respected German cultural position degenerates into an old roué with a homoerotic fixation on a young boy in Venice. Made into a much acclaimed film by Visconti (1971), the novel is an allegorical account of how the betrayal of knowledge for beauty leads to death. After *Basham and I* (1919, trans. 1923), came *The Magic Mountain* (1924, trans. 1927), which heralds the central theme of post-First World War Germany as the need to break out of decadence. Set in a sanatorium surrounded by mountains, the book explores how to share scepticism and insecurity and yet live an affirmation of life, and concludes that writing is a life-giving act in itself. *Mario and the Magician* (trans. 1930) was followed by the four volumes of *Joseph and His Brothers* (1933–1943, trans. 1934–1944), in which a journey into the biblical past formed an act of defiance in its homage to the Judaeo-Christian humanistic tradition, and was a reply to the crude and repressive procedure of Nazi mythologisation. He continued with *Lotte in Weimar* (1939, trans. 1940), *The Transposed Heads* (1940, trans. 1941), *The Table of the Law* (1944, trans. 1945), and *Doctor Faustus* (1947, trans. 1948), which was an attempt to comprehend Germany's political lapse into diabolism in a new version of the Faust legend, focused upon the protagonist, artist and composer Adrian Leverkühn. Other novels are *The Holy Sinner* (trans. 1951), and *The Black Swan* (1953, trans. 1954), and his final work, *Confessions of Felix Krull, Confidence Man* (1954, trans. 1955), a semi-autobiographical parody of the role of the writer and the ambivalence of fiction. His non-fiction consists of *Reflections of a Non-political Man* (1918, trans. 1983), A

Sketch of My Life (trans. 1930), *Past Masters and Other Papers* (trans. 1933), *This Peace* (trans. 1938) and *This War* (trans. 1940). Numerous volumes of essays, and letters, for example with his brother and with Hermann HESSE, have also been published. With a fascination for decadence – the cult of beauty against a background of decline – he creates a duality of comedy and pathos in his early fiction, in which doomed artists are seeking release from their society. His fiction depicts the individual as incomplete, a fragment broken away from the whole, and the critical insight of the outsider who has realised the self-deceiving motivation of human conduct. Widely honoured in Europe and throughout the world, he was awarded the Nobel Prize for Literature in 1929.

R. Hollingdale, *Thomas Mann: A Critical Study* (1971); H. Bloom, ed., *Thomas Mann* (1986).

Manning, Olivia (1908–1980) Born in Portsmouth, England, she went to London at the age of 18, where she worked in a department store during the day and wrote at night. Her first success was *The Wind Changes* (1937), set in Dublin during the Troubles. She travelled to Romania with her husband just as the Second World War broke out, and they escaped to Greece before the Italian invasion. These experiences were the basis for her most famous work, *The Balkan Trilogy* (1981) – *The Great Fortune* (1960), *The Spoilt City* (1962) and *Friends and Heroes* (1965) – which portrays the lives of Harriet and Guy Pringle and others caught up in the early events of the war. Other novels include *The Remarkable Expedition* (1947), about the explorer Stanley in Africa, *Artist Among the Missing* (1949), set in Cairo, *School for Love* (1951), *A Different Face* (1953), about a teacher in Portsmouth, *The Doves of Venus* (1955), *The Playroom* (1969), and *The Rain Forest* (1974), set on a fictitious north African island. *The Levant Trilogy* (1982) featured the next stage of the couple's wartime adventures, when Manning was press officer at the US Embassy in Cairo and then in Jerusalem, and consists of *The Danger Tree* (1977), *The Battle Lost and Won* (1978), and the posthumously published *The Sum of Things* (1980). As with much of her fiction, these narratives were partly autobiographical. Writing for magazines like *Vogue*, *Punch*, *New Statesman* and the *Spectator*, collections of sketches and short stories include *Growing Up* (1948), *My Husband Cartwright* (1956) and *A Romantic Hero* (1967).

Mansfield, Katherine (1888–1923) The pseudonym of Katherine Mansfield Beauchamp, she was born in Wellington, New Zealand, and spent her early life travelling backwards and forwards to England, before settling into a complex and various emotional life in London in 1908. Her first work was *In a German Pension* (1911), and she began to write for *Rhythm*, edited by John Middleton Murray. She lived with Murray, in what was an unconventional relationship, and under his influence, began to experiment with short fiction, moving towards the free indirect discourse of her best stories. The deaths of friends in the First World War, and her contraction of tuberculosis in 1918, had a profound impact, and she was supported in her deterioration in health by her lifelong companion Ida Baker. Her short story collections include *Prelude* (1918), *Bliss* (1920), *The Garden Party* (1922), *The Doves' Nest* (1923) and *Something Childish* (1923), while her poems were collected in 1988. Her unconventional life excited much interest, and she has become something of a cultural icon as a displaced woman artist. Central to European modernism, associated with the Bloomsbury circle and such writers as D.H. LAWRENCE and Virginia WOOLF, she has also been claimed by regional New Zealand litera-

ture, where all her major stories are set. However, she had an ambiguous attitude towards New Zealand, and many of her stories demonstrate a sense of dual location and diversity as she explores selfhood, gender and class identities. Volumes of letters and journals were edited after her death by Murray.

A. Alpers, *The Life of Katherine Mansfield* (1980).

Maraini, Dacia (1936–) Born in Florence, Italy, and brought up in Sicily, she was held in a Japanese concentration camp during the Second World War. A founder of feminist theatre in Rome (in 1973), Maraini is one of Italy's leading feminist writers, and has published a considerable number of books. Her novels include *The Holiday* (1962, trans. 1966), looking at the last phases of fascism, *The Age of Discontent* (trans. 1963), *Memoirs of a Female Thief* (1972, trans. 1973), which was based upon work carried out on the appalling conditions of Italian female prisons in the 1970s, *Women at War* (1975, trans. 1984), about the period after the industrial boom, *Letters to Marina* (1981, trans. 1987), *The Train* (1984, trans. 1989), *Isolina* (1985, trans. 1993), and *The Silent Duchess* (1990, trans. 1992), set in Palermo in the eighteenth century, concerning an aristocratic deaf-mute woman who communicates by messages. Other works include *Bagheria* (1993, trans. 1994), a bitter-sweet memoir of Sicily, *Voices* (trans. 1994), a murder-mystery novel, *Stowaway on Board* (1996, trans. 1999), and a study of Flaubert in *Searching for Emma* (1993, trans. 1998). Formal experimentation accompanies the political analysis in each novel, as she unremittingly exposes the androcentric and oppressive nature of society, which, with her commitment to a new socialism in post-war Italian literature, has made an inestimable contribution to modern Italian and European feminism.

Marechera, Dambudzo (1952–1987) Born in Rusape, Zimbabwe, he had a poverty-stricken childhood, before going to the University of Zimbabwe where he was expelled for student activism. He then went to Oxford University, but was again forced to leave, living on the bread-line in Britain before returning to Zimbabwe. His first novel was *The House of Hunger* (1978), about the pain of life in the ghetto, written in a non-realist style, with brilliant fractured shards connected by feelings of anger and bitterness. Depicting a sense of dispossession and alienation, it received accolades in 1979, yet he gave contemptuous drunken demonstrations and castigated participants for their hypocrisy at the awards ceremony. The modernist prose collection *Black Sunlight* (1980) followed, which was a critical statement about the outcasts of British society. *Mindblast* (1984) was a collection of poetry, plays and prose, again relentlessly dissident and experimental. Posthumous publications include *The Black Insider* (1990), a collection of prose and poetry, and his collected poems in *Cemetery of Mind* (1992). Writing in English, he always sought to subvert this medium, and despite his challenging and erractic behaviour, his early death has elevated him to legendary status.

F. Veit-Wild, *Dambudzo Marechera: A Source Book on His Life and Works* (1992).

Marías, Javier (1951–) Born in Madrid, Spain, he became a writer in 1971 at the age of 20, since when he has become widely honoured. The novels that have been translated into English are *All Souls* (1989, trans. 1992), based upon his romance and experiences as a Spanish lecturer for two years at Oxford University, *A Heart So White* (1992, trans. 1995), a first person narrative about complex family and emotional fears and anxieties, and *Tomorrow in Battle Think on Me* (1994, trans. 1997), about an affair between a young man and a married woman

in Madrid called Marta. When she dies in his company, he is placed in a difficult situation, eventually sharing secrets with Marta's husband in a climactic ending. The latter was hugely acclaimed. Short stories occur in *When I Was Mortal* (1996, trans. 1999). One of a young cohort of Spanish writers who refuse to use their work for political or social commentary, opting instead for topics like love, he has also translated several writers into Spanish, such as Sterne, CONRAD, Hardy and Yeats.

Markandaya, Kamala (1924–) The pseudonym of Kamala Purnaiya Taylor, she was born in Mysore, in south India, and attended the University of Madras, although did not complete her degree. She emigrated to England in 1948 and became a freelance writer. Her first published novel was *Nectar in a Sieve* (1954), a much praised depiction of Indian village life, which was followed by *Some Inner Fury* (1955), *A Silence of Desire* (1960), *Possession* (1963), *A Handful of Rice* (1966), *The Coffer Dams* (1969), *The Nowhere Man* (1972), about an elderly Brahmin suffering racism in a London suburb, *Two Virgins* (1973), about girls' lives in India and the oscillation between Eastern and Western perspectives and fashions, *The Golden Honeycombs* (1977), and *Pleasure City* (1982), which presents a comprehensive picture of western technologists' attempts to modernise India. Her novels cover a wide range of social groups, and in the main depict the minutiae of social life in India.

Márquez, Gabriel García (1928–) Born in Aracataca, Columbia, he studied law and journalism at the National University of Columbia, Bogota (1947–1948) and then at the University of Cartagena. He worked as a journalist in the 1950s, living abroad until his return in 1982. A prolific writer, his first novel was *In Evil Hour* (1962, trans. 1980), a satire exposing corruption and foregrounding writing and textual self-referentiality, which was to become a feature of his fiction. There followed his widely renowned *One Hundred Years of Solitude* (1967, trans. 1970), an epic history and mythic narrative about fatalism in the destruction of a family, and whose exploration of the limits of fiction made magic realism a common critical term. *The Autumn of the Patriarch* (1975, trans. 1976) analyses the desire for power in a study of a dictator, and *Chronicle of a Death Foretold* (1981, trans. 1982) is a murder story which shows a fascination for Greek tragedy. *Love in the Time of Cholera* (1985, trans. 1988) celebrates a love affair, *The General in His Labyrinth* (1989, trans. 1990) traces Bolivar's journey down the Magdalena river and the destruction around him, and *Of Love and Other Demons* (1994, trans. 1995) is set in eighteenth-century Columbia. Short stories occur in *No One Writes to the Colonel* (1957, trans. 1968), *Innocent Erendira* (1978, trans. 1979), and *Strange Pilgrims* (1992, trans. 1993, retitled *Bon Voyage, Mr. President*, 1995). In addition to plays and screenplays, other books include conversations in *The Fragrance of Guava* (1982, trans. 1983), and anthologies in *Collected Novellas* (1990) and *Collected Stories* (1991). The non-fiction *News of a Kidnapping* (1996, trans. 1997) deals with hostages and drug-trafficking. The most significant and influential writer of the Latin American 'boom' period, the fashionable South American magic realist literature of the 1960s, his novels combine the natural and supernatural, humour and ironic juxtaposition, and they explore the ambiguous relationship between narrative and history. Like many Latin American novelists, he is also interested in national self-definition in the face of an imperial past and present-day cultural diversity. In a widely honoured career, he was awarded the Nobel Prize for Literature in 1982.

S. Minta, *Gabriel García Márquez, Writer of Columbia* (1987); A. Penuel, *Intertextuality in García Márquez* (1994).

Marsh, Ngaio (1895–1982) Born Edith Ngaio Marsh, in Christchurch, New Zealand, she pursued interests in painting, journalism and the theatre, before travelling to England in 1928. Her novel *A Man Lay Dead* (1934) was the first of thirty-two detective novels, and by the 1950s, she had become one of the *grandes dames* of the genre, alongside novelists like CHRISTIE, Sayers and ALLINGHAM. Only four of her novels were set in New Zealand – *Vintage Murder* (1937), *Colour Scheme* (1943), *Died in the Wool* (1944) and *Photo-Finish* (1980) – although many of the others focus on New Zealanders abroad. In the 1940s and 1950s, she was linked to the new nationalist-realist sentiment in New Zealand literature, and moved in Christchurch's literary circles. Attending closely to character and realistic settings, her witty and allusive novels depict her detective-hero, Roderick Alleyne of Scotland Yard, as a patient, empirical investigator. Her autobiography, *Black Beech and Honeydew* (1965), portrayed her life in the 1930s between New Zealand and England, and her involvement in the New Zealand theatre, in which she played an important role. She published two books on drama, entitled *A Play Toward* (1946) and *Play Production* (1948).

K. McDorman, *Ngaio Marsh* (1991).

Marshall, Paule (1929–) Marshall was born and brought up in Brooklyn, New York, US, during the Depression, the daughter of parents who had emigrated from Barbados during the First World War. She studied at Hunter College in New York City, but left prematurely due to illness, although she later graduated from Brooklyn College (BA 1953). Her first novel, *Brown Girl, Brownstones* (1959), remains her most successful, and has become a classic in the African-American canon. It tells of Selina Boyce, the daughter of Barbadian immigrants living through the Depression, and is in many ways a coming-of-age novel. Her later works include *The Chosen Place, the Timeless People* (1969), which examines the exploitative mechanics and dynamics of colonialism and racism, *Praisesong for the Widow* (1983), which examines the position of African-American women in relation to their African heritage and culture, *Daughters* (1991), which combines political and historical analysis in an examination of an African-American woman's attempt to come to terms with her Caribbean heritage, and most recently, *Fisher King* (2000). Novellas occur in *South Clap Hands and Sing* (1961) and *Merle* (1983). Much of her work is committed to examining the various issues and tensions surrounding race, class and gender, and she became a major figure in the black feminist writing that gained prominence in the 1980s.

M. Evans, ed., *Black Women Writers 1950–1980* (1984).

Martinson, Harry (1904–1978) Harry Edmund Martinson, was born in Jaemshoeg, Sweden. He worked as a seaman and stoker from 1918, before turning to full-time writing in 1927. A prolific writer, a large body of his work remains untranslated into English. First popular as an autobiographer and lyric poet, he is largely unfamiliar to readers outside Sweden, although of great importance to the Swedish literary world. His works include *Cape Farewell* (1933, trans. 1934), *Flowering Nettle* (trans. 1935), and *The Road* (1948, trans. 1955), which is one of the most popular novels in Sweden, and is about a vagabond traveller in Sweden told in a rambling narrative. Poetry includes the epic allegorical poem *Aniara: A Review of Man in Time and Space* (1956, trans. 1963), and a compilation of works in *Friends You Drank Sane Darkness* (trans. 1975). He was the co-winner of

the Nobel Prize for Literature in 1974 with Eyvind JOHNSON, although the Swedish Academy was strongly criticised for honouring them owing to their relative lack of international standing.

Mason, Anita (1942–) A British novelist, born in Bristol, England, and educated at Oxford University (1963). Her first novel was *Bethany* (1981), set in Cornwall in the 1960s, about betrayal in the battle of wills when a lesbian relationship is threatened by the appearance of a Zen guru. Shortlisted for the Booker Prize, her best-known novel, *The Illusionist* (1983), is set in biblical Judaic times and recounts the idiosyncratic religion and adventures of the magician Simon Magus against the background of the growth of Christianity. This was followed by *The War Against Chaos* (1988), a dystopian vision of a futuristic unnamed city, *The Racket* (1990), about two Brazilian cousins who run afoul of corrupt and criminal elements, and *Angel* (1994). She currently lives in Leeds in England.

Mason, Bobbie Ann (1940–) A highly regarded American novelist, born in Mayfield, Kentucky, and educated at the universities of Kentucky (BA 1962), SUNY-Binghamton (MA 1966) and Connecticut (Ph.D. 1972). Regarded as a southern regional writer, her fiction has tended to focus on the people and country of rural Kentucky, chronicling the changes to the region brought about by modernisation. *Shiloh and Other Stories* (1982) is about the working-class people and places in western Kentucky, as rural folk come to terms with change. *In Country* (1985), perhaps her most famous novel, and filmed in 1989, explores the dislocation wrought on the same region by the Vietnam War, as Samantha Hughes, a 17-year-old, has to deal with the death of her father, and her mother's and uncle's respective relationships. *Spence and Lila* (1988) is a Kentucky farm couple's love story, while *Feather Crowns* (1993) is a historical novel set at the turn of the twentieth century, about the changes brought to a farm family. Regarded as a strong short story writer, *Love Life* (1989) and *Midnight Magic* (1998) collect stories about the dignity vested in small-town lives, as they adjust to the daily encroachments of popular culture and increasing mechanisation. A memoir occurs in *Clear Springs* (1999), and *The Girl Sleuth* (1975) is a witty, nostalgic observations on popular culture, childhood and the pleasures of reading.

Massie, Allan (1938–) Born in Singapore, Allan Johnstone Massie went to Cambridge University, and taught in England and Italy (1960–1975), before becoming a writer and a columnist for various newspapers. Since his first novel, *Change and Decay in All Around I See* (1978), set in 1950s seedy London, he has written prolifically, including *The Last Peacock* (1980), set in Scotland, *The Death of Man* (1981), loosely based on the murder of the Italian politician Aldo Moro, and *A Night in Winter* (1984), set in contemporary Scotland. The histories of Scotland and Rome feature prominently in his fiction, notably in the fictional biographies of *Augustus* (1986), *Tiberius* (1991), *Caesar* (1993) and *King David* (1995). Other novels include *A Question of Loyalties* (1989), about the complexities of patriotism in contemporary Scotland, *The Hanging Tree* (1990), *The Sins of the Father* (1991), *These Enchanted Woods* (1993), *The Ragged Lion* (1994), *Shadows of Empire* (1998), about the different lives of four Scottish brothers in the 1930s, and *Nero's Heirs* (1999). Non-fiction includes *The Caesars* (1983), *Colette* (1986), *101 Great Scots* (1987), *Byron's Travels* (1988) and *Glasgow* (1989). Dealing with history and politics, his popular fiction often positions the personal within larger events.

Masters, John (1914–1983) Born in Calcutta, India, he attended the Sandhurst Military Academy (1933–1934), and then served with the British army until his retirement as a lieutenant colonel in 1948. His early novels, which are invariably set in India, include *Nightrunners of Bengal* (1951), about the Indian Mutiny in 1857, and focusing upon the Savage family, *The Deceivers* (1952) and *The Lotus and the Wind* (1953), which were later published as *An Indian Trilogy* (1978). Other novels include *Bhowani Junction* (1954), about events prior to Indian emancipation in 1947 (filmed in 1956), *Coromandel!* (1955), *Far, Far the Mountain Peak* (1957), these last two again about the Savage family, *To the Coral Strand* (1962), *Fandango Rock* (1959), *The Rock* (1970) and *The Ravi Lancers* (1972). The 'Loss of Eden' trilogy consists of *Now God Be Thanked* (1979), *Heart of War* (1980) and *By the Green of Spring* (1981). Other novels include *Man of War* (1983), and the posthumously published *High Command* (1984). Non-fiction includes the biography *Casanova* (1969), and several volumes of autobiography in *Bugles and a Tiger* (1956), *The Road Past Mandalay* (1961) and *Pilgrim Son* (1971). Although Masters' fiction manifests a great appreciation of Indian history, its landscape, culture and experience, his later fiction is set in the US, where he lived after he naturalised in 1954.

Matthiessen, Peter (1927–) Born in New York City, US, he studied at the Sorbonne, University of Paris (1948–1949) and Yale University (BA 1950), when he turned to writing. He returned to France, where he mixed with US expatriate writers, such as BALDWIN, WRIGHT, SHAW and SOUTHERN, and in 1951, co-founded the influential journal *Paris Review*, which he also edited. His early novels are *Race Rock* (1954), *Partisans* (1955) and *Raditzer* (1961). His fiction increasingly turned to the themes of greed, exploitation and the vulnerability of nature. His most widely acclaimed novel, *At Play in the Fields of the Lord* (1965), set in a remote jungle village in the Amazon, depicts the misguided efforts by four American missionaries to 'save' a local tribe. This was followed by *Far Tortuga* (1975), a portrayal of the fictitious voyage of a Caribbean schooner, and *Midnight Turning Gray* (1984). His 'Florida trilogy' consists of *Killing Mister Watson* (1990), *Lost Man's River* (1997) and *Bone by Bone* (1999), which present different accounts of a murder in the Florida Everglades in the nineteenth century. One of the most important wilderness writers of the twentieth century, his prolific non-fiction deals with natural and geographical explorations. These include *Wildlife in America* (1959), the widely acclaimed semi-autobiographical *The Snow Leopard* (1978), which presents contemplations of a spiritual nature, *In the Spirit of Crazy Horse* (1983), *Indian Country* (1984), *African Silences* (1991) and *East of Lo Monthong* (1995). Exploring the natural environment and human cultures threatened by encroaching technology, the popularity of his non-fiction has tended to overshadow his fiction.

W. Dowie, *Peter Matthiessen* (1991).

Matute, Ana María (1926–) Born in Barcelona, Spain, she suffered illness in her youth and an unhappy time spent in a convent school run by French nuns. Associated with Juan GOYTISOLO and the Turia literary group in 1951, in later life she became a lecturer in various US universities. Her prize-winning fiction engages with the processes of growing up and the loss of innocence in anguished adolescents, against the background of a materialistic, petrified Spain. Her themes concern the conflict between idealism and reality, the tragic effects of passing time, and the grotesqueness and cruelty of human existence and loneliness. From her vast output in Spanish, only a few works have been translated into English. These include *Celebration in the Northwest* (1953, trans. 1997); *The Lost Children*

(1958, trans. 1965), her most complex and ambitious novel, which deals with the generation gap, the tragic legacy of the Spanish Civil War, and the lack of love and charity; *School of the Sun* (1959, trans. 1963 and 1991), the first volume of a trilogy, the rest of which is untranslated into English, about a young girl who loses her innocence but remains silent in the face of injustice. A further trilogy, set in the Spanish Civil War, and exploring how childhood shapes our future lives, consists of *The Trap* (1973, trans. 1996), *Soldiers Cry By Night* (1977, trans. 1995), and a third volume which has yet to be translated into English. Other works include the novel *Fireflies* (1993, trans. 1998), and the collection of short stories in *The Heliotrope Wall* (1968, trans. 1989). Her style is modernist, although her many exaggerated descriptions have led to criticism for rhetorical excesses, and her protagonists often dream of a lost paradise.

J. Díaz, *Ana María Matute* (1971).

Maugham, W. Somerset (1874–1965) Born William Somerset Maugham, in Paris, France, he was educated as a doctor at St. Thomas' Medical School, London. He is best-known for his detached approach in recording, especially in his short stories, the lives of British colonial civil servants and expatriates living abroad in remote places during the disintegration of the British Empire. His first novel was *Liza of Lambeth* (1897), a grim portrait of slum London. His four most widely acclaimed novels are *Of Human Bondage* (1915), about a young medical student, *The Moon and Sixpence* (1919), a story about an unconventional artist living a bohemian life, *Cakes and Ale* (1930) and *The Razor's Edge* (1944). Other novels include *Mrs Craddock* (1902), *The Painted Veil* (1925) and *Ashenden* (1928). He was recruited into the British Secret Service during the First World War and travelled to Russia. In later life, his home in the south of France became a great literary destination; he left France for the US at the outbreak of the Second World War, returning after the war. His short stories include *The Casuarina Tree* (1926), *East and West* (1934), *The Round Dozen* (1939), *Creatures of Circumstance* (1947) and *East of Suez: Great Stories of the Tropics* (1948), many of which were made into films. In addition to his fiction, he wrote many plays, of which *Lady Frederick* (1907), *The Circle* (1921) and *The Breadwinner* (1930) are perhaps his most famous. *Looking Back* (1962) was a memoir. His writing suffered from criticism of his superficial characterisation, and although he was financially successful and enormously popular, he never really enjoyed critical acclaim.

F. Raphael, *Maugham and His World* (1976).

Maupin, Armistead (1944–) Full name Armistead Jones Jr. Maupin, he was born in Washington DC, educated at the University of North Carolina (BA 1966), and has worked in journalism and served in Vietnam. He is principally known for his 'Tales of the City' series, initially serialised from the mid-1970s in the *San Francisco Examiner*. *Tales of the City* (1978), *More Tales of the City* (1980) and *Further Tales of the City* (1982) have been collected in *28 Barbary Lane* (1990) and *The Complete Tales of the City* (1991). Adapted for television by Channel 4 in 1993 with acclaim, the cycle of stories charts America's shifting cultural landscape – gay and straight, male and female, rich and poor. It focuses on the inhabitants of a San Francisco boarding-house at 28 Barbary Lane, as they search for love and security in an increasingly uncertain world with the rise of AIDS in the 1980s. In addition to insights into the film and television business in *Maybe the Moon* (1992), and various dialogues for stage productions, other novels include *Babycakes* (1984), *Significant Others* (1987), *Sure of You* (1989) *Back to Barbary Lane: The Final*

Tales of the City Omnibus (1991) and *The Night Listener* (2000). Often placing gay characters within a tolerant and accepting society in San Francisco, his social satires depict the tangled motivations, longings and desires of the entire Bay Area community.

P. Gale, *Armistead Maupin* (1999).

Mauriac, François (1885–1970) Born François Charles Mauriac, in Bordeaux, France, he went to the University of Bordeaux. Under the pseudonym Forez, he worked as a Resistance journalist during the German Occupation, and later for *L'Express* (1954–1961). He is one of the major Roman Catholic novelists of twentieth-century France, blending psychology and theology in his fiction. An outstanding practitioner of realism, his many books frequently explore the claustrophobic geography of south-west France, in a continuing love-hate relationship with the region. In a deep seam of regionalism, his characters are from Bordeaux and the Landes area. In such works as *The Kiss to the Leper* (1922, trans. 1923), *The River of Fire* (1923, trans. 1954), *The Desert of Love* (1925, trans. 1929), *Thérèse* (1927, trans. 1928), *Destinies* (1928, trans. 1929) and *Viper's Tangle* (1932, trans. 1933), he generally criticises the materialism and hypocrisy of the provincial bourgeois family and examines its constraints and spiritual barrenness. Other works include *The Frontenac Mystery* (1933, trans. 1952), *A Woman of the Pharisees* (1941, trans. 1946), *The Lamb* (1954, trans. 1955) and *Maltaverne* (1969, trans. 1970). SARTRE famously attacked Mauriac in 1935 for his god-like authorial stance, which Sartre perceived as preventing the freedom of the fictional characters. He was awarded the Nobel Prize for Literature in 1952.

J. Flower, *Intention and Achievement: The Novels of François Mauriac* (1969).

Michener, James A. (1907–1997) Born in New York City, US, James Albert Michener attended Swarthmore College (BA 1929) and the University of North Colorado (MA 1936), before working variously as an actor, teacher, editor and freelance writer. During the Second World War, he was a naval officer in the Pacific, the experiences of which led to his first book, *Tales of the South Pacific* (1947, Pulitzer Prize 1948). It was adapted by Rodgers and Hammerstein as the musical *South Pacific*, itself filmed in 1958. He was a widely published and prolific author of fiction and non-fiction, and many of his books have been adapted for television and film. Although much of his earlier fiction was set in the South Pacific and the Far East, with travel sketches and non-fiction about these regions, he gradually developed what came to be a tremendously successful formula for his fiction. This was a series of large popular fictionalised histories of different countries, epic narratives in which generations of families were woven into documented facts and events. Beginning with *Hawaii* (1959), among these narratives are included such countries and regions as Israel in *The Source* (1965), the history of Colorado from the beginning of time to 1974 in *Centennial* (1974), Maryland in *Chesapeake* (1978), South Africa in *The Covenant* (1980), the work of NASA in *Space* (1982), and *Poland* (1983). *The World Is My Home* (1992) is an autobiography and *Literary Reflections* (1993) collects essays.

M. Severson, *James A. Michener: A Critical Companion* (1996).

Miller, Henry (1891–1980) An American writer, born in Brooklyn, New York, Henry Valentine Miller attended the City University of New York (1909). He worked for a cement company and, later, for the Western Union Telegraph (1909–1924). He travelled to Paris in 1930, where he moved in avant-garde literary circles and had an affair with Anaïs NIN, before eventually settling in Big Sur, California in 1944, where he turned to painting. He is best remembered for his books *Tropic of Cancer* (1934), *Black Spring* (1936) and *Tropic of Capricorn* (1939), which portrayed life's seamier side and were largely based upon his experiences in Paris and elsewhere. They were censored in the US for sexual obscenity and not published until the 1960s, when they became immediate best-sellers. His other well-known books were 'The Rosy Crucifixion' trilogy, developed from expanding the *Tropic of Capricorn*, consisting of *Sexus* (1949), *Plexus* (1953) and *Nexus* (1960). His wide variety of other writings include *Max and the White Phagocytes* (1938), *The World of Sex* (1940), *The Colossus of Marousi* (1941), which depicts a quest for spiritual illumination in Greece, *Big Sur and the Oranges of Hieronymous Bosch* (1957), and the autobiographies in *Quiet Days in Clichy* (1956) and *My Life and Times* (1971). A novel entitled *Crazy Cock* was posthumously published (1991). Short stories occur in *The Air-conditioned Nightmare* (1945), *Nights of Love and Laughter* (1955), and in addition to two volumes of *Selected Prose* (1965), he published numerous editions of his letters, essays and occasional writings. He always held that life should be revered over all other considerations, and championed freedom over materialism and individuality over social conformity. However, his notion that sexual drives are a necessary form of masculine self-expression, caused him to be fiercely castigated by feminists, most notably Kate Millett.

K. Millett, *Sexual Politics* (1970); R. Ferguson, *Henry Miller: A Life* (1991).

Millin, Sarah Gertrude (1889–1968) Born in Lithuania, she went to South Africa as a small child, and grew up and was educated in Kimberly. She spent most of her adult life in Johannesburg and wrote prolifically from the mid-1920s to the mid-1960s, during which time she established herself as an acclaimed author. Of her early novels, *God's Step-Children* (1924) is perhaps her most celebrated outside of her country, about a missionary who travels to South Africa in the early nineteenth century and marries a young black woman from his village. It explores the subsequent politics of miscegenation and the struggle of four generations of the family for self-respect and dignity. Other novels include *Mary Glenn* (1925), *An Artist in the Family* (1928), *The Fiddler* (1929), *Adam's Rest* (1930), *The Sons of Mrs Aab* (1931), *What Hath a Man?* (1938), *The Dark Gods* (1941), *The Herr Witchdoctor* (1941), *King of the Bastards* (1949), *The Burning Man* (1952), *The Wizard Bird* (1962) and *Goodbye, Dear England* (1965). She also wrote biographies of Cecil Rhodes (1933) and Jan Smuts (1936), as well as an autobiography entitled *The Measure of My Days* (1955).

M. Rubin, *Sarah Gertrude Millin: A South African Life* (1977).

Mishima, Yukio (1925–1970) The pseudonym of Kimitake Hiraoka, he was born in Tokyo, Japan, studied jurisprudence at Tokyo University (1947), and after time as a civil servant in 1948, turned to writing. He is renowned for his flamboyant personality, eccentric political beliefs and spectacular ritual suicide. A literary genius of post-war Japan, creating a dazzling impression as a *tour de force* young writer, his first work was *Confessions of a Mask* (1949, trans. 1958), a chronicle of his life from childhood to wartime and his growing homosexuality. A prolific author, other works of significance include *Thirst for Love* (1950, trans. 1969), which is the story of a widow who becomes the mistress of her father-in-law and then of a servant boy, *Forbidden Colours* (1954, trans. 1968), which explores homosexuality, *The Sound of Waves* (1954, trans. 1957), and *The Temple of the Golden Pavilion* (1956, trans. 1959), one of his masterpieces, based on a true case about a young Buddhist priest who burns a temple to the ground, and is an exploration of obsession, self-destruction and private pathology. Later works include *After the Banquet* (1960, trans. 1963), *Sun and Steel* (1968, trans. 1971), and *The Sailor Who Fell from Grace with the Sea* (1963, trans. 1966), about youthful hero-worship and disappointment. His last work was the *Sea of Fertility* tetralogy (1969–1971), which consists of *Spring Snow* (trans. 1972), *Runaway Horses* (trans. 1973), *The Temple of Dawn* (trans. 1973), and *The Decay of the Angel* (trans. 1974). His magnum opus, it spans Japanese history of the twentieth century, as the central character, Kiyoaki, is reincarnated in each new volume in keeping with the Buddhist metamorphosis of the soul, and explores the beauty of nothingness, the dissolution of the individual and the old aristocratic cultures. He also published ten short stories and plays in *Death in Midsummer* (1966), and *Acts of Worship* (trans. 1989). Fascinated with death and suicide in the old Samurai tradition, he believed in 'sepukku' (the old Samurai suicide custom) as the ultimate expression of one's beliefs, which he carried out by committing ritual suicide in front of assembled soldiers after a failed coup attempt. A mixture of exhibitionism and the impulse towards self-destruction, he is regarded as one of the major writers of the twentieth century.

J. Nathan, *Mishima: A Biography* (1974).

Mistry, Rohinton (1952–) Born in Bombay, India, he emigrated to Canada in 1975, and attended the University of Toronto. *Tales from Firozsha Baag* (1987) and *Swimming Lessons and Other Stories from Firozsha Baag* (1989) established his reputation. They are a linked set of stories centred upon a Bombay apartment block inhabited by a Parsi community, which depict their various dislocated social and cultural experiences. His novel *Such a Long Journey* (1991), short-listed for the Booker Prize, is set in Bombay in the crucial year 1971, and again focuses on a Parsi community, linking India's turbulent political situation with the family of Gustad Noble. His second novel *A Fine Balance* (1996) continues the themes of Indian history and its effects upon individuals. Exploring the relationships between self-community and identity, he highlights the heterogeneity of identity *within* community, as well as the traumas of change from outside pressures.

Mitchell, Margaret (1900–1949) An American novelist, born in Atlanta, Georgia, who was educated at Smith College. She is most famous for writing America's most celebrated romantic best-seller, *Gone with the Wind* (1936, Pulitzer Prize 1937), which is set in Georgia during the American Civil War, and depicts the struggles of Scarlett O'Hara to keep her family together at Tara, despite the war and its concomitant difficulties. The epitome of a headstrong young heroine who causes her own downfall, Scarlett drives her lover Rhett Butler to a rejection made famous in the film version (1939). After the publication of the novel, she lived in the legend she had constructed, until her death in a road accident.

Mitchell, W.O. (1914–1998) Full name William Ormond Mitchell, he was raised in Weyburn, Saskatchewan, and educated at the universities of Manitoba and Alberta. One of Canada's best-known writers, he began as a teacher and then on the success of his short stories, became editor of *Maclean's* (1948–1951). He held a series of writer-in-residence positions until his retirement to Calgary. His first two books are the most popular, establishing a sense of regional identity in Canadian literature. The famous *Who Has Seen the Wind* (1947) is an endearing story of a prairie boy's discovery of his spirituality, and Mitchell became some-

thing of a national celebrity for his public broadcasts of his earlier short stories, collected in *Jake and the Kid* (1961) and *According to Jake and the Kid* (1989), which were nostalgic portraits of small-town prairie life. He continued his theme of resistance to oppression and the celebration of the wisdom, vitality and simplicity of prairie life in *The Kite* (1962), and *Vanishing Point* (1973), which deals with the treatment of the Native-Canadian population and features the protagonist Archie Nicotine, who returns in *Since Daisy Creek* (1984), a satire of university life. Other works include *How I Spent My Summer Holidays* (1981), *Ladybug, Ladybug ...* (1988), and the uglier realism of *Roses Are Difficult Here* (1990) and *For Art's Sake* (1992). He has written for radio, television, film and the theatre, with several of his plays collected in *Dramatic W.O. Mitchell* (1982). Often humorous in his representations of the prairie landscape and the link of the people to the land, his fiction champions an ethic of practical self-reliance.

M. Peterman, *W.O. Mitchell* (1980).

Mitchison, Naomi (1897–1999) Born Naomi Mary Margaret in Edinburgh, Scotland, and educated at Oxford University, she is the daughter of the philosopher John Scott Haldane and the brother of the geneticist J.B.S. Haldane. She is best known for her historical novels, for example *The Conquered* (1923), which is about her experience of the war years. This was followed by *Cloud Cuckoo Land* (1925), *The Corn King and Spring Queen* (1931), *The Blood of the Martyrs* (1939) and *To the Chapel Perilous* (1955). Active in the women's movement and birth control, the peace and the Labour movements, she wrote *We Have Been Warned* (1935), which was censored by her publishers for its open references to birth control, while *The Hare* (1934) analyses the position of women as property in western patriarchy. Her later novels tended towards science fiction in *Memoirs of a Spacewoman* (1962), *Solution Three* (1975), a post-nuclear fantasy, and *Not By Bread Alone* (1983). In addition to *Mucking Around* (1981), a travelogue about her journeys from the 1920s onwards, there are several volumes of autobiography in *Small Talk* (1973), *All Change Here* (1975) and *You May Well Ask* (1979), and diaries in *Vienna Diary* (1934) and *Among You Taking Notes* (1985).

Mo, Timothy (1950–) An Anglo-Chinese writer, born in Hong Kong, Timothy Peter Mo graduated from Oxford University after his family emigrated to England. His first novel was *Monkey King* (1978), a widely praised expatriate's narrative about Hong Kong culture, while *Sour Sweet* (1982, filmed 1987) was a depiction of an immigrant's experience from the viewpoint of a Chinese family in London, who open a restaurant but live under threat from the Triads. There followed *An Insular Possession* (1986), about the Opium Wars and the founding of Hong Kong, and *The Redundancy of Courage* (1991), a thinly veiled narrative based upon the guerrillas in East Timor. Despite his wide commercial success, he published *Brownout and Breadfruit Boulevard* (1995) under his own imprint Paddless Press, owing to his disillusionment with conglomerate editing and publishing. A satirical political comedy set in the Philippines, the novel contains a graphic description of coprophilia and offers a complex investigation of imperial domination. His most recent work is *Renegade or Halo* (1999), set in the streets of Manila and London and narrated by a Black Amerasian, exploring themes of globalisation, decolonisation and migration. Scrutinising the representation of racial stereotypes in the culture clash between East and West, Mo's fiction has had considerable acclaim and been awarded many prizes.

Momaday, N. Scott (1934–) Full name Navarre Scott Momaday, and born in Lawton, Oklahoma, US, he went to the University of New Mexico (BA 1958) and Stanford University (MA 1960, Ph.D. 1963). He has held various teaching positions in English, dedicating much of his time to researching and writing about his Kiowa Indian heritage. His first book, *The Journey of the Tai-me* (1967), was a retelling of Kiowa folktales, and *The Way to Rainy Mountain* (1969) relates the history of the Kiowa's journey 300 years ago from Yellowstone to the plains. Yet his fame came with his widely acclaimed novel *House Made of Dawn* (1968, Pulitzer Prize 1969), which is a discontinuous sequence of events centred upon Abel's return to his reservation area after the Second World War, and the problems arising from the mixing of Native-American and Anglo cultures. As with much of his work, it demonstrates a strong reverence for the landscape and the tribal mythic heritage. *The Names: A Memoir* (1976) is composed of tribal tales, boyhood memories and a genealogical quest for roots, which covers his own Kiowa and Anglo-American heritage, while *The Ancient Child* (1989) is built on the legend of his Kiowa name, Tsoaitalee, and is about a modern Kiowa artist in search of artistic identity in San Francisco. Short stories and poems are collected in the volumes *Angle of Geese* (1974), *The Gourd Dancer* (1976) and *In the Presence of the Sun* (1992), essays occur in *Man Made of Words* (1997), while *Circle of Wonder* (1994) is a children's story. His latest work is *In the Bear's House* (1999). His major achievement is to have participated in squarely placing Native-American experience within the trajectories of contemporary American fiction.

Monsarrat, Nicholas (1910–1979) An English novelist, Nicholas John Turney Monsarrat, was born in Liverpool, and educated at Cambridge University. His first novel was *Think of Tomorrow* (1934), although he is best known for his vivid novels *H.M. Corvette* (1942) and *The Cruel Sea* (1951), in which he drew on his experiences with North Atlantic convoys during the Second World War. The latter became a best-seller and was made into a popular film (1953). Later books include *The Story of Esther Costello* (1953), *The Tribe That Lost its Head* (1956), about the struggle for independence of an African state, and *Smith and Jones* (1963), based on the defections to the USSR of the spies Burgess and McLean, *The Kapillan of Malta* (1973), and the unfinished two volume *The Master Mariner* (1978, 1980). He also wrote two volumes of autobiography (1966, 1970).

Montgomery, L.M. (1874–1942) A widely honoured Canadian novelist, born in Clifton (now New London), Prince Edward Island, her full name was Lucy Maud Montgomery. After her education at Dalhousie University, Halifax, she taught for several years, before working in journalism. She is most famous for *Anne of Green Gables* (1908), a world-wide bestseller, which is about an adolescent girl's search for self-knowledge that results in liberation from adult authority and success in the male–female struggle. There were seven sequels owing to adoring public demand, following Anne Shirley's life and development. This became the pattern for her wish-fulfilment romances about adolescent girls' developments, which are invariably optimistic and humorous narratives. The more autobiographical 'Emily' series followed, beginning with *Emily of New Moon* (1923), charting Emily's development as a woman and writer, with two sequels. Her adult novels, such as *The Blue Castle* (1926) and *A Tangled Web* (1931), were less successful, and these were followed with new adolescent girl heroines in *Pat of Silver Bush* (1933), *Mistress Pat* (1945) and *Jane of Lantern Hill* (1937). Short stories are collected in *The Story Girl* (1911), and the posthumous *The Road to Yesterday*

(1974) and *The Doctor's Sweetheart* (1979), with a volume of poems in *The Watchman and Other Poems* (1916). Various volumes of letters and diaries, as well as early magazine articles, have been published posthumously.

Montherlant, Henry de (1896–1972) Born in Paris, France, into minor aristocracy, Henry Milon de Montherlant fought in the French army (1914–1918), and then worked as a bullfighter and a writer, and travelled extensively in the 1920s. Despite serving in the French army, he controversially adulated the arrival of fascism during the Second World War. Beginning early, he created a vast output of writing, examining the irrationality and unpredictability of human behaviour in his fiction. Novels include *The Dream* (1922, trans. 1962), in which the protagonist finds fulfilment in the fraternity of war, *The Matador* (1926, trans. 1957), about heroism in the bullring, and *Lament for the Death of an Upper Class* (1934, trans. 1935). *The Girls* tetralogy (two vols, trans. 1968), consists of *Young Girls* (1936, trans. 1937), *Pity for Women* (1936, trans. 1937), *The Demon of Good* (1937, trans. 1940) and *The Leppers* (1939, trans. 1940). It explores the simultaneous or alternating presence of opposites in human motivation, and the male protagonist studiously avoids women, rejecting the passivity of a man in love. Other novels include *Desert Love* (1954, trans. 1957), *Chaos and Night* (1963, trans. 1964), which is a cynical rejection of unmanly qualities, and shows a bitterness about useless service, and *The Boys* (1969, trans. 1974). Although he began as a novelist, arguably his greatest successes were his plays, such as *The Master of Santiago* (trans. 1947).

J. Cruickshank, *Montherlant* (1964).

Moore, Brian (1921–) Born in Belfast, Northern Ireland, he emigrated to Canada and naturalised in 1948, and later moved to the US. His earliest serious work and best-known novel is *Judith Hearne* (1955), about a lonely Belfast spinster who resorts to alcohol. Together with *The Emperor of Ice-cream* (1956), *The Feast of Lupercal* (1957), and *The Luck of Ginger Coffey* (1960), about an Irish immigrant to Canada, these early novels feature characters who rebel against the essentially closed society of Northern Ireland and the claustrophobia of Belfast. Other novels include *Intent to Kill* (1956), *An Answer from Limbo* (1962), *I am Mary Dunne* (1968), *Catholics* (1972), *The Doctor's Wife* (1976), *The Mangan Inheritance* (1979), *The Temptation of Eileen Hughes* (1981), *Cold Heaven* (1983), *The Colour of Blood* (1987), *Black Robe* (1985), about a French priest during the early exploration of Ontario, and *Lies of Silence* (1990), about Irish terrorism and politics. More recent novels are *No Other Life* (1993), *The Statement* (1996), which is a fictional treatment of a historical event about ex-Nazis in France in 1989, and *The Magician's Wife* (1997), about the life of a French illusionist sent by Napoleon III to persuade the Arabs not to go to war with France. Short stories appear in *Two Stories* (1978), and he has also written plays and screenplays. With an economy of style, characterisation and description, his works reflect his multinational wanderings, a fascination with Catholicism's influence on modern life, and interpersonal relations.

R. Sullivan, *A Matter of Faith: The Fiction of Brian Moore* (1991).

Moorhouse, Frank (1938–) An Australian novelist, born in Nowra, New South Wales, after a period of journalism he became a full-time writer in the late 1960s. An activist for writers' causes and organisations, he has become the doyen of Australian short story writers. He found difficulty in getting his early work accepted owing to its sexual explicitness, and it occasionally appeared in men's magazines. *Futility and Other Animals* appeared in 1969, and was notable for its discontinuous narrative, a style continued in *The Americans, Baby* (1972), which established his reputation as a leading short story writer, *Forty-Seventeen* (1988) and *Lateshows* (1990). Describing daily life, and in particular recording the banalities of contemporary life and language, his stories often seek to revivify the moribund and to rework the discarded. *Days of Wine and Rage* (1980) is a non-fictional documentation of Sydney in the 1970s, while in addition to film collaborations and screenplays, other fiction includes *The Elemental Experience* (1974), *Conference-Ville* (1976), *Tales of Mystery and Romance* (1977) and *The Everlasting Secret Family and Family Secrets* (1980). More recent works include *Room Service* (1987), *Woman of High Distinction* (1993), *Ground Days* (1993), which is set in Geneva and explores the interwar European idealism, and *Loose Living* (1995). He was associated with the Balmain writers, a radical group who gathered in the Sydney suburb in the 1960s, and he co-founded the experimental magazine *Tabloid Story* with Michael WILDING. Exploring the connection between the fragment and the whole, his narrative discontinuities create a sense of uncertainty and ambiguity as they question social attitudes and absolutes.

Moravia, Alberto (1907–1990) Born Alberto Pincherle, in Rome, Italy, he was a writer and part-time editor. An Italian Jew and anti-fascist, he fled persecutions, and came to be regarded as the leader of the neo-realist school of fiction in Italy. His novels include *The Time of Indifference* (1929, trans. 1953), about a brother and sister sliding into moral indolence, which was a great success and is regarded as the first existentialist novel in Italian. Numerous other works include *Mistaken Ambitions* (1929, trans. 1955), *The Fancy Dress Party* (1941, trans. 1947), *Two*

Adolescents: Agostino and Disobedience (1944, trans. 1952), *The Woman of Rome* (1947, trans. 1949), about a young girl who turns to prostitution, *The Conformist* (trans. 1951, filmed by Bernardo Bertolucci in 1969), *The Empty Canvas* (1963, trans. 1965), *The Two of Us* (1971, trans. 1972), *1934* (trans. 1982), *The Voyeur* (1985, trans. 1986), which described the disaffection of a left-wing Italian academic and his struggles to come to terms with his identity, and *Journey to Rome* (trans. 1990), about the homecoming of a young boy raised in France and haunted by the psychic distress of his childhood. Short stories occur in *Conjugal Love* (1949, trans. 1951), *The Wayward Wife* (1952, trans. 1960), *Roman Tales* (1954, trans. 1956) and *Erotic Tales* (1983, trans. 1985). In addition to plays and screenplays, his essays appear in *Man as an End* (1964, trans. 1965). His frank treatment of sexual obsession and dysfunction in his early novels caused moral outrage, although his studies of amorality in contemporary Italy depicted a world of bourgeois decadence, peopled by alienated and indifferent characters.

T. Peterson, *Alberto Moravia* (1996).

Morris, Wright (1910–1998) Born in Central City, Nebraska, US, he attended Crane College, Chicago and Pomona College, California, and after travelling in Europe, held various university teaching positions. A fine if somewhat neglected writer, his work explores what it means to be American. He wrote a wide number of novels about the Nebraska landscape, and the plains appear as constitutive of most of his characters in his re-creations of the pioneer roots and spirit. His novels include *My Uncle Dudley* (1942), about a young boy and uncle who make a cross-country trip in the vein of John STEIN-BECK, *The Man Who Was There* (1945), about a painter seeking to understand the US, and the two novels about Clyde

Muncy, who returns to his childhood home from New York City to discover a clash of values between prairie and modern culture in *The Home Place* (1948) and *The World in the Attic* (1949). With acute observations about character and quests for meaningful human relationships, more recent fiction includes the typical Nebraska setting of *Ceremony in Lone Tree* (1960), *The Field of Vision* (1956), *Fire Sermon* (1971), *The Huge Season* (1975) and *Plains Song* (1981). Short story collections include *Green Grass, Blue Sky, White House* (1970), *Here is Einbaum* (1973), *The Cat's Meow* (1975), *Real Losses, Imaginary Gains* (1976) and *Collected Stories 1948–1986* (1986). Autobiographical volumes include the story of his early life in *Will's Boy: A Memoir* (1981), his young adulthood in *Solo* (1983), and *The Cloak of Light* (1985). He published two noteworthy photography books of the US, *The Inhabitants* (1946) and *Structure and Artifacts* (1981), and a book of literary essays, *The Territory Ahead* (1958). Sadly, despite prolific publications, popularity constantly eluded him.

L. Howard, *Wright Morris* (1968).

Morrison, Toni (1931–) Born Toni Chloe Anthony Morrison, in Lorain, Ohio, US, she began her career lecturing in English at universities in the States, before becoming an editor at Random House publishing company, where she worked from 1965 to 1984, and from where she aided the careers of several African-American writers. During this time, she continued with various distinguished lecturing positions at several universities, including Yale, Berkeley and Princeton. Her writing career began with *The Bluest Eye* (1970), which changed the way that the complex lives of black women within the African-American community was represented, and which she regarded as 'important because I had to bear witness to what was not recorded'. In this one act of writing, she laid bare the emotional landscape of African-American women, which had been persistently obscured and sidestepped. This focus on a marginalised culture was continued in a succession of widely acclaimed novels: *Sula* (1974), *Song of Solomon* (1977) and *Tar Baby* (1981). Arguably, her most celebrated work is *Beloved* (1987, Pulitzer Prize 1988; and filmed in 1999, starring Oprah Winfrey), which engages with the African-American past, narrating the harrowing history and circumstances of the inhabitants of a house on the edge of Cincinnati, Ohio, in 1873. Purportedly a 'ghost story', it relates how a mother is forced to cut the throat of her child rather than allow it to be taken into slavery. Years later, the spirit of the slain returns as a child called Beloved, who is fully embraced by the mother as her lost child. As the past interrupts and literally haunts the present, the novel explores how the effects of slavery have devastated the African-American community, even decades after its abolition. *Jazz* (1992) focuses on black culture in Harlem in the 1920s and, as with much of her other fiction, the novel urges African-Americans to reclaim and rewrite their own history. Her latest novel, *Paradise* (1998), depicts a tiny farming community called Ruby, Oklahoma, which was settled by African-American clans during the 1940s. Set in 1976, it weaves the history of the town with post-war African-American history, exploring self-reliance and community, race and gender. In 1993, she was awarded the Nobel Prize for Literature, which instated her in the first rank of international authors. In addition to fiction, Morrison has written several texts which elaborate her political arguments concerning racial prejudice. These are *Playing in the Dark* (1992) and *Race-ing Justice, En-gendering Power* (1992), both of which address themselves to her lifelong exploration of the social and political situation of African-Americans in the

US. She has also written a play, entitled *Dreaming Emmett* (1986).

S. Willis, *Specifying: Black Women Writing the American Experience* (1990); B. Rigney, *The Voices of Toni Morrison* (1991).

Mortimer, John (1923–) A widely honoured British novelist and playwright, born in London, John Clifford Mortimer went to Oxford University (BA 1947), before distinguishing himself as a barrister often defending cases of press freedom. He is principally known for his creation of the endearing, eccentric barrister Rumpole, featured in *Rumpole of the Bailey* (1978), *The Tricks of Rumpole* (1979), *Rumpole's Return* (1980), *Rumpole for the Defence* (1982), and several further volumes including *Rumpole à la Carte* (1990) and *Rumpole on Trial* (1992), collected in omnibus volumes in 1983 and 1987. A prolific playwright, he has written theatre, radio and television plays, notably the popular television series *Rumpole of the Bailey*. Other novels include *Charade* (1947), *Rumming Park* (1948), *Paradise Postponed* (1985), about an aspiring politician, and its sequel, *Titmuss Regained* (1990), *Summer's Lease* (1988), *Dunster* (1992), and *The Sound of Trumpets* (1998), which is about political collaboration between Tories and New Labour. Autobiographical volumes occur in *Clinging to the Wreckage* (1982) and *Murderers and Other Friends* (1994). Interested in character, atmosphere and social humour, his fiction is marked by cerebral dialogue, linguistic nuance and verbal urbanity, and often involves mystery and sleuths. His fiction delights in pricking the pretensions of the pompous and exposing repression and hypocrisy. He was formerly married to the novelist Penelope MORTIMER.

Mortimer, Penelope (1918–1999) Born in Rhyl, Wales, Penelope Ruth Mortimer attended London University, and worked as a film critic for the *Observer* (1967–1970), and subsequently as a columnist for the *Daily Mail* under the pseudonym Ann Temple. Her first novel, under the name Penelope Dimont, was *Johanna* (1947), and was followed by other titles under her own name. These include *A Villa in Summer* (1954), *The Bright Prison* (1956), *Daddy's Gone A'Hunting* (1958), *The Pumpkin Eater* (1962), *My Friend Says It's Bullet-Proof* (1967), *The Home* (1971), *The Handyman* (1973), about a woman recently widowed who is suddenly forced to face the new challenges of ageing and solitude, and *Long Distance* (1974). Her non-fiction consists of a travel book jointly written with her ex-husband John MORTIMER, *With Love and Lizards* (1957), a biography of the Queen Mother which drew mixed reviews in *Queen Elizabeth* (1986), short stories in *Saturday Lunch with the Brownings* (1960), and autobiographies in *About Time* (1979), *About Time Too* (1990) and *Autobiography* (1999), and several screenplays. With a precision and economy of style and all-encompassing female figures dominant in her fiction, her novels often focus on the strained relationships of men and women.

Mphahlele, Ezekiel (later Es'kia) (1919–) Born in Marabastad Township, Pretoria, South Africa, he was educated at the University of South Africa (BA 1949, MA 1956) and the University of Denver (Ph.D. 1968). He worked as a clerk, a teacher in Orlando Township, Johannesburg (1945–1952), and when he was banned from teaching for his protests against the segregationist Bantu Education Act, he became the first editor of the prominent black writing magazine *Drum* (1955–1957). While in exile, he held various university posts in Nigeria, Kenya, Colorado, Zambia and Pennsylvania, before becoming a professor at the University of Witwatersrand (1978–1983). He began his prolific writing with short stories, collected in *Man Must Live* (1947), *The Living and the Dead* (1961)

and *In Corner B* (1967). His first novel was the autobiographical *The Wanderers* (1971). Upon his return to South Africa in 1978, he produced a series of works, including the novels *Chirundu* (1981), about a man torn between African traditions and English law, and *Father Come Home* (1984), a collection of selected writings in *The Unbroken Song* (1981), the autobiographical *Afrika My Music* (1984), and letters in *Bury My Heart at the Marketplace* (1984). In a remarkable story of moving from slum-life to becoming an internationally acclaimed professor of English, he developed a high reputation for literary criticism, and essays appear in *The African Image* (1964) and *Voices in the Whirlwind* (1972). Other writings include an anthology in *Modern African Short Stories* (1964), and an early autobiography *Down Second Avenue* (1959), which is continued in *Exiles and Homecomings* (1983) and *Renewal Time* (1988). Much of his influential writing, often angry and impassioned, deals with dispossession, exile, racism, and corruption in African politics.

U. Barnett, *Ezekiel Mphahlele* (1976).

Mukherjee, Bharati (1940–) Born in Calcutta, India, she went to the University of Calcutta (BA 1959) and the University of Iowa (MFA 1963, Ph.D. 1969), before moving to Canada in 1968 with her husband. She later returned to the US (1980), where she now resides, and worked in various universities, and she now teaches at the University of California at Berkeley. Her first novel, *The Tiger's Daughter* (1972), is about an expatriate's difficult visit to her hometown in India, and was followed by *Wife* (1975) and *Jasmine* (1989), the latter her most significant novel to date, about an illegal immigrant's struggle to find her identity in the US. There followed *The Holder of the World* (1993), which is a feminist reworking of the historical novel, as one American women researches the life of an earlier American woman in India, and *Leave It to Me* (1997), a bleakly comic postmodern exploration of personal identity within contemporary California's hybrid cultures. Short stories are collected in *Darkness* (1985) and *The Middleman* (1988), and she has co-authored non-fiction in *Days and Nights in Calcutta* (1977) and *The Sorrow and the Terror* (1987), about the Air India tragedy. A significant figure in Asian-American literature, her fiction consistently deals with Asian immigrants to the West, charting the search for identity undertaken by semi-assimilated Indians and the multicultural underclass in the US.

E. Nelson, *Bharati Mukherjee: Critical Perspectives* (1993).

Mungoshi, Charles (1947–) Born in Manyeye Communal land in Zimbabwe, he attended Cambridge University, and has forged a career as a novelist, poetry editor and actor. He worked for a booksellers in Harare (1969–1974), and then became a highly influential literary editor at the Zimbabwe Publishing House in the 1980s. Fluent in his native Shona and English, he has written award-winning and critically admired work in both languages. His first work in English was a short story collection, *Coming of the Dry Season* (1972), collected with *Some Kinds of Wounds* (1980) in *The Setting Sun and the Rolling World* (1987). Other short stories appeared in *One Day, Long Ago: More Stories from a Shona Childhood* (1991). His only novel to date is *Waiting for the Rain* (1975), which deals in a realistic and unflinching way with the difficulties and conflicts of tribal life adjusting to a post-industrial society. His work was banned sometimes by the white government when the country was Rhodesia, and a continent wrenched in two different directions underpins his collection of poetry *The Milkman Doesn't Only Deliver Milk* (1980), which experiments with the condensation of meaning.

Munro, Alice (1931–) Born in Wingham, Ontario, Alice Laidlaw Munro began writing in her early teens. After two years at the University of Ontario, in 1963 she moved to Vancouver and Victoria, before returning to western Ontario in the 1970s. She has published one novel, *Lives of Girls and Women* (1971), although this reads as a series of stories; and it is as a writer of short stories that she is most famous. Her collections include *Dance of the Happy Shades* (1968), *Something I've Been Meaning to Tell You* (1974), *Who Do You Think You Are?* (1978), *The Moons of Jupiter* (1982) *The Progress of Love* (1986), *Friend of My Youth* (1991), *Open Secrets* (1994), *Selected Stories* (1994), and *The Love of a Good Woman* (1998), which brings the lives of women and their hidden desires to the surface. She explores the depth and complexity of ordinary people, often through the perspective of young girls who feel they are 'different' due to their creative potential, and who evince a searching, critical quality. Despite living in the west of Canada, she is most closely identified in her fiction with rural south-western Ontario. In addition to television scripts, she has written a book about her television documentary on Irish immigrants to Canada, entitled *The Newcomers* (1979).

W. Martin, *Alice Munro: Paradox and Parallel* (1987).

Murakami, Haruki (1949–) Born in Ashiya City, Japan, he was educated at Waseda University, Tokyo (BA 1975), and ran a Tokyo jazz bar until 1981, when he turned to writing. His first two novels, *Hear the Wind Sing* (1979, trans. 1987) and *Pinball, 1973* (1980, trans. 1985), pioneered a new Japanese literary style in their depiction of post-war alienation, which was a blend of science fiction, metaphysics, and 'hard-boiled cool'. Further influence from cyberpunk science fiction is evident in *A Wild Sheep Chase* (1982, trans. 1989), a trendy, postmodern work about a search for a supernatural sheep, and its postmodern sequel, *Dance, Dance, Dance* (1988, trans. 1994). *Hard-boiled Wonderland and the End of the World* (1985, trans. 1991), a major success in Japan, is set in the Japanese subway system, and extends his interest in science fiction by presenting alternating narratives that gradually coalesce. This was followed by the realist *Norwegian Wood* (1987, trans. 1989), about youth troubles and the drug culture, and *The Wind Up Bird Chronicle* (1994, trans. 1997), which is a searingly graphic account of the Japanese-Chinese War retrospectively remembered by participants. His most recent novel is *South of the Border, West of the Sun* (trans. 1999), a less fantastic novel then his earlier work, about adolescent feelings of love re-emerging in 30-year-olds. Short stories occur in *A Day in the Life* (trans. 1983) and *The Elephant Vanishes* (trans. 1993), and *Underground* (2000) is a collection of interviews with survivors of the Aum cult's 1995 gas attack in the Tokyo underground. A leading representative of the 'hip' Japanese – the post-war generation – his fiction depicts their disenchantment with traditional culture and the search for freedom in US popular culture. Projecting a cool image with ironic observations, he is a brash yet significant and widely honoured contemporary talent in Japanese literature.

Murdoch, Iris (1919–1999) A widely honoured English writer and philosopher, Jean Iris Murdoch was born in Dublin, Ireland. She attended Oxford University (BA 1942), and later worked as a civil servant, and during the Second World War, worked for the United Nations relief organisation, before eventually returning to lecture at Oxford University (1948–1963). Her first published novel, *Under the Net* (1954), was the sixth she wrote, and contained many of the philosophical preoccupations which were to become characteristic of her later fiction. Subse-

quent novels include *Flight from the Enchanter* (1956), *The Sandcastle* (1957), *The Bell* (1958), *A Severed Head* (1961), *An Unofficial Rose* (1962), *The Unicorn* (1963), *The Italian Girl* (1964), *The Red and the Green* (1965), *The Nice and the Good* (1968), *Bruno's Dream* (1969), *A Fairly Honourable Defeat* (1970), *The Black Prince* (1973), *The Sacred and Profane Love Machine* (1974), *The Sea, the Sea* (1978, Booker Prize), about a young obsessional love, *The Philosopher's Pupil* (1983), *The Good Apprentice* (1985), *Acastos* (1986), *The Book and the Brotherhood* (1987), *The Message to the Planet* (1989), *The Green Knight* (1993) and *Jackson's Dilemma* (1995). Often writing about intellectual and professional people, her fiction embraces the humanist-realist tradition in narratives that are concerned with the nature of morality, freedom, determinism and language. In addition to three plays and a volume of poetry, she has written several philosophical works, including a book on Jean-Paul SARTRE (1953), *The Sovereignty of Good* (1970) and *Metaphysics as a Guide to Morals* (1992). Her husband John Bayley, a distinguished Oxford don, wrote a controversially frank account of their married life and her final years in *Iris* (1998). Her fiction often has something of a dream-like quality, displaying an amused and comic tolerance for the foibles and absurdities of human sexual behaviour.

D. Johnson, *Iris Murdoch* (1987).

Murnane, Gerald (1939–) An Australian novelist, he was born in Melbourne but spent his childhood in rural Victoria. Initially characterised as a 'Catholic novelist' for his novels *Tamarisk Row* (1974), which depicted a Catholic childhood in the 1940s, and *A Lifetime on Clouds* (1976), a tragi-comedy about experiences as a Catholic youth in the 1950s, he has since branched out into other areas. *The Plains* (1982), *Landscape with Landscape*

(1985), which is a series of six stories, *Inland* (1988), the stories in *Velvet Waters* (1990) and *Emerald Blue* (1995), are generally postmodernist, in which language works metaphorically and deconstructs reality, producing visionary and hallucinatory fictions. His narratives defer meaning for the play of language and desire, and focus on the perceiving self, especially the pleasures and boredoms of suburban life. He lectures on fiction at Victoria College, Melbourne.

Musil, Robert (1880–1942) Full name Robert Edler von Musil, he was born in Klagenfurt, Carinthia, Austria, and was educated at military academies in Vienna, Brno and Berlin, before becoming a mechanical engineer and then a librarian. He fought in the Austrian army during the First World War, and turned to writing full-time in 1922. His most significant work is the unfinished three-volume masterpiece, *The Man without Qualities* (1930–1933 and 1943, trans. 1954), which has been compared to the work of James JOYCE and Marcel PROUST in its immense scope and ambition. Set in 1913 Vienna, on the eve of war, it follows society's plans to celebrate the Kaiser Wilhelm's and Emperor Franz-Josef's periods of rule, seen through the eyes of Ulrich, a man without distinguishing features. Examining all aspects of Viennese society, the later volumes develop Ulrich and his sister Agatha's retreat into an incestuous mystical union. Other works include *Young Toerless* (1906, trans. 1955), about the inner conflicts of a cadet who participates in the torture of another cadet, *Posthumous Papers of a Living Author* (1936, trans. 1987), *Selected Writings* (trans. 1986) and *Precision and Soul* (trans. 1990). In addition to an acclaimed play, entitled *The Enthusiasts* (1921, trans. 1983), short stories occur in *Tonka* (trans. 1965). One of the leading figures in European modernist literature, his fiction straddles the worlds of science and art and explores the conflicts and

political harmonies of the two. Investigating what he believed to be the rational and affective dualism of human consciousness, his fiction deals with the psychological, sexual and social disorder in a doomed Central European culture.

P. Payne, *Robert Musil's 'The Man without Qualities'* (1988).

Mwangi, Meja (1948–) Born in Nanyuki, Kenya, he studied advanced level science at Kenyatta College. He worked as a sound technician for French television, and later for the British Council, before turning to full-time writing. In 1990, he studied English at the University of Leeds. His life in Nanyuki during the Mau Mau struggle for independence, provides much of the impetus for his fiction. Both *Carcase for Hounds* (1974) and *Taste of Death* (1975) are set during the Mau Mau conflict, vividly depicting the sufferings of both sides. Elsewhere, he depicts characters trying to escape the trap of urban poverty and despair in *Kill Me Quick!* (1973), *Going Down River Road* (1976) and *The Cockroach Dance* (1979). Later titles include *Bushtrackers* (1979), *Bread of Sorrow* (1987) and *Return of Shaka* (1989). Using urban street jargon in his narratives to generate a fiction of mass appeal, he nevertheless remains an ideologically committed writer. This ethos is exemplified in *Weapon of Hunger* (1989), which focuses on the protracted civil unrest and collapse of communal ethical values in African societies.

Mzamane, Mbulelo (1948–) Born in Port Elizabeth, South Africa, and brought up in Brakpan and on the Witwatersrand, Mbulelo Vizikhungo Mzamane went to the University of Botswana, Lesotho and Swaziland and gained a Ph.D. from the University of Sheffield, England. From 1976, he lectured on English literature in Botswana, England and Nigeria, and has emerged as a prominent critic of African literature. His first work was the lively account of events and characters in South African townships, focused upon the protagonist Jola, in *Mzala, the Stories of Mbulelo Mzamane* (1980), republished as *My Cousin Comes to Johannesburg* (1981). The stories depict Jola adapting to the urban environment of Johannesburg with ingenuity and cunning. *The Children of Soweto* (1982) presents three stories recounting the upheavals of the 1976 student riots. His fiction is often similar in content and style to the black South African writers of the 1960s and 1970s in its focus upon radical politics. He also edited the volumes of poetry of Mongane Wally Serote (1982), Sipho Sepamla (1984), and a collection of short stories by South African writers in *Hungry Flames* (1986).

N

Nabokov, Vladimir (1899–1977) Born Vladimir Vladimirovich Nabokov in St. Petersburg, Russia, he was a White Russian emigré who travelled through Germany and Europe before arriving in the US in 1940, where he was naturalised in 1945. He took a degree at Cambridge University (BA 1922), and held various positions teaching Russian and literature at Stanford and Cornell universities. One of the most brilliant and deceptive novelists of the twentieth century, he was also a translator and renowned lepidopterist. However, he began as a poet, and linguistic play is a characteristic of all his works. He started to write fiction early, under the pseudonym V. Sirin, including *Korol, Dama, Valet* ('King, Queen, Knave', 1928), *Zashchita Luzhina* ('The Defence', 1930) and *The Gift* (1936, trans. 1963), and these novels remained in Russian until later years, when he translated many with his son. His first English book was a novel he translated into English himself in 1937, *Despair*, although the first novel he wrote in English was *The Real Life of Sebastian Knight* (1941), which chronicles a search for the 'essence' of the narrator V's half-brother. This was followed by *Lolita* (1955, filmed 1962 and 1997), about the seduction of a 12-year-old girl, Dolores Haze, by a middle-aged man, Humbert Humbert, whose theme of perversion provoked a moral outcry. *Pale Fire* (1962) is a difficult work, with its emphasis on form and structure, constructed as a 999-line poem in four cantos composed by a recently assassinated US poet, and with footnotes which are keyed to the lines of the poem, forcing the reader to flick backwards and forwards. *Ada or Ardour* (1969), written in a variety of styles, is about an incestuous affair between Van Veen and his cousin (revealed to be his sister) Ada, which takes place on Earth's parallel world, Antiterra or Demonia. Other novels include *Laughter in the Dark* (1932), *Bend Sinister* (1947), about a professor in a totalitarian state seeking to maintain his integrity, *Pnin* (1957), *Transparent Things* (1972) and *Look at the Harlequins!* (1974). *Conclusive Evidence* (1951) is a memoir of life in Imperial Russia, later extended in *Speak, Memory!* (1966), and he translated *The Song of Igor's Campaign* (1960) and Pushkin's *Eugene Onegin* (1964). His studies of literature appear in *Lectures on Literature* (1980), *Lectures on Russian Literature* (1981), and a study of Nikolai Gogol (1947), while his poetry is in *Poems* (1959) and *Poems and Problems* (1971). Much critical work has been written which seeks to understand the relationship between his early Russian works and the later English fiction, much of which is now regarded as classic examples of anti-realist, postmodern metafiction, marked by disjointed temporalities, unstable narrators and collage juxtapositions.

A. Field, *V.N.: The Life and Art of Vladimir Nabokov* (1986).

Nahal, Chaman (1927–) Born in Sialkot, India (now Pakistan), Chaman Lal Nahal was educated at Delhi University (MA 1948) and Nottingham University in England (Ph.D. 1961). He returned to lecture at Delhi University in 1963, where he is now professor. His novels include *My True Faces* (1973), *Azadi* (1975), which translated means 'freedom', and narrates the divisive effects of the Partition in 1947, *Into Another Dawn* (1977), *The English Queens* (1979), and *Sunrise in Fiji* (1988). *The Crown and the Loincloth* (1981), *The Salt of Life* (1990) and *The Triumph of the Tricolour* (1993) comprise a trilogy which engages with modern Indian history, in a fictional treatment of Mahatma Ghandi and the freedom movement. Short stories occur in *The Weird Dance* (1965), and he has edited *Drugs and the Other Self* (1970). His non-fiction includes *D.H. Lawrence: The Eastern View* (1970), *The Narrative Pattern in Ernest Hemingway's Fiction* (1971), *The New Literatures in English* (1985) and *The Bhagavad-Gita* (1987). His largely realist fiction tends to focus on the under-privileged in society, concentrating on social problems and eschewing the metaphysical novel.

Naipaul, Shiva (1945–1985) Born Shivadhar Srinivasa Naipaul, in Port of Spain, Trinidad, he is a widely honoured writer, and the younger brother of the novelist V.S. NAIPAUL. He attended Oxford University (1964–1968), and then became a lecturer at Aarhus University, Denmark (1972). His first novel, *Fireflies* (1970), was a critically acclaimed account of the demise of Trinidad's Hindu community's leaders, resulting from family squabbles. There followed *The Chip-Chip Gatherers*

(1973), set in Trinidad and examining the relationships between two families where a marriage fails to bring them together, like the futility of gathering food on a beach, to which the title refers. His final novel was *A Hot Country* (1983), a pessimistic portrayal of the complex problems of a bleak fictional South African state called Cuyama. Short stories appear in *A Man of Mystery* (1984) and *Beyond the Dragon's Mouth* (1985), while non-fiction occurs in *North of South: An African Journey* (1978), about Kenya, Zambia and Tanzania, *Black and White* (1980), attempting to understand the mass suicide of the Jonestown Massacre in Guyana, 1978, and *An Unfinished Journey* (1987). He died in London.

Naipaul, V.S. (1932–) Full name Vidiadhar Surajprasad Naipaul, born in Chaguanas, Trinidad, he is the older brother of the novelist Shiva NAIPAUL. He was educated at Oxford University (BA 1953), and worked as a freelance writer for the BBC (1954–1956), and then went on to publish the novels *The Mystic Masseur* (1957), *The Suffrage of Elvira* (1958) and *Miguel Street* (1959). These are variations on a West Indian comedy of manners, often farcical and humorous treatments of Trinidadian society in the movement from colonial to independent status. There followed arguably his best novel, *A House for Mr Biswas* (1961), a psychological realist narrative which deals with Mr Biswas' desire to own his own house as a sign of his assertion of personal identity. Later novels include *Mr Stone and the Knights Companion* (1963), *The Mimic Men* (1967), *In a Free State* (1971, Booker Prize), which is about self-exiled people who have become displaced and rootless souls, *Guerrillas* (1975), which was a widely acclaimed treatment of West Indian politics, *A Bend in the River* (1979), *The Enigma of Arrival* (1987) and *A Way in the World* (1994). Short stories occur in *The Perfect Tenants and the Mourners* (1977) and *A Flag on the*

Island (1967). He has increasingly turned to non-fiction in recent years, drawing parallels between Trinidad and other cultures and the exploration of an ancestral homeland. Non-fiction includes *The Middle Passage* (1962), *An Area of Darkness* (1964), *The Loss of El Dorado* (1970), *India: A Wounded Civilisation* (1977), *The Return of Eva Peron* (1980), *A Congo Diary* (1980), *Among the Believers: An Islamic Journey* (1981), *Finding the Center* (1986), *A Turn in the South* (1989), *India* (1991) and *Beyond Belief* (1998). Recent works are *Letters Between a Father and Son* (1999), which chronicle his time at Oxford University, and *Reading and Writing: A Personal Account* (2000). Considered by many as a highly gifted writer, his fiction explores rootlessness, and the majority of his stories take place in emerging Third World countries. However, he has been vilified by some critics for his disparaging remarks about the absence of development and lack of social order in the West Indies.

B. King, *V.S. Naipaul* (1993).

Narayan, R.K. (1906–) Born in Madras, India, Rasipuram Krishnaswami Narayan was educated at the University of Mysore (BA 1930). After working as a teacher and a journalist in the early 1930s, he turned to writing with his first novel, *Swami and Friends* (1935), an episodic account of a group of friends as they begin high school. Together with Raja RAO and Mulk Raj ANAND, he has become one of the best-known Anglo-Indian writers of the twentieth century. Almost all his novels and short stories are set in the fictional backwater town of Malgudi. His novels include *The Bachelor of Arts* (1937), *The Dark Room* (1938), *The English Teacher* (1945), *Mr Sampath* (1949), *The Financial Expert* (1952), *Waiting for the Mahatma* (1955) and *The Guide* (1958). The stories depict characters involved in the chaos of life and human relations, who are desperately

seeking their own identities, which become reflections of the life of India at large. Other novels include *The Man-eater of Malgudi* (1961), which features a fanatical taxidermist, *The Vendor of Sweets* (1967), *The Painter of Signs* (1976), *A Tiger for Malgudi* (1983), which is narrated by a tiger, Raja, who confronts Malgudi, *Talkative Man* (1986), and *The World of Nagaraj* (1990), which depicts an easy-going townsman whose life is bedevilled by various events. Short stories include *Malgudi Days* (1943), *Dodu* (1943), *Lawley Road* (1956), *Under the Banyan Tree* (1985), *Salt and Sawdust* (1993) and *The Grandmother's Tale* (1994), while essays and sketches are collected in *Next Sunday* (1956), *A Writer's Nightmare* (1988) and *A Story-Teller's World* (1989), and a memoir appears in *My Days* (1974). His influence has been partly disclaimed by younger contemporaries, arguing that he has deliberately pandered to the western taste for exoticism and foreign quaintness.

S. Krishnan, ed., *Malgudi Landscapes: The Best of R.K. Narayan* (1992).

Narogin, Mudrooroo (1939–) An Australian Aboriginal novelist, born Colin Johnson in Beverley, Western Australia, he was brought up in an orphanage. He began writing while living in Melbourne working for the Victorian public service, and his *Wild Cat Falling* (1965) was the first novel to be published by an Aboriginal writer. It tells of the search of a young Aboriginal for a meaningful existence in the white world which excludes him. He spent several years in India, some of the time as a Buddhist monk. Returning to teach in Australian universities, he spent various periods working on fiction and Aboriginal histories and documentaries. As he identified further with Aboriginal culture and politics, he adopted the name of Mudrooroo Narogin, and later, Mudrooroo Nyoongah. *Long Live Sandawara* (1979) is about a youth inspired to start his own Aboriginal resistance group in the slums of Perth, and subsequent novels include *Doctor Wooreddy's Prescription for Enduring the Ending of the World* (1983), about race relations in Tasmania, *Doin Wildcat, a Novel 'Koori' Script* (1988), about adapting his first novel into a film written in Aboriginal English, *Master of the Ghost Dreaming* (1991), *Wildcat Screaming* (1992), and *The Kwinkan* (1993), which tells of white corruption and white paranoia about Aboriginal culture. Essays studying modern Aboriginal literature are collected in *Writing from the Fringe* (1990), a seminal work on Third World regional indigenous writing, while *Aboriginal Mythology* (1994) and *Indigenous Literature of Australia = Milli Milli Wangka* (1997) are studies in cultural history. Mythology and traditional song-cycle forms appear in the poetry collections *The Song Cycle of Jacky* (1986), *Dalwurra* (1988) and *Garden of Gethsemane* (1991). A highly regarded novelist who interweaves character and event with adroitness, he has sustained the subversive quality of Aboriginal writing, making particular use of the Aboriginal philosophy of dreaming and the inscription of their experience of the landscape.

Naylor, Gloria (1950–) An African-American novelist, born in New York City, US, and educated at Brooklyn College (BA 1981) and Yale University (MA 1983). She has worked as a missionary for the Jehovah's Witnesses (1968–1975) and as a hotel telephone operator (1975–1981). Since graduating from Brooklyn College, she has been a professional writer, and has also taught and studied African-American literature and culture at various prestigious US universities. Her first novel was the critically praised *The Women of Brewster Place* (1983), which in a combination of fantasy, folklore and social comment explores the black female experience of seven strong-willed African-American women; this was followed by a later companion novel, *The Men of Brewster Place* (1998). Her other works include *Linden Hills* (1985), which deals in magic realist mode with the affluent end of the socio-economic African-American experience, *Mama Day* (1989), which alternates male and females voices in an exploration of social conformity and historical heritage, and *Bailey's Café* (1992), in which the café becomes a focal point for eccentric characters who exchange their stories revealing hidden black histories. *The Children of the Night* (1995) is an edition of African-American stories. The novels are set in the present, against the backdrop of a depressing era in African-American history, and located in the same (fictional) urban/suburban environment. Naylor's work consciously echoes that of her role model, Ann PETRY, and other African-American novelists like Toni MORRISON, in her exploration of aspects of the African-American experience within the wider context of the US.

Ngũgĩ, wa Thiong'o (1938–) Born James Ngugi, at Kamiriithu, near Limuru town, Kenya, he is East Africa's most famous and accomplished novelist to date. He studied economics at Makerere University in Uganda, but later changed studies and graduated in English Literature (1964), and wrote *Weep Not Child* (1964). This was the first novel to be published in English in East Africa, and explores the effect of the Mau Mau war on the peasants and the destruction of family and personal relationships. Although the second to be published, the first to be written was *The River Between* (1965), which presents the cultural conflict between traditional and Christian values in rural Kenya, issues which recur throughout his later work. After postgraduate studies at Leeds University, England, he returned to Kenya (1967) and became a lecturer at Nairobi University. During the revolutionary period of the 1970s, his reflections upon literature, culture and politics led to his decision to write in his native tongue of Gikuyu rather than English. He embraced revolutionary Marxism and adopted theatre as a powerful means of informing and educating the public. He was imprisoned by the government in 1977 after staging his Gikuyu play, co-authored with Ngugi wa Mirii, entitled *I Will Marry When I Want* (1980, trans. 1982). After his release in 1978, he was refused his job at the university and has lived in self-exile since 1982. His early book *Penpoint: The New Africa and Origin East Africa. A Makerere Anthology* (1965), shows a preoccupation with family stability and the social effects of its disruption. Following his early student novels, he wrote *A Grain of Wheat* (1967), which reflected the effects of the Kenyan Emergency and the destruction of the old life depicted in *Weep Not Child*; it also fully embraced Marxist thought and projected a socialist vision for Kenya. After *The Trial of Dedan Kimathi* (1976), written with Micere Githae Mugo, there followed *Petals of Blood* (1977), arguably his most accomplished novel, which extends the exploration of the legacy of the Mau Mau struggle, the sufferings and hopes that culminated in 'Uhuru' or Independence (1963), and Kenya's accompanying political and social crises. *Matigari* (1987) pursues the unrealised hopes and disillusions of 'Uhuru'. Other work has drawn upon folk tales, like *Devil on the Cross* (1982), while *Detained* (1981) and *Barrel of a Pen* (1983) comment on the oppression of the people and the suppression of thought by the Kenyan authorities. He has published several volumes of critical essays on the cultural and political reactions to British cultural domination in *Homecoming* (1972), *Writers in Politics* (1981), *Decolonizing the Mind* (1986) and *Penpoints, Gunpoints, and Dreams* (1998). His writing displays a deep passion to instil humanistic values in a society obsessed with material aggrandisement, and he regards the author's role as one of participant rather than a mere observer in social conflicts.

J. Ogude, *Ngugi's Novels and African History* (1999).

Nin, Anaïs (1903–1977) Born in Paris, France, she was taken to the US in 1914 where she was naturalised. Self-educated, she worked as a fashion and artist's model, lived in France from 1935 to 1939, where she moved in the 'Villa Seurat' circle of avant-garde writers, which included Henry MILLER, and later studied psychoanalysis and practised in Europe and New York. A prolific writer, her fiction began with *Winter of Artifice* (1939), which probes dreams to nourish conscious reality, as it explores the psychological relationship between a father and daughter. There followed *This Hunger* (1945), and then a series of novels, later published as *Cities of the Interior* (1959): *Ladders to Fire* (1946), *Children of the Albatross* (1947), *The Four-Chambered Heart* (1950), *A Spy in the House of Love* (1954) and *Solar Barque* (1958). These explore the feminine psyche, following the inner flows of her characters' drives and motivations, in an experimental style. Arguably her most acclaimed work were the seven volumes of *The Diary of Anaïs Nin* (1966–1980) and the four volumes of *The Early Diary of Anaïs Nin* (1985), along with the later unexpurgated 'The Journal of Love' volumes, which described the full emotional and sexual drama of her life. Short stories occur in *Under a Glass Bell* (1944), *Waste of Timelessness* (1977), and erotic fiction in *Delta of Venus* (1977) and *Little Birds* (1979). Non-fiction includes a study of D.H. LAWRENCE (1932), *Realism and Reality* (1946) and *The Novel of the Future* (1968). A controversial figure of the feminist movement, she has been denounced for her archaic feminine values, as much as she has been praised for her uniquely feminine perspective.

D. Bair, *Anaïs Nin: A Biography* (1995).

Niven, Larry (1938–) Full name Laurence Van Cott Niven, he was born in Los Angeles, US, and graduated from Washburn University in Kansas (AB 1962). He became a freelance writer in 1964. A prolific author of science fiction, his first book, *World of Ptavvs* (1966), was about psionic powers. Apparently flying in the face of the 'New Wave' science fiction of the 1960s, with his belief in 'hard' science as efficient and problem-solving, he became the leading practitioner of 'hard' science fiction, in which his books speculate about the technologies of the future. This can be seen in the trilogy *Ringworld* (1970), *The Ringworld Engineers* (1980) and *The Ringworld Throne* (1996), in which he extrapolates from current scientific explanation about artificial planets to imagine Ringworld, an artificial planet built in a massive hoop, with a range of diverse inhabitants. Since the 1970s, much of his work has been collaborative, and his most famous partner is Jerry Pournelle, producing *The Mote in God's Eye* (1974), a novel about first contact, and its sequel *The Gripping Hand* (1993), *Lucifer's Hammer* (1977), *Footfall* (1985), *The Legacy of Heorot* (1987) and *The Burning City* (2000). His other writing partner has been Steven Barnes, with whom he wrote *The Descent of Anansi* (1982) and *Dream Park* (1981). Other novels include *The Integral Trees* (1984), *The Smoke Ring* (1987), *Destiny's Road* (1997) and *Rainbow Mars* (1999), with short stories occurring in *Neutron Star* (1968), *The Shape of Space* (1969), *N-Space* (1990), *Playgrounds of the Mind* (1991) and *Flatlander* (1995). Widely celebrated for his invention of grandly scaled worlds that dwarf their inhabitants, he created a future history and popular mythology called 'Known Space', which he uses for much of his fiction. Other writers have contributed novels using 'Known Space' as a setting.

Nkosi, Lewis (1936–) Born in KwaZulu-Natal, South Africa, he worked as a journalist for *Drum* magazine in Johannesburg (1956–1960). He left South Africa to study journalism at Harvard University (1961–1962), and when banned under the all-embracing Suppression of Communism Act in 1966, went into exile in Britain and studied at the University of London (Dip. Lit, 1974) and the University of Sussex (1977). He worked for various newspapers and journals (1956–1968), as well as for the BBC (1962–1965). His only novel to date is *Mating Birds* (1983), about a young South African Zulu on death row for allegedly raping a white woman. As one of the foremost African literary and cultural critics, his vigorous essays occur in *Home and Exile* (1965), *The Transplanted Heart* (1975), *Tasks and Masks* (1981), *Underground People* (1993) and *In Defence of the Study of Literature* (1997), which examine the relevance of African literature in the modern world. Other works include a play, *The Rhythm of Violence* (1964), and various short stories.

Nobbs, David (1935–) Born in London, England, he was educated at Cambridge University (1955–1958), and worked as a reporter until 1962. He is an acclaimed comic writer, famous for his 'Reginald Perrin' books (1975–1978), published as one volume in *The Complete Reginald Perrin* (1990), and culminating in *The Legacy of Reginald Perrin* (1995). Depicting a company executive who attempts to surmount a mid-life crisis, the novels present hilarious perspectives on middle-class England, and were made into a successful BBC television series starring Leonard Rossiter. Other novels include *The Itinerant Lodger* (1965), about a drifter who desperately wishes to start life anew, *Ostrich Country* (1968), *A Piece of the Sky Is Missing* (1969), *Second from Last in the Sack Race* (1983) and *Pratt of Angus* (1988). *A Bit of a Do* (1986) is a social comedy focused upon set-piece events – weddings, a party and a beauty contest – and the characters reappear in the sequel *Fair Do's* (1990). *The Cucumber Man* (1994) is a sequel to *Second from Last*, and *The Complete Pratt* (1998) is an omnibus volume. *Kate* (2000) is his latest novel.

Nwapa, Flora (1931–) Born in Oguta, central Nigeria, she was educated at the University of Ibadan (BA 1957) and the University of Edinburgh. She has worked as an education officer, teacher, assistant registrar and commissioner in Nigeria, and managed her own publishing press, Tana Press, in Enugu. She emerged as the first Nigerian woman writer with the publication of *Efuru* (1966). Strong women characters who survive by economic independence, and Oguta, the trading town on Lake Oguta, figure prominently in her fiction, as in *Efuru* and *Idu* (1970), both of which concern the lives of two women in Oguta, who find new strength of purpose after being abandoned by their husbands. This female perspective on Nigerian life continues in *One Is Enough* (1981), *Never Again* (1975), about the Nigerian civil war, and *Women Are Different* (1986), which explores the experiences of modern Nigerian women. As well as her earlier preoccupations of maternity, motherhood and economic independence, she explores urban themes, such as sexual exploitation in the work force, materialism and corruption. Her many short stories occur in *This Is Lagos* (1971), *Emeka-Driver's Guard* (1972) and *Wives at War* (1980), and she has written two plays, *The First Lady* (1993) and *Conversations* (1993). Among her defiant feminist statements, her major contribution is the portrayal of a more convincing and articulate African female perspective in literature.

C. Davies and A. Graves, eds, *Ngambika: Studies of Women in African Literature* (1986).

O

Oates, Joyce Carol (1938–) A widely honoured and prolific American writer, she was born in Lockport, New York, and attended Syracuse University (BA 1960) and the University of Wisconsin (MA 1961). She is also an academic, and currently teaches at Princeton University. Her first publications were short stories in *By the North Gate* (1963), and the novel *With Shuddering Fall* (1964), which like much of her other work is set in the fictional 'Eden County'. At the age of 31, she was the youngest writer to receive the National Book Award for fiction, for *Them* (1969), depicting the Wendall family in the violence and poverty of Detroit. She has since published almost two dozen novels, including *The Garden of Earthly Delights* (1967), *Expensive People* (1968), the surreal *Wonderland* (1971), about the pitfalls of the modern medical community, *Do With Me What You Will* (1973), which is about the legal profession, *The Assassins* (1975), which attacks political corruption in Washington DC, *The Childwold* (1976), *Unholy Loves* (1979), about shallowness and hypocrisy in the academic community, and *Cybele* (1979). Not limited to one literary style or genre, her writing has embraced realism, metafiction and parodic epics, like the Gothic tales of *Bellefleur* (1980), *A Bloodsmoor Romance* (1982) and *Mysteries of Winterthurn* (1984), which are suspenseful tales of the ordinary infused with terror, and probing the darker side of American life. Demonstrating a wide range of protagonists and exploring the moral and social conditions of American society, her more recent novels include *Marya: A Life* (1986), *You Must Remember This* (1987), *American Appetites* (1989), *The Rise of Life on Earth* (1991), *Foxfire* (1993), which recounts in retrospect the destructive sisterhood of a group of teenage girls in the 1950s, *We Were the Mulvaneys* (1996), *Man Crazy* (1997), *My Heart Laid Bare* (1998), *Blonde* (1999), a fictional retelling of the life of Marilyn Monroe, and *Broke Heart Blues* (1999), set in the mid-1960s, about the effects of a bad boy who moves into a town. As well as publishing several collections of short stories, such as *The Wheel of Love* (1970), *Will You Always Love Me?* (1995) and *Collector of Hearts* (1999), there are also poems, essay collections, like *Contraries* (1981), and plays. In addition, she wrote *On Boxing* (1987), reflecting a lifelong preoccupation. Under the pseudonym Rosamund Smith, she has recently written *Nemesis* (1990), *Snake Eyes* (1992) and *You Can't Catch Me* (1995).

E. Bender, *Joyce Carol Oates* (1987).

O'Brien, Edna (1936–) Born in Tuamgraney, Co. Clare, Ireland, she worked briefly as a pharmacist, before settling in London in 1959. Her early novels, entitled *The Country Girls* (1960), *The Lonely Girl* (1962) and *Girls in Their Married Bliss* (1963), were a literary sensation for their socially and psychologically realistic treatment of a young girl's coming-of-age in puritanical and hypocritical Irish society. Although initially banned under the Censorship Act, all three novels were republished as *The Country Girls Trilogy and Epilogue* (1986). Subsequent work typically deals with affairs of the heart from a female protagonist's point of view. *August Is a Wicked Month* (1964) is about a separated woman, having an affair in France, whose husband and son are killed in a car crash, and her subsequent recovery. From the 1970s onwards, she became a deliberate stylist after her early untutored freshness, a change evident in *A Pagan Place* (1971), *Night* (1972), about a woman's reconstruction of her past, *Johnny I Hardly Knew You* (1977), *The High Road* (1988), set on a Spanish island, when murder follows a love affair, *Time and Tide* (1992), dealing with separation, custody and loss, and *House of Splendid Isolation* (1994), about a relationship between an IRA terrorist and a woman whose house he commandeers. Recent novels are *Down By the River* (1996), a crime of passion in rural Ireland, and *Wild Decembers* (1999), about murder, revenge and landownership in contemporary Ireland. As well as writing plays and screenplays, her short stories appear in *The Love Object* (1968), *A Scandalous Woman* (1974), *Mrs Rheinhardt* (1978), *Returning* (1982), *The Fanatic Heart* (1982), *Lantern Slides* (1988) and *Tales for the Telling* (1997). Her short story 'X, Y and Z' was filmed starring Elizabeth Taylor (1972). She has also written an iconoclastic travelogue and commentary with photos, entitled *Mother Ireland* (1976), and a study of James JOYCE (1999). She is regarded as one of Ireland's pre-eminent contemporary writers.

O'Brien, Flann (1911–1966) The pseudonym of Brian O'Nolan, he was born in Strabane, Co. Tyrone, Ireland, and grew up speaking Irish. He moved to Dublin in 1923, and attended Blackrock College (1927–1929), and then University College, Dublin, where he became involved in literary activities, developing what would later be recognised as his distinctive satirical journalistic voice. He joined the civil service in 1935 and rose to become town planning officer. His first novel was the ingeniously complex and self-reflexive *At Swim-Two-Birds* (1939). Although critically well received, it sold poorly, but was reissued in 1962 to tremendous acclaim. His next work was *The Third Policeman*, which was repeatedly rejected by English publishers; it was finally published posthumously in 1967, and is now generally regarded as his masterpiece. In 1940, he began his humorous column, 'Cruiskeen Lawn', in the *Irish Times*, which ran until his death, and was published under the name 'Myles na Gopaleen', one of his many pseudonyms. He wrote puns, parodies and satires of Irish politics, bureaucrats and other mediocrities, and this became the basis for his contemporary fame. *An Beal Bocht* (1941), an Irish novel later translated into English as *The Poor Mouth* (1964), was followed by a play called *Faustus Kelly* (1943), a wordy satire that was staged at the Abbey Theatre. Following bouts of drunkenness, and owing to his literary attacks on establishment figures, he was persuaded to retire from the civil service in 1953, although his confidence was restored with the re-release of *At Swim-Two-Birds*. The best-sellers *The Hard Life* (1961) and *The Dalkey Archive* (1964) caused a scandal due to their irreverent attitude towards the Catholic Church. His unfinished novel *Slattery's Sago Saga* was included in *Stories and Plays* (1974), and a selection of his newspaper columns appear in *The Best of Myles* (1968), *Further Cuttings from Cruiskeen Lawn* (1976) and *The Hair of* *the Dogma* (1977). His reputation as one of the most important twentieth-century Irish writers to follow James JOYCE seems assured.

A. Cronin, *No Laughing Matter: The Life and Times of Flann O'Brien* (1989).

O'Brien, Tim (1946–) A highly regarded American novelist and short story writer, he was born William Timothy O'Brien in Austin, Montana, and graduated from Macalester College, St. Paul (BA 1968). After serving as an infantryman in Vietnam, he undertook graduate studies at Harvard, and then worked as a journalist for the *Washington Post*. Frequently self-reflexive in his work about the status of truth and fiction, his first book, *If I Die in a Combat Zone* (1973), is a compelling, anecdotal account of his own tour of duty in Vietnam, and was followed by *Northern Lights* (1975), about the complexities faced by a soldier returning home from the war. The Vietnam War theme was continued in the highly praised *Going After Cacciato* (1978), an allegory of war and peace, part dream and part reality, in a description of a soldier who goes AWOL and his comrades who go to fetch him, while *The Nuclear Age* (1981) is about a civilian's perspective of the war and nuclear paranoia. *The Things They Carried* (1990) is a sequence of stories concerning soldiers in Vietnam and the futility of the war, and *In the Lake of the Woods* (1994) is a tense mystery story based upon the effects of the My Lai massacre. More recently, *Tomcat in Love* (1998) shows a new departure, a black comedy about an academic's sexual relationships.

S. Kaplan, *Understanding Tim O'Brien* (1994).

O'Connor, Flannery (1925–1964) Born Mary Flannery O'Connor, in Savannah, Georgia, US, she studied at Georgia College (AB 1945) and the State University of Iowa (MFA 1947). A Catholic from the Bible-belt South, she wrote about the power of God's grace in a fallen world. Her novels are *Wise Blood* (1952), about a man who tries to establish a church without Christ in his southern town, and *The Violent Bear It Away* (1960), about a crazed grandfather bringing up his grandson to think of himself as a prophet. Short stories appeared in *A Good Man Is Hard to Find* (1955) and *Everything That Rises Must Converge* (1965). Posthumous publications include *Mystery and Manners: Occasional Pieces* (1969), *The Complete Short Stories* (1971), *The Habit of Being: Letters* (1979) and *Collected Works* (1988). Her fiction has been characterised as Southern Gothic because of the grotesque, bizarre and misanthropic figures who suffer agonies and people her stories. With violent, shocking stories, which demonstrate an interest in the uncannily strange and sadistic, she is a widely acclaimed writer who has achieved almost cult status in the American South. Her early death was due to a life-long illness with lupus.

M. Friedman and B. Clark, eds, *Critical Essays on Flannery O'Connor* (1985).

Oë, Kenzaburo (1935–) Born in Ose village, Shikoku Island, Japan, he was educated at Tokyo University (BA 1959), and became a freelance writer. As early as 1958, when he was still a student, he was recognised as one of Japan's most important writers, known for his works celebrating the marginal and outcast, often in violent opposition to a central establishment. His first novel, *Nip the Buds, Shoot the Kids* (1958, trans. 1995), showed an interest in the political and the absurd and highlighted his rural past in his village and valley on Shikoku Island, as he explored the possibilities inherent in folk legends. His brain-damaged son, born in 1963, figures in several semi-autobiographical books of father–son relationships, such as *A Personal Matter* (1964, trans. 1968), about the divisive birth of a brain-damaged son and the gradual reunification of the family. Other works include *The Silent Cry* (1967, trans. 1974) and the four short novellas in *Teach Us to Outgrow Our Madness* (trans. 1977), which consists of the title story, 'The Day He Himself Shall Wipe My Tears Away', a brilliant and savage attack on the emperor system that lay behind Yukio MISHIMA's suicide, 'Prize Stock', and 'Aghwee the Sky Monster', a surreal fantasy story. *The Pinch Runner Memorandum* (1976, trans. 1994) is a carnivalesque epic, about a father and son leading an army of marginal characters against the Japanese establishment, *An Echo of Heaven* (1989, trans. 1996) narrates the determination and relentless devotion of a woman, and *A Quiet Life* (1990, trans. 1996) concerns a mentally handicapped, brilliant musician in the midst of family crises. He edited *The Crazy Iris and Other Stories of the Atomic Aftermath* (trans. 1984), and his short stories appear in *The Catch* (1958, trans. 1981). *Hiroshima Notes* (trans. 1981) contains essays about Hiroshima and Nagasaki, and *A Healing Family* (1995, trans. 1996) is a portrait of his handicapped son and the courage of his family. Much other writing remains untranslated into English. Politically controversial and highly imaginative, he rejected the delicacy of traditional Japanese writers and confronted the Japanese emperor system, which crumbled in 1945 when, in surrendering to the Americans, the Japanese emperor admitted he was not a god. Kenzaburo espoused the democratic principles of the US, and his early realism gives way to mythical treatments, with an increasingly elegiac rather than angry tone in later books. He was awarded the Nobel Prize for Literature in 1994, and his speech and other lectures are reprinted in *Japan, the Ambiguous, and Myself* (trans. 1995).

S. Napier, *Escape from the Wasteland* (1991).

O'Faolain, Sean (1900–1991) Born John Whelan, in Cork, Ireland, he went to study at University College, Cork in 1918, but instead ended up joining the Republican cause and the Irish Volunteers. His early encounters as a child with nationalist idealism and the galvanising effect of the 1916 Easter Rising are described in the autobiography *Vive Moi* (1964). He went to Harvard University (1926–1929), and taught for a while in London, before returning to Ireland in 1933 as a writer. His fiction arises from these early experiences, and the historical novels *A Nest of Simple Folk* (1934), *Bird Alone* (1936) and *Come Back to Erin* (1940) depict a family saga from the Fenian Rising to the War of Independence and the following years, in a fictional study of idealism and the divisive effects of war. Other novels include *The Man Who Invented Sin* (1949), *I Remember, I Remember* (1948), *The Heat of the Sun* (1966), and a late novel *And Again?* (1979), which explores time, fate and free will. Often considered better than his novels, his short stories appear in *Midsummer Night Madness* (1932), *A Purse of Coppers* (1937), set in the bleak conditions of 1930s Ireland, *Teresa* (1947), *The Talking Trees* (1971) and *Foreign Affairs* (1976). As editor of *The Bell* in the 1940s, he encouraged many young Irish writers, and in his editorials challenged the complacent Catholic conservatism of the new Irish state. He wrote a study of the liberal tradition of Catholicism in *Newman's Way* (1952), travel books in *A Summer in Italy* (1949) and *South to Sicily* (1953), a study of national character in *The Irish* (1948), literary studies in *The Short Story* (1948) and *The Vanishing Hero* (1956), and biographies of Eamon De Valera (1933), Constance Markievicz (1934), Daniel O'Connell (1938) and Hugh O'Neill (1942), in which he put forward a critique of Irish leadership. His *Collected Stories* (1980–1983) appeared in three volumes.

M. Harmon, *Sean O'Faolain: A Life* (1994).

O'Flaherty, Liam (1896–1984) An Irish writer, born in Inishmore, in the Aran Islands, he had a Catholic education, and abandoned his studies in 1915 to join the Irish Guards. Wounded in 1917, he suffered a period of war melancholia, recounted in his memoirs *Two Tears* (1930) and *Shame the Devil* (1934). Involved in radical Irish politics on the Republican side, he fled to London in 1923. His first novel was *Thy Neighbour's Wife* (1923), which was a detailed description of life on Aran, as was *The Black Soul* (1924). There followed *The Informer* (1925), *Mr Gilhooley* (1926), *The Assassin* (1928) and *The Puritan* (1931), rather sombre novels, displaying the influence of Dostoevsky and Gogol. After a nomadic existence in the 1920s, he wrote several travel books, including *I Went to Russia* (1931) about communism, and an acerbic view in *A Tourist's Guide to Ireland* (1930). Other work includes two regional novels, *The House of Gold* (1929) and *Skerrett* (1932), *The Return of the Brute* (1930), *The Martyr* (1935) and *Hollywood Cemetery* (1935). His last novels formed a historical trilogy – *Famine* (1937), *Land* (1946) and *Insurrection* (1950) – and trace the rise of Irish nationalism. Short stories appear in *Spring Sowing* (1924) and *The Tent* (1926), which offer insights into peasant life. He was linked with James JOYCE, as one of the new realists challenging the romantic writers of the Irish literary revival. He became a recluse in later years, although he found a new audience from the 1920s to the 1950s with his short stories in Irish, collected in *Dúil* ('Desire') (1953).

P. Sheeran, *The Novels of Liam O'Flaherty* (1976).

O'Hara, John (1905–1970) Born in Pottsville, Pennsylvania, US, John Henry O'Hara held a variety of jobs during his early life, eventually becoming a screenwriter, journalist and novelist in the 1930s. His first book, *Appointment in Samarra* (1934), about the tensions between Protestant and Catholic communities in a fictional Pennsylvanian town in the 1920s, established him as a novelist of significant potential. His next two novels, *Butterfield 8* (1935, filmed 1960) and *Hope of Heaven* (1938), were bestsellers, and were followed after the Second World War by his most ambitious novel, *A Rage to Live* (1949), about a marriage that is destroyed after the wife commits adultery. His prolific career includes *Ten North Frederick* (1955), about the rise and fall of a successful Pennsylvania lawyer, which was banned for its obscenity, *From the Terrace* (1958), *Elizabeth Appleton* (1963), *The Lockwood Concern* (1966), and the posthumous *The Ewings* (1972). A successful writer of short stories for *The New Yorker*, collections include *The Doctor's Son* (1935), *Pal Joey* (1940) and *The Good Samaritan* (1974). He also wrote plays, essays in *Sweet and Sour* (1954), newspaper columns, lectures, and *Selected Letters* was published in 1978. One of the most successful writers of the 1950s and 1960s, his stories focus upon the American upper-middle class. A realist-naturalist writer, he concentrated upon the materialist aspirations and sexual exploits of his characters, in his stated attempt to chronicle every aspect of twentieth-century America.

M. Bruccoli, *The O'Hara Concern: A Biography of John O'Hara* (1975).

Okri, Ben (1959–) Born in Minna, northern Nigeria, he lived in England (1961–1966), and went back to Nigeria where he was educated, and returned to England in 1978. He worked for *Afroscope* (1978), studied literature at the University of Essex (1980), was poetry editor of *West Africa* (1983–1986), worked as a BBC broadcaster (1983–1985) and was a Visiting Fellow at Cambridge (1991–1993). His novels *Flowers and Shadows* (1980) and

The Landscape Within (1981) were followed by two books of short stories,
Incidents at the Shrine (1986) and *Stars
of the New Curfew* (1988). *The Famished
Road* (1991, Booker Prize) is his biggest
success, and concerns the story of a young
man, but also the recurrent patterns of
African mythology, history and politics.
The attempt to escape the pattern becomes symbolic of a recurring history that
must be resisted in order to live fully and
to improve the future of Africa. Later
novels are *Astonishing the Gods* (1995),
which is set on an enchanted island, and
Infinite Riches (1999), about a spirit child
who breaks a pact at death. Poems occur
in *An African Elegy* (1992) and the epic
Mental Fight (1999), which celebrates
humanity's achievements at the end of
the millennium, and essays are collected
in *A Way of Being Free* (1993). His wide
range of subject matter encompasses satires of contemporary life and explorations of supernatural, often dream-like,
sequences. Many of his stories are impressionistic, transforming the world into a
strange inner reality, and concern the
cruelty, corruption and injustice perpetrated in contemporary Nigeria, including
the horrors of the Nigerian civil war. He
frequently scrutinises relationships struggling to survive in a society that has
become brutalised through the harshness
of survival. However, while lamenting the
humiliations of colonialism and racial
prejudices, he looks optimistically to
Africa for its own solutions and means of
reconciliation. Okri's use of symbolism,
literary traditions, and forms from various
ethnic groups, results in a style that is
highly intertextual and which explores the
ways in which art is related to social
traditions.

B. Cooper, *Magic Realism in West African
Fiction* (1998).

Olsen, Tillie (1913–) Born into a poor
family, in Omaha, Nebraska, US, she was
politically active from a young age, began

writing for the Young People's Socialist
League and *Partisan Review*. She has
worked in a variety of industrial jobs and
as an office typist and university teacher.
Since 1987, has been writer-in-residence
at Kenyon College, Ohio. Her writing
demonstrates her long-held conviction
that literature marginalises women and
the working class; it is her belief that
people have been denied the opportunity
to express and develop themselves due to
the restrictive circumstances placed upon
them by sex, race and class. She began her
only novel, *Yonnandio* (1974) – the Iroquois word for 'lament for the aborigines'
– at the age of 19, but was forced to put it
aside for some years due to the pressures
of raising her family and working. It
describes a family's life during the Depression, narrated from the perspective of the
child and the mother, as the father moves
from a Wyoming mine to a Chicago meat-
packing factory. Her collection of three
stories and a novella, *Tell Me a Riddle*
(1961), has received critical acclaim and
attention from feminists. The title story,
'Tell Me a Riddle', centres upon the
antagonism and collapse of two Jews after
thirty-seven years' of marriage, as the wife
undergoes a slow death from cancer.
Silences (1978) is a collection of essays
about the difficulties of writing due to the
prejudices of social circumstances, and
she has written an introduction to the
1972 reprint of Rebecca Harding Davis'
Life in the Iron Mills (1861), in which she
describes Davis' thwarted career following marriage. A politically motivated
author, she has also edited a collection of
women's writing, *Mother to Daughter,
Daughter to Mother* (1984).

A. Martin, *Tillie Olsen* (1984).

Omotoso, Kole (1943–) Born in Akure,
Nigeria, he attended the universities of
Ibadan and Edinburgh, specialising in Arabic drama. He has worked as a freelance
journalist, and has been an ardent champion of indigenous African publishing. He

has published mainly in Nigeria, and this includes the novels *The Edifice* (1971), *The Combat* (1972), *Fella's Choice* (1974), *Sacrifice* (1974), *The Scales* (1976), *To Borrow a Wandering Leaf* (1978) and *Memories of Our Recent Boom* (1982). *Just Before Dawn* (1988), his most important novel, depicts a Nigeria enmeshed in a net of its own contradictions, and its large historical sweep shows the country being systematically exploited by the greed and ambition of the ruling minority capitalists, often in association with foreign economists. His publications also include the short story collection *Miracles* (1973), a travelogue about the USSR in *All This Must Be Seen* (1986), *The Form of the African Novel* (1979), a study in *Achebe and Soyinka* (1996), as well as critical books on African theatre and several plays. Employing allegorical characters and plots taken from African oral tradition, he frequently warns of the consequences of oppression in society.

Ondaatje, Michael (1943–) A Canadian poet and novelist, born Philip Michael Ondaatje in Colombo, Sri Lanka, his family is of Dutch, Tamil and Sinhalese origins. He moved to England in 1954, and emigrated to Canada in 1962, where he went to the University of Toronto (BA 1965) and Queen's University, Ontario (MA 1967). He first made his name as a poet, with a surrealistic juxtaposition of gruesome images in *The Dainty Monsters* (1969), *The Man with Seven Toes* (1969), *The Collected Works of Billy the Kid* (1970) and *Rat Jelly* (1973). His later poetry is to be found in *There's a Trick with a Knife I'm Learning to Do* (1979), *The Cinnamon Peeler* (1990) and *Handwriting* (1998). He has twice, in 1970 and 1979, won the prestigious Canadian prize, the Governor General's Award for Literature, for his poetry. His novels deliberately blur generic distinctions, often mixing fiction with factual, fabulous and mythical elements, as well as including prose, poetry and visual representations. They are *Coming Through Slaughter* (1979), about the legendary New Orleans jazz trumpeter Buddy Bolden, *Running in the Family* (1982), a semi-autobiographical novel about a visit to Sri Lanka, *In the Skin of a Lion* (1987), concerning the early history of Toronto in the 1920s and 1930s, and *Anil's Ghost* (2000), about a revelatory journey. His best-known work, *The English Patient* (1992, filmed 1996) – a more conventional novel than his other work, and essentially a love story that takes place in the aftermath of the Second World War – shared the 1992 Booker Prize with Barry UNSWORTH. It was successfully filmed in 1996 by Anthony Minghella. Ondaatje has also written and directed three short films, *Sons of Captain Poetry* (1970), *Carry On Crime and Punishment* (1972) and *The Clinton Special* (1972), and edited books of poetry and short stories. A central figure in Canadian postmodernist literature, he is concerned with the construction of private and public histories, issues which link him with Canadian contemporaries like Margaret ATWOOD and Robert KROETSCH. Since 1971, he has been Professor of English at York University, Toronto.

W. Siemerling, *Discoveries of the Other* (1994).

Onetti, Juan Carlos (1909–1994) Born in Montevideo, Uruguay, he lived in Buenos Aires in the 1930s and 1940s, and worked in advertising and as an editor for Reuters News Agency. He was imprisoned by the dictatorship in 1974, and after being forced to move to Madrid, became a Spanish citizen in 1975, and did odd jobs until his death. Although he began writing in the 1930s, he only gained significant attention in the 1960s. His novels include *The Pit* (1939, trans. 1991), *No Man's Land* (1941, trans. 1994), which is set in the fictional town of Santa Maria, as an escape from 'real' life, and the rest of his fiction is also set in this town, such as *Tonight* (1943, trans. 1991), *A Brief Life* (1950, trans. 1976), *A Grave with No Name* (1959, trans. 1992), *The Shipyard* (1961, trans. 1968) and *The Body Snatcher* (1964, trans. 1991). Short stories occur in *Farewells* (1954, trans. 1992) and *Past Caring* (1993, trans. 1995), while *Goodbyes* (1990) is an anthology of stories. Encouraging the promotion of Argentinean urban consciousness while editor of *Marcha* (1939–1942) in Buenos Aires, he instigated the South American urban novel. With an elliptical style, sinuous prose and characters who are frequently daytime dreamers imagining their realities, he is the most distinguished Uruguayan writer of the twentieth century.

M. Adams, *Three Authors of Alienation* (1975).

O'Rourke, P.J. (1947–) Full name Patrick Jake O'Rourke, he was born in Toledo, Ohio, US, and educated at Miami University in Ohio (BA 1969) and Johns Hopkins University (MA 1970), after which he wrote for an underground newspaper in Baltimore (1968–1971). He then worked as a journalist for various newspapers, including the *New York Herald* (1971–1973), and as an editor for the magazines *The National Lampoon* (1973–1981) and *Rolling Stone*. A humorist and provocative writer, he is associated with the 'new journalism' of such writers as Tom WOLFE and Hunter S. THOMPSON, in which journalistic objectivity gives way to unbridled subjectivity. His various parodies and spoof books include *The 1964 High School Yearbook* (1974), *Sunday Newspaper Parody* (1978), *Modern Manners* (1983), *The Bachelor's Home Companion* (1987), the essays of a hip conservative libertarian in *Republican Party Reptile* (1987), *Holidays in Hell* (1988), which gathers his reports from the world's trouble-spots, *Parliament of Whores* (1991), which is an attack on modern US politics, and *Give War a Chance* (1992). *Age of*

Guile Beat Youth, Innocence, and a Bad Haircut (1995) celebrates twenty-five years of his writings, and in which, as a fiercely proud Republican, he calls for a 'New McCarthyism' in the US. *Eat the Rich* (1998) is his latest work, about a journalist flying around the world gleefully recording all the economic mistakes of poorer capitalist countries.

Orwell, George (1903–1950) The pseudonym of Eric Arthur Blair, he was born in Bengal, India, where his father was a civil servant. After his education in England, he joined the Imperial Indian Police and spent five years in Burma, which caused him to be thoroughly disillusioned about imperialism. Upon his return to England, he disguised himself as a tramp, slept in the doss houses of London's East End and lived with the under classes in Paris. Changing his name to protect his parents from his views, he published an account of his experiences in *Down and Out in London and Paris* (1933). He wrote reviews for the *New Adelphi*, and taught for a period of time. *Burmese Days* (1934) was based upon his military experiences, and was followed by the novels *A Clergyman's Daughter* (1935), *Keep the Aspidistra Flying* (1936) and *Coming Up for Air* (1939), a heady mixture of nostalgia and social philosophy. A politicised, plain-speaking Orwell appeared in *The Road to Wigan Pier* (1937), about industrial poverty in Wigan, Sheffield and Barnsley. His account of fighting for the Republican side against Franco in the Spanish Civil War was published in *Homage to Catalonia* (1937), in which his beliefs in democratic socialism and the inhumanity of totalitarianism were expressed. He served with the Home Guard during the Second World War, and joined the BBC in 1941, resigning in 1943 to become the literary editor of the *Tribune*. His reputation as a novelist was established with his famous allegory of anti-Stalinist totalitarianism in *Animal Farm* (1945), a fable about animals on a farm.

He lived out the remainder of his life on the Scottish island of Jura, while suffering from tuberculosis, and finishing *Nineteen Eighty-Four* (1948), his equally famous dystopian view of futurist power-blocs and the dangers of totalitarianism, which has firmly established him as one of the major British writers of the twentieth century. He was a highly reputable journalist who wrote numerous essays on such diverse subjects as boys, comics, pornography, imperialism, obscenity, nationalism, and literary topics, collected in *Inside the Whale* (1940), *The Lion and the Unicorn* (1941), *Critical Essays* (1946), *The English People* (1947), *Shooting an Elephant* (1950), *England, Your England* (1953) and *Decline of the English Murder* (1965). Four volumes of the *Collected Essays, Journalism and Letters of George Orwell* were published in 1970.

B. Crick, *George Orwell: A Life* (rev. edn. 1992).

Ousmane, Sembène (1923–) Born in Ziguinchor, Casamance, Senegal, he was educated at a technical school and later at the Gorki Film Studios in Moscow. He worked as a fisherman, plumber, mechanic's mate and bricklayer before the Second World War, when he served with the Free French forces in Africa (1942–1946). He then became a docker and stevedore in Marseilles from 1948, and was involved as a union official for black workers in France. During this period, he established himself as a significant francophone writer, with such novels as *Black Docker* (1956, trans. 1987), an account of the exploitation of young black migrant workers in French shipyards, *God's Bits of Wood* (1960, trans. 1962), which is a compelling social and economic epic of the life of a railway strike in Senegal, and *Xala* (1981, trans. 1983, filmed 1974), which analyses a Senegalese businessman and his curse of impotence, or 'xala'. Short stories occur in *Tribal Scars* (1962, trans. 1974), while other fiction includes

The Money Order; White Genesis (1965, trans. 1972), a political thriller in *The Last of the Empire* (1981, trans. 1983), and *Niiwam and Taaw* (1990, trans. 1992). Constantly demonstrating a compassion for the dispossessed and underprivileged of Senegal, he has adopted a critical attitude towards West African culture, arguing that it is not only colonialism but the post-independence institutions which have stunted individuals' growths. In recent decades, he has established a reputation as one of Africa's most important film directors, with eleven films, from *Borom Sarret* (1963) to his most recent, *Guelwaar* (1992), and has won several awards. Whereas Ousmane's fiction is written in French, though widely translated, his films employ French and African languages, including Wolof and Diola. The majority of his work chronicles the psychological legacies of colonialism and the problems attendant on the transfer of power to indigenous rule.

J. Peters, *Ousmane Sebene, Contemporary Griot* (1990–1991).

Oz, Amos (1939–) Born Amos Klausner, in Jerusalem, Israel, he was educated at the Hebrew University (BA 1963) and Oxford University (MA 1970), and has been a widely honoured writer since 1962. He served in the Israeli Army (1957–1960), and since 1986, has been a professor at Ben Gurion University, Negev. His first novel was *Elsewhere, Perhaps* (1966, trans. 1973), which is one of the best representations of communal kibbutz life to emerge from Israel. This was followed by *My Michael* (1968, trans. 1972), a best-seller in Israel, dealing with the psychological disintegration of a young Israeli housewife symbolically depicting the country under siege, *Touch the Water, Touch the Wind* (1973, trans. 1974), *Soumchi* (1978, trans. 1995), about a boy's love in contemporary Jerusalem, *A Perfect Peace* (1982, trans. 1985), *Black Box* (1987, trans. 1988), *To Know a*

Woman (1989, trans. 1991), and *Don't Call It Night* (1994, trans. 1996). Short stories occur in *Where the Jackals Howl* (1965, trans. 1981), and two novellas in *Unto Death* (1971, trans. 1975), which examines the hatred that surrounds the Jews. Essays about Middle East politics appear in *Under This Blazing Light* (1979, trans. 1995), *The Slopes of Lebanon* (1987, trans. 1989) and *Israel, Palestine and Peace* (trans. 1995), and literary studies occur in *The Silence of Heaven* (1993, trans. 2000), which is a study of AGNON, and *The Story Begins* (1996, trans. 1999). *Panther in the Basement* (1995, trans. 1997) is a memoir of his childhood. Written in Hebrew, most of his novels describe a populace under siege and a society threatened by internal contradictions and contentions. The worlds of his novels are often symbolic landscapes and his central concern is the conflict between idealistic Zionism and the realities of a pluralistic society. He has lived most of his life as a member of Kibbutz Hulda, and much of his fiction is based on these experiences and the national struggles of Israel.

Ozick, Cynthia (1928–) Born in New York City, US, she studied at New York University (BA 1949) and Ohio State University, Columbus (MA 1951). Her first book was *Trust* (1966), a novel of American manners, about trust in a family and religion. An immense, intricately plotted novel, it is a mixture of Jewish, Christian and pagan cultures, isolating her conviction that Hellenism versus Hebraism is one of the central conflicts in the West. This was followed by several novels: *The Cannibal Galaxy* (1983), about the interaction between Europe and America, as a Holocaust survivor establishes a school in the Midwest; *The Messiah of Stockholm* (1987), a search for the identity of a father, set in Europe; and *The Puttermesser Papers* (1997), which depicts a woman who is prisoner of her own imagination in a series of misadventures. Short stories have been collected in *The Pagan Rabbi* (1971), which continues the Pan versus Moses theme, *Trust, Bloodshed and Three Novellas* (1976), about Jewish issues, *Levitation* (1982), set in New York and acting as a three-part pun on levitation, levity and the priestly tribe of Levi, and *The Shawl* (1989), about an incident in the Holocaust. Her journal contributions on Jewish American culture appear in *Art and Ardor* (1983) and *Metaphor and Memory* (1989), literary essays occur in *What Henry James Knew* (1993) and *Portrait of the Artist as a Bad Character* (1994), and other essays in *Fame and Folly* (1996) and *Quarrel and Quandary* (2000). Her writing generally combines mysticism, history, Judaic law, comedy and satire, as she explores the conflicts of the sacred and the profane and the ambiguous marginality of the Jew in American culture.

S. Cohen, *Cynthia Ozick's Comic Art* (1994).

P

Pagnol, Marcel (1895–1974) Born in Aubagne, France, Marcel Paul Pagnol served in the French army (1914–1917), and then took a degree in letters at the University of Montpellier, after which he held various teaching posts, including the Lycée Condorcet (1922–1929). He is principally famous for his evocations of the people and vocabulary of the Midi in southern France. He wrote the tragicomic 'Marseille' trilogy of plays (1929–1936), and in the 1940s and 1950s became a successful film-maker, writing and directing *Manon des Sources* (1952). A light-hearted writer of satirical regional pieces, he turned to prose in the 1950s with two autobiographical works, *My Father's House* (1957, trans. 1986) and *My Mother's Castle* (1958, trans. 1986). Published together as *The Days Were Too Short* (trans. 1960), they recalled his summers as a boy on a farmhouse near Marseille, and were followed by *The Time of Secrets* (1960, trans. 1962), a memoir about his growth into manhood. His best-known novels are *Jean de Florette* (trans. 1962) and *Manon of the Springs* (trans. 1963), the latter an adaptation of his earlier film, and later published together as *The Water of the Hills* (trans. 1988). A tragicomic celebration of the myth of water, it depicts a family struggling to create an ideal life in Provence, thwarted by the machinations of the local people and Manon's later revenge,

and was filmed to wide acclaim by Claude Berri in 1986. Posthumous memoirs occur in *The Time of Love* (1968, trans. 1979).

C. Caldicott, *Marcel Pagnol* (1977).

Paley, Grace (1922–) An American short story writer and poet, she was born into a Russian Jewish family in the Bronx, New York, and attended Hunter College, New York (1938–1939). She has taught at a variety of universities, and at City College, New York, since 1983. Known for her poetry as well as her short stories, her poetry is collected in *Leaning Forward* (1985) and *New and Collected Poems* (1991), and deals with many of the themes evident in her fiction. Her stories began to appear in such magazines as *Esquire*, *Atlantic* and the *New American Review* in the mid-1950s, and her first collection was *The Little Disturbances of Man* (1959), probing loneliness and escapism across wide social strata, typically reflecting upon the ordinariness of quotidian life. Other collections include *Enormous Changes at the Last Minute* (1974), which is more impressionistic in style and largely set in the New York slums, *Later the Same Day* (1985), *Long Walks and Intimate Talks* (1991) and *The Collected Stories* (1994). Her autobiography is entitled *Just As I Thought* (1998). Invariably set in New York, and often with a Jewish background, her stories display wit and grace, a sophisticated realist technique, an ear for the idiosyncratic speech of New York, and draw upon a family legacy of political activism and pacifism.

J. Taylor, *Grace Paley: Illuminating the Dark Lives* (1990).

Parker, Dorothy (1893–1967) Dorothy Rothschild Parker was an American short story writer, poet and critic, born in West End, New Jersey, who was well-known for her acerbic wit and one-liners, such as: 'Men seldom make passes at girls who wear glasses'. A founder member of the Algonquin Club in New York in the 1920s, she began writing for famous magazines like *Vogue* and *Vanity Fair*, before becoming a reviewer and writer for *The New Yorker*, which made her into something of a literary guru. She was involved with the Communist Party in 1934, and her support for radical causes led her to be blacklisted under McCarthyism. Her volumes of light verse – *Enough Rope* (1926), *Sunset Gun* (1928) and *Death and Taxes* (1931) – were best-sellers. She co-authored three plays, *Close Harmony* (1924) with Elmer Rice, *The Coast of Illyria* (1949) and *The Ladies of the Corridor* (1953), as well as numerous scripts and screenplays for Hollywood between 1925 and 1930, which she later dismissed. Her epigrammatic, sparse style of dialogue with its pervasive irony attacking the pretensions of society and the constraining gender roles of both sexes, is particularly evident in her collections of short stories, *Laments for the Living* (1930), *After Such Pleasures* (1933) and *Here Lies* (1939). *The Portable Dorothy Parker* (1944) was revised and reissued by her friend Lillian Hellman in 1977, and *The Uncollected Dorothy Parker* (1999) collects unpublished poetry.

M. Mead, *Dorothy Parker* (1988).

Pasternak, Boris (1890–1960) Born in Moscow, Russia, Boris Leonidovich Pasternak graduated from Moscow University (1913), and worked as a private tutor, clerk and librarian, before turning to writing. Principally a post-Revolutionary poet, held in high regard in Russia for works like *My Sister, Life: Summer 1917* (1923, trans. 1967), he is nevertheless most famous to English-speaking readers for his single novel *Doctor Zhivago* (1957, trans. 1958, filmed 1965). Banned as anti-Soviet, and not published in Russia until 1988, it begins with the suicide of Yuri Zhivago, and then recounts his life during the Revolution, in the Urals, his service in the Second World War and his return to Moscow. Affirming the values of individuality and the indomitable human spirit, it received huge acclaim in the West, although it brought him harassment in the USSR. Pasternak's autobiography, *The Last Summer* (1934, trans. 1959), was adapted by the English poet Craig Raine for his opera *The Electrification of the Soviet Union* (1986). *Letters to Georgian Friends* (1967, trans. 1968) and other volumes of letters have been published, in addition to the omnibus volumes of *The Collected Prose* (trans. 1945) and *Selected Poems* (trans. 1946). Pasternak also translated Shakespeare, Goethe and Schiller among others into Russian. He declined the Nobel Prize for Literature in 1958 after a controversy over the award.

G. de Mallac, *Boris Pasternak: His Life and Art* (1981).

Paton, Alan (1903–1988) A widely honoured writer, Alan Stewart Paton was born in Pietermaritzburg, South Africa, and educated at the University of Natal (B.Sc. 1923). He was a schoolteacher at Ixopo, Natal (1925–1928), and then taught in Pietermaritzburg and later at the Diepkloof Reformatory school in Johannesburg (1935–1948). His first novel, *Cry, the Beloved Country* (1948), was a landmark publication in its day as the first novel by a white South African writer of liberal conscience to draw attention to the devastation wrought on black lives by the policies of apartheid. It describes how the protagonist Kumalo's act of murder cannot be judged until one takes into consideration the context of racial oppression and hostility. *Too Late the Phalarope* (1953) centres upon an Afrikaner whose youthful idealism ends with tragic consequences, exploring the politics of the Immorality Act which prohibited interracial sexual relations. The later novel *Ah, But Your Land Is Beautiful* (1982), an unflinching treatment of the struggle against apartheid in the 1950s, and the short stories in *Tales from a Troubled Land* (1961), both deal with institutionalised racism in South Africa. His non-fiction includes *The Land and People of South Africa* (1955) and *The Long View* (1968), dealing with apartheid. He also wrote a biography of Hofmeyr (1964), *Apartheid and the Archbishop* (1973) about Geoffrey Clayton, Archbishop of Cape Town, and *Knocking on the Door* (1975) is an edition of his shorter writings. Autobiographies appeared in *Towards the Mountain* (1980) and *Journey Continued* (1988). One of the earliest white proponents of racial equality in South Africa, he was a founder and president of the Liberal Party of South Africa until it was banned in 1968.

P. Alexander, *Alan Paton: A Biography* (1994).

Patterson, Glenn (1961–) Born in Belfast, Northern Ireland, he was educated at the University of East Anglia (BA 1985, MA 1986), and then became a community writer in Craigavon and Lisburn. After working in northern England, he became writer-in-residence at Queen's University, Belfast in the 1990s. His first novel, *Burning Your Own* (1988), looks at the Northern Ireland Troubles from a Protestant perspective, and was followed by *Fat Lad* (1992), about a lower-middle-class prota-

gonist managing a bookshop in Belfast against the background of conflict in Northern Ireland. *Black Night at Big Thunder Mountain* (1995), is a fantasy about the construction of Euro-Disney, and *The International* (1999), an apolitical novel set in the International Hotel in Belfast on the eve of the Troubles and tracing the lives of a disparate group of characters, has maintained his reputation as a bright, up-and-coming young novelist.

Pavese, Cesar (1908–1950) Born in Santo Stefano, in Piedmont, Italy, he became a novelist, poet and translator. Imprisoned by the fascists in 1935 for his political activities, the themes of confinement, solitude, detachment and death recur throughout his writing. He resisted the stifling cultural pressures of fascism by bringing US and British works to Italy in translation, although his reputation rests upon his fiction, which transforms his homeland into scenes of violence and primordial actions. His main novels form two interlocking series, about the individual's participation in society, seen in the very precise geographical and historical setting of contemporary Piedmont. The 'Beautiful Summer' trilogy consists of *The Devil in the Hills* (1948, trans. 1990), *Among Women Only* (1948, trans. 1953) and *Beautiful Summer* (1949, trans. 1955), and investigates the region's psychic mechanisms and social mores. His other trilogy consists of *The Political Prisoner* (1948, trans. 1955), *The House on the Hill* (1948, trans. 1956) and *The Moon and the Bonfire* (1950, trans. 1952), and provides a political history of Italy and the political responses of its individuals. Other fiction includes *The Harvesters* (1941, trans. 1962), *Dialogues with Leucò* (1947, trans. 1989), which are dialogues between Greek deities about human mortality, and *The Leather-Jacket Stories* (trans. 1980). His fiction suspends time, and through submersion into peasant society, strives to capture the essence of the conflicts between city and country. He committed suicide in 1950.

D. Heiney, *Three Italian Novelists: Moravia, Pavese, Vittorini* (1968).

Peake, Mervyn (1911–1968) Mervyn Laurence Peake was born in Kuling, China, the son of a missionary. He went to England in 1923, and became an author, poet and painter. Excelling in portraiture, he served as a military illustrator during the Second World War, and depicted Belsen in 1945 for the *Leader* magazine, an experience which had a major impact upon him. His first novel was *Captain Slaughterboard Drops Anchor* (1942), a fantasy pirate story. He is perhaps most famous for the *Gormenghast Trilogy* (1967), which consists of *Titus Groan* (1946), *Gormenghast* (1950) and *Titus Alone* (1959), a singular Gothic fantasy about the Gormenghast castle and its environs and its eccentric characters. It chronicles the life of Titus Groan from his birth to maturity in a closed world of fantasy, and his struggle with a challenge from a servant for his crown and freedom. Peake illustrated the novel himself, and it was made into a lavish BBC series in 2000. Among his other works are *Mr Pye* (1953), an allegorical novel set on the island of Sark, *Boy in Darkness* (1956), several volumes of poetry published posthumously as the *Selected Poems of Mervyn Peake* (1972), and *Peake's Progress* (1979), a posthumous edition of his selected writings and drawings.

J. Batchelor, *Mervyn Peake* (1974).

Percy, Walker (1916–1990) Born in Birmingham, Alabama, US, he was educated at the University of North Carolina (BA 1937) and Columbia University (MD 1941), and became a writer in 1943. Known as 'the Dixie Kirkegaard', his fiction explores the twentieth-century angst of the individual adrift in an existential Catholicism, influenced by his conversion in 1946. His first novel was

The Moviegoer (1961), set in New Orleans, in which Binx Bolling, an alienated outsider, finds himself cut-off from the activities of those around him. Establishing him as a major writer of the Deep South, this was followed by *The Last Gentleman* (1966), *Love in the Ruins* (1971), set in the near future, about a character named Dr. Tom More and modelled on his renaissance namesake Sir Thomas More, *Lancelot* (1977), which is the confessions of an inmate in a mental hospital, *The Second Coming* (1980), and *The Thanatos Syndrome* (1987), featuring Dr. Tom More again and dealing with ethical issues. His non-fiction includes philosophical essays in *The Message in the Bottle* (1975) and *Lost in the Cosmos* (1983). His fictional environment is the country clubs and fairways of the Deep South; yet the novels explore the nature of the cosmos and humans' position within it, as his protagonists realise their alienation and inauthenticity in the malaise of everyday existence.

J. Tolson, *Pilgrim in the Ruins: A Life of Walker Percy* (1994).

Perec, Georges (1936–1982) Born in Paris, France, of Polish Jewish parents, his mother was killed in a Nazi concentration camp. He attended the Sorbonne, University of Paris (1954), and worked as a public opinion pollster (1959–1961), and a research librarian in neurophysiology (1962–1979), as well as compiling crossword puzzles for the French magazine *Point* (1976–1982). *Les Choses: A Story of the Sixties* (1965, trans. 1968) is a study of Parisian materialism, as two protagonists seek to fill up their spiritually empty lives with 'things', and was regarded in France as a pioneering sociological novel. *A Man Asleep* (1967, trans. 1990) is a serious psychological study of a young man's emotional crisis, and *W, or the Memory of Childhood* (1975, trans. 1988) deals with the horrifying realities of the Holocaust in the form of an experimental fiction. In 1967, he joined OULIPO ('The Workshop for Potential Literature'), founded by Raymond QUE-NEAU, which was dedicated to problems of form in literature. This prompted him to write such works as *La Disparition* (1969), a lipogram, in which the letter 'e', the most commonly used letter in French and English, was omitted from the text, with a plot which was a model of self-reference, since it hinges upon a character's mysterious disappearance; and *Les Revenentes* (1972), which used no vowel other than 'e'. These and other character-istic word puzzles, allusions, linguistic games and experiments make his fiction very difficult to translate, and much remains untranslated into English. His most significant novel, *Life: A User's Manual* (1978, trans. 1987), is a minute description of characters, objects and events at an apartment at 11 Rue Simon-Crubellier, Paris, just before 8 p.m. on 23 June 1975, deftly constructed with a complex numerological and literary archi-tecture and clarity of style. Stretching language to its limits, he was a major figure in French literature from the 1960s onwards, noted for his diversity of forms and styles, his structural and verbal in-genuity, and the many-layered depths of learning brought to his narratives.

D. Bellos, *Georges Perec: A Life in Words* (1993).

Petry, Ann (1911–1997) Born in Old Saybrook, Connecticut, US, Ann Lane Petry graduated from the University of Connecticut (Ph.D. 1931), and initially worked as a pharmacist in her parents' drugstore. She moved to Harlem in 1938 and became a journalist for newspapers, writing about Harlem's middle classes, before turning to fiction in the 1940s. Regarded as a masterpiece of African-American realism, *The Street* (1946) is her most acclaimed work, a best-selling naturalist-feminist novel about a mother who tries to provide a better life for herself and her son in the bleak urban slum environment. Thereafter she wrote *Country Place* (1947), about class and gender in a New England community, *The Narrows* (1953), which is a complex narrative of psychological realism, and two children's books about well-known slaves in *Harriet Tubman* (1955) and *Tituba of Salem Village* (1964). *Miss Muriel* (1971) collects short stories depict-ing urban and small-town American char-acters, while *The Drugstore Cat* (1949) is another children's book. She is noted for a versatile style, an eye for detail, and early feminist politics in her characters of the 1940s and 1950s, as well as her explora-tion of interracial relationships.

Phillips, Caryl (1958–) Born in St. Kitts, West Indies, he went to Leeds, England in 1958 and was educated at Oxford Uni-versity (BA 1979). He began in theatrical work, with such plays as *Strange Fruit* (1981) and *Where There Is Darkness* (1982), and has held various lecturing and writer-in-residence positions, working at Amherst College, Massachusetts since 1990. His first novel was *The Final Passage* (1985), about leaving the Carib-bean for England in the 1950s, and explores cross-Atlantic relations, identi-ties, racial abuses and prejudices. This was followed by *A State of Independence* (1986), exploring the contradictions of a British West Indian on an island like St. Kitts, *Higher Ground* (1989), which is a trilogy of stories covering 200 years, examining uprootedness from one's home-land, *Cambridge* (1991) and *Crossing the River* (1993), two historical novels of contrasting racial views dealing with slav-ery and its various legacies, and *The Nature of Blood* (1997), an epic of linked stories about persecution and loss ranging from the Holocaust to Renaissance Ve-nice. His latest novel is *The Atlantic Sound* (2000), exploring the slave-triangle between Liverpool, Emina in Ghana, and Charleston, US. In addition, he has writ-ten various plays, screenplays and radio plays, edited the anthologies *Extravagant Strangers* (1997) and *Right Set: A Tennis Anthology* (1999), and written essays on racism and place-identity in *The European Tribe* (1987). The compromised identity of West Indians is a common theme in his work, and his fiction reflects a multinational identity and consciousness.

Phillips, Jayne Anne (1952–) Phillips was born in Buckhannon, West Virginia, US. She attended the University of West Virginia at Morgantown (BA 1974) and the University of Iowa (MFA 1978), and has taught English at Boston University. Her first works were collections of short stories in *Sweethearts* (1976), *Counting* (1978) and *Black Tickets* (1979). The latter, her first major collection, is a series of stylistic exercises, sketches and interior monologues about the street worlds of prostitution, destitution and drug addiction. Further collections emerged as *How Mickey Made It* (1981) and *Fast Lanes* (1984), about isolation from the past and the discontinuity of the itinerants and destitute from her earlier stories. Her first novel was *Machine Dreams* (1984), an expansive, sprawling story about disorientation in modern life, following different narrators of the Hampson family through two generations, from the Depression to the 1970s. This was followed by the tighter *Shelter* (1994), about the loss of childhood innocence, set in a West Virginia summer camp for girls in 1963, and four campers' stories, and her latest novel *MotherKind* (2000), about a woman caring for her terminally ill mother and bringing up her daughter in a young marriage. Her focus on seedy, small-town America and its dropouts, has earned her an acclaimed reputation of being a 'dirty realist', along with Raymond CARVER, Tobias WOLFF and Richard FORD.

Piercy, Marge (1936–) An American novelist and poet, born in Detroit, Michigan, she was educated at the University of Michigan (AB 1957) and Northwestern University (MA 1958), and has subsequently taught at several universities. Her writing has a strong feminist theme, evident from her first novel *Going Down Fast* (1969), and in *Small Changes* (1973) and *Vida* (1980), which document the challenges faced by student activists in an increasingly conservative 1970s America. She is best known for *Woman on the Edge of Time* (1976), a science fiction narrative which contrasts a future utopia with the economic, environmental and gender wasteland of contemporary America. Later novels include *Braided Lives* (1982), *Fly Away Home* (1984), *Gone to Soldiers* (1987), which depicts the pervasive effects of the Second World War, *He, She and It* (1991), *Longings of Women* (1994), *City of Darkness, City of Light* (1996), and *Storm Tide* (1998), about a man retiring from baseball who gets involved in several affairs in Cape Cod before coming to terms with his new life. She has also published poetry, including *The Moon Is Always Female* (1980), *Available Light* (1998) and *Early grrrl* (1999). Essays have appeared in *The Grand Coolie Dam* (1970) and *Parti-Colored Blocks for a Quilt* (1982). Politically active since the 1960s and associated with the women's movement since 1969, she writes about the oppression of individuals, and many of her novels feature female characters caught in the matrix of sexual liberation and political radicalism.

Pieyre de Mandiargues, André (1909–1991) Born in Paris, France, he was relatively unknown outside French literary circles until the publication of his celebrated *The Margin* (1967, Prix Goncourt, trans. 1969), which traces the two-day wanderings of a man who has denied himself knowledge of the full details of his wife's untimely death. A study of intense psychological exile, love and death, it is meticulously realistic. Thereafter, he gained a wider audience for his novels, poetry and short stories. Other works include the novels *The Girl Beneath the Lion* (1956, trans. 1958) and *Arcimboldo the Marvellous* (1977, trans. 1978), the short stories in *Blaze of Embers* (1959, trans. 1971), the novelette *The Motorcycle* (1963, trans. 1965), which tells of a young girl's fantasies about her motorbike as she journeys to her tryst with her lover, and poetry in *Hyacinths* (trans. 1976). A prolific writer, much of his work remains untranslated into English. His writing reflects his involvement with Surrealism in the 1940s, as he juxtaposes the terrifying with the appealing, and the erotic and the grotesque, combining fantasy and allegory in his fiction.

D. Bond, *The Fiction of André Pieyre de Mandiargues* (1982).

Pinget, Robert (1919–1997) Born in Geneva, Switzerland, he studied law at the Collège de Genève, and subsequently practised law until 1946, when he went to France as a painter, and taught drawing. He became a freelance writer in Paris in 1951, with short stories in *Between Fantoine and Agapa* (1951, trans. 1983), and the novel *Mahu: Or, the Material* (1952, trans. 1966), which evokes the perplexed and paradoxical situation of the artist seeking truth through falsehood. *Baga* (1958, trans. 1967) introduced fantastic, absurdist invention, including treacheries of memory, threatened identities, comic clips and snatches of everyday gossip. Subsequent works like *Monsieur Levert* (1959, trans. 1961), *The Inquisitory* (1962, trans. 1966), *Someone* (1965, trans. 1984), *The Libera Me Domine* (1968, trans. 1972), *Recurrent Melody* (1969, trans. 1975), *Fable* (1971, trans. 1980), *That Voice* (1975, trans. 1982), *The Apocrypha* (1980, trans. 1987, *Monsieur Songe* (1982, trans. 1989), *The Enemy* (1987, trans. 1991) and *Théo, or, the New Era* (1991, trans. 1994), established him as one of the distinctive voices of the so-called French 'new novel', which explored forms and patterns in the novel

cut adrift from its traditional supports. Investigating the slippery nature of language, his fiction resists closure and myths of completeness, and rather than merely becoming narcissistic narratives, he explores the dilemmas and contradictions of human communication.

R. Henkels, Jr., *Robert Pinget: The Novel as Quest* (1979).

Pirandello, Luigi (1867–1936) Born in Agirgenti, Sicily, Italy, he attended the University of Palermino, Rome (1886–1887), the University of Rome (1887–1889) and gained a doctorate from the University of Bonn. While working as a teacher (1897–1922), he turned to writing fiction and drama. His novels include *The Late Mattia Pascal* (1904, trans. 1923), a naturalistic story about a man who fakes his identity to escape life's circumstances, *The Outcast* (1906, trans. 1925), *The Naked Truth* (1910, trans. 1934), *The Old and the Young* (1913, trans. 1928), *Tu Ridi* (1914, trans. 1920), *Shoot! The Notebooks of Serafino Gabbio* (1916, trans. 1926), *The Horse in the Moon* (1918, trans. 1932), and *One, None, and a Hundred Thousand* (1926, trans. 1933), another narrative concerned with definitions of the self, as the protagonist seeks to free himself from social identity. His short stories occur in *Tales of Madness* (1932–1937, trans. 1984), *Better Think Twice About It* (trans. 1934) and *The Oil Jar* (trans. 1995). In addition to poetry, he was one of the most important twentieth-century dramatists, whose innovative use of stagecraft, philosophical themes and dramatic structure was evident in such plays as *Six Characters in Search of an Author* (1921, trans. 1922) and *Henry IV* (trans. 1922). Concerned with sanity and madness, appearance and reality, he dealt with relativism and anti-rationalism in provocative formulations. He was awarded the Nobel Prize for Literature in 1934.

O. Budel, *Pirandello* (1966).

Pirsig, Robert M. (1928–) Robert Maynard Pirsig was born in Minneapolis, Minnesota, US. He went to the University of Minnesota (BA 1950, MA 1958), and has since been an instructor at Montana State University (1959–1961) and the University of Illinois, Chicago (1961–1962). After acting as a technical writer to various firms, he became a member of the board of directors of the Minnesota Zen Meditation Center in 1973. A novelist and metaphysician, his first novel was *Zen and the Art of Motorcycle Maintenance: An Inquiry into Values* (1974), which was part autobiographical, telling the story of a man's motorcycle journey across the US with his 11-year-old son in 1968, contemplating philosophy, life, technology and himself. A great hunt after identity, the book became a cult success in the 1970s. A more recent edition of *Zen and the Art of Motorcycle Maintenance* has an appendix, in which he tries to come to terms with the death of his son with whom he made the original journey. *Lila: An Inquiry into Morals* (1991) was his second novel, which again uses the image of a journey, this time travelling by boat in the company of Lila, a middle-aged woman of loose morals, in whom the narrator Phaedrus, his protagonist of the first novel, sees something of himself and is forced to reassess his entire philosophical basis for being.

Pohl, Frederik (1919–) A prolific American science fiction writer and editor, born in New York City, who has published under a variety of pseudonyms, principally James MacCreigh until 1953. In the 1950s, his collaborations with Cyril Kornbluth pioneered a new science fiction, known as sociological science fiction, which presented alternate futures on Earth through the exaggeration of current social trends and forces. Perhaps the best of these collaborations was *The Space Merchants* (1953), about a world ruled by advertising, but they also include *Search the Sky* (1954) and *Gladiator-at-Law*

(1955). As editor of *Galaxy* magazine and later Bantam Books, he was a significant supporter and helper into print of the 'New Wave' writers of the 1960s, like Joanna RUSS and Samuel DELANY. His second long-term collaboration occurred with Jack Williamson, which was best known for the *Undersea* stories for juveniles, and the space opera *Starchild* novels, collected as *The Starchild Trilogy* (1977). For novels written under his own name, he is most famous for the prize-winning *Gateway* (1977), about a discovery of the spaceport of the long-dead Heechee civilisation. This presaged a series following human exploration of the galaxy using the abandoned alien technology, including *The Annals of Heechee* (1988) and *The Gateway Trip* (1990). *JEM* (1979) is about a near-future Earth and the colonisation of an alien world, and other novels include *Syzygy* (1981), *Years of the City* (1988), *The Voices of Heaven* (1994), and the recent *The Eschaton Sequence* (1999), consisting of *The Other End of Time* (1996), *The Siege of Eternity* (1997) and *The Far Shore of Time* (1999). His short stories are slickly ironic satires with twists of black humour, and include *Alternating Currents* (1954) and *The Man Who Ate the World* (1960). *The Way the Future Was* (1978) is his autobiography.

Potok, Chaim (1929–) Originally born Herman Harold Potok, he is an American writer, born in New York City, and educated at Yeshiva University, the Jewish Theological Seminary, and the University of Pennsylvania. He is an ordained rabbi, and served in this capacity as a chaplain during the Korean War. Most of his writing concerns Hassidic and Orthodox Jewish themes. His novels include *The Chosen* (1967), *The Promise* (1969), *My Name Is Asher Lev* (1972), about a young Hasidic Jew with a prodigious talent for art, for which his ultra-conservative parents can see no use, and a sequel entitled *The Gift of Asher Lev* (1990), *In the Beginning* (1975), *The Book of Lights*

(1981), about a New York rabbi who is attracted by the mysticism of the Kabbalah, and *Davita's Harp* (1984). He began to write more auto-biographically based works in the late 1980s, and these include *I Am the Clay* (1992), *The Tree of Here* (1993), *The Sky of Now* (1994), and *The Gates of November: Chronicles of the Slepak Family* (1996), a non-fiction account of a family who emigrate to the US from Russia and then return to the USSR. He has also written a history of the Jews entitled *Wanderings* (1978), and short stories occur in *Zebra* (1998). His fiction usually examines the tensions between traditional and modern Jewish life, and the mystical and rational elements within Judaism.

E. Abramson, *Chaim Potok* (1986).

Powell, Anthony (1905–2000) Born in London, England, Anthony Dymoke Powell went to Oxford University (BA 1926), and became a writer in 1930. He worked for Duckworth Publishers (1926–1935), and for the Intelligence Corps during the Second World War. His early novels, for example *Afternoon Men* (1931) and *Venusberg* (1932), were satires of upper-middle-class society and distinguished him as one of the most significant novelists of his generation. He is most famous for the twelve volumes of 'A Dance to the Music of Time' series, beginning with *A Question of Upbringing* (1951) and concluding with *Hearing Secret Harmonies* (1975). The complete cycle was published as *A Dance to the Music of Time* (1995) and it follows a group of characters from adolescence in 1914 to old age and death in the late 1960s. Based on a picture by Nicholas Poussin, an allegory of time and death, the sequence is a comedy of manners told by the protagonist Nicholas Jenkins, and chronicles the changing fortunes and extinction of the British upper class in the twentieth century. In addition, he wrote a biography, *John Aubrey and His Friends*

(1948), a four-volume memoir *To Keep the Ball Rolling* (1983), and a novel entitled *The Fisher King* (1986), which is a mythological allegory about a group of characters on a round-Britain educational cruise. Other non-fiction includes literary essays in *Miscellaneous Verdicts* (1990), *Under Review* (1994), and several volumes of journals covering the period 1982 to 1992. During his life, he developed close friendships with Evelyn WAUGH, Cyril Connolly and George ORWELL.

N. McEwan, *Anthony Powell* (1991).

Powys, John Cowper (1872–1963) Born in Shirley, Derbyshire, England, and educated at Cambridge University, he was the brother of Llewellyn POWYS and T.F. POWYS. He wrote several books of poetry before his first novel, *Wood and Stone* (1915), but his first substantial novel was *Wolf Solent* (1929). He became something of a cult author, writing massive books with a strong mystical element deriving from Welsh, Arthurian and Blakean mythologies, and often featuring the West Country of England, which appealed only to a limited readership. He lived in the US until 1934, when he settled in North Wales. Among his novels are *A Glastonbury Romance* (1933), perhaps his most famous work, and involving the legend of the Holy Grail, *Weymouth Sands* (1934), *Maiden Castle* (1936), *Owen Glendower* (1940), *Porius* (1951), *The Brazen Head* (1956) and *All or Nothing* (1960). Non-fictional works include *Autobiography* (1934), *The Meaning of Culture* (1930), *The Pleasures of Literature* (1938), *The Art of Growing Old* (1943) and *Rabelais* (1948). Often developing the conflict between pagan and Christian cultures, other dominant themes include vivisection, mental illness and sexual energy. Visionary and idiosyncratic, his fiction champions individual potential and cosmic oneness, and criticises technological and industrial society.

R. Graves, *The Brothers Powys* (1983).

Powys, Llewellyn (1884–1939) An English writer, born in Dorchester, Dorset, and the brother of John Cowper POWYS and T.F. POWYS, he was educated at the University of Cambridge. His first book, *Confessions of Two Brothers* (1916), was written in collaboration with his brother John. Among his twenty-six books, he wrote a novel, *Apples be Ripe* (1930), and what he termed an 'imaginary biography', *Love and Death* (1939), but his travel writing is considered to be his best work. This comprises sketches of Africa in *Black Laughter* (1924), and *A Pagan's Pilgrimage* (1931), about Palestine. He also wrote two autobiographical books, *Skin for Skin* (1925), an account of his tuberculosis, and *The Verdict of Bridlegoose* (1926). *Earth Memories* (1934) contains essays, and he wrote a biography of Henry Hudson. Of the three brothers, he was the most cheerful and the most at ease, and his writing blends description, reminiscence and polemic.

R. Graves, *The Brothers Powys* (1983).

Powys, T.F. (1875–1953) Full name Theodore Francis Powys, and born in Shirley, Derbyshire, England, he was the brother of John Cowper POWYS and Llewellyn POWYS. He lived nearly all his life in Dorset, and his books are redolent of the village life of that county, and in particular of the area between Wareham and Weymouth. His novels include *Black Bryony* (1923), *Mr Tasker's Gods* (1925), *Innocent Birds* (1926), *Mr Weston's Good Wine* (1927), which is often regarded as his finest novel, *Kindness in a Corner* (1930), *Unclay* (1931) and *The Only Penitent* (1931). His fiction is suffused with a deep religious belief, outlined in *An Interpretation of Genesis* (1907) and *The Soliloquies of a Hermit* (1916), often producing parables of human morality and meditations on the nature and purposes of God. His unorthodox version of Christianity derives from a blend of the Bible, mysticism, pantheism and quietism,

and his works explored themes of love, death, good and evil within the microcosm of the rural world.

H. Coombes, *T.F. Powys* (1960).

Price, Reynolds (1933–) Born Edward Reynolds Price, in Macon, North Carolina, US, he was educated at Duke University (AB 1955) and Oxford University (B.Litt. 1958), after which he taught at Duke University, where he is currently Professor of English. His first novel was the much praised *A Long and Happy Life* (1962), which depicts the life of a country girl, Rosacoke Mustian. Thereafter, he wrote prolifically, and is best known for his novels which feature the carefully drawn characters, back roads and small towns of North Carolina. These include *A Generous Man* (1966), *Love and Work* (1968), *The Surface of the Earth* (1975) and *The Source of Light* (1981), both of which depict the life of the Mayfield family in a broad scope, and *Mustian* (1983). *Kate Vaiden* (1986) was a much acclaimed novel about a woman coming-of-age in the South during the Depression and war years, and subsequent novels include *Good Hearts* (1988), which returns to the Mayfields, *The Tongues of Angels* (1990), about a precocious young boy's stay at summer camp, *Blue Calhoun* (1992), *Michael Egerton* (1993), *The Promise of Rest* (1995), which concludes the Mayfield family saga in the 1990s and deals with AIDS, *Roxanne Slade* (1998) and *A Perfect Friend* (2000). Short stories occur in *The Names and Faces of Heroes* (1963), *Permanent Errors* (1970), *The Foreseeable Future* (1990), *An Early Christmas* (1992) and *The Collected Stories* (1993). In addition to plays, volumes of poetry, and essays in *New and Selected Essays* (1988), he has written a memoir entitled *Clear Pictures* (1989) of the first twenty-one years of his life, and *A Whole New Life* (1994), which is an account of his battle with spinal cancer. Exploring the tensions in families, and often manifesting a religious sensibility in his writing, he is heavily influenced by the oral traditions of the American South.

J. Schiff, *Understanding Reynolds Price* (1996).

Prichard, Katherine Susannah (1883–1969) An Australian novelist, born in Levuka, Fiji, she spent her childhood in Tasmania and went to South Melbourne College. After working for the Melbourne *Herald*, she went to London in 1912, where she published short stories and poetry. Her first novels, *The Pioneers* (1915) and *Windlestraws* (1916), were poorly received romances. She moved to Western Australia in 1919, where she wrote *Black Opal* (1921), acclaimed in Australia for its study of the opal-mining community at Fallen Star Ridge. Her involvement with the Communist Party increased in the 1920s, before her most influential novel, *Coonardoo* (1929), which caused such a domestic political storm due to its frank treatment of sexual relationships between white men and black women, that it was not published in Australia until 1965. Her other major work, the 'Goldfields trilogy' – *The Roaring Nineties* (1946), *Golden Miles* (1948) and *Winged Seeds* (1950) – concentrates upon social and sexual politics in a gold-mining community. Further novels and short story collections include *Haxby's Circus* (1930), *Kiss on the Lips* (1932), *Intimate Strangers* (1937), *Moon of Desire* (1941), *Potch and Colour* (1944), *N'Goola* (1959) and *Subtle Flame* (1967). Much of her writing depicts social injustice and the oppression of working people. In addition to hundreds of essays and articles, some collected in *Straight Left* (1982), she wrote plays, poetry, children's books and short stories. Many of her short stories dealt with the harsh environment and the lives of Aboriginal women. Her autobiography is entitled *Child of the Hurricane* (1963).

H. Drake-Brockman, *Katherine Susannah Prichard* (1963).

Priestley, J.B. (1894–1984) An English novelist, playwright and essayist, born in Bradford, Yorkshire and educated at Cambridge University (BA 1922), his full name was John Boynton Priestley. His first successes were with essays collected in *The English Comic Characters* (1925) and *The English Novel* (1927). His most entertaining novels were *The Good Companions* (1929), about a troupe of travelling actors, and *Angel Pavement* (1930), concerning the lives of a group of office workers in London. Other novels include *Let the People Sing* (1939), *Three Men in New Suits* (1945), *Bright Day* (1946), *The Magicians* (1954), *Lost Empires* (1965) and *It's an Old Country* (1967). His last years saw renewed interest in his work, and the publication of *Found, Lost, Found, or the English Way of Life* (1976). He was also a prolific playwright and experimented with expressionist psychological drama in *Time and the Conways* (1937), although one of his most popular plays was the mystery *An Inspector Calls* (1946), involving an intriguing dislocation in time. An adept broadcaster, he had wide audiences for his radio programmes during the Second World War, collected in *Britain Speaks* (1940) and *All England Listened* (1968). Other works include travel books, a trilogy of historical studies of Regency, Victorian and Edwardian England, and post-war journalism, as well as several autobiographical volumes.

J. Atkins, *J.B. Priestley: The Last of the Sages* (1981).

Pritchett, V.S. (1900–1997) Full name Victor Sawdon Pritchett, born in Ipswich, England, he left school at 15 and worked as a bookkeeper (1916–1920), a freelance journalist (1923–1926), and then as a literary critic for various journals (1926–1965), working in universities along the way. Regarded as one of Britain's premier twentieth-century men of letters, he was principally associated with two forms – the short story and essay. His short stories occur in *The Spanish Virgin* (1930), *You Make Your Own Life* (1938), *It May Never Happen Again* (1945), *The Sailor, Sense of Humour* (1956), *When My Girl Comes Home* (1961), *Blind Love* (1969), *The Camberwell Beauty* (1974), *A Careless Widow* (1989), and two volumes of *Complete Collected Stories* (1991). An acute observer, economical with language, and with a strong sense of the comic, his essays occur in *Complete Collected Essays* (1992), with travel essays in *Marching Spain* (1928), and *At Home and Abroad* (1989). His vast output of non-fiction includes biographies of Balzac, Turgenev and Chekov, literary essays in *The Myth Makers* (1979) and *The Tale Bearers* (1980), and autobiographies in *A Cat at the Door* (1968) and *Midnight Oil* (1971). Less distinguished but still technically accomplished, his novels include *Clare Drummer* (1929), *Elopement into Exile* (1932), *Nothing Like Leather* (1935), *Dead Man Leading* (1937) and *Me Beluncle* (1957), about a restless father desperately associating with various religious sects.

J. Stinson, *V.S. Pritchett: A Study of the Short Fiction* (1992).

Proulx, E. Annie (1935–) A highly praised American writer, Edna Annie Proulx was born in Norwich, Connecticut, US, and attended the University of Vermont, Burlington (BA 1969) and Sir George Williams University, Montreal (MA 1973). After working as a freelance journalist and writer of DIY books, she wrote her first novel *Postcards* (1991), a tale about the decline and fall of an American farm, in which each chapter is tied to a postcard to the protagonist Loyal Blood, an aimless wanderer. She confirmed her position as one of the great talents in contemporary American fiction with *The Shipping News* (1993, Pulitzer Prize 1994), a best-seller, set in Killick-Claw, a remote coastal village in Newfoundland, and depicting the adventures of Quoyle, a hapless journalist. The delightful *Accordion Crimes*

(1996) was equally as successful, a set of stories about various immigrants to America, linked together by an accordion. She has also written short stories set in New England, in *Heart Songs* (1988), and her latest work is *Close Range: Wyoming Stories* (1999), a series of stories set in the harsh and unforgiving state that is now her home. Often situated in hostile environments, her stories are inventive, funny and explore the resilience of humanity.

Proust, Marcel (1871–1922) Born Valentin-Louis-George-Eugene-Marcel Proust, in Auteuil, France, he graduated from the Sorbonne, University of Paris (1895), and became a writer and librarian (1895–1900). Considered by many to be one of the greatest novelists of the twentieth century, his reputation derives exclusively from his seven-volume novel, *Remembrance of Things Past* (1913–1927, trans. 1922–1931). The seven parts are: *Swann's Way* (1913, trans. 1922), *Within a Budding Grove* (1919, Prix Goncourt, trans. 1924), *The Guermantes Way* (1920–1921, trans. 1925), *Cities of the Plain* (1922, trans. 1927), *The Captive* (1923, trans. 1929), *The Sweet Cheat Gone* (1925, trans. 1930) and *The Past Recaptured* (1927, trans. 1934). *Swann in Love* (1919, trans. 1984) features one chapter from *Swann's Way*. All seven volumes centre upon the narrator, Marcel, telling his life story with its errors and successes, its bourgeois family life and his friend Swann. It is most significant for exploring the power of involuntary memory, which can break down habit and restore sensory and emotional impressions of years ago, which famously happens when Marcel eats a madeleine cake, thus prompting the novel's recollections. Told in a subjective first person narrative, the novel stresses the relativism of perception, manipulates narrative chronology and shows it patterned by image, association and coincidence. Depicting the power of recollection and the ability to shape memories into a compelling account of one man's search for his past, taking him into a world of charm, deceit, virtue and perversion, the novel is meticulously observed, dealing with love, memory, class politics, and sexuality. Other works include the three volumes of the posthumously published *Jean Santeuil* (1952, trans. 1956), various volumes of collections of letters, prose and poetry in *Pleasures and Reports* (1896, trans. 1948), and the art and literary essays in *By Way of Saint-Beuve* (1954, trans. 1958), which challenged the aesthetic principles of Saint-Beuve.

S. Beckett, *Proust* (1931); W. Carter, *Marcel Proust: A Life* (2000).

Puig, Manuel (1932–1990) Born in General Villegas, Argentina, he went to the University of Buenos Aires (1950–1951), and then studied film in Italy and around Europe. He returned to Argentina in 1967, although following persecution by Péron, lived variously in Brazil and the US in later life. A post-'boom' writer like Antonio SKÁRMETA, his fiction is marked by the uncertainty, ambivalence and impossible reconciliations associated with postmodernism. His novels include *Betrayed by Rita Hayworth* (1968, trans. 1971), a *bildungsroman* about a child protagonist who finds escape in Hollywood films, *Heartbreak Tango: A Serial* (1969, trans. 1973), which imitates the conventions of serial romance, and *The Buenos Aires Affair* (1973, trans. 1976), which is a parody of a detective novel. One of his more famous books is *Kiss of the Spider Woman* (1976, trans. 1979, filmed 1985), which gradually explores the developing relationship between a homosexual hedonist and a Marxist revolutionary forced together in a prison cell. Further novels include *Pubis Angelical* (1979, trans. 1980), which exposes the sexual exploitation of three women, *Eternal Curse on the Reader of These Pages* (1980, trans. 1982), *Blood of Requited Love* (1982, trans. 1984), and *Tropical*

Night Falling (1988, trans. 1991), set in Brazil. Finding Marxism and psychoanalysis inadequate for providing an intellectual framework for personal happiness, many of his novels contain cinematic references and dismiss the division between 'high' and 'low' art. Although wider recognition came posthumously, he is now considered one of the more significant Latin American writers of the post-'boom' period.

P. Bacarisse, *The Necessary Dream* (1988).

Purdy, James (1923–) James Amos Purdy was born in Fremont, Ohio, US. He attended the University of Chicago and the University of Puebla, Mexico. His career was launched when Edith Sitwell took an interest in his work in 1957, since when he has become a prolific writer of poetry, short stories, novels and plays. Often exploring the crippling effects of the American family on its children, his early novels developed the subject of orphans and runaways, as in *63: Dream Palace* (1957), about two orphaned brothers and their tragic life in Chicago, and *Malcolm* (1959), about the sad life of a 15-year-old boy abandoned at a posh hotel. Other novels of this time include satires on American life, in *Cabot Wright Begins* (1964), about a Wall Street heir who becomes a rapist and writes his memoirs, and *Eustace Chisholm and the Works* (1967), about homosexual love, set in 1930s Chicago. There followed a series of novels set in rural Ohio and the inhabitants of a small town and its regional concerns: *Jeremy's Version* (1970), *The House of the Solitary Maggot* (1974), and *Mourners Below* (1981). Later novels include *I Am Elijah Thrush* (1972), *In a Shallow Grave* (1976), *Narrow Rooms* (1978), *On Glory's Course* (1984), *Out with the Stars* (1992), about gay artists and musicians in New York City in 1965, and *Gertrude on Stony Island Avenue* (1997), about a woman who realises the emptiness of her own life after the death of her daughter. Short story collections include *Don't Call Me By My Right Name* (1956), *Children Is All* (1962), *Mr. Evening* (1968), *On the Rebound* (1970) and *The Candles of Your Eyes* (1987). His later fiction combines the real and the fantastic, in an exploration of consuming narcissism. However, he is little known to a wider audience in the US.

S. Adams, *James Purdy* (1976).

Puzo, Mario (1920–1999) Born in New York City, US, and educated at Columbia University, he is famous for his novels set in the Italian-American underworld. His two early novels, *The Dark Arena* (1955), about law and corruption in occupied Germany, and *The Fortunate Pilgrim* (1964), met with little commercial success despite critical praise. He made his name with *The Godfather* (1969), about the rise of Don Vito Corleone and the fall of his sons, the peculiar Mafia honour system, and the power struggles between rival 'families'. Selling 13 million copies, it was the best-selling novel of the 1970s. This was followed by *Fools Die* (1978), about ambition, power and corruption in the worlds of gambling, publishing and movie-making, and *The Sicilian* (1984), again about the Corleone family. *The Fourth K* (1991) is a political thriller set in the first decade of the twenty-first century, the title referring to a fictional President Kennedy, and *The Last Don* (1996), is another crime-family novel. The posthumously published *Omerta* (2000), yet another Mafia tale, focuses on the betrayal of *omerta*, the Italian for code of silence. He wrote the screenplays for Coppola's famous films of *The Godfather* (filmed 1972) and *The Godfather, Part II* (1974), as well as the screenplays for *Superman* (1978), *Superman II* (1981) and *Earthquake* (1974). His other books include *The Godfather Papers and Other Confessions* (1972) and *Inside Las Vegas* (1977).

R. Green, *The Italian-American Novel* (1974).

Pym, Barbara (1913–1980) An English writer, born in Oswestry, Shropshire, Barbara Mary Pym was educated at Oxford University (BA 1934). Seeing duty with the Women's Royal Naval Services in England and Italy (1943–1946), she then worked for the International African Institute in London until 1974. Her early novels, such as *Some Tame Gazelle* (1950), *Excellent Women* (1952), *Jane and Prudence* (1953), *Less Than Angels* (1955), *A Glass of Blessings* (1958) and *No Fond Return of Love* (1961), depict the lives of the younger generation of the British middle class, with a veneer of humour covering more serious issues. A quietly successful novelist of manners in the genteel world of drawing rooms and the professions in the 1950s, she found publishers uninterested in her work in the 1960s. After suffering a period of neglect, *Quartet in Autumn* (1977), regarded by many as her best work, launched her comeback, with its focus on four individuals, and the drudgery of their working lives and their relationships. Thereafter she published steadily, including *The Sweet Dove Died* (1978), *A Few Green Leaves* (1980), *An Unsuitable Attachment* (1982), *Crampton Hodnet* (1985) and *An Academic Question* (1986). *Civil to Strangers* (1988) collected her unpublished fiction, and *A Very Private Eye* (1984) is an autobiographical collection of letters and journals. With a growing posthumous reputation, much of her work focuses on single, lonely women, with care and attention given to the details of daily routine in a wry and observant style.

Pynchon, Thomas (1937–) Thomas Ruggles Jr. Pynchon is an American novelist and short story writer, born on Long Island, New York, and educated at Cornell University (BA 1958). Regarded as the archetypal postmodern novelist, and often compared to BARTH, COOVER, GADDIS and GASS, his work describes an America wracked by confusion and paranoia and systematically manipulated by multinational corporate capitalism. Protecting his privacy with care and determination, he is a mysterious character around whom all sorts of speculative stories have developed. His earliest stories were written between 1958 and 1964 in Greenwich Village, New York, and subsequently published as *Slow Learner* (1984), exploring ideas such as entropy, which were to be significant in his later novels. After working as a technical writer for Boeing in Seattle, he published his first large novel, *V* (1963). Concerning the search by a band of eccentric characters for the elusive and mysterious woman known as 'V', who appears in various guises at critical moments throughout European history, the novel demonstrates Pynchon's characteristic combination of slapstick humour, enigmatic puzzles, narrative complexity, images from popular culture, and the proliferation of linguistic signs. This was followed by another quest narrative – *The Crying of Lot 49* (1966) – a more compact investigation of the acts of interpretation, reading and decipherment, in a devastating critique of Californian cultural excesses which become symbolic of American decadence in the 1960s. He develops many of these themes and styles in his most sophisticated and complex novel, *Gravity's Rainbow* (1973), which utilises a large array of narrative modes and specialist information in an allegorical narrative about the V-2 rockets, set during the final months of the Second World War, to explore a wide variety of issues concerning the impact of corporate capitalism on contemporary society. After a long silence, which increased speculation about his mysterious character, he published *Vineland* (1990), a quest novel for Frenesi Gates, the estranged wife of Zoyd Wheeler, who has turned her back on her radical past and become involved with Brock Vond, a Justice Department official. A critique of the conservative years of the Nixon–Reagan era, it demonstrates all the characteristics of the typical erudite and allusive Pynchon narrative. His most recent novel is *Mason and Dixon* (1997), another long and complex novel about the adventures of the two British topographers who charted the state lines of Pennsylvania and Maryland. Written in imitation of an eighteenth-century novel, it deals with the origins of modernity, in a satirical and farcical fusion of history, fable, science and science fiction. He has also written an essay about Los Angeles, entitled 'Journey into the Mind of Watts' (1983).

D. Seed, *The Fictional Labyrinths of Thomas Pynchon* (1988); J. Dugdale, *Thomas Pynchon: Allusive Parables of Power* (1990).

Q

Queneau, Raymond (1903–1976) Born in Le Havre, France, he graduated from the University of Paris (1926), and after serving as a Zouave in Morocco in 1927, he worked as a bank clerk, and then from 1938 for the publishing house Gallimard. He was editor of the *Encyclopédie de la Pléiade* (1955–1975), and in 1960 he founded OULIPO ('The Workshop of Potential Literature'), which was dedicated to problems of form in literature, and which counted writers like Georges PEREC among its members. Early novels include *The Bark Tree* (1933, trans. 1968), *A Hard Winter* (1939, trans. 1948), *Pierrot* (1943, trans. 1950) and *The Skin of Dreams* (1944, trans. 1948). His blend of complex linguistic patterns, colloquial language and humour is demonstrated in *Exercises in Style* (1947, trans. 1958), which describes an ordinary encounter on a bus in ninety-nine different ways, styles and genres, and *Zazie in the Métro* (1959, trans. 1960), which brought him international attention, about an 11-year-old girl visiting her Parisian uncle and her comic and zany language use. The latter novel was turned into a film by Louis Malle in 1960, entitled *Zazie dans le Métro*. Other novels include *The Sunday of Life* (1951, trans. 1976), *One Hundred Million Poems* (1961, trans. 1983), *Between Blue and Blue* (1965, trans. 1967), and *The Flight of Icarus* (1968, trans. 1973), which is a series of spoof mystery stories and a play in seventy-four scenes. His poetry occurs in *Raymond Queneau: Poems* (trans. 1971). His writing is indebted to his involvement in the 1920s with André Breton and the Surrealists, and their emphasis on the irrational forces of the unconscious mind. The problems of language became the most important feature of his writing, and he strove to reproduce spoken rather than written French. Owing to his linguistic playfulness, translation of his work is difficult, and a large body of work remains untranslated into English.

R. Barthes, *Critical Essays* (1972).

R

Raddall, Thomas H. (1903–) Full name Thomas Head Raddall, he was born in Hythe, England, and went to Halifax, Canada in 1913. After a period sailing, he settled as a bookkeeper in Nova Scotia, developing an interest in Native-Canadian culture and local history. His early works *Saga of the Rover* (1931) and *The Markland Sagas* (1934) were adventure tales, and he wrote many short stories for *Blackwood's Magazine*, collected in *The Pied Piper of Dipper Creek* (1939). He is best known for his historical fiction, the first of which was *His Majesty's Yankees* (1942), set in Nova Scotia at the time of the American Revolution, followed by *Roger Sudden* (1944) and *Pride's Fancy* (1946), set in Nova Scotia in the eighteenth century. Additional historical novels include *The Rover* (1958), *The Governor's Lady* (1960) and *Hangman's Beach* (1960). He also wrote three fictional romances with twentieth-century settings: *The Nymph and the Lamp* (1950), which is considered a Canadian classic, *Tidefall* (1953) and *The Wings of the Night* (1956). One of Canada's leading writers of the 1950s, he was also an established authority on the history of Nova Scotia, with such books as *Halifax: Warden of the North* (1948) about the provincial city. After his memoir *In My Time* (1976), he retired as a writer, although recent years have seen the publication of *The Dreamers* (1986) and *Courage in the Storm* (1987).

A. Young, ed., *Time and Place: The Life and Works of Thomas H. Raddall* (1991).

Rao, Raja (1909–) A highly regarded writer, who, together with Mulk Raj ANAND and R.K. NARAYAN, is considered to be one the most distinguished Anglo-Indian novelists of the twentieth century. Born in Hassan, Mysore, India, he was educated at the Aligarh Muslim University (1926–1927) and the University of Madras (BA 1929). He undertook postgraduate study at the Sorbonne, University of Paris (1929–1933), and spent his post-Second World War life in France until he became Professor of Philosophy at the University of Texas, Austin (1966–1980). His first novel, *Kanthapura* (1938), is his most famous, and tells how a young Brahmin influences a village to abandon their old ways and to embrace Ghandi's non-violent movement for Indian independence. There followed *The Serpent and the Rope* (1960), a highly acclaimed semi-autobiographical narrative about the dissolution of a marriage between a Brahmin and his French wife, examining the incompatibilities of East and West figured in the archetypes of the title. Other novels include the light-hearted *The Cat and Shakespeare* (1965), *Comrade Kirilov* (1976), and *The Chessmaster and His Moves* (1978), the first of a projected trilogy, preoccupied with the question of truth, as various people debate philosophical issues. Short stories appear in *The Cow of the Barricades* (1947), about Ghandism in south India, *The Policeman and the Rose* (1978) and *On the Ganga Ghat* (1989). He edited *Changing India* (1939), *Whither India?* (1948) and *Soviet Russia* (1949). One of the most celebrated modern Indian writers, his fiction explores the philosophical significance of India's religions, traditions and values and the contrasts with western societies.

S. Narayan, *Rao: The Man and His Works* (1989).

Raven, Simon (1927–) Born Simon Arthur Noël Raven, in London, England, he studied classics at Cambridge University (MA 1955), and after a period of service with the British army, in 1957 became a writer, critic and dramatist. His first book, *The Feathers of Death* (1959), portrays a homosexual scandal in the army, and since then he has written many more novels, including *Brother Cain* (1959), *Blood of My Bone* (1989), *In the Image of God* (1990) and *Islands of Sorrow* (1994). *The Rich Pay Late* (1964) marked the beginning of the ten-volume 'Alms for Oblivion' series, completed with *The Survivors* (1975). Written in a satiric style reminiscent of Anthony POWELL or Evelyn WAUGH, the series portrayed the English upper-middle class since the Second World War, and focuses upon a luckless anti-hero, Fielding Gray (something of a raffish self-portrait), with various characters involved in funny sexual incidents. A second sequence, 'The First Born of Egypt', which includes *Morning Star* (1984), *The Face of the Waters* (1985) and *The Troubadour* (1992), reaffirmed his reputation for cynical black comedy dealing with traditional subjects like cricket and public schools. He has also written several volumes of

scabrous memoirs in *The Old Gang* (1988), *Bird of Ill Omen* (1989) and *'Is There Anybody There?' Said the Traveller* (1990), a volume of short stories in *Remember Your Grammar* (1997), and numerous radio plays and television work, including the script for *The Palliser* television series (1974).

Rechy, John (1934–) Born in El Paso, Texas, US, of Mexican-American heritage, John Francisco Rechy studied at the University of Texas at El Paso. *City of Night* (1963) was his first novel, a controversial best-seller which traces the journey of a sexual adventurer through the homosexual night-life of suburban America, with its drug addiction, prostitution, and hustlers. The sequel to this was entitled *Numbers* (1967). He creates alternative gay worlds in contrast to 'straight' society, and shows a preoccupation with criminality and violence. Other novels explore form as well as content, and include *This Day's Death* (1969), *The Vampires* (1971), *The Fourth Angel* (1973) and *Rushes* (1979). *The Sexual Outlaw* (1977) documents Hollywood suburban homosexual lifestyles; *Bodies and Souls* (1983) is about three runaways who go to Los Angeles to search for the realisation of their dreams, and experience only isolation and loneliness; *Marilyn's Daughter* (1988) is about Normalyn Morgan, a possible daughter of Marilyn Monroe, searching for the truth about her mother; *The Miraculous Day of Amalia Gomez* (1991) is the tragic life of a Mexican-American woman in Los Angeles; and *Our Lady of Babylon* (1996), set in eighteenth-century Europe, is about a woman's religious fantasies. His latest novel is *The Coming of Night* (1999), another evocation of gay desire just before AIDS, set in one day in Los Angeles in 1981. Often writing novels about finding patterns in life, Chicano culture influences much of his fiction.

Reed, Ishmael (1938–) A widely honoured writer, Ishmael Scott Reed was born in Chattanooga, Tennessee, US, and attended the State University of New York at Buffalo (1956–1960). He has been a long-time resident in Berkeley, California. A founder of the Before Columbus Foundation, which promotes and encourages multicultural American writing, he has persistently focused on the social circumstances that inhibit the development of African-Americans in US society, and he has been very influential as a contemporary African-American writer. His first novel, *The Freelance Pallbearers* (1967), offers a critique of Western/European/Christian traditions, but stirred up controversy for its negative portrayals of African-American figures as well. *Yellow Back Radio Broke-Down* (1969) is the first instance of his influential use of Hoodoo (or Voodoo) methods and folklore, which he argues is based upon the two aspects of syncretism and synchronicity, or combination and temporality. Hoodoo methods are continued in *Mumbo Jumbo* (1972), set in 1920s New Orleans and Harlem, and which seeks to define the origin of an African-American aesthetic in Hoodoo and Egyptian myths, *The Last Days of Louisiana Red* (1974), *Flight to Canada* (1976), and *The Terrible Twos* (1982), a parody of racism and greed in the Reagan era. Following the satiric allegory *Reckless Eyeballing* (1986), he published *The Terrible Threes* (1989), a parody of white supremacism, and *Japanese By Spring* (1993), which satirises the factional struggles of faculty on a fictional Oakland college campus. Poems are collected in *Conjure: Selected Poems* (1972) and *New and Collected Poems* (1988), while non-fiction includes essays and reviews in *Shrovetide in Old New Orleans* (1978), *God Made Alaska for the Indians* (1982), *Writin' is Fightin'* (1988) and *MultiAmerica* (1997). *Airing Dirty Laundry* (1993) confronts the media for its misrepresentations of African-Americans, and *A Reed Reader* (2000) offers a selection of his work. With preposterous plots marked by fantasy and surrealistic elements, much of his fiction makes use of orthographic, stylistic and rhetorical techniques, such as capitalisation for emphasis, as he imaginatively manipulates the language and beliefs of African-American folk culture for the purposes of a black protest literature.

R. Martin, *Ishmael Reed and the New Black Aesthetic Critics* (1987).

Reeman, Douglas Edward (1924–) Born in Thames Ditton, Surrey, England, he joined the Navy during the Second World War, and then worked for the Metropolitan Police until 1950, when he became a children's welfare officer in London until 1960. He began by writing short stories, but turned to adventure novels about the sea and naval battles, with his first novel *A Prayer for the Ship* (1958). He continued to write formulaic historical novels about naval adventures, often set in the Second World War, under his own name, the latest of which are *Battlecruiser* (1997) and *Dust on the Sea* (1999). However, under the pseudonym Alexander Kent, he writes the equally prolific 'Richard Bolitho' series, beginning with *To Glory We Steer* (1968) and continuing through to the most recent, *The Only Victor* (2000), about a popular sea captain in the eighteenth-century British navy, undergoing adventures in the French and American revolutions and the Napoleonic Wars. During the series he moves up the ranks to the position of admiral. The heir to C.S. FORESTER's stories of Horatio Hornblower, these novels are highly researched and realistic in their accounts of sea-life and battles.

Remarque, Erich Maria (1898–1970) Born Erich Maria Remark, in Osnabrück, Germany, he changed his name in 1923. He served in the German army between 1914 and 1918, and then held a variety of jobs. He went to Switzerland in 1931 to escape the Nazis, and after moving to the US in 1939, was naturalised there in 1947. He is principally remembered for his best-selling novel *All Quiet on the Western Front* (trans. 1929), which depicts vividly the lives and deaths of German soldiers during the First World War in the front-line trenches. An indictment of the war's pointlessness and its creation of a 'lost generation', the novel polarised German society in its representation of the soldiers. *The Road Back* (trans. 1931) was a sequel about the no road back for the surviving soldiers, and was followed by many more novels, including perhaps his best in *Arch of Triumph* (trans. 1945), about disruption, as characters survive by hanging on to a shred of their lives, two novels about the Second World War in *The Spark of Life* (trans. 1952) and *A Time to Love and a Time to Die* (trans. 1954), both of which depict the political corruption of Nazism destroying the fabric of society. Other novels are *The Black Obelisk* (1956, trans. 1957), *The Night in Lisbon* (1962, trans. 1964) and *Shadows in Paradise* (1971, trans. 1972), which recounts the shattered illusions of émigrés in the US and their lack of cultural adjustment. He enjoyed a flamboyant lifestyle in exile after the success of his first novel, and his fiction is always dogged by a strain of sentimentality.

R. Firda, *Erich Maria Remarque: A Thematic Analysis of His Novels* (1988).

Rendell, Ruth (1930–) Born in London, England, Ruth Barbara Rendell had an early career as a reporter and sub-editor working on West Sussex newspapers, before becoming a writer. Rendell is a highly acclaimed crime novelist, with over fifty novels and short stories to her name. Her first novel was *From Doom with Death* (1964). Her most successful novels are the 'Wexford' novels, which are police procedural novels set in the Sussex town of Kingsmarkham, depicting the cases of the compassionate and intelligent CID officer, Chief Inspector Reginald Wexford, and his associate Mike Burden. Among these novels are *Some Die and Some Lie* (1973), *A Sleeping Life* (1978), and *The Speaker of Mandarin* (1983), *Simisola* (1994), *Road Rage* (1997), *A Sleeping Life* (1998) and *Harm Done* (1999). They focus on middle-class crimes in southern England, and many of them have been adapted for television. Other novels of a psychological nature include *Demon in My View* (1976), *The Killing Doll* (1984), *The Veiled One* (1988; televised 1989) and *Crocodile Bird* (1993). She also writes thrillers under the pseudonym Barbara Vine, which tend to be dark psychological analyses of the motivations for violent crimes, sexual perversities, extreme fantasy lives and familial conflicts. Many of these thrillers have been televised, including *A Dark-Adapted Eye* (1985), *Fatal Inversion* (1987; televised 1992), *Gallowglass* (1990; televised 1993), *The Brimstone Wedding* (1996), and *Chimney Sweeper's Boy* (1998). *The Grasshopper* (2000) is also written under the name of Barbara Vine. *Piranha to Scurfy* (2000) is a collection of short stories. She has received many awards and accolades during her career, including the Crime Writers Association Cartier Diamond Dagger Award (1991). She also edited *The Reason Why: An Anthology of the Murderous Mind* (1995).

Rhys, Jean (1890–1979) A West Indian novelist, born Ella Gwendolen Rees Williams, in Roseau, Dominica, Windward Islands. After leaving home at 16, she lived in London, and then in Paris. Her earlier works have a strong autobiographical element and are often about bohemian life and women who are badly treated by manipulative men. Her first book was a collection of short stories, *The Left Bank* (1927), followed by the novels *Postures* (1928), *After Leaving Mr McKenzie* (1931), which is about a woman struggling to survive in a patriarchal world, *A Voyage in the Dark* (1934), and

Good Morning Midnight (1939), which displays the characteristics of modernist fiction in its style. Her final and most celebrated novel, written nearly thirty years later, was *Wide Sargasso Sea* (1966), which imagines the early life of Bertha Mason, the mad Creole first wife of Rochester in Charlotte Brontë's *Jane Eyre*, thus juxtaposing the contrasting world-views of Bertha and Rochester. In addition to the short stories in *Sleep It Off Lady* (1976), an unfinished autobiography, *Smile Please* (1979), was published after her death. Her fiction depicts a subtle yet ambiguous understanding of racial politics, and her exploration of colonisation and recolonisation has placed her work at the centre of postcolonial debates about 'English' literary politics.

C. Angier, *Jean Rhys* (1990).

Rice, Anne (1941–) Born in New Orleans, Louisiana, US, she was educated at San Francisco State University (BA 1964, MA 1971), and has since held a variety of jobs. She is perhaps most famous for her 'Vampire Chronicles', beginning with *Interview with the Vampire* (1976, filmed 1994), in which Louis, a vampire, tells a young reporter his life story, and continues with *The Vampire Lestat* (1985), *The Queen of the Damned* (1988), *The Tale of the Body Thief* (1992) and *Memnoch the Devil* (1995). Infused with a new consciousness and perspective, her books display an unusual treatment of vampires. In addition, she has written a series entitled 'Lives of the Mayfair Witches', which consists of *The Witching Hour* (1990), *Lasher* (1993) and *Taltos* (1994), and 'The Sleeping Beauty Novels', three sadomasochistic erotic books, written under the pseudonym A.N. Roquelaure (1983–1985). More contemporary mainstream fiction is written under the pseudonym of Anne Rampling in *Exit to Eden* (1985) and *Belinda* (1986); and under her own name, *The Feast of All Saints* (1980),

a historical novel involving non-whites in nineteenth-century Louisiana, *Cry to Heaven* (1982), about the world of Italian castrati, *The Mummy* (1989) and *Servant of the Bones* (1996). More recent novels include *Violin* (1997), *Pandora* (1998), *Vampire Armand* (1998), and *Vittorio the Vampire* (1999), set in fifteenth-century Italy. *Merrick* (2000) is the seventh volume in her 'Vampire Chronicles'. She adopts different voices to account for what she regards as her divided self, and has gained a cult readership for her inventive stories and intricate plots with their bizarre, supernatural focus.

K. Ramsland, *Prism of the Night: A Biography of Anne Rice* (1991).

Richardson, Dorothy M. (1873–1957) A British writer, born Dorothy Miller Richardson, in Abingdon, Berkshire, she became a governess, and then a journalist, and moved in avant-garde literary circles with such people as John Cowper POWYS H.G. WELLS, and Hilda DOOLITTLE. She was a pioneer of psychological modernist fiction, and, together with James JOYCE, Marcel PROUST and Virginia WOOLF, was one of the first to conceive of and develop the interior monologue and stream-of-consciousness technique to reveal characters' inner reactions to experiences. In her portrayals of women's inner consciousness, she was influenced by the French philosopher Henri Bergson. Her most famous work is the semi-autobiographical thirteen-volume sequence entitled *Pilgrimage*, which presents the consciousness of her alter ego, Miriam Henderson, tracing her search for self-realisation through her relations with other women and writing. Considered one of the most significant novels of the twentieth century, it began with *Pointed Roofs* (1915) and concluded with the posthumous publication of *March Moonlight* (1967). *Pilgrimage* was released in four volumes in 1969, but despite recent feminist interest in her explorations of gender, identity and narrative, she still languishes in a certain degree of obscurity. Other works include *The Quakers Past and Present* (1914) and *John Austen and the Inseparables* (1930), and previously uncollected sketches and prose have been published in *Journey to Paradise* (1989).

E. Bronfen, *Dorothy Richardson's Art of Memory* (1999).

Richler, Mordecai (1931–) A widely honoured Canadian novelist, born in Montreal, and educated at Concordia University, Montreal for two years. He moved to London in 1951, but went back to Canada in 1972. His early novels are *The Acrobats* (1954), *Son of a Smaller Hero* (1955) and *A Choice of Enemies* (1957), which portray young idealistic protagonists disillusioned with the world, exploring crises of ethnic, national and artistic identities. His widely celebrated fourth novel, *The Apprenticeship of Duddy Kravitz* (1959), is an ambivalent portrait of an unreliable young Montreal-Jewish entrepreneur on the make. After a satire of Canadian nationalism in *The Incomparable Atuk* (1963), and *Cocksure* (1968), about amoral London in the 1960s, he attempted more ambitious novels. These are *St. Urbain's Horseman* (1971) and *Joshua Then and Now* (1980), companion works which examine the life of Jake Hersh, a Jewish-Canadian in London and Canada, which is structured in flashbacks; and *Solomon Gursky Was Here* (1989), which explores a financially powerful Jewish-Canadian family and attempts to encompass Canada's history in an epic style of magic realism and self-reflexivity. His most recent novel is *Barney's Version* (1998), a first person narrative about a television producer's life, which attacks Quebecois separatists, rabid feminists and self-deceiving Jews. He has also written film and television scripts for some of his novels, a travel book entitled *Images of Spain* (1977), an autobiographical account of his trip to Israel in *This Year in*

Jerusalem (1994), and journalism, some of which is collec-ted in *Hunting Tigers Under Glass* (1968). *Oh Canada! Oh Quebec!: Requiem for a Divided Country* (1992) is a scathing attack on Quebec separatism.

V. Ramraj, *Mordecai Richler* (1983).

Riley, Joan (1958–) Born in Hopewell, St. Mary, Jamaica, she went to the University of Sussex (BA 1979) and the University of London (MA and M.Sc. 1984). She worked as a drug researcher (1983–1985), and then as a social worker in London. Her first novel was *The Unbecoming* (1985), which centres upon an 11-year-old girl summoned to join her father in the UK, and is a quest for identity amid the city gloom and racial hostility. *Waiting in the Twilight* (1987) is about a woman looking back to the 1950s and 1960s after being crippled by a stroke. Other novels include *Romance* (1988), which deal with two sisters rethinking the orientation of their lives after the visit of their two Jamaican grandmothers, and *A Kindness to the Children* (1992), her most accomplished novel, which deals with different aspects of Caribbean reality and postcolonial politics. Short stories about exile and belonging occur in *Leave to Stay* (1996). Her fiction is noted for its scrupulous realism and her experiences with Caribbean women immigrants to Britain.

Roa Bastos, Augusto (1917–) A widely honoured novelist, Augusto Antonio Roa Bastos was born in Asuncíon, Paraguay. As a teenager, he fought in the Chaco War against Bolivia (1932–1935), and then worked as a bank clerk and on the editorial staff of *El País*. During the Civil War in 1947, he went into exile, living in Buenos Aires and then Toulouse, France, working variously as a writer and a teacher of South American studies at the University of Toulouse. At the end of Stroessner's dictatorship in 1989, he returned to Paraguay, while retaining

French citizenship. He began as a poet, renewing Paraguayan poetry in the 1940s, but turned to fiction in the 1950s. His novels include his first work *Son of Man* (1960, trans. 1965), which is the Paraguayan epic *par excellence*, embracing the nation's history from 1814 to 1935, weaving the dichotomies of freedom and oppression, justice and betrayal into his characters' lives, and embedding them within a 'theology of liberation'. *I the Supreme* (1974, trans. 1986) is his masterpiece, which focuses on the Paraguayan dictator Dr Francia, and is said to be 'compiled' by the author, thus seeming to allow the dictator to speak for himself. Creating broadly humorous works from regional and national crises in Paraguay and his own forty-year exile, he turned to narrative experimentation in his later novels. Widely regarded as one of Latin America's greatest authors, a great amount of his writing remains untranslated into English.

D. Foster, *Augusto Roa Bastos* (1978).

Robbe-Grillet, Alain (1922–) Born in Brest, France, he studied agronomic engineering, and then worked in an agricultural institute in Paris (1945–1950). He became an editor at the Minuit publishing house in the 1950s, and since then has been a writer and lecturer. His early novels, such as *The Erasers* (1953, trans. 1964), *The Voyeur* (1955, trans. 1958), *Jealousy* (1957, trans. 1959) and *In the Labyrinth* (1959, trans. 1960), introduced a new, flat, objective style of writing, largely attending to visual descriptions and eliminating figurative language, which creates a strange fictional instability. Emerging as the acknowledged leader of the French 'new novelists', along with Nathalie SARRAUTE, Claude SIMON and Michel BUTOR, he regarded the novel not as a tool but as a search. Introducing experimental techniques and concentrating upon vision and minute descriptions of matter-of-fact objects, he rejected rea-

lism, and specifically, Jean-Paul SARTRE's politically committed realism. However, with the screenplay for Alain Resnais' film *Last Year at Marienbad* (1961, trans. 1962) and his own film screenplay *The Immortal One* (1963, trans. 1971), he turned to more subjective texts of dream, fantasy and obsession. In later novels, such as *The House of Assignation* (1965, trans. 1966), *Project for a Revolution in New York* (1970, trans. 1972), *Dreams of Young Girls* (trans. 1971), *Belle Captive* (1975, trans. 1995), which takes themes from the surrealist painter Magritte, *Typology of a Phantom City* (1976, trans. 1977), *Recollections of the Golden Triangle* (1978, trans. 1984) and *Djinn* (1981, trans. 1982), he became more playful with language, incorporating repetitive scenes and sadomasochism. His essays in *Towards a New Novel* (1963, trans. 1965), theorised that phenomenology should replace traditional psychology, personality should be more fluid and indefinable, and moral judgements should be avoided in the 'new novel'. In addition to the short stories in *Snapshots* (1962, trans. 1968), he began an autobiographical series, *Ghosts in the Mirror* (1985, trans. 1988), which was something of a volte-face to his earlier claims that life and writing were unconnected. Always confrontational, his fiction poses radical questions about fantasy and anti-representational structures.

R. Ramsay, *Robbe-Grillet and Modernity* (1992).

Robbins, Harold (1916–1997) Born Francis Kane, in New York City, US, and raised as an orphan in the Hell's Kitchen area of the city, he worked for Universal Pictures in New York and eventually became part of the senior management. He is known for his best-selling novels, with sales in the billions, of which many have been screened or adapted for television. A typical Robbins' novel is long, intricately plotted, and usually includes illicit sex, graphic violence and powerful conflicts between members of the international jet-set. Often these take the form of exposés of a glamorous or respected business or industry to reveal secret behind-the-scenes corruption. Robbins has discerned two types of plot in his work: the adventure novel, about the power machinations of influential men, and the Depression novel, about tough kids fighting their way out of slums to success, power and wealth. His first novel, *Never Love a Stranger* (1948), was an example of the latter: partly autobiographical, it is about a tough New York orphan who comes of age and becomes very successful. Other popular novels include *A Stone for Danny Fisher* (1952), about a poor New York Jewish boy's struggle to succeed in the 1930s and 1940s, *79 Park Avenue* (1953), *The Carpetbaggers* (1961) and its sequel, *The Raiders* (1994), *The Adventurers* (1966), *Dreams Die First* (1977), and *The Betsy* (1985), an exposé of the movie industry and its sequel, *The Stallion* (1996). Although his novels are usually adept, fast-paced narratives, he has nevertheless been accused of superficiality and for creating clichés, and shallow stereotypes.

Robbins, Tom (1936–) Born Tom Thomas Eugene Robbins, in Blowing Rock, North Carolina, US, he attended Washington and Lee University (1950–1952), before working as a journalist on the West Coast. His first novel was *Another Roadside Attraction* (1971), in which plot is secondary to his eccentric and outlandish characters. *Even Cowgirls Get the Blues* (1976, filmed 1994), is his best-known novel, about Sissy Hankshaw and her extraordinary hitchhiking abilities due to her enormous thumbs, and her adventures with the Rubber Rose Ranch cowgirl community. Fame came when these two early novels were released as paperbacks in the mid-1970s, elevating him to cult status among a young readership. He tapped into the California counter-cul-

ture, along with the 'West Coast' school of writers like Ken KESEY and Richard BRAUTIGAN, whose fictional characteristics are a search for personal integrity, an interest in higher states of being rooted in Eastern mysticism, and escape from the confinements of suburban California. *Still Life with Woodpecker* (1980), which is a romance between a princess and an outlaw, was followed by *Jitterbug Perfume* (1984), about a waitress devoted to the development of the ultimate perfume, and *Skinny Legs and All* (1990), set in New York City, about the art world aspirations of Ellen Charles. *Half-asleep in Frog Pyjamas* (1994), about four days in the life of a Seattle stockbroker and introducing a parade of unusual characters, is followed by his latest work, *Fierce Invalids Home from Hot Climates* (2000), about the contradictory and rascally character Switters. Despite having written only a few novels, Robbins has exerted a large influence on the West Coast literary scene, with his linguistic play, puns and black humour.

M. Siegel, *Tom Robbins* (1980).

Rolland, Romain (1866–1944) Born Romain Edme Paul-Émil Rolland, in Clamency, France, he was an educator, musicologist, biographer, novelist and essayist. He is best remembered for his ten-volume novel cycle, *Jean-Cristoph* (1903–1912, trans. 1910–1913), which depicts the life of a romantic, courageous, simple German musician who moves to France and attempts to reconcile his background with his adopted culture. *Above the Battlefield* (1915, trans. 1916) was a collection of his articles opposing the First World War aggression between Germany and France, which made him many enemies. He taught musicology in Paris and wrote several biographies of musicians, artists, and other illustrious men, such as Beethoven, Handel, Michelangelo, Mahatma Ghandi and Tolstoy. Many further works remain untranslated into English.

He was committed to art with a social statement, and his abhorrence of violence spurred him to advocate international understanding, pacifism and socialism. He was awarded the Nobel Prize for Literature in 1915.

F. Harris, *A. Gide and R. Rolland: Two Men Divided* (1973).

Romains, Jules (1885–1972) Born Louis-Henri-Jean Farigoule in Cevannes, France, he changed his name in 1953. He graduated from the École Normale Supérieure (1909), and taught philosophy in France until 1919, when he became a full-time writer. Hugely prolific, he is perhaps most noted for his enormous twenty-seven volume epic of the twentieth century, entitled *The Men of Good Will* (1932–1946, trans. 1933–1946). Intricately designed, it encompasses twenty-five years of western European history, and depicts 400 characters intertwined with the events and times, as the protagonists Jeraphanion and Jallez aspire to change the world in their different ways. Other novels include *The Death of a Nobody* (1911, trans. 1914), *The Boys in the Back Room* (1913, trans. 1937), *Lucienne* (1922, trans. 1925), the three volumes of *The Body's Rapture* (1922–1929, trans. 1933), *The Lord God of Flesh* (1928, trans. 1953), *Tussles with Time* (1951, trans. 1952), *As it Is on Earth* (1954, trans. 1962) and *The Adventuress* (1957, trans. 1958). In addition to a large amount of work untranslated into English, he wrote several plays, including *Donogoo* (1930, trans. 1937). Describing his search for a single, universal spirit as 'Unanimism', he chose exile in the US during the Second World War, where his writing received wide acclaim.

D. Boak, *Jules Romains* (1974).

Rooke, Daphne (1914–) Daphne Marie Rooke, born in Boksburg, South Africa, was a prolific author of novels, written mainly during the 1950s and 1960s. These include *A Grove of Fever Trees* (1950), *Apples in the Hold* (1950), which was written under the pseudonym Robert Pointon, her most famous book entitled *Mittee* (1952), which depicts violence rather than the pastoral in South Africa, as two young women face up to living under apartheid, *Ratoons* (1953), *Wizard's Country* (1957), *Beti* (1959), *A Lover for Estella* (1961), *The Greyling* (1962), *Diamond Jo* (1965), *Boy on the Mountain* (1969), and *Margaretha de la Porte* (1974), the first in a proposed trilogy. In addition to various contributions to anthologies, she has also published children's books. Her fiction offers serious examinations of South Africa's political and social mores, and locates miscegenation in social prejudice and legal statute.

Ross, Sinclair (1908–) A Canadian novelist, born James Sinclair Ross, near Prince Albert, who worked in banking until his retirement in 1968. His first and best-known novel, *As For Me and My House* (1941), was largely ignored upon publication, but it has since become a Canadian classic. Depicting the conflict between the Bentleys and narrow-minded prairie town values, it is a dense and complex novel which typifies the world of limited understanding and communication that permeates his fiction. His other novels are *The Well* (1958), about an escaped convict hiding on a Saskatchewan farm; *Whir of Gold* (1970), about the development of a young struggling musician named Sonny McAlpine; and *Sawbones Memorial* (1974), about four generations and their values in a small prairie community. Short stories are collected in *The Lamp at Noon* (1968) and *The Race* (1982), which display an economy and precision in their representation of the isolation and poverty in 1930s prairie environments. Noted for his metaphoric use of landscape, his stories depict the harsh, impoverished life of prairie farmers and townspeople during the Depression.

L. McMullen, *Sinclair Ross* (1980).

Rossner, Judith (1935–) Born in New York City, US, and educated at the City University of New York, she has written a range of fiction concerning such themes as childbirth, child-rearing, ambition, love and friendship, and the fluctuating roles of women in an era of constantly changing expectations. Her first novel was *To the Precipice* (1966), a coming-of-age novel about a young Jewish woman raised in the 1940s and 1950s in a New York City tenement building and her marriage and social roles. This was followed by *Nine Months in the Lie of an Old Maid* (1969), about a self-absorbed, isolated woman, and *Any Minute I Can Split* (1972), about a woman who leaves her husband and joins a 1960s-style commune, exploring the nature of the family and its alternative modes. *Looking for Mr. Goodbar* (1975, filmed 1997) brought her wide popular acclaim, and is based on the true story of a murderer of a teacher who haunts singles bars. *Attachments* (1977) explores the tensions and conflicts of two friends married to a pair of Siamese twins, and was followed by several novels about women caught in dramatic circumstances, reflecting the conflicts of their gender and era: *Emmeline* (1980), set in the 1880s, and about the tragic consequences of a 13-year-old who is seduced in the Massachusetts cotton mills; *August* (1983), about psychoanalysis; *His Little Women* (1990), concerning an absent father and his daughters and the trials and tribulations of domestic affairs; and more recently, *Olivia, or, the Weight of the Past* (1994), about a mother and daughter relationship in New York.

Rosten, Leo C. (1908–1997) Born Leo Calvin Rosten, in Lodz, Poland, he was educated at the University of Chicago (Ph.D. 1937), and held a variety of jobs teaching political science, working in the motion picture business and editorial work. He is best known for creating the character Hyman Kaplan, an immigrant whose fractured attempts to learn English at the Night Preparatory School for Adults, are the basis of many comic stories which play upon words, puns, dialect and linguistic illogic. Under the pseudonym Leonard Ross, he wrote *The Education of H*Y*M*A*N K*A*P*L*A*N* (1937), which was continued, under his own name, with the sequel *The Return of H*Y*M*A*N K*A*P*L*A*N* (1959) and *O K*A*P*L*A*N, My K*A*P*L*A*N* (1976). Amid a wide variety of other writing, he has written a study of journalism in *The Washington Correspondents* (1937), a sociological study of the movie industry in *Hollywood: The Movie Colony, the Movie Makers* (1941), edited *A Guide to the Religions of America* (1955), and written several comic books about language, including *The Joys of Yiddish* (1968), *Rome Wasn't Burned in a Day* (1972) and *The Joys of Yinglish* (1989). Stories are collected in *The Many Worlds of L*E*O R*O*S*T*E*N* (1964), and there are several novels, including a witty story about an army psychiatrist in *Captain Newman, M.D.* (1961), a spy story in *A Most Private Intrigue* (1967), and the detective stories involving much Yiddish, *Silky!* (1979) and *King Silky!* (1980). A writer of versatile talent, essays occur in *Passions and Prejudices* (1978) and travel reminiscences in *The 3:10 to Anywhere* (1976).

Roth, Henry (1906–1995) Born in Tysmenica, Austria-Hungary, he was brought to the US at 18 months old and grew up on the Lower East Side in New York City. Educated at the City University of New York (BS 1928), he worked for the Works Progress Administration in 1939, as well as teaching and metal grinding over the years. *Call It Sleep* (1934) received laudatory reviews on publication, but it soon went out of print; it was reprinted in the late 1950s and became a popular success in the 1960s. Regarded as the best of the American Jewish ghetto novels, it involves a young Jewish boy growing up in New

York's Lower East Side before the First World War, and concerns his development, political activism and the domestic milieu of the Jewish immigrant community. Broken only by the memoir *Nature's First Green* (1979), sixty years of silence occurred before his next fiction in *Shifting Landscapes: A Composite 1925–1987* (1987), which is short stories written since 1934. This was shortly followed by his highly praised and much-awaited autobiographical sequence, *Mercy of a Rude Storm*, comprising *A Star Shines Over Mt. Morris Peak* (1994), about the boyhood years of Ira Stigman who withdraws into the world of literature, *A Diving Rock on the Hudson* (1995), in which Stigman is expelled from school and goes through adolescent crises before turning to writing, and *From Bondage* (1996), about his college years and sexual relationships.

B. Lyons, *Henry Roth: The Man and His Work* (1977).

Roth, Joseph (1894–1939) Born in Brody, Austria (now the Ukraine), he went to the University of Lemberg, Vienna (1914–1916), and served in the Austrian army during the First World War. He worked as a journalist (1919–1928), before fleeing to Paris in 1933 to escape the Nazis. He had a stellar literary career in the interwar years, with the novels *Hotel Savoy* (1924, trans. 1986), which is a sketch of displaced war veterans in Poland, *Right and Left* (1929, trans. 1991), *The Radetzky March* (1932, trans. 1933), which is an epic saga of generations, spanning the years 1859 to 1914, *The Ballad of a Hundred Days* (trans. 1936), which uses the story of Napoleon Bonaparte to assess events in Roth's Austria, *Weights and Measures* (1937, trans. 1982), and *The Emperor's Tomb* (1938, trans. 1984), a monumental novel which explores the psychological collapse of a First World War veteran of Slovenian descent and the social deterioration of the Habsburg em-

pire. Much of his fiction reflects the fragmentation of Austrian and Jewish identity as a result of the escalating anti-Semitism at the end of the nineteenth century. Although he rejected Zionism and Jewish orthodoxy, he actively opposed all forms of anti-Semitism, and some of his novels specifically deal with Jewish culture, like *Job* (1930, trans. 1931), *Tarabas* (1934, trans. 1987) and *The Legend of the Holy Drinker* (1939, trans. 1989). Posthumous publications include *The Silent Prophet* (1966, trans. 1979) and *The Spider's Web* (1967, trans. 1988), a novel about the collapse of social hierarchy and the moral system in post-First World War Austria, providing the breeding ground for National Socialism. He believed in the resurrection of the Danube monarchy as a means of protecting the minorities against Nazism.

C. Mathew, *Ambivalence and Irony in the Works of Joseph Roth* (1984).

Roth, Philip (1933–) Born in Newark, New Jersey, US, Philip Milton Roth was educated at Bucknell (BA 1954) and Chicago (MA 1955) universities, since which time he has been an instructor at the universities of Chicago, Iowa, SUNY at Stony Brook, and CUNY. Often compared to such Jewish American writers as Bernard MALAMUD and Saul BELLOW, he is one of the leading American twentieth-century writers, with careful and biting satires of American society. His first book, *Goodbye Columbus, and Five Short Stories* (1959), was an immediate success, utilising his childhood memories of being in a first generation Jewish community. *Letting Go* (1962) and *When She Was Good* (1967) emerged before his famous *Portnoy's Complaint* (1969, filmed 1972), a wildly comic yet controversial novel, which dealt with conflict and repression in young Jewish Alex Portnoy's obsession with Gentile girls and his war with his overbearing mother. Descriptions of sexual activity and Portnoy's frequent mas-

Roussel, Raymond   Rubens, Bernice

turbation to alleviate his frustration, made the book into a scandalous sensation. Other novels include *Our Gang* (1971), which satirises the Nixon administration, *The Breast* (1972), which is a Kafkaesque tale of transformation, about a man turned into a six-foot breast, *The Great American Novel* (1973), which is a burlesque and allegory of American political events set in the environment of a baseball league, and *The Professor of Desire* (1977), which is about a romance involving the professor who was the subject of *The Breast*. Roth is also known for the semi-autobiographical Nathan Zuckerman novels: *The Ghost Writer* (1979), opening in the 1950s, with the life and fantasies of Nathan Zuckerman, a struggling writer in Newark; *Zuckerman Unbound* (1981), about the writer's later years of fame; and *The Anatomy Lesson* (1983), dealing with themes of art and the artist's life. All three novels are collected in *Zuckerman Bound* (1985), which also includes the epilogue, 'The Prague Orgy', and was continued with *The Counterlife* (1986), a postmodern display in which Zuckerman contrasts his life with that of his brother. Later novels are *Deception* (1990), exploring the relationship of fact and fiction in an ambiguous tale about a Jewish writer's diary; *Operation Shylock: A True Story* (1993), in which a writer called Philip Roth is involved in a complex, self-reflexive narrative of identity, partly set in Israel; *Sabbath's Theater* (1995), about Mickey Sabbath and his course to suicide which he eventually avoids; *American Pastoral* (1997); and *The Human Stain* (2000), an account of an academic scandal over racism in which Zuckerman makes another appearance. Autobiographical memoirs about his childhood, adolescence and the gradual death of his father occur in *The Facts* (1988) and *Patrimony* (1991), with critical essays in *Reading Myself and Others* (1975). Drawing on personal experience for much of his fiction, he has achieved notoriety for blurring fact and fiction, and

yet is a widely honoured novelist of originality and variety.

A. Milbauer and D. Watson, eds, *Reading Philip Roth* (1988).

Roussel, Raymond (1877–1933) Born in Paris, France, he committed suicide in Italy. Convinced he was a genius, he became depressed when his first work, a long book in verse, written when he was 19, failed to earn instant acclaim. His principal works are *Impressions of Africa* (1910, trans. 1966), with a circular narrative structure, and *Locus Solus* (1914, trans. 1970), both prose novels which displayed his fastidious obsession with detail and elaborate textual embeddings and forestallings of sentences by parentheses. Although much admired by the Surrealists and avant-garde artists, and a significant influence on the French 'new novelists', such as Alain ROBBE-GRILLET, he never gained the popular attention he desired.

M. Foucault, *Raymond Roussel* (1963).

Roy, Arundhati (1961–) An Indian writer, born in Bengal, India, raised in Aymanam, Kerala State, and educated at the Delhi School of Architecture. Her only novel to date is the critically acclaimed *The God of Small Things* (1997, Booker Prize), a moving story set in Kerala, involving intra-family jealousies, the divisiveness of caste and the loss of childhood innocence. She has also written *Soviet Intervention in Afghanistan: Causes, Consequences and India's Response* (1987). More recently, she has developed a campaigning journalist career, writing *The End of Imagination* (1998), which deplores India's nuclear tests, and *The Greater Common Good* (1999), which criticises India's dam-building projects, particularly in the Narmada Valley, and both of which are collected in *Cost of Living* (1999).

Rubens, Bernice (1923–) Born in Cardiff, Wales, into a musical Jewish family, Bernice Ruth Rubens graduated from the University of Wales, Cardiff, in English, and after teaching in Birmingham (1948–1949), became a freelance film director and scriptwriter. Her novels include *Set on Edge* (1960), *Madame Sousatzka* (1962, filmed 1988), about a music teacher and a young Jewish boy, *Mate in Three* (1966), and *The Elected Member* (1969, Booker Prize 1970), which explores the link between sanity and madness in the context of Jewish family life and matriarchy. Other novels include *Sunday Best* (1971), *Go Tell the Lemming* (1973), *I Sent a Letter to My Love* (1975), *The Ponsonby Post* (1977), *Spring Sonata* (1979), which deals with child prodigies again, *Birds of Passage* (1981), *Mr Wakefield's Crusade* (1985), about a lonely paranoid middle-aged man who becomes involved in a murder mystery, *Our Father* (1987), *A Solitary Grief* (1991), *Autobiopsy* (1993), and *Yesterday in the Black Lane* (1995), in which a protagonist presents Gothic reflections on her past life and actions. Recent works are *The Waiting Game* (1997), about the goings-on at an old people's home as they wait out their lives, and *I, Dreyfus* (1999), a narrative about betrayal as a headmaster is found guilty of murdering a child. Her fiction draws heavily upon her Jewish background, and examines the ambiguities of identity and sexuality, non-communication between people, and the connections between the changing definitions of sanity and madness, deriving from her documentary films on victims and mental handicap in the 1960s.

Rule, Jane (1931–) Born in Plainfield, New Jersey, US, she studied at Mills College, California (BA 1952), and has worked periodically as a lecturer. She lives in British Columbia, and most of her fiction is set in the Vancouver area. She has established a reputation as a writer on lesbian themes in her novels and stories, and in a major study *Lesbian Images* (1975). Concerned more with local and

regional communities than with landscapes, her fiction usually depicts alienation and expatriation or people forming communities outside conventional family life. Her early fiction includes *Desert of the Heart* (1964, filmed as *Desert Hearts*, 1985), about a lesbian relationship, set in Reno, and written in alternating voices, and *This Is Not For You* (1970), written in the form of a self-justifying letter, and about a woman whose entrapment in conventional attitudes prevents her love for another woman. Her realist writing continually explores women's relationships and their responsibilities and pleasures, in such works as *Against the Season* (1971), *The Young in Another's Arms* (1977), *Memory Board* (1987), and *After the Fire* (1989). One of her better known novels is *Contract with the World* (1980), in which the lives of six Vancouver artists are told in chronological sequence, and which offers an interesting structural form. Short stories and essays occur in *Theme for Diverse Instruments* (1975), *Outlander* (1981), *A Hot-Eyed Moderate* (1985) and *Inland Passage* (1985). Despite being widely read, her unapologetic and clear-eyed depictions of lesbianism as a natural form of human expression and the increasing irrelevance of traditional family life have received little formal or critical attention.

M. Schuster, *Passionate Communities: Reading Lesbian Resistance in Jane Rule's Fiction* (1999).

Rulfo, Juan (1918–1986) Born in Apulco, Mexico, he studied law at university in Mexico City (1934–1935), and worked for the government immigration department (1935–1946), a rubber company (1947–1954), wrote television and screenplays, and then became an academic. He is principally known for his one novel *Pedro Páramo* (1955, trans. 1959), whose main theme is a search for the father. It transformed the Mexican novel in a radical way, including fantastic, surrealistic elements as the story is told by a dead man from his tomb. One of the best-known Mexican novels of the twentieth century, it acts as a deconstruction of political power, and a critique of economic and social reforms by the new bourgeoisie after the Revolution. His other works include the short stories in *The Burning Plain* (1953, trans. 1967), and *Infamundo* (1980, trans. 1983), a series of his photos of Mexico.

L. Leal, *Juan Rulfo* (1983).

Runyon, Damon (1884–1946) Born Alfred Damon Runyon, in Manhattan, Kansas, US, he became a reporter and sportswriter, and one of the most popular columnists of the Jazz Age of the 1920s until the Second World War. His short stories about the life of Broadway in New York, in the first person idiom dubbed 'Runyonese', featured urban colloquialisms and an assortment of comical gamblers and gangland characters, albeit painting a highly romanticised version of their world. The hoodlum heroics of Frank Loesser's Broadway musical 'Guys and Dolls' (1950), later filmed starring Frank Sinatra and Marlon Brando, was based on Runyon's fiction, and derived from a story in the collection *Guys and Dolls* (1931). Other collections include *Blue Plate Special* (1934), *Money from Home* (1935) and *Take It Easy* (1935). *Runyon on Broadway* (1955) is an omnibus edition of his work.

J. Breslin, *Damon Runyon* (1991).

Rushdie, Salman (1947–) A widely honoured novelist, born Ahmed Salman Rushdie, in Bombay, India, he was educated at Cambridge University (MA 1968). He began working in fringe theatre, and became a freelance advertising copywriter in the 1970s. His first novel, *Grimus* (1975), about a man who quests for the meaning of life after the gift of immortality has been bestowed upon him, characteristically combines fable, fantasy and magic realism. His second novel was *Midnight's Children* (1981, Booker Prize), an allegory which chronicles the history of modern India in the lives of 1,001 children born in the first hour of Independence from Britain in 1947. A magic realist fantasy with postmodern reflections upon narrative, history and postcolonial India, it has been unanimously celebrated and was voted the best novel to have received the Booker Prize in the first twenty-five years of the prize's history. There followed *Shame* (1983), a serious-comic novel which explores violence and responsibility set in a fictionalised Pakistan, with his characteristic blend of fantasy and history. *The Satanic Verses* (1988) is a complex narrative which tells stories within stories about the clash of good and evil in a fantastic, allegorical style. It caused a widespread furore: outraged Muslims charged Rushdie with blasphemy for his irreverent use of Islam, and a death sentence, or fatwah, was passed by Ayatollah Khomeini of Iran. The issue has since become a major case of international civil liberties and political concern. Despite having to go into hiding, he continued to write, and *The Moor's Last Sigh* (1995) is a satirical view of India's politics, this time parodying Hindu fundamentalism, and was followed by his recent novel *The Ground Beneath Her Feet* (1999), a love story which reworks the myth of Orpheus in its examination of the East and West. Other works include *The Jaguar Smile* (1987), which is a travel book about Nicaragua, the juvenile stories in *Haroun and the Sea of Stories* (1990), short stories in *East, West* (1994), collected essays in *Imaginary Homelands* (1991), and *The Rushdie Letters* (1993). A writer of considerable stature in the late twentieth century, his fiction frequently deals with pressing issues of cultural mongrelisation and hybridity, and explores the intersection of history, narrative, and national and racial identity in a manner which is both challenging and engaging.

L. Appignanesi and S. Maitland, eds, *The Rushdie File* (1989); C. Cundy, *Salman Rushdie* (1996).

Russ, Joanna (1937–) Born in New York City, US, she was educated at Cornell (BA 1957) and Yale (MFA 1960) universities, after which she became Professor of English at the University of Washington, Seattle (1977–1990). Her science fiction combines a feminist perspective with a sophisticated style, often exploring the oppositions between self and society, and male and female. Her early novels are *Picnic on Paradise* (1968) and *And Chaos Died* (1970), but her most famous work is *The Female Man* (1975). Now a feminist classic, this novel articulated her feminist ideas most completely, depicting four different lives for the female protagonist, each from a different time and place, representing four alternative possibilities for women in society, which all converge on the utopian female planet, Whileaway. This was followed by *Alyx* (1976), *The Two of Them* (1978), *Kittatinny: A Tale of Magic* (1978), *On Strike Against God* (1980), and short stories in *The Zanzibar Cat* (1983) and *The Hidden Side of the Moon* (1988), embracing thirty years of her science fiction. Feminist studies include *We Who Are About to...* (1977), *How to Suppress Women's Writing* (1983) and *What Are We Fighting For?* (1998), while literary criticism includes *To Write Like a Woman: Essays in Feminism and Science Fiction* (1995), covering different genres as well as diverse writers. Seen as a pathfinder for women writers of science fiction, her fiction varies from the experimental to the conventional with equal assurance.

S

Sackville-West, Vita (1892–1962) Full name Victoria Mary Sackville-West, she was born at Knole Castle, Sevenoaks, England, into a socially prominent family. She established herself at the heart of literary circles with her poetry, fiction and plays, and married the politician Harold Nicholson in 1913, with whom she had a long-lasting, albeit unconventional, marriage. Associated with the Bloomsbury set in the 1920s, her lesbian relationship with Virginia WOOLF inspired the eponymous central figure of Woolf's novel *Orlando* (1928). From her first novel *Heritage* (1919), she quickly achieved a reputation for her re-creations of the English aristocratic society at the turn of the twentieth century, as in *The Edwardians* (1930), the best-sellers *All Passion Spent* (1931) and *Family History* (1932), which depict the social dramas of upper-class England, and *No Signposts in the Sea* (1961). Experimental novels, such as *Seducers in Ecuador* (1924), published by the Woolfs' Hogarth Press, also emerged. Short stories appeared in *The Heir* (1922) and *Thirty Clocks Strike the Hour* (1932), while her letters to Virginia Woolf appeared in 1984 and her letters to Harold Nicholson in 1992. She also published numerous volumes of poetry, including the highly praised epic rural poem *The Land* (1927) and *The Garden* (1946), whose pastoral and nature themes were continued in her gardening column for the *Observer* for fifteen years. Indeed, she also wrote many gardening books, designed the famous all-white garden at Sissinghurst Castle, her home, and achieved an international reputation as a landscape designer. She also wrote several biographies, including those of Aphra Behn, Andrew Marvell and Joan of Arc.

V. Glendinning, *Vita: The Life of Vita Sackville-West* (1983).

Sagan, Françoise (1935–) Born Françoise Quoirez, in Cajarc, France, she attended the Sorbonne, University of Paris, and became a writer under her pseudonym. Her prolific output began with her first novel, written when she was just 18, *Bonjour Tristesse* (1954, trans. 1955, filmed 1957), which stunned the world with its bitter-sweet story of a girl, Cecile, who plots to break her father's philandering habit. There followed the novels *A Certain Smile* (trans. 1956), *Those without Shadows* (trans. 1957), *Wonderful Clouds* (trans. 1961), *A Few Hours of Sunlight* (1969, trans. 1971), *Scars on the Soul* (1972, trans. 1974), which intermingles fiction, personal reflection and autobiography, *Lost Profile* (1974, trans. 1976), *Salad Days* (1980, trans. 1984) and *A Reluctant Hero* (1985, trans. 1987). In addition to writing plays and film scripts, her short stories include *Silken Eyes* (1975, trans. 1977) and *Incidental*

Music (1981, trans. 1985). Her autobiographical works include *Toxique* (1964, trans. 1977) and *The Autobiography of Françoise Sagan* (1974, trans. 1979), and she was acclaimed for *Dear Sarah Bernhardt* (1987, trans. 1988). There followed *Painting in Blood* (1987, trans. 1988), *Evasion* (1991, trans. 1993), and *A Fleeting Sorrow* (1994, trans. 1995), a story of a man in his thirties who learns he has terminal cancer. Emerging as a post-war spokesperson for a generation of bored and blasé young adults, her fiction usually depicts a confrontation between the young and old, usually a man and a woman, often in a place frequented by the idle rich, such as Parisian night-clubs. Focusing upon the interrelationships between characters, with an atmosphere of sadness and pessimism reigning over her fiction, she has been plagued by descriptions of her work as superficial and 'pulp fiction'.

J. Miller, *Françoise Sagan* (1988).

Sahgal, Nayantara (1927–) Born Nayantara Pandit Sahgal, in Allahabad, India, she was educated at Wellesley College, Massachusetts (BA 1947), and over the years has worked as a freelance journalist and novelist. Her first novel was *A Time to Be Happy* (1958), about the dawn of Indian independence, while *This Time of Morning* (1965) is set later, when the rosiness of independence has worn off. Other novels include *Storm in Chandigarh* (1969), which deals with the partition of the Punjab on linguistic lines, *The Day in Shadow* (1972), *A Situation in New Delhi* (1977), *Rich Like Us* (1985), which is regarded as her best novel and looks at the social problems in India during the Emergency, *Plans for Departure* (1986), which evokes the Raj, and *Mistaken Identity* (1988). A keen analyst of Indian politics, non-fiction studies include *The Freedom Movement in India* (1970), *A Voice for Freedom* (1977), *Indira Ghandi's Emergence and Style* (1978), *Indira Ghandi: Her Road to Power* (1982) and essays in *Point of View* (1997). She has written two autobiographies in *Prison and Chocolate Cake* (1954) and *From Fear Set Free* (1962) and edited *Sunlight Surround You* (1970). The niece of the renowned Indian politician Jawaharlal Nehru, a political background suffuses her fiction, as she analyses the characters of India's affluent upper classes from an intimate knowledge of the complexities of India's politics.

M. Narendra, *Microcosms of Modern India* (1998).

Saint, Dora Jessie (1913–) Born in Surrey, England, she attended Oxford University (1931–1933), and became a prolific writer of tales of village life in England. She writes under the pseudonym of 'Miss Read', and from her first novel, *Village School* (1955), to *Fairwell to Fairacre* (1993), she has sought to portray the lives of ordinary people in their daily rural activities, centring upon various fictional English villages. Among her characters are Dorothy Watson and Agnes Fogarty, who appear in the Cotswold village of Thrush Green in such novels as *The School at Thrush Green* (1987), and the Howards of Caxley market town, recently collected in the omnibus volume *The Caxley Chronicles* (1999). Resisting the parochial, her work appears simple and light-hearted, although this disguises the extent to which the novels chart the daily negotiation with the pressures of everyday life and history.

Saint-Exupery, Antoine (1900–1944) Born Antoine Jean Baptiste Marie Roger Saint-Exupery, in Lyons, France, he worked as a pilot in the 1920s and 1930s, and became a lecturer and freelance writer in the late 1930s and 1940s in the US. His fiction includes *Southern Mail* (1929, trans. 1933), a semi-autobiographical account of a pilot who finds comfort in duty after a failed romance, and *Night Flight* (1931, trans. 1932), which portrays a director of a postal airline and the hazardous night flights over South America. His essays and non-fiction include *Wind, Sand and Stars* (trans. 1939), an autobiographical account about crashing in the Libyan desert and being rescued by the Bedouin, *Flight to Arras* (trans. 1942), and the posthumously published *The Wisdom of the Sands* (1948, trans. 1950), about a society of desert dwellers and the proclamations of their leader about responsibility and independence, *A Sense of Life* (1956, trans. 1965) and *Wartime Writings 1939–1944* (1982, trans. 1986). Praised for the lyricism with which he evokes the exhilaration of flight, he generally depicts duty and responsibility as a necessary element of love. He was reported missing in action, presumed shot down, while on a reconnaissance flight in southern France in 1944.

R. Rumbold and M. Stewart, *The Winged Life* (1953).

Salinger, J.D. (1919–) Full name Jerome David Salinger, he was born in New York City, US. He attended New York University and Columbia University in 1939, and served with the US army in Europe during the Second World War. He first came to prominence with *The Catcher in the Rye* (1951), about Holden Caulfield's adolescent rebellion against the world of 'phoniness' and conventionality, which has become a modern classic of the teenage rejection of the cultural values of the adult world. Never quite achieving the same level of success again, he published short stories in *Nine Stories* (1953), and the long awaited *Franny and Zooey* (1961), two stories previously published in *The New Yorker*, about crises in the lives of the two youngest members of the Glass family, who lived in New York and were of Jewish and Irish descent. *Raise High the Roof Beam, Carpenters; and Seymour: An Introduction* (1963), were two more stories about the Glass family.

A recluse who lives in New Hampshire, which has made him something of a mysterious figure, he has retired from public and refuses to discuss his work. He was much angered by the unauthorised publication of uncollected short stories in 1974. However, he successfully blocked the publication of an unauthorised biography by Ian Hamilton in 1987, and only after extensive revision was the biography published, entitled *In Search of J.D. Salinger* (1988).

Salkey, Andrew (1928–1995) Born Felix Andrew Alexander Salkey, in Colon, Panama, and raised in Jamaica, he graduated from the University of London (BA 1955), and worked as a BBC broadcaster, teacher, freelance writer and, later, a lecturer at Hampshire College, Amherst, Massachusetts. His fiction was inspired by the folk tales, myths and legends of Jamaica and the Caribbean, and his novels include *A Quality of Violence* (1959), about a violent cult in Jamaica, *Escape to an Autumn Pavement* (1960), *The Shark Hunters* (1966), *The Late Emancipation of Jerry Stover* (1968), *The Adventures of Catullus Kelly* (1969), *Come Home, Malcolm Heartland* (1976), *Danny Jones* (1980), *The River That Disappeared* (1980) and *Joe Tyson* (1991). Much of his fiction examines alienated protagonists who assert themselves through violent confrontations and manoeuvres for power. A contemporary urban version of the folkloric spider-trickster figure appears in the short stories in *Anancy's Score* (1973), *One* (1985), *Anancy Traveller* (1992) and *In the Border Country* (1998), and in addition to volumes of poetry, edited anthologies and children's books, his non-fiction includes *Caribbean Essays* (1973) and travel writing in *Havana Journal* (1971).

Sapper (1888–1937) The pseudonym of Herman Cyril McNeile, an English writer of adventure stories, born in Bodmin, Cornwall, who served in the British Army until 1919. Albeit exciting books, they were xenophobic, chauvinist, racist and sexist: his villains are always 'fiendish' foreigners, 'Dagoes', the 'Boche', the 'Bolshevists', or in fact anyone he perceived to be the enemy of a certain type of Englishman (upper class, rich and idle). His *Bulldog Drummond* (1920) was an immediate success, and was followed by several other Drummond stories, among which are *The Black Gang* (1922), *The Female of the Species* (1928), *The Return of Bulldog Drummond* (1932) and *Bulldog Drummond at Bay* (1935). Among his short stories are *Sergeant Michael Cassidy, R.E.* (1915) and *The Human Touch* (1918).

Saramago, José (1922–) José de Sousa Saramago was born in Azinhaga, Portugal. After leaving school, he worked as a technician, journalist, translator, and later, turned to writing. He joined the banned Communist Party of Portugal in the 1970s, and supported himself mostly by translation works. Since 1979, he has been a prolific writer, publishing plays, short stories, novels, poems, libretti, diaries and travelogues. Written in his late fifties, his first novel was *Manual of Painting and Calligraphy* (1976, trans. 1977), concerning the genesis of the artist and the relationship between life and art, championing creativity over material rewards. He gained an international reputation with his satirical novel *Baltasar and Blimunda* (1982, trans. 1987), set in the first half of the eighteenth century, depicting the conflicting reality of visionaries and the authorities of the Church and monarchy. *The Year of the Death of Ricardo Reis* (1984, trans. 1991), one of his most ambitious novels, set in Lisbon in the 1930s, takes the form of a dialogue between the great Portuguese poet Fernando Pessoa and his alternative fictional personality from his poem collection *Odes de Ricardo Reis* (1946). The symbolic *The Stone Raft* (1986, trans. 1995) tells a story of Portugal's exclusion from

Europe: a series of supernatural events culminates in the severance of the Iberian peninsula so that it starts to float into the Atlantic. His most controversial novel, *The Gospel According to Jesus Christ* (1991, trans. 1994), like KAZANTZÁKIS' *The Last Temptations of Christ*, interprets the key episodes from the Gospels from an untraditional view. In the novel, God and the Devil negotiate about evil, and Jesus questions his role and challenges God. Other works include *Blindness* (1995, trans. 1997), about an epidemic of blindness in a city, the short fable entitled *The Tale of the Unknown Island* (1997, trans. 1999), and *All the Names* (1997, trans. 1999), about an official archivist who reconstructs people's lives from his records. He also wrote *Journey to Portugal* (1985, trans. 2000) and *The History of the Siege of Lisbon* (1989, trans. 1996). His latest novel is *All the Names* (2000). The most distinguished man of letters from Portugal, his panoramic works view European existence within an artistic framework, which melds myth, history, and fiction. He was awarded the Nobel Prize for Literature in 1998, and currently lives in the Canary Islands.

Sargeson, Frank (1903–1982) Born Frank Norris Davey, in Hamilton, New Zealand, he trained as a solicitor. After realising his homosexuality, he dropped out of conventional living, changed his name, and settled in a suburb of Auckland, where he lived for the rest of his life and became a writer. He rejected the New Zealand literary tradition as unrelated to the New Zealand experiences of the Depression in the early 1930s, and focused on language and speech. With vignettes and fables in *Tomorrow* (1935), and a small collection entitled *Conversation with My Uncle* (1936), his early stories were concerned with people on the margins of society, and *A Man and His Wife* (1940) established him as the leading New Zealand fiction writer with an international readership. *That Summer* (1946) recounted the fugitive lives and experiences of homosexuals in the Depression. His first novel was the autobiographical *I Saw in My Dream* (1949), followed by the diary of an unmarried female schoolteacher in *I for One...* (1954), and *Memoirs of a Peon* (1965), a picaresque reminiscence of a wayward youth and a breakthrough novel in terms of its style. There followed *The Hangover* (1967), *Joy of the Worm* (1969), *Man of England Now* (1972) and *Sunset Village* (1976). His *Collected Stories 1935–1963* (1964) and *The Stories of Frank Sargeson* (1973) cemented the vernacular Sargeson of the 1930s and 1940s as the best known to the New Zealand public. Three volumes of autobiography, entitled *Once Is Enough* (1973), *More Than Enough* (1975) and *Never Enough!* (1977), were published in *Sargeson* (1981), a major work about ordering and recreating a life. A mentor to a wide range of younger writers and a major influence in post-war New Zealand literature, his plays of the 1950s, articles and reviews were collected in *Conversation in a Train and Other Critical Writing* (1983).

D. McEldowney, *Frank Sargeson in His Time* (1976).

Saro-Wiwa, Ken (1941–1995) Full name Kenule Beeson Saro-Wiwa, born in Bori, Rivers State, Nigeria, he graduated from the University of Ibadan (BA 1965). He lectured at the University of Lagos (1967–1973), was affiliated to a number of government ministries in the late 1960s and 1970s, and then managed the Saros publishing company. As well as writing radio plays and poetry, his novels are *Sozaboy* (1985), often considered his best work, which describes the hardships and futility of the Nigerian civil war, and *Prisoners of Jebs* (1988), a satirical farce set on an island prison full of intellectuals and leaders from all over Africa, which leads to a commentary on the political and social manoeuvrings of the continent.

Short stories appear in *A Forest of Flowers* (1986), *Adaku* (1989) and *The Singing Anthill* (1991), which is a collection of Ogani folk tales. He became well known for his 'The Adventures of Mr. B' series, which includes eleven books about Basi (1987–1992), satirising Nigerian life. His non-fiction documents the Nigerian civil war in *On a Darkling Plain* (1989), and also his increasing concern for the Ogani people, who suffered the oppression of the rest of Nigeria and multinational oil companies as they sought to extract the oil lying under the tribal lands, in *Similia* (1991) and *Nigeria: The Brink of Disaster* (1991). His political activism on their behalf led to imprisonment and eventual execution by the military regime, causing an international outcry. His period of detention is described in the posthumously published diary smuggled out of Nigeria, *A Month and a Day* (1995).

Sarraute, Nathalie (1900–1999) Born in Ivanovo, Russia, she graduated from the Sorbonne, University of Paris (1925), and after additional study at Oxford and Berlin, worked as a barrister (1926–1932). Her early novels include *Tropisms* (1939, trans. 1967), and *Portrait of a Man Unknown* (1948, trans. 1958), in which a nameless narrator speaks, dreams or reflects upon a father and daughter couple with whom he is obsessed. However, attention only came in the 1950s and 1960s, when she emerged as one of the outstanding practitioners and theorists of the French 'new novel', along with SIMON, BUTOR and ROBBE-GRILLET. *Martereau* (1953, trans. 1959), which is a complex narrative using pronouns rather than characters' names, *The Planetarium* (1959, trans. 1960), written in free indirect discourse, *The Golden Fruits* (1963, trans. 1964), *Between Life and Death* (1968, trans. 1969) and *Do You Hear Them?* (1972, trans. 1973), all demonstrate the self-examining features of the 'new novel', with their complex studies of human interaction that question the traditional aspects of plot and character. Other novels, such as *Fools Say* (1976, trans. 1977), the sketches in *The Use of Speech* (1980, trans. 1983), *You Don't Love Yourself* (trans. 1990) and *Here* (1995, trans. 1997), push fiction to its limit and explore self and identity. In addition to a few plays and the autobiographical work *Childhood* (1983, trans. 1984), she wrote literary essays, collected in *The Age of Suspicion* (1956, trans. 1963), which develop many of her theories of fiction. Her innovative writing constantly tries to apprehend the psychological reality beneath the surface of daily events.

B. Knapp, *Nathalie Sarraute* (1994).

Sarton, May (1912–1995) Born Eleanor May Sarton, in Wondelgem, Belgium, she became a US citizen in 1924, and from 1937 held various posts at universities in creative writing. She published many volumes of poetry, from the meditative *Encounter in April* (1937) to the lyrical *Coming Into Eighty* (1994), as well as a *Collected Poems: 1930–1993* (1993). She also wrote many works of fiction, beginning with *The Single Hound* (1938), a tale of two poets, and followed with twenty-one novels. Exploring such issues as human qualities, feminism and sexuality, her novels include *The Bridge of Years* (1946), about a Belgian family resisting fascism, *Faithful Are the Wounds* (1955), about the suicide of an eminent Harvard scholar during McCarthyism, *The Birth of a Grandfather* (1957), about coming to terms with middle age, *The Small Room* (1961), about women at a New England college, and *Mrs Stevens Hears the Mermaids Singing* (1965). Among several volumes of autobiography is *I Knew a Phoenix* (1959), which tells of her meeting with Virginia WOOLF and her friendship with Elizabeth BOWEN, and many volumes of journals were published be-

tween 1973 and 1996, which deal with old age, friends and self-reflections.

M. Peters, *May Sarton: A Biography* (1997).

Sartre, Jean-Paul (1905–1980) Born in Paris, France, he graduated in philosophy from the École Normale Supérieure (1930), and became a professor of philosophy at various institutions in the 1930s and 1940s. A prisoner of war between 1940 and 1941, upon his release he joined the Resistance, and wrote for underground newspapers like *Combat*. In 1944, he founded *Les Temps Modernes* with his lifelong companion Simone de BEAUVOIR. A widely honoured writer and philosopher, he is principally associated with the development of French Existentialism during the 1940s, which stressed the primacy of the thinking person and of concrete individual experience as the source of knowledge, and analysed human anguish and solitude in making choices. Associated with CAMUS and the French philosopher Maurice Merleau-Ponty, his existential ideas are put forth in his major philosophical works, such as *Being and Nothingness* (1943, trans. 1956), *Existentialism and Humanism* (1946, trans. 1948), *Critique of Dialectical Reason* (1960, trans. 1976) and *Between Existentialism and Marxism* (1962, trans. 1974). One of the major intellectuals of the twentieth century and a huge influence in France, he was a prolific writer. His novels frequently use fiction as a critical tool for his philosophical ideas. These include *Nausea* (1938, trans. 1949), in which the hero's discovery of the absurdity of life and feelings of repulsion are allayed through aesthetic creation, and 'The Roads of Freedom' series: *The Age of Reason* (1945, trans. 1947), *The Reprieve* (1945, trans. 1947), and *Iron in the Soul* (1949, trans. 1950). Written with simultaneous plots and jumping narrative threads, this trilogy deals with an ineffectual protagonist before the war in France, and the ordeals and events demonstrate how inauthentic French life had been. Other writing includes the short story collections *The Wall* (1939, trans. 1948) and *Intimacy* (trans. 1956), and a large number of successful plays, such as *The Flies* (1942, trans. 1947), *No Exit* (1944, trans. 1946), *The Devil and the Good Lord* (1951, trans. 1953) and *The Condemned of Altona* (1959, trans. 1961). His literary criticism includes such well-known works as *What Is Literature?* (trans. 1949), an analysis of Jean GENET in *Saint Genet: Actor and Martyr* (1952, trans. 1963), and psychological studies of Baudelaire and Flaubert. Essays occur in *Portrait of an Anti-Semite* (1946, trans. 1948), *Literary Essays* (trans. 1957), and autobiographical works in *Sartre by Himself* (1959, trans. 1978) and *Words* (1963, trans. 1964), with *The War Diaries of Jean-Paul Sartre* translated in 1985. He held strong political views, and strongly opposed western capitalism, although he also criticised the USSR over the invasions of Hungary and Czechoslovakia. He refused the Nobel Prize for Literature in 1964, claiming that this was merely middle-class recognition.

P. Caws, *Sartre* (1979); C. Howells, *Sartre: The Necessity of Freedom* (1988).

Sciascia, Leonardo (1921–1981) Born in Racalmuto, Sicily, Italy, he worked as a functionary in the Fascist party, requisitioning farm produce, before becoming a schoolteacher in Palermo (1949–1968). He turned to writing in 1968, and was considered one of the finest Italian novelists of his day. He wrote mainly about the Sicilian people and their culture, although his wider project makes the sad corruption of Sicily, ruled by the Mafia, a microcosm for the larger world's problems. His fiction includes *Salt in the Wound* (1956, trans. 1969), which is fictional essays constituting a social biography of an imaginary Sicilian town, *Sicilian Uncles* (1958, trans. 1986), *Mafia*

Vendetta (1961, trans. 1963), which in long sequences of dialogue narrates a policeman's efforts to solve a murder, *The Council of Egypt* (1963, trans. 1966), which raises questions about the reliability of written history, *To Each His Own* (1966, trans. 1989), concerning a professor's attempt to solve the murder of his friend, and *One Way or Another* (1974, trans. 1977), which deals with an investigation of a mysterious sign on a road. Other works include *Candido; or, a Dream Dreamed in Sicily* (1977, trans. 1979), *The Day of the Owl and Equal Danger* (trans. 1983) and *1912 + 1* (trans. 1987). Developing an anti-detective novel, which reshapes the genre with metaphysical questions, his innovations have earned him the description of a postmodernist. Much of his work remains untranslated into English.

S. Tani, *The Doomed Detective* (1984).

Scott, Paul (1920–1978) Born in Palmers Green, England, Paul Mark Scott served with the British army in India and Malaya during the Second World War, after which he worked in publishing and with a literary agency, and turned to freelance writing in 1960. Many of his novels are based upon his knowledge of India, beginning with his first, *Johnnie Sahib* (1952), a war novel concerning the personnel of an air supply unit. He is most famous for his complex and exhaustive fictional survey of India under British colonial rule in *The Raj Quartet* (1976), consisting of *The Jewel in the Crown* (1966), *The Day of the Scorpion* (1968), *The Towers of Silence* (1971) and *A Division of the Spoils* (1975), which vividly chronicles the decline of the British occupation of India in a fragmentary narrative form. Other novels include *The Alien Sky* (1953), *A Male Child* (1956), *The Mark of the Warrior* (1958), *The Chinese Love Pavilion* (1960), *The Birds of Paradise* (1962), *The Corrida of San Feliu* (1964), which is set in Spain, and *Staying On* (1977, Booker Prize), a coda to the quartet with its poignant evocation of the aftermath of Indian independence. He also wrote *The Making of 'The Jewel in the Crown'* (1983) and *On Writing and the Novel* (1987), and several radio and television plays. Critical acclaim came late, partly due to the slow pace of his novels with their gradual accumulation of detail.

Selby, Jr., Hubert (1928–) Born in Brooklyn, New York, US, he dropped out of school and signed on with the US Merchant Marine Service until 1946, but was invalided out with tuberculosis, during which time he developed an addiction to morphine. After recovery, he served as an insurance analyst from 1950 to 1964. Meanwhile, encouraged by his childhood friend Gilbert SORRENTINO, he began to read, observe and write, and his stories started to appear in magazines like *Kulchur*. His first work is his best-known and most controversial book, the stories depicting the horrors of a loveless world in *Last Exit to Brooklyn* (1964, filmed 1989). It explores the world of drugs, prostitutes and criminals in graphic detail, and was banned in several European countries for what was regarded as its pornographic content. This was followed by *The Room* (1971), a violent stream of consciousness from an incarcerated criminal about revenge on the system, and *The Demon* (1976), about a young businessman's dark consciousness and sexual impulses. *Requiem for a Dream* (1979) is about heroin addiction and people frustrated in their dreams, and *The Willow Tree* (1998) is about an African-American teenager whose psychological wounds are healed through a friendship with a Holocaust survivor. *Song of the Silent Snow* (1986) is a collection of short stories. In 1987, he began to perform spoken shows in Los Angeles to wide popularity. Brutality, shock and alienation characterise all of Selby's work, as he explores the American psyche in a frank writing style.

Self, Will (1961–) Born in London, England, he graduated from Oxford University (MA 1982), and after work as a clerk and a labourer, became a journalist and writer. He produced the cartoon series 'Slump' in *The New Statesman* in the 1980s. His short stories occur in *The Quantity Theory of Insanity* (1991), the two linked novellas in *Cock and Bull* (1992), in which two characters metamorphose into the other sex in a surreal exploration of gender, *Grey Area* (1994) and *Tough, Tough Toys for Tough, Tough Boys* (1998). His novels are *My Idea of Fun* (1993), which explores madness and sexual confusion with deliberately shocking images, *The Sweet Smell of Psychosis* (1996), *Great Apes* (1997), about the metamorphosis of a man's girlfriend into a chimpanzee, and *How the Dead Live* (2000), about a woman's thoughts as she dies of cancer in a London hospital. *Junk Mail* (1995) is a collection of his writings, cartoons and essays. Characterised by black humour and uncompromising themes, such as madness, altered states, and the sinister authority of psychiatric institutions, his writing has been praised for its clever use of language and its persistently macabre tone.

Selvon, Sam (1923–1994) Born Samuel Dickson Selvon, in Trinidad, West Indies, he was a journalist in the 1940s, and emigrated to England in 1950, where he worked for the BBC. After a brief spell as a civil servant, he became a freelance writer in the 1950s, and later naturalised as a Canadian citizen in the 1970s. His first novel, *A Brighter Sun* (1952), received considerable acclaim, and dealt with a rural Indian couple in Trinidad who grow together during the aftermath of the Second World War. This was followed by *An Island Is a World* (1955), *The Lonely Londoners* (1956), an ironic and comic depiction of the culture clash, poverty and racism experienced by West Indian immigrants to London in the post-Second World War years, *Turn Again*

Tiger (1958), *I Hear Thunder* (1962), which looked at the native educated bourgeoisie in Trinidad and interracial marriage, *The Housing Lark* (1965), about white prejudice and exploitation in Trinidad, *The Plains of Caroni* (1970) and *Those Who Eat the Cascadura* (1972). More recent novels include *Moses Ascending* (1975) and *Moses Migrating* (1983), continuing the narration of *The Lonely Londoners*. In addition to writing a large number of radio plays, short stories occur in *Ways of Sunlight* (1957) and *Foreday Morning* (1989). With a refreshing voice and a keen ear for everyday speech, much of his fiction seeks to capture changing cultures, evoking life in the Caribbean and exploring the ramifications of colonialism and the racial tensions between Africans and Indians in the West Indies.

S. Nasta, *Critical Perspectives on Sam Selvon* (1989).

Seth, Vikram (1952–) A widely honoured writer, he was born in Calcutta, India and went to Oxford University (MA 1978), Stanford University (MA 1977), and later studied at Nanjing University, China (1982). After working as an editor for Stanford University Press (1985–1986), he became a poet, travel writer and novelist. Early volumes of poetry include *Mappings* (1980) and *The Humble Administrator's Garden* (1985), and a novel in verse entitled *The Golden Gate* (1986). Hailed as a *tour de force*, it contains nearly 600 sonnets, set in San Francisco and involving the lives of urban yuppies, in an attempt to revitalise traditional narrative poetic forms. Other poetry includes *All You Who Sleep Tonight* (1990), verse fables in *Beastly Tales from Here and There* (1992) and translations of Wang Wei, Li Bai and Du Fu in *Three Chinese Poets* (1992). His *magnum opus* is his novel *A Suitable Boy* (1993), an epic which tells the story of an upper-class Indian woman rebelling against an arranged marriage to 'a suitable boy'. Ex-

ploring the traditional customs of Indian society, the plot focuses on four families in the 1950s and postcolonial India and its troubles. His other works include *From Heaven Lake* (1983), an account of his hitchhiking adventure from Nanjing University back to India, and an opera and play *Arion and the Dolphin* (1994). He has achieved something of a literary 'pop star' status, and his latest novel is *An Equal Music* (1999), a story of lost love set in the world of classical music performance.

Shadbolt, Maurice (1932–) Born in Auckland, New Zealand, he was educated at the University of Auckland, and then turned to journalism, scriptwriting and documentary-making. After spending a brief time in Europe, he published short stories about contemporary New Zealand in *The New Zealanders* (1959) and *Summer Fires and Winter Country* (1963). *Among the Cinders* (1965) was his first novel, and was followed by *The Presence of Music* (1967), *This Summer Dolphin* (1969), *An Ear of the Dragon* (1971), *Strangers and Journeys* (1972) and *A Touch of Clay* (1974), many of which are about New Zealanders coming to terms with modern New Zealand. Writing in distinction to Frank SARGESON's work, in turning away from the Depression and examining contemporary New Zealand, his books between 1965 and 1976 attempt to deal with the new interest and change in Pacific culture and politics. Later novels include *Danger Zone* (1975), about French nuclear testing, *The Lovelock Version* (1980), which is an encyclopaedic account of New Zealand myths and motifs, *Season of the Jew* (1986), the acclaimed historical novels *Monday's Warriors* (1990) and *The House of Strife* (1993), and *Dove on the Waters* (1996), which is a story of relationships between an unlikely threesome. His revisionist accounts of history depict a New Zealand in which the Maoris have been defeated by European victors who are not portrayed as champions of 'culture' or 'progress'. Autobiography and memoir appear in *One of Ben's: A New Zealand Medley* (1993) and *From the Edge of the Sky* (1999), while short stories occur in *The Short Stories of Maurice Shadbolt* (1998).

Sharpe, Tom (1928–) Born Thomas Ridley Sharpe, in London, England, he was educated at Cambridge University (MA 1951), and worked as a teacher and photographer in South Africa (1951–1961). He was a history lecturer at Cambridge College of Arts and Technology (1963–1971), before turning to writing in 1971. His first two novels, *Riotous Assembly* (1971) and *Indecent Exposure* (1973), dealt with his experiences and observations of the callousness and stupidities of apartheid South Africa. Although an outstanding satirist, he never quite attained the same degree of farce as these first two books. Thereafter, he published a large number of satires of contemporary British life: of academia in *Porterhouse Blue* (1974), and its sequel *Grandchester Grind* (1995), *Wilt* (1976), *Vintage Stuff* (1982) and *Wilt on High* (1984); and of bureaucrats and other authority figures in *Blott on the Landscape* (1975), *The Throwback* (1977) and *The Wilt Alternative* (1979). Other satirical novels include *The Great Pursuit* (1977), which assaults the publishing world, *Ancestral Vices* (1980), which depicts the excesses of the English upper classes, and *The Midden* (1996), a farce about a British rural family and the Lloyd's of London fiasco. His books contain biting caricatures, which are comically vulgar and gruesome, and are often aimed at the petty illusions of social progress. Several of his novels have been made into successful films and television series.

Shaw, Irwin (1913–1984) A prolific American playwright, author and screenwriter, he was born in Brooklyn, New York, studied at Brooklyn College (BA 1934), and, at the age of 21, began to write the popular *Andy Gump* and *Dick Tracy* radio shows. He wrote many plays, including the pacifist play *Bury the Dead* (1935), *Retreat to Pleasure* (1940) and *Sons and Soldiers* (1944). His first screenplay was *The Big Game* (1936), and he continued to write short stories for *The New Yorker* and *Esquire* throughout the late 1930s, which were praised for their characterisation, plotting and ease of narration. His experiences during the Second World War led to the best-selling *The Young Lions* (1948), an epic, ambitious novel about the ethical and military consequences of a German's and two Allied soldiers' actions in wartime. Thereafter, he devoted most of his time to writing novels, including *The Troubled Air* (1951), about radio actors harried in the anti-communist witch-hunts, *Lucy Crown* (1956), the romance of a middle-aged woman, *Tip on a Dead Jockey* (1957), the popular *Two Weeks in Another Town* (1960), *Voices of a Summer Day* (1965), *Evening in Byzantium* (1973), about a young Hollywood producer, *Nightwork* (1975) about a confidence man, *The Top of the Hill* (1979) and *Bread Upon the Waters* (1981). *Rich Man, Poor Man* (1970), perhaps his most successful novel, was turned into a television mini-series, and was followed by the sequel *Beggarman, Thief* (1977). In addition, he published the essays in *Paris, Paris!* (1977) and short stories in *Mixed Company* (1950) and *Stories of Five Decades* (1982).

Shields, Carol (1935–) Born in Oak Park, Illinois, US, she was educated at Hanover College (BA 1957) and the University of Ottawa (MA 1975), since when she has been a freelance writer, and from 1980, a lecturer at the University of Manitoba. Although she has written poetry and criticism, she is best known for her fiction. Her early novels, such as *Small Ceremonies* (1976), *The Box Garden*

(1977), *Happenstance* (1980) and *A Fairly Conventional Woman* (1982), are portrayals of everyday life, in which the protagonists struggle to define themselves and make human connections in their relationships. With the mystery *Mary Swann* (1987), she began to experiment with different voices, and explored art, creation, textuality and language in a postmodernist style. This continued in *Swann* (1989), *Departures and Arrivals* (1990), *A Celibate Season* (1991), the romance novel *The Republic of Love* (1992), and *The Stone Diaries* (1993, Pulitzer Prize 1995), which was published to overwhelming acclaim, and is a fictional biography of Daisy Goodwill since her birth in 1905, exploring loneliness, banality, inner and outer selves, and the relations between fiction and biography. Her most recent novel is *Larry's Party* (1997): set in Winnipeg, in the 1970s, it is about an ordinary guy who becomes a builder of mazes, and culminates in a dinner party. Short stories appear in *Various Miracles* (1985), *The Orange Fish* (1989) and *Dressing Up for the Carnival* (2000). Her critical acclaim mostly came when she began to experiment with form. She is now a leading novelist in Canada with an international reputation, and is frequently compared to MUNRO and ATWOOD.

Sholokov, Mikhail (1905–1984) Born in Kruzhlino, Russia, the region of the Cossacks, Mikhail Aleksandrovich Sholokov worked in a variety of jobs – as a teacher, a musician, and as a war correspondent during the Second World War. A prolific writer, he is primarily known for his epic series of narratives about life in a Cossack village from 1912 to 1922, consisting of the short stories in *Tales from the Don* (1926, trans. 1961), and the novels *And Quiet Flows the Don* (1928–1932, trans. 1934) and *Harvest on the Don* (1955, trans. 1960). Focusing upon the power and resilience of human love under adversity, this became the most widely read work of Soviet fiction. *Seeds of Tomorrow* (1932, trans. 1935) explores the Soviet collectivisation of agriculture, while other works are *Hate* (trans. 1942), *The Fate of a Man* (1943, trans. 1957), and the short stories in *One Man's Destiny* (1965, trans. 1967), *Early Stories* (trans. 1966), *Fierce and Gentle Warriors* (trans. 1967) and *At the Bidding of the Heart* (1970, trans. 1973). Awarded many prizes in the USSR, he has been accused by some as an apologist for the Soviet Communist Party and a defender of socialist realism, a realist art designed to glorify socialism. He was awarded the Nobel Prize for Literature in 1965.

Shreve, Anita (1947–) An American writer, she attended Tufts University, and after acting as deputy editor of *Viva* magazine, became a freelance writer in 1986. Her novels include *Eden Close* (1989), set in upstate New York, about two friends growing up and their relationship after she has been raped and he returns from college to help her recover, *Strange Fits of Passion* (1991), about journalistic integrity, battered women and emotional abuse, *Where or When?* (1993), which twists the love story of Romeo and Juliet and moves to a shocking conclusion, *Resistance* (1995), a love story between a Belgian and a USAAF pilot, set in Belgium during the Second World War, *Weight of Water* (1997), in which a reporter explores a double murder plot, and *Pilot's Wife* (1998). Her non-fiction concerns motherhood and feminist consciousness-raising movements in *Remaking Motherhood* (1987) and *Women Together, Women Alone* (1989). Her fiction often explores women's issues, such as violence and loss, physical abuse and women's struggles for jobs. Her latest novel is *Fortune's Rocks* (1999), in which a young woman tests the limits of her enclosed life in a wealthy Boston family in 1899.

Shute, Nevil (1899–1960) An English writer, born Nevil Shute Norway in Ealing, Middlesex, he studied at Oxford University (B.Sc. 1922), and became an aeronautical engineer and developed an aircraft manufacturing company. Combining his business with writing fiction, he gradually established a reputation for adventure and romance novels, such as his first novel, *Marazan* (1926), which was followed by *So Disdained* (1928), *Lonely Road* (1932), *What Happened to the Corbetts* (1939), *Pied Piper* (1942) and *Most Secret* (1945). After settling in Australia in 1945, he continued with *No Highway* (1948), about metal fatigue and aircraft fuselage failure, his famous novel *A Town Like Alice* (1950), which deals with the war in the Far East, while *Round the Bend* (1951), *The Far Country* (1952), *In the Wet* (1953) and *Beyond the Black Stump* (1956) all have Australian outback settings. Among his other famous books, are *On the Beach* (1957), a bleak story about the survivors of an atomic holocaust, and *The Trustee from the Toolroom* (1960). His fast-paced novels usually illustrate moral themes and many of them have been adapted for film.

Silko, Leslie Marmon (1948–) Born in Albuquerque, New Mexico, she is of mixed Laguna, Mexican and Anglo descent, and was raised on the Laguna Pueblo reservation in New Mexico. Educated at the University of New Mexico (BA 1969), her writing is founded in Laguna traditions and stories, issues of ethnic and cultural identity and the southwestern desert landscape. Her best-known novel is *Ceremony* (1977), about a young Pueblo war veteran, struggling to come to terms with his experiences, which won considerable critical acclaim and established her as one of the most significant contemporary Native-American novelists. Her other novels include *Almanac of the Dead* (1991), in which the Native-American people retake their ancestral lands in the face of an Anglo-American cultural,

spiritual and ecological collapse, and her latest novel is *Gardens in the Dunes* (1999), set in the Wild West borders, about Native-Americans coming into conflict with the paternalistic white culture, and also dealing with emerging women's rights, female sexuality, medicine and mystery. Her poetry collections include *Laguna Woman* (1974), and she has also published an autobiographical text, *Storyteller* (1981), which weaves together personal and family history, photography, contemporary and traditional Laguna stories. In addition to essays on Native-American life in *Yellow Woman* (1993) and *Yellow Woman and a Beauty of the Spirit* (1996), she has also written a screenplay, for Marlon Brando, entitled *Black Elks*, and an edited collection of her correspondence with the American poet James Wright occurs in *The Delicacy and Strength of Lace* (1985).

P. Seyerstad, *Leslie Marmon Silko* (1980).

Sillanpää, Frans Eemil (1888–1964) Born in Hämeenkyrö, Finland, he went to Helsingfors Universitet (1908–1913) to study natural science, where his friendship with the composer Jean Sibelius changed him to arts, causing him to leave and become a writer. Generally regarded as the finest Finnish writer of the twentieth century, much of his fiction remains untranslated into English. Among those that have been translated is *Meek Heritage* (1919, trans. 1971), which established his reputation throughout Europe with its stark presentation of peasant life in the wake of Finland's bitter civil war, in which the Red Army was defeated by the Whites. Other works are *The Maid Silja* (1931, trans. 1974), published to international acclaim, which depicts a girl and a father who are icons of a dying generation and the old world in the Finnish civil war, and *People in the Summer Night* (1934, trans. 1966), regarded by many as his most exquisitely composed work, in which poetic sketches document the impact of events of a summer's night on a variety of characters. His lyrical prose works generally depict unsophisticated people struggling to exist in a changing and confounding world, and who seek to maintain the balance between reality and idealism. He was awarded the Nobel Prize for Literature in 1939.

Sillitoe, Alan (1928–) Born in Nottingham, England, he left school at 14 and worked in a bicycle plant and various factories, before turning to freelance writing in 1948. *Saturday Night and Sunday Morning* (1958, filmed 1960) catapulted him into the literary limelight, with a robust depiction of the English working class and the rebelliousness of the young factory-hand Arthur Seaton, and made him a significant figure of the 'angry young men' of the 1950s. He married the poet Ruth Fainlight in 1959. There followed *The General* (1960), which was a political fable about militarism; and his reputation rests upon these first two novels, despite his subsequent prolific output. After *Key to the Door* (1961), a sequel to his first novel, he wrote a trilogy, consisting of *The Death of William Posters* (1965), *A Tree on Fire* (1967) and *A Start in Life* (1970), focusing upon another Nottingham factory-worker; and a later second trilogy, consisting of *The Flower of Life* (1974), *The Widower's Son* (1976) and *The Storyteller* (1979). Other novels include *Travel in Nihilon* (1971), *Down from the Hill* (1984), *The Open Door* (1988), which returns to characters from the early books, *Snowstop* (1994), *The Broken Chariot* (1998) and *The German Numbers Woman* (1999). Many of his stories centre upon the class fate of individuals isolated from society in the grim world of Midlands factories. Short stories appear in famously frank representations of working-class life in *The Loneliness of the Long Distance Runner* (1959, filmed 1962), *The Ragman's Daughter* (1968), *Guzman Go Home* (1968), *The Second Chance* (1981), *Collected Stories* (1995) and *Alligator Playground* (1997). In addition to various screenplays and his *Collected Poems* (1993), travel books include *Road to Volgograd* (1964) and *The Saxon Shore Way* (1983), while *Life without Armour* (1995) is an autobiography.

J. Hawthorn, ed., *The British Working-Class Novel in the Twentieth Century* (1984).

Simenon, Georges (1903–1989) Born Georges Jacques Christian Simenon, in Liège, Belgium, he worked at a variety of jobs, including a baker and reporter. He went to Paris in 1922, where he began writing 'pulp' fiction under various pseudonyms, although he is best known for his Inspector Jules Maigret series. Beginning with *The Strange Case of Peter the Lett* (1931, trans. 1933), he departed from the conventional super-sleuth with his portrayal of the heavy-set, pipe-smoking policeman who uses intuition rather than deduction to solve his cases. Rarely carrying a gun, Maigret rises to become a high-ranking policeman in France, and demonstrates extraordinary patience and compassion for the victim and the murderer. Without the flamboyant traits of Sherlock Holmes, Perry Mason or Hercule Poirot, Maigret is generally regarded as standing alone in detective fiction. One of the world's most prolific writers, with a career that spanned over five decades and in excess of 500 books, he has been widely translated and there have been many films and television adaptations of his novels. He retired from fiction writing in 1974, devoting himself to his diaries, non-fiction and autobiographies, like *Letter to My Mother* (1974, trans. 1976), and he wrote *Intimate Memoirs* (1981, trans. 1984), which was a best-selling account of his daughter's suicide.

T. Young, *Georges Simenon* (1976).

Simon, Claude (1913–1984) Born in Antananarivo, Madagascar, he was brought up in France. He served with the French cavalry in 1939, became a prisoner of war and then escaped. Thought by many to be one of the most important 'new novelists', together with such writers as SARRAUTE, BUTOR and ROBBE-GRILLET, his novels include *The Wind* (1957, trans. 1959), *The Grass* (1958, trans. 1960), *The Flanders Road* (1960, trans. 1961), *The Palace* (1962, trans. 1963), and *Histoire* (1967, Prix Medicis, trans. 1968), which is a history of the narrator's family depicted in various ways, with the past and present interwoven. The latter four novels form part of a connecting work with recurrent characters and incidents. His numerous other novels include *The Battle of Pharsalus* (trans. 1971), *Conducting Bodies* (1971, trans. 1974), *Triptych* (1973, trans. 1976), *The World About Us* (1975, trans. 1983) and *The Georgics* (1981, trans. 1989), in which the texts are assemblages of interrelated elements. His fragmented, disconnected, innovatory fiction, seeks to create an awesome awareness of reality through experimentation with perspective, exploring the possibilities of language; and in so doing, the writing aims to reproduce the flux and simultaneity of perceptual experience. Belated recognition came for his work when he was awarded the Nobel Prize for Literature in 1985.

J. Loubèe, *The Novels of Claude Simon* (1975).

Sinclair, Andrew (1935–) Andrew Annandale Sinclair was born in Oxford, England. After completing National Service with the Coldstream Guards (1953–1955), he was educated at Cambridge University (BA 1958, Ph.D. 1962). His early novels are light-hearted attempts to capture significant moments of the 1950s, like the adventures of a young Guards officer in *The Breaking of Bumbo* (1959), later continued in *Beau Bumbo* (1985), life at Cambridge University in *My Friend Judas* (1959), and an American car adventure in *The Hallelujah Bum* (1962). Subsequent novels include 'The Albion

Triptych', based upon the mythical British giant and offering a panoramic history of Britain from prehistoric Stonehenge to the Second World War, and consisting of *Gog* (1967), and the sequels *Magog* (1972) and *King Ludd* (1988). There followed *The Surrey Cat* (1976), *A Patriot for Hire* (1978), while *The Far Corners of the Earth* (1991) began the 'Empire Quartet', a fictionalised account of the Sinclair family. It was continued in *The Strength of the Hills* (1992). In addition to a few plays, he has written a large amount of non-fiction, mostly historical studies and biographies, and *In Love and Anger* (1994), which is a memoir of the 1960s.

Sinclair, Upton (1878–1968) Born Upton Beall Sinclair, in Baltimore, Maryland, US, and educated at the College of the City of New York and Columbia University, he was a prolific novelist (writing some ninety books) who held strong socialist convictions. For the most part, his novels were written with a polemical intent and to criticise US economic and social issues stemming from the industrial system. His best-known work is *The Jungle* (1906), which exposed the appalling conditions in the Chicago stockyards and led to new Federal legislation in the meat-packing industry. Other novels include *King Midas* (1901), *The Metropolis* (1908), which explores fashionable New York City, *King Coal* (1917), which describes a Colorado miners' strike, *Jimmie Higgins* (1919), *They Call Me Carpenter* (1922) and *Oil!* (1927). His novel *Boston* (1928) deals with the infamous Sacco and Vanzetti case in the 1920s in the US, in which two Italian immigrants and known Anarchists, arrested for murder, were eventually executed on circumstantial evidence. He ran unsuccessfully for governor in California in 1934, on the famous EPIC (End Poverty in California) manifesto. He also wrote a ten-novel sequence, starting with *World's End* (1940), including *Dragon's Teeth* (1942, Pulitzer Prize 1943), and ending with *O Shepherd, Speak!*

(1949), about Lanny Budd, an American secret agent, which are set against the backdrop of world politics and political intrigue, especially the descent of Germany into Nazism during the 1930s. Famous for his social concern in his novels, he also wrote *The Autobiography of Upton Sinclair* (1962).

I. Scott, *Upton Sinclair: The Forgotten Socialist* (1997).

Singer, Isaac Bashevis (1904–1991) A Polish-American writer, born in Radzymin, Poland, he emigrated to the US, settling in New York City, and naturalised as an American citizen in 1943. His books were all written initially in Yiddish, but were translated later into English, some by Singer himself. His first novel was *Satan in Goray* (1935, trans. 1955), about the brutal massacre of Polish Jews by Cossacks in pogroms in the 1600s. Later books are *The Family Moskat* (trans. 1965), *The Magician of Lublin* (trans. 1960), *The Slave* (trans. 1962), *The Manor* (trans. 1967), *The Estate* (trans. 1969), *Enemies* (trans. 1970), *Shosha* (trans. 1978), *The Penitent* (trans. 1983), and *Scum* (trans. 1991), and the posthumously published *The Certificate* (trans. 1992) and *Meshugah* (trans. 1994), about Holocaust survivors in New York. Singer also wrote several books of short stories, notably those in *Gimpel the Fool* (trans. 1957), *The Spinoza of Market Street* (trans. 1961), *Short Friday* (trans. 1964), *The Séance* (trans. 1968), *A Friend of Kafka* (trans. 1970), *A Crown of Feathers* (trans. 1973), *Collected Stories* (1982) and *The Death of Methuselah* (trans. 1985). Among his stories written for children are *A Day of Pleasure: Stories of a Boy Growing Up in Warsaw* (1969) and *Stories for Children* (1984). *Yentl the Yeshiva Boy* (1983) was turned into a film by Barbra Streisand, called *Yentl*. Singer wrote two autobiographical books, entitled *In My Father's Court* (1966) and *Love and Exile: A Memoir* (1984). He

was awarded the Nobel Prize for Literature in 1978. Dealing with old age, loneliness and a sense of Jewish alienation in a Gentile world, his fiction draws heavily upon Jewish folklore, mysticism and religion.

I. Makin, *Singer* (1972).

Skármeta, Antonio (1940–) Born in Antofagasta, Chile, he went to university in Chile and to Columbia University (MA 1966), after which he became an academic in Latin American literature at the University of Chile in Santiago. He left after the military coup in 1973, and worked as a screenwriter and film-maker in Berlin until his return to Chile in 1989, where he became a popular television personality. His first novel was *I Dreamt the Snow Was Burning* (1975, trans. 1985), about a protagonist who aspires to become a professional soccer player, and which inaugurated the novels of the South American post-'boom' era, the period of fashionable South American magic realist literature of the 1960s. After *Chileno!* (trans. 1979), he wrote *The Insurrection* (1982, trans. 1983), a revolutionary novel set in Nicaragua during the Sandinista uprising, which depicts the fall of the Somoza regime, and then *Burning Patience* (1985, trans. 1987), upon which the highly acclaimed Italian film *Il Postino* (1994) was based, depicting a love story in which the Nobel Prize-winning poet Pablo Neruda acts as a protective father-figure to two young lovers. Recent work includes *Match-ball* (trans. 1989), *Love-fifteen* (trans. 1996), which narrates a love story for a young tennis star, and short stories in *Watch Where the Wolf Is Going* (trans. 1991). His fiction during the post-'boom' period was a major contribution to South American literature, as chaos and absurdity gave way to reconciliation.

D. Shaw, *Antonio Skármeta and the Post-boom* (1994).

Skvorecký, Josef (1924–) Born in Nachod, Czechoslovakia, he worked in the Messerschmitt factories during the Nazi occupation. After studying philosophy at Charles University, Prague (Ph.D. 1951), he worked in editing, translating and teaching. A central figure in the Czech underground in the 1950s, his first novel, *The Cowards* (1958, trans. 1970), was attacked as decadent and anti-socialist, causing his later works to be banned until the 1968 Prague Spring. Upon the 1968 Russian invasion, he emigrated to Toronto, where he and his wife founded the resistance publishing house Sixty-Eight, before becoming Professor of English at the University of Toronto (1971). *The Cowards* began a cycle whose protagonist Danny Smiricky, obsessed with girls and jazz, is an anti-hero, and whose very existence subverts socialist ideologies. Translated out of chronological order, the cycle is continued in *The Swell Season* (1975, trans. 1982), in the widely praised wry and sceptical comic novel *The Engineer of Human Souls* (1977, trans. 1984), which seeks to reveal the true Czech history suppressed by Stalinism, juxtaposing the 'old' and 'new' worlds of Czechoslovakia and Canada, as Danny becomes Skvorecký's political mouthpiece, *Miracle Game* (1972, trans. 1991), *Republic of Whores* (1971, trans. 1993) and the *Tenor Saxophonist's Story* (1993, trans. 1997). *Dvorak in Love* (1983, trans. 1986) is a lyrical novel that establishes a faith in creativity, and was awarded the prestigious Neustadt Prize for Literature. Other works include the short stories in *The Mournful Demeanour of Lieutenant Bonurka* (1974), *Miss Silver's Past* (1975), *The Bass Saxophone* (1977), *Emoke* (1977), the novel *The Bride of Texas* (1992, trans. 1995), which depicts nineteenth-century emigrés in Texas amid the American Civil War, and *Headed for the Blues* (trans. 1996), a memoir and short stories. Interweaving the tragic and comic, he insistently explores man's fate in history and the function played by art as a metaphor for freedom and liberation.

S. Solecki, ed., *The Achievement of Josef Skvorecký* (1994).

Smiley, Jane (1949–) An American novelist, born in Los Angeles, Jane Graves Smiley grew up in St. Louis, and studied at Vassar College and the University of Iowa. Since 1981, she has taught at Iowa State University. She has made the American Midwest and family life in the prairie landscape the focus of much of her fiction. *At Paradise Gate* (1981) concerns a family and its attempts to come to terms with a dying father, and was followed by *Barn Blind* (1980), about a farm in Illinois, *Duplicate Keys* (1984), which is a mystery set in Manhattan, and *The Age of Grief* (1987), a collection of short stories about the perils of domestic life. *The Greenlanders* (1988) was a slight departure in that it was an historical novel about a fourteenth-century Norse community and the problems of survival in a harsh climate and remote culture. However, the novellas *Ordinary Love and Good Will* (1989), returned to domestic family issues; and the successful *A Thousand Acres* (1991, Pulitzer Prize 1992), returned to the Midwest with a contemporary rendering of the King Lear story set on a farm in the fictional Zebulon County in Iowa. Her more recent work includes a satire of contemporary American mores in *Moo* (1995), which is a campus novel set in a fictional Midwestern University called Moo, while *The All-True Travels and Adventures of Lindie Newton* (1998) depicts homesteading in Kansas in the 1850s with abolitionist and pro-slavery tensions, and *Horse Heaven* (2000) is a comic novel about horse-breeding and racing.

N. Nakadate, *Understanding Jane Smiley* (1999).

Smith, Wilbur (1933–) Born in Broken Hill, in what is now Zambia, Wilbur

Addison Smith was educated at Rhodes University (B.Sc. 1954), and now lives in South Africa. He worked for Goodyear Tyres (1954–1958), and then worked in Harare, Zimbabwe (1958–1963), since when he turned to full-time writing. A prolific writer of historical adventure novels in colourful African settings, his novels include *When the Lion Feeds* (1964), *The Train from Katanga* (1965), *Shout at the Devil* (1968), *Gold Mine* (1970), *The Diamond Hunters* (1971), *The Sunbird* (1972), *Eye of the Tiger* (1974), *Cry Wolf* (1975) and *The Leopard Hunts in Darkness* (1984). A series of related novels about the European conquest of Zimbabwe and the fictional Ballantyne family's challenge to Cecil Rhodes is recounted in *A Falcon Flies* (1979), *Men of Men* (1980) and *The Angel Weeps* (1983). Recent novels include *Rage* (1987), which focuses upon three generations of a South African diamond-mining family, *River God* (1994), an epic love story set in ancient Egypt, *The Seventh Scroll* (1995), a sequel set in the present and a search for lost pharaohs' tombs, and *Birds of Prey* (1997) and *Monsoon* (1999), which depict the swashbuckling adventures in the early eighteenth century off the coast of South Africa. Despite masterful popular and pacy narratives, he has been criticised for formulaic writing and for his simplistic depiction of African politics.

Snow, C.P. (1905–1980) Full name Charles Percy Snow, born in Leicester, England, he was educated in chemistry at the universities of Leicester and Cambridge, and became a scientist and a novelist. He engaged in scientific work in the 1930s but soon moved into scientific administration. He became chief of scientific personnel for the Ministry of Labour during the Second World War, and was knighted in 1957 and made a life peer in 1964. His earliest novels were the detective stories, *Death Under Sail* (1932), *New Lives for Old* (1933), and *The*

Search (1934), about the frustrations of a scientific life. He is best known for a sequence of nine novels, beginning with *Strangers and Brothers* (1940) and ending with *Last Things* (1970), which chronicles English social, academic and political life over a period of about thirty years as perceived by a barrister, Lewis Eliot. Other novels in the sequence include his best-known novel, *The Masters* (1951), concerning a Cambridge college in dispute over the election of a new Master, *Corridors of Power* (1964), about the machinations of parliamentarians, and *The Sleep of Reason* (1968), centring upon the trial of the Moors murderers. In addition to a biography of Anthony Trollope (1975), he also published a controversial lecture, entitled *The Two Cultures and the Scientific Revolution* (1959), which lamented the isolation of science and literature and led to a furious response by the literary critic F.R. Leavis.

Sokolov, Sasha (1943–) Born Alexander Vsevolodovich Sokolov, in Ottawa, Canada, he was educated at Moscow University (BA 1971), and worked as a journalist until 1976, when he emigrated to Canada. He worked as an instructor in Russian in Michigan, before returning to Russia in 1989. He has written three novels, two of which have been translated into English: *A School for Fools* (1976, trans. 1977), which explores the confused yet delicate world of a schizophrenic youth in a special school near Moscow, and is a psychological *tour de force*; and *Astrophobia* (1985, trans. 1989), a comic, picaresque extravaganza, parodying many aspects of Soviet life and literary emigrés. Widely regarded as one of the most outstanding contemporary Russian prose writers, language and style are paramount to his fiction.

Soldati, Mario (1906–1999) Born in Turin, Italy, he went to the University of Turin (1927) and undertook graduate study in Rome and at Columbia University

(1928). He developed a reputation as a screenwriter in the 1930s and 1940s, and worked as an assistant film director on *War and Peace* (1956) and *Ben Hur* (1959). Developing a special talent for narrative and description, he has written novels, poetry, screenplays and short stories. After the stories in *The Commander Comes to Dine* (1950, trans. 1952), which involve the human mysteries of the heart and mind, his interest in American–Italian relations emerged in *The Capri Letters* (1954, trans. 1955), an award-winning novel about a young American couple travelling in Italy and their affairs with Italians, as it explores the perversities of the puritan conscience. This theme was continued in *The American Bride* (1977, trans. 1979), which looks at the psychology of US and Italian relations. Other fiction includes *The Confession* (1955, trans. 1958) and *The Orange Envelope* (1966, trans. 1969), both of which investigate the psychology of sex, guilt and Catholicism, *The Real Silvestri* (1957, trans. 1960), *The Malacca Cane* (1964, trans. 1973) and *The Emerald* (1974, trans. 1977).

Solzhenitsyn, Aleksander I. (1918–) Full name Aleksander Isaevich Solzhenitsyn, born in Kislovodsk, Russia, he graduated from the University of Rostov (1941) in mathematics and physics, and fought in the Red Army until 1945. Arrested in 1945, he underwent a series of imprisonments for treason in labour camps and the notorious Lubyanka Prison in Moscow, and internal exile in Kazakhstan, until 1974. Deported and exiled from the USSR, he emigrated to the US, where he lived until his return to Russia in 1994. A prolific writer, he came to overnight fame with his novella *One Day in the Life of Ivan Denisovich* (1962, trans. 1963), centring on the concentration camps in which millions died under Stalin, narrating a day in the life of a simple prisoner and seeking to elicit the reader's feelings rather than imposing them as socialist realism sought

to accomplish. After *For the Good of the Cause* (1963, trans. 1964) and the two short novels in 'We Never Make Mistakes' (trans. 1963), he wrote *The First Circle* (trans. 1968), which drew upon his experiences of an isolated *sharashka* (a special prison) in the late 1940s, and *The Cancer Ward* (1968, trans. 1969), which was inspired by his stay in a Tashkent hospital where he was treated for cancer in the 1950s. One volume of a four-volume novel called 'The Red Wheel' has been translated, entitled *August 1914* (1971, trans. 1972), which focuses upon the Battle of Tannenberg through the eyes of two men. *The Gulag Archipelago 1918–1956* (1973, trans. 1974–1979) is his most important work of non-fiction, and is a detailed account of Stalinist oppression. Other non-fiction includes *Letter to the Soviet Leaders* (trans. 1974), *The Oak and the Calf* (1975, trans. 1980), *The Mortal Danger* (trans. 1980), *Rebuilding Russia* (trans. 1991), and *The Russian Question Toward the End of the Century* (trans. 1995), which grapples with his country's future. Engaged in an on-going attempt to restore unity to Russian society, his principal theme has been the dissolution of an anachronistic, deeply-divided society under great stress and the responses of individuals to that dissolution. He was awarded the Nobel Prize for Literature in 1970.

A. Rothberg, *Aleksander Solzhenitsyn: The Major Novels* (1971); M. Scammell, *Solzenhitsyn: A Biography* (1984).

Sontag, Susan (1933–) An American intellectual and writer, born in New York City, and brought up in Tucson, Arizona and Los Angeles. She went to the universities of Chicago (BA 1951) and Harvard (MA Philosophy, 1954, MA English, 1955), before undertaking doctoral work at Harvard and Oxford, and has since taught at various universities. Doyenne of the US academic left, her radical yet élitist politics have led her to demystify the ideologies of marginalised areas of American culture. She is best known for her non-fiction essays, which include *Against Interpretation* (1966), the directly political writing of *Trip to Hanoi* (1968), *Styles of Radical Will* (1969), and after suffering from a near fatal case of cancer in the 1970s which interrupted her writing life, she wrote *Illness as Metaphor* (1978), about the cultural myths that surround certain diseases, *Under the Sign of Saturn* (1980) and *AIDS and Its Metaphors* (1989). Exploring the politics of style, the representations of sexuality, issues of identity, and the interrelationship of self with social, political and historical circumstances, she has been a controversial writer. Her novels are situated within a European tradition recast in an American mould, and include *The Benefactor* (1963), about dreams invading the male protagonist's life, *Death Kit* (1967), *The Volcano Lover* (1992), which is a romance about Admiral Nelson and Lady Hamilton in Italy, dealing with ideas about history, aesthetics, politics and feminism, and *In America* (2000), which depicts the travails of a late nineteenth-century Polish actress who emigrates to the US. Short stories are collected in the innovative and much praised *I, etcetera* (1978) and *The Way We Live Now* (1991), while a play about Alice James, the invalid sister of William and Henry James, occurs in *Alice in Bed* (1993). She has directed films, edited *Commentary* in 1959, written about modernity in *On Photography* (1976), and edited selections of work by Antonin Artaud and Roland Barthes.

F. Sayres, *Susan Sontag: The Elegiac Modernist* (1990).

Sorrentino, Gilbert (1929–) Born in Brooklyn, New York, US, he has had a variety of jobs, including editing, publishing and university teaching, and was made Professor of English at Stanford University in 1982. Despite his reputation for innovative fiction, he is equally known as a poet and has published a variety of collections of poetry, often showing the influences of the Black Mountain poets, a sample of which can be read in *Selected Poems 1958–1980* (1981). His early novels are *The Sky Changes* (1966), about an unhappy married couple's journey across America, and *Steelwork* (1970), which depicts sites and characters from his Brooklyn childhood. *Imaginative Qualities of Actual Things* (1971), a satire of the New York avant-garde in the 1960s, which is written in a resolutely anti-realist, fragmented style, was followed by *Splendide-Hôtel* (1973), whose twenty-six sections are based on the letters of the alphabet. His most acclaimed work, *Mulligan Stew* (1979), an avant-garde text which mocks the processes of fiction in a self-reflexive fashion, is regarded by some as one of the most important works of American postmodernist fiction. Other novels include *Aberration of Starlight* (1980), which is more conventional in form, and is set on the New Jersey coast during the Depression, *Crystal Vision* (1981), and a trilogy of experimental novels in *Odd Number* (1985), *Rose Theater* (1987) *Misterioso* (1989), which are collected in *Pack of Lies* (1997), and *Red the Fiend* (1995). Essays occur in *Something Said* (1984). Always treating form and structure as more significant than content, he has earned considerable critical praise for his technical virtuosity and attention to the operations of language.

J. Klinkowitz, *Literary Disruptions* (1975).

Soseki, Natsume (1867–1916) Born Natsume Kinnosuke, in Tokyo, Japan, he went to Tokyo Imperial University (1890–1893), and held various academic posts. One of the leading writers responsible for forming modern Japanese prose fiction, he is widely read and highly revered. His fiction includes *The Tower* *of London* (1905, trans. 1992), the two volumes of *I Am a Cat* (1905–1907, trans. 1971 and 1980), *Botchan* (1906, trans. 1968) and *The Three-Cornered World* (1906 trans. 1965). His early works demonstrate a youthful buoyancy and energy, and an obsession with the modern crisis of alienation, involving brooding heroes, and the themes of isolation and cultural insularity. Later works include *The Wanderer* (1914, trans. 1967), *Grass on the Wayside* (1915, trans. 1969) and *Light and Darkness* (1917, trans. 1971). His fiction explores the rapid change of Japan after exposure to western culture, although he remains convinced of Japan's distinctiveness and orientalness. A major motif in the novels is the struggle to make the competing claims of the East and West compatible, although his attachment to the old culture is evident. With a style both traditional and experimental, his fiction acts as a bourgeois critique of Imperial Japan.

Van C. Gessel, *Three Modern Novelists: Soseki, Tanizaki, Kawabata* (1993).

Soupault, Philippe (1897–1990) Born in Chaville, France, he was educated at the Sorbonne, University of Paris, and was a founder of Surrealism with André Breton and Louis ARAGON, and co-founded the magazine *Littérature* in 1919. He travelled extensively in the 1920s, and founded the radio service of Tunisia in 1938. After the Second World War, he worked for the United Nations. His numerous novels include *Last Nights of Paris* (1928, trans. 1929), a characteristic Surrealist work, which relates the activities of socially marginalised Parisians in the 1920s, presenting a night-time landscape of the city, and *The Age of Assassins: The Story of Prisoner No. 1234* (1945, trans. 1946), an account of his imprisonment by the Nazis and regarded by many as his best book. Among various literary studies and essays are many volumes of poetry, and a recent *Selected*

Poems of Philippe Soupault (trans. 1984). Concerned with human psychology, he was a widely honoured writer, much of whose work remains untranslated into English.

Southern, Terry (1924?–1995) Born in Alvarado, Texas, US, he graduated from Northwestern University (BA 1948), and became a writer who helped define the youth culture of the 1960s with several classic screenplays. He began with three novels which established his cult following: *Flash and Filigree* (1958); *Candy* (1958), written with Mason Hoffenberg under the joint pseudonym of Maxwell Kenton, which was a send-up of conventional porn and a modern pastiche of Candide's *Voltaire*; and *The Magic Christian* (1959), a picaresque satirical tale exposing materialism and snobbishness. He then wrote the screenplays for the films *Dr. Strangelove; or How I Learned to Stop Worrying and Love the Bomb* (1963), starring Peter Sellers, *The Loved One* (1965), *The Cincinnati Kid* (1965), *Barbarella* (1968) and *Easy Rider* (1969), satires which defined the Cold War climate and the counter-culture in America. He published only two more novels, *Blue Movie* (1970) and *Texas Summer* (1991), a coming-of-age novel about race relations, set on the stark north Texas prairies. Short stories occur in *Red-Dirt Marijuana and Other Tastes* (1967). His fiction and screenplays handle the futility of life and the idea of freedom from convention.

Soyinka, Wole (1934–) Born Akinwande Oluwole Sonyika, in Aké, western Nigeria, he attended the University of Ibadan (1952–1954) and went to the University of Leeds (1957). He worked as play-reader at the Royal Court Theatre, London, before returning to Ibadan in 1960 to play a leading role in the development of Nigerian theatre. He has held various university appointments in Nigeria, Ghana, England and the United

States, and he has been involved in the political crises of Nigeria in different ways, having been imprisoned and in self-imposed exile as a result. Among his considerable achievements in drama are *The Lion and the Jewel* (1963), *Kongi's Harvest* (1967) and *The Road* (1965), which show techniques imbibed from Shakespeare, the Absurdists, as well as his native Yoruba rituals and idioms. Other drama includes *A Dance of the Forests* (1963), *The Swamp Dwellers*, *The Trials of Brother Jero* and *The Strong Breed* (published as *Three Plays*, 1963). In the 1970s and 1980s, his drama derived its inspiration from and against western writers: he adapted Euripides in *The Bacchae of Euripides: 'A Communion Rite'* (1973), while *Opera Wonyosi* (1981) was an adaptation of Brecht's *The Threepenny Opera*, and *Requiem for a Futurologist* (1985) adapts Swift. His later plays include *A Play of Giants* (1984), *A Scourge of Hyacinths* (1992) and *From Zia, with Love* (1992), the latter two returning to contemporary African politics. Although primarily a playwright, he has used a variety of different literary forms. His collections of poetry are *Ibandre* (1967), *Ogun Abibiman* (1976) and *Mandela's Earth* (1988), although the most famous and widely anthologised poem is his lightly satirical work about racial prejudice, 'Telephone Conversation' (1958). He has translated work from Yoruba, written a great deal of journalism for television, radio and film, and recorded and composed songs. His first novel, *The Interpreters* (1965), was a complex, poignant revelation of the crises of the youthful Nigerian generation; while his second novel, *Season of Anomy* (1973) reworks the myth of Orpheus and Eurydice against the background of the Nigerian civil war, exploring ideas of sacrifice and the impact of a small ideologically committed group on the wider society. After his imprisonment during the civil war, he published his prison notebooks, *The Man Died* (1972), an important contribution to African prison literature. Autobiography and memoirs include *Aké: The Years of Childhood* (1981) and *Isara: A Voyage Around 'Essay'* (1989), a re-creation of his father's world, and literary and political essays occur in *Myth, Literature and the African World* (1976), *The Credo of Being and Nothingness* (1991), *Art, Dialogue and Outrage* (1993), *Open Sore of a Continent* (1996) and *Burden of Memory, the Muse of Forgiveness* (1999). An intense commitment to human rights has motivated his politics, whilst his eloquent command of voice, energy and versatility as a writer, has established him as a dominant writer of his generation among anglophone African writers, duly acknowledged by the award of the Nobel Prize for Literature in 1986.

O. Maduakor, *Wole Soyinka: An Introduction to His Writings* (1986).

Spark, Muriel (1918–) Born Muriel Sarah Spark, in Edinburgh, Scotland, after studying at Heriot Watt University she taught for a short period, and worked for British Intelligence during the Second World War. One of contemporary Britain's more under-appreciated writers, she first gained prominence as a poet and critic and has been hugely prolific over the years. *The Comforters* (1957) deals with coming to terms with her conversion to Catholicism in 1954, and subsequent novels reflect her religious beliefs and her Scottish identity. *Memento Mori* (1959) was followed by *The Ballad of Peckham Rye* (1960) and her famous novel *The Prime of Miss Jean Brodie* (1961), about an Edinburgh school and its teachers' influence over its pupils. Subsequent novels include *The Mandelbaum Gate* (1965), which looks at her Jewish heritage, *The Girls of Slender Means* (1963), and *The Abbess of Crewe* (1974), set in a convent but inspired by the Watergate hearings. More recent novels are *Loitering with Intent* (1981) and *A Far Cry* *from Kensington* (1988), both about London in the 1950s, *Symposium* (1990) and *Reality and Dreams* (1996) about an injured film-maker watching his friends' lives from a hospital bed. Her latest novel is *Aiding and Abetting* (2000), a brisk fantasia on the Lord Lucan affair. Short stories occur in *The Go-Away Bird* (1958), *Collected Stories* (1994) and *Open to the Public* (1997), with an autobiography of her early life in *Curriculum Vitae* (1992). She has also written plays for radio, edited collections of English writers' letters and poems, and published her *Collected Poems I* (1968). Many of her short, sharp, witty novels consider the social roles people ought to play, and explore the morality of the upper class in England, and in Italy where she settled in the 1960s.

R. Whittaker, *The Faith and Fictions of Muriel Spark* (1982).

Spillane, Mickey (1918–) Born Frank Morrison Spillane, in Brooklyn, New York, he is an American writer, mainly of 'hard-boiled' crime fiction. He was a fighter pilot instructor in Mississippi during the Second World War, and then turned to writing stories, mostly for pulp magazines, before writing full-length novels. He is the creator of private-eye Mike Hammer, who appeared in thirteen novels, beginning with *I, the Jury* (1947), and including, among others, *Vengeance Is Mine* (1950), *The Big Kill* (1951), *Kiss Me Deadly* (1952, filmed 1955), *The Snake* (1964), *The Killing Man* (1989) and *Black Alley* (1996). His non-Hammer crime books include *The Long Wait* (1951), *Bloody Sunrise* (1965), *The Delta Factor* (1967), *The Tough Guys* (1969) and *The Last Cop Out* (1973). He has also written short stories, for example, in *Me, Hood* (1969) and *Tomorrow I Die* (1984), and children's stories in *The Day the Sea Rolled Back* (1979) and *The Ship That Never Was* (1982). Along with writers like CHANDLER, HAMMETT and

LEONARD, his fiction has helped to define the American detective genre.

Stead, Christina (1902–1983) Born in Sydney, Australia, Christina Ellen Stead studied psychology and then travelled to London in 1928. She worked as a bank clerk in Paris in the 1930s, where she published her first book, *The Salzburg Tales* (1934). After going to the US during the war, she returned to England to live with her husband, who died in 1968. In 1974, she went back to Australia, and remained there until her death. She published fifteen books, but most attention is directed to the three novels regarded as her masterpieces, based upon her Australian experience, entitled *Seven Poor Men of Sydney* (1934), *The Man Who Loved Children* (1940) and *For Love Alone* (1944). Other novels include *The House of All Nations* (1938) and *Cotter's England* (1967), which give political insights into English and European values at moments of historical crisis, *Letty Fox: Her Luck* (1946), *A Little Tea, a Little Chat* (1948), *The People with the Dogs* (1952), *The Little Hotel* (1973) and *Miss Herbert* (1976). Written largely in the 1940s, *I'm Dying Laughing* (1986) spans three decades and two continents as it re-creates to chilling effect the political turbulence of the American left and the menace of the McCarthy right. Many of her novels show the influence of her communist politics and modernism, but she resisted the formulaic novels of proletarian realism. Tending to be more aware of the limitations of communist realism, her long novels, which focused upon the politics of the personal – personal relations and domestic issues – have recently begun to gain the attention of feminist critics and she is emerging as one of Australia's greatest women novelists.

S. Sheridan, *Christina Stead* (1988).

Steel, Danielle (1947–) Born in New York City, Danielle Fernande Steel attended

New York University (1963–1967), and worked in public relations (1968–1971) and advertising (1973–1974) before becoming a full-time writer. A writer of popular and historical romances and novels, generally dismissed by critics but embraced by readers in their millions, she has written over forty novels, many of which have been adapted for television and achieved massive popularity. Her first novel was *Going Home* (1973), and among her many best-selling novels are *Palomino* (1982), *Secrets* (1986), *Daddy* (1989), *Star* (1990), *Jewels* (1992), *No Greater Love* (1992), *Special Delivery* (1997) and *Bittersweet* (1999). Her latest novel is *The Wedding* (2000), about a Hollywood couple and their daughter's wedding. Her novels tend to be about women in powerful or glamorous positions, forced to choose between priorities in their lives. They focus upon the difficulties women face, such as juggling a career with familial responsibilities, coping with bereavement, divorce, disability, or fame. Her heroines usually triumph in difficult circumstances, often achieving wealth or happiness against difficult odds.

Stegner, Wallace (1909–1993) A widely honoured American novelist, he was born Wallace Earle Stegner in Lake Mills, Iowa, and attended the University of Utah (BA 1930) and the State University of Iowa (MA 1932, Ph.D. 1935), since when he held various university positions in creative writing. The American West figures prominently in his work, especially as the setting for quests for personal and regional identity, and explorations of the influence of the past on the present. He published prolifically, with early novels like *Remembering Laughter* (1937), *The Potter's House* (1938), *On a Darkling Plain* (1940) and *Fire and Ice* (1941). His first popular and critical success came with the wide-ranging *The Big Rock Candy Mountain* (1943), which chronicles the life of Bo Mason and his family from 1906 to 1942, and their search for

their fortune in the West. Thereafter he published *Second Growth* (1947), *The Preacher and the Slave* (1950), which is based upon the life of the radical Joe Hill, *A Shooting Star* (1961), *All the Little Live Things* (1967), and his most praised novel, *Angle of Repose* (1971, Pulitzer Prize 1972), about a professor in California who is researching his grandmother's life, who was an illustrator and writer about the old West. His last novels were *The Spectator Bird* (1976), another search for the past as the protagonist Joe Allston goes through his earlier journal of a trip to Denmark looking for family roots, *Recapitulation* (1979) and *Crossing to Safety* (1987). His short stories occur in *The Women on the Wall* (1948), *The City of the Living* (1956) and *The Collected Stories of Wallace Stegner* (1990), while essays on the West appear in *The Sound of Mountain Water* (1969), *One Way to Spell Man* (1982) and *Where the Bluebird Sings* (1992). A variety of other books on the West include two major works on the Mormons in *Mormon Country* (1941) and *The Gathering of Zion* (1964), a biography of the western explorer John Wesley Powell in *Beyond the Hundredth Meridian* (1954), and a memoir of his childhood in Saskatchewan, *Wolf Willow* (1962).

C. Rankin, ed., *Wallace Stegner: Man and Writer* (1996).

Stein, Gertrude (1874–1946) An influential and prolific modernist American writer, she was born in Allegheny, Pennsylvania, and grew up in Oakland, California. She was educated at Radcliffe College, Harvard (BA 1897), during which time she developed a primary interest in the psychology of William James, and then attended Johns Hopkins Medical School (1897–1901). She moved to France in 1903 with her brother Leo, and immediately became a central figure in the Parisian art world, promoting the avant-garde in her salon shared with her lifelong companion, Alice B. Toklas, which became the gathering place for the 'new moderns' like Juan Gris, Pablo Picasso and Henri Matisse, and the American and English writers like James JOYCE, Ernest HEMINGWAY, F. Scott FITZGERALD and Sherwood ANDERSON, whom she dubbed the 'lost generation'. A bold experimenter, she developed James' psychological theories by rejecting linear, time-oriented writing in favour of a spatial, process-oriented writing, in dense poems and fiction devoid of plot and dialogue. These narrative experiments began in *Three Lives* (1909), a set of three tales investigating the essential nature of each of the central characters, of which 'Melanctha', about a young mulatto girl, is often singled out for praise. *The Making of Americans, Being a History of a Family's Progress* (1925), written between 1906 and 1908, is regarded as a milestone for her technique of 'a continuous present', and is a 900-page novel without dialogue or action, beginning as a chronicle of a family life and evolving into a history of the human race. *Tender Buttons* (1914), which includes passages of automatic writing, is a series of paragraphs about objects which revels in syntactic and grammatical play and is often described as an example of 'cubist' prose. *Composition as Explanation* (1926) and *How to Write* (1931) practice the theory of her writing techniques and the abstraction of language. In response to a lack of money, she wrote her only popular best-seller, *The Autobiography of Alice B. Toklas* (1933), which is her own autobiography, and takes the form of a more conventional narrative style. She also wrote librettos for music, notably for operas with Virgil Thompson, entitled *Four Saints in Three Acts* (1934) and *The Mother of Us All* (1949), as well as many plays. Later works include her 1934 lecture series in the US in *Lectures in America* (1935), *Everybody's Autobiography* (1937), a portrait of Picasso (1938), *Ida* (1941) and *Brewsie and Willie* (1946), the latter two set in the war.

Many volumes of her lectures, letters and poetry have been posthumously published. The eight-volume Yale edition of her unpublished writings, published between 1951 and 1958, is a definitive work. Recent research has regarded her writing as a precursor of poststructuralist and feminist theories, while performance artists have been attracted to her experiments in the 'invention' of language. She died in France and is buried in Père la Chaise cemetery in Paris.

S. Neuman and I. Nadel, eds, *Gertrude Stein and the Making of Literature* (1988).

Steinbeck, John (1902–1968) An American novelist, born John Ernst Steinbeck, in Salinas, California, and educated at Stanford University, although he never took a degree. Steinbeck's most enduring theme is the dignity of the common man, especially the small farmer, and his stories are often about migrant farm workers who are exploited by ruthless farm owners. His first three books, *Cup of Gold* (1929), about the seventeenth-century pirate Sir Henry Morgan, *The Pastures of Heaven* (1932), short stories about California farmers, and *To a God Unknown* (1933), were largely unsuccessful. His first acclaim was for *Tortilla Flat* (1935), a sympathetic story about Mexican Americans, set near Monterey, California. This was followed by *In Dubious Battle* (1936), a sombre story about a strike by migrant fruit pickers, and *Of Mice and Men* (1937), another tragic story about two migrant farm labourers. His most affecting book, which became a best-seller, was *The Grapes of Wrath* (1939, Pulitzer Prize 1940, and filmed in 1940 by John Ford), about a family dispossessed of their farm in the Oklahoma Dust Bowl during the Depression of the 1930s and their enforced trek to California in order to find work, under exploitative conditions, on fruit farms. During the war, he wrote *The Moon Is Down* (1942), about Norway under the Nazis. Other novels include *Cannery Row* (1945), a collection of stories set in Monterey Bay about a group of diverse characters and their humorous escapades, *The Wayward Bus* (1947), *Burning Bright* (1950), *East of Eden* (1952, filmed 1955), about a California farmer and his sons, *Sweet Thursday* (1954) and *The Winter of Our Discontent* (1961). He also wrote *Travels with Charley* (1962), a light-hearted autobiographical chronicle of a trip which he made across the US with his dog. With his friend E.F. Ricketts, Steinbeck wrote the non-ficion *The Sea of Cortez* (1941), about a trip they made together to study the local fauna of the Gulf of California. His final book, a modernisation of the Arthurian legends, *The Acts of King Arthur and His Noble Knights* (1976), was published posthumously. He also wrote short stories, collected in *The Lost Valley* (1938). Steinbeck was awarded the Nobel Prize for Literature in 1962. A master of realist fiction, he is generally acclaimed for his depictions of the effects of the Depression upon American working class and migrant life during the 1930s and 1940s.

J. Parini, *John Steinbeck* (1994).

Sterling, Bruce (1954–) Born in Brownsville, Texas, US, he attended the University of Texas at Austin (1972–1976), and became a professional writer in 1983. In the vanguard of the science fiction development of cyberpunk, a loosely bound alliance of techno-visionaries, pop culture and street-level anarchists, his work generally explores the implications of computer technology in near-future worlds dominated by corporate capitalism. Novels include *Involution Ocean* (1977), *The Artificial Kid* (1980), *Schismatrix* (1985), *Islands in the Net* (1988), *Heavy Weather* (1994) and *Holy Fire* (1996). His latest novel is *Distraction* (1998), about political intrigue and the sour American Dream, set in 2044. These novels deal with worlds tightly knit by computer networks, in which sites of resistance spring up among communities of anarchists, criminals or fanatics. Short stories occur in *Crystal Express* (1989) and *Globalhead* (1992), and he has edited the influential cyberpunk anthology, *Mirrorshades* (1986). He also co-wrote *The Difference Engine* (1990) with William GIBSON, which belongs to the 'alternative worlds' sub-genre of science fiction, in which steam-driven computers in the English Victorian nineteenth century are threatened by a virus. In addition to numerous stories published in magazines and anthologies, his non-fiction includes *The Hacker Crackdown* (1992), a study of law and disorder in the electronic world.

Storey, David (1933–) A widely honoured British writer, born in Wakefield, Yorkshire, David Malcolm Storey worked at various jobs, including as a postman, teacher and bus conductor, before signing to play with Leeds Rugby League Club (1952–1956). During this time, he commuted to London to attend the Slade School of Art (Diploma 1956), the two pressures of which are combined in his first novel *This Sporting Life* (1960), which depicts the differences between northern working-class and southern intellectual lifestyles. This was followed by *Flight into Camden* (1960), about the art world in which family ties threaten an ambiguous relationship, and other novels, including *Radcliffe* (1963), which examines class conflicts and a homosexual relationship, *Pasmore* (1972), *A Temporary Life* (1973), and *Saville* (1976, Booker Prize), his most highly acclaimed novel, about a Yorkshire miner's son gradually alienated from his family and village by his education, providing a chart of the social and economic changes in post-war Britain. Subsequent novels include *A Prodigal Child* (1983), *Present Times* (1984), which chronicles the life of a professional rugby player, and *A Serious Man* (1998), about a successful artist whose collapsed life is rescued by his daughter. Despite his success with fiction, he prefers the dramatic form, and has written a large number of plays and several screenplays, among which are *The Changing Room* (1971) and *Stages* (1992). A volume of *Collected Poems* was published in 1992.

J. Taylor, *David Storey* (1974).

Stow, Randolph (1935–) A highly regarded Australian novelist, born in Geraldton, Western Australia, and educated at the University of Western Australia. After periods of lecturing at various universities, he travelled and worked in a number of jobs, including a stint as a cadet patrol officer in New Guinea, before settling permanently in Suffolk, England in 1966. His first novel remains his most popular novel in Australia, *The Merry-Go-Round in the Sea* (1965), which is a semi-autobiographical account of a boy's growth and adolescence in 1940s Geraldton. There followed *A Haunted Land* (1956) and *The Bystander* (1957), both of which deal with the disjunctions of English culture in the Australian environment, *To the Islands* (1958, rev. 1982), *Tourmaline* (1963), an exploration of power in an isolated community and drawing upon Taoist philosophy, *Visitants* (1979), set in Papua New Guinea in 1959, *The Girl Green as Elder-flower* (1980), a traditional romance merging with medieval myth, and *Suburbs of Hell* (1984), about a series of English village murders. In addition, he has written two libretti for operas with Peter Maxwell Davies – *Eight Songs for a Mad King* (1969) and *Miss Donnithorne's Maggot* (1974) – a popular children's book *Midnite* (1967), several collections of poetry, and edited *Australian Poetry* (1964). He demonstrates an adept handling of different narrative techniques, mingling realism, symbolism, myth, allegory and romance, and his fiction often explores human metaphysical isolation, and the relationships between England and her colonies.

A. Hassall, *Strange Country: A Study of Randolph Stow* (1986).

Stuart, Francis (1902–2000) Born Henry Francis Montgomery Stuart, in Townsville, Australia, of Ulster parents, he returned to Antrim as a child. In 1920, he married Iseult Gonne, the daughter of Maud Gonne. He took part in the Irish Civil War on the Republican side, and was captured and interned in 1923. His first novel was *Women and God* (1931), about the erosion of Irish society by materialism and scientific rationalism, and the narrator seeks to counter this by a mystical union of flesh and spirit. There followed *Pigeon Irish* (1932) and *The Coloured Dome* (1932), which reveal anxieties about life in modern Ireland, where the romantic mysticism of an ancient past is repressed by the mediocrity of mass commercialism. In a prolific career, other early novels include *Try the Sky* (1933), *Glory* (1933), *In Search of Love* (1935), *The Angel of Pity* (1935), *The White Hare* (1936), *The Bridge* (1937), *Julie* (1938) and *The Great Squire* (1939). Despite hostile accusations, he took a post at Berlin University in 1939, and during the war years broadcast to Ireland from Germany. He was arrested and imprisoned by the Allies until 1946, when he went to London and wrote his trilogy. Consisting of *The Pillar of Cloud* (1948), *Redemption* (1949) and *The Flowering Cross* (1950), it was based on wartime experience, with a brooding intensity over the painful experience of gaining personal and spiritual understanding. Other novels of this middle period of his life include *Good Friday's Daughter* (1952), *The Chariot* (1953), *The Pilgrimage* (1955), *Victors and Vanquished* (1958) and *The Angels of Providence* (1959). Returning to Ireland in 1958, the publication of his memoir *Black List, Section H* (1971), heralded a new literary phase in which he turned to more experimental fiction, in *Memorial* (1973), *A Hole in the Head* (1977), *The High Consistory* (1981), *Faillandia* (1985), *A Compendium of Lovers* (1990) and *King David Dances* (1996). These novels use structural and narrative techniques to undermine textual stability and reliability, and form a series of novels which gave him international critical acclaim in the 1980s and 1990s. *States of Mind* (1984) collects short prose, while the memoir, *Things to Live For* (1934), is an account of the events which shaped his philosophies and beliefs.

G. Elborn, *Francis Stuart: A Life* (1990).

Styron, William (1925–) Born in Newport News, Virginia, US, he served with the US Marines during the Second World War, and subsequently went to Duke University (BA 1947). Widely honoured for his fiction, his first novel was *Lie Down in Darkness* (1951), which narrates the tragic life and suicide of a girl from a rich Virginian family. *The Long March* (1957) is about a forced march leading to the deaths of eight marines, and *Set This House on Fire* (1960) is about US expatriates in France and Italy in search of creativity. *The Confessions of Nat Turner* (1967, Pulitzer Prize 1968) won him major acclaim, and is a meditation on history based on the transcript of a testimony by a slave victim of oppression who led a brief revolt against the Virginia state. Although widely praised, it also led to protests from African-Americans against the alleged white stereotyping. Thirteen years later, he wrote the famous *Sophie's Choice* (1979, filmed 1982), about the life of a concentration camp survivor who loses two children in Auschwitz, travels to Brooklyn after the war, and settles into a tempestuous relationship with her lover. Other works include the essays and memoirs in *This Quiet Dust* (1982) and *Darkness Visible* (1990), the latter about his struggle to overcome clinical depression, a comic play about venereal disease in the navy, entitled *In the Clap Shack* (1973), and the three long stories in *A Tidewater Morning* (1993).

J. West, III, *William Styron: A Life* (1998).

Sukenick, Ronald (1932–) Born in Brooklyn, US, and educated at the universities of Cornell (BA 1955) and Brandeis (MA 1957, Ph.D. 1962), after a variety of university teaching posts, in 1975 he became director of the creative writing programme at the University of Colorado at Boulder. The metafictional *Up* (1968) is a satirical novel of autobiography and fantasy about attempts to write a first novel, while *Out* (1973) is about disaffected New Yorkers of the 1960s trying to find a better life in California, and makes typographical innovations with space and fragmentation. Iconic and visual experimentation continued in 98.6 (1975), about life on a far western commune, set in three parallel spaces, *Long Talking Bad Conditions Blues* (1979), which is one long sentence broken into paragraphs, and *Blown Away* (1987), a curious tale about Hollywood. More recent fictional works are *Doggy Bag* (1994) and *Mosaic Man* (1999), which is a mosaic of stories about the roots of Jewish and western traditions. Short stories appear in *The Death of the Novel* (1969) and *The Endless Short Story* (1986), which demonstrate radical innovation in style and structure. *Wallace Stevens: Musing the Obscure* (1967) is a study of the American poet, and *In Form* (1985) and *Narralogues* (2000) are essays on literature. *Down and In* (1987) is an exploration of 1980s counter-culture through a personal view of Manhattan bars. One of the founders of the Fiction Collective, he is regarded as being one of the principal postmodern invigorators of fiction since the 1960s. His turn away from the aesthetics of realism towards typographical and linguistic experiment has created a writing which represents itself rather than 'reality'.

J. Kutnik, *Fiction as Performance* (1986).

Süskind, Patrick (1949–) Born in Germany, he studied at Munich University and Aix-en-Provence, and became a television scriptwriter, playwright and novelist. He is best known for *Perfume: The Story of a Murderer* (1985, trans. 1986). Set in eighteenth-century Paris, it portrays the life of Grenouille, a man with an uncanny sense of smell who becomes a serial killer. Remarkable for its descriptions of the perfume manufacturing industry in the eighteenth century, it explores evil, obsession and vengeance. He has also written the novellas *The Double Bass* (1984, trans. 1987), *The Pigeon* (1987, trans. 1988), about a day in the life of a man whose life is unnerved by a pigeon landing on his window-sill, and *The Story of Mr Sommer* (1991, trans. 1992), about a boy's glimpse of mortality, in a bleak post-Second World War Germany, and more recently, *Three Stories and Reflection* (trans. 1996). Creating a balance between comedy and tragedy, he writes an evocative prose.

Svevo, Italo (1861–1928) Born Aron Hector Schnitz, into a Jewish family in Trieste, Italy, he attended the University of Trieste (1874–1880) and then worked as a bank clerk and an industrialist. He adopted his pseudonym to underline the dual aspects of his Italian and Swabian (German) roots. His early fiction includes *A Life* (1892, trans. 1963), which takes the hypocrisy and mediocrity of the Triestine middle classes to task, developing the themes of identity, frustration and the crisis of modern humanity, a subject continued in *As a Man Grows Older* (1898, trans. 1932), about an unhappy love affair between people from different classes, and inquiring into the irrational motivations of modern people. One of the first Italian writers to make use of Freudian ideas, *Confessions of Zeno* (1923, trans. 1930) is regarded as his best book, a psychoanalytical novel about the fictional life of Zeno Corsini, a business man in Trieste, which is depicted through diary extracts and explores the recesses of the unconscious. His style paved the way for the new Italian novel, as he used imagination to take the reader out of the modern condition of illness, alienation, moral uncertainty and social deterioration. Other fiction includes the short stories in *The Hoax* (trans. 1929), the novella *The Nice Old Man and the Pretty Girl* (1929, trans. 1930), and the fragments and drafts of his unpublished sequel, *Further Confessions of Zeno* (trans. 1969). *The Works of Italo Svevo* (trans. 1967–1980) have been published in five volumes. A major figure in European modernism, an experimenter in style, language and narrative techniques, his fame came late in the 1920s in Italy and France, with the aid of James JOYCE, who befriended him while teaching at the University of Trieste.

C. Russell, *Italo Svevo, the Writer from Trieste* (1978).

Swift, Graham (1949–) Born Graham Colin Swift, in London, England, he graduated from Cambridge University (MA 1975) and attended York University (1970–1973). A part-time teacher between 1974 and 1983, he turned to full-time writing with *The Sweet-Shop Owner* (1980), portraying the memories and opinions of an industrious shopkeeper in his final hours. *Shuttlecock* (1981) is another analytical tale of the past, in which a police archivist, obsessed with the past, tries to make connections between his records and crimes, and gradually discovers the truth about his father's wartime past. *Waterland* (1984, filmed 1992) is his best-known novel, and is set in the Fens region of eastern England. It is a complex account of a history teacher narrating his past in the first person, mixed with a murder story, and philosophically explores the relationships between narrative, fiction and history. *Out of this World* (1988) once again develops the interplay of history and the present, examining the reconciliation of an estranged father and daughter, while *Ever After* (1992) considers the past life recounted by a depressed academic. *Last Orders* (1996, Booker Prize) is set in Thatcherite Britain, as four ageing friends take the ashes of a fifth friend to scatter at Margate Pier, gradually allowing the portrait of the dead man to emerge through their memories and stories. This novel became embroiled in a controversy over the similarity of the plot to William FAULKNER's novel *As I Lay Dying*. Short stories have appeared in *Learning to Swim* (1982), and he co-edited *The Magic Wheel: An Anthology of Fishing in Literature* (1985) with David Profumo. Widely acclaimed and honoured, he has established himself as one of Britain's foremost contemporary novelists, exploring the psychological motivations of people and the complex interrelationship of the present and the past.

Symons, Julian (1912–1994) Born in London, England, the brother of the British biographer and essayist A.J.A. Symons, Julian Gustave Symons left school at 14, and worked as a secretary in his early years while writing poetry. He edited the influential magazine *Twentieth Century Verse* (1937–1939), introducing the work of new US poets to Britain. He became a Trotskyite in the 1930s and retained moderate left-wing sympathies. After war service, he became a journalist and freelance writer in 1947, and established a reputation for his detective fiction. His first novel was *The Immaterial Murder Case* (1945), and his numerous novels thereafter include *The Colour of Murder* (1957), *The Progress of a Crime* (1960), *The End of Solomon Grundy* (1964), *The Man Who Killed Himself* (1967), *The Players and the Game* (1972), *Murder Under the Mistletoe* (1993) and *Playing Happy Families* (1994). He brought a new psychological depth to detective fiction and was at his best when he combined detection with social comment. He also wrote an influential history of the genre, entitled *Bloody Murder* (1972), as well as biographies of Charles Dickens, Arthur Conan DOYLE, George ORWELL and Dashiell HAMMETT, among others, and general works of history, true crime and criticism, such as his lively history of modernism in *Makers of the New* (1987). An autobiography, *Notes from Another Country* (1972), details his early life.

T

Tan, Amy (1952–) A Chinese-American novelist who lives in San Francisco, Amy Ruth Tan was born in Oakland, California after her parents emigrated to the US. She was educated at San José State University, California (BA 1973, MA 1974), and in Switzerland, and has subsequently worked as an administrator of programmes for disabled children, a reporter and an editor. Widely regarded as one of the pre-eminent Asian-American women novelists, her first novel, *The Joy Luck Club* (1989, filmed 1993), swiftly became a best-seller, narrating the struggle of four mothers and their first-generation Chinese-American daughters who are trying to come to terms with their hybrid cultural identity. There followed the equally successful *The Kitchen God's Wife* (1991), which continued her exploration of mother and daughter relationships, examining the position of women in pre-Revolutionary China. Her third novel was *The Hundred Secret Senses* (1995), which focuses upon the relationship between two half-sisters, Olivia and Kwan, and makes use of the supernatural. Blending the styles of the literary and the popular, her fiction is frequently compared to that of Bharati MUKHERJEE and Louise ERDRICH. Her principal focus is the contrast between the Chinese past and contemporary America, especially for first-generation immigrants to the US, and this has also placed her within a tradition of Asian-American writing closely associated with Maxine Hong KINGSTON. She is also the author of the children's books *The Moon Lady* (1992) and *The Chinese Siamese Cat* (1994).

Tanizaki, Jun'ichiro (1886–1965) Born in Tokyo, Japan, he attended Tokyo Imperial University (1908–1910), and became a playwright, novelist and short story writer after discovering a talent for writing as an undergraduate. Revelling in western influences, thought and practices in the 1920s, he was a committed aesthete in his youth and something of a flamboyant 'bad boy', shocking Japanese society and culture. His early works include *A Spring-Time Case* (1915, trans. 1927), *Naomi* (1925, trans. 1985), *Quicksand* (1931, trans. 1994), which deals with lesbian characters and promiscuity, *A Portrait of Shunkin* (1933, trans. 1965), and *Some Prefer Nettles* (1936, trans. 1955), which is a psychosexual analysis of a domestic crisis in a marriage between a couple from the East and West. Later fiction consists of *The Makioka Sisters* (1949, trans. 1957), which is a novel of manners, and the two minor masterpieces, entitled *The Key* (1957, trans. 1960) and *Diary of an Old Man* (1962, trans. 1965), the latter depicting an impotent old man receiving erotic pleasures from a young girl. Other works include *Seven Japanese Tales* (trans. 1963) and the essay *In Praise of*

Shadows (trans. 1977), while many more plays, short story collections and fiction remain untranslated into English. After the Tokyo earthquake in 1923, he turned to a more traditional Japanese life, and became critical of western values and industrialisation. Preoccupied with the dichotomy of eastern and western values in his writing, he summoned the 'shadows' of the past, although his later writings were condemned as indecent and pornographic. Regarded as one of the masters of Japanese narrative, he was spontaneous and versatile, blending the factual with fantasy in plot and theme.

Van C. Gessel, *Three Modern Novelists: Soseki, Tanizaki, Kawabata* (1993).

Tarkington, Booth (1869–1946) A prolific American novelist, essayist and playwright, born Newton Booth Tarkington, in Indianapolis, Indiana, he attended Princeton University (1891–1893). With 171 stories, over forty novels, nineteen plays and several screenplays, many of his narratives describe middle-class life in the American Midwest of the early part of the twentieth century. His first novel was *The Gentlemen from Indiana* (1899), in which he sought to correct New York perceptions of men from the Midwest, however, popular acclaim came with *Monsieur Beaucaire* (1900), an eighteenth-century romance. Other novels include his most famous work, *The Magnificent Ambersons* (1918, Pulitzer Prize 1919), about the fall and reclamation of the old and wealthy Amberson family through the son and heir George Amberson, and made into a classic film by Orson Welles (1942); and *Alice Adams* (1921, Pulitzer Prize 1922), about a young girl brought up with middle-class aspirations to achieve social and material success. He was also well known for his chronicles of youth in the 'Penrod' series, about Penrod Schofield's adventures and antics whilst growing up, and *Seventeen* (1916), a collection of short stories for

children. His later fiction continued to narrate stories about the economic and historical development of the US, such as the 'Growth' trilogy, comprising *The Magnificent Ambersons*, to which he added *The Midlanders* (1925), written later but the second in his sequence, and *The Turmoil* (1915). He published the autobiographical *The World Does Move* (1928), and many of his books were adapted for the cinema. However, in the age of modernist aesthetics, his adherence to realism and regionalism appeared somewhat conservative.

K. Fennimore, *Booth Tarkington* (1974).

Taylor, Elizabeth (1912–1975) Born in Reading, Berkshire, England, she worked as a governess and librarian, but became a prolific writer whose reputation has been secured by the publication of her work by the feminist Virago Press. Her first novel was *At Mrs Lippincote's* (1945), and others include *Palladian* (1946), *A View of the Harbour* (1949), *A Wreath of Roses* (1949), *A Game of Hide-and-Seek* (1951), *The Sleeping Beauty* (1953), *Angel* (1957), *In a Summer Season* (1961), *The Soul of Kindness* (1964), *The Wedding Group* (1968), *Mrs Palfrey at the Claremont* (1971) and *Blaming* (1976). Highly regarded for her short stories, these are collected in *Hester Lilly* (1954), *The Blush* (1958), *A Dedicated Man* (1965), *The Devastating Boys* (1972) and *Dangerous Calm* (1995). Her witty writing focuses upon the issues of sexuality and sexual tensions between characters, the routine aspects of everyday life, and domestic relationships, which have led some to compare her work to that of Jane Austen and Elizabeth BOWEN.

F. Leclerq, *Elizabeth Taylor* (1985).

Tennant, Emma (1937–) Born in London, England, into an aristocratic family, Emma Christina Tennant attended finishing school and became a debutante in London. She worked as a journalist for

Queen and *Vogue*, contributed to the *Listener* and *New Statesman*, and founded *Bananas* in 1975, a magazine to encourage new writing. Her first novel, *The Colour of Rain* (1964), published under the pseudonym of Catherine Aydy, was about upper-class London. Nine years later, under her own name, saw *The Time of the Crack* (1973), a futuristic and apocalyptic fable about a fissure in the Thames. Other novels include *The Last of the Country House Murders* (1974), *Hotel de Dream* (1976), *The Bad Sister* (1978), about a young woman's alter ego, *Wild Nights* (1979), *Queen of Stones* (1982), *Woman Beware Woman* (1983), *Black Marina* (1985), *The Adventures of Robina, by Herself* (1987), *Two Women of London: The Strange Case of Ms Jekyll and Mrs Hyde* (1989), *Sisters and Strangers* (1990) and *Faustine* (1991). 'The Cycle of the Sun' sequence, examining contemporary English life from the 1950s to the 1980s, so far consists of *House of Hospitalities* (1987) and *A Wedding of Cousins* (1988). Often magic realist in style, characteristically full of black humour and bizarre events, as many of her titles suggest, much of her fiction consciously reworks earlier styles and novels from a feminist perspective, often retold in the form of pastiche and parody. This can be seen in more recent works such as *Pemberly – A Sequel to Pride and Prejudice* (1993), *Tess* (1993), a reworking of Hardy's novel, *An Unequal Marriage – Pride and Prejudice Continued* (1994), *Emma in Love* (1996) and *Elinor and Marianne* (1996), while her most recent novel is *The Lost Brother* (2000). She has written a series of memoirs in *Strangers* (1998), *Girlitude* (1999) and *Burnt Diaries* (1999), the latter describing her affair with Ted Hughes, and the film script for *Frankenstein's Baby* (1990), directed by Robert Bierman.

Tharoor, Shashi (1956–) A widely honoured Anglo-Indian writer, he was born in London, but brought up in Bombay. After

going to the University of Delhi (BA 1978) and Tufts University (MA 1976, Ph.D. 1978), he began work for the UN Commission for Refugees, in Geneva in 1978. He has since become a significant figure at the UN Headquarters in New York for his work on refugees, which has curtailed his writing career. His first novel, *The Great Indian Novel* (1989), recasts the traditional Indian epic *Mahabharata* as a means to satirise India's political history, and in which an elder statesman of the Nationalist Movement, Ved Vyas, presents an allusive and intertextual narration. *Show Business* (1991) is a satire of 'Bollywood', centring upon an actor catapulted to fame in the Indian film business. Demonstrating all the features of self-reflexivity in fiction, these two novels present an irreverent treatment of major Indian issues, such as the nature of society and the nation, and its history and politics, featured in a style which makes full use of linguistic tricks and games. Short stories occur in *The Five-Dollar* (1990), reflecting the consciousness of a male adolescent in urban India, while *Reasons of State* (1982) and *India: From Midnight to Millennium* (1997) are non-fiction studies of India's history and politics. He was appointed executive assistant to UN Secretary General Kofi Annan in 1997.

Theroux, Paul (1941–) A prolific and eclectic American writer, Paul Edward Theroux was born in Medford, Massachusetts, and attended the University of Massachusetts (BA 1963). He taught at universities in Malawi (1960–1965), Uganda (1965–1968) and Singapore (1968–1971), after which he became a full-time writer. Although he is known for his non-fiction, he has written many novels, the first of which was *Waldo* (1967). Other novels include *Saint Jack* (1973), *The Family Arsenal* (1976), following the exploits of a group of terrorists awaiting orders in the London slums, *Picture Palace* (1978), *The Mosquito*

Coast (1982), about an inventor and his family from Massachusetts leaving for the jungles of Honduras, and *Half Moon Street* (1984). His writing continued with *Doctor Slaughter* (1984), *O-Zone* (1986), about a post-apocalyptic American culture in the future, the autobiographical *My Secret History* (1989), *Dr. DeMarr* (1990), *Chicago Loop* (1990), a disturbing murder story about a Chicago businessman, *Millroy the Magician* (1994), about television evangelism, *My Other Life* (1996), which is part novel and part memoir, and *Kowloon Tong* (1997), a business thriller set in the last days of British rule in Hong Kong. Like his fiction, his non-fiction recounts the anomalies of post-imperial life in exotic locales, which has often caused him to be compared to novelists like Joseph CONRAD, Graham GREENE and V.S. NAIPAUL. Works which recount his many travels include *The Great Railway Bazaar* (1975), about a train journey through Asia, *The Old Patagonian Express* (1979), about a train journey through the Americas, *Sailing Through China* (1984), *The Kingdom By the Sea* (1985), about a journey around the coast of Great Britain, *Riding the Iron Rooster* (1988), about a train journey through China, and *The Pillars of Hercules* (1993), about a Mediterranean tour. In addition to autobiographical essays in *Sunrise with Seamonsters* (1985), he has written a controversial memoir of V.S. Naipaul in *Sir Vidia's Shadow* (2000), and recent travel writings have been collected in *Fresh-air Fiend* (2000).

Thomas, D.M. (1935–) Full name Donald Michael Thomas, he was born in Redruth, Cornwall, but spent much of his childhood in Australia. He was educated at Oxford University (MA 1961), after which he became a teacher (1960–1964), and then a lecturer in Hereford (1964–1979). He began as a poet and has published many volumes of poetry over the years, which can be sampled in

Selected Poems (1983). His first two novels, *The Flute-Player* (1979), a fantasy-like meditation on art, and *Birthstone* (1980), about a woman seeking to create a stable identity out of fragments, proved to be unsuccessful. *The White Hotel* (1980, Booker Prize 1981), a blend of real and surreal narratives, combining Freud, the Holocaust and a train journey, brought him huge success in the US, and was infamous for its sensational sexual subject matter. *Flying to Love* (1992) is about the assassination of John F. Kennedy, and was later followed by *Pictures at an Exhibition* (1993), *Eating Pavlova* (1994), and *Lady with a Laptop* (1996), a satire about a mediocre novelist writing a mystery novel. He has also published the 'Russian Nights' quintet, set in post-war eastern Europe, consisting of *Ararat* (1983), *Swallow* (1984), *Sphinx* (1986), *Summit* (1987) and *Lying Together* (1990), which is a series of stories within stories calling into question the distinction between truth and fiction, and in which sex and psychoanalysis form the principal ingredients. He has translated the Russian poets Yevtushenko, Akhmatova and Pushkin, and has written a biography of Aleksander SOLZHENITSYN (1998), and an experimental memoir entitled *Memories and Hallucinations* (1988).

Thompson, Hunter S. (1939–) Born Hunter Stockton Thompson, in Louisville, Kentucky, US, he studied journalism at Columbia University, and became a writer and journalist, working for *Rolling Stone* magazine (1970–1984) and the *San Francisco Examiner* (1985–1990). One of the foremost practitioners, along with Tom WOLFE and Gay Talese, of the 'new journalism' that evolved in the 1960s, he called his brand of writing 'Gonzo Journalism'. This was a series of mad, drug-ridden forays into the heart of complacent America, in a style which indulged in insult and invective, as he chronicled the disillusionment and delirium of the volatile era of the 1960s and the souring of the 'American dream'. His first work was *Hell's Angels: A Strange and Terrible Saga* (1966), about the infamous Californian motorcycle gang, with whom he rode for almost a year while researching the book. *Fear and Loathing in Las Vegas* (1972, filmed 1998) followed, and still remains his best-known book. It is basically a confession of the persona Raoul Duke's failure to report on some Las Vegas conferences, detailing instead his drug-induced hallucinations and fantasy adventures, which become symbolic of the state of the American nation. *Fear and Loathing on the Campaign Trail '72* (1973) is an account of George McGovern's presidential campaign, and collections of essays, including journalism about the Watergate Scandal, appear in *The Great Shark Hunt: Gonzo Papers Volume I* (1979). After *The Curse of Lono* (1983), which tells of his antics in Hawaii with his friend Ralph Steadman, he continued to mine his vein of personal, high energy reporting from his columns in the *San Francisco Examiner* for further volumes of the 'Gonzo Papers', in *Generations of Swine* (1988), which lambastes the American conservatism of the 1980s, and *Songs of the Doomed* (1990), which among other things gives an account of his arrest and charge for five felonies in 1990. Other volumes include *Silk Road* (1990), *Untitled Novel* (1992) and *Better Than Sex: Confessions of a Political Junkie* (1994), the publication of a novel written in 1959 about the fears of a dead-end journalism career in *The Rum Diary* (1998), and a selection of letters from 1955 to 1967 in *The Proud Highway* (1997). A controversial figure, he provided the cartoonist Garry Trudeau with the inspiration for his character 'Uncle Duke' in his *Doonesbury* cartoon strip.

C. Jean, *Hunter* (1993).

Tlali, Miriam (1933–) Born in a designated black suburb of Johannesburg, South Africa, she attended the University of the Witwatersrand, before being forced out by apartheid legislation, whereupon she went to Roma University in Lesotho. Owing to financial difficulties, she dropped her studies and worked as an electrical clerk in Johannesburg. This experience formed the basis for her first autobiographical novel, *Muriel at Metropolitan* (1975), which describes the degrading treatment of the black female protagonist Muriel at an electrical store. Describing the daily indignities, oppressions and inequalities suffered by black South Africans, parts of the book were banned under apartheid. Her second novel, *Amandla!* (1980), meaning 'power is ours', was also banned, due to its harrowing depiction of the Soweto uprising in 1976. *Mihloti* (1984), meaning 'tears', includes various pieces from her experiences as a journalist in the late 1970s for the magazine *Staffrider*, an influential and important journal for black writers which she co-founded, while *Soweto Stories* (1989, also published as *Footprints in the Quag*), deals with racial and sexual oppression and the tensions derived from relocation from rural to city environments.

M. Schipper, ed., *Unheard Words* (1984).

Tóibín, Colm (1955–) Born in Wexford, Ireland, he was educated at University College, Dublin, and has since worked as a columnist for various newspapers. His first novel was *The South* (1990), depicting the relationship between an Irish Protestant woman and a Spanish Civil War activist in the aftermath of 1939. This was followed by *The Blazing Heather* (1992), about a judge and his relationship with his wife after his retirement, *The Story of the Night* (1996), which is about a gay man coming-of-age in Argentina during the Falkland's War, and his latest novel is *The Blackwater Lightship* (1999). An articulate essayist and writer of travelogues, his non-fiction includes *Walking Along the Border*

(1987), *Homage to Barcelona* (1990), and *The Sign of the Cross* (1995), a book about Catholic Europe. Emerging as a distinctive and confident new voice in Irish writing, his fiction keys in with contemporary events.

Tolkien, J.R.R. (1892–1973) Full name John Ronald Reuel Tolkien, born in Bloemfontein, South Africa, he went to England in 1895 and was educated at Oxford University (MA 1919). An author and academic scholar, he lectured at Leeds (1920–1925) and Oxford (1925–1973) universities, where his wide variety of research into Anglo-Saxon and Medieval English culture and literature made him the leading philologist of his age, producing seminal Middle English texts in *A Middle-English Vocabulary* (1922), *Sir Gawain and the Green Knight* (1925) and *Beowulf: The Monsters and the Critics* (1936). He is most famous for the creation of his own world, called Middle-Earth, complete with its own creatures, heroes, history and language, and drawing upon his knowledge of ancient literatures and cultures. It began with *The Hobbit* (1937), and continued in *The Lord of the Rings* trilogy, consisting of *The Fellowship of the Ring* (1954), *The Two Towers* (1954) and *The Return of the King* (1955), which can be seen as an allegory of good and evil in the context of the Second World War, and in which Frodo the hobbit quests for the Ring of Power in order to bring peace to the Land. Other novels include the satirical *Farmer Giles of Ham* (1949), *Tree and Leaf* (1964), *Smith of Wootton Major* (1967), *The Silmarillion* (1977), *Unfinished Tales of Numenor and Middle-Earth* (1980) and a volume of poetry in *The Adventures of Tom Bombadil and Other Verses from the Red Book* (1962). *Pictures by J.R.R. Tolkien* (1979) and *Letters* (1981) appeared posthumously, along with *The Book of Lost Tales* (2 vols, 1983–1985). His Middle-Earth creations have proved to be some of the most

unique, enduring and influential fantasy stories, and have sparked a host of imitations.

H. Carpenter, *J.R.R. Tolkien: A Biography* (1977).

Toole, John Kennedy (1937–1969) Born in New Orleans, Louisiana, he was educated at Tulane (BA 1958) and Columbia (MA 1959) universities. He then undertook some graduate study at Tulane in the mid-1960s, and taught at colleges in New York and Louisiana between 1959 and 1968. He committed suicide in Biloxi, Mississippi. Famous for his one novel, *A Confederacy of Dunces* (1980, Pulitzer Prize 1981), it was written in the 1960s when he was stationed as a soldier in Puerto Rico, and remained unpublished until his death. His mother tried to get it published, and after several rejections, took it to Walker PERCY who championed the book, and it subsequently became a best-seller. It depicts the farcical and humorous exploits of Ignatius J. Reilly, a misfit, liar, raconteur and mother's boy, and is regarded by some to be one of the funniest novels ever written. Many believe that if he had lived, he would have been one of the South's most significant novelists.

Toomer, Jean (1894–1967) Born Nathan Pinchbeck Toomer, in Washington DC, he attended the University of Wisconsin (1914) and the City University of New York (1917–1918). He worked as a teacher in Georgia (1920–1921), but was otherwise a professional writer, changing his name to Jean Toomer and acting as an important bridge between the Harlem renaissance writers and the literary scene of Greenwich Village in the 1920s. His principal book is *Cane* (1923), an experimental work collecting sketches, poetry and drama, depicting the black experiences in the South and urban, northern life, in a search for meaning that is at the core of American modernism. Although a search for wholeness was the central theme of his writing, he never again dealt with African-Americans as his subject. He fell under the influence of the Russian mystic and psychologist Gurdjieff's writings, and his later work became propaganda on behalf of Gurdjieff's theories. Consequently, he fell into obscurity after 1923, although he published *Essentials* (1931), a collection of aphorisms that express his philosophy of life, and the epic *The Blue Meridian* (1936). Writers such as Alice WALKER and Gloria NAYLOR have claimed him as a significant influence on their work, and his selected previously unpublished writings appeared in 1993.

N. McKay, *Jean Toomer, Artist* (1984).

Tournier, Michel (1924–) Born in Paris, France, Michel Edouard Tournier attended the universities of Paris and Tubingen, and worked as a producer and director in French radio (1949–1954), as a journalist (1955–1958), and for Plon publishers (1958–1968). A prolific writer, his novels include *Friday; or, the Other Island* (1967, trans. 1969), which deviates from the Robinson Crusoe story by stressing the alternatives to rationalism and technical order, showing Crusoe going native with Friday as his teacher; *The Erl King* (1970, Prix Goncourt, trans. 1972), based upon Goethe's poem, and set in Nazi Germany, it presents issues of morality to do with fascism; *Gemini* (1975, trans. 1981), which depicts the experiences of identical twins; *The Four Wise Men* (1980, trans. 1982), which retells the story of the Magi, albeit departing from orthodox Christian belief; *Gilles and Jeanne* (1983, trans. 1987); *The Ogre* (1984, trans. 1997), about an innocent man sucked into the Nazi machine and the Holocaust; *A Garden at Hammamet* (trans. 1985); *The Golden Droplet* (1986, trans. 1987), about a quest for identity in a world where images are more valued than realities; and *The Midnight Love*

Feast (1989, trans. 1991). A considerable variety of other works include an autobiography in *The Wind Spirit* (1977, trans. 1988), essays in *Waterline* (trans. 1994) and *The Mirror of Ideas* (1994, trans. 1998), and short stories in *Fetishist* (trans. 1983). A radical social critic, his novels consist primarily of philosophical speculations combined with fiction in unexpected ways, and are densely packed with complex webs of symbols and allusions.

D. Colin, *Michel Tournier: Philosophy and Fiction* (1988).

Trapido, Barbara (1941–) Born in Cape Town, South Africa, Barbara Louise Trapido went to the University of Natal (BA 1963) and the University of London (Dip.Ed. 1967). She worked as a schoolteacher from 1964 until 1970, when she turned to writing full-time. Her first novel was *Brother of the More Famous Jack* (1982), nominated for the Whitbread Award, a satirical romance about fifteen years in the life of a father-fixated woman and her relationships. *Noah's Ark* (1984) explores the fragile and precarious nature of contemporary family life in the lives of Alison and her husband Noah, set in the political climate of apartheid South Africa in the 1960s, while *Temples of Delight* (1990) contains shrewdly observed classroom experiences and a portrayal of the *nouveau riche*. *Juggling* (1994) adapts Shakespearean comedy in its depiction of twins growing up in New York, while her latest novel, *The Travelling Horn Player* (1998), presents three different narrators in contemporary England in a tale of loss and grief. A contemporary novelist of psychological and emotional tension amidst comic circumstances, she has also contributed to the *Sunday Telegraph*, the *Sunday Times* and the *Spectator*.

Tremain, Rose (1943–) Born in London, England, she was educated at the Sorbonne, University of Paris, and the University of East Anglia (BA 1967), where she later became a lecturer in English. She turned to writing in 1970, and has built up a steady reputation as one of the best contemporary British fiction writers. Her first novel was *Sadler's Birthday* (1976), about an English butler's life, which was followed by *Letter to Sister Benedicta* (1978), about a woman trapped in an unhappy marriage after her husband's stroke, *The Cupboard* (1981), *The Swimming Pool Season* (1985), about the interconnections between the lives of expatriates in a French provincial town, *Restoration* (1989), which is a historical novel set in the court of Charles II in the late 1600s, dealing with the social adjustments and the excesses of aristocratic life, and *Sacred Country* (1992), about transsexuality, sexual identity and gender. More recent novels are *Way I Found Her* (1997), a coming-of-age thriller set in Paris, and *Music and Silence* (2000), which is a series of interlocked stories centring upon a young English lutenist who joins the court orchestra of Christian IV of Denmark in 1629. Short stories occur in *The Colonel's Daughter* (1984), *The Garden of the Villa Mollini* (1987), *Evangelista's Fan* (1994) and *Collected Short Stories* (1996). As well as writing radio and television plays, her other books include *Freedom for Women* (1971) and a biography of Stalin (1974). Often tinged with descriptive irony, her characters tend to be lonely and unfulfilled, and her diverse fiction constantly offers new departures and challenges.

Tressell, Robert (1870–1911) The penname of Robert Noonan, born in Dublin, Ireland, he was educated in London, and then went to South Africa for two years in 1893. In 1902, he worked as a housepainter and sign-writer in Hastings, Sussex. He eventually died of tuberculosis in Liverpool while on his way to Canada. Active in the early British Labour movement, he is principally remembered for his novel *The Ragged Trousered Philanthro-*

pists (1914), which was published initially in a bowdlerised version by his daughter, the complete version not appearing until 1955. Seen as a twentieth-century fable and social documentary, it is regarded now as one of the outstanding working-class novels of the twentieth century. Powerfully satirical, it reflects the attitudes of philanthropists (the working class) towards their capitalist exploiters.

J. Mitchell, *Robert Tressell and the Ragged Trousered Philanthropists* (1969).

Trevor, William (1928–) Born William Trevor Cox, in Michelstown, Cork, Ireland, he was educated at Trinity College, Dublin (BA 1950). After teaching in Ireland and England, he turned to sculpture and then writing, and settled in England in 1953. His first novel was *A Standard of Behaviour* (1958), since which time, he has written a large number of black comedies, distinguished by a rogues' gallery of eccentric, aged, orphaned, sexually perverted and marginally insane characters who hilariously disrupt society, and where institutions such as boardingschools and beach resorts act as representations of the world at large. Some of these novels are *The Old Boys* (1964), *The Love Department* (1966), *The Children of Dynmouth* (1976) and *Other People's Worlds* (1980). Several of his novels in the 1980s explored the turbulent Irish political history and condition, such as *Fools of Fortune* (1983), *The Silence in the Garden* (1988), and the widely praised and prize-winning *Felicia's Journey* (1994), which tells of an Irishwoman's emigration to England. More recently, *Death in Summer* (1998) depicts an obsessive relationship between a widower and a nanny. With novels set in England, Ireland and Europe with equal assurance, he straddles the two literary traditions of Dickensian middle-class England and Elizabeth BOWEN's knowledge of the Anglo-Irish ascendancy. His short stories occur in *The Ballroom of Romance*

(1972), *Family Sins* (1990), *The Collected Stories* (1992), *After Rain* (1996) and *Cocktails at Doney's* (1996), and his collected essays appear in *Excursions in the Real World* (1993). He has also edited the *Oxford Book of Irish Short Stories* (1989). Many of his later novels depict characters burdened with the weight of the past and seeking to adjust to contemporary Irish life. Regarded as a master of traditional forms, he is not averse to modernist techniques of collage and fragmentation.

G. Schimer, *William Trevor: A Study of His Fiction* (1990).

Trollope, Joanna (1943–) Born in Gloucestershire, England, she studied at Oxford University (MA 1965), and after working in the Foreign Office and as an English schoolteacher for twelve years, became a writer. Her prolific output of novels include *Eliza Stanhope* (1978), set in the English Regency period, *Parson Harding's Daughter* (1979), *A Village Affair* (1989), *A Passionate Man* (1990), *The Rector's Wife* (1991), about a woman's troubled relationship with her minister husband, *The Man and the Girls* (1992), *A Spanish Lover* (1993), and *Next of Kin* (1996), about a dairy farmer's family coping with their mother's death. More recent novels include *Other People's Children* (1998), about painfully divided affections when a stepfamily is formed, and *Marrying the Mistress* (2000), about family reactions when a judge leaves his wife to marry his younger mistress. She has recently begun a series of historical novels, written under the pseudonym Caroline Harvey, beginning with *The Brass Dolphin* (1999), which is set in Malta during the Second World War. A descendant of the famous Victorian novelist Anthony Trollope, her best-selling novels are set in the English countryside, and many of them have been adapted for television in the US and Britain. With provincial settings and witty

dialogue, and depicting family crises with sympathetic characters, her novels are usually carefully researched and full of good cheer.

Troyat, Henri (1911–) Born Lev Tarassoff in Moscow, Russia, he settled in Paris in 1920 after the Russian Revolution and changed his name. After working for the government (1935–1941), he became a prolific writer. His novels include *One Minus Two* (1936, trans. 1938), *The Web* (1938, trans. 1984) and *Judith Madrier* (1940, trans. 1941), all short psychological works which established his reputation. He gained worldwide renown for his multi-volume best-selling historical sagas, which use realist fiction to examine world crises in history. These include the trilogy – *My Father's House* (1947, trans. 1951), *The Red and the White* (1948, trans. 1956) and *Strangers on Earth* (1950, trans. 1958) – which cover the years leading up to the First World War in Russia and his move to France, the five-volume *The Seed and the Fruit* (1953–1958, trans. 1956–1962), and the five-volume *The Light of the Just* (trans. 1959–1963), which cover Napoleon's rise to power during the early nineteenth century. Other novels include *The Mountain* (1952, trans. 1953), *An Intimate Friendship* (1963, trans. 1967), the three volumes of *Sylvie* (1980–1989, trans. 1982–1989) for younger readers, which is about a young girl in mid-twentieth-century Paris, *The Children* (1982, trans. 1983) and *An Act of Treachery* (1988, trans. 1990). He is perhaps best known to English-speaking readers for his various biographies of, for example, Dostoevsky (trans. 1940), Pushkin (trans. 1946), Tolstoy (trans. 1965), Gogol (trans. 1971), Catherine the Great (trans. 1977), Peter the Great (trans. 1979) and Turgenev (trans. 1985).

Turner, George (1916–1997) An Australian writer, born and educated in Melbourne, he served in the Australian army during the Second World War. His first novel was *Young Man of Talent* (1959), about soldiers in New Guinea during the Second World War, and was suceeded by 'The Treelake saga' – *A Stranger and Afraid* (1961), the widely acclaimed *The Cupboard Under the Stairs* (1962), *A Waste of Shame* (1965) and *The Lame Dog Man* (1967) – a tetralogy which examined social dilemmas and conflicts in the town of Treelake. Following the publication of these realist novels, in 1967 he suffered from acute depression and a period of creative silence. However, 1970 saw him take a new turn as a science fiction reviewer for the Melbourne *Age*, and he wrote his first science fiction novel in 1978, since when he has established himself as Australia's premier science fiction writer and critic. Regarded as his best work, his science fiction includes the 'Ethical Culture' novels, *Beloved Son* (1978), *Vaneglory* (1981) and *Yesterday's Men* (1983), which examine the twenty-first century's blindnesses and psychological experiments, *Transit of Cassidy* (1978), about the corrosive effects of unrestrained egotism, and *The Sea and Summer* (1987), an important novel which traces the details of a family's collapse as a result of the greenhouse effect. More recent novels include *Brain Child* (1991) and *Destiny Makers* (1992), both of which are sequels to *Beloved Son*, *Genetic Soldier* (1994), and the posthumously published *Down There in Darkness* (1999). *In the Heart or in the Head* (1984) is a memoir, and short stories occur in *Pursuit of Miracles* (1990).

Turow, Scott (1949–) Born in Chicago, Illinois, US, he was educated at Amherst College (BA 1970) and Stanford University (MA 1974), while working as a lecturer in creative writing (1972–1975). He then studied law at Harvard University (JD 1978), during which time he wrote *One L* (1977), an insider's view of the Harvard Law School, which has become almost required reading for all new applicants.

He has since worked as an Assistant US Attorney, and is now a practising attorney in a Chicago law firm. His first novel, written at odd hours on the way to work, was *Presumed Innocent* (1987, filmed 1990), followed by *The Burden of Proof* (1990), which were widely praised for the depiction of the murky terrain of urban justice. There followed *Pleading Guilty* (1993), about a law firm's internal investigation after a financial scandal, *The Laws of Our Fathers* (1996), and most recently, *Personal Injuries* (1999), about a corrupt lawyer who agrees to aid the FBI in exchange for leniency. Turow uses his insider knowledge of the US legal system to form the basis of his best-selling suspense novels of intrigue and corruption in the legal environment, and is especially famous for his staged courtroom scenes.

Tutuola, Amos (1920–1997) Born in Abeokuta, western Nigeria, he received limited formal education, and worked as a coppersmith before entering the colonial civil service in 1948. Taking up writing to relieve his boredom, he jotted down tales from the Yoruba folk repertoire. Faber and Faber published *The Palm-Wine Drinkard* (1952), a series of loosely and randomly connected episodes, involving humans and weird creatures from the non-human world. This was followed by *My Life in the Bush of Ghosts* (1954), in which a boy enters the 'Bush of Ghosts', where he has twenty-four years of adventures, wandering from town to town before finding his way back to the land of the living. Further books, such as *Simbi and the Satyr of the Dark Jungle* (1955), *The Brave African Huntress* (1958), *Feather Woman of the Jungle* (1962), *Ayaiyi and His Inherited Poverty* (1967) and *The Witch-Herbalist of the Remote Town* (1981), retained the quest structure, as well as inverting common-sense logic, giving them a surreal flavour. Despite Tutuola's success in Europe, he suffered for years from poor comparison with other Nigerian writers, and there was only belated acceptance by the Yoruba readership. However, continued acceptance came with *Yoruba Folk-tales* (1986), *Pauper, Brawler, Slanderer* (1987), which showed the enduring influence of D.O. Fagunwa (a Yoruba folk-teller and writer), although radical revisions and rewritings raised questions about their Yoruba origins, *Feather Woman in the Jungle* (1988) and *Village Doctor* (1988). Despite an international following, his work has received an ambivalent critical reception, and he has remained a somewhat marginal figure within African literature.

O. Owomoyela, *Amos Tutuola Revisited* (1998).

Tyler, Anne (1941–) Born in Minneapolis, Minnesota, US, she grew up in the Quaker community, and attended Duke University (BA 1961), where she studied Russian. She is a prolific and widely honoured best-selling novelist. After her early *If Morning Ever Comes* (1964), and three other novels, wider acclaim came with *Celestial Navigation* (1974), about an agoraphobic artist in Baltimore and his female relationships, and *Searching for Caleb* (1976), about four generations of the Peck family. There followed *Earthly Possessions* (1977), about a woman held hostage by a bank robber on the run and their relationship, *Morgan's Passing* (1980), *Dinner at the Homesick Restaurant* (1982), the tragedy and farce of a family's life recounted from a deathbed, and *The Accidental Tourist* (1985, filmed 1988), a comic book about American insularity and xenophobia. The widely praised *Breathing Lessons* (1988, Pulitzer Prize) explores the themes of marriage, love and regret in a day in the life of a mother; *Saint Maybe* (1991) is about religion; *Ladder of Years* (1995) looks at the new-found independence of a middle-aged woman, and her past life; and *A Patchwork Planet* (1998) is about a terrible loser who tries to get his life in order, despite encountering pitfalls along the way. Often compared to Carson MCCULLERS, Flannery O'CONNOR and Eudora WELTY for her urban Southern scenarios and the social misfits who populate her fiction, she writes about the obdurate endurance of the human spirit, and the effects of everyday life, grounded in generally slow-paced, circular plots.

E. Evans, *Anne Tyler* (1993).

U

Undset, Sigrid (1882–1949) Born in Kalundborg, Denmark, she was brought up in Norway, and graduated from the Commercial College, Oslo (1898). Undset worked in the office of an electrical firm in Oslo, and turned to writing in 1909. She moved to the US during the Second World War. Her first novel was *Gunnar's Daughter* (1909, trans. 1936), followed by *Jenny* (1911, trans. 1920), about a young working girl facing the pressures of modern society. *Images in a Mirror* (1917, trans. 1938) was followed by her most successful work, a trilogy set in the fourteenth century, collected in *Kristin Lavransdatter* (trans. 1930), consisting of *The Garland* (1920, trans. 1922), *The Mistress of Husaby* (1922, trans. 1925) and *The Cross* (1922, trans. 1927). Regarded as her finest achievement, its realism in a wealth of detail tracks the development of the young woman's life against the political history of Scandinavian kingdoms and emergent Christianity. A prolific writer, her other novels include *The Master of Hestviken* (1925, trans. 1935), set in the thirteenth century, *The Wild Orchid* (1929, trans. 1931), *The Longest Years* (1934, trans. 1935) and *Madame Dorothea* (1939, trans. 1941). A chronicler of past ages, Norwegian history acted as a foundation for a number of her medieval historical novels, which frequently involved religious themes. She stood against Nazism during the 1930s, and her move to the US brought an end to her career as a novelist. She was awarded the Nobel Prize for Literature in 1928.

M. Brunsdale, *Sigrid Undset: Chronicles of Norway* (1988).

Unsworth, Barry (1930–) Born Barry Forster Unsworth, in Durham, England, he studied English at Manchester University (BA 1951), and since 1960, has lectured in many cities, including London, Athens and Istanbul. From his first novel, *The Partnership* (1966), which is set in an artists' colony in Cornwall, he has written a variety of novels. These include: *The Greeks Have a Word For It* (1967), *The Hide* (1970), *Mooncranker's Gift* (1973), *Pascali's Island* (1980), *The Idol Hunter* (1980) and *The Rage of the Vulture* (1982), both of which are set at the turn of the century in Constantinople, *Stone Virgin* (1985), set in Renaissance Venice, and *Sugar and Rum* (1988), about a writer blocked while trying to write a novel about slavery. *Sacred Hunger* (1992, joint winner Booker Prize), set on an eighteenth-century slave-ship, is a harrowing utopian social adventure in Florida, while *Morality Play* (1995) is set in fourteenth-century Yorkshire, about a monk errant who joins a troupe of actors, whose dramatic innovations prefigure the development of western drama's psychological realism. His most recent work includes *After Hannibal* (1996), which is set in rural Umbria, Italy, concerning three expatriates who become ensnared in dangers of greed, perfidy and deceit, and *Losing Nelson* (1999), about a historian obsessed with Horatio Nelson, which examines the darker side of patriotism. He has received wide critical acclaim for his historical novels and his exploration of imperial power and ethical dilemmas since the 1970s.

Updike, John (1932–) John Hoyer Updike was born in Shillington, Pennsylvania, US, and went to Harvard University, and the Ruskin School of Drawing and Fine Art in Oxford, England. He worked as a staff writer with *The New Yorker* magazine (1955–1957), before turning to full-time writing. Many of his stories are set in Pennsylvania or Massachusetts. His first novel, *The Poorhouse Fair* (1959), about an insurrection by the inhabitants of an old people's home, received much critical acclaim. Perhaps his best-known books are a sequence of four novels which follow the fortunes of Harry 'Rabbit' Angstrom during the changes taking place in America from the 1960s to the 1980s. These are *Rabbit Run* (1960), *Rabbit Redux* (1971), *Rabbit Is Rich* (1981; Pulitzer Prize, 1982) and *Rabbit at Rest* (1990; Pulitzer Prize, 1991), and are collected in *Rabbit Angstrom: A Tetralogy* (1995). Other novels include *The Centaur* (1963), *Of the Farm* (1965), concerning the tensions between a man's wife and his mother, *Couples* (1968), about the infidelities of suburban neighbours, *Bech: A Book* (1970), about a writer seeking recognition, and a sequel, *Bech Is Back* (1982), *A Month of Sundays* (1975), *Marry Me* (1976), *The Witches of Eastwick* (1984, filmed 1987), and *Brazil* (1994). More recent novels include *In the Beauty of the Lilies* (1996), *Toward the End of Time* (1997), *Bech at Bay* (1998), which continues the ongoing sagas of the philandering Jewish-American Henry Bech, and *Gertrude and Claudius* (2000),

which is a witty prequel to Shakespeare's *Hamlet*. Updike has also written many short stories, most of which are collected in *The Same Door* (1959), *Pigeon Feathers* (1962), *The Music School* (1966), *Museums and Women* (1972), *Too Far to Go* (1979), *Problems* (1979) and *The Afterlife* (1994). In addition to a compendium of book reviews, interviews and essays, entitled *Picked Up Pieces* (1975), *Golf Dreams* (1996) and *More Matter* (1999), he has also written poetry, in *The Carpentered Hen and Other Tame Creatures* (1958), *Telephone Poles* (1963), *Midpoint* (1969), *Seventy Poems* (1972) and *Tossing and Turning* (1977). Producing sophisticated analyses of American middle-class life, he is regarded as something of a doyen of contemporary American literature.

J. Newman, *John Updike* (1988); J. Schiff, *John Updike Revisited* (1998).

Upward, Edward (1904–) Born in Romford, Essex, England, Edward Falaise Upward was educated at Cambridge University (MA 1925), and was a schoolmaster until 1962. At school, he befriended Christopher ISHERWOOD, with whom he wrote *The Mortmere Stories* (1994), set in an imaginary place. He was also closely associated with W.H. Auden and Stephen Spender in the 1930s. A novelist of promise in the 1920s and 1930s, his first novel, *Journey to the Border* (1938), examined Marxism through interior monologue. After joining the Communist Party, his political affiliations hindered him from writing for almost twenty-five years. He began to write again in 1954, having left the Party, and produced his major work, *The Spiral Ascent* (1977), which is a trilogy using autobiographical elements, and consists of *In the Thirties* (1962), *The Rotten Elements* (1969) and *No Home But the Struggle* (1977). It depicts a frustrated poet and schoolmaster, Alan Sebrill, who joins the Communist Party only to find his artistic ideals incompatible with his politics. Short story collections occur in *The Railway Accident* (1969), *The Night Walk* (1987), *An Unmentionable Man* (1994) and *The Coming Day* (2000), and memoirs in *Christopher Isherwood: Notes in Remembrance of Friendship* (1996) and *Remembering the Earlier Auden* (1998).

Uris, Leon (1924–) Born in Baltimore, US, Leon Marcus Uris has written several best-sellers, based upon events and details drawn from history. In eleven novels written over four decades, he has chronicled the unceasing fight of committed individuals against the forces of oppression, in particular fascism, communism and imperialism. In the tradition of the historical novel, his plots bear witness to political and social tensions as well as personal conflicts. *Battle Cry* (1953) emerged out of his Second World War experiences in the US Marines, *The Angry Hills* (1955) is about the Palestine Brigade's service in Greece, while the thoroughly researched *Exodus* (1958) is the tale of the establishment of Israel. Other novels include *Mila 18* (1961), about the Warsaw Ghetto uprising against the Nazis, *Armageddon* (1963), set in Berlin after the war, and *Topaz* (1967), about Soviet espionage in France. His recent novels include *QB VII* (1970), a legal narrative about Nazi experimentation, *Trinity* (1976), and the sequel *Redemption* (1995), about conflicts in Northern Ireland, *The Haj* (1984) about relationships between Palestinians, Arabs and Israelis, *Mitla Pass* (1988), a love story set during the 1956 Sinai War, *Redemption* (1995), which is a sequel to *Trinity*, and *A God in Ruins* (2000), an epic novel set on the eve of the 2000 US presidential election, in which the Irish-American front-runner discovers that he is Jewish. Non-fiction includes *Ireland: A Terrible Beauty* (1975) and *Jerusalem* (1981), a history of Israel. His themes include the indomitability of the human spirit, the power of patriotism, and the restorative capacity of romantic love. He developed a style of panoramic historical, fast-paced fiction, with a mass audience appeal, to rank alongside that of James MICHENER and James CLAVELL.

V

Valenzuela, Luisa (1938–) Born in Buenos Aires, Argentina, she graduated from the University of Buenos Aires, and went to work as the assistant editor on the newspaper *La Nación* in Buenos Aires (1964–1969). She has also worked as a freelance journalist, and from 1980, has held various academic posts. Her novels are *Clara: 13 Short Stories and a Novel* (1966, trans. 1976), which is a feminist exploration of gender stereotypes, centred upon a young prostitute's desire to 'use her head', *The Lizard's Tail* (trans. 1983), which for the most part engages with Péronist politics, *Bedside Manners* (1990, trans. 1995), and *Black Novel with Argentines* (1990, trans. 1992), a thriller set in New York among paranoid Argentine exiles. Her short stories appear in *Strange Things Happen Here* (1975, trans. 1979), *Other Weapons* (1982, trans. 1985), *Open Door* (trans. 1988), *The Censors* (trans. 1988), *He Who Searches* (1977, trans. 1987) and *Symmetries* (1993, trans. 1998). A feminist, her writing pushes against the barriers of all kinds of censorship, searching for a new language in her use of shifting narrators and humorous linguistic games.

S. Magnarelli, *Reflections/Refractions: Reading Luisa Valenzuela* (1988).

Van Herk, Aritha (1954–) A Canadian writer, born in Wetaskiwin, Alberta, and educated at the University of Alberta (BA 1976, MA 1978), she teaches creative writing at the University of Calgary. She began with the novel *Judith* (1978), which depicted a heroine defined by her environment in rural Alberta, and this was followed by *The Tent Peg* (1981), set in the stark and forbidding Yukon landscape, *No Fixed Address* (1986), about a character who explores and maps the vast spaces of western and northern Canada, and *Restlessness* (1998), a novel about suicide. She has edited *Due West* (1996), a collection of stories from the great plains states in Canada. Focusing upon young women's attempts to establish their independence and autonomy through spiritual quests, her fiction teeters on fantasy, yet remains anchored in the familiar world. In a self-reflexive fiction about the nature of the relationship between author and character, the novels reshape traditional classical myths of female identity, and they display a striking sense of national and geographic identity. This is a strong element in her three books of criticism and ficto-criticism – *Places Far from Ellesmere: A Geografictione* (1990), which considers how we read landscape through literature, *A Frozen Tongue* (1991) and *In Visible Ink* (1991) – which often blur the boundaries between fiction and criticism in typical postmodernist fashion.

Vargas Llosa, Mario (1936–) Born in Arequipa, Peru, he was brought up in Bolivia and Peru by his grandparents. He studied literature and law at the University of San Marcos (1955–1957) and gained a doctorate from the University of Madrid (1959). After working as a journalist and co-editor, he went to Paris as a teacher and broadcaster, returning to Peru in 1975. He has since held various academic posts around the world, and stood as an unsuccessful candidate for the presidency of Peru in 1990. His first phase of writing includes *The Time of the Hero* (1963, trans. 1966), *The Green House* (1966, trans. 1968) and *Conversation in the Cathedral* (1969, trans. 1975), and displays a geometric progression, formal patterning, interwoven plots and a range of characters, all motivated by the concept of the 'total novel'. His second phase tends to the political and a re-elaboration of autobiographical events. Such works as *Captain Pantoja and the Special Service* (1973, trans. 1978), *Aunt Julia and the Scriptwriter* (1977, trans. 1982, filmed 1990), *The War of the End of the World* (1981, trans. 1984), *The Real Life of Alejandro Mayta* (1984, trans. 1986), *Who Killed Palomino Molero?* (1986, trans. 1987), *The Storyteller* (1987, trans. 1989), *In Praise of the Stepmother* (1988, trans. 1990) and its sequel in *The Notebooks of Don Rigoberto* (1997, trans. 1998), and *Death in the Andes* (1993, trans. 1996), are less concerned with the 'total novel' ideal, and are less realistic and more postmodern in their shifting terrain of language. Often reflecting upon Peruvian politics and the dilemma of writing a novel about such a subject, they are full of humour and parody. Short stories appear in *The Cubs* (1959, trans. 1979), and newspaper articles in *Making Waves* (trans. 1996). An important literary critic, his critical works include a study of Gabriel García MÁRQUEZ, and Flaubert in *The Perpetual Orgy* (1975, trans. 1986). *A Fish in the Water* (1993, trans. 1994) is a memoir. One of the most influential writers of the 'boom' period of the Latin American novel in the 1960s, his experimental writing shows a predilection for false certainties and the exploration of the fissures in life as it is lived and reconstructed by memory and desire.

M. Booker, *Vargas Llosa among the Postmodernists* (1994).

Vidal, Gore (1925–) Born Gore Eugene Luther Vidal, in West Point, New York, US, he served in the US army between 1943 and 1946, and lived in Italy between 1967 and 1976. He has demonstrated great versatility with a wide range of writing, including scholarly novels about ancient world emperors, plays, short stories, screenplays, essays on contemporary America, and memoirs. With a terseness of style derived from HEMINGWAY, his first novel, *Williwaw* (1946), was set on an army transport during the Second World War. However, he made his name with *The City and the Pillar* (1948), a *succès de scandale* about a young man's gradual discovery of his homosexuality. There followed many historical fictions, the more famous of which are *A Search for the King* (1950), an imaginative reconstruction of twelfth-century history, describing the search for Richard the Lionheart; his first major novel, *Julian* (1964), purporting to be the autobiographical memoir of the Roman Emperor Julian; and his trilogy about the vagaries of American political life – *Washington D.C.* (1967), a wry comedy of political manners, *Burr* (1973), about the political figure Aaron Burr, and *1876* (1976), about the political scandals of Grant's presidency. Other works include the cult success of *Myra Breckenridge* (1968, filmed 1970), a farce about transsexuality and Hollywood; *Creation* (1981), a tour of fifth-century historical figures; *Lincoln* (1984), considered by many to be his best work, about the sixteenth president's life through the eyes of various people associated with him; *Hollywood* (1990); *Live* *from Golgotha* (1992); *The Smithsonian Institution* (1998), a fantasy about experiments in time travel in the Smithsonian Institute; and *The Golden Age* (2000), which completes the 'American chronicles', picking up after *Washington D.C.*, from the Second World War to the present. Short stories are collected in *A Thirsty Evil* (1956), and essay collections include *Sex, Death and Money* (1968) and *United States: Essays 1952–1992* (1993). He has also written detective novels under the name Edgar Box. Despite the grand epic quality of much of his fiction, he is able to combine small-scale minutiae with significant stylistic wit, aplomb and elegance. *Palimpsest: A Memoir* appeared in 1995. He now lives permanently in Italy.

R. Kiernon, *Gore Vidal* (1982).

Vittorini, Elio (1908–1966) Born in Syracuse, in Sicily, Italy, he began work in construction, but then became an editor, adviser and proofreader to several publishers. In the early 1930s, he was employed by the newspaper *La Nazione* as a proofreader. He has translated many US and British writers into Italian. During the war, he ran into trouble with Italy's fascists, was imprisoned, and then went underground. His fiction includes his major novel *In Sicily* (1941, trans. 1949), about a young man who returns to Sicily to reunite with his family, but meets friends divided by fascism and anti-fascism; *Men and Not Men* (1945, trans. 1986), about the violent conflicts between the Germans and the Italian resistance; *Tune for an Elephant* (1947, trans. 1955), about an idle patriarch who threatens a house with starvation owing to his insatiable appetite; *The Red Carnation* (1948, trans. 1952), about an adolescent's love for a prostitute and his attraction to fascism; and *Women of Messina* (1949, trans. 1973) and *Women of the Road* (1956, trans. 1961), two novels about the class system. He is among Italy's most

distinguished writers of the mid-twentieth century.

D. Heiney, *Three Italian Novelists: Moravia, Pavese, Vittorini* (1968).

Vollmann, William T. (1959–) Full name William Tanner Vollmann, he was born in Santa Monica, California, US. He went to Cornell University (BA 1981) and studied at the University of California at Berkeley (1982–1983). His first novel, *You Bright and Risen Angels* (1987), was a study of political power struggles in a fantasy of an inane war between insects and inventors of electricity, and was followed by *The Rainbow Stories* (1989), set mainly in the slums of San Francisco, focusing on the prostitutes, derelicts and criminals, where each story is determined by a colour of the spectrum. His major fictional work is a multi-volume project entitled *Seven Dreams: A Book of North American Landscapes*, which is a symbolic history of North America drawing upon mythological and historical sources. It so far comprises volume I, *Ice-Shirt* (1990), about the colonisation of North America by the Vikings, volume II, *Fathers and Crows* (1992), about the missionary endeavours of Jesuits in Canada, and volume VI, *The Rifles* (1994), about the life of Sir John Franklin, the British explorer searching for the Northwest Passage. Other novels include *Whores for Gloria* (1991), a documentary-novel about the Tenderloin area in San Francisco, *Thirteen Stories and Thirteen Epitaphs* (1991), recounting fictitious travels in the US and abroad, *An Afghanistan Picture Show* (1992), about his post-college trip in the early 1980s to aid the Afghanistan rebels against the Soviet invasion, *Butterfly Stories* (1993), about the peregrinations of an unnamed narrator, *Open All Nights* (1995), *The Atlas: People, Places and Visions* (1996), which contains more travel writing and autobiography, and *The Royal Family* (2000), with familiar depictions of low-life, seekers, vigilantes, prostitutes, in a haunting series of parallel lives. Regarded as an innovative, postmodern novelist, his epic novels have complicated plots, numerous character types, and generally focus on social misfits, prostitutes and down-and-outs.

Vonnegut, Kurt (1922–) A widely acclaimed, influential and provocative American writer, born in Indianapolis, Indiana, and educated at Cornell (1940–1942) and Chicago (1945–1947) universities. During the Second World War, he served in the USAF, and following his capture by the Germans, survived the fire-bombing of Dresden in 1945. In the late 1940s, he worked as a reporter and a public relations writer, before turning to fiction. His first novel, *Player Piano* (1952), a science fiction satire on modern automation and its dehumanising effects, was followed by *The Sirens of Titan* (1959), *Mother Night* (1962), *Cat's Cradle* (1963), which is a fantasy about an apocalyptic end to the world, and *God Bless You, Mr. Rosewater* (1965), a satire about an idealistic philanthropic foundation and its encounter with greed. His most famous novel, *Slaughterhouse Five* (1969), is an attempt to re-create his experiences as a captive in Dresden in fictional form, producing a searing attack on the cruelty and destructiveness of war. The book was taken up as a counter-cultural, pacifist 'manifesto' in the early 1970s in the US. Other novels include *Breakfast of Champions* (1973), *Slapstick* (1976), a farce about a future American president, *Jailbird* (1979), *Deadeye Dick* (1983), *Galápagos* (1985), *Bluebeard* (1987) and *Hocus Pocus* (1990). His other principal works includes the short story collections *Canary in a Cat House* (1961) and *Welcome to the Monkey House* (1969); several plays and screenplays, including *Happy Birthday, Wanda June* (1970); essays in *Wampeters, Foma, and Granfallons: Opinions* (1974); and the autobiographical *Palm Sunday* (1981) and *Fates Worse Than Death* (1991). His most recent work is *Timequake* (1994), a science fiction adventure novel about a 'timequake' which forces people to relive the decade between 1991 and 2001, uncollected short fiction in *Bagombo Snuff Box* (1999), and *God Bless You Dr. Kevorkian* (2000), which is comic, irreverent vignettes of death and the afterlife. His innovative blend of science fiction, fantasy and realism has produced many celebrated works and established a cult following for their anti-institutional parodies and critiques. Regarded as a major postmodern novelist, his constantly innovative explorations of narrative structure, the politics of representation, the destructiveness of technology, the art world and the nature of comedy, have elevated him to the first rank of contemporary American writers.

J. Klinkowitz, *Kurt Vonnegut* (1982).

W

Wagoner, David (1926–) Born in Massillon, Ohio, US, David Russell Wagoner went to Pennsylvania State University (BA 1947) and Indiana University at Bloomington (MA 1949). After various university teaching posts, he was made Professor of English at the University of Washington at Seattle in 1966. A highly regarded poet, he has published a number of volumes of poetry, including *Dry Sun, Dry Wind* (1953), *In Broken Country* (1979), *Collected Poems 1956–1976* (1976), *Through the Forest* (1987), *Walt Whitman Bathing* (1996) and *Travelling Light* (1999). Although principally known for his poetry, he has also written several novels, from his first entitled *The Man in the Middle* (1954), to *Money, Money, Money* (1955), *Rock* (1958), *The Escape Artist* (1965), *Baby, Come on Inside* (1968) and *The Hanging Garden* (1980). His fiction mixes the tragic with comic and satiric devices, and tends to focus on lonely, doomed individuals, exploring their sense of alienation and entrapment. He also edited *Straw for the Fire* (1972), which is selections from the notebooks of Theodore Roethke.

R. McFarland, *The World of David Wagoner* (1997).

Wain, John (1925–1994) Born in Stoke-on-Trent, Staffordshire, England, John Barrington Wain went to Oxford University (BA 1946) and pursued an academic career at Oxford and Reading universities until 1955, when he became a writer and critic. A prolific author of fiction, poetry, plays, non-fiction and edited works, for which he garnered many honours, his first novel was *Hurry on Down* (1953), a satire about the 1940s and 1950s, and involving the individual rebellion of Charles Lumley, a man who cynically chooses to avoid the cosy middle-class lifestyle. This caused Wain to be associated with the 'angry young men', such as Alan SILLITOE and John Osborne. Other novels include *Living in the Present* (1955), *Strike the Father Dead* (1962), *A Winter in the Hills* (1970), about a philologist in North Wales involved in local politics, *The Pardoner's Tale* (1978), *Young Shoulders* (1982), and the trilogy based on his life at Oxford and the necessary social adjustments – *Where the Rivers Meet* (1988), *Comedies* (1990) and *Hungry Generations* (1994). Short stories are collected in *Nuncle* (1960), *Death of the Hind Legs* (1966), *The Life Guard* (1971) and *King Caliban* (1978), while memoirs and autobiography occur in *Sprightly Running* (1962) and *Dear Shadows* (1986). In addition to critical work on Gerard Manley Hopkins, Arnold BENNETT and an acclaimed biography of Samuel Johnson, he was one of the leading younger poets of 'the Movement', a loose grouping of anti-romantic and ironic poets in the 1960s, exemplified in his *Poems, 1949–1979* (1981). As Oxford Professor of Poetry (1973–1978), he published his lectures in *Professing Poetry* (1978). His fiction concerns contemporary English manners and largely depicts disillusioned Englishmen, and like many of the 'angry young men', he developed a bluff, more right-wing stance in his later work.

Walker, Alice (1944–) A widely honoured African-American writer of fiction, poetry and literary criticism, she was born Alice Malsenior Walker, in Eatonton, Georgia, to a poor black family and was educated at Spelman College, Atlanta (1961–1963) and Sarah Lawrence College (BA 1965). She subsequently worked in welfare in the South and in New York City, before taking various university positions. Her best-selling novel *The Color Purple* (1983, Pulitzer Prize) has won numerous accolades, and was adapted for film by Steven Spielberg (1985). An epistolary novel set in the Deep South between the wars, it is a stark narrative of abuse, oppression and self-discovery, centring upon the experiences of two sisters. Her other novels include *The Third Life of Grange Copeland* (1970), *Meridian* (1976), which deals with her Civil Rights experiences in the 1960s, *The Temple of My Familiar* (1988), *Possessing the Secret of Joy* (1992), which examines the subject of female circumcision and is linked through its characters to *The Color Purple*, and *By the Light of My Father's Smile* (1999), which crosses conventional boundaries in its exploration of a woman regaining her self through her denied sexuality. Her short story collections include *In Love and Trouble* (1973), *You Can't Keep a Good Woman Down* (1981) and *The Complete Stories* (1994). Among her poetry volumes are *Revolutionary Petunias* (1973) and *Good Night, Willie Lee, I'll See You in the Morning* (1979), and her poems have been collected in *Her Blue Body Everything We Know: Earthl-*

ing Poems 1965–1990 (1991). Her essay collections, *In Search of Our Mothers' Gardens: Womanist Prose* (1983) and *Living by the Word: Selected Writings 1973–1987* (1988), explore such issues as black women's creativity, 'womanist' prose, the impact and legacy of the Civil Rights movement, and her own memories. In addition to her edition of the writings of Zora Neale HURSTON in *I Love Myself When I Am Laughing...* (1979), she has published a memoir, entitled *The Same River Twice: Honoring the Difficult* (1996), in which she documents her struggle to come to terms with almost overnight literary celebrity status, while *Anything We Love Can Be Saved: A Writer's Activism* (1997) is autobiography and essays. Her most recent work is *The Way Forward Is with a Broken Heart* (2000).

M. Evans, ed., *Black Women Writers 1950–1980* (1984).

Wallace, Edgar (1875–1932) Born Richard Horatio Edgar Wallace, in London, England, he is known mainly for writing mystery and suspense stories. After leaving school at the age of 12 with little formal education, he performed various odd jobs before enlisting in the British Army at 18 and serving in South Africa during the Anglo-Boer War until 1899. He subsequently became a journalist and prolific writer, publishing 175 books and fifteen plays, which helped him to become one of the most popular mystery and crime writers of all time. His mystery books include *The Four Just Men* (1905), *The Crimson Circle* (1922), *The Green Archer* (1923), *The Dark Eyes of London* (1924), *The Hand of Power* (1927), *The Flying Squad* (1928) and *The Terror* (1930). In addition to a series of books featuring the detective J.G. Reader (*The Mind of Mr. J.G. Reader*, 1925, and others), he wrote a series about a British Native Commissioner in Africa, the first of which was *Sanders of the River* (1911, filmed 1935). He died in Hollywood, California, while working on the film script for *King Kong*.

M. Lane, *Edgar Wallace: The Biography of a Phenomenon* (1938, rev. 1964).

Walser, Martin (1927–) Born in Wasserburg, Germany, he served in the German army (1944–1945) before going to the University of Tübingen (1948–1951), and then worked in radio and television (1949–1957). A widely honoured novelist, at the beginning of his career he was associated with Gruppe 47 and writers like Heinrich BÖLL. His early novels include *The Gadarene Club* (1957, trans. 1960, later translated as *Marriage in Philippsburg*, 1961), and *The Unicorn* (1966, trans. 1971), which is part of the 'Kristlein' trilogy, about Anselm Kristlein's life against the backdrop of the German 'economic miracle' and an analysis of post-war German values. Other novels include *Beyond All Love* (1976, trans. 1982), *Runaway Horse* (1978, trans. 1980), which explores marriage and exposes male attitudes towards women, *The Inner Man* (1979, trans. 1985), *The Swan Villa* (1980, trans. 1982), *Letter to Lord Liszt* (1982, trans. 1985), *Breakers* (1985, trans. 1987), which adopts the model of the American campus novel, and *No Man's Land* (1987, trans. 1989). Often reformulating genres, his fiction explores the post-war German legacy and the social and sexual mores of the affluent middle classes, although his refusal to use literature for political ends has at times led him into public controversy.

Warner, Marina (1946–) Born in London, England, she was educated at Oxford University (MA 1967), since when she has become a writer, historian and scholar of female mythology. Her first work was *The Dragon Empress* (1972), a biography of Tzu Hsi of China, and was followed by *Alone of All Her Sex* (1976), a study of the cult of the Virgin Mary in fields as diverse as religion, art and literary criticism. She continued her studies of representations of the female in *Joan of Arc* (1981), and then in *Monuments and Maidens* (1985), a study of the female form as allegory in art and public life. She turned to monsters and fairy tales in *Managing Monsters* (1994) and *From the Beast to the Blonde* (1995), and most recently, wrote a study of our commonest fears and myths which define human sensibilities in *No Go the Bogeyman: Scaring, Lulling and Making Mock* (1998). This interest in legend, folklore and female symbolism recurs in her novels, which began with *In a Dark Wood* (1977), and continued with *The Skating Party* (1983), *The Lost Father* (1988), which is her most successful novel, set in Mussolini's Italy and which spans the twentieth century as a female narrator pieces together her family history, and *Indigo; or, Mapping the Waters* (1992), a retelling of *The Tempest* within seventeenth- and twentieth-century time frames and which explores the colonial terrain implicit in Shakespeare's play. In addition to short stories in *The Mermaids in the Basement* (1993) and various children's books, she has edited a collection of myths and fables in *Wonder Tales* (1994). She has also written for the *Times Literary Supplement* and the *Independent* newspaper.

Waterhouse, Keith (1929–) Keith Spencer Waterhouse is a British writer, born in Leeds, who has been a screenwriter, novelist, playwright, and journalist for the *Daily Mirror* (1970–1986). His novels began with *There Is a Happy Land* (1957), but he is most famous for *Billy Liar* (1959), about a daydreaming undertaker's assistant who has trouble distinguishing fantasy from reality, which went on to become a huge success on stage and television (1973–1974). There followed the black comedy *Jubb* (1963), *The Bucket Shop* (1968), a sequel to the earlier success with *Billy Liar on the Moon*

(1975), *Mondays, Thursdays* (1976), *Office Life* (1978), *Maggie Muggins* (1981), *Mrs Porter's Diary* (1984), *Bimbo* (1990) and *Unsweet Charity* (1992), which was a satire about large-scale charity campaigns. Associated with the 'angry young men' of the 1950s, such as Alan SILLITOE and John Osborne, he is a brilliant satirist and caricaturist, whose relentless mordant ridicule of the world emerges in a wide range of styles. In the 1960s, he collaborated with the playwright Willis Hall, and both are well known for their adaptation for British children's television of the Worzel Gummidge scarecrow character. He is also the author of influential books on newspapers, such as *Waterhouse on Newspaper Style* (1989), and an authority on correct English usage in *English Our English* (1991). Two memoirs of his life in Leeds occur in *City Lights* (1994) and *Streets Ahead* (1995).

Waugh, Evelyn (1903–1966) Born Evelyn Arthur St. John Waugh, in Hampstead, London, he was educated at Oxford University (1921–1924) and became part of a literary circle which included Anthony POWELL, Henry GREEN and Cyril Connolly. His travel and career experiences provided much of the material for his novels: school teaching in North Wales, journalism with the *Daily Express*, acting as a war correspondent in Ethiopia, and his war service (1939–1945). *Decline and Fall* (1928) was his first comic novel, about an innocent schoolteacher in Wales who is caught up in Mayfair's nefarious activities. This was followed by *Vile Bodies* (1930), *Black Mischief* (1932), inspired by the coronation of Haile Selassie, *A Handful of Dust* (1934), and *Scoop* (1938), his comic account of Fleet Street – all of which capture the cynicism of the post-First World War generation. His war service was the basis for *Put Out More Flags* (1942) and the *Sword of Honour* (1965) trilogy, which charted the increasing disillusionment of a romantic middle-aged Catholic gentleman during the

Second World War, and consisted of *Men at Arms* (1952), *Officers and Gentlemen* (1955) and *Unconditional Surrender* (1961). *Brideshead Revisited* (1945), a lush and nostalgic deference to the aristocracy and the Catholic faith, was made into a television series by the BBC in 1980. Other novels include *The Loved One* (1948), a comedy about farcical Californian funeral services, and *The Ordeal of Gilbert Pinfold* (1957). Short stories appeared in *Mr Loveday's Little Outing* (1936), *Work Suspended* (1942) and *Tactical Exercise* (1954), while the *Diaries* (1976) and *Letters of Evelyn Waugh* (1980) have widened the perspective on his life. His travel books include *Remote People* (1931), *Ninety-Two Days* (1934) and *Waugh in Abyssinia* (1936). Other non-fiction includes a work on the pre-Raphaelites (1926), and biographies of Ronald Knox and Edmund Campion. An ardent convert to Roman Catholicism in 1930, he made his name as the chronicler of the 'bright young things' of the 1920s, with satires and comedies influenced by Ronald FIRBANK. Frequently depicting the battle between civilisation and barbarism, not only in Africa but also in London's Mayfair and in California, he became increasingly irascible in later life, and espoused anti-egalitarian views.

I. Littlewood, *The Writings of Evelyn Waugh* (1983).

Wedde, Ian (1946–) Born in Blenheim, New Zealand, he was educated at the University of Auckland (MA 1968), and was associated with the university-based magazine *The Word Is Freed* (1969–1972). He was at the forefront of the New Zealand poets in the late 1960s and early 1970s, introducing the freshness of American literary traditions and writers like Thomas PYNCHON and William GADDIS, as well as the Beats and the Black Mountain School. He published many volumes of poetry and translations, and after a period spent in Otago (1972–1975), he moved to Wellington and became a script-writer. Technically astute and prolific, his novels include the experimental, intertextual *Dick Seddon's Great Dive* (1976), the comic novel *Survival Arts* (1981), and the epic novel *Symmes Hole* (1986). Much of his writing in the 1970s and 1980s was related to his detailed research into the whaling culture. Short stories occur in *The Shirt Factory* (1981), and he co-edited *The Penguin Book of New Zealand Verse* (1985) and *The Penguin Book of Contemporary New Zealand Poetry* (1989), which included poems by Maori writers and hitherto marginalised women poets. His collected writings were published in *How to be Nowhere* (1995), and he has extended critical discourse beyond the merely literary, with his art criticism and historical researches.

Weidman, Jerome (1913–1998) Born in New York City, US, he studied at the City University of New York and New York University Law School (1931–1937), during which time he worked as a clerk. Since then he has been a professional writer, and has published a range of novels which frequently include explicit, unpleasant portraits of Jewish characters. His first novel, *I Can Get It For You Wholesale* (1937), received critical acclaim, and was later dramatised as *Tenderloin* (1961). Together with its sequel, *What's In It For Me?* (1938), they tell of an unscrupulous New York dress-manufacturing business. Thereafter, he wrote a variety of novels, such as *Other People's Money* (1967) and *A Family Fortune* (1978), about the rise and fall of a Jewish racketeer. His travel books include *Letter of Credit* (1940), about a world tour, and *Traveler's Cheque* (1954), while *Back Talk* (1963) collects essays and magazine sketches. He also wrote a number of successful plays, among which was the collaboration with George Abbott, *Fiorello!* (1960, Pulitzer Prize). His short stories are collected in *The Captain's Tiger* (1947) and *The Death of Dickie*

Draper (1965), while *Praying for Rain* (1986) is an autobiography. Writing about commonplace rather than heroic events in a realist vein, his fiction has often suffered criticism for its thinness.

Welch, James (1940–) Part Blackfoot and part Gros Ventre Indian, he was born in Browning, Montana, US, and went to the University of Montana. The American West features in much of his writing. His first work was a volume of poetry, *Riding the Earthboy Forty* (1971), and his first novel was *Winter in the Blood* (1974), about a young Native-American boy's development on a Montana reservation. *The Death of Jim Loney* (1974) focused upon an alienated, alcoholic half-breed of white and Native-American parents, and his search for identity and purpose. *Fools Crow* (1986) was a huge success and brought him significant attention; it deals with a band of Blackfoot Indians in Montana territory in the 1870s, and how the lead character, Fools Crow, grows from a young warrior to become the tribe's medicine man, with his bleak vision of the end of the Indian prairie culture. *The Indian Lawyer* (1990) returns to a contemporary setting and corruption involving an Indian attorney, Sylvester Yellow Calf, and the conflicts and complexities of a multicultural existence. His latest novel is *Heartsong of Charging Elk* (2000), a historical narrative about the Oglala Indians and the Wild West. After research for a film collaboration, he wrote *Killing Custer* (1994), a non-fictional mixture of narrative, history and rumination concerning the Battle of Little Bighorn. His work shows a commitment to depicting the Native-American search for identity in their land.

R. McFarland, *James Welch* (1986).

Weldon, Fay (1931–) A British writer, born in Alvechurch, Worcestershire, she spent several early years in New Zealand, returning to England in 1936. She was educated at the University of St. Andrews (MA 1954), and became a copy-editor for an advertising agency. She gained recognition for the sardonic wit displayed in her early novels like *The Fat Woman's Joke* (1967), *Down Among the Women* (1971), *Female Friends* (1974), *Remember Me* (1976) and *Praxis* (1978), and has since written prolifically in a variety of genres and modes. Her more recent novels include *Puffball* (1980), which deals with the supernatural and witchcraft, themes that recur throughout her work, *The Life and Loves of a She-Devil* (1983), which depicts a woman's fantastic revenge on her faithless husband, *The Cloning of Joanna May* (1989), *Life Force* (1992), *Trouble* (1993), *Affliction* (1994), *Splitting* (1995), and *Worst Fears* (1996), in which a female protagonist realises late in life that her world is not as rosy as she thought. Her latest novels are *Big Girls Don't Cry* (1997), a comic, clever narrative which provides a long-term view of feminism since the 1970s, and *Godless in Eden* (2000). Short stories occur in *Moon Over Minneapolis* (1991), *Wicked Women* (1995), *Angel, All Insurance* (1995) and *A Hard Time to Be a Father* (1998). She has also written a study of Rebecca WEST, and collected essays in *Godless of Eden* (1999). Many of her works depict the anxieties of women in loveless marriages and men's unreasonable expectations of women. Often labelled a feminist writer, her major subject is the complex experience of women, and she displays a caustic perspective on the battle between the sexes at the centre of many of her novels.

Wells, H.G. (1866–1946) A prolific English writer, famous for his science fiction novels, he was born Herbert George Wells, in Bromley, Kent. After a period of apprenticeship to a draper, he was educated at the Normal School of Science, London (B.Sc. 1890). A schoolmaster until 1893, he thereafter settled to writing. His

science fiction novels include *The Time Machine* (1895), about time travel, *The Island of Doctor Moreau* (1896), *The Invisible Man* (1897), *The War of the Worlds* (1898), about the invasion of Earth by Martians, *When the Sleeper Wakes* (1899), *The First Men in the Moon* (1901) and *The Shape of Things to Come* (1933). His science fiction romances have had a considerable effect on modern literature and popular culture, with their cosmic panorama and somewhat pessimistic assessment of technology's impact on the world. His growing friendships with and influence among writers like Arnold BENNETT, Joseph CONRAD and Henry James made him a major novelist in British Edwardian literature. Novels of character include *Kipps* (1905), drawing on his experience as a draper's apprentice, and *The History of Mr Polly* (1910). Wells also wrote polemical novels, such as *Ann Veronica* (1909), championing women's rights, and *Tono-Bungay* (1909), an attack on rampant capitalism. His later fiction took the form of the novel of ideas, such as the famous war novel *Mr Britling Sees It Through* (1916), and he appears to have anticipated the First World War in his novel *The War in the Air* (1908) and the atomic bomb in *The World Set Free* (1914). His nonfiction includes *The Outline of History* (1920) and a *Short History of the World* (1922). His later life was taken up with increasing efforts on his behalf to work for human rights and world peace, although his pessimistic views of the future appeared to be confirmed at Hiroshima.

M. Foot, *The History of Mr. Wells* (1995).

Welsh, Irvine (1958–) A Scottish novelist, born in Edinburgh, he left school at 16, lived in London during the 1980s, and gained an MBA at Heriot-Watt University in Edinburgh. His first novel, *Trainspotting* (1993, filmed 1996), was a huge success, and turned him into a cult writer for its uncompromising and frank, yet humorous and comic, portrayal of Edinburgh's dispossessed and marginalised youth involved in drug-addiction and self-obsession. The same themes were handled in the novel *Marabou Stork Nightmares* (1995), which is narrated by a football casual whose consciousness moves between hallucinations, rave culture and his ornithological preoccupations in Africa, while his latest novel, *Filth* (1998), depicts a loathsome, corrupt Edinburgh policeman on the trail of a murder mystery, infused with his usual deeply peeved sense of humour. *The Acid House* (1994) collects short stories about drugs, violence and sexual perversion, while *Ecstasy* (1996) is three novellas dealing with the grotesque.

Welty, Eudora (1909–) Born in Jackson, Mississippi, US, she attended Mississippi State College for Women (1926–1927) and the University of Wisconsin (BA 1929), although she returned to Jackson during the Depression. Working for the Works Progress Administration, she travelled Mississippi writing stories and articles, later published in *One Place, One Time* (1971), along with her photographs of the South during the Depression in *Photographs by Eudora Welty* (1990). The speech and locality of the Deep South preoccupies her entire work, evident from her earliest stories published in such magazines as the *Atlantic Monthly* and the *Hudson Review*. Her first volume of short stories appeared in *A Curtain of Green* (1941), and other volumes include *The Wide Net* (1943), *The Golden Apples* (1949), *The Bride of Innisfallen* (1955), *Collected Stories* (1980) and *The First Story* (1999). Although principally known for her technically versatile stories, with crisp prose, individual perceptions, and vibrant narratorial voices, she has also written many novels. These include her first novel, *The Robber Bridegroom* (1942), set in the pre-revolutionary period during the last years of Spanish domina-

tion, *Delta Wedding* (1946), set in 1923 on a modern plantation in the Mississippi Delta on the occasion of a wedding, *The Ponder Heart* (1954), which depicts a trial of an alleged murder during which people manifest their inner selves, *Losing Battles* (1970), and *The Optimist's Daughter* (1972, Pulitzer Prize), a short novel about a funeral and family hatred. In addition to children's books, poetry, and some astute criticism and essays, including her key piece 'Place in Fiction' collected in *The Eye of the Story* (1978), she has written the autobiographical *One Writer's Beginnings* (1984) and compiled *Stories, Essays, and Memoir* (1998). Wide recognition occurred late in her life, after a long period of neglect, and she is now regarded as one of the principal writers of the American South.

L. Westling, *Eudora Welty* (1989).

Wendt, Albert (1939–) Born in Apia, Western Samoa, he was educated at Victoria University, Wellington, New Zealand (MA 1964). He returned to Samoa in 1965, becoming the principal of Samoa College in 1969, and then a lecturer in English at the University of the South Pacific, Fiji in 1974, before being made a Professor of Pacific Studies at the University of Auckland (1988). His editorial and publishing work, such as *Nuana: Pacific Writing in English Since 1980* (1995), has helped establish a renaissance in South Pacific regional writing. His first novel was *Sons for the Return Home* (1973), an allegorical story of love between a young Samoan student and a *papalagi* (white) New Zealand girl, with the resulting ambivalent cultural experiences. This was followed by *Pouliuli* (1977), described as a Samoan *King Lear*, in which a powerful chief tests the loyalty of his family and friends; *Leaves of the Banyan Tree* (1979), which follows a Samoan family through several generations and becomes an allegory of capitalism in Samoa; *Ola* (1991), which won the Commonwealth

Writers Prize, with its depiction of a woman's self-assessment on a journey to Israel; and *Black Rainbow* (1992), an allegorical thriller set in an Orwellian New Zealand. Short stories occur in *Flying-Fox in a Freedom Tree* (1974), *The Birth and Death of the Miracle Man* (1986) and *The Best of Albert Wendt's Short Stories* (1999), and poetry with *Inside Us the Dead* (1976) and *Shaman of Voices* (1984). Often preoccupied with the impact of white civilisation and Protestant religion on Samoa, his stories explore the modernisation of and racial prejudices in the South Pacific.

Werfel, Franz (1890–1945) Born in Prague, Czechoslovakia, he studied at the universities of Prague, Leipzig and Hamburg. He fought with the Austrian army on the Russian Front (1911–1912), and then became a reader for publishers, the co-founder of the expressionist journal *Der Jüngste Tag* (1913–1921) and a freelance writer in 1917. After marrying Alma Mahler, the widow of the composer Gustav Mahler, in 1929, he emigrated to France in 1938, and then the US with Heinrich MANN in 1940. He gained early fame with expressionist verse, but shifted to fiction and drama in the 1920s. A prolific novelist, his works include *Verdi: A Novel of the Opera* (1924, trans. 1925), which was a best-selling fictional encounter between Verdi and Wagner, *The Man Who Conquered Death* (trans. 1927), set in the petit bourgeois milieu of post-First World War Vienna, *The Hidden Child* (1929, trans. 1931), which is a vivid evocation of turbulent post-war Vienna, *The Forty Days of Musa Dugh* (1933, trans. 1934), about the persecution of the Armenians in the Turkish empire, *Hearken Unto the Voice* (1937, trans. 1938), which displays his interest in both Judaic and Christian cultures, and *The Song of Bernadette* (1941, trans. 1942), which is a best-selling portrayal of the Catholic saint of Lourdes. In addition to verse in *Poems* (trans. 1945) and plays,

his essays occur in *Between Heaven and Earth* (1946, trans. 1947).

L. Huber, *Franz Werfel: An Austrian Writer Reassessed* (1988).

Wesley, Mary (1912–) The pseudonym of Mary Wellesley, a descendant of the Duke of Wellington's family, she was born in Englefield Green, England. She attended the London School of Economics (1931–1932) and worked for the War Office during the Second World War. She made her debut as a novelist at the age of 70, with a string of best-selling and critically acclaimed novels. Her first novel was *Jumping the Queue* (1983), which depicts a middle-aged widow on the brink of suicide re-evaluating her life. There followed perhaps her best novel, *The Camomile Lawn* (1984), about the tangled relations between five cousins during the Second World War and into their old age, which was made into a television series, and which was controversial for its uninhibited writing. Other novels include *Harnessing Peacocks* (1985), *The Vacillations of Poppy Carew* (1986), *Not That Sort of Girl* (1987), *Second Fiddle* (1988), *A Sensible Life* (1990), *A Dubious Legacy* (1992), a novel written in a more comic vein, *An Imaginative Experience* (1995), in which a series of coincidences bring together a variety of characters, and *Part of the Furniture* (1996), set in 1941 during the Blitz and in the West Country, depicting a marriage which transforms a woman's life. Her fiction portrays gutsy and convention-defying women from privileged backgrounds and presents lively depictions of historical periods, especially the idiosyncratic English middle classes of the Second World War.

West, Morris (1916–1999) Born in St. Kilda, Melbourne, Australia, he graduated from the University of Melbourne (1937), and worked as a schoolteacher in Tasmania and New South Wales. A member of the Christian Brothers, he left in

1939 before taking orders. He worked in radio until 1954, and then left Australia to pursue his writing, since which time he has lived all over the world and only recently returned to Australia. His first novel, *Moon in My Pocket* (1945), was written under the pseudonym Julian Morris, and was followed by *Gallows on the Sand* (1956), *Kundu* (1956), *Children of the Sun* (1957), which, in its factual account of the slum conditions in Naples, established his reputation as a writer, and *The Devil's Advocate* (1959), about the Catholic Church's investigation into the case for the beatification of an alleged Italian partisan, which made him a best-selling novelist. Other novels include *The Big Story* (1957), *Daughter of Silence* (1961), and the so-called 'Vatican trilogy', consisting of *The Shores of the Fisherman* (1963), *The Clowns of God* (1981) and *Lazarus* (1990). More recent novels are *The Ringmaster* (1991), an international business thriller, *The Lovers* (1993), *Vanishing Point* (1996), and *Eminence* (1998), about politics in the Vatican. *A View from the Ridge* (1996) is his Christian memoir. He has dramatised a number of his novels, and some have been produced as films. Although his early novels were potboilers, he has had a string of international best-sellers that have sometimes astutely anticipated world events, and which depict world-weary figures struggling to rediscover their sense of 'belonging'.

West, Nathanael (1903–1940) An American novelist and screenwriter, born Nathan Weinstein in New York City, he was educated at Brown University (Ph.B. 1924). After living in Paris, he returned to New York to manage a hotel, where he met several writers, such as William Carlos Williams with whom he co-edited the journal *Contact* (1931–1932). During this period, he wrote three short novellas: *The Dream Life of Balso Snell* (1931), which is a surreal tale of characters living in a Trojan horse; *Miss Lonelyhearts*

(1933), which is about a despairing agony aunt columnist who seeks security in religion in the midst of materialist and moral corruption; and *A Cool Million: The Dismantling of Lemuel Pitkin* (1934), a savage satire on the Horatio Alger myth and a critique of the illusory pillars of American society. He moved to Hollywood in the mid-1930s, where he adapted *Miss Lonelyhearts* for the cinema (filmed as *Advice to the Lovelorn*, 1933) and wrote several other screenplays. His increasing despondency about social and institutional problems emerges in his only full-length novel, *The Day of the Locust* (1939), which exposes the cynicism and excesses of Hollywood, and by implication the whole of American society, with a prophetic anticipation of the rise of fascism. His fiction combines images of sex and violence with an idiosyncratic blend of pathos, realism and comedy, in a surreal representation of a degraded and desperate world. He was killed in a car crash in California.

J. Martin, *Nathanael West: The Art of His Life* (1970).

West, Paul (1930–) Born in Eckington, Derbyshire, England, he was educated at the universities of Birmingham (BA 1950) and Columbia (MA 1953). He has been a university lecturer at several universities, including Penn State since 1963. In addition to poetry and essays on modern fiction, he has written numerous novels: *A Quality of Mercy* (1961); a trilogy consisting of *Alley Jaggers* (1966), *I'm Expecting to Live Quite Soon* (1970) and *Bela Lugosi's White Christmas* (1972); *Caliban's Filibuster* (1971); and *Gala* (1976), which tests the limits of art and imagination. Several of his novels are historically based, such as *The Very Rich Hours of Count von Stauffenberg* (1980), about the man who orchestrated the attempted assassination of Hitler in 1944; *Rat Man of Paris* (1986), based upon a man who haunted Paris flashing a rat at passers-by, which becomes an exploration of Nazi war atrocities; *The Women of Whitechapel and Jack the Ripper* (1991); and *Dry Danube: A Hitler Forgery* (1997), which purports to be Hitler's 'memoir' as a failed student in Vienna before the First World War. However, he associates himself primarily with experimentalists like William GASS and the Latin American innovators, and his other works include the explorative *Colonel Mint* (1973); *Love's Mansion* (1992), a semi-autobiographical exploration of his parents' lives before he was conceived; *The Place in Flowers Where Pollen Rests* (1988), a narrative of Joycean intricacy about a northeastern Arizona Hopi settlement; and more recently, *Sporting with Amaryllis* (1997), *Terrestrials* (1997) and *OK: The Corral, the Earps and Doc Holliday* (2000). His autobiographical *A Stroke of Genius* (1995) explores his several diseases, *Life with Swann* (1999) is a fictionalised account of his courtship and marriage to Diane Ackerman, and short stories are collected in *The Universe, and Other Fictions* (1988).

D. Madden, *Understanding Paul West* (1993).

West, Rebecca (1892–1983) Born Cicily Isabel Fairfield, in Co. Kerry, Ireland, she attended the Royal Academy of the Dramatic Arts. After playing the part of Rebecca West in Ibsen's *Rosmersholm* in 1911, she adopted the name. She had a child in 1914, through her long liaison with H.G. WELLS. As a journalist, critic and writer for the *Freewoman, Clarion, New Statesman* and *Nation*, some of her best work appears in *The Young Rebecca* (1982). She wrote several acclaimed biographies, including *Henry James* (1916), *D.H. Lawrence* (1930), *Arnold Bennett* (1931) and *St. Augustine* (1933). Her first novel, *The Return of the Soldier* (1918), portrayed the effects of amnesia and shell-shock in the First World War, and was followed by *The Judge* (1922), about the ways in which men frustrate women's

aspirations. After *Harriet Hume* (1929), again about gender battles, there followed *The Thinking Reed* (1936), which many reviewers felt was contrived and sterile. Her reputation for fiction picked up with the later *Cousin Rosamund: The Fountain Overflows* (1956) and *The Birds Fall Down* (1966), often regarded as her two best novels, and both about growing up before the Great War. In addition, the novels *This Real Night* (1984) and *Sunflower* (1986) and the short stories in *The Only Poet* (1992) were published posthumously. A committed suffragette, she became a socialist and a fine essayist, her literary essays occurring in *The Strange Necessity* (1928) and *Ending in Earnest* (1931). Other works include a travel book about Yugoslavia in *Black Lamb and Grey Falcon* (1942) and the memoir, *Family Memories* (1987). In recent years, West has been championed by feminists for her fiction of psychological insight and detailed historical descriptions.

V. Glendinning, *Rebecca West* (1987).

Wharton, Edith (1862–1937) An American novelist, poet and short story writer, Edith Newbold Wharton was born in New York City and was privately educated. The most celebrated American woman novelist of her generation, her fiction tended to portray characters who sought to escape society's pressures to conform, and like her good friend Henry James' work, was laced with observant details of characters' lives. She wrote many novels, and her first mature work was *The House of Mirth* (1905, filmed 2000), a social satire which depicts the philistinism of old New York society. This was followed by *Ethan Frome* (1911), set in rural New England, in which a protagonist is tragically caught between his wife and love for another woman, *The Reef* (1912) and *The Custom of the Country* (1913), both of which concern Americans in France. Her best-known novel was *The Age of Innocence* (1920,

Pulitzer Prize 1921, filmed 1993), set in old New York society, and in which the passionate character Newland Archer finds himself hemmed in by his desire to belong to society when he falls in love with a European divorcée. Other novels include *Hudson River Bracketed* (1929), and its sequel, *The Gods Arrive* (1932), *The Mother's Recompense* (1925), *Twilight Sleep* (1927), *The Children* (1928), and the unfinished *The Buccaneers* (1938). Her short stories occur in many collections, including *The Greater Inclination* (1899), *Critical Instances* (1901), *The Descent of Man* (1904), *The Hermit and the Wild Woman* (1904), *Xingu* (1916) and *Certain People* (1930). She was awarded the Cross of the Legion of Honour for her war relief work in France during the First World War, and her account of the war occurs in *Fighting France* (1915) and in the novels about the war, *The Marne* (1918) and *A Son at the Front* (1923). Other work includes travel writing, an autobiography entitled *A Backward Glance* (1934), volumes of poetry in *Artemis to Actaeon* (1909) and *Twelve Poems* (1926), and essays, including *The Writing of Fiction* (1925).

M. Bell, ed., *The Cambridge Companion to Edith Wharton* (1995).

Wharton, William (1925–) The pseudonym of John Franklin Wharton, in order to protect his privacy, he was born in Philadelphia, Pennsylvania, US, and attended the University of California, Los Angeles. He is a painter and a novelist who now lives in seclusion in France. His best-known novels are *Birdy* (1978), a tale of a psychological case in an army mental asylum and its protagonist's obsession with birds and flying, and *Dad* (1981). Other work includes *A Midnight Clear* (1982), which is about youth and war in the Ardennes during 1944, *Scumbler* (1984), *Tidings* (1987), *Franky Furbo* (1989), which is dedicated to his daughter who was killed in a car accident, and *Last*

Lovers (1991), which is about a complex relationship between a businessman and a blind Parisian spinster. *Ever After: A Father's True Story* (1995) is an acclaimed memoir about the family tragedy of his daughter's death, while *Houseboat on the Seine* (1996) is about his attempt to rebuild and re-float a rotten houseboat. His fiction frequently pits the creative self against the oppressions of a mad social world.

Wheatley, Dennis (1897–1977) Born in London, England, Dennis Yates Wheatley worked as a wine merchant between 1919 and 1931, when he inherited the business after his father's death. Following the liquidation of the business during the Depression, he turned to freelance writing in 1932. He is principally known for his crime fiction, and after his first novel, *The Forbidden Territory* (1933), he wrote a stream of thrillers and became a best-selling author. Many of his novels were inspired by the adventures of Alexander Dumas, and he created modern musketeers in many of his thrillers. He also wrote in other genres: his spy stories are set during the Second World War, while his historical melodramas, featuring the spy protagonist Roger Brook, are set in the context of early nineteenth-century Napoleonic France. Other writings manifest his intense interest in the macabre, occult and Satanism, such as *The Devil Rides Out* (1935), *The Haunting of Toby Jugg* (1948), *The Ka of Gifford Hillary* (1956), *The Satanist* (1960), *Gateway to Hell* (1970), *The Irish Witch* (1973) and *Murder Off Miami* (1980). His memoirs occur in three volumes, entitled *The Time Has Come* (1977–1979).

White, Antonia (1899–1980) The pseudonym of Eirene Botting, she was born in London, England, and attended the Royal Academy of Dramatic Arts (1919–1920) before becoming an actress. She later went into copywriting (1924–1931) and freelance journalism and editing. *Frost in May* (1933) recounts her troubled experiences at her convent school leading to her expulsion, and has become something of a minor classic. Her subsequent torrid and tormented life as a result of her early difficulties arising from her Roman Catholic education, led to a history of psychoanalytical treatment, breakdowns and collapsed marriages. As a consequence, her next novel was not written until 1950, *The Lost Traveller*, which along with *The Sugar House* (1952) and *Beyond the Glass* (1954), formed a trilogy about Clara Batchelor's experiences, again largely autobiographical, and which form a sequel to *Frost in May*. Short stories occur in *Strangers* (1954), while *The Hound and the Falcon* (1966) is an account of her reconversion to Catholicism, and *As Once in May* (1983) is a collection of her essays and memorabilia. As a consequence of her psychological difficulties, most of her novels take the form of 'writing therapy'. She also developed a reputation as a translator, especially for her translations of COLETTE's work. Upon her death, a bitter literary controversy broke out between her daughters about their conflicting memoirs of their mother, in S. Chitty, *Now to My Mother* (1985) and L. Hopkinson, *Nothing to Forgive* (1988).

White, Edmund (1940–) An American writer, born in Cincinnati, Ohio, Edmund Valentine White was educated at the University of Michigan (BA 1962). His insightful non-fiction and acclaimed novels on gay society in the US, have made him a prominent spokesperson for American homosexuals. His early, somewhat fantastic novel, *Forgetting Elena* (1973), was a first person narrative of an amnesiac victim struggling to determine his identity, and was followed by *Nocturnes for the King of Naples* (1978), about a man's older, dead lover. *A Boy's Own Story* (1982), perhaps his most famous novel, is a first person narrative of a homosexual boy's adolescence in the 1950s and his struggle with society's

judgements. The latter book forms a trilogy with *The Beautiful Room Is Empty* (1988), set in the 1960s, which met with criticism for its depictions of casual homosexual liaisons, and *The Farewell Symphony* (1997), which is set in the 1970s in New York and deals with the onset of the AIDS epidemic. Other novels are *Caracole* (1985), set in the nineteenth century, about two rural lovers and their sexual escapades in a large city, and most recently, *The Married Man* (2000), about the difficulties in a gay relationship between an American man and a married French architect. In addition to the short stories in *Skinned Alive* (1995), he has written essays on gay society, homosexuality and the impact of AIDS in the US in *The Burning Library* (1994), works on gay issues in the US in *The Joy of Gay Sex* (1977), *States of Desire: Travels in Gay America* (1980) and *The Darker Proof* (1987), and biographies of Jean GENET (1993) and PROUST (2000).

White, Patrick (1912–1990) An internationally acclaimed Australian novelist, he was born Patrick Victor Martindale White, in London, England, and was educated partly in Australia, and later at Cambridge University, where he graduated in 1935. He is the only Australian novelist to have received the Nobel Prize for Literature (1973). During the Second World War, he served as a British intelligence officer, and met his lifelong companion, Manoly Lascaris. After concentrating on poetry and drama in the early part of his career, he wrote his first novel, *Happy Valley* (1939), which is set in the cold regions of Australia rather than in the clichéd sun-baked territories. His next novel, *The Living and the Dead* (1941), set in 1930s London, continues this concern with sterility. *The Aunt's Story* (1948) dramatised his return to Australia in 1948, and was followed by *The Tree of Man* (1955). Reworking the myth of the pioneer by focusing on his two protagonists, Stan and Amy Parker, *The Tree of*

Man's epic narrative marked his increasing interest in exploring the Australian consciousness and the philosophical gap between self and the world. It was followed by the equally epic *Voss* (1957), based upon the story of Ludwig Leichhardt who disappeared while attempting to cross Australia from east to west in 1848, pitting a man of powerful will against the land in a spiritual and emotional struggle. Eschewing the Australian penchant for naturalism in the 1940s and 1950s, his early fiction is indebted to the European modernists. *Riders of the Chariot* (1961) is a study of four visionaries, all social misfits, and began his exploration of a fictional Sydney suburb, Sarsaparilla, reminiscent of William FAULKNER's Yoknapatawpha country. Sarsaparilla figures again in *The Solid Mandala* (1966), the psychodrama of twin brothers who are two sides of the same consciousness, and was followed by *The Vivisector* (1970), *The Eye of the Storm* (1973), *A Fringe of Leaves* (1976), which explores the savagery behind civilised life in 1840s Queensland, *The Twyborn Affair* (1979), and *Memoirs of Many in One* (1986), which develops his interest in transsexuality. Short stories occur in *The Burnt Ones* (1964), *The Cockatoos* (1974) and *Three Uneasy Pieces* (1987), while his drama is collected in *Four Plays* (1965). An autobiography is entitled *Flaws in the Glass* (1981), and *Patrick White Speaks Out* (1990) contains speeches and essays. White's preoccupations have been form and language, and the psychic as well as physical effects of the landscape. With a fresh perspective in each new novel, his fiction seizes details and gives them a transcendent significance, thus endowing his fiction with a Jungian and Blakean vision in which objects often take on revelatory illumination.

D. Tacey, *Patrick White: Fiction and the Unconscious* (1988).

Wideman, John Edgar (1941–) Born in Washington DC, he went to the universities of Pennsylvania (BA 1963) and Oxford (B.Phil. 1966), and taught at a variety of universities before gaining a position as Professor of English at the University of Massachusetts at Amherst in 1986. A widely honoured writer, his first novel, *A Glance Away* (1967), was about the life of a drug addict and the harsh realities of Pittsburgh's ghetto Homewood. Subsequent complex novels sharply contrast his highly literate style with this gritty content of street-life desolation. After *Hurry Home* (1970) and *The Lynchers* (1973), he wrote the short stories in *Damballah* (1981), and the novels *Hiding Place* (1981) and *Sent For You Yesterday* (1983), the last three works collected in *The Homewood Trilogy* (1985). These are narratives set in Homewood, and blend myth, superstition and dream sequences to create elaborate portraits of the lives of ordinary black people. After the moving memoir, *Brothers and Keepers* (1984), an attempt to come to terms with his brother's street and drug life in his childhood, there followed *Reuben* (1987), again dealing with the drug problems in Homewood, and *Philadelphia Fire* (1990), in which two stories are brought together, blending fact and fiction about racial and social problems in Philadelphia. *Fatheralong* (1994) is about his strained relationship with his son who is serving a life sentence for murder, and *The Cattle Killing* (1996) joins history, religion and race in a story about the plight of African-Americans in eighteenth-century Philadelphia woven with the Xhosa tribe in South Africa. Structured on musical forms of various sorts, his recent novel, *Two Cities* (1998), is about an African-American woman's new lease of life after deaths in her family, and is set in Pittsburgh and Philadelphia.

D. Mbalia, *John Edgar Wideman: Reclaiming the African Personality* (1995).

Wiebe, Rudy (1934–) A Canadian novelist, born in Fairholme, Saskatchewan, Rudy Henry Wiebe was educated at the University of Alberta (BA 1956, MA 1960), and from 1967 taught English at the University of Edmonton. Wiebe descended from a German family, and his early fiction explored the culture of the small Mennonite religion, in such works as *Peace Shall Destroy Many* (1964), which caused controversy in the Mennonite community for its suggestion that a quest for personal independence conflicts with one's relationship with God, and *First and Vital Candle* (1966). *The Blue Mountains of China* (1970) was less heavily dogmatic and achieved a more three-dimensional style in its account of the Mennonite diaspora, but a wide readership came with *The Temptations of Big Bear* (1973), which offered white Canadian and Native-Canadian perspectives on existence on the Canadian prairies. *Riel and Gabriel* (1973) was followed by *The Scorched-Wood People* (1977), an account of a nineteenth-century rebellion led by Louis Riel to aid Native-Canadians in preserving their land. Other works include the novels *The Mad Trapper* (1980), *My Lovely Enemy* (1983), exploring physical lust and religious love, and *A Discovery of Strangers* (1994), about the first encounter between the Yellowknife Indians and whites in Canada. Short stories occur in *Where Is the Voice Coming From?* (1974), *Alberta* (1979) and *The Angel of the Tar Sands* (1982), while essays and reminiscences appear in *Playing Dead* (1989) and *River of Stone* (1995). *Stolen Life: The Journey of a Cree Woman* (1998) narrates the events and injustices that led to the imprisonment of Yvonne Johnson, a descendent of the Cree Chief Big Bear. Remaining a staunch Christian throughout his life, his fiction explores personal religious beliefs, modern society and the character of western Canada. He has been widely honoured for his representations of the Canadian prairies, moving from the obscure minority Mennonite group to articulate the wider experiences of the Canadian West.

W. Keith, *Epic Fiction: The Art of Rudy Wiebe* (1981).

Wilding, Michael (1942–) An Australian novelist born in Worcester, England, and educated at Oxford University. Since 1972, he has been a Reader in English at the University of Sydney. His early fiction was short stories, collected in *Aspects of the Dying Process* (1972), *The West Midland Underground* (1975), *The Phallic Forest* (1978), *Reading the Signs* (1984), *The Man of Slow Feeling* (1985), *Under Saturn* (1988), *Great Climate* (1990), *This Is For You* (1994), *The Book of Reading* (1994) and *Somewhere New* (1996). His novels include *Living Together* (1974), *The Short Drive Embassy* (1975), *Scenic Drive* (1976), which was an answer to Frank MOORHOUSE's *Tales of Mystery and Romance*, *Pacific Highway* (1982), about a small community on the north coast of New South Wales which retreats into nature, and *The Paraguayan Experiment* (1990), which tells the story of the New Australia Movement in documentary sources. He is also an important editor, co-editing, among other works, the anthology *Australians Abroad* (1967) and, with David MALOUF, the anti-war anthology, *We Took Their Orders and Are Dead* (1971). He established with Pat Woolley an alternative publishing house, Wild and Woolley, and was associated with the short fiction supplement *Tabloid Story*, as well as becoming an important critic of Australian literature with several critical works, including a monograph on *Paradise Lost* (1969) and the literary studies *Political Fictions* (1980), *Dragon's Teeth* (1987) and *Social Visions* (1993). *Wildest Dreams* (1998) is a bleakly comic fictional memoir of the literary world in Sydney from the 1960s. One of the Balmain writers who gathered in the Sydney suburb of that name in the late 1960s and documented its radical lifestyle, he rejects the realist mode and is an experimental writer who employs a variety of forms in stories about the way people's identities are defined through narratives and fictions.

Williams, Nigel (1948–) Born in Cheadle, Cheshire, England, he graduated from Oxford University (BA 1969) and became a writer and television executive with the BBC. He has written a number of plays, notably *Class Enemy* (1978). His novels are *My Life Closed Twice* (1977), *Jack Be Nimble* (1980), *Star Turn* (1985) and *Witchcraft* (1987). *The Wimbledon Trilogy* (1995) consists of *The Wimbledon Poisoner* (1991), which targets suburban life with black satire, in which a lawyer, Henry Farr, tries to poison his wife but instead accidentally kills other people, *They Came from SW19* (1992), which continues the focus on the bizarre in the suburban world, and *East of Wimbledon* (1993). Farr returns to do further battle for survival against his wife, family and neighbours in the stories in *Scenes from a Poisoner's Life* (1994). *Stalking Fiona* (1997) and *Fortysomething* (1999) are his most recent novels. Focusing primarily upon the lower classes abandoned by the established middle classes, his comic narratives are marked by social commentary and are generally praised for their dialogue. He has also written the travel books, *2½ Men in a Boat* (1992), retracing Jerome K. Jerome's trip on the Thames, and *From Wimbledon to Waco* (1995), about a family trip to the US.

Wilson, A.N. (1950–) A widely honoured English writer, he was born Andrew Norman Wilson, at Stone, Staffordshire, and went to Oxford University (MA 1976). After a spell as a teacher and Oxford University lecturer (1975–1980), he became literary editor of the *Spectator* (1980–1983). His prolific fiction writing began with *The Sweets of Pimlico* (1977), about the eccentric life of a young woman and a mysterious German aristocrat, and

was followed by *Unguarded Hours* (1978), and its sequel *Kindly Light* (1979), the misadventures of an innocent protagonist in the worlds of academia and organised religion. Other novels include the highly acclaimed *The Healing Art* (1980), *Wise Virgin* (1982) about a blind scholar editing a medieval book about virginity, *Gentlemen in England* (1985), *Love Unknown* (1987), *Stray* (1987), which is the autobiography of an 'alley-cat', *The Vicar of Sorrows* (1993), and *Dream Children* (1998). The 'Lampitt Papers' sequence consists of *Incline Our Hearts* (1988), *A Bottle of Smoke* (1990), *Daughters of Albion* (1991), *Hearing Voices* (1995) and *A Watch in the Night* (1996). His non-fiction includes biographies of Walter Scott in *The Laird of Abbotsford* (1980), *The Life of John Milton* (1983), *Hilaire Belloc* (1984), and also of Tolstoy (1988), C.S. Lewis (1990) and Jesus (1992). The non-fiction work *God's Funeral* (1999), charts the decline of religious certainty in Victorian times rooted in eighteenth-century scepticism. He has written several books about the state of Christianity, for example *How Can We Know?* (1985), and a collection of literary journalism in *Penfriends from Porlock* (1988), although he is best known for his Tory satires in wide-ranging farcical novels about British life and the absurdities of British social institutions.

Wilson, Colin (1931–) Born in Leicester, England, Colin Henry Wilson left school at 16 and has worked at a variety of jobs since 1947, spending a year in France in 1950. Begun in 1954, his first novel was *Ritual in the Dark* (1960), about a young writer drawn into the world of a mass murderer. A voracious reader, Wilson slept on Hampstead Heath and wrote in the British Museum, determined to produce a substantial contribution to European thought. His first non-fiction and best-known work was *The Outsider* (1956), a study of existentialism and the figure of the 'outsider', which tended to associate him with the 'angry young men' of the 1950s. Thereafter he produced a formidable body of work on philosophical, criminal, sociological and psychological issues, among which are *Religion and the Rebel* (1957), *The Strength to Dream* (1962) and *The Essential Colin Wilson* (1985). In addition to this wide body of non-fiction, he wrote several plays, and a variety of lesser-known novels, which include *Adrift in Soho* (1961), *Necessary Doubt* (1964), *The Black Room* (1971), the 'Spider World' sequence – *The Delta* (1987), *The Tower* (1987) and *The Magician* (1992) – *The Desert* (1988), *The Sex Diary of a Metaphysician* (1988) and *Fortress* (1989). Among a large number of books on the supernatural, arcana, mysteries and the occult, is the recent *The Devil's Party* (2000), a study of charismatic leaders and their psychology.

Winterson, Jeanette (1959–) An acclaimed English novelist, born near Manchester, she graduated from Oxford University (MA 1981), and worked in a variety of jobs (including in a funeral parlour) before turning to writing full-time. Her first novel was the controversial autobiographical novel, *Oranges Are Not the Only Fruit* (1985), a coming-of-age story about a young girl, the daughter of Pentecostal Evangelical parents in Yorkshire, who encounters difficulties and tensions with her emerging lesbian sexuality. The book was turned into an acclaimed television film. Her other fictional works include a disavowed early novel, *Boating for Beginners* (1985), which reworks the Biblical narrative of the Flood; *The Passion* (1987), a fantasy love story between Henri and a web-footed girl, Villanelle, set in Napoleonic France and Venice; *Sexing the Cherry* (1989), largely set in England in the 1660s, combining fairy tale and fantastical figures like the gargantuan Dog-Woman; *Written on the Body* (1992), which deliberately blurs the gender of the narrator who is having an

affair with a married woman dying of leukaemia; and *Gut Symmetries* (1997), another fantasy love story, combining contemporary physics and metaphysical theories of chance. Her latest novel, *The Powerbook* (2000), combines fantasy and alternative times and spaces, as she investigates cyberspace and shifting realities. All her work concerns issues of gender, sexuality and fantasy. Her cultural criticism includes *Art and Lies* (1994), a set of essays with a loosely connected plot centring upon Sappho, Picasso and Handel, *Art Objects: Essays on Ecstasy and Effrontery* (1996) and *The World and Other Places* (1999). She has also written a screenplay, *Great Moments in Aviation* (1994), and collected short stories in *World and Other Places* (1998).

H. Grice and T. Woods, eds, '*I'm telling you stories*': *Jeanette Winterson and the Politics of Reading* (1998).

Wiseman, Adele (1928–1992) A Canadian novelist, born in Winnipeg, Manitoba, to Jewish emigrant parents from the Ukraine, she graduated from the University of Manitoba (BA 1949). She is principally known for her two novels, entitled *The Sacrifice* (1956), based upon the biblical story of Abraham, and *Crackpot* (1974), set in a Jewish ghetto in Winnipeg during the Depression, and using unconventional sentence and language structures. Both novels interpret modern Jewish experience as it is reflected in emigrants to the Canadian prairies between the two world wars, depicting their hardships and the ways in which they were exploited. *Old Woman at Play* (1978) tells her life story, and in addition to short stories, she wrote two plays of social criticism, *Testimonial Dinner* (1978) and *The Lovebound* (1981).

Wodehouse, P.G. (1881–1975) Full name Pelham Grenville Wodehouse, he was born in Guildford, England, of aristocratic ancestry. On leaving school, he worked for a bank in London until 1903. His early stories, which were published in *Punch* and the *Strand Magazine*, remain uncollected. It was with his first book, *The Pothunters* (1902), a school story, that he became known as a writer of children's books, focusing on the character Psmith (the 'P' is silent), an Old Etonian dandy, who emerged in these early books as his first great comic character. Psmith appears with other comic characters in the Blandings books, which include *Something New* (1915), *Leave it to Psmith* (1923), *Blandings Castle* (1935) and *Sunset at Blandings* (1977, unfinished). However, first appearing in short stories in 1919, his most famous characters are Bertie Wooster, the archetypal aristocratic silly ass, and his unflappable manservant Jeeves, who extricates him from all manner of embarrassing situations. Jeeves and Wooster appear in such novels as *Carry On, Jeeves* (1925), *Right Ho, Jeeves* (1934) and *Much Obliged, Jeeves* (1971). Wodehouse's popularity soared in the 1920s, and after increasing transatlantic visits, he also turned to musical comedy, collaborating with Jerome Kern and Guy Bolton in the US. In 1934, he moved to the south of France, and in the 1940s, after internment, was forced by the Nazis to make broadcasts in Berlin, which caused an uproar in Britain. Although later publication showed them to be somewhat innocuous, these scandalous activities nevertheless forced him to settle in the US after the war, and he naturalised in 1955. A prolific novelist and playwright, with approximately 120 books to his name, his humorous stories caricatured eccentric aristocratic Edwardian England and have been widely adapted for film and television.

F. Donaldson, *P.G. Wodehouse* (1982).

Wolf, Christa (1929–) Born in Landsberg an der Wartle, Germany, now Gorzow, Poland, she went to the universities of Jena and Leipzig (1949–1953), after which she worked as a technical assistant and a reader for publishers, and turned to freelance writing in 1962. A member of the German Communist Party from 1949, she resigned in 1982. *Divided Heaven* (1963, trans. 1965) is about ill-fated love and is a differentiated critique of the German Democratic Republic, but her reputation was established with *The Quest for Christa T* (1968, trans. 1970), which developed her style of 'subjective authenticity', implicitly challenging the Party's socialist realism and its claim to have an objective view of history. In the course of writing about a dead friend, the female protagonist is forced to challenge her own political past. There followed *A Model Childhood* (1976, trans. 1980), an autobiographical projection of her upbringing under Nazism, *No Place on Earth* (1979, trans. 1982), about her loss of faith in the GDR's socialist project, and *Cassandra* (1983, trans. 1984), a 'revision' of the classical legend of Troy and an allegory of Wolf's own loss of loyalty to the GDR's ruling ethos, as well as concerning the exclusion of women from cultural agency and the rationalism of the technocratic age. Her most recent novel is *Medea* (1996, trans. 1998), which rewrites the Greek myth, representing her as a fiercely independent woman ensnared in a brutal political battle. Other works include *Accident: A Day's News* (1987, trans. 1989), a response to the Chernobyl disaster, and short stories in *What Remains* (1990, trans. 1993). *The Reader and the Writer* (1972, trans. 1977) is an essay to accompany *The Quest for Christa T* and is a pivotal text in the development of GDR literature, and *The Fourth Dimension* (1986, trans. 1988) and *The Writer's Dimension* (1987, trans. 1993) are collections of interviews and essays. Internationally acknowledged as a leading literary figure of the former GDR, and the foremost woman writing in German, she has critically engaged with the rigid structures of the Communist regime and established herself in the vanguard of formal and stylistic innovation. Despite this and her position as a significant figure within feminist debates, she has been embroiled in controversy, accused of propping up the Communist regime by her continued presence as a prestigious intellectual in the GDR without speaking out against its oppressions.

M. Love, *Christa Wolf: Literature and the Conscience of History* (1991).

Wolfe, Thomas (1900–1938) Born in Asheville, North Carolina, US, Thomas Clayton Wolfe was educated at the University of North Carolina at Chapel Hill (BA 1920) and Harvard (MA 1922). His major contribution is four sprawling, highly autobiographical novels of youthful exuberance, which fictionalise his early life in the somewhat romanticised Blue Ridge Mountains, and recount his trips to the North, to Europe and back again. The ponderous manuscripts were judiciously edited and shaped by Maxwell Perkins at Scribner's and Edward Aswell at Harper's. The first of these is *Look Homeward, Angel* (1929), about the protagonist Eugene Gant and his Southern family, followed by *Of Time and the River* (1935). Although the protagonist in *The Web and the Rock* (1939) changes to George Webber, the novel continues the autobiographical narrative and tells of the snares of experience, environment and ancestry and the search for a secure foundational rock, and is followed in *You Can't Go Home Again* (1940). His other works include the novella, *A Portrait of Bascom Hawke* (1932), and short stories collected in *From Death to Morning* (1935), *The Hills Beyond* (1941) and *The Complete Short Stories of Thomas Wolfe* (1987). In addition to several plays, he wrote a travelogue about his 1938 trip to the national parks of the West in *A Western Journal* (1951), and numerous essays, the most interesting of which is *The Story of a Novel* (1935), which lays out his writing theories and working

relationship with Perkins. *The Letters of Thomas Wolfe* appeared in 1956, and a final novel, *The Lost Boy* in 1965. His characteristic intensity of emotional evocation, and his sometimes swollen and frenzied rhetoric mixed with more meditative passages, make for a fiction which is an unaffected celebration of America. He died of tuberculosis.

D. Donald, *Look Homeward: A Life of Thomas Wolfe* (1987).

Wolfe, Tom (1930–) Born Thomas Kennerly Wolfe, in Richmond, Virginia, US, he attended Washington and Lee (BA 1951) and Yale (Ph.D. 1957) universities. As a journalist and social commentator, he has been a leading chronicler of US social trends, for which he has been widely honoured. Originating as articles for his newspaper, *The Kandy-Kolored Tangerine-Flake Streamline Baby* (1965) collects a series of essays on early 1960s trends, with studies of the custom-car pop culture in California, heroes like Cassius Clay and Phil Spector, and art galleries. He emerged as a leader of the 'new journalism', along with such writers as Gay Talese and Hunter S. THOMPSON, which is characterised by extensive dialogue, shifting perspective, detailed descriptions, complex character development and linguistic innovation. Its aim is to bring the reader as close as possible to the material, and is frequently termed an 'aural' style of writing. He wrote a series of culture-defining works, such as *The Electric Kool-Aid Acid Test* (1968), about the author Ken KESEY and his Merry Pranksters and their psychedelic experiences with LSD, *The Pump House Gang* (1968), and *Radical Chic and Mau Mauing the Flak Catchers* (1970), two essays about the ambivalent style and politics of cultivated intellectuals. After editing the anthology *The New Journalism* (1973), he continued to write studies of American culture: *The Painted Word* (1975) explores the art world; *The Right Stuff*

(1979, filmed 1983), often regarded as his best work, is a black comic study of the early years of the US space programme; and *From Bauhaus to Our House* (1981) looks at modern architecture. Other collections of essays appear in *In Our Time* (1980) and *The Purple Decades* (1982), while short stories occur in *Mauve Gloves and Madmen* (1978). He has published two novels: *Bonfire of the Vanities* (1987, filmed 1990), a best-seller about the greed and hatred seething in New York City in the 1980s, when a smug Wall Street executive's life is crushed after killing a young African-American in a hit-and-run accident, and *A Man in Full* (1998), which is also on an epic scale, dealing with political machinations and incipient racial tensions in Atlanta, Georgia, in the 1990s. His unorthodox style and unpopular opinions have led him into frequent controversy; yet he remains one of America's leading satirists, caricaturists and coiner of phrases, such as 'radical chic', with his kaleidoscopic descriptions and painstaking research.

Wolff, Tobias (1945–) Born in Birmingham, Alabama, US, Tobias Jonathan Ansell Wolff served with the American Special Forces in Vietnam (1964–1967), and then attended Oxford University (BA 1972) and Stanford University (MA 1978). After working as a journalist, he was made Professor of English at Syracuse University in 1980. A highly regarded writer, he is associated with the so-called 'dirty realists', like Raymond CARVER and Richard FORD, in a range of fiction which mixes fastidious realism and uncompromising protagonists with the grotesque and the lyrical. His first novel was *Ugly Rumours* (1975), since which time he has published the short story collection *In the Garden of North American Martyrs* (1981), which scrutinises the disorders of daily life for some significance, the widely praised novella *The Barracks Thief* (1984), which deals with an event involving paratroopers at Fort Bragg during

the Vietnam War years, and *Back in the World* (1985), short stories about the disillusionment and powerlessness felt upon returning from the Vietnam War. The three latter works are collected in *The Stories of Tobias Wolff* (1988). He has also written *This Boy's Life* (1989), a memoir about growing up and leaving Utah for Washington with his mother to escape her abusive boyfriend, *In Pharaoh's Army* (1994), another memoir about the author's one year tour of duty in Vietnam, and *The Night in Question* (1996). In addition to his many stories, published in such magazines as *Atlantic Monthly* and *The New Yorker*, he has edited the short story collection, *Matters of Life and Death* (1983).

J. Hannah, *Tobias Wolff: A Study of the Short Fiction* (1996).

Woolf, Douglas (1922–) Born in New York City, US, he was educated at Harvard University (1939–1942), and after serving in the US army during the war, at the University of New Mexico (BA 1950). He has been variously employed as an itinerant worker and freelance writer, and published his first novel, *The Hypocritic Days*, in 1955. Remaining relatively obscure, he has nevertheless developed a small but loyal readership. His novels include *Fade Out* (1959), about two men seeking to escape the claustrophobia of suburban life, *Wall to Wall* (1962), *Ya! John-Juan* (1971), *Spring of the Lamb* (1972), *On Us* (1977) and *The Timing Chain* (1985). His short stories include the collections *Signs of a Migrant Worrier* (1965) and *Future Pre-Conditional* (1978).

Woolf, Virginia (1882–1941) Named Adelaide Virginia Stephen, she was born in London, England, into an intellectual Victorian family. Her father was Sir Leslie Stephen, the founder of the *Dictionary of National Biography*. Woolf's childhood was rocked by a series of emotional shocks and family crises that left her with serious mental instability, and caused her to suffer from emotional breakdowns throughout her life. She set up house in Bloomsbury with her sister Vanessa and her brothers, and this became the nucleus of the famous Bloomsbury group, attracting such writers, painters and intellectuals as Lytton Strachey, Clive Bell, Roger Fry and E.M. FORSTER. She wrote for the *Times Literary Supplement* in 1905, and married Leonard Woolf in 1912, with whom she founded the Hogarth Press in 1917, which published their own work and that of many of their friends, for example T.S. Eliot. She had a series of lesbian relationships, most notably with Vita SACKVILLE-WEST, who was her inspiration for *Orlando* (1928) and its exploration of androgyny. Her first novel, *The Voyage Out* (1915), was somewhat traditional in its form, and was followed by *Night and Day* (1919). It was with the short stories collected in *Monday or Tuesday* (1921) and the novel *Jacob's Room* (1922) that her impressionistic style emerged, establishing her reputation as one of the leading modernist writers. This style of representing interior mental states was developed in her major novels, *Mrs Dalloway* (1925), *To the Lighthouse* (1927) and *The Waves* (1931), and established Woolf as a writer to rival the modernist experiments in fiction of Marcel PROUST, James JOYCE and D.H. LAWRENCE. She also wrote a series of seminal essays on fiction, such as 'Modern Fiction' (1919) and 'Mr Bennett and Mrs Brown' (1923), which were subsequently collected in *The Common Reader* (1925). Her last novels were *The Years* (1937) and *Between the Acts* (1941), which turned towards an exploration of history. Other works include numerous essays and sketches, and a biography of Roger Fry (1940). Several volumes of her letters (1975–1979) and diaries (1977–1984) were published posthumously, as were the essays in *The Death of the Moth* (1942), *The Captain's Death Bed* (1950), *Granite and Rainbow* (1958) and *Col-*

lected Essays (1966–1967). She committed suicide at Rodmell, her house in Sussex. She was adept at catching moments of experience, developing an aesthetic practice which presented epiphanies of insight, although her fiction tended to be somewhat restricted in subject matter, milieu and character. Her reputation has been further enhanced by feminist criticism, which sees *A Room of One's Own* (1929) and *Three Guineas* (1938), for example, as seminal feminist texts.

Q. Bell, *Virginia Woolf: A Biography*, 2 vols (1972); R. Bowlby, *Virginia Woolf: Feminist Destinations* (1988).

Wouk, Herman (1915–) An American writer, born in New York City, and educated at Columbia University, where he graduated in 1934. During the Second World War, he served in the US navy, an experience which informed much of his writing. He began work as a writer for comic radio, and his earliest novels were *Aurora Dawn* (1947), a satirical story about the advertising business, and *The City Boy* (1948), about a boy's life in New York in the 1920s. There followed *The Caine Mutiny* (1951, filmed 1954), concerning a revolt against the unstable captain of a Pacific minesweeper, and *Marjorie Morningstar* (1955), about a Jewish girl's bid for a stage career. Later came *Youngblood Hawk* (1962), about a talented writer, *Don't Stop the Carnival* (1965), and two panoramic novels, *The Winds of War* (1971) and *War and Remembrance* (1978), set against many of the theatres of the Second World War. *Inside, Outside* (1985) is the life of an orthodox Jew during the twentieth century, and *The Hope* (1993) and *The Glory* (1994) both chronicle the birth of the state of Israel. His plays are *The Traitor* (1949) and *Nature's Way* (1957). His non-fiction is *This Is My God* (1959), about Judaism, while *This Will to Live On; This Is Our Heritage* (2000) is a religious autobiography.

Wright, Richard (1908–1960) Richard Nathaniel Wright was born in Natchez, Mississippi, US. His expression of the African-American voice in his writings, and his challenge to white stereotypes of African-Americans, changed the landscape of possibilities for African-American writers. He moved to Chicago and worked for the Post Office, whose character and life he sketched in the posthumously published *Lawd Today* (1963). He also became involved with the Communist Party, and his association and break with the Party and its failure to address race relations became the subject of much of his later fiction, signalled in his article, 'How I Tried to Be a Communist' (1944) in the *Atlantic Monthly*, and *The God That Failed* (1950). Working for the Federal Writers' Project (1935–1937), his first work *Uncle Tom's Children* (1938) was a collection of short stories about a young black man growing up in the violent South under the Jim Crow segregation laws. Yet it was with the acclaimed *Native Son* (1940) that his major influence began, in which he deals with the life of Bigger Thomas and his move North in search of freedom. *12 Million Black Voices* (1941) was a folk history, and was followed by *Black Boy* (1945), an autobiography which remembered his childhood and adolescence and the fear and dread engendered by racism and its restrictive nature. Despite his success as one of the most famous African-American writers, he still felt beset by racism and left for Paris in 1947, where his work was better received than in the US. In France, he published the novels *The Outsider* (1953), about a black man's fatal involvement with the Communist Party in Chicago and New York, *Savage Holiday* (1954), and *The Long Dream* (1958), which is a social protest against racism and corruption, set in Mississippi. His non-fiction includes *Black Power* (1954), which is a diary of a visit to the Gold Coast, *The Color Curtain* (1956), a report on the multiracial Bandung conference in Indonesia in 1955, the travelo-

gue *Pagan Spain* (1956), and *White Man, Listen* (1957), a series of four lectures on racial issues. Posthumous publications include *American Hunger* (1977), which continues his autobiography from *Black Boy*, short stories collected in *Eight Men* (1961), and the two novellas in *The Man Who Lived Underground* (1971), and *Rite of Passage* (1994), set in the 1940s. A writer who is concerned with the roots of racial oppression, he has achieved international stature and fame, and his influence on American literature has been considerable.

H. Gates, Jr and K. Appiah, eds, *Richard Wright: Critical Perspectives Past and Present* (1993).

Wyndham, John (1903–1969) The pseudonym of John Wyndham Parkes Lucas Beynon Harris, an English writer of science fiction and fantasy, he was born in Knowle, Warwickshire. His novels include *The Day of the Triffids* (1951, filmed 1962), in which a shower of meteors blinds much of the Earth's population and thus renders them vulnerable to attack by alien carnivorous plants, *The Kraken Wakes* (1953), again about an invasion of Earth by aliens, and *The Chrysalids* (1955), in which Britain is segregated into radioactive wastelands which breed mutations. *The Midwich Cuckoos* (1957) concerns an alien miasma which renders all the women of a village pregnant, after which they give birth to a race of alien children (filmed as *The Village of the Damned*, 1960), *Trouble with Lichen* (1960) and *Chocky* (1968). He also wrote short story collections, including *The Seeds of Time* (1956) and *The Infinite Moment* (1961). Other novels are *Foul Play Suspected* (1935), written under the name John Beynon, and *Love in Time* (1946), as Johnson Harris. He described his fiction as 'logical fantasy', and he became one of the most popular post-war writers of science fiction in Britain, influencing other science fiction writers, such as Brian ALDISS.

Y

Yerby, Frank G. (1916–1991) Born Frank Garvin Yerby, in Augusta, Georgia, US, he attended Paine College (BA 1937) and Fiske University, Nashville (MA 1938), where he began writing. He worked for the Federal Writers' Project in 1938, and met other aspiring writers, like Richard WRIGHT and Margaret Walker. After a brief time spent teaching, he worked in manufacturing. His stories began to be successfully published in the 1940s, and he abandoned his early protest fiction for historical period fiction, with works like *The Foxes of Harrow* (1946), *The Vixens* (1947) and *Pride's Castle* (1949), constituting a trilogy about the American Civil War and the reconstruction period, *The Golden Hawke* (1948) and *The Saracen Blade* (1952). Many of his novels have been made into successful movies, and he has achieved an unprecedented commercial success for an African-American writer, selling fifty-five million books over the years. Although many of his best-sellers eschewed contemporary social issues – the cause of critical hostility by some – his later work focused increasingly on race issues, the most famous of which is *The Dahomean* (1971), about slavery and set in nineteenth-century Africa, and *A Darkness at Ingraham's Crest* (1981). Other novels include *The Devil's Laughter* (1953), about the French Revolution, *The Serpent and the Staff* (1958), *The Garfield Honour* (1961), *Griffin's Way* (1962), the protest novel *The Tents of Shem* (1963), *Western* (1982), which is a saga of the Great Plains, *Captain Rebel* (1983), *Devilseed* (1984), *McKenzie's Hundred* (1985) and *A Woman Called Fancy* (1992). A highly successful manipulator of the conventions of popular fiction, his fiction is known for its demystification of historical myths and an uncompromising criticism of the romanticism of the Deep South. In 1955, he moved to Spain, where he lived out his life.

Yezierska, Anzia (1885?–1970) Born in Plinsk, Russian Poland, she emigrated to the US in 1901, and was naturalised in 1912. She worked as a seamstress in sweatshops (1900–1903), taught domestic science at schools (1908–1910), and from 1915, worked as a translator, screenwriter and novelist. Her first work was a collection of short stories, entitled *Hungry Hearts* (1920), which included the acclaimed story, 'The Fat of the Land'. About a newly affluent Jewish woman who yearns for the vibrancy of her former life in New York's East Side, the story shot her to fame when she sold it to Hollywood. As a Russian-born Jewish immigrant, her fiction examined the experience of the poor in New York, as female protagonists struggled with poverty and the restrictions of Judaic values. *Salome of the Tenements* (1923), a novel about an interclass and intercultural marriage which falls apart, was followed by the short stories in *Children of Loneliness* (1923). Thereafter came the novels *Bread Givers* (1925), *Arrogant Beggar* (1927), and *All I Could Never Be* (1932), about a doomed romance between an immigrant and a wealthy American. Apart from an autobiographical novel, *Red Ribbon on a White Horse* (1950), she lapsed into poverty and obscurity, but was rediscovered in the late 1960s. The posthumous edition *The Open Cage* (1979) is a collection of her unpublished writings. Conflict, tension and bitter disappointment mark many of her characters, as they seek to reconcile their old world heritage with the potential of the new land.

C. Schoen, *Anzia Yezierska* (1982).

Yglesias, Jose (1919–1995) Born in Tampa, Florida, US, after serving in the US navy during the war, he attended Black Mountain College in 1946, after which he became the film critic for the *Daily Worker* until 1950, and then worked for a pharmaceutical company until 1963. *A Wake in Ybor City* (1963) was succeeded by *The Goodbye Land* (1967), a narrative of self-discovery, which was the result of attempts to trace the details of his father's birth in Galicia, Spain. *In the Fist of the Revolution* (1968) captures the people embracing the optimism of the Cuban revolution, and was followed by other novels, including *An Orderly Life* (1968), *The Truth About Them* (1971), *Double, Double* (1974), *The Kill Price* (1976), *Home Again* (1987) and *Tristan and the Hispanics* (1989). Non-fiction includes *Down There* (1970), about the personal viewpoints of young revolutionaries in Brazil, Cuba, Chile and Peru, and *The Franco Years* (1977), about the effect of the dictator's regime on people's lives. Of bilingual Cuban and Spanish descent, his novels chronicle the lives of the American His-

panic peoples and the adjustments, dreams, and disappointments of the Cuban working-class immigrant families to the US.

Yourcenar, Marguerite (1903–1987) A Walloon writer, born Marguerite de Crayencour in Brussels, Belgium, she was educated in Flanders. In 1939, she settled in the US, and changed her name to Yourcenar when she naturalised in 1947. She taught at Sarah Lawrence College (1940–1950) and lectured at various American universities. Always writing in French, her first published works were of poetry. Her early novels, such as *Alexis* (1929, trans. 1984), *A Coin in Nine Hands* (1934, trans. 1982) and *Coup de Grace* (1939, trans. 1957), explored the contemporary world through tales of unrequited love, homosexuality and political assassination. However, these were dwarfed by her two major novels: *Memoirs of Hadrian* (1951, trans. 1954), a fictional autobiography of the Roman emperor, recreated in first person letters sent to his nephew Marcus Aurelius; and another thought-provoking historical novel, *The Abyss* (1968, trans. 1976), about the struggle of a physician and alchemist against prevailing superstition and religious dogma in the 1500s. A wide range of short stories include *Oriental Tales* (1938, trans. 1985), *Two Lives and a Dream* (1982, trans. 1987) and *A Blue Tale* (trans. 1995), while other work includes essays in *The Dark Brain of Piranesi* (1962, trans. 1984) and *That Mighty Sculptor Time* (1983, trans. 1989), and interviews in *With Open Eyes* (1980, trans. 1989). The first woman to be elected to the Academie Française, she writes of the tragedy of human destiny with profound philosophical meditation in a compact, poetic language.

J. Savigneau, *Marguerite Yourcenar: Inventing a Life* (1993).

Z

Zamyatin, Evgeny Ivanovich (1884–1937) Born in Lebedyon, Russia, he was educated at the St. Petersburg Polytechnic Institute in naval engineering (1902–1908), after which he worked as an engineer until 1911. He then lectured at the Institute, edited various journals, and went into exile in Paris in 1932, where he died. He began publishing stories as a student, and these include the novella and short stories in *The Dragon* (1913, trans. 1966), *A Godforsaken Hole* (1914, trans. 1988), which depicts military life as drunken and corrupt, and *The Islanders* (1922, trans. 1985), which offers a devastating assessment of English life. His only completed novel is *We* (1920, trans. 1924), an anti-utopian account of a totalitarian state which extinguishes individuals' imaginations, built upon diary entries of a rebel leader, the publication of which led him into trouble with the Communist Party. In addition to screenplays and plays, his non-fiction includes essays in the posthumously published *A Soviet Heretic* (1955, trans. 1970). A leading modernist writer of the early Soviet period, he was better known in the West than in the USSR due to his innovations in the neo-realist style, involving formal experimentation, satire, primitivism and linguistic play.

Zelazny, Roger (1937–1995) An American science fiction writer, Roger Joseph Zelazny was born in Cleveland, Ohio, and educated at the Western Reserve (BA 1959) and Columbia (MA 1962) universities. He worked for the US Social Security administration until 1969, when he became a full-time writer. As a leading re-presentative of the science fiction 'New Wave', his arrival in 1962, together with Ursula LE GUIN and Thomas DISCH, mar-ked the maturity of science fiction into a sophisticated literature. He has published a wide range of science fiction, but is best known for the ambitious 'Amber' series (1970–1991), about the Amber world which exists in all times and places at once, and of which the Earth and other worlds are mere reflections. In two sequences, the series charts the machinations of the ruling family as it vies for power. As well as contributing to many story collections, sometimes under the pseudonym Harrison Denmark, his other works include the novels *This Immortal* (1966), about a declining Earth and an immortal protagonist, *The Dream Master* (1966), *Lord of Light* (1967), *Jack of Shadows* (1971), *A Night in the Lonesome October* (1993), and several collections of short stories in *Four for Tomorrow* (1967), *My Name Is Legion* (1976) and *Frost and Fire* (1989). With a colourful prose style and innovative adaptations of ancient Egyptian and Hindu mythological characters, his work is marked by the themes of divinity and immortality.

J. Lindskold, *Roger Zelazny* (1993).

Zweig, Stefan (1881–1942) Born in Vienna, Austria, he was a prolific writer of biographies, novels, essays and historical works. He went into exile under National Socialism in 1934, and emigrated to England, before travelling to Brazil in 1941. His only novel is his best-known work, *Beware of Pity* (1939, trans. 1982), while short stories occur in *The Royal Game* (1942, trans. 1981). His outstanding accomplishments are generally regarded to be his biographies based upon psychological interpretation, and include *The Tide of Fortune* (1927, trans. 1955), *Erasmus and the Right to Heresy* (1934, trans. 1955), and *The Queen of Scots* (1935, trans. 1950), focusing upon such people as Marie Antoinette, Verlaine, Magellan and Balzac. He committed suicide in Petropolis, Brazil, and his autobiography was published posthumously as *The World of Yesterday* (1943).

E. Allday, *Stefan Zweig: A Critical Biography* (1972).

Appendix

Literary prizes

Booker McConnell Prize for Fiction

An annual award for the best novel by a British or Commonwealth writer, founded in 1969.

1969 P.H. Newby, *Something to Answer For*
1970 Bernice Rubens, *The Elected Member*
1971 V.S. Naipaul, *In a Free State*
1972 John Berger, *G*
1973 J.G. Farrell, *The Siege of Krishnapur*
1974 Nadine Gordimer, *The Conservationist*
     Stanley Middleton, *Holiday*
1975 Ruth Prawer Jhabvala, *Heat and Dust*
1976 David Storey, *Saville*
1977 Paul Scott, *Staying On*
1978 Iris Murdoch, *The Sea, the Sea*
1979 Penelope Fitzgerald, *Offshore*
1980 William Golding, *Rites of Passage*
1981 Salman Rushdie, *Midnight's Children*
1982 Thomas Keneally, *Schindler's Ark*
1983 J.M. Coetzee, *Life and Times of Michael K*
1984 Anita Brookner, *Hotel du Lac*
1985 Keri Hulme, *The Bone People*

1986 Kingsley Amis, *The Old Devils*
1987 Penelope Lively, *Moon Tiger*
1988 Peter Carey, *Oscar and Lucinda*
1989 Kazuo Ishiguro, *The Remains of the Day*
1990 A.S. Byatt, *Possession*
1991 Ben Okri, *The Famished Road*
1992 Michael Ondaatje, *The English Patient*
     Barry Unsworth, *Sacred Hunger*
1993 Roddy Doyle, *Paddy Clarke, Ha Ha Ha*
1994 James Kelman, *How Late It Was, How Late*
1995 Pat Barker, *The Ghost Road*
1996 Graham Swift, *Last Orders*
1997 Arundhati Roy, *The God of Small Things*
1998 Ian McEwan, *Amsterdam*
1999 J.M. Coetzee, *Disgrace*
2000 Margaret Atwood, *The Blind Assassin*

The Pulitzer Prize

One of several annual prizes, one of which is awarded to the best 'fiction in book form', inaugurated in 1917.

1917 No award
1918 Ernest Poole, *His Family*
1919 Booth Tarkington, *The Magnificent Ambersons*
1920 No award

1921 Edith Wharton, *The Age of Innocence*
1922 Booth Tarkington, *Alice Adams*
1923 Willa Cather, *One of Ours*
1924 Margaret Wilson, *The Able McLaughlins*
1925 Edna Ferber, *So Big*
1926 Sinclair Lewis, *Arrowsmith*
1927 Louis Bromfield, *Early Autumn*
1928 Thornton Wilder, *The Bridge of San Luis Rey*
1929 Julia Peterkin, *Scarlet Sister Mary*
1930 Oliver La Farge, *Laughing Boy*
1931 Margaret Ayer Barnes, *Years of Grace*
1932 Pearl S. Buck, *The Good Earth*
1933 T.S. Stribling, *The Store*
1934 Caroline Miller, *Lamb in His Bosom*
1935 Josephine Winslow Johnson, *Now in November*
1936 Harold L. Davis, *Honey in the Horn*
1937 Margaret Mitchell, *Gone with the Wind*
1938 John Phillips Marquand, *The Late George Apley*
1939 Marjorie Kinnan Rawlings, *The Yearling*
1940 John Steinbeck, *The Grapes of Wrath*
1941 No award
1942 Ellen Glasgow, *In This Our Life*
1943 Upton Sinclair, *Dragon's Teeth*
1944 Martin Flavin, *Journey in the Dark*
1945 John Hersey, *A Bell for Adano*
1946 No award
1947 Robert Penn Warren, *All the King's Men*
1948 James A. Michener, *Tales of the South Pacific*
1949 James Gould Cozzens, *Guard of Honor*
1950 A.B. Guthrie, Jr., *The Way West*
1951 Conrad Richter, *The Town*
1952 Herman Wouk, *The Caine Mutiny*
1953 Ernest Hemingway, *The Old Man and the Sea*
1954 No award

1955 William Faulkner, *A Fable*
1956 MacKinlay Kantor, *Andersonville*
1957 No award
1958 James Agee, *A Death in the Family*
1959 Robert Lewis Taylor, *The Travels of Jaimie McPheeters*
1960 Allen Drury, *Advise and Consent*
1961 Harper Lee, *To Kill a Mockingbird*
1962 Edwin O'Connor, *The Edge of Sadness*
1963 William Faulkner, *The Reivers*
1964 No award
1965 Shirley Ann Grau, *The Keepers of the House*
1966 Katherine Anne Porter, *The Collected Stories of Katherine Anne Porter*
1967 Bernard Malamud, *The Fixer*
1968 William Styron, *The Confessions of Nat Turner*
1969 N. Scott Momaday, *House Made of Dawn*
1970 Jean Stafford, *Collected Stories*
1971 No award
1972 Wallace Stegner, *Angle of Repose*
1973 Eudora Welty, *The Optimist's Daughter*
1974 No award
1975 Michael Shaara, *The Killer Angels*
1976 Saul Bellow, *Humboldt's Gift*
1977 No award
1978 James Alan McPherson, *Elbow Room*
1979 John Cheever, *The Stories of John Cheever*
1980 Norman Mailer, *The Executioner's Song*
1981 John Kennedy Toole, *A Confederacy of Dunces*
1982 John Updike, *Rabbit Is Rich*
1983 Alice Walker, *The Color Purple*
1984 William Kennedy, *Ironweed*
1985 Alison Lurie, *Foreign Affairs*
1986 Larry McMurtry, *Lonesome Dove*
1987 Peter Taylor, *A Summons to Memphis*
1988 Toni Morrison, *Beloved*
1989 Anne Tyler, *Breathing Lessons*

1990   Oscar Hijuelos, *The Mambo Kings Play Songs of Love*
1991   John Updike, *Rabbit at Rest*
1992   Jane Smiley, *A Thousand Acres*
1993   Robert Olen Butler, *A Good Scent from a Strange Mountain*
1994   E. Annie Proulx, *The Shipping News*
1995   Carol Shields, *The Stone Diaries*
1996   Richard Ford, *Independence Day*
1997   Stephen Millhauser, *Martin Dressler: The Tale of an American Dreamer*
1998   Philip Roth, *American Pastoral*
1999   Michael Cunningham, *The Hours*
2000   Jhumpa Lahiri, *Interpreter of Maladies*

The Nobel Prize for Literature

Founded in 1900, the prize is an annual award for the author of the most significant work 'of an idealistic tendency'.

1901   René-François-Armand-Sully Prudhomme
1902   Theodor Mommsen
1903   Bjørnstjerne Bjørnson
1904   José Echegaray / Frédéric Mistral
1905   Henryk Sienkiewicz
1906   Giosuè Carducci
1907   Rudyard Kipling
1908   Rudolf Eucken
1909   Selma Lagerlöf
1910   Paul Heyse
1911   Maurice Maeterlinck
1912   Gerhart Hauptmann
1913   Rabindranath Tagore
1914   No award
1915   Romain Rolland
1916   Verner von Heidenstam
1917   Karl Kjellerup / Henrik Pontoppidan
1918   No award
1919   Carl Spitteler
1920   Knut Hamsun
1921   Anatole France
1922   Jacinto Benavente y Martínez
1923   William Butler Yeats
1924   Wladyslaw Reymont
1925   George Bernard Shaw
1926   Grazia Deledda
1927   Henri Bergson
1928   Sigrid Undset
1929   Thomas Mann
1930   Sinclair Lewis
1931   Erik Axel Karlfeldt
1932   John Galsworthy
1933   Ivan Bunin
1934   Luigi Pirandello
1935   No award
1936   Eugene O'Neill
1937   Roger Martin du Gard
1938   Pearl S. Buck
1939   F.E. Sillanpää
1940–1943   No awards
1944   Johannes V. Jensen
1945   Gabriela Mistral
1946   Herman Hesse
1947   André Gide
1948   T.S. Eliot
1949   William Faulkner
1950   Bertrand Russell
1951   Pär Lagerkvist
1952   François Mauriac
1953   Winston S. Churchill
1954   Ernest Hemingway
1955   Halldór Laxness
1956   Juan Ramón Jiménez
1957   Albert Camus
1958   Boris Pasternak
1959   Salvatore Quasimodo
1960   Saint-John Perse
1961   Ivo Andrić
1962   John Steinbeck
1963   George Seferis
1964   Jean-Paul Sartre
1965   Mikhail Sholokov
1966   S.Y. Agnon / Nelly Sachs
1967   Miguel Ángel Asturias
1968   Yasunari Kawabata
1969   Samuel Beckett
1970   Aleksander Solzhenitsyn
1971   Pablo Neruda
1972   Heinrich Böll
1973   Patrick White
1974   Eyvind Johnson / Harry Martinson
1975   Eugenio Montale
1976   Saul Bellow

1977	Vincente Aleixandre	1989	Camilo José Cela
1978	Isaac Bashevis Singer	1990	Octavio Paz
1979	Odysseas Elytis	1991	Nadine Gordimer
1980	Czeslaw Milosz	1992	Derek Walcott
1981	Elias Canetti	1993	Toni Morrison
1982	Gabriel García Márquez	1994	Kenzaburo Oë
1983	William Golding	1995	Seamus Heaney
1984	Jaroslav Seifert	1996	Wislawa Szymborska
1985	Claude Simon	1997	Dario Fo
1986	Wole Soyinka	1998	José Saramago
1987	Joseph Brodsky	1999	Günther Grass
1988	Naguīb Māhfuz	2000	Gao Xingjian